Development Concerns in the 21st Century

ABOUT THE EDITORS

Prof. Sudesh Nangia is currently UGC-Emeritus Fellow at the Centre for the Study of Regional Development, Jawaharlal Nehru University, New Delhi. She has taught Geography and Population Studies for more than four decades. She has authored/edited a dozen books, published more than 60 articles and guided more than 100 research scholars for M. Phil / Ph.D. at JNU and other academic institutions. She has been Consultant to several International Bodies. She has been President of National Association of Geographers' India (NAGI); and Indian Association for the Study of Population (IASP). She has been a Member of the Commission on Population and Environment of the IUSSP and International Geographical Union.

Dr. Mrityunjay Mohan Jha received his Masters in Geography, M.Phil and Ph.D. in food security from the Jawaharlal Nehru University, New Delhi, besides receiving training in Geographic Information System from the Indian Institute of Remote Sensing, Dehradun. He has worked in the areas of social development, resettlement and rehabilitation (R&R), decentralized planning, and natural resource management. He has five books and about a dozen research papers to his credit. He has worked with national level institutes, reputed organizations and Consulting Groups. He is providing consultancy in the areas of resettlement, rehabilitation and social development.

Prof. Suresh Misra is Chair Professor (Consumer Affairs) and Chairman Centre for Consumer Studies, Indian Institute of Public Administration, New Delhi. He holds MA in Political Science from JNU, MHRM from Pondicherry Univeristy and D.Phil from Allahabad Central University. He has his advance training in rural management from Israel. His areas of interest include rural development and local governance, administrative restructuring and consumer affairs. He has authored/edited a number of books and brought numerous reports and papers.

Prof. H. Ramachandran is Professor of Geography at the Delhi School of Economics, University of Delhi. He held positions of Director, Institute of Applied Manpower Research; Executive Director, National Research and Resource Centre, Lal Bahadur Shastri National Academy of Administration, Mussoorie; Professor & Faculty Co-ordinator, Centre for Micro Planning and Regional Studies, LBSNAA, and stint at Institute for Social and Economic Change, Bangalore and the JNU, New Delhi. He has been Member to a numerous committees of the UN Bodies and Government of India. He has more than 37 years of teaching experience and guiding research and specializes in Quantitative Methods, Programme Evaluation, Urban and Regional Studies. He has authored/edited eight books and more than 60 research papers. He is also the Honorary Executive Chairman of the Bhoovigyan Vikas Foundation.

Dr. M. Velayutham, the current Chairman of the Bhoovigyan Vikas Foundation, Delhi (Foundation for Earth Sciences Development), is a distinguished Agricultural Scientist. During his career with the Indian Council of Agricultural Research for 33 years, he occupied important positions as National Project Coordinator, Assistant Director-General and Director, NBSSLUP, Nagpur. He was President of the Indian Society of Soil Science and was bestowed the Honorary Membership of the Society in 2008 and the President of the ISSSLUP. He has over 260 publications published in National and International Journals and presented in Seminars and Conferences. He served as National Project coordinator and Executive Director of the M.S. Swaminathan Research Foundation, Chennai, during 2002-2007. He has been a consultant to the FAO, Bangkok and the World Bank.

DEVELOPMENT CONCERNS
in the 21st Century

Felicitation Volume in Honour of
Dr. K.V. Sundaram

Edited by

Sudesh Nangia
Mrityunjay Mohan Jha
Suresh Misra
H. Ramachandran
M. Velayutham

CONCEPT PUBLISHING COMPANY PVT. LTD.
NEW DELHI-110059

ISBN: 13-978-81-8069-718-0

First Published 2010

Published and Printed by

Concept
Since 1974

Concept Publishing Company Pvt. Ltd.
Regd. Office:
A/15-16, Commercial Block, Mohan Garden
New Delhi-110059 (India)
Phones : 25351460, 25351794, ***Fax*** : 091-11-25357109
Email : publishing@conceptpub.com
Website: www.conceptpub.com

Editorial Office:
H-13, Bali Nagar, New Delhi-110 015, India.

Cataloging in Publication Data--*Courtesy:* D.K. Agencies (P) Ltd. <docinfo@dkagencies.com>

Development concerns in the 21st century : felicitation volume in honour of Dr. K.V. Sundaram / [editors], Sudesh Nangia ... [et al.].
p. cm.
Kavasseri Vanchi Sundaram, b. 1929, founder and chairman of Bhoovigyan Vikas Foundation; contributed articles.
Includes bibliographical references and index.
ISBN 9788180697180

1. Sustainable development--India. 2. Rural development--India. 3. Women in development--India. 4. Food security--India. 5. City planning--India. 6. India.--Economic policy--1991- I. Sundaram, K. V. II. Nangia, Sudesh, 1942- III. Title: Development concerns in the twenty-first century.

DDC 338.9270954 22

PROF. M.S. SWAMINATHAN
Member of Parliament (Rajya Sabha)
Chairman, M S Swaminathan Research Foundation
Third Cross Street, Taramani Institutional Area
Chennai - 600 113
Tel: +91 44 2254 2790 / 2254 1229 / 2254 1698;
Fax: +91 44 2254 1319
Email: chairman@mssrf.res.in / msswami@vsnl.net

Foreword

I am happy that a book is being released on Earth Day to commemorate the 80th Birthday of Dr. K.V. Sundaram, Leader of the Sustainable Development Movement. Dr. Sundaram has always emphasized that sustainable lifestyle. is the pathway to restoring harmony between humankind and nature. Dr. Sundaram's contributions to regional planning are truly monumental. Even today he is tirelessly working for rural renaissance and for the establishment of a Centre for Earth Care Policies in India.

The release of a book in his honour on Earth Day is very appropriate since Dr. Sundaram has shown that future belongs to the nations which take to the path of reducing human ecological footprint on natural resources and increasing agricultural production in an environmentally sustainable manner. I pray for his long life and leadership.

(M.S. Swaminathan)

Contents

SECTION II
FOOD SECURITY

SECTION III
RURAL-URBAN DEVELOPMENT

SECTION IV
INFRASTRUCTURE CONCERNS

Contributors

Amit Kumar Singh, Research Associate, Indian Institute of Public Administration, I.P. Estate, New Delhi-110002.

Gopal Krishan, Professor Emeritus, Panjab University and Senior Professor and Principal Advisor, Centre for Research in Rural and Industrial Development, Chandigarh. Email: gkrishan13@yahoo.com

Krishna Mohan, Reader and Chairman, Department of Geography, Panjab University, Chandigarh. Email: kmohan@pu.ac.in

K.S. Gopalakrishnan, Professor and Head (Rtd.), Department of Geography, University of Madras.

K.V. Raman, Former Member, Agricultural Scientist Recruitment Board, New Delhi. Email: kvraman100@yahoo.com

Madaswamy Moni, Deputy Director General, National Informatics Centre, Lodhi Road, New Delhi-110003. Email: moni@nic.in

M. Saktivel, Lecturer Senior Scale in Geography, University of Madras, Chennai-600005.

Mridula Singh, Additional Director, State Land Use Board, Planning Department, Government of U.P., 5th Floor, Yojana Bhawan, Lucknow-226001.
Email: mridula.06@gmail.com

Mrityunjay M. Jha, Principal Social Development Specialist, SMEC India, Gurgaon. Email: mrityunjayjha@yahoo.com

N.N. Singh, Vice Chancellor, Birsa Agricultural University Ranchi-834006, Jharkhand.

Nira Ramachandran currently Director, Research and Training, Bhoovigyan Vikas Foundation, New Delhi. Email: nira_ramachandran@hotmail.com

Nishith Srivastava, Urban Planner, Snowy Mountain Engineering Corporation (SMEC), India, Gurgaon. Email: nishith@smec.com

R. Sunil Kumar, Lecturer in Geography, Government Arts College, Coimbatore-16

R.P. Misra, Former Vice Chancellor, Allahabed University, 35/1, Stanley Road, Allahabad.

Ravi S. Singh, Associate Professor, Department of Geography, Faculty of Sciences, Banaras Hindu University, Varanasi-221005, U.P.
Email: ravisingh.geog@gmail.com, ravi_geog_bhu@yahoo.com

Shahab Fazal, Associate Professor, Department of Geography, Aligarh Muslim University, Aligarh, U.P. Email: essfazal@rediffmail.com

S.K. Pal, University Professor, Agronomy, Birsa Agricultural University, Kanke, Ranchi-834006, Jharkhand.

Sudesh Nangia, UGC Emeritus Fellow, CSRD, JNU, New Delhi.
Email: nangia42@hotmail.com

Suresh Misra, Chair Professor and Chairman, Centre for Consumer Studies, Indian Institute of Public Administration, New Delhi.
Email: drsureshmisra@gmail.com

Surya Kant, Professor of Geography, Panjab University, Chandigarh-160014.
Email:suryak@pu.ac.in

Sushma Bomjan: E-4, Foch Square, R.K. Ashram Road, Gole Market, New Delhi,
Email: sushmabomjan@yahoo.com

Dr. K.V. Sundaram: A Tribute to a World-class Geographer-cum-Development Planner

M. VELAYUTHAM
Chairman, Bhoovigyan Vikas Foundation
Former President, Indian Society of Soil Science
Former Director, National Bureau of Soil Survey and Land Use Planning (ICAR)
Former Executive Director, M.S. Swaminathan Research Foundation

---

I was fortunate to come in contact with Dr. K.V. Sundaram in 1999. He was then the president of the National Association of Geographers, India (NAGI). I was the Director of the National Bureau of Soil Survey and Land Use Planning (NBSS&LUP), Indian Council of Agricultural Research (ICAR). His passion for sustainable development and judicious management of Natural resources was so exhorting that we at the NBSS&LUP readily agreed to host the Annual Convention of NAGI and a National conference on sustainable development at Nagpur in January 2000.

The convention and the conference was inaugurated by Hon'ble Shri Sompal ji, Member of the Parliament. The Nagpur Declaration of the conference recommended for the establishment of a Non-Government Organization for promoting "caring for Mother Earth". Thus, Dr. Sundaram with the support of numerous delegates founded the "Bhoovigyan Vikas Foundation (BVF)—Foundation for Earth Sciences Development" and registered it as an NGO on *16th* August 2000 at Nagpur.

As Founder-Chairman of BVF, Dr. Sundaram has been the driving force for the various professional and advocacy activities and conferences towards. Saving our Mother Earth, Saving our Planet. The establishment of a Museum of Earth, Man and Environment, a model for which is already taking shape at Raipur; Growth-centre approach to Regional Development; Auto-Kinetic model of Rural Renaissance in India; Establishment of an independent National Centre for Earth Care Policies for which he has prepared a visionary Blue-print.

As Chief of the Multi-level Planning Division of the Planning Commission,

Government of India, as member of the State Planning Board, Karnataka (1998-99) and as Chairman, Committee on Decentralised Planning, Government of Tamil Nadu (1997), his contributions on Decentralised Bottom-up and inclusive planning process have been seminal and have become well institutionalised now in the country's planning process.

As a soil scientist and Co-Chairman of the BVF—it has been a learning experience for me to gain insights from him into "the Geography of Soil" for sustainable development from physical, Anthropological, Economic and Ecological perspectives.

His passion, zeal and advocacy for an independent centre for Earth Care Policies in India are so abiding, absorbing, inspiring and exhorting that I cannot but reproduce below the poem, "Heavenly Earth—A Prayer", written by him in the BVF Discussion paper (2004) entitled, "Policies for our Plundered Planet—Some Pathways to the Future":

Heavenly Earth—A Prayer

(*Adapted from Rabindranath Tagore's Gitanjali*)

Where the mind is without fear and the head is held high;
Where knowledge is free;
Where the world has not been broken up into fragments by narrow domestic walls;
Where the Earth retains its greenery, sanctity and natural beauty;
Where birds in freedom sing and chirp without fear;
Where all living species and life support systems co-exist without threat and extermination;
Where man's greed, does not overtake his need;
Where the Earth's diversity and vitality are preserved and protected;
Where man lives in perfect harmony with the bounties of nature, within the carrying capacity of the Earth;
Where man listens to the cry of an ailing Earth—"*Avani-Dhwani*" and acts with veneration and respect for natural laws;
Where man uses Vasundhara's resources with restraint and wisdom;
Where the Earth's precious resources and fragile ecosystems are managed with prudence and care for a sustainable future;
Where humans desist from causing air and water pollution and increasing economic toxicity;
Where tireless striving stretches its arms towards conservation, preservation and scientific management of natural resources;
Where governments, U.N. entities, the private sector and, the civil society march in unison, towards the goal of sustainable development;
Where man learns to produce and consume wisely and sustainably, and holds the Earth as a '*Treasure in Trust*' for the future generations;

Where a benign Science and Technology is truly harnessed for promoting sustainable development and a livable planet;
Where human leadership is able to rise above the narrow domestic walls of caste, religion, community and exploitation of Man by Man;
Where mega-cities, metropolises, slums and shanty towns yield place to a Micropolitan-centred sustainable human settlement pattern of development;
Where Nations share the bounties of Mother Earth in just and equitable proportions in the global system;
Where women's potentials are harnessed for environmental governance, through emancipation and participation in National and International ecosystems management, and control of environmental degradation;
Where the unsustainable use of our finite natural resources is effectively controlled to reduce their depletion;
Where "*water wars*" are averted by ensuring Water and Food security through a steady supply of water for safe drinking and productive irrigation;
Where equity and justice in the use and control of water are ensured through people-centred Watershed development approach and inter-linking of river basins;
Where "Village Swaraj", with the just devolution of powers and finances, manages all local affairs and the civil society takes over the management, and control of local projects with active public participation;
Where the voices of the poor and the disadvantaged groups are listened to with justice and freedom;
Where the clear stream of reason has not lost its way into the dreary desert sand of dead habit;
Where the mind is led forward by THEE into ever-widening thought and action towards sustainable development and sustainable lifestyles;
Into that *heavenly earth*, my *Father*, let our ecosystems awake.

(By K.V. Sundaram)

May Dr. Sundaram's dream of a centre for Earth Care Policies in India fructify with Public, Corporate and Political Support and come true soon. May his guidance and counsel inspire Bhoovigyan Vikas Foundation, Delhi for many more years.

Chennai
18-3-2010

M. Velayutham

Dr. K.V. Sundaram: A Journey

At the outset, I would like to start with a quote from Late Dr. K. Venkatasubramanian, an eminent scholar and educationist: "*covering over a period of half a century, Dr. Sundaram has traversed a bumpy road characterized by relentless striving towards greater accomplishments*". (*Foreword, The Trodden Path*). His journey witnessed major turning points in his career-migration from academic stream to the planning stream as a policy-planner in government and international organizations, and finally, as the Founder of an Earth Care Foundation. Spanning over close to six decades, his path is studded with contributions, which can be clearly seen through in each decade distinctly, covering vast spectrum of planning development paradigm. Through the prism of time, the following paragraphs bring out some important aspects of his journey as a planner, based on his narration of each instance on several occasions, which is captured in his landmark book titled—*The Trodden Path*.

1950s: CONCEPT OF SERVICE CENTRES AND COMMUNITY OF INTEREST AREAS

Born on 30th November 1929, Dr. K.V. Sundaram completed his Master's degree in Geography in 1951 and registered as a Research Scholar in the Department of Geography in the University of Madras. Hardly within a month, he was compelled to join a new college started at Karaikudi (Ramnad District) as a Lecturer in Geography. The college had been started by a great philanthropist of Tamil Nadu, Dr. R.M. Alagappa Chettiar, who donated a major portion of his wealth to building up a educational complex near his native town. He took up this job on the understanding from the University that he can continue his research work on "Agricultural Geography of Cumbam Valley". Incidentally, this research site was also close to his place of work, Karaikudi, and his Professor, Dr. George Kurien, also approved the arrangement of his working in the college and at the same time pursuing the research work. Professor V.L.S. Prakasa Rao, a well-known name in geography, was later appointed as Reader in Geography in the University of Madras and he became his research guide.

From 1952 to 1957, he worked on his Ph.D. thesis which was intensely fieldwork oriented. As in all socio-economic research, the first phase of the work was data collection and his guide had instructed that unit area of his study should be Taluk (Tehsil) and village. The very first task was "Spatial Cognition" through mapping techniques and to discover the "crop combination patterns" and then to select sample villages from each crop combination region for detailed study. In those days, data collection, mapping, and cartographic exercise were laborious methods in geographic research. Even the data collection was a highly rigorous and time consuming experience, since talukwise data had to be copied from the village-wise statistics maintained in the Tahsildar's office. Since he was a part-time researcher, this alone took three years. In any case, when he went through all these ordeals and more or less completed even the study of sample villages, it took nearly five years and he was ready to write the thesis. According to university rules, a research scholar was expected to intimate the university authorities six months in advance about the proposed date of submission of the thesis, duly certified by the Research Guide. A fee of Rs. 100 was also to be paid along with this intimation. When he did so, he received a prompt reply from the University Registrar saying that according to the statute of the university he was not qualified to submit a research work done as a faculty member from an affiliated college. The university rules (framed in 1860s) had stipulated that only members of the faculty working either in the university departments or in constituent colleges of the university were eligible to conduct research studies for Ph.D. degrees.

Meanwhile, in order to come out of that situation he had taken interest in the field of urban planning. He studied the Community travel pattern around the Karaikudi town, which was a market town with Saturday being the market day. He found that the surrounding villagers used to visit the town on the market day to sell their produce and buy their requirements and at the end of the day, they would complete their trip to the town by seeing a cinema show in one of the two picture halls available in that town. That was the only source of entertainment in those days. A bullock cart carrying the advertisement of the picture of the week used to make rounds, with the beating of drums, to the villages during the week days, announcing the picture being screened, distribute leaflets and paste the posters in those villages from which the clients used to come. This marked the area of influence of the town and it struck him that the mapping of that area would delineate the hinterland of the town. It was in those years that two studies appeared in the Annals of the Society of American Geographers, describing how the hinterlands of New York and Boston cities in USA were delineated using frequency of telephonic calls from rural hinterland, as the criterion for delineating their city regions he wrote a critique on these studies, saying that in developing countries like India, where telephonic communication in the rural areas was almost non-existent, simple methods like the one used for Karaikudi, would be appropriate.

That was the time when preparations were afoot for the first Master Plan of Delhi, a unique venture with technical assistance from the Ford Foundation. They were looking for an Indian counterpart to join the Master Plan team under the leadership of the famous American Planner, Albert Meyer. Dr. K.V. Sundaram was one among those selected for the job, on a "one year assignment". He was asked to come to Delhi in 1958 and since then, there were several developments. A Town Planning Organisation was set up under the Ministry of Health and he was fully drawn into the Central Government service.

The major task assigned to him in the First Master Plan of Delhi was to conduct a rural survey in the hinterland of urban Delhi consisting of more than 300 villages. He had the privilege to work directly under Albert Meyer, who also became the architect of the community development movement in India and was closely advising Prime Minister Pandit Jawaharlal Nehru.

For preparing the rural development plan, KVS submitted a note for rural surveys, which would lead to the perception of a hierarchically conceived rural development framework with service centres, on the basis of Christaller's concept advocated in Germany. Albert Meyer called this as the "village cluster" programme and guided in formulating the methodology and approach.

Thus, he moved from the deep South to the distant North, in search of a new profession and career. It marked a big change, a movement from the familiar academic path to that of development planning. In those days, for social scientists, job opportunities outside the realm of teaching were quite limited. Policy and planning studies in the developing countries were in their infancy. With an unknown future before him, his one of the favourite quotes justifies the beginning of his journey.

> "*Two roads diverged in a wood, and I took the one less travelled by*"
> —*Robert Frost*

The work on the First Master Plan of Delhi was completed in 1960. As a first exercise in Regional Metropolitan Planning accomplished by an interdisciplinary team of planners it was highly acclaimed as an innovative endeavour with great lessons for planning for the future. Taking lessons from this exercise, a similar venture was launched for Calcutta.Metropolitan Area.

As one who had participated in the Delhi exercise, KVS wrote a critique on the interdisciplinary teamwork experience. This idea was further reinforced and took shape when a new journal titled "*Interdiscipline*" appeared on the scene from the Gandhian Institute of Development Studies at Varanasi, edited by Prof. Hans Christopher of South Asian University at Heidelberg, West Germany.

1960s: ERA OF SPATIAL PLANNING

The Government of India took a decision that the Town and Country Planning Organisation, which prepared the First Master Plan for Delhi with the assistance of Ford Foundation, would continue as a Central Government organization to oversee the implementation of the Master Plan. Another organization called the "Central Regional and Urban Planning Organisation" (CRUPO) was set up. This was conceived as a multi-disciplinary organization with an economist, a geographer, a sociologist and a few architect planners. One of the first regional planning projects undertaken was the Rajasthan Canal Colonization Project. It was undertaken in the virgin area of the Thar Desert of Rajasthan, coming under the command of Rajasthan Canal which was under construction. In the wake of the development, a highly coordinated, balanced and functionally efficient hierarchical pattern of settlements, had to be planned for, consisting of villages and towns. He worked as Project Coordinator for this highly prestigious project under the leadership of the famous Town and Country Planner in India, Mr. C.S. Chandrasekhara.

For establishing the norms of planning for this area planning exercise, he studied the settlement pattern in an identical tract in the arid zone of Rajasthan, viz., The Ganga Canal of Ganganagar district, where development had come about automatically for the existing settlements. Thus, the Rajasthan canal planning was a great experience in adaptive and proto-type planning. The President of India, Dr. S. Radhakrishnan inaugurated the Rajasthan Canal Project and KVS had the good fortune to explain the Master Plan for the Development of this area.

In the late 1960s and early 1970s, the academic discussions centred around the role of Growth Poles and Growth Centres in regional development and planning. For alleviating regional inequalities in the developing countries and for restructing the rural regions and putting them in functioning order, it was felt by many regional planners that a deliberate process of decentralized concentration of functions in '*punctiform*' locations would be needed to spearhead spatial dynamics and development. This led to a number of studies on Spatial Planning. At the same time, some developments which were happening in some developing countries, such as the establishment of industrial complexes in backward areas, it was noted, had resulted in adverse 'back-wash effects'. In India, Roy Burman's study of the impact of Rourkela Steel project in the tribal area of Orissa brought out such adverse social process in the wake of economic change in backward areas. An international organization called "United Nations Research Institute of Social Development" (UNRISD) in Geneva (Switzerland) promoted a number of studies in different countries, both developed and developing, to get a better feel of the forces and determinants of spatial change. In India, this organization sponsored a study in 1963-64 to investigate the feasibility of Growth Centre Strategy in a backward tribal region. At that time, KVS was working in the Central Regional and Urban Planning Organisation (CRUPO) and was engaged in a study in the Dandakaranya region, a region of forest-tribal economy in Central India. KVS got associated with Prof. R.P. Misra, for the prestigious UNRISD Project.

It was a daring venture which took them to fieldwork in the Bastar district, referred to as "an unknown backwater of the river of Indian history" by a British collector W.V. Grigson, who made a long tour of the area and presented a detailed description of the area, the people, their customs, manners etc. in his book "*The Maria Gonds of Bastar*". These tribes occupy the rugged and mountainous area known as "*Abujhmarh*", meaning literally "the unknown highlands". It is a little known area inhabited by the *Abujhmarhias*, representing the "stone-age culture". Against official advice, they walked to this area and met the tribals and talked to them with the aid of an interpreter. They had few material possessions, consisting of their dress (just a loin cloth), earthen pots, baskets, wooden stools, knives, bows and arrows. They practiced shifting agriculture. Their requirements from the outside world were few—some salt, sugar and kerosene. They preferred to be left alone and objected to interference by outsiders.

The Bastar study proved to be a very interesting one. The conclusion was drawn that for the development of highly backward tribal areas, like the Bastar District, social development was more relevant and the spatial framework of settlement structure must be decided after taking note of the existing consumer travel patterns in the tribal society. The conclusion indicated that the spatial structure must be conceived in terms of a 5-tier decentralized pattern of "Social development nuclei", hierarchically conceived in terms of Central Villages, Service Towns, Market Towns, Growth Points and Growth Centres.

1970S: REGIONAL PLANNING AND SPATIAL INEQUALITIES

In the late 1970s, under the "Indo-Soviet Commission on collaboration in the field of Social Sciences", two Symposia were organized, one at Tblisi/Baku (USSR) in 1978 and the other at New Delhi in 1980. He was invited to both symposia. A select team of five social scientists under the leadership of Prof. Moonis Raza left for USSR for a 15-day seminar on Regional Development and Planning. KVS wrote this paper for the Tblisi Symposium. Since territorial division of labour is an outcome of the regional development process, the paper identified three important pace setters, viz. the structural changes in economy and society, spatial interaction and multiplier and linkage effects that promote regional development.

In the 1970s, Prof. V.L.S. Prakasa Rao, Head, Department of Geography, University of Delhi established close links with British Geographers in the various universities in Great Britain. This led to a bilateral agreement to hold Indo-British Geography Seminars alternatively in India and Britain at intervals of two to three years. The first Indo-British Seminar was held at New Delhi in December, 1972 with "Rural Urban Interaction" as the theme and with mutual participation of ten researchers from each side.

K.V. Sundaram was one of those invited for this seminar. In consultation with Prof. Prakasa Rao, who led the Indian Team, KVS chose an innovative theme, i.e. 'Urban Village', which had not been researched upon before by many Geographers. The term 'Urban Village' refers to a 'relict village' absorbed into the urban area during the course of urban expansion and thus transported 'into the urban setting' and undergoing transformation. One of the urban villages in New Delhi—Kotla Mubarakpur, for which a Re-development Plan was being drawn up by the Town and Country Planning Organisation was chosen for this study. It provided insights into certain important, but obscure aspects of urbanization, both from geographical as well as sociological point of view.

The focus of the study was on Rural-Urban Interaction and the resulting transformations in the village, both in the human habitat as well as in lifestyles and the social milieu of the local residents. The transformations included changes in (a) land use, (b) the major landscape elements of the village, (c) the occupational structure of the inhabitants, (d) the intensity of flows of people, goods and services, and (d) changes in life styles and social milieu.

The study of the Urban Village received great appreciation from the Britishers. Later in 1978-79, this research contribution paved the way for a prestigious Senior Fellowship of the status of a Visiting Professor by the Nuffield Foundation, London, to pursue his post-doctoral studies in the Centre of South Asian Studies, University of Cambridge at U.K. This enabled him to write a book "*The Geography of Underdevelopment—The Spatial Dynamics of Underdevelopment*".

The year 1970 was a defining moment and a turning point in his official career, when many events happened in quick succession. Generally speaking, the period 1970-80 represented an era characterized by an upsurge in urban and regional development research. In 1971, the United Nations Centre for Regional Development at Nagoya (Japan) was set up, in pursuance of the terms of ECOSOC Resolution 1086c (XXXIX) and 114 (XLI), which called for global action to promote regional development, and Resolution 1582(L) that provided guidelines for its establishment.

Although the bulk of his writing work was completed during his stay at Cambridge, he could finalise the manuscript of the study for publication only by 1983. It was published by the Concept Publishing Company under the title "Geography of Underdevelopment—The Spatial Dynamics of Underdevelopment". The book consists of two parts. Part I deals with the conceptual framework and Part II contains the case studies of five countries—Malaysia, the Philippines, Thailand, Indonesia and India. The concluding chapter of the book (Chapter 10) synthesizes the "lessons of experience".

Dr. B.H. Farmer wrote in his Foreword to the book as follows:

> "It is a great privilege, and gives me much pleasure, to be asked to write a Foreword for Dr. K.V. Sundaram's *magnum opus*, his *Geography of Underdevelopment: The Spatial Dynamics of Underdevelopment.*
>
> I first met Dr. Sundaram at the First Indo-British Geographical Seminar held in Delhi in 1972 (having been delayed for a year by the Bangladesh War of 1971). He impressed me, as he impressed other British participants previously unaware of him and his work, as a man of great ability destined to make a great contribution to geography, to the study of development, and to his country...

> Dr. Sundaram's book is to be warmly commended to geographers of development and of South and Southeast Asia (from which he drawn his case studies); to students of development in other disciplines (some of whom are still insufficiently aware of geographical and spatial dimensions in their work); and to planners, politicians and administrators of development. I hope that it will have the very considerable intellectual and practical impact that it deserves."

In October 1970, the Ministry of Works, Housing and Urban Development, Government of India, deputed K.V. Sundaram for a month-long International Seminar on "Physical and Town Planning in overall Development" organized by the German Foundation for Developing Countries in Berlin (West Germany). This programme had been conceived in the nature of a training programme for mid-career officials in government in the developing countries and provided a good exposure to them on how urban planning was being carried out in the Western countries. It contributed to a two-way learning process, by which the developed and developing countries were able to engage themselves in a "development dialogue", which gave new impetus to cooperation in the field of physical, regional and town planning. It widened his understanding of urban and regional planning and enabled him to contribute a number of research papers, bearing on innovative themes. In 1973, the United Nations Centre for Regional Development (UNCRD), Nagoya, Japan, invited him for a one-year assignment as Faculty Member/Consultant. During this period, he worked on a research study on "Growth of Medium Size Towns in relation to Rural Development: Selected case studies in Japan, the Philippines and India".

He spent two terms of residence at the Centre of South Asian Studies in the University of Cambridge from March to May 1978 and again from April to June 1979. This enabled him to complete a work. During 1973-74, he was a Consultant to the United Nations Centre for Regional Development (UNCRD) at Nagoya and later to FAO/UN. During this period he visited a number of countries in South and South-east Asia.

1980: MULTI-LEVEL PLANNING AND MICRO-LEVEL DEVELOPMENT

His interest in Decentralized Multilevel Planning has been kindled since the 1970s through many events and circumstances in his life. Among them, special mention goes to late Prof. Sukhumoy Chakravarti's seminal paper on the subject in 1970 and his subsequent appointment in the Indian Planning Commission in 1973, with the major responsibility for Multi-level Planning and area development. The seventies and eighties were critical times for the Planning Commission, when several ideas on multilevel/area development/micro level (district and block) planning were circulating. In this, he played a crucial role, by conducting policy analysis and studies and writing extensively on the subject. In this manner he furthered policy decision-making on several vital issues. This was also the period, when certain important National Committees were appointed by the Planning Commission to deliberate on the relevant issues of the time and advise the Centre and the States on taking several forward steps. These Reports have become milestones. These included the Working Group on Block Level Planning (known as Dantwala Committee,1977), the Working Group on District Planning (known as Hanumantha Rao Committee, 1982) and the Committee to review the existing arrangements for Rural Development and Poverty Alleviation Programmes (CAARD) (G.V.K. Rao Committee, 1985). In all these committees, KVS played a very important role as an actor, facilitator and scribe in various capacities as Division Chief/Member-convener/Permanent Invitee, etc. in preparing discussion papers, drafting reports, making case studies and preparing guidelines for state governments. During this period he also authored a book (with Prof. R.P. Misra) on Multi-level Planning and Integrated Rural Development in India, 1980, which was the first ever published document on this subject at that time. Gradually, a district planning process also evolved in some States in the country. It must be emphasized that those were the formative years and several actions pursued at the Planning Commission level acted as a 'catalyst' and served to push the process of multi-level planning in a meaningful direction.

During this period he brought out two significant papers. The first one titled "Multilevel Planning and the Two-way Planning Process" as a Concept Paper originally prepared for inclusion in a book edited by Lata Chatterjee and Peter Nijamp titled "*Urban and Regional Policy Analysis in Development Countries*" (Gower Publishing Co., England, 1983). Later, this paper underwent several changes, until a theory of multilevel planning emerged as a result of several experiments in local level planning. His book on "Multi-level Planning—Principles and Practice—Asian and African Countries" published in 1997, reflects the quintessence of his life-time work and experience in this field.

The second paper which is titled "The Chemistry of Micro-level Development" was written in 1985. The Planning Commission appointed him as the Leader of the Study Team to analyse the Kundrakudi experience. His report to the Planning Commission was published under the title "Towards Improved Local Level Planning for Rural Development—Lessons from some experience", (Planning Commission, New Delhi, 1986). The emphasis of this paper was on the peculiar combination or "mix" of factors and circumstances which he called as Technocratic, Academic and Democratic Mix (TADMIX) that led to the success of this story of rural development. His report on "Kundrakudi" was prescribed as an "Essential Reading" in the Training Programmes organized by the Lal Bahadur Shastri National Academy of Public Administration, Mussoorie. Later, when he joined the FAO, it was included as a training material in several training programmes on decentralized agricultural planning in Asian and African countries. In the year 1987, he rose to the level of Chief Technical Advisor (FAO) to Nepal and remained their till 1990.

1990s: DEVELOPMENT FROM WITHIN AND DECENTRALISED PLANNING

From 1991 to 1995, he was on various Consultancy assignments in African and Asian countries for FAO, CIRDAP, ESCAP, ICIMOD and the World Bank. These consultancies related to projects on development from below and bottom-up planning. It was while in African countries, that he realized that it was the continuing dependency of these countries on the developed industrial world (i.e. the 'dependency syndrome') that was responsible for their chronic state of underdevelopment. Many African leaders, with whom he interacted, agreed with this view.

In 1997, the National Association of Geographers, India, was holding its 19th Geography Congress at Thiruvananthapuram, Kerala State and he was invited to deliver the Prof. Prakasa Rao First Memorial Lecture. His lecture dealt with the theme of "Area Development", i.e. the systematic and scientific study of "areas" and their natural resources potentials and the spatial dimensions of development phenomena, which constitute the core or heart of Geographical Studies. India's programme interventions in backward area planning was critically analysed and a 'transition growth strategy' to take the backward area development through successive steps of radical changes over time was advocated. The lack of a 'collaborative or participatory mode' of planning was pin-pointed as one of the principal weaknesses in realizing the full potentials of area development. The hope for better performance in the planning and development of backward area was expressed in the wake of the democratic and institutionalization process undergoing transformation in India with the empowerment of local self-governments, following the enactment of the 73rd and 75th Constitutional Amendments in 1992. The lecture urged upon the professionals in Geography to orchestrate their efforts in a united and unified manner and to put their discipline to its most intensive practical use. Following this, the Congress unanimously elected him as their President for the two years 1998 and 1999. It was termed as "Return of the Native".

The 20th Indian Geography Congress held its Annual Convention at Gorakhpur during December 28-30, 1998 and he delivered the Presidential address on issues relating to 'Sub-National Development and Underdevelopment'. It encompassed a critical analysis of the economic reforms and the changing spatial structure of our economy, the strategies adopted in our Five Year Plans to overcome the backwardness in selected problem areas (the Hill areas, the Drought-prone areas, the Tribal areas, the North-East Region, the Irrigation Command areas, the Border areas and the Desert Areas) and the revitalization of Panchayats involving empowerment of the people and changes in the style, stance and substance of planning at the regional and micro levels. He also elaborated on the need for the Geography discipline to become qualitatively more different, scientifically sharper and fully equipped with more modern tools and techniques and thus respond to a changing globally integrated economy. He also outlined a vision and action programme for the development of backward areas.

In 1999 he was invited by the Prof. R.N. Dubey Foundation located at Allahabad to deliver a series of three lectures in memory of Professor R.N. Dubey, who was the first Professor of Geography (1953-1958) in Allahabad University. He delivered these lectures during 15-16, November 1999, titled as follows:

1. The Search for Spatial Order in Sub-National Planning
2. Removal of Regional Disparities
3. Planning in Oceanic Circles

During 19-21 January 1999, a workshop on "Decentralization, Local Governance and Rural Development" was organized by the Asian Institute of Technology (AIT), Bangkok and the United Nations Capital Development Fund (UNCDF) at the AIT, Bangkok. This workshop sought to bring together the two major sets of policy themes, viz., Decentralization, and Local Governance, as practiced in the countries of South and South East Asia. Policy-makers and Practitioners from these countries were invited for the sharing of experience, successes and failures and to understand the similarities and differences between country experiences. The Indian team for this Conference consisted of KVS, Prof. D.M. Nanjundappa, Deputy Chairman, State Planning Board, Government of Karnataka, Dr. S.S. Meenakshisundaram, Joint Secretary to the Prime Minister and Dr. M. Govinda Rao, Director, Institute of Social and Economic Change, Bangalore. The workshop enabled him to bring together and update earlier work and present the latest state-of-the-art of decentralized planning in the country. The workshop papers were first published in a special issue of the International Journal, "Regional Development Dialogue" of the United Nations Centre for Regional Development (UNCRD) in Nagoya, Japan (Vol. 20, No. 2, December 1999). Later, a book was published as the proceedings of the International Workshop: "Decentralization, Local Governance and Rural Development", H.D. Kammier and Harvey Demaine (eds.), AIT, 2000.

A NEW MILLENNIUM (2000 ONWARDS): SUSTAINABLE DEVELOPMENT AND RURAL RENAISSANCE

The Twenty-first Indian Geographical Congress held at Nagpur during 2-4 January, 2000, was a great turning point. The delegates who had gathered in large numbers (more than 400) vociferously expressed their deep concern about the neglect of

Earth Sciences and Earth Scientists by the Planning Commission and other policy making bodies of the Government of India and urged that something should be done to bring about a change in the situation. A vigorous dialogue ensued and a suggestion was put forward, that since the various Earth Sciences were splintered and fragmented into a large number of professional societies and association, an "Umbrella Organisation" should be setup, which could interact with policy-making institution in the country. The methods of enhancing the image of the Earth Sciences and protecting the interests of Earth Scientists were debated at length. At the end, the conference reposed faith and confidence in him to initiate necessary action in this context. This marked the genesis of the Bhoovigyan Vikas Foundation as a consortium of Earth Sciences and an autonomous research organization. After considerable discussions with a number of senior professionals the Foundation was registered as a professional association at Nagpur.

The Foundation has, as its patrons, many eminent personalities of the country including Bharat Ratna (Late) Shri C. Subramaniam, Dr. M.S. Swaminathan, Dr. Mohan Dharia, Dr. K.C. Pant and Dr. R.A. Mashelkar. It is managed by a Governing Board consisting of Parliamentarian, Planners, Academicians, Scientists and Policy-decision makers.

The major objectives of the Foundation are:

- Policy-moulding through a "Think-tank", to suggest policy options and development alternatives for Earth Care Policies and Human Development;
- Awareness creation about the sanctity of Earth's natural resources and the need for inculcating an ethic of sustainable development among the students and citizens, through Earth Care mission-oriented "Museums of Earth, Man and Environment; and celebration of significant event like the "Earth Day" to establish harmony with nature;
- Enhancing the image of the Earth Sciences and Earth Sciences and Earth Scientists through institution of prestigious awards and prizes; and
- Promoting various academic and support activities, such as research collaboration, exchange programmes, seminars etc.

The Foundation was launched at New Delhi on 21 April, 2001 with celebrations marking the First Earth Day of the millennium in which more than 5000 school children participated and took pledge as Earth Trustees. Three International Conferences have been held under the aegis of the Foundation both at New Delhi, one on "Sustainable Development and Sustainable Life Styles" during 22-23 April, 2001 and the Second International Conference on "Sustainable Agriculture, Water Resources Development and Earth Care Policies" held on 18-20 December, 2002. Third International Conference was organized in Hyderabad with a theme "Rural India Achieving MDGs and Grassroots Development" during November 10-12, 2005.

Another fall-out of the Nagpur Congress was the genesis of the idea of a "Geographical Museum" or "The Museum of Earth, Man and Environment." In his introductory remarks in the Congress, he referred to the great educational role that could be played by such museums in our country and particularly their contemporary relevance, which the Earth Eco-systems were under severe strain. He advocated the concept of Open Air Museums, which should bring out the cataclysmic problems and the stressed relationships that have emerged as a consequence of the interface of Man with Earth, resulting in great problems such as land degradation, water depletion, air pollution, loss of biodiversity, loss of eco-specific knowledge systems, loss of local conservation practices and the larger problem of climate change. Following this, the Chhattisgarh State Government decided to setup an Open Air Museum (Muktangan) and has earmarked a site of 350 acres of land for this purpose. The Muktangan has already been initiated at its designated place, close to Raipur, Chhattisgarh.

During December 28-30, 2001, the National Association of Geographers (India) held its 23rd Indian Geography Congress at the Department of General and Applied Geography of Dr. H.S. Gour University, Sagar (Madhya Pradesh). He was invited to deliver the first Prof. N.P. Ayyar Memorial Lecture in this congress.

For this lecture, he chose a theme relevant for the new millennium, viz. "Rural Renaissance" and called for a mass movement for bringing about changes in the theory and practice of rural development. In this context he advocated the concept of "Rural Space", i.e. 'village clusters' and a spatially oriented strategy of development. In this approach he sought to weave together many of his personal field experiences as well as lessons learnt in rural development from different countries—India, Nepal, Bangladesh, the Philippines, South Korea, Uganda, Ghana and Tanzania, advocating a methodology of rural development emerging as an auto-kinetic development process, by establishing locally integrated economic circuits and engineering circular flows, chain effects and recycling the primary produce of the villages into at least the first stage of secondary lines of production in the village itself. In this manner, each village cluster could become a 'mini territorial production complex', seeking to achieve full employment for its inhabitants and environmentally sustainable development through an eco-development approach.

He has been conferred with the Life Time Achievement Award (2004) by the Centenarian Trust, Chennai for his contribution to the cause of promoting Sustainable Development and Earthcare. The National Association of Geographers India (NAGI) conferred on him the "Vachaspati Samman" (2008) for his contribution to the domain of geography, planning and sustainable development. Besides, he has been felicitated by numerous institutions and universities in India and abroad.

He was felicitated in October 1989 by the National Association of Geographers

(India) during its 11th Geography Congress at Delhi and by the Centre for Land Use Management (CLUMA) at Hyderabad in August 2003 for his contributions in Regional and Local level Planning. On his Sixtieth Birthday (1989) he was honoured by release of a book on "District Planning", as a tribute to his contributions to the theory and practice of District Planning. He is included in "Learned India—Men and Women of Achievements and Distinctions", by Asia International, New Delhi. He has also figured in the International Directory of Distinguished Leadership (Second Edition) for outstanding professional performance by the American Biographical Institute, U.S.A.

KVS held several positions of repute. He was Member in the State Planning Board, Karnataka (1998-99). He was also the Chairman, Committee on Decentralised Planning, Government of Tamil Nadu (1997) and was Member, Editorial Board, Indian Council of Social Science Research (ICSSR), New Delhi (1998-2003). He has 20 Books and 200 Research Papers to his credit on subjects like Decentralised Planning, Rural Development, Urban and Regional Planning, Natural Resources Development and Management and Earth Care Policies.

And the journey continues.....

Dr. Mrityunjay M. Jha

Introduction

This book is a tribute to Dr. K.V. Sundaram, the geographer-planner, an institution builder and a person of inspiring qualities of heart and mind. This Volume consisting of papers with diversified themes in the realm of development and geography is a befitting tribute to Dr. K.V. Sundaram, who contributed significantly in the areas of decentralized planning, rural development, sustainable development and earth care policies. The limited time and space, however, forces us to narrow down on a few issues confronting our country and society, from the perspective of application of geographical knowledge in planning, policies and programmes of development.

The articles received from eminent scholars have been grouped into four sub-themes, viz., Development Issues, Food Security, Rural-Urban Development, and Infrastructure Concerns. They are summarized below for a quick overview of the content and quality of the text inside.

SECTION I: DEVELOPMENT ISSUES

The principle goal of development policy is to create sustainable improvements in the quality of life for all people. Last six decades have been marked by a mix of pessimism and optimism about prospects for development. In so far as rising per capita income improves people's living standards, it is one among many development alternatives. The overarching aim of lifting the standards encompasses a number of more specific goals: bettering peoples health and educational opportunities, addressing livelihood issues and employment generation, promoting gender equality, ensuring a clean environment, promoting participatory approach to development and much more. It is recognized that development planning in India has to concentrate on effective mechanisms and instruments to reduce poverty, inequality; in the process create purchasing power and with it generate economic and social equality.

Challenging the prosperity of India, is the unfortunate truth that a large percentage of the population still lives in high risk and unpredictable environment. The basic objective of development is to ensure a balanced and ecologically sound micro-regional economy and polity. The productivity and the service delivery mechanisms needed to be improved and targeted programmes should be implemented in full sincerity. Providing better access to services, technology, education, health care and drinking water will reduce inequality, alleviate poverty for hundreds of millions of citizen's and add an additional engine of growth to India's empowerment and capacity building to achieve a sustainable and inclusive development. In spite of several programmes and schemes the state of rural India has not improved substantially, therefore we need to reorient our development priorities and policies as well and find urgent solutions to the problems to empower the people more so those living in the rural areas. The papers in this section address the core issues of development and suggest appropriate strategies to ensure that India gets out of the vicious cycle of poverty and unemployment. They advocate a paradigm shift in development strategy.

R.P. Misra in his paper on "Overcoming Environmental Crisis: Indian Culture shows the Way", highlights that global warming poses far more danger to mankind, than even terrorism as global warming may eliminate all life from planet earth including human beings. In his view modern civilization is full of conflicts and contradictions and in this process nature is the first target of attack of this civilization.

Arguing that the Indian concept of progress is different from the one currently in vogue he argues that today's development essentially means economic development. It means higher GDP, per capita income, and more consumption of goods. A progressive society is one whose values do not clash with these developmental values. Highlighting the ecological foundations of Indian culture he looks towards Gandhi to solve the current crisis. In his view Gandhi's seminal contribution lies in the alternative paradigm of development. He excavated Indian civilization from overburden of ignorance, rebuilt a new structure on the old foundation, and left it to the future generations to adopt, adapt and innovate. His genius encompassed all religious traditions of the world, for they were one and the same as far as the essentials were concerned. Gandhi's philosophy centres on Truth and Nonviolence. Search for Truth is the ultimate task of humanity and this must be done using nonviolence in its broadest form. His oft-cited quotation: 'Earth has enough to meet everyone's need but not everyone's greed' is the centerpiece of the worldview of ecology and humanism that we are looking for.

Concluding his paper he asserts that the first step in taking the society back to incorporation of the time-honoured Indian values lies in the educational system in India. Mahatma Gandhi offered a new concept of education wherein head, heart and hand could be trained to work in unison and give rise to creative human beings. He termed it *Nai Talim* or New Education. It was new in the sense that it was completely different from the Western model of education in vogue. *Nai Talim* laid great stress on pupils' contact with nature through manual work and on the concept of unity of life. The need is to inculcate values in the younger generation so that they respect nature.

Suresh Misra in his paper 'Sustainable Rural Development in India: Towards a Gandhian Framework' asserts that India lives in villages but even after six decades of independence the rural sector continues to be neglected and is in distress. Successive Five Year Plans though focused on rural development, have not been able to address the problems of the rural sector. The model of development that we initiated after the British left to a large extent does not suit our requirements and the rural areas have remained underdeveloped with the destruction of the economy, environment and the community life. In the process of growth, the development of rural areas has remained skewed. We need to search for alternative models. He is of the view that Gandhi has answers to many of the problems that are prevalent in the rural areas. The basic objective of sustainable rural development is to ensure the development of the individual, community and the society at large using local resources and in a balanced manner. The paper discusses the causes and consequences of rural destruction and provides a Gandhian framework for ensuring a sustainable rural development.

Sustainable human development necessarily rests on the equitable distribution of development benefits between men and women. India, as the rest of South Asia is infamous for its deeply rooted gender discrimination argues Nira Ramchandran in her paper on "Are Women and Men Equal Partners in Development? : Reality Checks from Rural India". The paper attempts to perform a quick reality check in a sample group of villages—not remote and isolated, but located within easy reach of the state capital. The assumption is that the empowerment status of women in these rural settlements will reflect the situation in villages elsewhere in the country, which have attained a certain level of development with access to basic infrastructure and communication, and are also exposed to urban influence. By implication, it may be assumed that women's empowerment in the more remote and backward areas of the country is likely to be correspondingly low.

Most development indicators are heavily skewed against women, whether one assesses the economic characteristics such as assets, wages or employment or looks at social indicators like nutrition status, health and education. Nira opines that much has been written on the need for women's empowerment. Policies have been framed, countless schemes implemented and large scale budgetary allocations made. The introduction of micro credit schemes and the formulation of women's Self Help Groups have transformed lives in villages, where they have been implemented. Yet the scales remain heavily weighted against women and poverty, itself, is now being described as "feminised".

The study is based on a household survey of six villages of the Vikasnagar Block in Dehradun District, Uttarakhand. The study brings out that mere provision of services targeted to women does not ensure utilization and hence, the achievement of the desired outcomes. The study reveals that the number of female headed households is disproportionately higher in lower income, asset less group. Restrictions on female mobility and gender disparities in wages continue to exist. High levels of anaemia among women and children and stunting and underweight among young children persist.

'Integrating Gender into Development Policies and Programmes', the paper by Sudesh Nangia indicates that lately gender issues have become an integral part of development programmes and policies, and within them the status of women in terms of equity and equality continue to be crucially related issues for the world community. In India, women form a vital part of the economy, directly or indirectly.

Despite progress along several key indicators, socio-economic data still demonstrates that women in India continue to be relatively disadvantaged in matters of survival, health, nutrition, literacy, job opportunities and asset formation. Broadly, the problem of women can be grouped into four categories—education, health, employment and issue of gender discrimination. A very large percentage of women are unskilled, therefore, restricting them to low-paid occupations. They generally have no control over land and productive assets. It is not unknown that in the rural areas of the country, female agricultural labourers are among the poorest sections of Indian society and on an average their wages are thirty to forty per cent lower than that of men.

Beginning around 1800, there were a series of movements to reform aspects of social, culture and religious beliefs that were perceived as impinging on human welfare and dignity. A series of efforts have been made since then by the Indian political and social leadership to improve women's position in society. Since independence, the government of India's policy on women's development has undergone various shifts of emphasis. The most significant change occurred in the mid 1980s, when there was a move towards equality and empowerment. There was the time when the 'Department of Women and Child Development' and its counterparts were formed in several states were set up. At the same time, women's development corporations were formed in several states to implement a new strategy of economic development for facilitating access to training, entrepreneurship development, credit, technical consultancy services and marketing facilities.

The main objective of this paper is to understand how gender issues have been integrated into research, and policies and programmes related to gender equity and equality.

In 'Development Disparity and Emerging Governance Issues and Challenges in the Post-Reform India', Surya Kant has examined the changes in India's economic plicies since 1990s in the light of its impact on the regional pattern of income and inequalities, pattern of poverty at the state level and its implications, and challenges having links with administration and bureaucracy. His observation that in India social and regional inequalities in income and consumption are widening in the post-reform phase, leads him to suggest counter-measures to mitigate such inequalities. They are strengthening the regulatory role of the state apparatus; higher investment in health, education and infrastructure development, specially in backward regions and deprived classes, reorganization of administrative units, and decentralization of administrative powers.

Ravi S. Singh in his paper 'Recent Scenario of Gender Patterns in Arunachal Pradesh' focuses on the gender disparity, which is one of the major problems faced by India. According to him every domain in human life is gendered. Initially this aspect was not addressed explicitly, however, in the contemporary context, gender is considered as one of the major concerns, which needs to be addressed through appropriate interventions. Highlighting the fallouts of gender identity he points out that gender based discriminations deprive womenfolk in numerous ways and ultimately they find themselves at unequal footing *vis-à-vis* the male counterpart. It is a common belief that tribal societies are free from this social evil.

The existing gender disparity in Arunachal Pradesh, which is dominated by the tribal communities, presents a unique case of investigation. In his paper Ravi seeks to unravel the position of women in Arunachali society. He opines that Arunachali women are no better than fellow women in other parts of India. Though valued for agricultural production and reproduction of children, they have no property rights nor are they allowed to perform sacred rituals. The prevalent system of bride price clearly reflects the general perception in the state that women are purchasable commodities. Women are deprived of endowments-entitlements resulting into her poor capabilities. The findings of the study reinforce the saying that "women are discriminated from womb to tomb."

In 'Development and Environment: A Challenge for 21st Century', Sudesh Nangia feels that the relationship between the two, i.e. development and environment can be understood in terms of area/region, people, economy and technology. Development is a dynamic phenomenon and being time and space-specific, is best conceived when segmented into structure, process and stage. The major issues confronting the process of development and its consequential impact on environment revolve around high consumption; high population growth; mismanagement of natural and human resources; sustainable development; gender sensitivity of development policies and programmes etc. unbalanced regional development, formation of transitional zones like rural-urban fringe, formation of slums and changing land values point towards a highly variable quality of life and quality of environment. Last but not the least, the author stresses upon the basic human values, which need to be nurtured and dovetailed into development, to make development environment-friendly.

SECTION II: FOOD SECURITY

Food security refers to the availability of food and one's access to it. A household is considered to be "food secure", when its occupants do not live in hunger or fear of starvation. Food Security does not exist, when people are undernourished as a result of the physical unavailability of food, their lack of social or economic access to adequate food, and/or inadequate food utilization. This truncation of human development undermines a country's potential for economic development—for generations to come.There are strong, direct relationships among agricultural productivity, hunger, and poverty. Eradicating two injustices: hunger and poverty, requires an understanding of the ways in which they get interconnected. Hunger, and the malnourishment that accompanies it, prevents poor people from escaping poverty, because it diminishes their ability to learn, work, and care for themselves and their family members.

Between 1993-94 and 2004-05, the percentage of people living below poverty line fell from 36 per cent to 27.5 per cent, according to government data. But a large chunk of people who live just above the poverty line face the risk of sliding back to their earlier status. This is similar to what World Bank said: that "seven years worth of poverty alleviation" could be reversed by rising prices. Globally, the price rise could push 150 million people into poverty, it said.

India remains a poor country, despite a few years of 9 per cent GDP Growth, and India faces severe economic challenges: galloping inflation and a slowdown in growth (due to meltdown somewhere seven seas away). India's economic growth has not reached all sectors of the population, especially those living in rural areas (i.e. economic growth has not trickled down). India ranks 66 out of 88 countries on the 2008 Global Hunger Index (GHI), released by IFPRI, far behind comparable developing countries as well as smaller, less diverse and resource deprived nations.

The five papers presented in this section pertains to food and livelihood security, throwing light on the role of ICT, food security in our planning paradigm, impact of globalization, regional cooperation and the role of employment opportunities. These papers are presented as under.

'Food Security: Grassroots Concerns' by Madaswamy Moni indicates that economic growth and poverty reductions were unimpressive during the 1960s and 1970s, as India was weakly integrated into the global economy and had relied heavily on planning and licensing. A perfect storm of food scarcity, global warming, rocketing oil prices and the world population explosion is plunging humanity into the biggest crisis of the twenty-first century, by pushing up food prices and spreading hunger and poverty from rural areas into cities. As of late 2007, increased farming for use in biofuels, world oil prices at more than $100 a barrel, global population growth, climate change, loss of agricultural land to residential and industrial development, and growing consumer demand in China and India, have pushed up the price of grain. Around the World, protests against soaring food and fuel prices are mounting. The poor are seeing their incomes squeezed as the global economy entered a slow down. The Asian Development Bank said that the economic progress achieved by many Asian countries could take an about-turn because of high food prices.

Most states in India are net importers of foodgrains. Improving agricultural productivity would improve food security. However, even in green revolution states such as Punjab, the agricultural productivity has declined. Moreover, agriculture is widely considered to be a part of life rather than an economic undertaking in densely populated states. India is committed to ensure food security for its citizen, and following a twin-track approach: (a) strengthening productivity and livelihoods, and (b) implementing social safety nets for those unable to provide for themselves. Right to Food Approach complements food security, in terms of food availability, accessibility and utilization with human dignity and cultural acceptability. This paper discusses several dimensions of food security in India with a focus on agriculture and application informatics for achieving sustainable agriculture and food security. It dwells upon National Food Security Mission (NFSM), Comprehensive District Agricultural Development Plan (CDAP), role of Agricultural Technology Management Agency (ATMA), Krishi Vigyan Kendras

(KVKs), National Rural Employment Guarantee Act (NREGA) 2005, impact of Agricultural Debt Waiver and Debt Relief (ADWDF) Scheme, 2008, improving agricultural productivity with an integrated policy framework, AGMARKNET and National Knowledge Portal, linking information with facilitating food security. An attempt has also been made to evaluate Impact of Economic Reforms on Food Security, globalisation and sustainable urban food security system, towards achieving a hunger free India.

In 'Globalisation of Food Prices', Gopal Krishan states that it was hard to anticipate that the early years of the twenty-first century will witness such a scenario of growing food insecurity, especially when the race between the field productivity and human fertility had decisively gone in favour of the former for the last about half a century. By a sharp turn of events, the early years of the twenty-first century experienced a phenomenal rise in food prices. Only a few could believe that Malthus would resurrect himself, in the manner of speaking. The basic human right to food was seen as having come under threat. Today the world has nearly a billion souls who are food insecure. The highest incidence of such insecurity is in Sub-Saharan Africa but South Asia and East Asia carry the largest number of people in this category. Ironical is it that virtually all the agricultural based countries are net importer of food and food insecurity is concentrated in rural areas where food is produced. This paper explains the food insecurity through change in land use, cropping pattern in developed and developing countries. It reasons out the manifold increase in global prices and its impact on food security of developing countries. The agricultural production and the factors influencing it are linked with the changing agricultural geography, which has been discussed in this paper.

K.V. Raman in 'Livelihood Security Concern in India: Development and Sustainability' maintains that sustainable livelihoods cover a range of sustainable paradigms like sustainable lifestyles, sustainable agriculture, sustainable community, sustainable economy etc. About seventy per cent of the 106 million people in India live in the rural areas and derive their livelihoods directly or indirectly from the 329 million hectares of land resources. Since food is so basic to human well-being, sustainable livelihoods, especially of the rural population, should envisage sustainable development of agriculture by widening employment opportunities, increasing income, improving health and enhancing the quality of life.

To enable people have access to food and better living standards, employment opportunities will have to increase. An important consequence of population growth and demographic changes in future will be the most significant increase in the working age group 15-64. Providing employment to such a huge population will be the biggest challenge India will face in the first half of this century.

For sustainable growth, the growth process will have to be (i) technologically sound, (ii) ecologically sustainable, (iii) environmentally friendly, (iv) economically viable, and (v) socially acceptable. Some activities like horticulture and animal husbandry including aquaculture when practiced in common property resources, serve both growth and equity objectives. Such activities are suitable for small farmers and women, for whom they provide additional income and employment. Sets of possible approaches for finding solutions to the paradoxical challenge are outlined in this paper. These include: (a) primary value addition of commodities at the household level like production of semi-processed foods, pickle making, sun-drying, packaging, etc.; (b) utilization of locally available resources like paddy-straw for mushroom growing, sericulture, goat rearing, dairying and milk production, backyard poultry for eggs and meat; (c) community aquaculture, floriculture and horticulture that includes production of fruits and vegetables; (d) effective use of CPRs, use of waste and degraded lands and community aquaculture; (e) protecting community biodiversity; (f) establish rural industries; (g) strengthening capital formation in agriculture; (h) value addition to agricultural products; (i) and establish market interface and promotion of value added agro-food production.

'Food Security in Five Year Plans of India' by Mrityunjay M. Jha has cautioned that for India, the second decade of the twenty-first century is going to be more challenging than ever before in terms of food security for the country at all levels, covering aspects of production for self-sufficiency, sustained employment opportunities for accessibility to food, sustained income for access to nutrition for all and food absorption in the households. The struggle for it will become daunting in the light of sustaining the economic growth momentum, trade liberalization, and declining subsidies among others.

During the last 5 decades, there has been two divergent views on the political democracies *vis-à-vis* quality of life. One section argues that political democracies are vulnerable to political instability, and that strong authoritarian are better at regulating new demands and introducing the economic interventions needed for industrialization. The centralized development planning has been debating of its merits and demerits. It was unanimously agreed that a national plan has to be an expression of a basic unity of purpose in the community. It is this unity which would constitute the ultimate sanction behind the plan, give it driving force and evoke the necessary sacrifice and effort on the part of members. There is no doubt that development is a complex process. India, being a democratic country, adopted the Five Year Plan route and considered it to be the basis for all development efforts that would lead to economic growth and well-being of its people, removing regional and sectoral disparity.

This paper is an attempt to review different aspects and efforts of our Five Year Plans that determined and influenced food security in our country. It briefly discusses the basic concepts of food security and related issues and then moves on to review all Five Year Plans in terms of their focus, and food security related aspects.

In his article on 'Food Security in South Asia: Demographic Policy and Regional Cooperation Issues', Mrityunjay Mohan Jha states that judged by the criteria of food insecurity and poverty, South Asia has the distinction of being the worst affected region. A large majority of the poor and the food-insecure people live in this part of the world, where the incidence of malnutrition is very serious. The region is also backward in terms of other social development indicators.

Throughout the developing world and specially in the South Asian countries the population growth has been regarded as the most vital parameters in the development process. In the recent years, food production has increased satisfactorily. South Asia as a whole has managed to keep its food production just ahead of population growth. However, during the last decade, the production of foodgrains has stagnated, pushing India and Bangladesh once again into the uncomfortable zone of food self-sufficiency. Along with the fluctuation in food production there is wide nutritional gap. A country like India, which is close to the level of self-sufficiency in food production, is still facing the problem of accessibility to food in year of globalization and liberalization. While food security at the national level is a necessary condition, it is not sufficient to ensure automatically that all the people have enough to eat. With increasing pressure over the limited usable land and non-farm employment very hard to find the problem of food insecurity get accentuated. The countries of this region face similar problems. India being the largest country having border with almost every country, needs to take lead in the areas of cooperation for achieving food security. This paper attempts to examine the population dynamics, food production and nutritional status for all countries in this region, and also discusses population and agricultural policies and reviews the regional cooperation issues for improving food security.

SECTION III: RURAL-URBAN DEVELOPMENT

Krishna Mohan in his article on 'Revolving Tribal Space in India: Some Reflections' asserts that tribal area is a misnomer. In reality it does not exist. The term tribal area, frequently used, is a construct formulated by human agencies. It denotes a space predominantly occupied by the communities known in India as scheduled tribes. The scheduling of tribes is an ongoing and perhaps never ending process. The tribal space is, therefore, undergoing the process of evolution on every change in schedule.

The present paper raises the following questions: Does tribal space exist or is created? How is tribal space evolving and what is its spatial spread? Is tribal space objectively delineated? The reference of tribal areas find place in our very First Five-Year Plan. However it refers to scheduled areas or tribal areas.

The distribution of tribal population on space has undergone tremendous change consequent to inclusion of large number of new groups in many new areas. The number of groups included in the list increased from 245 in 1950 to over 750 (including sub-tribes) in 2001. The proportion of tribal population increased from 5.36 per cent in 1951 to 8.2 per cent in 2001. Therefore, the tribal map has changed. The new map is very pertinent for the planners in implementing various projects. The new map reveals new areas and finds that many old areas considered as tribal now do not withstand the objective delineation. It is also revealed that tribal population living in many areas is not enumerated for the simple reason that tribals were not found there historically. It is surprising that contemporary spatial changes are ignored in planning.

Amit Kumar Singh in his paper on 'Urbanisation and Tribal Development: A Case Study of Ranchi District, Jharkhand' attempts to study the growing disparity (measured in socio-economic terms) between tribes living in Ranchi city of Jharkhand and its hinterland. The rapid pace of urbanisation which started after independence caused enormous uprooting of tribal population from their habitats and they lost their agricultural and forest based occupations. Among those who migrated to the city got absorbed into the low wage jobs. Their standard of living, hence, is much lower than the general city population. But those who are still living in the rural areas are far from modern development processes and their standard of living is even lower than their fellow tribes, who have migrated to the city. While analysing data, a significant variation in the availability of infrastructure and basic amenities has also been found in Ranchi district. A large number of villages of Ranchi district do not have accessibility to schools, hospitals, roads and other services. It is an unpleasant truth of India's development that most of the economic activities and basic services have significant urban bias. Jharkhand is no exception and most of the services are located in urban centres. So the tribals in rural areas are not able to get these benefits. This paper is based on the analysis of primary data to bring out micro regional differences and also focuses on the interventions reducing the socio-economic gap. Aspects of their overall tribal development have been also studied in detail.

In 'Exploring Sustainable Urban Development: A Regional Planning Approach', Nishith Srivastava weighs Push and Pull factors that instigate migration of population from rural to urban areas. The lack of alternative employment opportunities for the rural population in their respective villages is the prime factor. Increased pressure of population on land, because of sheer population growth, is important factor responsible for urban problems. One of the problems faced by cities is the growth of slums, which the author has projected in detail in case of Raipur City, the capital of newly created state of Chhattisgarh. In the discussion, the scholar has argued how a regional planning approach can assure a sustainable development and how the concept and delimitation of planning region, based on natural and human resources, could be considered for sustainable urban and regional planning.

'Representing Towns of Coimbatore District by GIS', paper jointly written by M. Saktivel, R. Sunil Kumar and K.S. Gopalakrishnan, provides classification, distribution pattern and functional hierarchy of towns in Coimbatore district of Tamil Nadu. The study presents a brief account of population growth (between 1981-2001) and functional classification of towns. The authors have observed that there is a high frequency of small towns in the Industrial centres. In preparing maps, the Geographical Information System has been made use of. The functional hierarchy of towns has been worked out using GIS. The study reveals that the towns can be categorized into six levels of hierarchy, while the first three orders are found more in urban agglomeration, the next three are more or less widely distributed in the district. From the distribution and functional hierarchy of towns, the authors have concluded a strong relationship between population and the number of functional establishments in the towns of Coimbatore district.

S.K. Pal and N.N. Singh in their article on 'Use and Management of Natural Resources for Sustainable Agriculture and Rural Development of Jharkhand' have underlined high potentials of the state for development on account of its rich land and mineral resources; water resources; crop combination and crop diversification are rampant but the author stressed on the lack of resources to be invested for the required inputs. They suggest that the technological options for rice substitution and crop diversification in rain-fed uplands are rain-water management, off-season ploughing, early sowing, closer spacing, timely fertilizer application, plant protection measures, early harvesting and proper soil-inter-cultural practices, apart from crop varieties and cropping-systems in relation to rainfall pattern and crop-growth period.

SECTION IV: INFRASTRUCTURE CONCERNS

'Land Use Planning for Sustainable Development' by Mridula Singh defines land as a physical entity in terms of its topography and spatial nature. A broader integrated view also includes natural resources: the soils, minerals, water and biota that the land comprises. These components are organized in ecosystems which provide a variety of services essential to the maintenance of the integrity of life-support systems and the productive capacity of the environment. Land resources are used in ways that take advantage of all these characteristics. Land resources are used for a variety of purposes which interact and may compete with one another; therefore, it is desirable to plan and manage all uses in an integrated manner. In traditional societies, the concept of land extends beyond the production purpose but holds also important social and spiritual values. Land is often the only available resource on which rural families can rely to build their lives. With the growing population and limited land resources, the relevance of Land Use Planning assumes significance. Land use planning ensures the use of land resources in an organized fashion so that the needs of the present and future generations can be best addressed. This paper discusses the need for effective land use planning in order to address various dimensions of development issues in a sustainable manner. It brings out some of the important issues for land use planning and sustainable development.

In 'Planning for Future Residential Developments in a Growing Urban Centre: A Case Study', Shahab Fazal states that in the last few decades, urbanization process has been very active among developing countries and there is widespread concern regarding the expansion and land reorganization in and around urban centres. The rapid sprawl of cities, outside their administrative boundaries and beyond their real physical-cultural domain possesses several attendant conflicts and stresses and has also stimulated various adaptations of human activities. The planners are also confronting with new problems and possibilities regarding the expansion and land reorganization in and around urban centres.

The present study tries to investigate land use land transformation in an Indian city (Saharanpur city) and on the basis of present trend it estimates demand for residential land in the year 2015. Further, the study identifies spatial location for prospective residential land. The result shows that the Saharanpur city has recorded a gradual increase in its population and has experienced significant changes in its economy. These changes have their bearing on the expansion of urban areas. The urban land use of the city is characterized by increase in residential area recording a growth of 201 per cent. The regression analysis for future residential expansion for year 2015 was estimated of 2706.3 hectares (a demand of another 421.3 hectares to the 2004 land under residential use). The spatial allocation analysis showed that independent variables, such as mobility (distance from roads), population density and land value have responded negatively, meaning thereby, the lower the value greater would be the probability for residential use. While distance to markets, public facilities and parks have responded positively, meaning that nearer these location, the probability of residential use would be lesser. On the basis of statistical analysis, spatial allocation for residential land showed that 442.3 hectares of land comes under most likely prospective residential land from where the future demand can be met.

In 'Waste Disposal and Management: Case Study of a Darjiling Town', Sushma Bomjan states that solid waste management is one of the most challenging issues in urban cities, which are facing a serious pollution problem due to the generation of huge quantities of solid waste. The sanitary methods adopted for disposal of solid waste are, therefore, a serious health concern. The poorly maintained landfill sites are prone to groundwater contamination because of leachate production. Open dumping of garbage facilitates the breeding of disease vectors such as flies, mosquitoes, cockroaches, rats, and other pests. The disposal of solid waste has always been an intractable problem throughout the hilly areas of Darjiling. They are generally operated below the standards of sanitary practice. Municipal budgetary allocations for operation and maintenance are always inadequate. The result is substandard and unsafe facilities which pose public health risks and aesthetic burdens to the citizens they are meant to serve.

Established by the Britishers in late nineteenth century, the population of Darjiling since 1921 has been growing significantly. From 22 thousand in 1921 to 1.07 lakh in 2001, apart from taking the burden of lakhs of tourist every year, it is entirely dependent on natural springs for its water requirements and jhoras for waste disposal. Increasing urban population and unplanned urban growth have also resulted in increasing pile of wastes and, hence, its disposal has become a major problem. Waste disposal problem has two aspects: first, considering the large number of wards and its inhabitants but number of disposal baskets and central community vats is very less. Garbage and wastes disposed mostly in jhoras (natural channel) and litter all-around city too due to the lack of basic urban infrastructure. Secondly, topography and physical contour of the town accentuate the problem since many municipal wards do not have any access to vehicular means of waste disposal. This paper has attempted to analyse the waste disposal system in Darjiling town and has discussed the problems, perceptions and management issues.

SECTION I
DEVELOPMENT ISSUES

1

Overcoming Environmental Crisis: Indian Culture Shows the Way

R.P. MISRA

Global warming poses by far the most imminent danger to mankind, far more than even terrorism. While terrorism may lead to the death of all that man has tried to build ever since he emerged from his animal existence; global warming may eliminate all lives from planet earth, including humans. The forces of violence and nonviolence have run concurrently from times immemorial to bring peace on planet earth. Mahavir, Buddha, Christ, and in our own times, Mahatma Gandhi tried hard to lead humanity to a higher level of consciousness and thereby to the culture of peace and harmony. But those who used violence to bring peace were not few. Human history is full of conflicts and wars interspersed by love and compassion.

The so-called modern civilization is built on violence: violence against nature both inanimate and animate, and violence against fellow human beings. Violence against nature has now led humanity to the door steps of climatic change, which if not reversed in time may ultimately produce an inert earth; the one against the fellow humans would take the Homo sapiens back to the door steps of the animal world he left behind long ago. Interestingly, we call this civilization 'modern' pointing that it is latest that man has created to live in peace and prosperity. How selfish and shortsighted man has become!

Modern civilization is full of conflicts and contradictions. Nations are fighting against nations, individuals are fighting against individuals, even religions, the depository of humanism and spirituality, are fighting with each other. Nature is the first target of attack of this civilization. Instead of being treated as the womb in which all that lives can grow and prosper, it is being treated as resource for exploitation. Greater the exploitation of nature, more development, if the benefits derived from it are reaped only by a select few depriving the most needy of their wherewithal. So goes the theory and practice of progress.

So deep seated is the war mentality of man, that he has been fighting his fellow human beings ever since the dawn of civilization. There were times when men of wisdom descended on the earth to show the way to peace. But soon man reverted back to his animal past and waged wars to control natural resources, and other human beings. He developed the weapons of mass destruction and expanded the theatre of war to engulf the whole world. We already had two World Wars. While we are readying ourselves to wage the Third, and perhaps the last World War, the natural Nemesis, in the form of global warming, is on its way to devastate everything living, leaving nothing to fight for or against.

Once upon a time, nature—land, water, air, plants, animals, and outer space—was considered by practically all civilizations as sacred for they ensured human survival and development. It was the duty of man to use the nature without jeopardizing its inherent regenerative capacity. And this duty was not the outcome of any conscious and thought out plan; it was built in psyche and behaviour of man. Man's use of nature was circumscribed by its inherent capacity to recoup and regenerate or his own capacity to help nature recover its lost virginity. He used the land fertilizing it by enriching it with manures derived from plant and animal wastes; he used the water, without wasting and polluting it; he used the air without fouling it; he lived in small communities so that the waste generated was not too large for the nature to digest it; he cut the trees but planted them too. In fact, human behaviour was so much in tune with nature that all that he turned out as a producer or consumer of goods and services was recycled in nature. In other words violence against nature was un-human.

Then came the so-called modern era in Europe in seventeenth century. Europeans spread over the whole world capturing both land and the people inhabiting it. They became the masters of all they surveyed. Both became the resources for exploitation: forests were cut, soils were destroyed, waters were polluted, air was poisoned, rivers were dammed—all this for increased production and consumption. The mental disease afflicting the Europeans spread over to their colonies. A series of scientific discoveres and technological developments strengthened man's hands to control nature as well as human beings. It heralded the era of city-based industrial revolution using energy resources like coal, petroleum, natural gas which released greenhouse gases in the atmosphere. Our land, water, and air are no longer in their life supporting state. The result is: global warming and climate change that is threatening the very survival of life on planet earth. The disease originated in the West but it has now engulfed the whole world.

As we enter the twenty-first century, we realize that something went drastically wrong with the way we tried to modernize ourselves; and that our forefathers who interfered with nature only within the confines of the laws governing it on the one hand, and human craving for peace and harmony on the other, were perhaps right. This realization, even if within a limited circle of people and institutions, has led to a search for a paradigm of development that is devoid of violence against nature and fellow human beings. This search is, however, still within the framework of the basic tenets of modern civilization, which gives priority to material advancement even if it means making nature inert and human beings less human. It is clear from the applied meaning of the new concept of Sustainable Development. If development is equated with continuing economic growth, it cannot be sustainable for earth's capacity to keep itself livable is limited.

Dominant groups in all societies still subscribe to the view that human ingenuity will triumph in the future as it has triumphed in the past, and the environmental problems we face today would be resolved satisfactorily as other problems have been resolved in the past. Science and technology would come to our help; the climatic change threatening the very existence of the humanity would become a thing of the past as scientific ways of purifying the environment are accelerated, and more resources are made available for pollution abatement. Progress without tears is impossible, so goes the argument. Humanity has always paid price for development, and it must pay in future too. The environmental crisis that looms large today is nothing but a price of progress.

The argument advanced above is, however, no longer valid. Violence cannot be eliminated by violence, as fire cannot be extinguished by fire. Violence can be eliminated by nonviolence alone, says Gandhi. Development must be refined as human progress that means higher ethical standards and better quality of life. Material advancement must once again be treated as a means rather than the end of human development. This paper explores the potential of the Gandhian worldview in resolving the environmental challenges we face today.

THE INDIAN WORLD-VIEW

India's written history goes back to over 5,000 years. Archaeological records take this culture deeper in the past. Its philosophy, thoughts, values and ethics have always had reverence for all that exists in nature, so much so that it evolved the concept of *vasudhaiva kutumbakam*, i.e. all that is alive, from plants to human species, belongs to a single family. They have originated from a common source and are interdependent. This cultural dictum was accepted not only by the people whom we now call Hindus, but also by other Indian religionists like Buddhists and Jains. Islam and Christianity came later but they too were highly influenced by these Indian values. The question is: can the Indian world-view, as evident from its cultural heritage, be used as a paradigm for what Gandhi called a truly modern civilization, a civilization which treats nature not only as a source of livelihood but also as a source of life.

Indian culture is deeply rooted in two different but interacting traditions. The Aryans had their sway in the Indus and subsequently in the Ganga Valley; and the Dravidians to the south of the Vindhyas prospered in the valleys of Godavary and Kavery. The two interacted to produce not only the Vedic and post-Vedic cultures but also perhaps the Indus civilization, which preceded them. Many of statuettes and seals found in Mohenjo-Daro and Harappa, and later in part of Gujarat and Rajasthan, indicate that some of the concepts, which now constitute the core of Indian culture were present in their incipient stage even then. For example, the statuette of the Mother found in Mohenjo-Daro points to what later gave rise to the concept of Mother Earth or *Sakti.*

Origin of Life

True, many schools of thought propounded by *rishis* like Carvak deny the existence of God or *paramatma*. What has, however, gripped the mind of India is not the deviations but the cross-current that 'there is One without a second', or 'All this is Brahman'. 'Brahman is devoid of any attribute'. Nothing can be positively postulated about Him. He can be indicated only by 'not this, not this'.

Gandhi equated Truth with God; he also referred to God as 'Cosmic Law' that governs the existence and functioning of the universe. Truth is not what each individual holds to be so; Cosmic Law is something that is beyond the purview of science. Neither Truth nor Cosmic Law leads us closer to the concept of God. They do, however, lead us to the realization that the power that governs the universe is difficult to know by the means we have at our disposal. God is, therefore, perceived differently by people living in different cultural and geographical settings. These perceptions, when generalized and integrated give rise to various philosophies and religions. Religions offer the ways to reach God that is Truth. The concept of God unites all human beings into a single family. Nay, it unites all that exists in the universe—living and non-living—making them interdependent.

The *Brahma* reveals Himself in two ways: as unconscious or matter (*jada*) or conscious or live (*jiva*). It could also be called non-self (*achetana*) and self (*chetana*). While the non-self or unconscious is not eternal, the self or the conscious is eternal. The non-eternal ultimately ends as the atoms, which went to create it, do. The *atman* is indestructible as it is part of *parmatman (God, Truth, Cosmic Law),* which is not a physical entity.

The concept of unity of life is not limited to the Homo sapiens. It covers all forms of life whether:

1. *jarayuja* (viviparous)
2. *andaja* (oviparous)
3. *udbhija* (germinating)
4. *svedaja* (generated by heat and moisture)

The first are born of placenta, like human beings and animals; the second of eggs, like birds and reptiles; the third break through the earth, like plants; and the fourth are born of heat and moisture, like bacteria. Inorganic matter (*jada*) does not possess the above qualities even though the process of production of the two is the same.

Creation, according to Hindu thought, is not purposeless, nor is at random. Its goal is to take man to higher levels of consciousness i.e. *moksha* or bliss. Anything that endangers life on earth or interferes with the processes that take man to perfection (divinity), is undesirable. If there is anything that comes close to the Indian theory of evolution of life, it is the *Gian* theory.

Concept of Progress

The Indian concept of progress is different from the one currently in vogue. Development, as it is conceived at present, essentially means economic development. It means higher GDP, per capita income, and more consumption goods. A progressive society is one whose values do not clash with these developmental values. To receive development, people have to make certain sacrifices. They have to discard all those values, which come in the way of development. To see divinity in nature is anti-developmental, for divinity is unintelligible. To think of unity of life is anti-developmental, for all other life forms are resources to be used by man. He can use them the way he wants.

Indian culture has a different concept of development called *mangalya.* It means a state in which man has no insurmountable problems and the natural, cultural and social environment in which he lives is conducive to his overall welfare. *Mangalya* is not limited to an individual; it covers all those humans and other life forms in and around him. It is collective welfare. It carries man towards a blissful life. The collectivity includes all living and non-living entities the individual in question is linked to. Modern development can take place at the cost of other people and lives, and indeed at the cost of nature; but not *mangalya.*

There is another word that goes with *mangala,* that is *kusala.* It conveys general welfare. *Mangalya* means bliss, supreme happiness. Indian culture has always aspired to achieve *kusala* and *mangala.* True, it has at times deviated from this path, but the society after brief interludes of deviations, it returned to the path of sanity, if we may say so.

Indian culture goes beyond human beings to take care of all that is living, from plants to elephants. It does not prohibit the use of nature. Rather, it encourages its use but only to the extent that its vitality is not adversely affected. That is why it advocates simple living and high thinking, and calls upon the people to perform their duties, their rights would automatically be protected. A farmer has the right to cut a tree, but only if he fulfils his duty to plant five other trees. The idea is that if everyone performs his duties honestly, the rights of all will be automatically preserved.

ECOLOGICAL FOUNDATIONS OF INDIAN CULTURE

It is for this reason that ever since the Indus valley civilization and more so from Vedic times, Indian culture has preached reverence to nature. It never considered nature to be a resource for exploitation. It treated it as a source of sustenance, livelihood, and survival.

Nature is Sacred

All that exist in nature is essential for life. If nature were not evolved the way it has, there would have been no life, or life would have taken a different form.

Mountains, rivers, oceans, animals and plants are, therefore, sacred. They cannot be defiled. They should be used, but only with compassion and without jeopardizing their inherent capacity to recoup. Beliefs that all that is valuable has come from the ocean, that the Himalayas are the abode of Siva, that the Ganga's water purifies everything, that the Ganga is a mother for the teeming millions even today, that the cow is sacred, all these have philosophical and scientific bases. God has come down to earth in animal forms too, like fish, boar, half-lion and half-human. Ganesa, who is worshipped all over India, is half elephant and half human. Almost all gods and goddesses have animals as their *vahan* (vehicles). Even the snake deserves our protection and reverence. Trees have received very special consideration, for they are the source of fruits, medicines and oxygen. Concepts of *kalpavriksa*, the tree, which gives everything, and of *kamadhenu*, the cow, which fulfils all desires, represent our reverence to nature and life.

To say that all primitive societies had similar approaches to nature and that modern scientific world cannot depend on such ideas for progress is to exhibit utter ignorance of what lies behind these traditions and the systems approach to life and living that prevailed then and must prevail now and in future too. Modern man, proud as he is of his scientific and technological achievements, has been trying to develop methods and processes to uncover the mysteries of nature and use the knowledge so derived to control it and thus to induce higher productivity and secure a wide range of consumer goods and services. But any attempt to control nature can benefit man in the short run only. In the long run nature takes revenge, because nature including human beings, constitutes a system governed by the cosmic law of integration and balance.

The processes whose perpetual sameness or recurrence, give rise to the representation of order obey *R'ta* or their occurrence is R'ta, says Maurice Bloomfield. We read in the Vedas that 'the rivers flow R'ta. According to the R'ta the light of the heaven-born morning has come .... The year is the path of R'ta. The gods themselves are born of the R'ta or in the R'ta; they show by the acts that they know, observe and love the R'ta. In man's activity, the R'ta manifests itself as the moral law.'

To obtain nature's bounty, man must obey *R'ta*: 'for one who lives according to Eternal Law, the winds are full of sweetness; the rivers pour sweet. So may the plants be full of sweetness for us.' The Vedic poet Atharva thus clearly reveals the human dependence on the order of the cosmos and the human role in maintaining it by observing the ancient law. He was perhaps the first deep ecologist of the world.

The same concept later finds a place in Buddha's *dharmachakra*. When a Buddhist lama turns his prayer wheel, he reminds us all of the *R'ta*. As Jane Harrison notes, 'He finds himself in sympathetic touch with the Wheel of the Universe when he performs the act Dharma-Chakra-Pravartana (justice wheel setting in motion). He dare not turn the Wheel contrariwise lest that were to upset the whole order of nature.'

The concept of *vasudhaiva kutumbakam* still prevails among the indigenous peoples all over the world. It was also present in other great civilizations and cultures, which gave rise to the great religions of the world. Raphael Patai in *Man and Temple in Ancient Jewish Myth and Ritual* says:

> The fact that primitive man draws no strict line of cleavage between the animal, vegetable, and mineral kingdom on the one hand, and human beings on the other, has been so often emphasized that it can be regarded as [an] anthropological commonplace.

Jane Harrison in *Themis: A Study of the Social Origins of Greek Religion* says: 'To man, in the totemistic stage of thinking, Dike and Themis, natural order and social order, are not distinguished, not even distinguishable. Plants and animals are part of this group, a factor in his social structure. It is not that he takes them under his protection: they are his equals, his fellow-tribesmen; naturally they obey the same laws.'

This integrated approach to life continued in India until modern times, because Indian culture never became a matter of history and museums. We do not know when it began. It has been alive and vibrant ever since it began and is marked by continuity. That is why we call it eternal (*sanatana)*.

Concept of *Panchabhoota*

According to the Indian cultural traditions all that exists in the universe, whether organic or inorganic, has five constituent elements. These are:

1. Air (atmosphere)
2. Water (hydrosphere)
3. Fire (heat/energy)
4. Earth (lithosphere)
5. Cosmic forces (ether)

Everything comes from varying combinations of these five elements; and ultimately returns to them. When combined in varying proportions, they form a system, otherwise known as nature.

Concept of Mother Earth

When the disciple asks Atharva Risi about the nature of the relationship between man and Earth, he said: The earth is the Mother; and we are her children (*mata bhumi putro-aham prithivyah*). When the pupil asked 'what is the nature of the Earth', the *risi* replied: 'The Earth has hills and snow-covered mountains; it has dense forests and soils of different colours; it is the mother of herbs, it has fire inside, and also gets energy from the sun; it produces a special odour, which enriches all that exists and grows on it.' And he added, 'to protect us from all that is evil, the Earth contains pure water. It purifies all that is impure. It cleans everything that goes in it. Earth is a real purifier of all that is undesirable and unclean. Let us not hurt its vitals and its heart. Let us use it judiciously.'

The Rishi went on describing the earth, and said:

> *jana vibrati bahudha vivacasam*
> *nana dharmanam prthivi yathaukasam*
> *sahasra dhara dravitasya ye duham*
> *dhruvena dhamurenk pasphuranti*

> (The earth is full of variety; it contains people speaking different dialects and languages, of diverse religious customs, each living according to what they think is right. The earth contains innumerable valuable things. It bears trees and plants of great diversity. We should pay homage to that Earth).

The *Prthivi Sukta* of the *Atharvaveda* gives in nutshell the Vedic view of man's relations to the Earth. The post-Vedic literature of Hindu, Buddhist and Jain thought is also imbued with reverence, love, and compassion for nature; it boldly points to not only the unity of all that is living but also the unity of what is living (*chetana*) and non-living (*achetana*). The *Svetasvatara Upanisad* captures the essence of this integration and unity when it describes nature in the following terms:

> *yo devo agro yo apsu yo visvam bhuvanamavivesa*
> *yo osdhisu yo vanaspatisu tasme devaya namo namah*

> (The God who is in fire, who is in water, who pervades the whole universe, who is in medicines, who is in vegetation, we salute that God.)

Indian culture paid special attention to land. Soil conservation methods developed in India are still unmatched. Green manuring, barn manure, crop rotation, intercropping, ploughing, irrigation and other agricultural methods and practices were designed to maintain and enhance the fertility of the soil. Soil erosion and exhaustion did occur due to natural or human vagaries, but it was replenished manually by storing the rainwater carrying the topsoil in local ponds and lakes. The fertile soil carried by water and deposited in these water bodies was excavated in summer and taken back to the land again. And thus the cycle continued.

Water the Purifier

Pure and uncontaminated water has always commanded a very high value in Indian culture. No ceremony, from birth to death, is complete and perfect without *gangajal* (water of River Ganga). The mythological story of the descent of the Ganga forms the subject matter of many a books in India. In scientific terminology, it is a description of the hydrological cycle: ocean water evaporates, forms monsoon clouds bursting over the Himalayas. The water so released gets locked as snow. Snow flows through the glaciers, which ultimately form rivers like Ganga. Without Ganga and its tributaries, the land between the Himalaya and the Vindhya mountains would have not nurtured a civilization as rich as that of India. The same applies to other Indian rivers: Sind, Brahmaputra, Mahanadi, Godavari, Krishna, Kavery, Narmada and Tapti. Each one is treated sacred, and so should not be defiled.

India has the distinction of developing unique irrigation systems as early as 3,000 years ago, which conserved and replenished surface and ground water and improved the living environment. Those of us who are familiar with the Deccan plateau know that thousands of tanks which dot this region and around which villages are built provide an excellent example of how man can improve the environment. But for these artificial tanks, much of the plateau would have been barren and human existence precarious.

The little dams that our forefathers built across rivers in South India point to what could be done to avoid the human tragedies of the Sardar Sarovar and Tehri dams. Drinking water wells dotted the villages and towns of India. The water of these wells was kept clean by frequent withdrawal for irrigation. There was no chance of contamination.

One can give several examples of water management, particularly watershed planning and water harvesting. The choice of crops and trees depended on the climatic conditions, particularly rainfall. So even in desert and drought prone areas, people could raise crops. People knew the close relationship between trees, rainfall, water table and soil moisture. Cropping patterns were designed to conserve water.

The Forest: the Abode of Gods

Forests constitute a very important part of Indian culture. Most of the ancient books like the *Vedas*, *Puranas*, *Brahmanas* and *Aranyakas* were written by the *rishis* living in forests, sometimes high up in the mountains. One finds references to three main types of forests *(vana)* in ancient times. These are:

1. *Mahavana*
2. *Tapovana*
3. *Srivana*

Mahavana was a dense, and virgin forest covering large mountainous, hilly and low-lying areas. Such forests were devoid of human habitation; human interference was, therefore, negligible. They were rich in biodiversity. They were the main sources of medicines. Lord Siva (the God of Destruction) was considered the presiding deity of the *mahavanas*. No one dared to encroach upon them. They remained virgin and covered a large part of India.

The *tapovana*, as the very name, indicates was the forest where sages did *tapas* (penance and meditation). It had *ashramas* (hermitages) where *gurus* (teachers) taught their pupils. *Ashramas* were away from human habitation and in the interior, but people had access to them for religious and educational purposes. They were full of plants and trees, which gave edible and medicinal leaves, roots, fruits, shade and soothing weather. It was in these forests that our *Upanishadas* and *Aranyakas* were written. There are still some *tapovanas* like the one near Haridwar.

Most of the *tapovanas* were destroyed during the last 200 years or so. And thus the tradition of *rishis* and *saints* living detached from the common people and engaging themselves in meditation, writing, and teaching died. It is pertinent to note that the *tapovanas* abounded in wildlife, but none was allowed to kill animals. Even princes were punished for killing animals as game.

It was in these forests that training in the use of weapons was also imparted. It was part of the overall education of pupils. Thus matters pertaining to peace as well as war were really in the hands of saintly people. Trainees were prohibited from using arms for purposes, which were outside *dharma* or moral code of conduct. This is what ensured peace in society. People dejected with life went to the *tapovanas* instead of committing suicide as it happens today. Excommunicated criminals also went there for repentance and cleansing themselves under the feet of the *samnyasins*.

Srivanas were local (village or town) forests. They were not within human habitation; rather human habitation was within them. These forests were managed by village and town *panchayat*s. People depended on them for fuel, medicines, fruits and other day-to-day domestic needs. While they had access to these forests, they also had the duty to conserve, protect, replenish and enrich them. Enriching was done through planting of trees in replacement of trees cut.

Srivanas had various kinds of trees, depending on soil, climate and other environmental conditions and local needs. *Tulsi* (basil) was found in abundance, for it was medicinal and at the same time improved the fertility of the soil. No Hindu worship is complete without *tulsi* leaves. *Srivanas* abounded in fruit orchards. The concept of social forestry was not foreign Indian culture even in that deep past. We are now trying to import it from the World Bank.

Five species of trees were a must in the *Srivanas*. These were banyan, *peepal*, *asoka*, *bela* and *harada*. The banyan is a self-multi-plying tree that is why it is known as *Akshaya But* (eternal tree). It does not die on its own; in fact it acquires the form of a grove in course of time. It is, therefore, associated with fertility and longevity of life. It is the abode of Lord Siva and Devi Parvati. It is shady, healthful and medicinal. The *peepal* (*ficus religiosa*) is perhaps the most sacred tree in India. It is the only tree that gives oxygen for more than 20 hours a day. It is the incarnation of Lord Visnu, the preserver of life. Every part of this tree has medicinal value.

The *asoka* tree under which Sita, Lord Ram's consort, is supposed to have spent her time in Lanka, is a pain-killer, as the name indicates, apart from being shady. The *bela* (*aegle marmelos*) bears fruit of great curative value. It is useful in a large number of diseases. Its leaves are offered to Lord Siva. Close to practically all Siva temple, there are *bela* trees. The last of the five trees is the *harad* (*myrobalem terminalia shebual*). It is perhaps the most commonly used medicinal plant.

The name *panchavati* is derived from these five trees. Every village had a *panchavati* even if it did not have *srivana.* The trees were not necessarily the same as listed above, nor was the number of trees fixed. They differed from region to region and sometimes from place to place and community to community.

The Atmosphere Gives us *Pranavayu*

Clean air with plenty of Oxygen (*Pran Vayu*) was looked for while building houses, villages and towns. The *rishis* lived in forests with plenty of oxygen giving trees. Even today, the breathing exercises (*yoga* and *pranayamas*) were performed in open spaces. Love for open spaces, trees and plants is clear from the open spaces, the verandahs, the aspect of buildings, the windows, etc. as ingredients of Indian architecture. All religious ceremonies were performed in the open. People slept in the open except in winter. One has to go through the *slokas* of the *Rgveda*, the most ancient book of the world, to realize the importance Indian culture gave to ecology and environment. A glimpse at the miniatures of the Mughal period gives a clear indication of the importance that the Mughal rulers of India gave to trees, foliage, plants and animals.

INDIAN AND WESTERN WORLD-VIEWS COMPARED

As Richard St. Barbe-baker says, 'this generation may either be the last to exist in any semblance of civilized world or it will be the last to have the vision, the bearing and the greatness to say "I will have nothing to do with this destruction of life; I will play no part in this devastation of land; I am determined to live and work for peaceful construction for I am morally responsible for "the world of today and the generations of tomorrow".' Barbe-baker was addressing to the man in the West who 'has lost his way in the jungle of chemistry and engineering and will have to retrace his steps, however painful this may be. He will have to discover where he went wrong and make his peace with nature. In so doing, perhaps he may be able to recapture the rhythm of life and the love of the simple things of life which will be an ever unfolding joy to him.'

Many others have expressed similar views. But those who still think that man will ultimately triumphantly come out of the ecological mess he has put himself in by discovering the newest secrets of nature and inventing newest technologies are not in minority. In fact, the ruling elites all over the world subscribe to this view, and no amount of evidence can induce them to change their perspectives. They flow with the current. When the current has changed, they will flow with the new current provided that they are still there to catch the boat.

The Indian world-view cannot stand the test of today's modernity, a product of the western world-view. Within this paradigm, no argument in favour of an alternative paradigm gets acceptance. The whole structure and superstructure of society today is built and sustained by the paradigm of economic growth at any cost. A shift from this mindset would be as painful as forceful conversion to another religion. The whole pattern of life, mental constructs and images will have to change. The shift from the economic growth as the be all and end all to both inner (moral) and outer (socio-economic and technological) development of man leading to *Sarvodaya* of Gandhi is the need of the hour. But we know it is very difficult and painful to all those who have vested interest in the prevailing paradigm of economic growth centric development. The paradigm change will occur only when the dangers ahead and inherent to it become visible even to those who have are powerful and have vested interest in it.

It is the contention of this author that the danger signals have become so forceful and loud that even those who turn their faces backwards cannot ignore them. The catastrophes inherent in escalating Global Warming, Climatic Change, Terrorism, and Poverty, to name a few are now being felt even by the elites. In more concrete terms, we face ecological and ethical crises. The environmental crisis has gripped the whole world—rich and poor alike. Strong voices calling for a new style of life and a new paradigm of development have now become audible. Grassroots level movements, small to start with, have begun networking themselves to have universal appeal and impact.

In India too, rethinking has begun. More and more scientists, artists, scholars, men in public life, and people in general have started looking into the traditions which were lost as the western paradigm superseded Indian values. In fact, the Hindu, Buddhist and Jain philosophies have started getting new adherents all over the world. Any attempt to delink Indian society from *dharma* or even religion in that sense is resisted. Even the modern Carvaks, for whom religion is the opium of the people, are changing. The citadel of communism has already fallen. Religion has come back in what was the USSR. It is now only a matter of time before the Indian world-view is replanted in India again.

GANDHI INCULCATES AND INNOVATES ON INDIAN TRADITION

We have had the great fortune of having persons like Mahatma Gandhi, Aurobindo and Vivekanand in the twentieth century to guide the destiny of India. Gandhi's greatest contribution was not the Independence of India, for India could not have remained in bondage longer than it was, Gandhi or no Gandhi. His seminal contribution lies in the alternative paradigm of development he gave to India and through India to the whole world. He excavated Indian civilization from overburden of ignorance, rebuilt a new structure on the old foundation, and left it to the future generations to adopt, adapt and innovate. His genius encompassed all religious traditions of the world, for they were one and the same as far as the essentials were concerned. Rituals differed but the goals were the same, the methods were the same and the messages too were the same.

Gandhi's philosophy centres on Truth and Nonviolence. Search for Truth is the ultimate task of humanity and this must be done using nonviolence in its broadest form (*manasa-vacha-karmana*). His oft-cited quotation: 'Earth has enough to meet everyone's need but not everyone's greed' is the centrepiece of the world-view of ecology and humanism that we are looking for. It goes beyond the recently propounded concept of inclusive economic growth. It aims at moral and ethical development of man and since equality—economic, social, cultural, and political—is the inherent right of man irrespective of age, sex, religion, region, country he was born and lives in, a society based on inequity and indignity, and a model of development that promotes these, must be unacceptable. He goes further to assert that all life is sacred and interdependent, and hence the nature that supports life must also be treated sacred. The principles of nonviolence should be limited to human beings; they must extend to other life forms too. Nothing should be done that would disturb the natural system consisting of man, insects, birds, animals, and plants; and man must use the nature to produce goods and services, or build villages, towns, cities, factories etc. that pollute the nature the purification of the pollutants must be a part of the building programme as it was in the past.

Gandhi on Industrialism and its Consequences

Gandhi warned as early as 1928 God forbid that 'India should ever take to industrialism after the manner of the West. The economic imperialism of a single tiny island kingdom is today keeping the world in chains. If an entire nation of 300 million took to similar economic exploitation, it would strip the world bare like locusts.' (YI, 20.12, 1928, p. 422) And he added in 1931, 'India, when it begins to exploit other nations—as it must if it becomes industrialized—will be a curse for other nations, a menace to the world. And why should I think of industrializing India to exploit other nations? Don't you see the tragedy of the situation, viz. that we can find work for our 300 million unemployed, but England cannot find none for its three million and is faced with a problem that baffles the greatest intellects of England'. (YI, 21-11-1931, p. 355)

Further elaborating his views on dangers of western style development, Gandhi observed: 'I do not believe that industrialization is ecessary in any case for any country. It is much less so for India. Indeed, I believe that Independent India can only discharge her duty towards a groaning world by adopting a simple but ennobled life by developing her thousands of cottages and living at peace with the world. High thinking is inconsistent with complicated material life based on high speed imposed on us by Mammon worship. All the graces of life are possible only when we learn the art of living nobly....

Whether such plain living is possible for an isolated nation, however large geographically and numerically, in the face of a world armed to the teeth and in the midst of pomp and circumstance is a question open to the doubt of a skeptic. The answer is straight and simple. If plain life is worth living, then the attempt is worth making, even though only an individual or group makes the effort.'

Basic Education is a Must for a New Socio-Economic Order

The first step in taking the society back to incorporation of the time-honoured Indian values discussed above in the educational system in India has been stressed from time to time. Mahatma Gandhi offered a new concept of education wherein head, heart and hand could be trained to work in unison and give rise to creative human beings. He termed it *Nai talim* or New Education. It was new in the sense that it was completely different from the Western model of education in vogue. *Nai talim* laid great stress on pupils' contact with nature through manual work and on the concept of unity of life.

Somehow, the concept of Basic Education was completely rejected by India after Independence. The educational system which the British had created was not only retained but also strengthened. This was, however, not an isolated step. Other Gandhian concepts including that of development were also rejected. Now in the 1990, we hear more of Gandhi than we did in the 1960s through the 1980s.

As early as 1959, the Sri Prakasa Committee on Religious and Moral Education set up by the Ministry of Education stated,

"Many ills that our world of education and our society as a whole is suffering today resulting in widespread disturbance and dislocation of life are mainly due to the gradual disappearance of the hold of basic principles of religion on the hearts of the people . . . . The only cure, it seems to us, is in deliberate inculcation of moral and spiritual values from the earliest years of our lives."

Let us note here that in the Indian context, religious and moral education incorporate ecological and environmental education.

The Commission on Education (1964-66) chaired by the late Professor D.S. Kothari was more vocal on the issue of value education:

Modernization did not mean, least of all in our national situation, a refusal to recognize the importance of or to inculcate necessary moral and spiritual values and self-discipline. While a combination of ignorance with goodness may be futile, that of knowledge with a lack of essential values may be dangerous.

The weakening of social and moral values in the younger generation is creating many serious social and ethical conflicts in western societies and there is already a desire among great western thinkers to balance the knowledge and skills which science and technology bring with the values and insights associated with ethics and religion at its best, viz. a search for the knowledge of self, of the meaning of life, of the relationship of man to other human beings and the ultimate reality. In the situation that is developing, it is equally important for us to give a proper value orientation to our educational system.

India has a unique advantage with her great tradition of duty without self-involvement, unacquisitive temperament, tolerance, and innate love of peace and reverence for all living things. Too often are these precious assets forgotten and we tend to relapse into moods of pessimism, fears and forebodings, discord and destructive criticism. A new pride and a deeper faith expressed in living for the noble ideals of peace and freedom, truth and compassion are now needed.

Several other committees, commissions, seminars, conferences and plan documents have since then repeated these views. Not much, however, happened in policy and programme terms, and the educational system of the country continued as usual. The call for a new education policy, however, became so persistent that Parliament, under the 42nd Amendment Act of 1976, inserted Fundamental Duties to match the Fundamental Rights guaranteed by the Constitution of India. Among these duties, at least five were pertinent to the environment. These are:

1. to promote harmony and the spirit of common brotherhood amongst all the people of India transcending religious, linguistic and regional or sectional diversities; to renounce practices derogatory to the dignity of women;
2. to value and preserve the rich heritage of our composite culture;
3. to protect and improve the natural environment including forests, lakes, rivers and wild life, and to have compassion for living creatures;
4. to develop scientific temper, humanism and the spirit of enquiry and reform; and
5. to safeguard public property and to abjure violence.

The incorporation of environmental protection among the statutory duties of Indian citizens was perhaps inspired by the Stockholm conference on the environment in which Mrs. Indira Gandhi, the then Prime Minister of India, played a leading role.

The *National Education Policy Statement, 1986* included these points and suggested a national curricular framework which included:

> ...the history of India's freedom movement, the constitutional obligations and other contents essential to nurture national identity. These elements will cut across subject areas and will be designed to promote values such as India's common cultural heritage, egalitarianism, democracy and secularism, equality of sex, protection of environment, removal of social barriers, observance of small family norms and inculcation of scientific temper.

The Ramamurthy Committee, which reviewed this policy in 1990, had this to say:

> The hidden curriculum, as distinct from the explicit ones obtaining in the classroom situation, is much more important for the development of balanced personality amongst the students. It is also the role of value education to bring about integration of the hand, head and heart to ensure that education does not alienate the students from the family, community and life. One of the key roles of education should be creation of a work culture at all stages of education so that the individual develops into a

socially and economically useful human being with respect for the welfare of all living beings *(sarva bhoota hitha)*. Above all else, critical appreciation and concern for the cultural and artistic heritage of the country has to be instilled amongst the students. It is this package of values which will help the creation and sustenance of an enlightened and human society in the country.

The five-year plans of India have consistently upheld the need to promote value education. The Seventh Plan (1985-90) stated:

> Value orientation of education should constitute a special thrust in the Seventh Plan, teacher education particularly being oriented for this purpose.

Earlier, in 1981, a seminar on value education held at Shimla said:

> There should be an integrated approach in the value oriented education programme. Instead of tackling piecemeal with such areas as awareness of ecology, environmental protection, community development, productivity, population stabilization, aesthetic education, national integration and international understanding, etc., they should be handled in a comprehensive manner under the broad spectrum of social responsibility and inner development of human personality.

Light in the Darkness

Even though the educational system of the country has not yet responded favourably to the above recommendation and business of education is as usual, attempts at value education have not been lacking. A number of institutions have taken up this challenge with all earnestness and have shown quite encouraging results. Among these institutions, mention may be made of:

1. Institutions associated with Satya Sai Baba
2. Institutions associated with the Ramakrishna Mission
3. Institutions associated with the Aurobindo Ashram
4. Vanasthali Vidyapeeth, Rajasthan
5. Jain Vishva Bharati, Ladnun, and related institutions
6. The Saraswati Vidya Mandir System of Schools

A recent report on the workload on pupils in primary and secondary education (Yash Pal Committee Report, 1993) strongly recommended the Gandhian approach to learning (without mentioning Gandhi's name).

There are many other institutions in different parts of the country. Those listed above use different approaches and methodologies with the same end results. What runs through them all is the thread of spirituality and ecological thinking. All these institutions instil value education through coursework as well as practice. The fact that their network is expanding, and they are being voluntarily accepted by parents as the right institutions for their children, is indicative of the wind of change.

In addition to these institutions, a large number of NGOs and voluntary agencies have now entered the field of value education in India. Some of them have evolved innovative programmes, particularly in the area of environmental education. Recent attempts to learn from the environmental values of tribal and village communities are indicative of the approaching scenario. The great religious traditions are being explored again to distill much of the environmental values which are now lost or getting lost, and which need to be revived, to bring about an eco-development process. We do thus see some light in the darkness.

Let us not be perplexed; let us follow the Upanisadic exhortation:

uttisthan jagrat prapya varan nibodhat
dyurasya dhara nisita duretyaya
durgam patham tat kavayo vadanti

Get up, wake up, and learn from the knowledgeable. As it is difficult to walk on the razor's edge, so it is difficult to walk on a right path.

That the right path of development is the ecological path is the message of Indian culture.

REFERENCES

Archer, A.A., *et al.*, 1987, *Man's Dependence on the Earth: The Role of Geosciences in the Environment*. Nairobi: UNEP and Paris: UNESCO.

Banwari, 1992, *Panchavati: Indian Approach to Environment*. New Delhi: Sri Vinayak Publications.

Ciriacy, S.V., *et al.*, 1967, *Natural Resources: Quality and Quantity*. Los Angeles: University of California Press.

Eyre, S.R., 1978, *The Real Wealth of Nations*. London: Edward Arnold.

Gandhi, M.K., *Hind Swaraj*. Ahmedabad: Navajivan Press.

Goldsmith, Edward, 1992, *The Way: An Ecological World View*. London: Rider.

Harrison, Jane, 1927, *Themis: A Study of the Social Origin of Greek Religion*. Cambridge: Cambridge University Press.

Hira Lal, *Nature Cure*. Manuscript in press, 1993.

Mehta, Rohit, 1982. *The Fullness of the Void*. New Delhi: Motilal Banarsidass.

Ministry of Education, Government of India, 1959, *Report of Committee on Religious and Moral Education*.

——, *Education and National Development: Report of Education Commission (1964-66)*.

——, 1968, *National Policy on Education*.

Ministry of Human Resource Development, Government of India, 1985, *Challenge of Education: A Policy Perspective.*
——, 1986, *National Policy on Education.*
——, 1993, Towards an Enlightened and Humane Society: Report of Ramamurthy Committee.
Narang, Sudesh, 1993, *Atharva Vediya Prithivi Sukta.* New Delhi: Paridhi Prakashan (in Hindi).
NASA, 1969, *Resources and Man.* San Francisco: W.H. Freeman & Co.
Patai, Raphael, 1947, *Man and Temple in Ancient Jewish Myth and Ritual.* London: Thomas Nelson.
Swami Budhananda, 1980, *The Saving Challenge of Religion.* Madras: Ramakrishna Math.

2

Sustainable Rural Development in India: Towards a Gandhian Framework

SURESH MISRA

INTRODUCTION

India ranks 128 (out of 177) countries in overall HDI, just below Morocco and Guinea, in life expectancy at birth India ranks 125 just below Pakistan and Comoros, in adult literacy rate (ages 15+) India ranks 125 just below Rwanda and Malawi, in terms of combined primary/secondary/tertiary education enrollment, India ranks 122, just below Namibia and Vietnam and as far as GDP per capita (PPP US $) India ranks 114, just below Syria and Nicaragua. Nearly 46 per cent of the children below five years of age are underweight and only 33 per cent of the population has access to improved sanitation. In 2006-07 the GDP grew at 8.4 per cent, agriculture at 2.7 per cent, industry at 11 per cent and services at 11 per cent. The bulk of this population lives in the rural areas. These figures are after nearly two decades of economic reforms. The important question is has the rural sector really benefited from the wave of reforms sweeping the country in the name of globalization and liberalization or it has been exploited and the disparities have only increased. The question needs a detailed analysis and identification of the causes of underdevelopment of the rural areas and a search for an alternate model. This paper reflects the writings and the ideas of Sundaram and Misra on approaches to sustainable rural development.

A majority of the total Indian population live in the numerous villages, scattered throughout the country. The rural population in India comprises the core of Indian society and also represents the real India. According to the 2001 Indian census, there are 638,365 villages in India and about 74 per cent of Indian population live in these villages. The number of people living in each of the Indian villages also varies considerably. It is found that most of the Indian villages have a population less than 1,000, while there are only a few villages where more than 10,000 people live. Given the rapidity with which urban population is growing, this share may come down to 70 per cent by the turn of this century. But if we count out the section of the urban population which resides in towns and cities, but is rooted in villages, the rural population would stay at 75 per cent even in 2001 A.D. While a quarter (25.70%) of population of India is classified as urban (in 1991), only 20.83 per cent of the labour force lives in cities. Rural areas thus sustain four-fifth of the total labour force (main workers) of the country. More than two-thirds (63.2%) of the working population is engaged in agriculture and allied activities (as cultivators, agricultural labourers, live-stock farmer, etc.). The situation is not likely to change for decades to come.

The share of rural activities in the gross National Product of the country is, however, secularly declining. Agriculture's share in the GDP in 1951 was 65 per cent; it declined to 45 per cent in 1971. In 1990-91, the contribution of agriculture towards Gross Domestic Product (GDP) output was at 32 per cent, which has decreased to 20 per cent by 2005-06. If trends continue, the output would be expected to decrease further. This makes us think about the fact that the Indian economy is mainly dependant on agriculture, but in the future it would contribute to only 10-15 per cent of the GDP. We need to look into the reasons for this worrying trend. Agriculture is undoubtedly the most important sector from the point of view of inclusion, since it is the primary source of income for about half of the population even today. The slowing down of agriculture growth to less than 2 per cent per annum, since the late 1990s has undoubtedly been the root cause of much of the rural distress. Naturally, the per capita income of rural population is far lower than that of its counterpart living in urban areas.

There are more poor in rural than in urban areas whether one looks at poverty in terms of absolute number or in terms of per cent of population below the poverty line. A substantial number of urban poor have deep roots in rural areas. When we look at the question of poverty in terms of access to work, opportunities and basic needs, the rural parts of India are in far worse situation. Self-reliance which made rural people meet their basic needs in the most adverse circumstances stands totally destroyed. Government, which professed and promised to uplift them from the miserable living conditions, have failed to do much if the records of the last five decades are any indicator.

Mahatma Gandhi, perhaps the most important thinker and social activist of this century, showed India not only the way to win freedom from the British but also to get rid of the tyranny of modern civilization. He asked, "Does economic progress clash with real progress? By economic progress, I take it, we mean material advancement without limit, and by real progress we mean moral progress which again is the same thing. In a well ordered society, the securing of one's livelihood should be and is bound to be the earliest thing in the world. Indeed, test of orderliness in a country is not the number of millionaires it owns, but the absence of starvation among the masses. The only statement that has to be examined is whether it can be laid down as a law of universal application that material advancement means moral progress."[1] A development model which is unable to remove mass poverty, which fails to bridge the gap between rural and urban areas and between haves and have-nots, and which cannot guarantee even the basic needs (food, clothing, shelter, health, education, security and self-esteem) of the people, can be pursued only to invite chaos—social, economic and moral.

RURAL UNDERDEVELOPMENT: CAUSES AND CONSEQUENCES

Among the various causes of rural underdevelopment, the following three stand out most prominently. Of course, all these and many others are interrelated; at times the cause takes the form of consequence and the consequence of the cause. The choice of just a few factors is, therefore, arbitrary to some extent. We have selected what appear to be the most fundamental ones, leaving those in the realm of strategies, policies and programmes as the derivatives.

DEVELOPMENT: A DISTORTED NOTION

The most fundamental factor is the ruling paradigm of development in general and rural development in particular. Enough has been written on this theme, and several attempts have been made to redefine development far more broadly and comprehensively than done hitherto. Development for a long time (until 1970s) was coterminous with economic development as evident from per capita national income, industrial growth, urbanization, etc. How the income was distributed, what impacts economic growth had on the quality of life of the poor, and on ecology and environment were not pertinent concerns. On becoming independent, India adopted hybrid development styles of mixing the styles pursued in USA, Western Europe and the then Soviet Union. In this model of development, rural functions and villages were treated as historical relics of a dying civilization. Ultimate answer was industrialization and urbanization. As such rural development policies remained populist, designed to push agricultural production to feed the growing number of people and industries.

Given the above world-view, rural development was equated with agricultural development. The logic ran something like this. Increased agricultural production will generate surplus for export to urban markets, within and outside the country. The rural incomes and wages will go up. This in turn will promote consumption of goods and services in rural areas. Surplus agricultural labour will move to the urban industries making urban centres the engines of economic growth. In due course of time India will get urbanised and only a small percentage of labour force will be left in rural areas to take care of a highly mechanised agriculture.

RURAL-URBAN DIVIDE

Rural and urban places were treated as two different worlds inhabited by two different sets of people. A typical villager was considered to be a conservative, traditional peasant unwilling to change and adapt to urban ways of life. As against this, an urbanite was supposed to be dynamic, risk taking, rational and willing to learn and change. How wrong these stereotyped notions were need not take our time here. The outcome of these notions is the present hiatus between rural and urban development policies in India. Rural and Urban centres in reality constitute a continuum of human settlements. They are sub-systems of a single system with considerable amount of overlapping of functions, problems, and prerequisites of development. They are inter-dependent and complimentary too. To divide them into watertight compartments is to ignore their potentials and to subvert the future of both. Today the rural and urban worlds in India are too far away from each other in terms of income, assets, occupational structure and quality of life. True, there are rich as well as poor people in rural as well as in urban centres, and the depth of poverty in both the places is highly degrading. But the rural areas are much worse off; they are struggling hard to save their souls.

How has this Rural-Urban divide come into being? It is a phenomenon of the last two hundred years or so. In ancient and medieval times there was nothing of this sort. There were large cities earlier too yet they were few in number. The villages were self-reliant and were well-served by small townships. It is pertinent to note that most of the productive functions were rural based. Even the industrial goods were produced in rural areas. Large and intermediate size cities were clearing houses for these goods. The picture was not rosy, but it was not so depressing either. With the advent of the British and the capitalist enterprises, the situation changed drastically and a new rural- urban relationship mediated by international capital developed.

Lack of adequate and appropriate development in rural parts of India has had several consequences. Some of these have further deepened poverty in villages and some others have wider ramifications. A few of them are discussed below:

1. Decreasing Access to Land

Land in its broadest sense is the most vital resource of rural India. Its importance further increases in the context of rapid growth of population particularly in rural areas. The first task of any meaningful rural development policy is to ensure is access to land for all those who were denied the same. Another major task would be to diversify the rural economy to such an extent that dependence of the people on agriculture declined. Agricultural census returns have consistently shown iniquitous distribution of arable land in India. In 1971, the country had 71 million operational holdings which increased to 105 million in 1990-91. The average size of holdings however declined from 2.28 ha in 1970-71 to 1.57 ha in 1990-91 indicating increasing pressure of population on land resources. When we look at the size of distribution of holdings, we find that 69.9 per cent of holdings were small, i.e. less than 2 ha in 1970-71. The proportion increased to 78.9 per cent in 1990-91. The share of marginal holdings (less than one ha) also increased from 51 per cent to 59 per cent. In 1970-71, almost 70 per cent (69.90%) of the total operational holdings accounted for only 20.9 per cent of the area operated.

According to the NSS Report No. 492 on "Some Aspects of Operational Land Holdings in India, 2002-03," released in 2006, there were 101.3 million holdings operated during the kharif season of 2002-03 and 95.7 million holdings operated during the rabi season of the same agricultural year. The average area operated per holding in 2002-03 was 1.06 hectare compared to 1.34 hectares during

1991-92 and 1.67 hectares in 1981-82. Marginal holdings (of size 1 hectare or less) in 2002-03 constituted 70 per cent of all operational holdings, small holdings (size 1 to 2 hectares) constituted 16 per cent, semi-medium holdings (2 to 4 hectares), 9 per cent, medium holdings (4 to 10 hectares), 4 per cent, and large holdings (over 10 hectares), less than 1 per cent. The share of marginal holdings in total operated area climbed by 6-7 percentage points since 1991-92 to reach 22-23 per cent, drawing level with the shares of the semi-medium and medium holdings, which had the largest shares in 1991-92. Tenant holdings, that is, holdings with partly or wholly leased-in land, formed about 10 per cent of operational holdings during 2002-03 compared to 11 per cent in 1991-92. On an average, a tenant holding operated 0.7 hectares of tenanted land in 2002-03. The share of leased-in land in total operated area, which has been declining more or less steadily from 10.7 per cent in 1960-61, was 6.5 per cent for the kharif season of 2002-03. Today land has become the most valuable asset for the rural inhabitants due to lack of employment leading to serious protests as a result of land acquisition.

Even after six decades of Independence the disparities have increased. "Equity is the foundation on which our democratic polity rests and thrives. It is the basis on which our citizens develop a sense of ownership of the state and its organs. Inequality can lead to large scale migration, disaffection and discord. Both the centre and the states have failed to address the issues of achieving our common development and equity goals. The process of development should unite the people and not divide them. The alienation of the weaker and the marginalized sections of the society from the development process have only aggravated the situation in the rural areas.

2. Poor Quality of Life

Rural underdevelopment has produced a vicious circle of poverty and underdevelopment; it does not allow people to get out of it. It carries them downwards. A few migrate to over-crowded cities but the cities offer nothing better. Only those who are educated and skilled make migration a success story. The rest are condemned to live in slums and *jhuggi-jhopadies* and to eke out a living from what is known as informal sector of the urban economy.

No less than 50 per cent of the rural people of India live below the poverty line though the official estimates bring it down to 30 per cent or less. But even 30 per cent means 325 million people. It is more than the total population of all other countries of the world except China. These are the people without food security; who cannot afford to send their children to schools; who have no money for health care; who have just a roof over their head; and who are partially or completely dependent on government support direct or indirect. If we trace the history of poverty in India, we note that in ancient times, only those who were displaced by natural calamities were poor. Almost everyone had access to land. All natural resources were owned jointly by the village community. During the medieval times, the diseased and dispossessed were also added to army of the poor. Dispossessed were those whose lands were taken away by the State for one reason or the other and the diseased were those who suffered from incurable diseases. The community through charity and alms took care of these people. There was poverty but within manageable limits.

The British period is marked by large-scale landlessness among the people. All lands were alienated, commons became government property; a large number of people were dislodged from their hearth and home to give place to railways, factories, cantonments, hill-stations, ports, etc. The Scheduled Castes and Tribes were the worst sufferers. And with the spread of various kinds of contagious diseases, the sick had no choice but to beg. Thus a caste of beggars emerged.

Post-independence era further intensified the poverty syndrome. The number of dispossessed, dislodged and development rejects enormously increased as did the landless due to rising population and goalless development policies. To ameliorate the worsening situation, the government adopted the same means which were adopted in medieval and British times, i.e. to extend support (subsidies), charities (grants), food for work programmes and token relief (give land in small patches to a few, only to be sold later).

3. Urban Obesity

Urban obesity has become a serious problem in India. Large cities have grown fast, because of the distress migration of rural people. Having no avenues for a decent living in villages, the young—both males and females—go to large cities to join the army of informal workers. The slums and *jhuggi-jhopadies* of large cities are their residential colonies. Many of them reside on footpaths and in parks and historical monuments. They together contribute 30 to 35 per cent of income generated in cities but they are under constant threat of eviction. Housing agencies both public and private have no land to settle them. But there is enough land for farmhouses for those who rule the country.

4. Loss of Community

Rural India was known for community solidarity. Social relations were based on duties, not on rights, for if everyone performed one's duties well, the rights of all are automatically protected. Even as late as the first quarter of 19th century, "the inhabitants give themselves no trouble about the breaking up and the division of kingdoms, while the village remains entire; they care not to what power it is transferred or to what coverage it devolves, its internal economy remained unchanged. These villages functioned as little republics having nearly everything within themselves and almost independent of foreign relations—they seem to last where nothing else lasts. The union of the village communities each forming a little separate state in itself has, I conceive, contributed more than any other cause to the preservation of the people of India through all revolutions and changes which they have suffered and it is in a high degree conducive to their happiness and enjoyment of great portion of freedom and independence. I wish, therefore, that the village constitution may never be disturbed and I dread everything that has a tendency to break them up."[2]

Unfortunately, the village was sucked into the colonial mode of production. It lost its autonomy, its self-reliance, its self-governance, and self-management. Attempts were made from time to time to revive village governments, the most recent one being the Constitutional Amendment to institute a third tier in the territorial governance. But the spirit, which made village government a well self-managing institution, has been lost. Today it is no longer the community solidarity which guides village panchayats; it is the blind pursuit of self-aggrandizement and sectoral interests. The divisive forces have taken over governments almost everywhere. Unscrupulous politicians and the goons have captured the village panchayats. People are divided on caste, ethnicity and religious bases. The community solidarity is an exception, rather than a rule.

5. Environmental Degradation

Rural underdevelopment has left no option for the people but to consume natural resources in far larger amounts than ever before. Having no other sources of livelihood, they have encroached upon the forests, pastures and water bodies destroying the ecological balance which once was the hallmark of rural space. Many plant and animal species are lost for ever and many more are on the verge of extinction.

The situation is highly disturbing in region of fragile ecology such as the Himalayas, Western Ghats, coastal zones, deserts and riverine tracts and degradation, depletion of underground water resources, deforestation and loss of biodiversity have emerged as major concerns of the people. Rural areas are no longer the preservers of nature. Man's reach has extended to highest mountains and deepest oceans. So long as he remains cut off from nature and treats it as material resource to be used as and when needed to satisfy his ever increasing wants, ecological balance would remain disturbed. Francis Bacon said, "man can command nature only if he learns to obey it." He has learnt to command it but he refuses to obey it. It is as true of urban areas as of rural parts.

RURAL DEVELOPMENT UNDER FIVE YEAR PLANS

The independence saw the thrust of planners on rural development. It was during the fifties that the concept of planned development was accepted and Five Year Plans were launched. The First Five Year Plan was from 1951-52 in which agriculture and allied areas like irrigation and power generation received priority. The Second Five Year Plan (1956-60) laid emphasis on industry and particularly the heavy industries of the public sector. The Third Five Year Plan (1961-65) aimed at substantial rise in the national per capita income while expanding the industrial base and rectifying the neglect of agriculture during the Second Five Year Plan. But due to Chinese aggression the plan process was disrupted which had an impact on both agricultural growth and industrial production. The situation worsened due to war with Pakistan and the successive droughts.

The Fourth Five Year Plan (1969-73) continued to give adequate importance to agriculture including irrigation which received 23 per cent of public outlays. The Fifth Five Year Plan (1974-75) was for just one year providing guidance to investments. The Sixth Five Year Plan (1980-84) was a more ambitious plan, which focused on increasing employment especially in the rural areas and reduction in the level of poverty. The Plan allocated 24 per cent of public sector development funding to irrigation next only to energy which was given 29 per cent. The Seventh Five Year Plan (1985-89) shifted the focus on social sector and energy moving away from industry and agriculture. The Eighth Five Year Plan (1992-96) was affected by the new economic reforms and the change in government at the centre. However, the plans gave priority to agriculture and rural development.

The momentum for rural development came with the Ninth (1997-2001) and the Tenth (2002-2007) Five Year Plans. The period saw fresh initiatives as well as continuity of earlier ones. To bridge the rural-urban divide the allocation of funds for rural development programmes has been hiked to Rs. 76,774 crores for the Tenth Plan as against Rs. 42,874 crores during the Ninth Plan. There has been greater emphasis towards giving greater participation to people in development process through Panchayati Raj and self help groups. The annual average real GDP growth during 2003-07 was 8.75 per cent. The Eleventh Five Year Plan (2007-12) aims at nine per cent growth per annum. The Plan attaches highest priority to agriculture, education and health and the Plan earmarks more than half of the budgetary support towards these areas. The goal of the Plan is to invest in our people to enable them to become active participants in economic growth process. In spite of various schemes being launched under different plans including the recently launched Mahatma Gandhi National Rural Employment Guarantee programme, the problems in the rural areas continue to mount. The anticipated impact of various schemes has not been very encouraging due to several factors including corruption. Today the sustainability of the programmes is itself being debated.

MAKING RURAL DEVELOPMENT SUSTAINABLE

The near failure of the colonial model of rural development has forced people to think of an alternative development model, a model which will ensure a high quality of life to the present as well as future generations maintaining ecological balance, community solidarity and social equity.

What is sustainable and what is not sustainable? The answer to these questions depends on our views about human destiny. If man is just another living creature, unmindful of its future and its roles and missions in this whole creation, the question of sustainability would not arise. Nature takes care of everything. Civilization exists by geological consent subject to change without notice. But if man is the latest product of this creation and he has a mission not only to maintain this creation but also to evolve himself, further, he must not do such things which will jeopardize his future. Human survival is, therefore, the foremost requirement of development. And since man's survival is linked to the survival of the creation as a whole, he must work for the preservation of nature—both living and non-living.

Of course, man has to draw resource for development from nature. He has been endowed with intellect to use these resources in such a manner and in such quantity that the basic metabolism of the nature at the macro as well as the micro levels is not derailed. Man is a part of nature; he cannot live outside it. He gets his air, water, food, building materials, industrial raw material, etc. from nature. Activities that use nature beyond its capacity to maintain life sustaining processes have to be treated as unsustainable. Their continuation may jeopardize life on planet earth. Ecological stability is, however, only one aspect of sustainability. The others are economic and social. We will examine these in some more details.

Economic Dimensions

The population of the world has increased by about three times since 1900. Had the pressure of population on resources gone up in that proportion, there would have been practically no environmental problem today. While the population during the last 50 years increased by three times, the GDP of the world increased by 21 times, the consumption of fossil fuels by 30 times, and industrial production by 50 times. The average income of the one-fifth of the population living in the developed parts of the world increased by 20 times. The countries which have stabilized population use more resources and inflict greater damage to ecology and environment. An average American consumes far more resources, perhaps 40 to 50 times more than an average Ethiopian or Indian.

Presuming that perpetual economic growth is desirable and drive for increasing consumption is in the interest of the humans, is it possible to reach the American or European standards of living for all the people of the world? The population of the industrialized countries of the world constitutes only one-fifth to one-fourth of the total population of the world. With present level of consumption, it has practically denuded the earth of its natural resources. If all the 6 billion people of the world try to attain that standard we will have to go beyond the earth to the actor space. It was possible for the West to reach this level of economic development, as the rest of the world, for one reason or the other was not in competition against it. But today the one billion well off people of the West, stand like a rock against the worse off five billion as they strive to catch them up.

Economic growth and ecological destruction seem to go together. Their ill-effects remained unfelt for so long as they affected only the marginalized majority in the Third World countries. Once its repercussions became global and the politico-economic shield which protected the industrialised countries weakened, a rethinking began. Even then, there is no attempt to go to the roots of the problem. The feeling that there are technological solutions for all problems has gained ground. Despite clear indications that current style of development cannot be sustained and that man will have to limit his material wants, the business of development has not changed much.

Social Dimensions

A.T. Durnning has divided humanity into three ecological classes on the basis of per capita consumption of natural resources, average per capita income and life style. The poor—approximately one-fifth of the world population—have income of US$ 700 per annum and share only 2 per cent of the world income. The middle class who constitutes 60 per cent of the population and has per capita income between $700 and $7500 shares 33 per cent of the world's income; and the rich who get 60 per cent of the world's income constitute only 20 per cent of the population.[3] The poor live in the rural parts and in the slums and squatter settlements of these countries of Asia, Africa and Latin America. About 5 per cent of them live in cities of developed countries. Their food consists of cereals, root crops and legumes; they drink unclean water, live in houses made of locally available materials and their needs, even the survival needs, remain unfulfilled. The middle class consumes grains with a sprinkling of vegetables and animal products; it lives in moderate houses with electricity for lights, radios, televisions, refrigerators and washing machines. It travels by public transport system, motorbikes and cars.

The rich class has per capita income of $ 7500 or more per annum. Conspicuous consumption is the hallmark of its life style. Although its per capita income is very close to the poverty line of the USA, it offers a living standard never witnessed before. The members of this class dine on meat, processed foods, and beverages of various kinds; live in houses fitted with refrigerators, washing machines, microwave ovens and a plethora of electrical and electronic goods. They have private cars, travel by air. This class takes home 32 times more income than the poor class.[4]

The world is divided into Developed and Developing, North and South, Industrialised and Industrialising countries, Urban and Rural etc. on the basis of which these classes predominate. A deeper examination of the apparently economic classification of the world shows that it is almost coterminous with ecological classification. The low income group is ecologically least destructive; its impacts are confined to the localities and regions where it exists. The middle income group bitten by the bug of consumerism has a significant negative contribution to ecology and environment. The recent meet on Climate Change at Copenhagen is an ample proof that the developed nations will continue to exploit the developing countries, even at the risk of destroying the planet earth.

Realising the widening gap between the rich and the poor of the world, the United Nations declared 1961-1971 as the decade of Development and created UNDP to promote development cooperation. It also set up the Lester Pearson Commission in 1968 to suggest the ways and means of narrowing the gap. The Commission recommended among others that the industrialised countries contribute at least 0.7 per cent of their GDP as development assistance to the developing countries.[5] The goal, set in 1968, is yet to be reached, and the World Summit on Social Development held at Copenhagen in March 1995 failed to put any firm date for its implementation.

Then came the report of the Willy Brandt Commission in 1980 entitled 'North-South: A Programme for Survival'. It recommended the creation of a World Development Fund to provide aid to the developing countries through the contribution of the industrialised countries to the tune of one per cent of their GDP. Seeing that nothing tangible was forthcoming, the UN established yet another commission in 1983 popularly known as Brundtland Commission which recommended a new pattern of development—Sustainable Development.

The United Nations held a conference "Only One Earth" in 1972 at Stockholm to deliberate on the problem of environment. The conference recognised the close relationship between poverty and environmental degradation and established the UN Environment Programme with headquarters at Nairobi. It was followed by the Vancouver conference on Human Settlements in 1976 which discussed the problems of human settlements, both rural and urban, with particular reference to housing in its broadest sense. It led to the establishment of another agency called UN Centre for Human Settlements again at Nairobi. The latest in the series of such global conferences is the Earth Summit held at Copenhagen in 1995, and Habitat II held at Istanbul in 1986.

In spite of these conferences and follow up efforts at the global as well as national level, one-fifth of the world population continue to live below poverty line; 30 per cent of it do not get clean water to drink; and at least half the people of the world do not have appropriate sanitary facilities. New diseases like AIDS are at our door steps and several of the diseases we thought we have conquered are on their come back trail. Despite the ratification of the Convention on the Rights of the Child by practically all countries of the world, about 250 million children do not get enough food to eat; 15 million per year die of malnutrition before they attain the age of five; Vitamin A deficiency adversely affects forty million children and half a million child prostitutes cater to the lust of sex tourists from rich countries. The condition of the women is deplorable; they constitute 70 per cent of the poor and 66 per cent of the illiterates of the world.

Ecological Dimensions

Life exists on the planet earth alone and nowhere else, as far as our current knowledge goes. The thin shell of the earth, only a few kilometres thick, supports all the life we know. The conditions which synergically support life are also not uniformly distributed on the earth surface. Availability of light, water, temperature, nutrients and several other life supports varies from place to place giving rise to as many as 10-30 million species of organisms including a large number of microbes. These millions of species are not independent units of life. Each has evolved from an evolving environment at a specific junction of time and space and synergic presence of physical, chemical and biotic conditions. And no species has come into existence without the above pre-existing conditions including the presence of the species which evolved earlier. Species by nature live and thrive in community of species; they form a symbiotic relationship with each other and with the environment for mutual support and benefit.

The biota has not stopped evolving; more specialisation and diversification through branching and cross-breeding, greater interdependence, and adjustment with more diverse and complex environment, never stops. The tropical forests and coral reefs are the ultimate in evolutionary expression. One hundred species in a hectare is a common phenomenon in these forests and reefs. Once it is lost, it is lost for ever. We cannot create those associative conditions; it can come about only under the very special circumstances mentioned above. Destroy one species and you lose many other species associated with it.

Which species are more important and useful for man than other? Can we not manage the biosphere without some species? Attempts have been made to answer questions like these by finding out the economic costs of losing them. We do not, however, have the methodology to measure the unmeasurable, i.e. the contribution biodiversity makes to keep the biosphere ready to support life on the earth. The erosion of biotic resources begins in small bits, each apparently small enough to be acceptable at the moment but its cumulative effects impoverish the landscape and make it incapable of supporting life. While no single species may be indispensable for the normal functioning of the biosphere, all species together constitute the driving force that maintains it. Biosphere is thus the product of the evolution and continued interaction of the species. Environmental issue is thus not a simple issue of economic cost-benefit analysis; it is an issue of very survival of life on the surface of the earth.

Here lies the dilemma of development. An expanding population aspiring to catch up with industrialised countries is looking for space on the earth—the space whose potential for photosynthesis is turned to personal support. Of course, the aspirations are reasonable and legitimate, but the resources are limited. The space and resources mean biodiversity and biodiversity is both opportunity and essential function in maintaining biosphere. Use of resources should be circumscribed by the fact that we live in a matrix of natural systems that will continue to dominate and operate the biosphere at little or no expense to the society as long as the basic function of the matrix is maintained intact. Violation of it can prove disastrous.

Half of the land of the world is partially or fully degraded, water pollution is now a mass killer; and air pollution is maiming millions of people through lung diseases of various kinds. According to some estimates one-fifth of the plant and animal species would be lost for ever by the turn of this century. Our over-crowded cities with ever increasing slums and squatter settlements and rising unemployment have already become breeding grounds for crimes, psychopathic diseases, and lawlessness. The world appears to be passing through a period of cultural decay and man appears to have lost his dignity.[6]

Political Dimensions

One of the major contributions of the founding fathers of the Indian republic was the strengthening of the democratic institutions. In a heterogeneous society like ours only democracy can help us to live together. The electoral process is very important for participatory democracy. Grassroots democracy enables the development of leaders as well as ensuring that the development that takes place is based on a participatory mechanism. Power to the people will only ensure that people will have faith in democratic principles and strengthen the nation state. There is an urgent need to address the problems of local bodies and ensure that they become participatory in the true sense. The state governments need to transfer power along with the finances to the Panchayati Raj Institutions. The Right to Information Act should be used as a tool to build transparency in the execution of the schemes. For democracy to survive political mobilization and political processes have to be strengthened and it should begin from the grassroots level.

LEARNING FROM GANDHI: NEED *VS.* GREED

Mahatma Gandhi is perhaps the only great thinker of this century who could foresee the social and ecological consequences of the ruling model of development and offer an alternative model. Gandhi was not only a pioneer but also very original. He was not an academic theoretician, but a man of unparalleled wisdom. The gap between this man of wisdom and the men of knowledge that this century has produced in plenty still remains unbridged. He remained irrelevant to the twentieth century, if by relevance we mean currency of his views and thoughts. This has happened in spite of the fact that he not only propounded concepts and approaches but also put them into practice. The nonviolent struggle he successfully launched against the mightiest colonial power of the time was emulated elsewhere too but it has yet to make a major dent in the war machine of the world and the war mentality of the people. He demonstrated how a very high level of culture and civilization could be evolved without destroying the environment, and without exploiting nature and fellow humans. Yet, in his own country, India, leaders rejected his ideas. Perhaps he was born ahead of his time; he may be the man of twenty first century.

Gandhi was highly critical of modern civilization. He called it satanic. He says, "this civilization is such that one has only to be patient and it will be self-destroyed". And elsewhere he says, "I ventured utterly to condemn modern civilization" because I hold that the spirit of it is evil. It is possible to show that some of the incidents are good, but I have examined its tendencies in the scale of ethics.[7] He based his thoughts and actions on three basic premises: (1) violence cannot be curbed by violence, it can be curbed by nonviolence alone; (2) all lives on the planet earth has come from a common source; it is untied and interdependent; and (3) real progress means moral progress. Progress in other walks of life must subserve moral progress. After considerable amount of thinking and experimentation, Gandhi came to the conclusion that India had the potential of offering an alternative civilisation model to the world, a model which can ensure human dignity, economic progress, ecological balance and interpersonal and interspatial equity. "We are inheritors of a rural civilization. The vastness of our country, the vastness of its population, its situation and climate of the country have in my opinion defined it for a rural civilization. Its defects are well known, but not one of them is irremediable. To uproot it and substitute for it an urban civilization seems to me an impossibility.[8]

Gandhi felt convinced that major Indian cities were built to subserve British interests; that they had weakened the villages where much of India lived; and that they were the product of industrialism and could not be sustained for too long. He advocated a new system of human settlements with cities subserving the interests of the villages. By village he meant a micropolitian community consisting of approximately 1000-5000 people. It will have all the modern facilities of sanitation, housing, various infrastructures, and community organizations which the country at different stages of development would be able to afford. In his scheme of things much of the industrial activity would move back to the villages so that each village will be self-reliant in its basic needs like food, clothing, housing, education, health, recreation and community management. For other matters, it will depend on the neighbouring villages, the towns, the nation and the world as a whole. It will constitute the innermost circle in his theory of oceanic circle with man in the centre.

Gandhi's writings on the issue of industrialization and machinery show that he was not against either of the two *per se*. If machinery could provide creative employment to everyone, he would welcome that. And if industrialism could be pursued without exploiting the people and destroying the nature, he would support it. He felt that violence was built in modern industrialization and mechanization processes and hence it could not be devoid of exploitation of man and nature. "Mechanization is good when the hands are too few for the work intended to be accomplished. It is an evil when there are more hands than required for the work, as is the case in India." In other words, machinery must serve man, "it is good so long it is controlled by the human beings. But when it starts controlling human beings, it becomes evil".[9]

Echoing the same ideas, Charles Reich in Greening of America says "the new consciousness seeks to transform Science and Technology, to restore them to their proper place as tools of man rather than as determinants of man's existence. It is by no means anti-technological; it does not want to break machines, but it does not want the machine to run men. It makes the wholly rational assertion that machines should do the bidding of man, of man who knows and respects his own nature and the natural order of which he is a part. The new consciousness seeks the new ways to live in the light of what technology has made both possible and desirable."[10]

Much of what Gandhi stood for is capsuled in his views on human settlements. He was against cities in the form they exist and the roles they play today. He was, however, not for the dismantling of cities as he was not for the dismantling of the machines and everything else that modern civilization had produced. He was for their transformation for a new set of roles and functions. Gandhi was looking for a model of development India would need after gaining independence. Having come to the conclusion that in the long run the western model based on industrialization and urbanization would not work, he started exploring what India itself had to offer in this regard. He stumbled on the ancient village model which fitted well with his concept of humanized development he was looking for.

I believe that if India, and through India, the world is to achieve freedom then sooner or later we shall have to go and live in the village. In huts, not in palaces. Millions of people can never live in cities and palaces in comfort and peace. We can have the vision of truth and nonviolence only in the simplicity of the villages. The sum and substance of what I want to say is that individual person should have control over the things that are necessary for the sustenance of life. My ideal village still exists only in my imagination. After all every human being lives in the world of his own imagination. In this village of my dreams, the villager will not be dull he will be all awareness. He will not live like an animal in filth and darkness. Men and women will live in freedom prepared to face the whole world. Granting all this, I can still envisage a number of things that will have to be organized on a large scale. I do not know what things there will be or will not be. Nor am I bothered about it. If I can make sure of the essential thing, I give up everything. And this essential thing was the replacement of the ruling civilization.[11]

Behind Gandhi's insistence on village economy was his grand design of the new civilization based on sustainable development in the real sense of the term. He wanted the human intrusion into the functioning of the biosphere to be minimized by closing man dominated systems such as cities, agricultural and industrial activities to the point where their net effects on the biosphere approximated those of the natural systems they have replaced. No other system of human settlement can achieve this except the village in the form of an Urban Centre.

WADING THROUGH THE GLOBALIZATION PROCESS

With the globalisation and liberalization of Indian economy, a new development context has emerged in the country since 1990. Centralised planning which determined the amount, activity and place for investment started taking the form of indicative planning. With the new policy of liberalized economy, private sector became the prime mover. The growth rate of the economy went up to 7-8 per cent per annum, a quantum jump from the normal growth rate of 3 per cent. Capital and technology started moving from Europe, America and Japan making the industrial environment buoyant and encouraging. It is now hoped that the economy will have the capacity to grow at the rate of 8 to 10 per cent in the long run. In 1996-97 the industrial sector grew at the rate of 9-10 per cent and the agricultural sector at the rate of 3.9 per cent, so that the food output amounted to over 191 million tonnes.[12] During 1999-2000 it went up to 205 million tonnes.

The rosy picture drawn above will be accompanied by a number of disturbing features which if not corrected in time will pull the economy down. As stated earlier at least 30 per cent of the people of India are below the poverty line. According to the World Development Indicators, 2007 the poverty (at $ 1 a day, PPP, 2004-05) is 33.5 per cent. Would rapid industrialisation based on labour displacing technology help the rural poor improve their economic status? The economic distance between haves and have nots, whether seen in terms of regions or groups of people, is already too large to keep the poor peaceful. The liberalisation process is benefiting those regions and groups which is already better off. Would the widening developmental gap not generate social tension injurious to the growth of the economy? What is happening in Bihar is only a curtain raiser? And finally, what is going to happen to ecology and environment?

Given the above economic, social and ecological perspectives, we must change our approaches to rural development. The goal is to usher in a sustainable process development.

EXPANDING THE SCOPE OF RURAL

Rural development is often capsuled in agricultural development. Rural means areas which are dotted with small human settlements producing and processing agricultural commodities. It also includes non-urban artisanal and small scale modern industries and business enterprises. In environmental terms it is an open landscape with a great variety of plant and animal species. Socially, rural is relatively slow moving following the rhythm of nature. It is in constant touch with nature and life. Rural people have robust body and mind; very practical in attitude.

Rural is often set apart from urban. In many ways it is so, but in matters fundamental, the two constitute parts of a continuum, they are interdependent. In an ideal situation they should feed and support each other. In order that rural can stand equal to urban, the former should diversify itself and should not be confined to the production of foods, fibres and industrial raw material. It should embark on agricultural processing on a massive scale and in the present context on information technology related activities. Food processing is the largest industrial sector in the United States. In Canada, a quarter of the workforce is employed in post-production food sector (in processing, marketing, distributing, catering and related service industries) even though only 3 per cent of the workforce is engaged in agriculture. Processed food is valued at $400 billion in USA and $300 billion in Europe. In India, more than two million people work in food industries. This is the largest component of industrial workforce. In Bombay alone over 100,000 people are engaged in this sector. The Malaysian food processing industries comprise a fifth of all industrial activity, while in Thailand, 60 per cent of the industrial economy comprises food processing.

It is apparent that the potential of rural sector of the economy have not been fully harnessed in India and that the declining share of agricultural sector in the GDP is partly because of the neglect of the rural sector of the economy and partly because agriculture is equated with crop production alone. Climatic variations in India enjoin on farmers to produce food, vegetables and fruits in different climatic zones at different times creating fluctuations between abundance and scarcity. In the month of January, tomatoes are sold at Re. 1 per kg. in the Ganga plain. In June, they cost Rs. 25 per kg. Processing of such products, wherever they are produced in abundance, would help improve the earnings of the farmers; would provide employment to many, and make the product available in lean season.

With the demographic changes and accelerated urbanization, the demand for packaged foods is bound to increase. In India too, processed foods are reaching every middle class household. A good quantity of it is being exported. All this would generate additional income and employment but so long as 60 per cent of Indian population remain outside this new movement, agro-industrialization will not achieve its potentials. Market forces, if allowed a free reign, would ignore the poor and cater to the needs of just 300 million Indians out of the total population of 1000 million. India's prime natural resources land, water and agricultural crops will be used to provide value added food products which only the well-to-do in the country and consumers abroad can purchase. It is the task of the agro processing sector to reach not only the rich but also the poor, the latter in production as well as marketing and consumption.

Agro-industrial development from below is the need of the hour. Agro-industries have to embrace cottage and home industries. Each village has to be oriented to agro-processing activities operated individually or jointly by groups of people or the whole village community. It is found that community weaving, pisciculture, vermiculture, sericulture, mushroom cultivation, gobar gas plant, afforestation have increased incomes of the poor. Joint efforts of Mahila Mandals in processing goods have made vast changes in some areas.

DEBUREAUCRATIZING DEVELOPMENT

How to organize sustainable rural development? Unfortunately the governmental agencies as they are at present have failed to deliver the goods. Nor have the Panchayati Raj Institutions improved the situation. Yet at the same time, one has to take cognizance of these institutions, lest they become hindrances in the path of progress.

The first thing that is urgently needed is the revitalization of rural cooperatives. In fact, the Gram Panchayat's role should be limited to municipal functions. Each village should have cooperative for developmental purposes. In addition to these three institutions (Government, Panchayats and Cooperatives) there should be one or two NGOs for a group of villages to help the three technically and otherwise and to take initiative where others do not venture to tread. There is no shortage of funds for Rural Development. Funds are there but they are misused and mismanaged. Without the involvement of the civil society organizations in the monitoring of the implementation of the programmes, the current situation will not change. The task of the civil society is to organize the people for action; to train them for initiative; to make people aware of the funds available for various target groups and purposes; to help people secure funds; and to monitor the progress. They will also generate some activities on their own. The RTI (Right to Information) can be an effective instrument to bring about transparency and ensure accountability.

MICROPOLITAN PLANNING

Given the current rural-urban divide, sustainable rural development is a difficult task. During the last fifty years no conscious attempt was made in this direction. The market forces have, however, injected a number of non-farm functions in rural areas producing haphazard growth along highways and road crossings. This growth should be channelised in right direction to create a new spatial structure of rural habitat supportive of sustainable rural development. Spatial structure envisaged here has to begin with a central village around which exist feeder hamlets. A village in general has a population of about 1000 to 5000 people. The village should have the following institutions:

1. Government officials (for implementing official programmes).
2. Village Panchayat (for municipal functions and village planning).
3. Village Cooperative (for development functions).
4. NGO (for generating awareness, cooperation initiative, initial support, etc.).
5. Village School (for educating children).
6. Swadeshi Bhandar (store to sell village products and requirement of village people).
7. Health Education Centre.
8. Gramin Bank (on Bangladesh Model).

A group of five to ten villages should be served by a micropolis (service centre) with a cooperative union, higher secondary school, regional swadeshi bhandar, a training centre for agro-industrial activities, and primary health care centre apart from various other functions such as police chawki, and private business activities. A micropolis should ordinarily be located on a road preferably at a road crossing. India, in order to develop its rural areas, should have about 50,000 micropolises. To serve the micropolitan centres, there should be higher order centres. A micropolitan region is the area of five to ten villages with a micropolis. As far as possible the micropolitan region should be self-reliant and self-sufficient in basic minimum needs. Here self-sufficiency does not mean autonomy nor it means producing everything. It means maximum autonomy with maximum interdependence. To make India self-reliant the beginning has to be made from the lowest level, i.e. micropolis.

Handicrafts and agro-processing should be declared as essential elements of rural development and they together should be accorded the same priority as crop production. All households should be encouraged to diversify their activities but those who are marginal or small farmers, as also those who are landless should be brought within the fold of cottage and agro-industries within ten years. Whatever is locally produced should be purchased by the gramodaya shop to be sold within the micropolitan area or outside. The producers should get the price of the goods produced instantaneously.

Thus conceived each village will strengthen inter-dependence and self-reliance. The micropolis will link up the village with larger towns and cities. Micropolitan centres being agro-industrial centres will absorb much of the surplus rural population locally and thereby relieve the pressure of population, the large cities are facing today.

BUILDING UP FROM BELOW

As discussed earlier, sustainability has to be seen in ecological, economic and social terms. If forests are cut, what compensatory measures have been taken to replace them? If a group of individuals are deprived of their means of livelihood, what steps are taken to put them on their feet elsewhere? If minerals are being consumed to produce industrial goods, what is being done to develop substitutes when the mines are exhausted and what measures are adopted to check environmental degradation? If chemical fertilizers are used to increase agricultural productivity, what steps have been taken to check soil exhaustion? If canal irrigation is a must, are there accompaning measures to check salination of land due to excessive irrigation and rise in the underground water table? Even a minute activity has its own environmental, social and economic consequences.

Similarly, each area, rural or urban, each village and city has to see whether it can carry on its functions for ever without exploiting nature or without exploiting other people or without facing chaos. As an example, is it possible for Third World Countries to reach the American standard of living without destroying the earth? Americans cannot maintain their income, if the terms of trade between North and South become reasonable. Similarly, urban India cannot maintain its economic superiority, if the terms of trade between urban and rural products are rationalized.

Cities as they are today consume nature; generate social anomie and economic polarization. None of these are sustainable. It is not the size of cities that should be the concern of the people; it is the management and governance of its metabolism that is the issue. A city should be conceived of as an assemblage of smaller communities each linked organically with the other to form the whole. These communities like villages should be modular even though fitting within the larger frame of the city though transport, communication and power systems. Each neighbourhood should be self-managed; only the residues should be managed at the ward level; and only major issues should be left to the city corporation. Let each neighbourhood and ward produce its own power, arrange its own water supply and manage its own sanitation.

The same principles will apply to a micropolitan region. Each village will function as a modular unit of the micropolis. The micropolitan region will be like a ward, and a supra-micropolitan region with intermediate size urban centres as the metropolitan regions. Thus conceived, the governance of the rural and urban areas will be similar and based on same management principles.

MAKING SUSTAINABLE RURAL DEVELOPMENT WORK

Land Use Planning

Land is the most vital resource of rural areas. Rural land should be classified on the basis of its suitability for various uses—agriculture, forestry, pasture, public uses, habitation, etc. Each micropolitan region should have a land use plan and the same should be made a legal document. Each village should also have a landuse plan which should detail out the suitability of each piece of land (plot) for various crops, tillage practice, irrigation, and mix of chemical and organic manuring.

Each village should have a forest land, something like the Deoban of older days or biodiversity reserves of modern times. The forest land should cover at least 5-10 acres of land depending upon the size of the village. It should be a common property, only minor forest cover should remain on it, so that in due course of time minor wild animals can get shelter. And each micropolitan region should have a biodiversity reserve of 10-15 ha. Each village and micropolitan region should have water management plan, along with the landuse plan. Misuse of water has become a major problem in the world. In India water scarcity has assumed serious proportions. The first step in this direction would be revive/restore the dead ponds and other water bodies. The second step that is urgently needed is to ration canal water to discourage flow irrigation that is leading to rise in water table. Drinking water should get priority in water resource planning.

Each micropolitan region should evolve a production plan which should meet the following requirements: (1) Food requirements of the region; (2) Agro-industrial requirements of region; (3) export crops; (4) input requirements (water, chemical fertilizers, manuring etc.); and (5) Training of the people. Efforts should be made to persuade the farmers to follow the plan indicators. The production plan should also include potentials of energy, manure, and seed production. Potential markets for village products should get due attention. The objective of production planning should be to move towards natural principles of agricultural production so that use of chemicals and other inputs like water is minimized in consonance with the carrying capacity of nature.

Self-Reliance

Each village must produce its own food grains, vegetables, fruits, milk and milk products as well as red and white meat (wherever relevant). But in case it is not done because of the physical and ecological constraints, it should be achieved at the micro-politan level. Any residuals should be met at the supra-micropolitan level so that practically each district would be self-reliant in food and raw materials it needs to run its processing and service industries. Each micropolitan region should ultimately generate its own electricity, manage its waste, produce manure, and have its own marketing outlet; run its own school, gramin bank and health service. It should have its own water supply system as well as excreta disposal.

Each household in the village must be engaged in one or the other non-farm functions—services or processing of agricultural produce. Each village should aim at selling nothing without processing. This may never be achieved, because lot of agricultural commodities has to be consumed fresh (fruits and vegetables). But to keep such a perspective will be helpful in diversification.

Ecological Regeneration

It is yet to be realised that environmental reconstruction can become a highly paying proposition. Community forests with selective cuttings can generate lot of resources. Pasture land with regulated entry of animals can promote dairying, and leaving water bodies intact provides avenues for aquaculture of plants and fish. Rural areas should become green again and its sanitation should reach the standards of at least Harappa and Mohenjo-Daro which flourished in India over 4000 years ago, within the next two decades or so.

Micropolitan Planning

Indian planners should not be neglectful of villages and rural areas as they have been in the past. They should adopt the concept of modular cities and modular micropolitan regions and prepare plans for each city and village with sustainability as the basic requirement. Each district should have a sustainable micropolitan regional development plan of action, so that the message can spread out to other parts. And each state should have an experimental action plan for a city with modular units. Each micropolitan region will be self-governing; and so will each village unit in the region be. Governance will be the joint responsibility of elected representative of the people (Panchayats) and council of Pradhans of village panchayats, cooperatives and NGO concerned.

CONCLUSION

The basic objective of sustainable development is to develop a balanced and ecologically sound microregional economy and polity. In an ideal setting and within a span of 20 years (i.e. by 2025) the rural economy should derive 30 per cent of its income from crop farming, 25 per cent from processing activities, 30 per cent from services and 15 per cent from remittances from outside and government.

In country like India, each micropolitan region will have to evolve its own plan to suit local geography, culture and experience. In cities, this concept could be implemented first in selected small towns and in the periphery of large towns so that villages falling within the expanding urban boundary are able to cope up with urban challenges. The concept of micro-politicization of rural areas was enunciated by the senior author in 1966 at Mexico International Geographical Congress. Subsequently, it was further developed at the United Nations Research Institute for Social Development Geneva (1969) and published in Mouton series on 'Regional Development' edited by A.R. Kuklinski. It was further elaborated and substantiated by case studies in India and published in 1974 under the title 'Regional Development Planning in India: A New Strategy.'

A number of other scholars including the associate author have been thinking on similar lines. John Freedman in USA, Michael Douglas in UK, Taylor in Australia and many others have suggested ideal spatial structure for rural development. This paper draws from these thinkers also, and attempts to give the basic framework for sustainable Rural Development in India.

REFERENCES

1. M.A. Ali, "On Patterns of Operational Holdings in Chhattisgarh", in *Agricultural Situation in India*, May, 1996, pp. 73-79.
2. Minutes of East India Company 1812; and Minutes of Sir Charles Metcalfe (Acting Governor General of India), 1830.
3. A.T. Durnning, "Income Distribution is Worsening", in *Vital Signs*, N.T. Norton, 1992. See also his, "How much is enough?"
4. *Ibid.*
5. The report was well received as the environment for aid to developing countries at that time was favourable.
6. See Ram K. Vepa, *New Technology and Gandhian Concept,* specially chapter 7. New Delhi. Gandhi Book House, 1975; and Ramashray Roy, "Sustainable Development of Society: Imperatives and Perspectives", in the *Indian Journal of Public Administration,* Vol. 39, No. 3, July-September, 1993, pp. 221-28.
7. M.K. Gandhi, *Hind Swaraj*, p.34.
8. ——, *Harijan,* October 14, 1939
9. ——, *Harijan*, November 16, 1934.
10. *Ibid.*
11. M.K. Gandhi, *Young India,* 1928.
12. Speech of the Finance Minister of India in Lok Sabha on 1997-98 Budget on 28th February, 1997.

3

Are Women and Men Equal Partners in Development?: A Reality Check from Rural India

NIRA RAMACHANDRAN

BACKGROUND

Sustainable human development necessarily rests on the equitable distribution of development benefits between men and women. India, as the rest of South Asia, is infamous for its deeply rooted gender discrimination. Most development indicators are heavily skewed against women, whether one assesses economic characteristics such as assets, wages or employment or looks at social indicators like nutrition status, health or education. Much has been written on the need for women's empowerment. Policies have been framed, countless schemes implemented and large scale budgetary allocations made. Compulsory gender budgeting is on the anvil for all Ministries in the Government of India and is likely to be put into practice soon. The introduction of micro credit schemes and the formulation of women's Self Help Groups (SHGs) have transformed lives in villages, where they have been implemented. Yet the scales remain heavily weighted against women and poverty, itself, is now being described as "feminised".

This paper attempts to perform a quick reality check in a sample group of villages—not remote and isolated, but located within easy reach of the State capital. The assumption is that the empowerment status of women in these rural settlements will reflect the situation in villages elsewhere in the country, which have attained a certain level of development with access to basic infrastructure and communication, and are also exposed to urban influence. By implication, it may be assumed that women's empowerment in the more remote and backward areas of the country is likely to be correspondingly lower.

RESEARCH QUESTIONS

The paper will attempt to answer the following questions:

- Are there major variations in access to productive assets, livelihoods and incomes between females and males?
- Is there a difference in mobility and access to institutions such as banks and markets between males and females?
- What is the level of utilisation of Government provided Nutrition and Health Services by women?

METHODOLOGY

The study is based on a household survey of six villages of the Vikasnagar Block in Dehradun District, Uttarakhand conducted in December 2005. The survey covered 207 households, of which 93 were Below the Poverty Line, and 14 headed by females.

THE STUDY AREA

The state of Uttarakhand created in 2000, consists of the Himalayan mountain and sub-mountain districts of the erstwhile state of Uttar Pradesh in North India. The study focuses on the Rudrapur Cluster of six villages located in the western part of the Doon Valley, within the Vikasnagar Block of Dehradun District. The area lies within easy reach (40 kms.) of Dehradun, the state capital and as such has easy access to education and health facilities, markets, transport and communication. Located at an altitude of approximately 2,000 feet above sea level, the region is part of the "Doon" or valley enclosed between two distinct mountain ranges—the Himalayas to the north and the Shivaliks to the south. Dissected by fast flowing mountain streams (*chos*), which remain dry and boulder strewn for the major part of the year, it is nonetheless prone to sudden torrents, effectively cutting off the area from outside contact. Yet, lack of irrigation remains an issue and drinking water shortages persist.

Agriculture on small landholdings both on the valley floor and the terraced hillsides is the principal source of livelihood. Rice, especially the famed *Basmati* and market gardening are the main sources of income. The dense vegetation surrounding the villages and fields is a source of fuel, fodder and medicinal herbs and controls to a large extent, the daily schedule and time use patterns of the women.

The cluster of study villages extends from Rudrapur to Horawala *Panchayats*, with the highest densities in the north and centre of the cluster. Rudrapur is the largest village with a population of 2,207, while the smallest village Chandpur has only 391 people.

With the exception of Horawala, where the dominant community belongs to the general caste (84%), all the sample villages are pre-dominantly inhabited by the Scheduled Castes and/or Scheduled Tribes, which form the most vulnerable social groups.

Table 3.1: Demographic Characteristics of the Study Villages

Village	*Total Population*	*Sex Ratio*	*% SC/ST Population*	*No. of Sample Households*	*No. of Female Headed Sample Households*
Barwa	731	955	65	17	0
Chandpur	391	965	70	25	4
Horawala	1836	972	16	27	1
Langha	1466	882	83	26	3
Rudrapur	2207	856	67	81	3
Sorna	1820	978	59	31	3

Source: Field Survey December 2005.

As regards sex ratios, four of the six study villages record values above the national average of 933 (females per '000 males). Higher sex ratios in Uttarakhand, however, are not necessarily indicative of lower gender discrimination, but may, in fact, reflect the practice of large scale out migration of males to join the armed forces or take up other occupations. In the case of Langha and Rudrapur, however, sex ratios are considerably lower than the national average.

As regards the availability of infrastructure, Table 3.2 highlights the glaring shortage of health facilities even at primary healthcare level and also Fair Price Shops, which are the outlets of the Government's subsidised public food distribution system (PDS). Basic amenities like piped water supply and electricity are available in about 50 per cent of the villages, while only the largest village—Rudrapur has a bank. Educational facilities, on the other hand, seem to be well developed and evenly distributed.

Table 3.2: Village-wise Availability of Infrastructure

Village	*Primary School*	*Middle School*	*High School*	*College*	*Anganwadi*	*Primary Health Care Centre*	*Bank*	*Fair Price Shop*	*Piped Water*	*Electricity*
Barwa	y	y							y	
Chandpur	y	y								
Horawala	y	y	y	y	y	Ayurvedic Dispensary		y		
Langha	y	y							y	y
Rudrapur	y	y	y		y	Y (Add. PHC)	y		y	y
Sorna	y	y	y	y	y			y		y

Source: Field Survey December 2005.

The Households

A standard household survey often overlooks inequities in gender access to income, assets, education, health, food and mobility. While economic and social disparities are usually, factored into any analysis, gender is often ignored. The fact that gender disparities, usually cut across caste and class barriers makes it imperative to incorporate a gender analysis into household surveys, if accurate diagnosis and effective solutions to persisting issues are sought.

While the current questionnaire did not specifically aim at analysing gender disparities, the data sets do contain gender specific information on most aspects. It is commonly acknowledged that the growing number of female headed households in India, particularly rural India, is strongly associated with increasing poverty. The phenomenon is often referred to as "the feminisation of poverty" (BRIDGE, 2001; Marcoux, 1997; Moghadam, 1997). Female headed households, usually account for about 20 per cent of the total households at all-India level. Regional variations, however, do exist. In the current sample, female headed households account for only 7 per cent of the total surveyed households. While so small a sample may not permit observations which could be extended to the entire area, they may provide pointers to issues which are gender-derived and may underlie the low rate of success achieved by many interventions, even those specifically targeted at women.

Income Levels

Table 3.3: Income Patterns by Male and Female Headed Households

Type of HH	*Income Group*							
	>Rs.500,000	100,000-500,000	50,000-100,000	25,000-50,000	15,000-25,000	<15,000	N.R.	Total
FHH	1	0	1	2	5	5	0	14
MHH	0	14	19	30	62	66	2	193
Total	**1**	**14**	**20**	**32**	**67**	**71**	**2**	**207**

Source: Field Survey December 2005.

Over 70 per cent of the female headed households have an annual income of less than Rs. 25,000 as compared to only 66 per cent of the male headed households. In the lowest income group of below Rs.15,000 per annum, the proportion of female headed households (36%) and male headed households (34%) is, however, more equal. As income levels rise, the proportion of female headed households reduces more sharply than the proportion of male headed households, though the distribution is not significantly different. However, at the highest income level of above Rs. 500,000 per annum, the only household falling into the category is female headed. As this one household tends to distort the analysis, it will be excluded from the forthcoming analysis.

Livelihoods

Agriculture remains the most important source of income for the majority of the households, either from cultivation of their own lands or as wages from agricultural

Table 3.4: Major Source of Income

	Cultivation	Agricultural Wage Labour	Non-agricultural Wage Labour	Artisan/ Self-employed	Petty Shop/ Small Business	Salaried Employment	Income from Rent, Pension, etc.
FHHs	8 (64)	1 (7)	1 (7)	—	1 (7)	—	—
MHHs	148 (77)	7 (4)	9 (5)	9 (5)	3 (1)	16 (8)	1 (0.5)
THHs	157	8	10	9	4	17	2

Note: Figures in parentheses represent percentages.

Source: Household Survey December 2005.

labour. Of the female headed households, 71 per cent report agriculture as the main source of income, while in the case of male headed households it is as high as 80 per cent. The majority of the households, both male and female headed are engaged in cultivating their own lands (77% and 64%, respectively). However, the proportion of households engaged in wage labour, both agricultural and non-agricultural is considerably higher among female headed households. Income accrues to both female and male headed households from self-employment as artisans, owners of petty shops or businesses, salaries or pensions and rent from assets.

Table 3.5: Diversification of Livelihoods

	Number of HHs with Income from			
	Single Source	Two Sources	Three sources	Four or more Sources
FHHs	6 (46)	5 (38)	2 (15)	—
MHHs	62 (33)	93 (50)	26 (14)	6 (3)
THHs	67 (33)	98 (49)	28 (14)	7 (3)

Note: Figures in parentheses represent percentages.

Source: Household Survey, December 2005.

Poor households tend to resort to varied activities to make ends meet. However, of the female headed households in the sample, 46 per cent derive income from a single source, while only 38 per cent have two sources of income. On the other hand, half the male headed households derive income from two sources, indicating, perhaps, greater stability in income accrual. Overall, only 54 per cent of female headed households have multiple sources of income as against 67 per cent of male headed households.

Households Below the Poverty Line

A total of 93 households are Below the Poverty Line (BPL)[1]. Six of the 14 (43%)

female headed households fall in the BPL category, while in the case of male headed households, the ratio is 45 per cent. Not surprisingly, all the BPL female headed households have BPL cards, (which entitle them to subsidised food grain and sugar), as women decision makers are known to show greater concern for household food security, while only about 80 per cent of the male headed BPL households possess such cards.

Table 3.6: Number of BPL Households with BPL (Ration) Cards[2]

Household Type	*No. of BPL HHs*	*No. of BPL HHs with Card*	*No. of BPL HHs without Card*
FHH	6	6	0
MHH	87	70	17
Total	93	76	17

Source: Household Survey December 2005.

Ownership of Productive Assets

Differentials in ownership pattern of productive assets most clearly reflect gender variations and the limitations on the income generating capacities of female headed households in rural society. Table 3.7 reveals the total lack of productive assets in female headed households, except for sewing machines, which are owned by three of these households and a knitting machine by one. Sewing machines either come as part of the dowry during marriage or are a last resort for earning a livelihood when all other more profitable income generation avenues are closed to the individual. With the exception of a single female headed household in the highest income category which owns a harvester, a tractor and a bio-gas plant, none of the

Table 3.7: Ownership of Productive Assets by Gender of HH Head

Asset Type	*No. of FHHs owning asset*	*No. of MHHs owning asset*	*Total No. of HHs owning asset*
Pumpset		1	1
Generator		1	1
Thresher		11	11
Harvester	1	18	19
Winnower		3	3
Bullock cart		5	5
Biogas Plant	1	28	29
Cycle Rickshaw		9	9
Agro-processing Unit		1	1
Sewing machine	3	59	62
Knitting machine	1	14	15
Truck		1	1
Tractor	1	11	12
Petrol Pump		1	1

Source: Household Survey December 2005.

remaining female headed households owns any agricultural asset, though 80 per cent of them cite agriculture as a source of income.

Wage Differentials

Major differences in daily wages for male and female labour continue to prevail. The average daily wage for males is Rs. 70-80 as against Rs. 50-60 for females.

Gender Variations in Mobility

Restrictions on the mobility of females are particularly strong in rural areas. A comparison of the mobility of females and males in the study villages was attempted by selecting three popular destinations—the neighbouring village, the Block HQs at Vikasnagar at a distance of 25 kms. from Rudrapur, where the nearest *Mandi* (wholesale market), Primary Health Centre (PHC) and other amenities are situated, and the State Capital of Dehradun, located at a distance of 41 kms and a Class I city with a population of 496,871 (Census 2000) and a wide range of amenities.

Table 3.8: Gender Variations in Adult Mobility

	Neighbouring Village		*Vikasnagar (Block HQ)*		*Dehradun (State Capital)*	
	Regular	*Occasional*	*Regular*	*Occasional*	*Regular*	*Occasional*
Females	2	62	17	96	2	44
Males	31	68	36	133	12	26
Mobility Ratio Female/Male	0.06	0.91	0.47	0.72	0.17	0.67

Source: Household Survey, December 2005.

It is quite clear from the table that in terms of regular trips, women are extremely restricted, even when the visit involves the neighbouring village and would be social in nature. Women seem to make a slightly greater number of trips to Vikasnagar, than to Dehradun or even to the neighbouring village. The reasons most often stated were shopping and visiting the Doctor as the Primary Health Centre (PHC) is located at Vikasnagar, and it is also the nearest market. Even in terms of occasional trips, the decline in ratio is evident with the distance of the destination. Most trips to Dehradun were in the nature of outings or occasionally to access legal services or Government offices.

Female access to Banks, Post Offices and *Mandis*, which may be considered proxy indicators of empowerment, ranges from 0.5 to 0.6 of male access, underlining the fact that women are still far from achieving economic independence and the empowerment that comes in its wake.

Table 3.9: Access to Banks, Markets and Post Offices

	Banks	*Mandis*	*Post Office*
Males	67	57	72
Females	36	37	42
F/M Ratio of Access	0.5	0.6	0.6

Source: Household Survey, December 2005.

UTILISING GOVERNMENT NUTRITION AND HEALTHCARE SERVICES

A major source of concern for human development policy in India is the poor health status of women and children. Undernourished and unhealthy women are not only unable to achieve their full potential as productive workers, but are also prevented from fulfilling their more fundamental role as progenitors of a healthy new generation. The National Family Health Survey 2005-06 (NFHS 3) found that more than one-third of Indian women are underweight, and this proportion raises to as much as 41 per cent in rural areas. Additionally, over half of all women in the reproductive age group of 15-49 have iron deficiency anaemia. Among pregnant women, the incidence of anaemia goes up to nearly 59 per cent. However, nutrition indicators for women in Uttarakhand are significantly better than the average for the erstwhile state of Uttar Pradesh (Table 3.10). With the exception of a slightly higher proportion of women suffering from mild anaemia, which is offset by the lower proportions of women with more severe forms of the deficiency, on all other indicators the State performs better. However, with one third of the women having low BMIs, around 9 per cent below the minimum height for an adult female and 45 per cent being anaemic, female nutrition levels in Uttarakhand are still far below the desirable norms.

More alarming is the fact that while height and body mass status show marginal improvement between NFHS 1 and NFHS 3, i.e., 1998-99 and 2005-06, the prevalence of anaemia seems to have recorded a sharp increase both in Uttarakhand and in Uttar Pradesh, with Uttarakhand recording the most severe deterioration.

Table 3.10: Nutrition Indicators of Women in Uttarakhand and Uttar Pradesh

State	*% with height below 145 cms*	*% with BMI below 18.5 kg/m^3*	*% Women with any anaemia*	*% Women with mild anaemia*	*% Women with moderate anaemia*	*% Women with severe anaemia*
Uttarakhand	8.6 (7.5)	32.3 (30)	45.3 (55.2)	35.1 (40.4)	9.8 (13.3)	0.4 (1.5)
Uttar Pradesh	16.4 (14.4)	35.8 (36)	48.7 (49.9)	33.5 (39.1)	13.7 (13.2)	1.5 (1.6)

Note: Figures in parentheses are the latest available statistics from NFHS 3.

Source: NFHS 1 (1998-99) accessed at ***http://www.nfhsindia.org/data/up/upchap7.pdf***

Iron deficiency anaemia (IDA) is common across all age groups, but highest among children and pregnant and lactating women. The consequences of IDA in pregnant women include increased risk of low birthweight or premature delivery, peri-natal and neonatal mortality, inadequate iron stores for the newborn, lowered physical activity, fatigue and increased risk of maternal morbidity. It is also responsible for almost a quarter of maternal deaths.

Severe anaemia during pregnancy increases the risk of maternal mortality by up to 23 per cent in Asia (Ross and Thomas, 1996 cited in Gillespie and Haddad, 2003). Pregnancy anaemia has been reported to be associated with pre-term delivery and subsequent low birth weight (LBW) in many studies (Gillespie and Haddad, 2003).

Women's nutrition status is inextricably bound with the nutritional status of their children starting with the infant's birth weight and proceeding through accentuated vulnerability of undernourished children to childhood illnesses, often resulting in increased mortality.

Table 3.11 brings out the nutrition status of rural children between the ages of 1-5 years in Uttarakhand and in India. Both the percentage of underweight children and those who are stunted (low height for age) is considerably higher than the country average, 4.7 per cent points in the case of underweight and as much as 10 per cent points with reference to stunted children. It is only in the case of wasting (low weight for age), which results from sudden and severe deprivation of food, usually in emergency situations, that the region seems to perform better than the average for the country, with a positive deviation of 4.4 per cent points. The repercussions in terms of morbidity and mortality have been aptly summarised in a recent World Bank Report on Child Malnutrition in India (Gragnolati *et al.*, 2005). "Through precipitating disease and speeding its progression, malnutrition is a leading contributor to infant, child and maternal mortality and morbidity. It has been estimated to play a role in about half of all child deaths and more than half of child deaths from major diseases, such as malaria (57%), diarrhoea (61%) and pneumonia (52%), as well as 45 per cent of deaths from measles (45%). Pediatric malnutrition is a risk factor for 16 per cent of the global burden of disease and for 22.4 per cent of India's burden of disease."

Table 3.11: Nutrition Indicators for Children—Uttarakhand and India

Indicator	*Uttarakhand*	*India*
IMR (Rural) deaths per '000 live births	87.4	75.4
% Underweight children: 1-5 years (rural)	51.7	47
% stunted children: 1-5 years (rural)	55.5	45.5
% wasted rural children (1-5 years)	11.1	15.5

Source: GOI, Department of Women and Child Development (2002) *The Indian Child: A Profile.*

The same report disaggregates the 1998-99 national averages of nutrition for children under three in India, and reveals that there are certain groups that are more likely to be underweight than others. The determinants of child malnutrition (and by extension), female malnutrition are classed into:

Location

The rural underweight prevalence of 50 per cent exceeds that of urban areas. Rural areas bear a particularly large share of the total *severe* underweight prevalence.

Wealth

As expected, both underweight and severe underweight prevalence increases as household wealth falls, although at a decreasing rate. Underweight prevalence is as high as 60 per cent in the lowest quartile, but is so pervasive throughout the wealth distribution that even in the wealthiest fifth of the population 33 per cent of children are underweight and 8.5 per cent are severely underweight.

Gender

Underweight (and severe underweight) prevalence is slightly higher among girls, 48.9 per cent (18.9%), than among boys, 45.5 per cent (16.9%).

Caste

Both underweight (and severe underweight) prevalence is much higher among scheduled castes 53.2 per cent (21.3%), and scheduled tribes 56.2 per cent (26.3%) than among other castes, 44.1 per cent (15.7%).

Government attempts to address malnutrition in the rural areas of the country are a mix of feeding, supplementary nutrition, health care and education programmes. At the village level, four sections of the population are targeted:

1. Children in the age group of 6 months to 54 months through the *Anganwadis* (Early Childcare Centres),
2. Pregnant women and nursing mothers,
3. Adolescent girls also, through the *Anganwadi* centres,
4. School going children through the mid-day meal scheme, which functions in all Government run primary schools, and
5. In addition, the foodgrain requirements of the household, particularly, BPL households are partly met through the provision of subsidised foodgrain through the PDS.

The success of Government efforts to address food insecurity and malnutrition is dependent on the level of utilisation of the services offered. Are the services on offer accessed by all households? Is there a gender difference in access to these services? The table below seeks to answer these questions.

Table 3.12: Utilisation of Government Supplementary Nutrition, Subsidised Food and Health Services

	Anganwadi	*Fair Price Shop*	*Community Health Centre*
HHs with female users	21 (10)	83 (40)	53 (26)
All user HHs	21 (10)	117 (56)	59 (28)
Total HHs	207		

Note: Figures in parentheses are percentages to total respondent HHs.

Source: Household Survey, December 2005.

Based on a specific question regarding the use of these three facilities, the level of utilisation was assessed. Utilisation appears to be dismally low across the 207 households of the six study villages. The Fair Price Shop appears to be the most commonly accessed of the three amenities. Even in this case, however, only a little over half the households (56%) reported utilisation. Households, in which women directly access the FPS, are even fewer, only 40 per cent. The *Anganwadi* centre is used by only 10 per cent of all households. However, an accurate estimate of the level of utilisation of this facility can be made only in relation to the number of HHs with pregnant women or children below the age of 5 years. Usage of the Government run Community Health Centre is also dismal with only about one quarter of all HHs accessing the facility. It is likely that private doctors or traditional healers are used in preference to the Government facility.

MAJOR FINDINGS

The paper sought to explore the gender disparity in development indicators in rural India with a view to accessing women's status as an equal partner in development. Some of the important findings are listed below:

1. A larger proportion of Female Headed Households (71%) have an annual income below Rs. 25,000 as compared to Male Headed Households (66%).
2. Only 38 per cent of Female Headed Households have two main sources of income compared to 50 per cent of Male Headed Households.
3. All female headed BPL households have BPL cards, which entitle them to special subsidies on food, as compared to only 80 per cent of male headed BPL households.
4. There is a total absence of productive assets in Female Headed Households with the exception of sewing machines. With one exception, not a single Female Headed Household owns any productive agricultural asset, despite 80 per cent of these households citing agriculture as their main source of livelihood.
5. Wage differentials between male and female labour persist with female wages at about 70-75 per cent of the male wage rate.

6. Female mobility remains restricted, even in cases of social interaction with neighbouring villages and more so for work related movement.
7. Households with women directly accessing Government run schemes like the FPS and the Community Health Centre are even fewer, than the total households accessing these schemes.
8. Overall, the utilisation of Government Food, Supplementary Nutrition and Health services is poor. The highest level of utilisation is that of the Public Distribution System through the FPS, but even in this case, only 50 per cent of the households report utilisation. Usage of the Community Health Centre is even lower—a mere 25 per cent and the *Anganwadi*, just 10 per cent of all households.

CONCLUSIONS

To summarise, the study villages present a case typical of most of rural India—a few large landowners, who can access nutritious diets, and private health and education facilities, and a majority of marginal farmers and landless labour, who are heavily dependent upon public support systems, yet do not appear to utilise fully the services offered to them. The number of female headed households among these is disproportionately higher in the low income, assetless group. Restrictions on female mobility and gender disparities in wages continue to exist. High levels of anaemia among women and children and stunting and underweight among young children persist.

It is clear that mere provision of services targeted to women does not ensure utilisation and hence, the achievement of the desired outcomes. It is now time to enquire more deeply into the reasons behind this apparent anomaly between supply and demand. The focus needs to shift from expansion of services to demand generation. An approach which has proved successful in many developing countries is that of conditional cash transfers, targeting behavioural change. The resounding success of the *Janini Suraksha Yojana* in some states, especially, Madhya Pradesh, which provides a cash benefit of Rs. 900 to pregnant woman from BPL families for institutional deliveries and a small incentive of Rs.150 to the case worker escorting the patient, underlines the potential of this kind of approach. In a short period of time, hospital deliveries have increased manifold to the point where it is becoming difficult to cope with the demand. Why is it not possible to emulate this strategy in the case of other schemes aimed at empowering women, whether for education, health or income generation? Such an approach may yet ensure for women an equitable partnership in development.

NOTES

1. Among other indicators, anyone consuming less than 2400 calories in rural areas and 2100 in urban areas is classed below the poverty line.

2. Ration cards in India are divided into BPL (Blow Poverty Line) and APL (Above Poverty Line). A BPL card entitles the holder to foodgrain, sugar, edible oil and kerosene among other commodities at specially subsidized rates. APL cards provide lesser quantities of rations at prices nearer.

REFERENCES

BRIDGE (2001): Briefing Paper on the 'Feminisation of Poverty' prepared for the Swedish International Development Cooperation Agency, BRIDGE Report No. 59, IDS, Sussex.

Gillespie, S. and L.J. Haddad (2003): *The Double Burden of Malnutrition in Asia: Causes, Consequences and Solutions*, Sage Publications, New Delhi.

GOI, Department of Women and Child Development (2002): *The Indian Child: A Profile.*

Gragnolati, M., M. Shekar, M. Das Gupta, C. Bredenkamp and Y. Kyoung Lee (August 2005): *India's Undernourished Children: A Call for Reform and Action*, HNP Discussion Paper, The World Bank.

IFPRI (October 2006): *Global Hunger Index.*

Marcoux Alain (1997): *The Feminisation of Poverty: Facts, Hypotheses and the Art of Advocacy*, FAO, Population Programme Services, Women and Population Division, Rome.

Ministry of Health and Family Welfare, *NFHS 3*, India, Vol. I, International Institute of Population Sciences, Mumbai.

Moghadam, Valentino (1997): *The Feminisation of Poverty: Notes on a Concept and Trend*, Women's Studies Occasional Paper no. 2, Illinois State University.

Ramachandran, Nira (2000): *Review and Field Testing of Guidelines for Formulating and Implementing National Plans of Action for Nutrition*, Nutrition Planning, Assessment and Evaluation Service, Food and Nutrition Division, FAO.

Ramachandran, Nira (2006): Why Women Must be a Central Concern in Food Policy, *Indian Social Science Review* (Forthcoming issue).

Ross, J.S. and E.L. Thomas (1996): *Iron Deficiency Anaemia and Maternal Mortality.* Profile 3. Working Notes Series No. 3. Academy for Educational Development, Washington D.C. cited in Gillespie, S. and L.J. Haddad (2003): *The Double Burden of Malnutrition in Asia: Causes, Consequences and Solutions*, Sage Publications, New Delhi.

UNICEF (May 2006): *Progress for Children: A Report Card on Nutrition*, Number 4.

4

Integrating Gender into Development Policies and Programmes

SUDESH NANGIA

> *"I should treat daughters and sons on a footing of perfect equality.. Both are God's gifts. They have an equal right to live and are equally necessary to keep the world going."*
>
> —Mahatma Gandhi (*Young India* 1929/1938)

INTRODUCTION

Women form about 48 per cent of the population. In 2001, of the total population enumerated in India, 513.2 million were men and 495.7 million women. Laws of nature have maintained a natural balance with more male births but then higher male mortality. Because of their (M/F) approximately equal distribution, it is evident then that, men and women are equal natural partners in evolution and growth process. And hence, if the natural and human eco-systems have to function properly, it is necessary that, apart from numbers, the quality of both the men and women (gender) should be at par. Women should enjoy equal social, economic and political status as that of men in civil society, if it is to be recognized as progressive or developed. Since, there is a wide gap between men and women in India, in terms of their socio-economic status, the question of women's empowerment is raised again and again during the recent decades with a view to reduce the gender gap and improve our demographic, social, economic and political institutional set up.

This paper examines how and what kind of efforts are being made to understand the gender gap and how various gender issues have been integrated into research and policies and programmes.

The discussion of this paper is organized into four parts:

(i) Population and Gender issues as deliberated in research.
(ii) Population and Gender issues as dealt in the National Five-Year Plans.
(iii) Legislative measures introduced since Independence (Laws and Policies) to strengthen gender equity and equality and improve the status of women.
(iv) Parliamentary Concerns, viz., the questions raised in the Parliament (Upper House and Lower House) on various dimensions of population, gender and development.

I. POPULATION AND GENDER ISSUES IN RESEARCH

A plethora of themes and sub-themes have evolved around gender issues of which the three basic issues debated are the determinants and consequence of sex-ratio including age-specific sex-ratio; gender disparity in literacy and education; forms of employment and gender discrimination etc.

The Census of India statistics have shown relatively a consistent decline in the sex-ratio (female per thousand male) since 1872. Despite several efforts made in family welfare programmes, steps taken towards the improvement of the status of women, policies and programmes towards gender empowerment, the sex-ratio did not improve substantially; on the contrary, the sex-ratio between 0-6 age-group further alarmed the policy makers about aftermath of state's policies and programmes (reflected in female foeticide) and social and community preferences (including son preference). The statistics on sex-ratio in ten states of India (Table 4.1) reveal that all these states had a sex-ratio more favourable to female in

Table 4.1: Sex-Ratio (female per thousand male) of selected states: 1951-2001

India/State/UT	*Sex-ratio*	
	1951	*2001*
1. Bihar	1000	921
2. Manipur	1036	978
3. Mizoram	1041	938.
4. Orissa	1022	972
5. Chhattisgarh	1024	990
6. Daman & Diu	1125	709
7. Goa	1128	960
8. Lakshadweep	1043	947
9. Kerala	1028	1058
10. Tamil Nadu	1007	986
11. Pondichery	1013	1001
12. India	946	933
Other States		
Jharkhand: 1032 (In 1901)—941 (In 2001)		
Meghalaya: 1036 (In 1901)—975 (In 2001)		

Source: Provisional Population Totals 2001, p. 154.

1951 and by 2001, all except Kerala and Pondicherry have become deficient in women, compared to men.

The figure on crude literacy rate in India between 1901 and 2001 reveal an increase in gender gap from 9.23 in 1901 to 18.29 in 2001, with a continuous rise up to 1961, a fluctuating trend between 1961 and 1981 and a decline in trend thereafter (Table 4.2).

A vast discrepancy is observed in the work-participation rate of male *versus* female. While a large number of male in the productive age-group are reported working, most of the women are reported as non-workers due to census definition of 'worker'. Among the workers, the participation of female in the informal sector and as marginal workers is reported to be higher than their male counterparts (Table 4.3: Work-status). The gender gap in the work participation rate between 1991 and 2001 has increased in 11 States and UTs. These states extend across the country from Rajasthan to Nagaland and from Kerala to Delhi. Even the smaller states like Goa and Pondicherry and islands like Lakshadweep are not spared from these aftermath.

Table 4.2: Crude Literacy Rate in India by Sex: 1901-2001

Census Year	Persons	Males	Females	Male-Female gap in Literacy Rate
1901	5.35	9.83	0.60	9.23
1911	5.92	10.56	1.05	9.51
1921	7.16	12.21	1.81	10.40
1931	9.50	15.59	2.93	12.66
1941	16.10	24.90	7.30	17.60
1951	16.67	24.95	7.93	17.02
1961	24.02	34.44	12.95	21.49
1971	29.45	39.45	18.69	20.79
1981	36.23	46.89	24.82	22.07
1991	42.84	52.74	32.17	20.57
2001	55.30	64.13	45.84	18.29

Source: Provisional Population Totals 2001, Census of India.

The data collected during the National Family Health Surveys, Rapid Household Surveys, and other intervening surveys have thrown open a new vista of research issues like domestic violence, crimes against women, women employment; fertility and reproductive health; mortality, morbidity and health care, status of woman and the status of the girl child, son preference and neglect of the female child, female foeticide and infanticide, women empowerment and the right to decision-making etc. Further, the status of women in society is also being measured in terms of quality of services and amenities being provided in the household to relieve them from the drudgeries of physical labour and enable them to use their time and energy in pursuits of higher productivity and skill formation. Hence, the quality of housing and basic amenities (like water, electricity, toilet, kitchen, *pucca* housing, privacy in housing, security in house) are main issues of concern. Besides, decisions regarding one's fertility, right to physical and financial assets of the household; heredity rights on the immovable property and the economic and socio-political equity, equality and justice for women are some of the issues of concern in measuring the status of women in society, incorporated into research and teaching programmes.

Table 4.3: Work Participation Rate (Main + Marginal) by Sex (India and State), 1991 and 2001

	Per cent age of workers to total population							
	1991				*2001*			
	Total	*Male*	*Female*	*Gap = M - F*	*Total*	*Male*	*Female*	*Gap = M - F*
India	37.5	51.6	22.3	29.3	39.1	51.7	25.7	26.0
Assam	36.1	49.5	21.6	27.9	35.8	49.9	20.7	29.2
Goa	35.3	49.6	20.5	29.1	38.8	54.6	22.4	32.2
Kerala	31.4	47.6	15.9	31.7	32.3	50.2	15.4	34.8
Manipur	42.2	45.3	39.0	6.3	43.6	53.3	30.8	22.5
Mizoram	48.9	53.9	43.5	10.4	52.6	48.3	35.2	13.1
Nagaland	42.7	46.9	38.0	8.9	42.6	57.3	47.6	9.7
Rajasthan	38.9	49.3	27.4	21.9	42.1	53.6	19.1	34.5
Dadra & Naga Haveli	53.3	57.5	48.8	8.7	51.8	56.1	38.7	17.4
Delhi	31.6	51.7	7.3	44.4	32.8	65.5	18.6	46.9
Lakshadweep	26.4	44.2	7.6	36.6	25.3	52.1	9.4	42.7
Pondicherry	33.1	50.6	15.2	35.4	35.2	53.1	17.2	35.9

Source: Census of India, 1991 and 2001.

II. POPULATION AND GENDER: APPROACH IN THE FIVE-YEAR PLANS

Over the years, the planning strategy for women and children in the country has evolved from welfare to development to empowerment. The approach in the First Five-Year Plan (1951-56) was to provide adequate services to 'promote the welfare of women' so that they could play their legitimate role in the family and community. The plan document further noted that special organizations on the part of Central and State governments for promoting the welfare of the women had not been developed and therefore, stressed on the role of the private agencies. The Central Social Welfare Board was set up in 1953 to promote voluntary organizations at various levels to take up welfare related activities of women. The Board has networked with over 20,000 voluntary organizations across the country.

The second, third, fourth and fifth plans continued the same approach for the welfare of women. The concept of women's development was mainly welfare oriented and was clubbed with other categories of welfare as the old and the disabled. The schemes of condensed course of education and women and socio-economic programme were introduced during the Second Plan (1956-1961). The Working

Girl's Hostel and Short Stay Home schemes were introduced in the Fourth Plan (1969-1974). During the first twenty-eight years of planning, these were the only schemes specific to women.

It was only in the Sixth Plan (1980-1985) that there was some shift in the approach, from welfare to development; and recognition was given to the women as being more than objects of welfare. The Plan laid special emphasis on three core sectors—health, education, and employment. Priority was given to implementation of programmes for women under different sectors of agriculture and its allied activities of dairying and poultry, small animal husbandry, handlooms, handicrafts, small-scale industries etc. Women's employment programme was introduced in 1982. The Seventh Plan (1985-1990) continued to stress on generation of skilled and unskilled employment among women through proper education and vocational training. Two new schemes of Support to Training and Employment (STEP) and Awareness Generation Programme for Rural and Poor Women (AGP) were introduced. There were certain important reports, which were presented during this period—*shram shakti*, Report of the National Commission on Self-Employee Women and Women in Informal sector, National Perspective Plan on Women and the SAARC Guidebook on Women in Development.

The Eighth Plan (1992-1997) adopted the strategy to ensure that benefits do not bypass the women and special programmes were implemented to complement the general development programmes. Two new schemes were introduced during this period, Mahila Samridhi Yojana and Indira Mahila Yojana. During this period, there were other milestones reached. The National Commission for Women and The National Credit Fund for Women better known as the Rashtriya Mahila Kosh were set up. The 73rd and 74th Constitutional Amendments were also made during this period to reserve one-third seats in the rural and urban self-governing institutions for the women.

In the Ninth Plan (1997-2002), there were significant changes in the concept and planning strategies. First, the empowerment of women became the primary objective of this plan. During this time the "National Policy for the Empowerment of Women" was also approved. The plan directed the Centre and the States to adopt a special strategy of "women's Component Plan" through which not less than thirty per cent of funds should be earmarked in all the women related sectors. The plan was an attempt to adopt a holistic approach to the empowerment of women. The policy objectives of the Tenth Plan (2002-2007) are:

- To promote gender equity by ensuring that women have equal access to health care, quality education, employment and remuneration.
- Elimination of all discrimination through legal system.
- Maintenance of gender perspective in all development processes.
- Providing equal access to participation and decision making for women in social, political and economic realms.

The Eleventh Five Year Plan is emphasising on:

- Engendering Policies and Strategies,
- Violence against Women,
- Empowerment, Advocacy, Awareness Generation and Support Services for Women.
- Women's Component Plan and Gender Budgeting.

The philosophy of Empowerment for Eleventh Plan is inclusive and has integrated Economic, Social and Political empowerment with gender justice.

Basic Issues Related to Women's Empowerment

The programmes, which the government of India took up for the welfare, development and empowerment of women can be grouped under the following categories:

- Social and economic empowerment of women,
- Training, employment and education,
- Attitudinal change towards the girl child,
- Support services,
- Women's rights and the law,
- Miscellaneous programmes.

III. LEGISLATIVE MEASURES

1. General Laws and Policies

The backbone of all legislative measures and policies is the Constitution of India that came into force on 26th January, 1950. The Preamble reads India as a 'Sovereign, Socialist, Secular, Democratic Republic' that secures justice, liberty, equality and fraternity to all citizens. It further reiterates that there would be no discrimination on account of gender.

In 1953, Central Social Welfare Board was established with a view to mobilize voluntary organizations for social welfare services specially for women and children. Soon, it established a networking of 20,000 voluntary organizations.

In 1984 the 'Family Court Act' was passed. A number of states have established direct family courts under this act. These courts have a specific task to perform and that is to settle disputes related to marriage and family affairs. Family courts are headed preferably by female judges.

1987 Legal Services Authorities Act provides the establishment of institutions (at National/State/District level) for providing free legal services to the underprivileged section of the society including women.

The National Commission for Women, established in 1992, is given the task of reviewing and suggesting reforms in existing laws to include issues of gender.

73rd and 74th Amendments to the Constitution which were passed in 1992, confer constitutional validity and status to local governing bodies both in rural (Panchayats) and urban areas and reserve one-third seats in these local governing bodies for women. The matters related to 'family welfare' and 'women and child development' formed part of the sectors reserved for consideration by the Panchayats in rural areas.

The 'Women Reservation Bill' introduced in 1996 as the 81st Amendment to the Constitution, currently pending in Parliament, if passed, would entitle women to one-third of the seats in Parliament.

International Laws and Treaty Obligations

India also draws the framework for its laws through several international laws and treaty obligations. For example, 'Convention on the Elimination of All Forms of Discrimination against Women' (CEDAW) is one such convention to which India is a state party.

India is a signatory to several such laws and treaties. Some of them are listed as under:

(i) 1978—Alma Ata declaration's goal of "Health for All" by the year 2000.
(ii) 1979—Convention on the Elimination of All Forms of Discrimination against Women (CEDAW)—India is a state party.
(iii) 1994—International Conference on Population and Development (ICPD) Programme of Action I.
(iv) 1995—Beijing declaration and platform for action.
(v) 2000—United Nations Millennium Development Goals (MDGs). India is committed to these goals.

2. Reproductive Health and Women Rights

Since Bhore Committee Report (1946), India is committed to the primary health care as the basic right of all individuals, irrespective of their ability to pay for services or other socio-economic factors. It further adopted the 1978 Alma Ata Declaration's goal of health for all by the year 2000.

The National Health Policy 2002 has its main objective to realize an acceptable standard of good health among the general population. Some of the primary objectives of this policy are:

- To reduce maternal mortality and infant mortality rates to 100 per 100,000 and 30 per 1000 by the year 2010.
- To make special efforts to reach the basic health services to the women and other underprivileged sections.

The government is committed to give top priority for funding to programmes aimed at women's health.

Tenth Five Year Plan (2002-2007) gives special cognizance to the enhancement of human well-being through primary health care and providing quality health services. The Plan aims at providing essential primary health care, emergency life saving services, and services under government, disease control and family welfare programmes free of cost to all individuals.

Pre-conceptions and Pre-diagnostic Technique (Prohibition of Sex Selection) Act, 1994 (amended in 2003) is a further step towards women empowerment and save the girl child and building of a consensus towards raising the status of women in society. This Act prohibits the prenatal diagnostic tests for the sex-determination and sex-selection for birth. The 2002 Indian Medical Council (Profession, Conduct, Etiquette and Ethics) Regulations specifically prohibit medical practitioners from performing sex determination tests for the purpose of female foeticide.

3. Health Insurance

One of the major steps towards achieving health goals is the introduction of Health Insurance Schemes in one form or the other. It is essential, as at present, only 10 per cent of the population is covered by health Insurance in the government, and private sector and those covered are primarily from upper income groups. Central government, employees are entitled to Central Government Health Schemes.

Beside, the Employees, State Insurance Act, 1948 that introduced health insurance programme for industrial workers; 2000 Janashree Bima Yojana formed a Group Insurance Scheme covering all families below the poverty line in urban and rural areas. The Health Ministers Discretionary grant; Janraksha (Public Sector insurance for the needy population), are some of the schemes to assist the public to solve their financial burden of health facilities. The 'Jeevan Bharti' Insurance plan of 2003, launched by Life Insurance Corporation of India, is meant exclusively for women in the age-group 18-50 years. The benefits under this scheme include coverage of expenses under critical illness like various types of cancer, congenital defects of newborn babies etc.

4. Reproductive Health Laws and Policies

Though there is no comprehensive National Reproductive Health Policy in India yet, several aspects of reproductive and Child Health Programme are aimed at providing integrated health and family welfare services for women and children. The main components of the programme are:

- Prevention and management of unwanted pregnancies;
- Services to promote safe motherhood;
- Services to promote child survival;
- Prevention and treatment of Reproductive Tract Infection and STIs.

The programme is aimed at providing 'client-centred quality services' rather than achieving contraceptive targets.

The programme envisions decentralized participatory approach involving Panchayats, women and community groups in planning and monitoring reproductive and child health services.

The reproductive and child health programmes, National Population Policy, 2000 and National Health Policies, 2002, establish the framework for the government's delivery of the family welfare services. Tenth Five Year Plan further lays emphasis on maternal health services by including the following aspects of women's health care:

- Essential obstetric care through early registrations of pregnant women to discover risk factors;
- Identification and management of high-risk mothers;
- Referral care for at-risk mothers.

On the occasion of the International Women's Day (March 8th) in 2003, the Ministry of Health and Family Welfare initiated a programme that compensates pregnant women's travel cost to health centres. The programme also provides a token of Rupees 1000 for birth of a daughter and Rs. 500 for the birth of a son.

Many of the earlier programmes initiated through national five year plans and health policies from time to time, have been incorporated into the Reproductive and Child Health Programme, for example, Universal Immunization Programme of 1985; Child Survival and Safe Motherhood Programme of 1992; training programme for midwives. Besides, the government has also launched nation-wide scheme of women's health groups called Mahila Swasthya Sanghs in villages, which act as agents for discussing women's health concerns and issues.

The 1993 National Nutrition Policy gives special priority to at-risk mothers, women and children. The Integrated Child Development Scheme (ICDS) launched in 1975, is a major intervention in combating malnutrition and providing food supplements to children with a special emphasis on the girl child below the age of six and to expectant and nursing mothers.

Similarly, abortion has been given legal status through 1971 Medical Termination of Pregnancy Act, when there is a risk to women's life; there is chance of a grave injury to women's physical and mental health and where there is a substantial risk of foetal impairment. The National AIDS Prevention and Control Policy, 2002 is formulated to contain HIV/AIDS transmission and reduce the impact of the disease of the infected person's health and on the socio-economic well being of the general population. The National Population Policy 2000 is formulated to address the unmet needs for contraception, health care infrastructure and provide integrated service delivery for basic reproductive and child health care, apart from several other goals and objectives listed in the policy documents.

5. Legal Status of Women

A number of laws have been enacted to provide women with reasonable health status, family-status, access to education, means of livelihood, age at first marriage, rape laws, laws related to sexual assault/domestic violence etc. which not only indicate the concern for women's rights but their capacity/capability to take independent decisions.

6. Rights to Gender Equality

The principle of gender equality is firmly established in the Constitution in the sense that there would be no discrimination against any citizen on grounds of sex, religion, race, caste or any other basis. It empowers states to take affirmative action in favour of women.

The Constitution prescribes several fundamental duties of citizens, among which is the duty to renounce practices derogatory to the dignity of women.

A number of national/state level institutions and policies aim at advancing gender equality. The development of women and children development is the principle of the national policies for the advancement of women.

National Commission for Women established in 1992 (in pursuant to National Commission for Women Act, 1990) advises government on all policy matters affecting women, reviews relevant laws and regulations and ensures the implementation of constitutional rights of women.

The task force on Women and Children, 2000 established by the Department of Women and Child Development reviews and makes recommendations with regard to legislations relating to women. In 2001, National Policy for the Empowerment of Women was adopted to eliminate all forms of discrimination against women, ensure gender justice and empower women both socially and economically. Tenth Five-Year Plan (2002-2007) sets forth broad policy objectives to promote gender equity and equality.

- The approach is to continue with the major strategy of "Empowering women" as Agents of Social Change and Development.
- To adopt a Sector-Specific 3-Fold strategy for empowering women, based on the prescriptions of the National Policy for Empowerment of Women. They include:

  (1) *Social Empowerment*—to create an enabling environment through various affirmative developmental policies and programmes for development of women besides providing them easy and equal access to all the basic minimum services so as to enable them to realize their full potentials;

  (2) *Economic Empowerment*—to ensure provision of training, employment

and income-generation activities with both 'forward' and 'backward' linkages with the ultimate objective of making all potential women economically independent and self-reliant; and

(3) *Gender Equality*—to eliminate all forms of gender discrimination and thus, allow women to enjoy not only the *de jure* but also the *de facto* rights and fundamental freedom at par with men in all spheres, viz. political, economic, social, civil, cultural etc.

IV. Parliamentary Concerns on Population and Gender

One of the ways to assess the state commitment towards various problems and dimensions of population and gender issues is to observe the concern expressed by the Parliamentarians in their parliamentary debates.

The Indian Association of Parliamentarians on Population and Development (IAPPD) set upon itself the talk of identifying the concern of the Parliamentarians (both in Lok Sabha and Rajya Sabha) on population and gender development issues. The issues in Parliament are discussed in detail through debates when any policy or programme is on the anvil. The members also monitor the progress of various policies and programmes/schemes through raising questions during "Question Hour" in both Houses of Parliament. Question hour was introduced to ensure accountability of the executive to the elected people's representatives. There are starred and un-starred questions. Starred questions are given in advance in writing and the government is expected to place its reply on the table of the House. In contrast, un-starred questions can be raised during the "question hour" itself and no written reply is expected from the government.

To know the types of questions (both starred and un-starred) raised in the parliament, it was decided to concentrate on questions raised in the two Houses during 2000-2003 covering a period of four years. Specific objectives of this analysis were:

- To identify the major concern areas of elected representatives with respect to population issues;
- Identify gaps in their awareness and knowledge of population related issues with a view to incorporate those in their training modules;
- Identify those members of Parliament who are deeply concerned about the population issues. They will then be approached for intensive training so that they are better able to advocate the cause of population both in the Parliament and in their respective constituencies and become resource persons for future training of Parliamentarians.

SCOPE OF ANALYSIS

Population related questions are mostly the concern of Ministry of Health and

Family Welfare and are addressed to the Minister of Health. It may be noted here that, in the distribution of the 'subjects' besides health, population development and family welfare have been assigned to the Ministry of Health and Family Welfare. However, there are other issues relating to education, especially population education, that fall in the realm of Ministry of Human Resource Development. Similarly, questions raised on women empowerment, even though they impinge on population and development issues, are normally directed to Department of Women and Child Welfare. The IAPPD decided to analyse the questions directed to the Ministry of Health and Family Welfare. For analysis, all the questions raised in Rajya Sabha and Lok Sabha during 2000, 2001, 2002 and 2003 were selected. These questions, put to the Ministry of Health and Family Welfare during that last four years, along with their answers were downloaded from the internet and they included both starred and un-starred questions.

PLAN OF ANALYSIS

Considering the variety of questions that was on several topics, the questions were telescoped into following categories:

- Population Policy/National Health Policy
- Population Growth Control and Family Planning
- Health Care—(i) Rural and (ii) Urban
- Reproductive and Child Health including Infant, Child and Maternal Mortality
- Morbidity
- Drugs and Pharmaceuticals
- HIV/AIDS
- Financial Allocation for Health Programmes including External Assistance
- Expenditure on Health Programmes
- Role of NGOs/Corporate Sector
- Alternative System of Medicines
- Miscellaneous

In all 326 questions were retrieved from the internet for the years 2002-03. Of these 172 questions were from Rajya Sabha members and 154 from Lok Sabha members. Year-wise distribution of questions separately for the two houses is given in the following Table 4.4.

Theme-wise Analysis of Questions

1. National Population Policy 2000 and National Health Policy 2002

The questions related to the following issues:

Table 4.4: Number of Questions in Rajya Sabha and Lok Sabha (2000-2003)

Year	Rajya Sabha	Lok Sabha
2000	70	28
2001	23	9
2002	28	32
2003	51	85
Total	172	154

- Role of incentives in controlling population.
- Whether population policy was Anti-women?
- Scope of introduction of Health Insurance in National Health Policy 2002.
- Introduction and training in alternative system of medicine.

2. Population Growth, its Control and Family Planning

- Relationship between population growth and development.
- Compensation for the family planning acceptors.
- Two-child norm for candidates contesting elections for MLA/MPs seats.
- Reasons for failure to control population growth.
- Any specific policies to handle poor performing states in family welfare programme.

3. Health Care

The questions on general health care related to

- medicinal education and possibility of opening new colleges; infrastructure, manpower and resources in hospitals and CGHS, Mental Health Institutes; sanction of private medical colleges and financial assistance to them; any development of indigenous technology for detecting hormonal imbalances, Community based insurance; ill-treatment of patients at CGHS; proposal to start new dispensaries and upgrade the medical institutions; improvement in medical colleges and state policy in this regard etc.
- in rural health care, shortage of manpower and medicines was the main concern.
- Disparities in rural and urban health services and how to narrow rural-urban gap were the main issues of concern.

4. Reproductive and Child Health

- The members have shown keenness about the details of RCH programme, its implementation and number of beneficiaries over time. They also

Table 4.5: Number of Questions (Theme-wise) in Lok Sabha and Rajya Sabha

Sl. No.	*Theme*	*Rajya Sabha*	*Lok Sabha*
1.	National Population Policy and National Health Policy	12	3
2.	Population Growth/Control and Family Planning	13	22
3.	General Health Care	30	29
	Urban Rural	19	18
4.	Reproductive and Child Health	9	13
5.	Morbidity and Disease Control Drugs and	17	15
	Medicines	9	9
6.	HIV/AIDS	8	16
7.	Financial Allocations	8	20
	Expenditure on Health Care	14	3
8.	Role of NGO/Corporate/Private Sector in Health	8	7
9.	Alternative System of Medicine	7	5
10.	Miscellaneous	30	10

wanted to know whether 'sex-education' was part of this programme.

- They wanted to know about the funds earmarked for BIMARU states under this programme and also the details of "family welfare" linked insurance plan.
- Questions were raised about the levels of CDR, IMR, Life-Expectancy and change overtime.
- The question on the new 'injectable' contraceptives and viewpoint of women's organisation even in respect of their experimental trials was also raised.
- The members showed concern over the Maternal Mortality Rate (MMR) and wanted to know whether the deaths due to delivery and abortion were on the increase in India, and if so, what remedial measures were being taken to control them.
- 'Polio Vaccination Scheme', malnutrition among children, nutrition to the expectant mothers were the other areas of concern. The members also wanted to know if govt, had taken any steps to legitimize 'test-tube' babies by using wombs and semen of willing donors, and their likely social-status, propriety and rights of such children.

5. *Morbidity, Disease Control and Drugs and Medicines*

- Questions under this head related specifically to tuberculosis, malaria, cancer and kalazar and campaign to eradicate/lower the incidence of disease and the measures taken to discover indigenous methods of treatment.
- Concern about Hepatitis A and B were expressed with questions about governments' special initiative to control it.

- Questions were also raised about heart-ailments.
- Referring to the newspaper item regarding cancer being caused by certain types of Shampoo and toothpaste, one member asked the government to furnish details and if any action was contemplated.
- Gujarat epidemic in earthquake-affected areas also drew the attention of the House and one member wanted to know as to what steps were being taken to eradicate the epidemic.
- Awareness of Government with respect to deaths due to dengue fever was another concern expressed in Lok Sabha.

6. HIV/AIDS and other Diseases

Although HIV/AIDS is part of morbidity, because of special concern regarding its spread among the youth and high incidence of mortality, this disease has been treated separately. Moreover, the United Nations, WHO and many other international organizations have been deeply concerned about the spread of this disease. The Government of India has given special treatment to HIV/AIDS in NPP-2000 and NHP 2002; hence, the significance of this disease.

In all 22 questions were raised in the Rajya Sabha and Lok Sabha during 2000-2003 relating to HIV/AIDS. Members showed their concern about the UNAID-WHO estimates of the spread of the disease in India, especially in Maharashtra and Tamil Nadu. They wanted to know the details and steps undertaken by the Government to control the disease. The members were concerned about a newspaper item that India was the second country with largest number of AIDS patients. They also wanted to know if Bangladesh, Pakistan and Sri Lanka were more successful in controlling AIDS and, if so, what were the reasons; and details of any new scheme in operation or proposed by the Government, especially regarding free (or subsidized) treatment of HIV/AIDS patients and if the demand for free treatment was growing.

There was a question in the Rajya Sabha asking if India was on the verge of developing AIDS control vaccine, the details thereof and any timeframe to market the drug at affordable price.

A question in the Rajya Sabha related to the initiatives and projects undertaken by NACO since its inception, project-wise details of the progress and if projects were behind schedule, the reasons thereof. The members were concerned about the AIDS control policy; they wanted to know the sex-age distribution of the infected persons and if the policy was lopsided in denying care to the infected persons.

The members wanted to know if India has its own reliable estimates of AIDS prevalence, statewise details thereof and if the Government has developed any surveillance system regarding AIDS.

The members were concerned about exorbitant payment to an NGO for monitoring HIV/AIDS control when NIHFW had competence to conduct programme in this regard. Specific questions were raised about AIDS infected persons in Delhi, their number and socio-economic status; and the sex abuse of street children and the incidence of AIDS. The members also wanted to know if any survey had been conducted in coastal areas regarding the incidence of AIDS.

7. Financial Allocations for Health Programmes

Financial allocations have been one of the major concerns of the Parliamentarians (29 Questions):

- Members were interested in knowing about the details of World Bank funding for Family Welfare activities.
- About specific funds available for Madhya Pradesh, Rajasthan, West Bengal, Orissa and Uttar Pradesh.
- Details of government assistance to hospitals repair and renovation of facilities.
- Reservation of beds in hospitals for the poor.
- Details of financial assistance received from European Union, WHO, DNIDA and other international agencies for improving the quality of primary and secondary health care services in the country.
- There were specific questions relating to assistance for health projects in Kerala, Karnataka and Orissa.
- Members also wanted to know the details of funds allocated for health programmes and disease control in the Tenth Plan.

8. Expenditure on Health Programmes

Spending on health has been another concern of the members. A total of sixteen questions were put in respect of expenditure on health. The members wanted to know the relationship between economic growth and health expenditure and if health expenditure in India was very low some members wanted to know the relative situation of India as compared to other countries, specially compared to China, Japan, USA, France and England. They also wanted to know if the expenditure has remained static or if it was going down as percentage of GDP. The members wanted to know the reasons for poor spending on health by the government and the steps that the government proposes to take to increase the same, and whether private component would continue to be the largest component of health care spending?

The analysis of the questions indicates the direction of the concern on the issues of population, gender and development of the parliamentarians. The gender dimension of these questions appears to be lopsided so far.

EPILOGUE

The educational curricular programmes of various universities have introduced gender dimensions to the behaviour sciences, apart from establishing special cells on women studies, for further research and dissemination of knowledge on gender equity, equality, status of women and gender empowerment. The mandatory formation of committees to look into the sexual harassment at work place, has been instrumental in furthering gender sensitization among the co-workers. The commitment to raise the status of women of the government is reflected in its multi-dimensional approach in the National Five Year Plans. The plans are well supported by appropriate legislative measures, further revealed in formulation of laws, acts and sector-oriented policy framework. The awareness is stepped up among the elected representatives through constant advocacy programmes, which is reflected in the types of questions raised by them in the Parliament, during the last few years.

Thus, with the multi-thronged approach, the gender issues are being integrated into research (including teaching), policy and programme development.

REFERENCES

Annual Budget, 2001-2002, Department of Women and Child Development, Ministry of Human Resource Development, Government of India.

Kumar, A. K. Shiv; the Path to Population Stabilization, Presented at the Conference of Inter Agency Working Group on Population and Development, September 2000.

National Policy for the employment of women, department of women and Child Development, Ministry of Human Resource Development, Government of India 2001.

Paula Kantor, *Women's Empowerment through Homebased Work: Evidence from India*, University of Wisconsin-Madison, 2001.

Policy Notes, 2002-2003, Demand No. 43, Chapter 2, Social welfare and Nutritious Meal Programme Department, Ministry of Social Welfare, Government of Tamil Nadu.

Premi, Kusum; *Population and Development Issues: Content Analysis of Questions raised in Parliament*. Report prepared for IAPPD, New Delhi, 2005. p. 27.

Proceedings of the meeting of the National Council—Hunger Project, India, Bangalore, August 9-10, 1997.

Programme of Action for Women and Children, Government of India.

Nangia, Sudesh, Abhay Kumar and Sadananda Mitra, Regional Disparity in Work-Participation in India. *Annals of the National Association of Geographers*, India, Vol. XXV, No. 2, December 2005.

The Largest Women's Self-Help Initiative: A Success Story from Andhra Pradesh, India, Women's Empowerment and Self-Employment, Department of Rural Development, Government of Andhra Pradesh.

Towards Equity, Report of the Committee on the Status of Women in India, Department of Social Welfare, Ministry of Education and Social Welfare, New Delhi, 1974.

Women's Economic Empowerment through Co-operative Farming, Vocational Training and Business Development, George Foundation.

5

Development, Disparity and Emerging Governance Issues and Challenges in Post Reforms India

SURYA KANT

INTRODUCTION

It is now widely known that India made sweeping changes in its economic policies following the Balance of Payment (BOP) crisis, which hit badly the Indian economy towards the last quarter of the year 1990 and continued during the first half of 1991. The new government, which took over in June 1991 under Shri P.V. Narsimha Rao, as the Prime Minister and Dr. Man Mohan Singh, as the Finance Minister, made radical changes in trade, investment, industrial, fiscal, energy, agricultural and human resource development policies. A Structural Adjustment Programme (SAP) with support from the World Bank (WB) and the International Monetary Fund (IMF) was initiated with the objective of making Indian economy more efficient and globally competitive. In fact, the international funding agencies, such as WB and IMF found favour with the market as a panacea for the contemporary economic problems faced in developing world.

Nevertheless, it is to be stated here that the history of process of change in Indian economic policy goes back to the decade of 1980s after Mrs. Indira Gandhi returned to power following the Mid-term elections to Indian Parliament in 1980. A detailed study of changes in economic policy and its political implication are available in several studies (*see,*Kohli, 2006; Nayyar, 2001; Sengupta, 2004; Aseema, 2004; Frankel, 2005).

The changes initiated in the Indian economic policy after 1991 have thrown a variety of challenges as well as opportunities before the country. The new policy has wide social, economic, political, administrative and institutional, environmental, and geographical implications. Regional and inter-personal income disparities and widening, national security and law and order situation is under tremendous pressure due to growing social and political conflicts, and growing corruption in political and personal life is gradually eating out the social and political fabric in the country from within.

All this raise a variety of questions and challenges before the policy-makers, planners, administrators, academicians and even the awakened masses to find solutions to current problems and challenges thrown by the post-reforms scenario. This paper, which is my tribute to Dr. K.V. Sundaram, a planner, a thinker and a visionary, attempts to examine the emerging scenario of disparities in regional development, inter-state pattern of poverty, and some important issues relating to governance emerging in the post-reforms India?

In the following, to begin with the changes in India's economic policy have been examined followed by a discussion on regional pattern of income and inequalities, pattern of poverty at the state level and its implications, and emerging issues and challenges having links with administration and governance, in a sequential order.

I

New Economic Policy

The measures adopted under the new economic policy, announced by the Government of India in July 1991, can broadly be grouped into: (i) the stabilization programme and (ii) the structural adjustment programme (SAP). The former, aimed at restoring the balance of payments equilibrium and controlling inflation, is a short-term measure. The latter, geared to achieve higher economic growth and make the Indian economy competitive in the world market, is a medium-term policy instrument.

To fill the gap between imports and exports and to reduce the deficit in the Union Government Budget to a manageable level exports have been encouraged, monetary and exchange rate policy rationalized, the rupee was devalued and a convertibility scheme introduced. Secondly, there has been curtailment in public expenditure and the considerable reduction in subsidies on various items, including food and fertilizers. The measures designed under the structural adjustment included: (i) the deregulation and privatization of domestic economic activities by de-bureaucratization and induction of competition in the domestic market, and (ii) the globalization of the Indian economy. The major changes were effected in existing policies relating trade and industrial development, and new policies were framed for agricultural, human resource and energy sectors. The policy has also been changed to open the insurance sector to foreign investors. Earlier, India joined the World Trade Organization (WTO). All quantitative restrictions on imports were lifted from April 2001. In addition, government announced several measures to encourage exports from the agriculture sector. By now, a change in economic policies on regular interval has become a part of government agenda in India. Officially, it is claimed that India has now entered the 'second generation reforms'.

The new policy looks at the market as a determinant of prices of commodities, labour, capital, land and exchange rate of currencies; privatisation as a means to improve efficiency and reduce fiscal deficit; and globalization as a way to do away with protective measures, to boost exports and to attract foreign direct investment (FDI) for rapid industrialization and economic growth.

In contrast, the focus of the pre-reform economic development strategy was to insulate the Indian economy from the world market and promote industrialisation by assigning the dominant role to the State in the economy. The market, by itself, was not perceived sufficient to meet the aspirations of a latecomer to industrialisation. Such a strategy of development was implemented through the system of controls.

The changes in the Indian economic policy have to be seen in the context of the following factors. India, a country with enormous diversities, has a federal democratic system with multiplicity of political parties. The state governments, competing with each other in all matters of importance, implement macro-economic policies decided at the national level; and formulate different welfare policies in consonance with their political ideologies, electoral base and realities at the local level. As expected in a federal system, inter-state competition for greater share of resources in the backdrop of significant inter-state disparities have often been fuelling movements for greater autonomy. There are urban-rural cleaves, besides communal, caste and lingual divisions. Nearly one-third of India's population lives below the poverty line and the problem of unemployment and underemployment of the educated have acquired alarming proportions. Widening inter-regional and social inequalities have made things worse. All these have culminated into erosion of state-sponsored institutions leading to problems of governance, especially in the periphery (Kohli, 1991).

Moreover, India has been experimenting/experiencing a number of new political and social ideas during the 1980s. These include social and political empowerment of former *dalit* (oppressed) castes, encouragement to caste and region based political parties and communal politics. Reservation of government jobs and seats in educational institutions for OBC castes, resurgence of dalit castes in electoral politics, emergence of regional parties, demolition of Babri Masjid, and 73th and 74th Constitutional Amendments for creating third tier in the hierarchy of development planning at the local level are some of the examples of new experiments. From the economic, it is interesting to note that by opening the macro economy to global market forces we created a level field for the domestic and foreign investors in Indian economy. On the other side of the scale, strengthening of planning process at the local level amounted to discouraging market forces to operate at the local level. Such a situation is full of socio-economic and political implications.

II

Regional Responses to New Policy

Following the change in economic policy in 1991, the transfer of financial resources from the Centre to State governments have been declining. The different state governments are now remodelling their investment policies to attract private investment from either domestic investors or foreign investors. They are competing with each other to attract private invest investment especially the direct foreign investment. The geographical and sectoral distribution of direct foreign investment is changing the regional pattern of development in India.

The information available from various issues of the Newsletter, published by the Secretariat for Industrial Assistance (SIA), reveal that the pattern of (proposed) foreign direct investment (FDI) in India, coming under the new investment policy, has diversified recently both in spatial and sectoral terms. However, there is a significant bias for the states having big metropolitan centres, well-developed physical and social infrastructure, political stability, and high return potential. Of the total FDI approvals between August 1991 and July 2005, six states, namely Maharashtra, the National Capital Territory of Delhi, Tamil Nadu, Karnataka, Gujarat and Andhra Pradesh, in combine, grabbed more than half (56.5%). In contrast, only a few FDI proposals have been finalised for troubled states of Jammu and Kashmir, Manipur, Nagaland, Mizoram, Sikkim, and Meghalaya. The combined share of ten backward states of Uttar Pradesh, Bihar, Assam, Orissa, Madhya Pradesh, Jammu & Kashmir, Rajasthan, Chhattisgarh, Jharkhand, Uttarakhand make less than one-tenth or 9.7 per cent of total FDI. The whole investment amount proposed in these states made only 56.6 per cent of total investment in single state of Maharashtra. Further, the coastal states have benefited more from FDI investment than the hinterland states. Based on FDI investment received in different states, states can be classified into FDI magnet states and FDI lagged states.

Industry-wise, the break-up of FDI reveals that the basic industries, including power, chemicals, oil refining and ferrous metals rank first with 37.5 per cent, followed by the services including computer software, telecommunications, financial services, tourism and hotel industries with about 35 per cent. These are followed by consumer non-durable industries, including food products, textiles and fermentation industries, received another about 8 per cent. In this way, more than 80 per cent of total (approved) investment went to these groups of services and industry. At the level of individual industry, telecommunications and paging received as high as about 20.4 per cent of the total amount involved in investment approved, followed by power with 16.4 per cent, oil refinery 9.3 per cent, and computer software 6.4 per cent. This shows that FDI is being invested largely in the core sectors of Indian economy. Among others, the pattern of FDI in India, discussed above, has significant implications for regional income growth and population redistribution.

On development impact of the new economic policies, various scholars and agencies have conducted studies. Their views differ on growth behaviour of various states in India. Some of the scholars are of the view that economic growth of different states is converging in post-reforms period, resulting in reduction of regional income inequality. In contrast, other group of scholars is emphasizing on divergence hypothesis. According to them, regional economic growth of different states in India is highly divergent leading to widening of disparity among different states. According to another conclusion, Indian economy is emerging as a 'service economy' in post-reforms period. They point out to rapidly increasing share of service sector in Indian economy. According to them, the fastest growing sector being the service sector, where salary structures differ widely, hence it has become a major cause for widening inter-personal, intra- and inter-regional disparities in the country. As per another interesting conclusion, the East-West economic divide existing in pre-reforms period has been reshaping into north-south divide in post-reforms period. According to them, Southern India is emerging as economic growth tiger, Western India as investment hub, Northern India as consumption boom and Eastern India as pimple on the face of resurgent India, and North-Eastern India a law and order headache. Still another important finding is that the size (area and population) is becoming a factor in economic development. In other words, states have relative small and manageable area size and having controlled over population growth are doing much better in economic growth terms than other states in post-reforms period.

According to a study by Kurian (2000) the forward states as a group accounted for about two-thirds (65.9 per cent) of the total private investment during 1991-1998, against only 28.1 per cent by the group of backward states. Maharashtra and Gujarat together received 36.7 per cent, significantly higher than the aggregate share of backward states in total private investment proposals. A grouping of fourteen major states into coastal and hinterland states reveals that the former have benefited more from the FDI investment than the latter for the locational advantage. Aggregate per capita FDI investment during August 1991 and June 2001 in the former has been Rs. 2797 as compared to only Rs. 965 in the latter. Further, as revealed in high value of co-efficient of correlation ($r = 0.52$) between growth rates of per capita SDP of states and per capita FDI investment received by them, the economic growth has been faster in states receiving higher FDI investment proposals during 1991-2001.

Locationally, the export-oriented industries are concentrated in and around big urban centres. The new industrial policy imposes almost no restrictions on the location of new industrial units; also permits the expansion of the existing ones. Consequently, the export-oriented industrial units are continuing to concentrate in the big urban industrial centres. Further, the port cities, in addition to existing export processing zones (mentioned earlier), are growing at a faster rate. Those cities lending transit facilities also growing rapidly.

Evidently, the new policy made the big urban industrial centres the hubs of higher industrial investment, and greater job opportunities, attracting large number of rural job seekers. This will result in population redistribution in favour of the big urban industrial centres, requiring efficient management of and investment in the urban infrastructure for accommodating the new developments. Industrial licensing almost abolished, the Monopoly and Restrictive Trade Policy (MRTP) Act lifted all restrictions on investment by and the growth of industrial houses, and the Foreign Exchange Regulation Act (FERA) amended to allow foreign investment in a large number of industries and investment of large foreign equity (even up to 100%) in select cases, especially for export-oriented production.

The new industrial policy, oriented towards achieving higher economic growth and efficiency, has opened the doors for large inflow of foreign direct investment. However, the regional inequalities in industrial and overall economic development are bound to accelerate at least in medium terms.

III

Emerging Issues and Challenges

While it is true that growth rates of State Domestic Product (SDP) has always been growing differently but these differentials have never being so wide as in post-reforms period. As revealed in Table 5.1, growth rates of SDP ranged from a high of 7.17 per cent (at constant prices) in case of Rajasthan to a low of 3.91 per cent in Assam during 1980-1990 decade. Against this, it varied from a high of 8.28 in Gujarat state to a low of 2.47 in Assam during 1990-2000. The co-efficient of variation value, which was only 0.14 during 1980-1990 decade, jumped to 0.29 during 1990-2000. With few exceptions, developed states experienced higher growth rates in comparison to less developed states. This is a clear evidence of growing income inequality among different states in the country.

Table 5.1: India: Growth Rates of SDP at Constant Prices (per cent per annum)

State	1980-1990	1900-2000	1980-2000
Andhra Pradesh	4.81	5.12	5.05
Assam	3.91	2.47	3.49
Bihar	5.20	3.46	3.85
Goa	5.71	8.23	7.47
Gujarat	5.71	8.28	6.80
Haryana	6.68	6.71	7.80
Himachal Pradesh	6.10	6.91	7.80
Karnataka	6.10	7.07	6.53
Kerala	4.50	6.00	5.97
Madhya Pradesh	5.18	5.45	5.89
Maharashtra	5.98	6.80	6.30
Orissa	5.85	3.60	3.90
Punjab	5.14	4.63	4.70
Rajasthan	7.17	6.46	6.95
Tamil Nadu	6.35	6.65	6.51
Uttar Pradesh	5.88	4.33	5.15
West Bengal	5.20	7.24	6.11
All India	5.60	6.03	5.68
Co-efficient of variation	0.14	0.29	0.22

A comparative picture of growth rates of SDP in per capita terms is more revealing than the SDP growth rates as such. States, which could have a control on population growth during the post-reforms decade (1990-2000) did perform much in per capita growth rates of SDP in comparison to their performance in this regard during 1980-1990. Three southern states of Kerala, Tamil Nadu and Karnataka, where growth rates of population declined sharply during 1990-2000 over 1980-1990, enjoyed higher growth rates of per capita incomes in comparison to several other states as well as their previous performance during 1980-1990. Notable exceptions in this regards, however, are Maharashtra and Orissa. Maharashtra's economy could perform well during 1990-2000 in per capita terms in spite of relatively higher population growth in the state during 1990-2000. On the other side of the scale, Orissa's economy could not perform well during 1990-2000 in per capita terms in spite of relatively low population growth in the state during 1990-2000 (see Tables 5.2 and 5.3). In overall, it is evidently clear that growth rates of population in Indian states have started now impinging upon their economic performance.

Table 5.2: India: Growth Rates of Per Capita SDP (per cent per annum)

State	*1980-1990*	*1900-2000*	*1980-2000*
Andhra Pradesh	2.56	3.62	3.09
Assam	1.74	0.65	1.38
Bihar	2.97	1.86	1.92
Goa	4.08	6.84	6.01
Gujarat	3.62	6.38	4.85
Haryana	4.12	4.42	5.32
Himachal Pradesh	4.36	5.11	4.29
Karnataka	4.00	5.27	4.63
Kerala	3.04	4.78	4.64
Madhya Pradesh	2.74	3.22	3.08
Maharashtra	3.60	5.04	4.83
Orissa	3.96	2.12	2.15
Punjab	3.19	2.71	2.73
Rajasthan	4.41	4.09	4.20
Tamil Nadu	4.79	5.40	5.10
Uttar Pradesh	3.46	1.98	2.92
West Bengal	2.93	5.41	3.99
All India	**3.36**	**4.07**	**3.54**
Co-efficient of variation	0.22	0.43	0.34

Source: Bhattachaya, B.B. and S. Sakthivel (2004), "Regional growth and disparity in India: Comparison of pre- and post-reform decades", *Economic and Political Weekly*, March 6, pp.1071-77.

(i) Widening Inter-Regional Income Inequalities

The impact of differential growth rates of economy in various states in India has reflected in widening inter-state income inequalities. Notwithstanding the fact that wide regional income inequalities have always existed in India, but this has accelerated under the impact of the new investment, industrial and trades policies initiated in 1991. The gap between the highest (Punjab, Rs.6487) and the lowest (Bihar, Rs.2253) per capita income states, which was 2.88 times in 1988-89 increased to 4.75 times in 1996-97 and further to 5.50 in 2003-04. Earlier in 1960-61, this gap has been of 1.90 times, increased to 2.66 times in 1970-71, to 2.92 in 1980-81, and then declined marginally to 2.88 times in 1988-89 (a stable financial year before the start of new economic policy). Obviously, the latest upward movement in regional income inequalities has been the biggest jump ever-since 1960-61 (Table 5.4).

Table 5.3: India: Population Growth Rates (per cent per annum)

State	*1980-1990*	*1900-2000*	*1980-2000*
Andhra Pradesh	2.19	1.36	1.77
Assam	2.05	1.74	1.90
Bihar	2.14	2.43	2.28
Goa	1.57	1.30	1.38
Gujarat	1.94	1.59	1.77
Haryana	2.45	2.50	2.48
Himachal Pradesh	1.91	1.62	1.76
Karnataka	1.93	1.60	1.77
Kerala	1.35	0.90	1.13
Madhya Pradesh	2.41	2.05	2.23
Maharashtra	2.32	2.06	2.19
Orissa	1.84	1.49	1.67
Punjab	1.91	1.83	1.87
Rajasthan	2.53	2.53	2.53
Tamil Nadu	1.44	1.07	1.25
Uttar Pradesh	2.30	2.30	2.30
West Bengal	2.22	1.67	1.94
All India	2.44	1.94	2.19

Source: Computed from Census of India, 1981, 1991 and 2001.

Recent studies also confirm such trend in regional income inequalities (*see* Nagaraj, 2000; Kurian, 2000; Ahluwalia, 2000). Nagaraj using data on per capita SDP across major states concludes, 'more significantly the divergence in per capita income between the top three and the bottom three states has widened sharply since 1986-87. The average per capita SDP of the bottom three states (Bihar, Orissa and Assam), which made 43 per cent of the top three states (Punjab, Haryana and Maharashtra) in 1980-81, fell down to 27 per cent in 1995-96. Even in absolute terms, the per capita SDP of the bottom three states was lower in 1995-96 than that of 1988-89.' Ahluwalia after analyzing SDP growth rates of the fourteen major states during 1981-1991 and 1992-1998 noted a significant increase in the degree of dispersion in growth rates across states in the 1990s. The variation in annual growth rate of SDP, which was in the ratio of less than 2 between the lowest (3.6 per cent in Kerala) and the highest rate (6.6 per cent in Rajasthan) in the 1980s, increased to more than 3.5 in the 1990s: (Bihar, 2.7 per cent) and (Gujarat, 9.6 per cent). These differences in performance across states get more marked with inclusion of growth rates of population and evaluation of performance in terms of growth rates of per capita SDP: from a ratio of 1:2 in the 1980s to 1:7 in the 1990s. However, Ahluwalia does not agree with the thesis of geographical polarization of high performance. Kurian opines that 'the ongoing economic reforms since 1991 have further aggravated the inter-state disparities'.

Table 18.4: India: Widening per capita Income Gap among Major States

Period	*Highest Per Capita State*	*Lowest Per Capita State*	*Ratio*
1960-61	Maharashtra (Rs. 409)	Bihar (Rs. 215)	1.90
1970-71	Punjab (Rs. 1070)	Bihar (Rs. 402)	2.66
1980-81	Punjab (Rs. 2674)	Bihar (Rs. 917)	2.92
1988-89	Punjab (Rs. 6487)	Bihar (Rs. 2253)	2.88
1996-97	Punjab (Rs. 18213)	Bihar (Rs. 3835)	4.75
2003-04	Haryana (Rs.29504)	Bihar (Rs. 5362)	5.50

Source: Economic Survey of Different Years, Government of India, Ministry of Finance, New Delhi.

If the current trend in regional income inequalities continues, the existing demographic, social, and economic divides between the rich and the poor states will sharpen to explode into inter-regional and intra-regional conflicts. Already, political discontentment is intense in the least developed states for their perceived neglect in the development process. The least developed regions are expressing anger for the perceived neglect and the developed ones for a check on their potential. The latter is represented by a demand for Sikh homeland *(Khalistan)* in the prosperous Punjab and the former by a demand for *Uttaranchal* in Uttar Pradesh. *Uttaranchal* (now *Uttrakhand*) has already been granted the statehood.

Already growth rates are quite low in backward states such as Uttar Pradesh, Bihar and Orissa. There will be serious implications if low growth rates continue into the future in these states, representing almost a third of the total population, while the rest of the country is enjoying robust growth. 'The continuation of low growth rates will accentuate inter-state disparities and poverty will further concentrate in some such regions, leading to socially and politically more explosive situations. It would not only affect the politics of these parts of the country but, because of their size, it would undoubtedly have a debilitating impact on the politics of the country as a whole' (Ahluwalia, 2000, p.1642). Corruption both inside and outside the government establishment is increasing in post-reforms phase. Government machinery entrusted with regulatory authority, which was supposed to act as watchdog in post-liberalization and globalization phase of Indian economy, is getting corrupt and ineffective.

(ii) Poverty: Declining but Getting Regionally Concentrated

It is heartening to note that the number of persons living below poverty line has declined from 320 million in 1993-94 to 260 million in 1999-2000. However, the geographical distribution of the people living below poverty line is undergoing a radial change. Majority of them were getting concentrated in certain states and the least developed parts within them. The four states—Uttar Pradesh, Bihar, Madhya Pradesh, and Maharashtra—had nearly 57 per cent of the total number of the poor in the country, against their combined share of 45 per cent in the total population of the country in 2001. Moreover, their combined share in all-India poverty has been increasing over the period: 44.6 per cent in 1972-73, 47.3 per cent in 1977-78, 51.0 per cent in 1983-84, 51.5 per cent in 1987-88, 53.1 per cent in 1993-94 and 56.9 per cent in 1999-2000. Meanwhile, the number of the poor in these states has grown to 148.2 million from 129.96 million (Table 5.5). While more than two-fifths of Bihar's population (42.6%) lives in poverty, almost the same situation prevails in eastern Uttar Pradesh and eastern Maharashtra. Already social tensions, due to the repression of the underprivileged castes and rivalry among anti-social groups, are intense in the states of Bihar and Uttar Pradesh. This has serious repercussions in maintaining law and order.

(iii) Poverty Declining but Vulnerability Increasing

Notably, regional inequalities in economic growth have been widening at a time when political power in India is drifting from the Centre to the States and from the upper to the backward and lower castes. In a democracy, such a tendency may be taken as a desirable outcome. But given the state's limited capacities for redistribution of wealth and the intensity with which electoral support has been courted, these mobilized but dissatisfied groups are highly potent agents in contributing to the growing political turmoil (Kohli, 1991, p.18). These new players may be 'uninitiated in the etiquette of parliamentary democracy and in the social graces of modernity, but are quite astute in pursuing the interests of their constituencies and, of course, their own self-interest'(Bardhan, 1998, p.132). If the enlarging inequalities are not halted by corrective measures quickly, Indian society may have to pay a huge political price for it (Nagaraj, 2000, p. 2836). Enlarging and intensifying Naxal activities in several states and increasing incidence of suicides by the farmers are the clear cut manifestation of the political price mentioned by Nagaraj. According to official statistics there were 8,900 suicides by farmers between 2001 and 2006 in the four states of Andhra Pradesh, Karnataka, Kerala and Maharashtra.[1]

Table 5.5: India: Increasing Concentration of Poverty

(Figures in millions)

State	1972-73	1977-78	1983-84	1987-88	1993-94	1999-2000
Uttar Pradesh	47.95	50.60	53.00	44.83	60.45	52.99
Bihar	31.71	36.42	36.55	33.64	49.33	42.56
Madhya Pradesh	25.48	28.58	25.49	22.49	29.85	29.85
Maharashtra	24.82	29.62	23.20	21.41	30.52	22.80
Total	129.96	145.22	138.24	122.37	170.15	148.20
Percentage in all-India Poverty	44.57	47.33	51.01	51.49	53.12	56.90
Percentage in all India Population	43.2[1]	43.2[1]	43.3[2]	43.3[2]	43.8[3]	45.0[4]

Notes:

1. Percentage share as per 1971 Census figures
2. Percentage share as per 1981 Census figures
3. Percentage share as per 1991 Census figures
4. Percentage share as per 2001 Census figures

Source: (i) Government of India (1993) *Report of the Expert Group on Estimation of Proportion and Number of Poor*, Planning Commission, New Delhi.

According to the information available from the Planning Commission, New Delhi the number persons living below the poverty line (BPL) has declined during 1993-94 and 2004-05 from 30.7 per cent during 1993-94 to 21.8 per cent during 2004-05. Numerically speaking, the number of poor and extremely poor population came down to 237 million in 2004-05 from 274 million in 1993-94. Nevertheless, during the same period, proportional share of marginal and vulnerable population (living on daily per capita consumption between Rs. 12 and Rs. 20) increased from 51.2 per cent to 55.0 per cent. In other words, the number of vulnerable section in Indian society increased to 392 million in 2004-05 from 290 million in 1993-94. Evidently, though BPL population declined but population just above BPL increased in the country. They are the people, who will be the hardest hit if the train of India's booming economy gets derailed any time. If the number of poor and vulnerable sections of population in India is added, they together make 836 million in 2004-05, making 77.0 per cent of total population. Composition of the poor and vulnerable groups of population within respective population groups is highly revealing. The 88 per cent of the total Scheduled Castes, 85 per cent of Scheduled Tribes, 85 per cent of the Muslims and 80 per cent of other backward castes (OBC) population fall in this category of poor and vulnerable section of Indian society. All these and some other startling facts reporting in the following paragraphs records the Report of the National Commission for Enterprises in Unorganised Sector, chaired by Professor Arjun Sengupta.

On the other side of the scale, the combined number of middle and rich population went up to 253 million in 2004-05 from 162 million in 1993-94, registering 56 per cent increase in just 10 years. Separately, the share of the Middle Income group (defined those having per capita daily consumption being Rs. 37 in 2004-05) has gone to 19.3 per cent in 2004-05 from 15.5 per cent in 1993-94. And that of the High Income group population (per capita per day consumption being Rs.93 plus in 2004-05) to 4.0 per cent in 2004-05 from 2.7 per cent in 1993-94.

Growth rates of consumption of different classes/groups in India during this period given below in a tabular form are highly revealing.

Serial Number	*Class/Group*	*Growth rate of Consumption (in per cent)*
1.	Poor	1.0
2.	Poor and vulnerable	2.8
3.	Middle Class	4.3
4.	High	6.2

Total consumption expenditure of middle and high income groups in India is estimated to the tune of 48 billion US dollars, which is higher than the total GDP of several developing countries in the world. Only 1.0 per cent of Scheduled Castes/Tribes population, 2.2 per cent of the Muslims and 2.4 per cent of other backward castes (OBC) fall in this group of population. Another social characteristic of poor and vulnerable social group is that 86 per cent of them are illiterate, 79 per cent are below primary level of education, and 79 per cent are working in unorganized sector. Of total India's population of 1090 million in 2004-05, 836 million were poor and vulnerable, 210 million middle income, and remaining 44 million rich/high income bracket.

Over 394.9 million workers, who make 86 per cent of the total working population and working under 'utterly deplorable' conditions with 'extremely few livelihood options', have very low consumption expenditure. In this way, over consumption by neo-rich upper middle class and rich people, on the one hand, and malnutrition among poor and extremely poor sections of Indian society will pose danger to the environment and economy in their own way.

Maximization of profits should not be the sole aim of economic growth. It has lead cutthroat competition, where is made no distinction between the fair and foul rules of game as eyes always remain on winning the game. Planning has to occupy itself entirely with the improvement of vulnerable regions and sections of society through geographical and social engineering. Otherwise, regional and social tensions will intensify further.

The way socio-economic and political processes have been operating in post-reforms period of India, a number of issues and problems have come to fore. Some of the important issues include: (i) widening of the gap between haves and have-nots (both at regional and societal level), (ii) regional concentration of poverty, (iii) growing unemployment among the youth, (iv) North-South and Urban-Rural economic divides, (v) corruption, (vi) ethnic divide, and (vii) ecological and environmental degradation. The leadership, policy-makers and planners have dealt with all such issues and problems giving the highest priority. Before leaving this issue, I will cite a few examples of political and bureaucratic corruption in the country in the following lines. The *Times of India*, a daily news paper, reported in news item on September 17, 2007 that foodgrains worth Rs. 31,500 crore earmarked for public distribution system (PDS) have been stolen in three years. About 53 per cent of wheat and 39 per cent of rice, meant for distribution among the poor through PDS, were diverted to the open market. Six worst offending states included Uttar Pradesh (Rs.3289.71 crore), West Bengal (Rs.1913.76 crore), Madhya Pradesh (Rs.1038.69 crore), Assam (Rs.958.75 crore), Rajasthan (Rs.665.71 crore) and Maharashtra (Rs.435.80 crore). The newspaper commented on the issue in the following words, "It is not mere inefficiency. It is a shocking crime. It means that instead of serving the poor, government is subsidising corrupt babus and middlemen to the tune of over Rs. 10,000 crore a year". *Krishi Pandit,* Gold Medals, giving some time back to BT cotton growers by the Maharashtra Government have been found impure. It is rather a national shame, speaking of declining morality even on the part of the State in India. The scam in Hyderabad based company, Satyam Computers, is not only shocking but also it has shaken the faith of millions of corporate sector investors in India. Mr. Ramalinga Raju, Promoter Chairman of the Company, in a letter send to Board of Directors on January 7, 2009 admitted of more than Rs. 7000 crore fraud in balance sheet of the Company. The comments of one of our former Vice Presidents, Shri Bhairon Singh Shekhawat, over the political corruption in India are worth noting. He stated corruption is making 'India's democracy and its political parties irrelevant'.[2]

SOME SUGGESTIONS

Finally, the paper put forward the following suggestions for discussion and debate:

1. Strengthening of regulatory role of the State apparatus involved in regulatory and supervising work;
2. Higher investment in health, education and infrastructure development especially in backward regions and to benefit specially the backward social groups in developed regions;
3. Reorganization of administrative units both at the state and district levels to facilitate higher level of economic development;
4. Decentralization of the administrative power to democratically elected bodies at the local level.

At the time when size (population and area) of administrative units has started impinging upon the development process operating in administrative units at different hierarchical level, it is imperative to reform administrative organization of space in a manner that it helps in acceleration of development process operating in them. Now, area and population sizes at different hierarchical levels differ very widely. For example, the largest area size state (Rajasthan, 342.2 thousand square kms) is ninety-three times larger than the smallest size state (Goa, 3.7 thousand square kms) of the Indian Union. The largest population size state (Uttar Pradesh, 162 million) is more than 300 times populous of the smallest population size state (Sikkim, 5.4 lakh).

At the district level, leaving aside Ladakh and Kuchchh districts of their peculiar situations, the third largest area size district (Jaisalmer, 38,428 square kms) is four hundred times larger than the smallest district (Mahe, 9 square kms) in the country. The largest population size district (Medinipur, 96.10 lakh) is more than two thousand times populous of the least populous district (Kuchchh, 45.6 thousand) in the country.

Obviously, there is an urgent need for administrative area reforms. In my opinion, to begin with all the 36 million plus cities in India along with their hinterlands must be carved into states. We need at least 80-100 states in Indian union. This will also considerably reduce the manipulative political power game now played by certain populous states in electoral politics.

CONCLUDING REMARKS

In India, social and regional inequalities in income and consumption are widening in post-reforms phase. If the current trend in regional income inequalities continues, the existing demographic, social and economic divides between the rich and the poor states will sharpen to explode as inter-regional and intra-regional conflicts. Already, political discontent is intense in the least developed states for their perceived neglect in the development process. In addition, information technology and mass media, that have entered India *via* the globalization route, is having westernizing impact on the life styles of elite groups and the youth. It has also created awareness and increased expectations among masses for material well-being. With increased mobility under the impact of the reform process, affluence and poverty are fast polarizing into separate geographical and social spaces within the country. A new dividing line is thus emerging in India between small groups of beneficiaries and vast sections of victims of globalization process. On one hand, the majority of vulnerable sections, which is at the receiving end of the globalization process, belong to the oppressed social groups of the Indian society. On the other hand, the balance of political power in Indian politics is shifting towards these social groups. The emerging paradox between the economic power, in the hands of the upper castes, and the political power, in the hands of the middle and lower castes, is highly potent of internal political instability and uncertainty about the continuity of the current economic reform process in India.

Massive and unplanned in-migration to booming metropolitan centres, and deterioration in quality of infrastructure with expanding urban-industrial activities placed new challenges before the administration in different states. In addition, rapidly growing casteism, religious fundamentalism, regionalism, and use of muscle power in electoral politics are the dangerous viruses, fast engulfing our democracy. This is shaping India into a paradox of successful elections and failed democracy.

Fortunately, the size of Indian middle class is increasing, since the 1980s. The growing spatial spread and numerical strength of the middle class is bound to have a significant impact on both economic and political process in India. Given the hard working, professional and rational character of the Indian middle class, their increasing influence will strengthen Indian economy and stabilize the political process. 'The Indian middle class, growing at the rate it is, will be the most formidable influence on Indian political economy for the rest of the twenty-first century making India a major political and economic global power' (Pai Panandiker, 1998, p. 394). Moreover, the foreign investors in Indian markets also have a stake in keeping India united and politically stable. They will not allow political stability in India to crumble so easily.

In sum, how to make it compatible with our culture, polity and economy is the real question. While the necessity of achieving fast economic growth and modern technology cannot be denied, the questions relating to poverty, regional and social inequalities, unemployment, empowerment of the weaker and unprivileged sections of Indian society cannot easily be brushed aside. We have to look for a globalization that includes rather than marginalises the poor. We need to evolve a strong and responsive system of governance.

NOTES

1. Briefing by Agriculture Ministry officials in Hyderabad on April 10, 2006, DNA, April 11, 2006 (quoted in *Economic and Political Weekly*, April 22-28, 2006, p.1523).
2. *The Hindu*, daily newspaper, Delhi edition, Friday, January 9, 2009, p.1.

REFERENCES

Ahluwalia, Montek S. (2000), 'Economic performance of states in post-reforms period', *Economic and Political Weekly,* May 6, pp.1637-1648.

——. (2000), *op. cit*, p.1642.

Assema, Sinha (2004), "Ideas, interests, and institutions in policy change: A comparison of Gujarat and West Bengal," in Rob, Jenkins (ed.) *Regional Reflections: Comparative Politics across India's States*, Oxford University Press, Delhi.

Bardhan, Pranab (1998), *The Political Economy of Development in India*, expanded edition, Oxford University Press, Delhi.

Frankel, Francine (2005), *India's Political Economy, 1947-2004: The Gradual Revolution*, Oxford University Press, Delhi.

Kohli, Atul (1991), *Democracy and Discontent: India's Growing Crisis of Governability*, Cambridge University Press, Cambridge.

—— (1991), *op. cit.,* p. 18.

—— (1991), *op. cit.,* pp. 305-338.

—— (1991), *op. cit.,* pp. 305-338.

Kolhi, Atul (2006), "Politics of economic growth in India, 1980-2005:Part-I-The 1980s," *Economic and Political Weekly*, Vol. XLI, No.13, April 1, 2006, pp. 1251-1260.

Kurian, N.J. (2000), 'Widening regional disparities in India: some indicators', *Economic and Political Weekly,* February 12, p. 545.

Kurian, N.J. (2000), *op. cit.*, pp.538-550.

Nagaraj, R. (2000), 'Indian economy since 1980: virtuous growth or polarisation?' *Economic and Political Weekly*, August 5, p. 2831.

—— (2000), *op. cit*, p. 2838.

—— (2000), *op. cit*, pp. 2831-38.

Nayyar, Deepak (2001),"Economic and political democracy: Interaction of economics and politics in Independent India, in Niraja, Gopal Jayal (ed.) *Democracy in India*, Oxford University Press, New Delhi, pp. 362-96.

Pai Panandiker, V.A. (1998), The Political Economy of Centre-State Relations in India, In Ahluwalia, Isher Judge and I.M.D. Little eds. *India's Economic Reforms and Development—Essays for Manmohan Singh*, Oxford University Press, Delhi, p.394.

Sen, Abhijit and Himanshu (2004), "Poverty and Inequality in India," *Economic and Political Weekly*, in two parts, September 18 and 25, pp.4247-63 and 4361-75.

6

Recent Scenario of Gender Patterns in Arunachal Pradesh*

RAVI S. SINGH

INTRODUCTION

One need not try hard to appreciate the changing perception and heightening response to gender issues. Sensitivity to it may vary interpersonally as much as inter-community; nevertheless the change is perceptible and well captures—reflected by the data. The contemporary development concerns recognize the need to ensure gender equity in policies, processes, and participation with reference to opportunities, access, and freedom. Real life experiences reveal enough that contested spaces and resource (rights) within household and hence community too is disfavourable to womenfolk. As rightly concluded by many researcher-scholars, gender is cultural construct in the true sense. That is how prevalent realities, here the gender, are product of the inherited practices, values and norms from the past and the contemporary behaviour too. Valuing the complimentary and contributory roles of men-women in due development processes, since quite some years, women-empowerment is advocated equivocally.

GENDER STUDIES: A SELECT OVERVIEW

The terms, 'Women' and 'gender' issues, are used almost as co- terminous. Gender unquestionably is a larger issue. In simple way, gender is about 'on not holding half the sky' by women. Being a socio-cultural construct, it requires deeper and wider focus involving all that inhibits equal footing (of women *vis-à-vis* men) and

*It is the revised version of a paper presented at "Human Development in Multi-Religious and Multi-Cultural Societies: South Asian Experience", Nalanda Open University, Patna (March 30-31, 2008).

implications of such inequalities. Every society necessarily contains two domains, two sets of desires...... The social world of humanity, split into innumerable parts, is primarily dichotomous. Of late, one finds over arching concerns to discern this truth that varies vertically and horizontally in our social experiences. The whole gamut of our contemporary knowledge, particularly human and social sciences is engaged in this discourse as this issue has caught our attentions along with other contemporary concerns of just development, sustain ability and environment. The ethical viewpoints well address valid questions like nature and source of (gendered) injustice the contested notions of it, norms and values for men-women, etc. (*see* Annas, 1993; O'Neill, 1993). Similarly, the welfare economists (like Amartya Sen) look at the missing of social opportunities on account of gender, and the effect of this phenomena on well-being, development and finally, on the health of economy (of developing countries) and laments the blatant reality of our times.

In geography, gender studies are late comer, especially in the Indian context. As it happens with any new sub-field, professional geographers gave habitual cold shoulder to it (cf. Raju, 2004). Clear emergence of gender studies is seen since the late 1980s. In the years to follow, there is satisfactory frequency of gender related works. The published work covers apparently north to south and west to east up to the northeast. Singh (2001) and Kar (2002) have attempted to understand gender geography of the northeast states of India. Lahiri-Dutta (2001) has worked on the coal mining communities, Bhagat and Sharma (2001) and Hasan (2000, 2002) have addressed the problem in Haryana, Joshi (2003) on Rajasthan and Samanta (2003) on West Bengal. An interesting study drawing comparison between two Bengals, i.e. West Bengal (India) and Bangladesh with respect to women's (health) status reports that the religious-gap for all indicators considered in the study is "pretty high" in West Bengal than Bangladesh (cf. Chattopadhyay and Goswami, 2007). A survey of literature sufficiently indicates predominance of quantitative and descriptive attempts. And, as it is the general weakness of ailing geography in India, there is lack of sufficient critical engagements in this area too. However, some recent works give reason to be hopeful (cf. Raju and Dutta, 2004).

The concurrent development concerns do take cognizance of the need to equalize processes, participations and policies in all contemporary issues concerning opportunities, access and freedom, in terms of gender. The contested spaces and resources are not favourable to womenfolk (e.g. access to resource and its role in capacity building is discussed by Sen, 1995). The deprivation and discrimination against womenfolk range from pre-natal abuse (read 'female foeticide') to crime and violence against women. Often one witnesses highly gendered domestic social (including political) and economic spaces with particular reference to opportunities within these recognized spaces. Majority of the existing works in this field do not include the North-East (NE) region, probably in view of the fact that this region as such constitutes a small proportion of the national population and it is predominated by the scheduled tribes (STs) considered free of the evil of gender discrimination (cf. Ahmad, 1999:16). This existing state of the affairs provides opportunity to venture into gender (deprivation) situation in NE India.

The basic issue of gender deprivation (that goes against womenfolk) highlighted rather prominently and conspicuously in the writings of Amartya Sen and fellow-scholars (cf. Nussabaum & Sen, 1993; Drèze & Sen, 1990, 1995; Sen, 2000) is undisputed concern of the contemporary civic societies. Many views may be there to justify and deny this dimension and it seems difficult to reject its existence in all societies. However, the 'known dimensions' and 'measurable degrees' of the problem do vary across ethnic communities (see Annas, 1993, for a lucid elaboration in this regard). On this account some societies are considered better and many more as worse. The means and manifestations of gender deprivation do vary but also share similarities in the basic sense. What should be the general outlook to this undeniable part of our realities?

Objective, Methodology and Data Base

The general understanding (or assumption?) is that tribal societies are 'women-friendly' (cf. Ahmad, 1999). How far this belief is true? What are the existing realities (reflected by data generated by government agencies) and many such questions shall be interesting to analyse. In the backdrop of observations made above, the primary concern of present paper is to seek some understanding of the place of women (*vis-à-vis* men) in Arunachal Pradesh (ArP). In fact, it is an attempt to highlight women's social status with reference to exiting gender gaps in demography, education and participation in economic activities.

The conventional practice to consider sex-ratio (number of females per 1000 males) as the primer in any gender discussion is used here too. As far as educational scenario is concerned, the gender-gap at primary, middle, secondary and senior/higher secondary level is considered. The participation in economic activities is discussed with reference to the Census of India's categorization of works. Determination of the gender gap is done simply on the basis of percentage difference. Some aspects are mapped to appreciate geographic dimension in a better manner. The district level data have been used. Further disaggregating is not undertaken for the lack of required data. It is worth mentioning here that though sixteen districts existed during 2005 (cf. Fig. 6.1), only thirteen of them reportedly existed during 2001 Census. Therefore, the present discussion is restricted to these districts to some extent. Changing district boundaries and erratic nature of data compilation forbids any temporal comparisons at the district level.

The data sources used are Census of India reports and the *Statistical Abstract of Arunachal Pradesh,* an annual volume published by the Directorate of Economics and Statistics, Government of Arunachal Pradesh (Itanagar).

The Region and the People

The state of ArP lies in the extreme north-eastern part of India between the

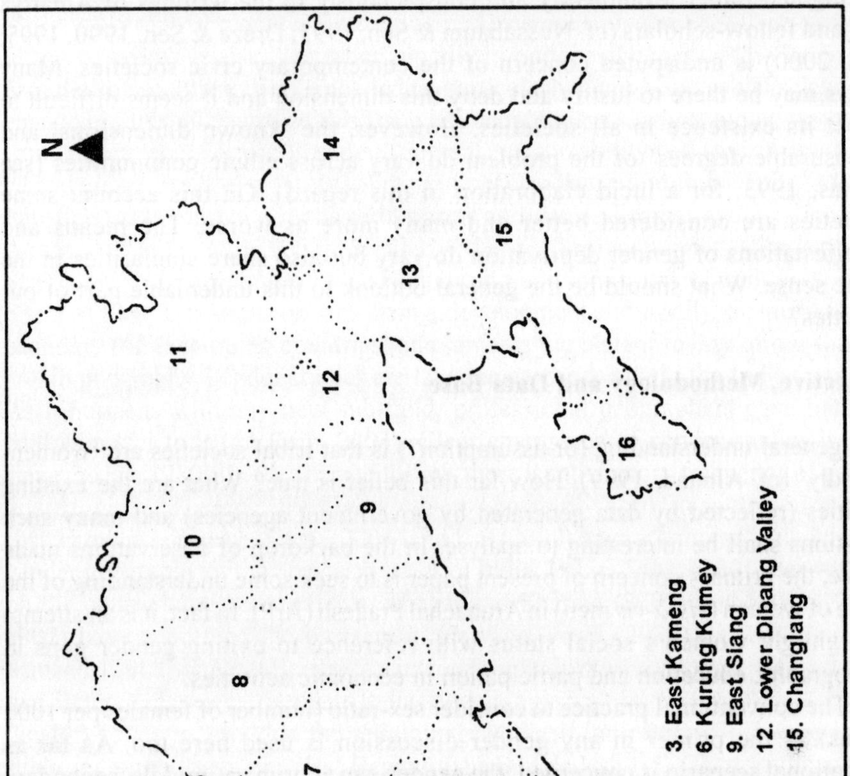

Fig. 6.1: Arunachal Pradesh: Location of Districts, 2005

26° 28'N to 29°31'N latitudes and 91°31'E to 97°30'E longitudes. Prior to attaining full statehood in 1987, it was one of the Union Territories of the Indian Union since 1972. This state was known as the North East Frontier Tract prior to 1954 and North East Frontier Agency (NEFA) during 1954-1972. It shares international boundary with Bhutan in the west, Tibet (China) in the north and the north-east, and Burma (Myanmar) in the east; Assam and Nagaland surround it in the south west and south respectively. This state is by and large mountainous as 80 per cent of the geographical area is above 600m of height. On aggregate some 61.57 per cent of the geographical area is forested. The region experiences (hot-humid) sub-tropical conditions in the southern foothills to the alpine type climate in the northern high-altitude mountains (Singh, 2005).

The total population was reported to be 10,97,968 persons (2001) distributed over 83743 sq. km geographical area. This population size could be further disaggregated as (scheduled) tribes 64.22 per cent and non-tribal 35.78 per cent; rural 79.25 per cent and urban 20.75 per cent. Thirty-one communities are identified as permanent inhabitants and majority of them are disaggregated into sub-tribes and clans. Considerable variation in terms of their respective socio-cultural practices is found; however, larger similarity is noticed in occupational pattern. Diversity in ethnic composition could be better captured with respect to linguistic aspect. Forty-two languages and sixty-one dialects of all varieties are spoken by just thirty-one communities. On top of that six scripts are in simultaneous use, viz. Devanagari, Assamese, Hingna, Mon, Roman and Tibetan. Indigenous faith, Christianity, Buddhism and some variants of Hinduism (e.g. Vaishnavism) are professed by the people.

Why to select Arunachal Pradesh?

As mentioned earlier, majority of the available literature on development issues discuss the 'mainland India' and thus North East region is often left unattended. Comparatively speaking, studies on this region are limited; the condition appears appallingly bad if one considers the aspects covered. Actually keeping a few exceptions aside, all studies are ethnographical and anthropological in orientation (particularly in the case of ArP). The geographically peripheral location and smaller population size probably have been the reasons for such neglect. Nevertheless, in order to integrate this part with mainstream, scholars (especially living/working in this region) need to undertake studies focusing development experiences. More so, the contemporary socio-political unrest that is allegedly projected as angry men reaction to underdevelopment could also be understood in right perspective through such studies.

As far as the selection of Arunachal Pradesh for the present analysis is concerned, the extremely lower level of development in one hand and conspicuous gender discrimination observed by the researcher at grassroots level encouraged to look for some answers. Answers to such questions are difficult to find in the published and known materials. And, thus this elementary exercise is undertaken to know what is the state of social opportunities and how are they shared between men and women of the society. Needless to mention, the conclusions drawn here would be aggregate ones and they need to be disaggregated further on many possible lines—potential areas of future work in this field.

GENDER INEQUALITY: SOME DEMOGRAPHIC EVIDENCES

On aggregate, the proportion of women in a population is taken as indicator of general inequality. The often-used variable for this purpose is sex ratios defined as number of females per 1000 males. The constantly decreasing sex ratio has sufficiently attracted scholars' attention. Many alternative explanations with effect to the problem of 'missing women' (to use Sen's phrase, 1992) are known today (see Agnihorti, 2000 for a comprehensive and fuller analysis on the sex ratio in India) and this controversy is yet to be settled. However, it is agreed upon that the sex-ratio of a population shows relative position of womenfolk and it summarises the popular attitude of the society towards women.

If sex-ratio figures of India and Arunachal Pradesh are compared two sets of facts are revealed. First, we find similarity with respect to the total population's sex-ratio—gradually declining. Secondly, divergent facts are seen with regard to the STs category and the general population. In the case of STs sex-ratio at India level, there was marginal improvement in 1981 than previous Census (cf. Table 6.1); else, their SR is declining throughout. Nevertheless, the rate of decline is slower in comparison to the total population. There is gross incoherence with regard to the behaviour of general population at India level. The experience of Arunachal Pradesh is quite different; a consistently smooth decline in the STs sex-ratio is evident at the same time, the sex-ratio of general population is steadily progressing. During initial phase the in-migration was by and large male-selective and thus highly imbalanced sex composition of the general population was unavoidable. The male- selective migration was natural response to the difficult living conditions. With the peopling of non-economic areas; expansion of transportation-communication network; and easier living conditions, migrant workers (which form bulk of general population) have brought their families. The matter of concern remains change in SR of the STs against the womenfolk. Though for now it is a marginal decrease, but the question is why this unknown development taking place? One may tentatively speculate it to be the consequence of 'demonstration effect' of non-tribal social norms and value system that are prejudiced against females?

Table 6.1a: India and Arunachal Pradesh: Sex Ratio (females per 1000 males)

Year	India			Arunachal Pradesh		
	Total Population	ST Population	General Population	Total Population	ST Population	General Population
1961	941	987	934	894	1013	299
1971	930	982	924	861	1007	460
1981	934	983	930	862	1005	599
1991	927	972	923	859	998	658
2001	933	NA	NA	893	1003	723

Source: compiled by the author.

Table 6.1b: Sex Ratio among Religious Communities, 2001

Religious communities	*Total*	*Workers*	*Non-Workers*
All	893	645	1148
Hindu	749	989	1310
Muslim	625	187	1326
Christian	1003	925	1068
Sikh	264	45	1601
Buddhist	970	833	1111
Jain	662	278	1138
Others	1001	938	1049
Religion not stated	1032	1087	978

Source: SAAP, 2005.

Table 6.2a: Arunachal Pradesh: Sex Ratio by Districts

District	*Sex Ratio*				*%age of ST Population*
	Total	*Juvenile (0-6 years)*	*STs*	*General Population*	
1. Tawang	844	964	1036	371	78.61
2. West Kameng	822	970	984	669	52.99
3. East Kameng	962	1036	1030	638	85.55
4. Lower Subansiri	931	970	1015	669	70.91
5. Upper Subansiri	867	1005	988	360	85.92
6. West Siang	872	997	1007	506	78.47
7. East Siang	748	997	1003	613	68.57
8. Dibang Valley	787	994	999	642	45.44
9. Lohit	797	968	981	701	37.31
10. Changlang	863	987	960	815	34.84
11. Tirap	862	946	980	450	80.43
12. Arunachal Pradesh	859	982	958	658	63.65

Note: General Population is used to denote the non-ST and SC Population.
Source: Compiled by the author.

It is worthwhile to look into the district level scenario in this respect. Tables 6.2a and 6.2b reflect that there is no regularity in the spatiality of sex-ratio either for total/STs/general population, and the variation in sex ratio of general population is higher. In case of the SR of STs, southern districts, namely Changlang (972), Tirap (977), and Lohit (863) perform most badly being the lowest sex ratio areas (Fig. 6.2).

As far as the total population's SR is concerned, one many understand it to be the outcome of greater concentration of non-bachelor population. The positive correlation between percentage of STs and total population's SR supports this argument.

Table 6.2b: Arunachal Pradesh: Sex Ratio, 2001

	District/State	Sex Ratio		
		Total	Tribal	Non-Tribal
1.	Tawang	982	1050	280
2.	West Kameng	754	975	580
3.	East Kameng	985	1037	111
4.	Papum Pare	901	1020	765
5.	Lower Subansiri	960	1037	635
6.	Kurung Kumey	1013	1033	387
7.	Upper Subansiri	960	1019	569
8.	West Siang	912	999	600
9.	East Siang	931	1002	768
10.	Upper Siang	848	987	476
11.	Dibang Valley	697	942	358
12.	Lower Dibang Valley	858	994	764
13.	Lohit	863	975	813
14.	Anjaw	814	970	43
15.	Changlang	906	972	870
16.	Tirap	910	977	625
	Arunachal Pradesh	893	1003	723

Source: Based in *SAAP, 2005*.

SOCIAL OPPORTUNITIES AND GENDER: CASE OF EDUCATION

Education is a social instrument capable of changing a person's life (positively) and overhauling customary social practices for development. Scholars argue in favour of raising literacy (and education), particularly of women, to give desirable direction to the development process. The value of education to a person is identified as follows:

1. *Intrinsic importance:* Being education and healthy are valuable achievements in themselves, and the opportunity to have them can be of direct importance to a person's effective freedom;
2. *Instrumental personal roles*: A person's education (and health) can help him or her to do many things — other than just being educated and healthy — that are also valuable. They can, for instance, be important for getting a job and more generally for making use of economic opportunities. The resulting expansion in incomes and economic means can, in turn, add to a person's freedom to achieve functioning that s/he values;
3. *Instrumental social roles:* Greater literacy and basic education can facilitate public discussion of social needs and encourage informed collective demands (e.g. for health care and social security); these in turn can help to expand facilities enjoyed by public, and contribute to the better utilization of the available services;
4. *Instrumental process roles*: The process of schooling can have benefits

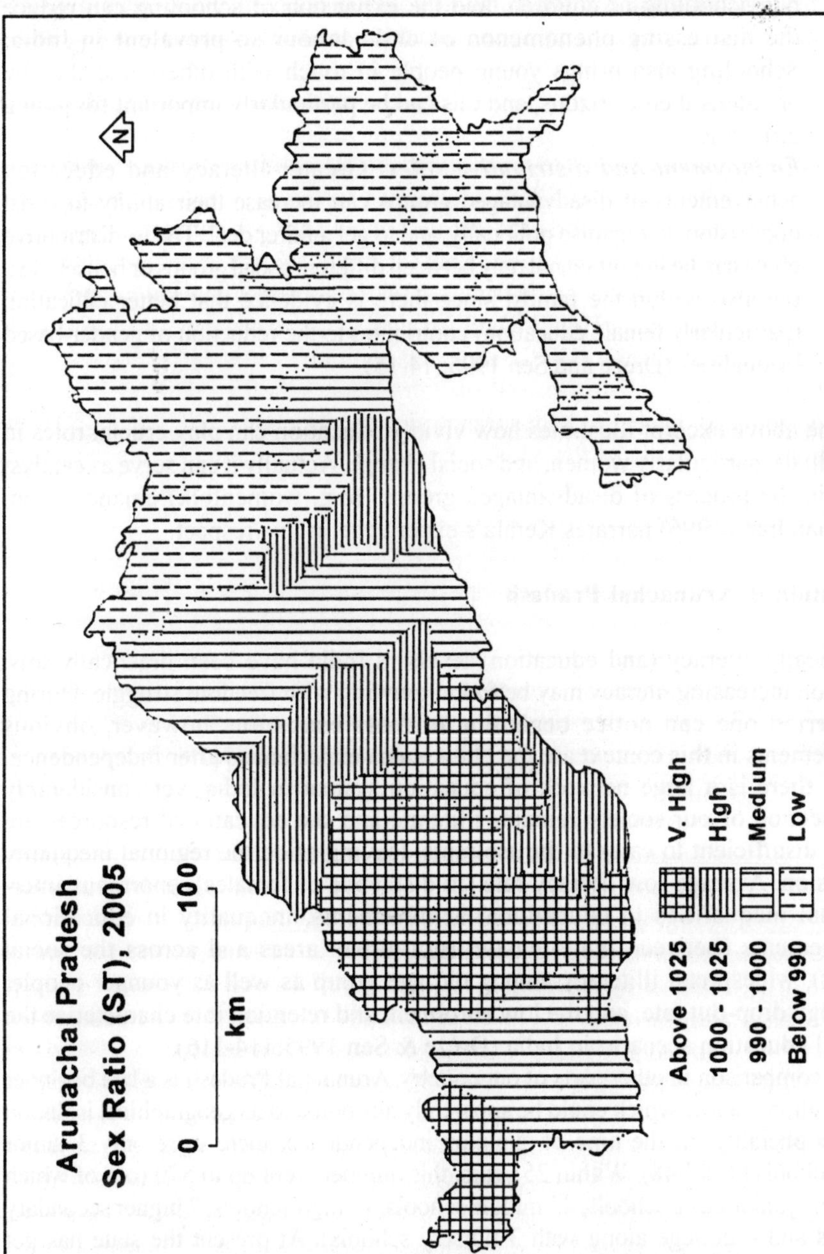

Fig. 6.2: Arunachal Pradesh: Sex Ratio (ST), 2005

even aside from its explicitly aimed objectives, namely, formal education. For example, the incidence of child labour is intimately connected with non-schooling of children, and the expansion of schooling can reduce the distressing phenomenon of child labour so prevalent in India. Schooling also brings young people in touch with others and thereby broadens their horizons, and this can be particularly important for young girls; and

5. *Employment and distributive roles*: Greater literacy and education achievements of disadvantaged groups can increase their ability to resist oppression, to organise politically, and to get a fairer deal. The re-distributive effect can be important not only between different social groups or households, but also within the family, since there is evidence that better education (particularly female education) contributes to the reduction of gender-based inequalities (Drèze and Sen 1995: 14-15).

The above excerpt illustrates how vividly education can play crucial roles in individuals, particularly women, and social change. Actually it can serve as catalyst agent in the process of disadvantaged groups' (e.g. womenfolk) emancipation. Ramchandran (1996) narrates Kerala's experience in this respect.

Education in Arunachal Pradesh

Historically, literacy (and education) levels in India have been drastically low. Focus on increasing literacy may be found growing with freedom struggle. During this period one can notice beginning of mass education; however, obvious achievements in this context are the phenomena experienced after independence. Today, there is a large network of education system in India, yet considerably large section of our society remains illiterate and the educational resources are highly insufficient to cater to the aspirants; leaving aside the regional inequality dimension. Average low literacy rate (in disfavour of females), enormous inter-personal inequalities in educational achievements, inequality in educational achievements (between male-female, rural-urban areas and across the social groups), widespread illiteracy among old age group as well as younger people, very high drop-out rate, and the low enrolment and retention rate characterise the general education scenario in India (Drèze & Sen 1995:114-116).

In comparison to other parts of our country, Arunachal Pradesh is a late beginner in education—a fact which could be apparently attributed to its geographical isolation and peripherality. At the time of attaining independence, there were only 3 junior basic schools (1947-48). Within 25 years, this number went up to 570 (out of which 503 were junior basic schools, 45 middle schools, 11 high schools, 7 higher secondary schools and 1 college along with 3 nursery schools). At present the state has got several institutions, totalling to 2,090 (including 242 non-governmental institutions) to impart education. This explains the stride taken by Arunachal Pradesh in creating infrastructure to spread education. No doubt, the government initiatives have yielded fruits over the years and today nearly 42 per cent population is reported literate; yet this figure is considerably small compared to many North East states (e.g. Mizoram, Manipur, etc.). Now, the main question in which we are interested is what is the gender-wise distribution of literacy and education?

Question of Female Education

Questioning poor state of female education is a very new happening to India and therefore, at first appallingly poor performers (BIMARU combination) have caught researchers' attention for they being 'burden of inertia' to use Drèze & Gazdar's (1997) nomenclature that is why so far the state of female education in Arunachal Pradesh is yet not addressed there is no known social reservation against any section of society to attain education in Arunachal Pradesh (ArP), as found to some extent in the so called Brahminical tradition that does not give equal opportunity to lower rungs and females, but still one finds gap between male-female literacy (see Tables 6.3a and 3b). Though the gap is consequence of gender relations and less valued female education, however the other links talked about (e.g. in Drèze & Saran, 1995, quoted in Drèze & Sen, 1995) do not appear relevant in case of ArP. Despite the prevalent bride-price system (essentially opposite to dowry system) women's status is subordinate to the men. Of course, the gender division of labour and patrilocal residence in the post-marriage period play decisive role in making options limited for the womenfolk. The system of bride-price 'commodifies' females, once the bride-price is paid the woman concerned becomes part of her husband's (and his family's) asset! And, hence, ordained to live as the husband decides. Naturally, her freedom to decide is ceased after marriage. Her inferior social standing becomes handicap in the process of domestic resource allocation. And, as argued by others, in the competition for domestic resource she meets discrimination and her

Table 6.3a: Arunachal Pradesh: Gender Gap in Literacy, 1991

District/State	*Total Literacy*		*ST Literacy*	
	Total	*Gender Gap*	*Total*	*Gender Gap*
Tawang	29.80	-14.66	20.80	-06.82
West Kameng	46.31	-17.95	36.42	-08.80
East Kameng	26.20	-12.20	20.01	-10.41
Lower Subansiri	41.57	-13.19	31.08	-09.62
Upper Subansiri	38.31	-13.49	35.52	-10.56
West Siang	45.64	-12.91	40.77	-08.05
East Siang	44.30	-13.08	42.26	-08.08
Dibang Valley	46.88	-18.60	45.31	-13.07
Lohit	49.21	-18.07	45.12	-10.88
Changlang	43.20	-16.32	47.86	-13.76
Tirap	32.06	15.14	21.89	-10.17
Arunachal Pradesh	41.59	-14.67	34.45	-09.45

Source: Based on General Population Tables, Census of India, 1991.

brothers get larger share on her cost (cf. Bhatty, 1998b). Agarwal (1998) too says 'In India... (gender) inequalities are revealed most starkly in the allocation of basic necessities such as health care, education...'

Table 6.3b: Arunachal Pradesh: Gender Gap in Literacy, 2001

District/State	*Literacy*	
	Total	*Gender Gap*
1. Tawang	47.32	–30.28
2. West Kameng	40.92	–23.83
3. East Kameng	40.64	–23.77
4. Papum Pare	69.32	–16.92
5. Lower Subansiri	72.86	–20.91
6. Kurung Kumey	31.43	–21.16
7. Upper Subansiri	50.34	–18.84
8. West Siang	59.47	–15.06
9. East Siang	60.73	–15.97
10. Upper Siang	49.61	–20.20
11. Dibang Valley	62.28	–16.56
12. Lower Dibang Valley	73.39	–21.26
13. Lohit	73.26	–23.72
14. Anjaw	47.26	–35.88
15. Changlang	52.32	–22.89
16. Tirap	41.73	–24.52
Arunachal Pradesh	54.34	–20.31

Source: Based on General Population Tables, Census of India, 2001.

ON GENDER GAP, (SCHOOL) EDUCATION: DISTRICT LEVEL REFLECTIONS

We noted above that there is lesser degree of deprivation of females in ArP (in comparison to mainland India) as reflected by sex-ratio like demographic evidences; in the field of literacy, however notice worthy gender gaps do exist. Whereas given the low literacy fact this situation should not have cropped up. This indicates prevalence of gender inequality (leading to deprivation afterwards) which one may not be able to catch in the light of better sex-ratio scenario and non-existence of dowry system (instead, the system of bride-price is in vogue in this region). Hence, the gender deprivation in literacy is a serious concern and a curious question arises that is it the same at all stages of education? In order to find answer to it, we will have to look into disaggregated education data. For this purpose, one may look at gap at four levels of school education.

It is evidently found that at all levels of school education the female students are outnumbered by male counterparts, at the state level (cf. Fig. 6.3 and Tables 6.3a & 6.3b). As far as district level picture is concerned, there is one case where female students are marginally (0.36 per cent) more, that is during middle level in West Siang district.

Table 6.4: Gender Gap in School Education

	District/State	*Primary Level*		*Middle Level*		*Secondary Level*		*Sr. Secondary Level*	
		All	*ST*	*All*	*ST*	*All*	*ST*	*All*	*ST*
1.	Tawang	–17.99	–10.62	–17.16	–10.92	–18.02	–09.96	–30.16	–34.78
2.	West Kameng	–08.94	–08.88	–13.44	–13.08	–16.32	–18.82	–14.84	–32.46
3.	East Kameng	–20.64	–20.44	–34.96	–35.02	–39.18	–48.88	–64.06	–67.08
4.	Lower Subansiri	–10.40	–07.86	–07.56	–09.58	–09.86	–16.10	–12.46	–13.26
5.	Upper Subansiri	–15.26	–06.72	–07.74	–08.72	–44.82	–44.60	–39.16	–39.92
6.	West Siang	–04.78	–00.58	–07.18	–00.36	–17.70	–16.44	–31.04	–41.40
7.	East Siang	–00.20	–00.40	–07.96	–03.40	–18.22	–16.96	–39.14	–43.36
8.	Dibang Valley	–15.68	–06.76	–14.24	–10.96	–18.20	–19.36	–43.48	–46.12
9.	Lohit	–11.60	–10.33	–18.06	–15.38	–22.80	–30.88	–28.08	–41.18
10.	Changlang	–12.34	–10.42	–16.64	–11.08	–19.94	–12.32	–29.88	–30.86
11.	Tirap	–26.18	–29.44	–25.48	–27.82	–24.78	–32.12	–39.44	–53.84
	Arunachal Pradesh	–11.02	–08.60	–12.40	–10.16	–21.48	–19.22	–5.64	–30.40

Source: Compiled and computed by the author.

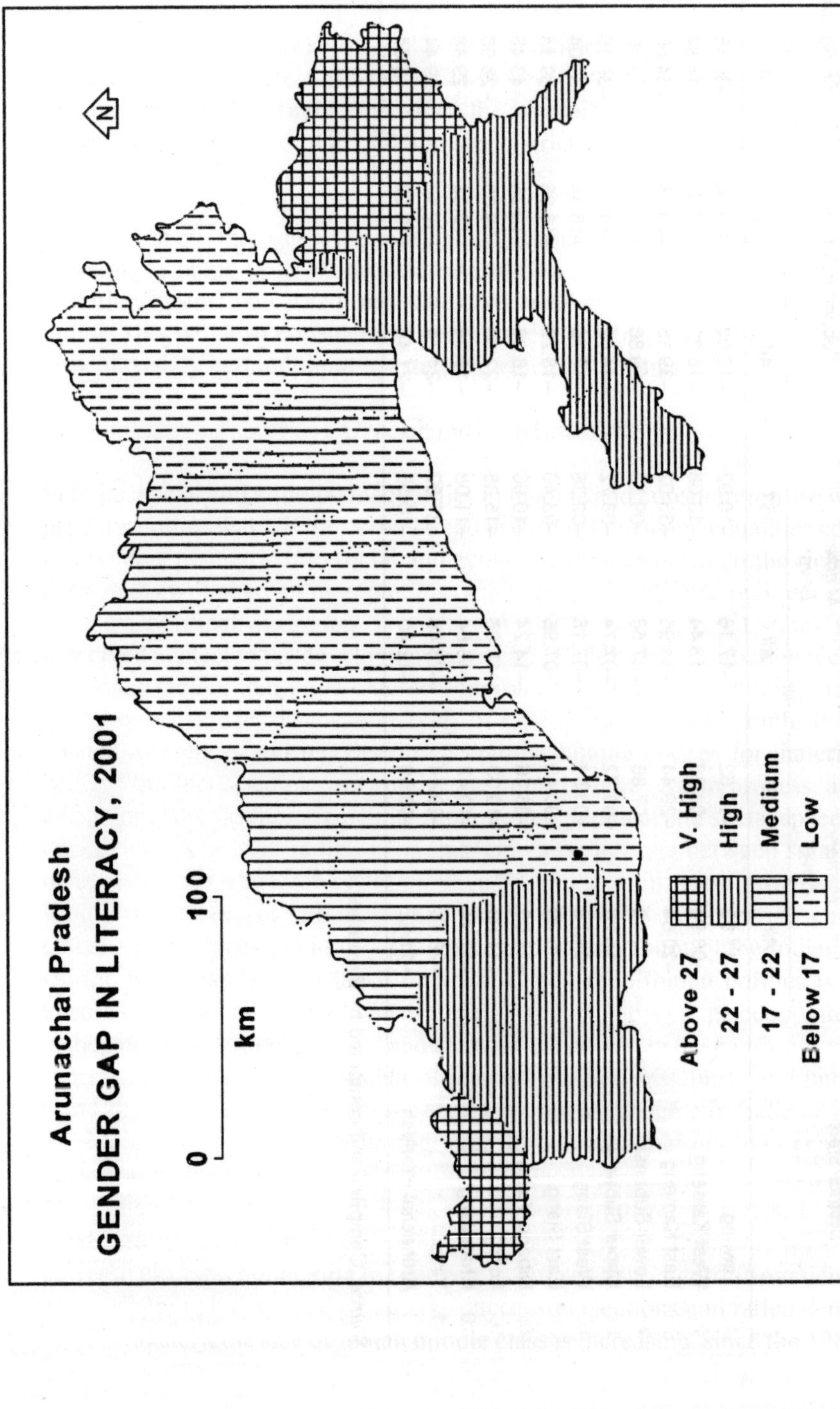

Fig. 6.3: Arunachal Pradesh: Gender Gap in Literacy, 2001

Some other major reflections of Table 6.4 are (i) lowest gender gap is at the primary level for both tribal and all population groups, (ii) the gender gap tends to increase towards higher classes, (iii) the gender gap at senior/higher secondary level is exorbitantly high. On the basis of school enrolment it is difficult to conclude that gender-gap is outcome of gender discrimination. Lower enrolment may be the outcome of higher dropouts, higher percentage of failure in previous examination (and their cumulative effect), lack of motivation (especially after secondary education), and patrilocal residence of females after marriage. To understand this reality undertaking of extensive primary survey is required. Even the resource capability and intra-household distribution of the same appears playing lesser role as the education for tribal students is free (in addition they are entitled to get free uniform, text books and on top of these stipend at higher education levels).

Table 6.5 gives as synoptic view of the first three best performing and worst performing districts with respect to the gender gap. It appears, East Kameng and Tirap districts experiencing larger incidence of gender-deprivation. But female-friendly districts do not make consistent good performance, e.g. West and East Siang districts show remarkably better up to middle level, but at secondary and senior/higher secondary level none of these two appear among best performers.

Table 6.5: Gender Gap in Education[1] and the Performance of Districts[2]

Category	Primary			Middle			Secondary			Sr. Secondary		
	I	*II*	*III*	*I*	*II*	*III*	*I*	*II*	*III*	*I*	*II*	*III*
Female Friendly	7	6	5	6	7	5	1	10	4	4	10	2
Female Non-Friendly	11	3	1	3	11	9	3	5	11	3	11	8

Notes: 1. ST population only considered, 2.The numbers in the table refer to district name as is Tables 6.3 & 6.4 and the Roman numerals are the ranks of districts.
Source: Compiled by author.

ECONOMIC ACTIVITIES, FEMALE PARTICIPATION: PRELIMINARY REMARKS

What one can achieve depends on his/her 'capabilities', Sen through his works (particularly 1985; and chapter 4 in 1999) elaborately deals the issue and 'poverty as capability deprivation' is highlighted. Actually, it is incomplete to use 'capability' if we are viewing the subject in Sen's framework, in the absence of 'endowment-entitlement' dimension. 'Endowment-entitlement-capability' continuum makes us clear that how endowment (may) decide entitlement which in turn plays crucially important role in defining one's capability. To me, the process of 'capability building' is most significant, that differs depending upon the (potential) command a person has over resources ('entitlements') and the means through which such a command could be established (e.g. skill, capital, etc.) termed as 'endowments'. Therefore, 'endowments' themselves are affected by various exogenous factors (e.g. income) and indigenous factors (e.g. health). The argument here is the extent and (effective) quality of endowment is closely linked with (economic) earnings and expenditure capacity. That is how ultimately participation in economic activities (through which income may be generated) becomes meaningful in defining endowment. It is on these lines that female participation in economic activities is being considered here to comprehend gender issue.

Considerable gender gap exists among workers. In a quite simple manner, we can explain realities as revealed by Tables 6.6a and 6.6b and Fig. 6.4. At the state level, the main workers' category has 17.95 per cent less women than their male counterparts. Among the districts, this female disadvantage varies between (-)7.81 (Lower Subansiri) to (-)29.14 (Lohit). Whereas in case of marginal workers, general female advantage (?) is clear. As far as the non-workers are concerned again female's preponderance is evidently clear. As the data used in for the whole population, probably higher percentage of non-ST population may inflate non-working female's percentage and in such districts under-reporting of working women might have been taken, e.g. in order to show their women are as good as the non-tribals, many STs might have concealed the fact that their womenfolk have every reason to be reported as workers; place for reasons, resulting into highly distorted enumeration of non-workers. As per the recent data, gap is higher in the districts like Tawang, West Kameng, Papum Pare and Lohit.

Table 6.6a: Gender Gap among Workers and Non-workers, 1991

	District/State	*Main Workers*	*Marginal Workers*	*Non–Workers*
1.	Tawang	13.60	00.27	13.33
2.	West Kameng	–26.97	00.81	26.16
3.	East Kameng	–08.40	01.85	06.55
4.	Lower Subansiri	–07.81	00.63	14.86
5.	Upper Subansiri	–12.80	04.21	08.60
6.	West Siang	–15.45	00.28	15.16
7.	East Siang	–18.20	00.77	17.43
8.	Dibang Valley	–23.64	00.19	23.46
9.	Lohit	–29.14	03.92	25.22
10.	Changlang	–20.37	03.92	16.14
11.	Tirap	–10.20	01.43	08.77
	Arunachal Pradesh	–17.95	01.68	16.27

Source: Compiled by the author.

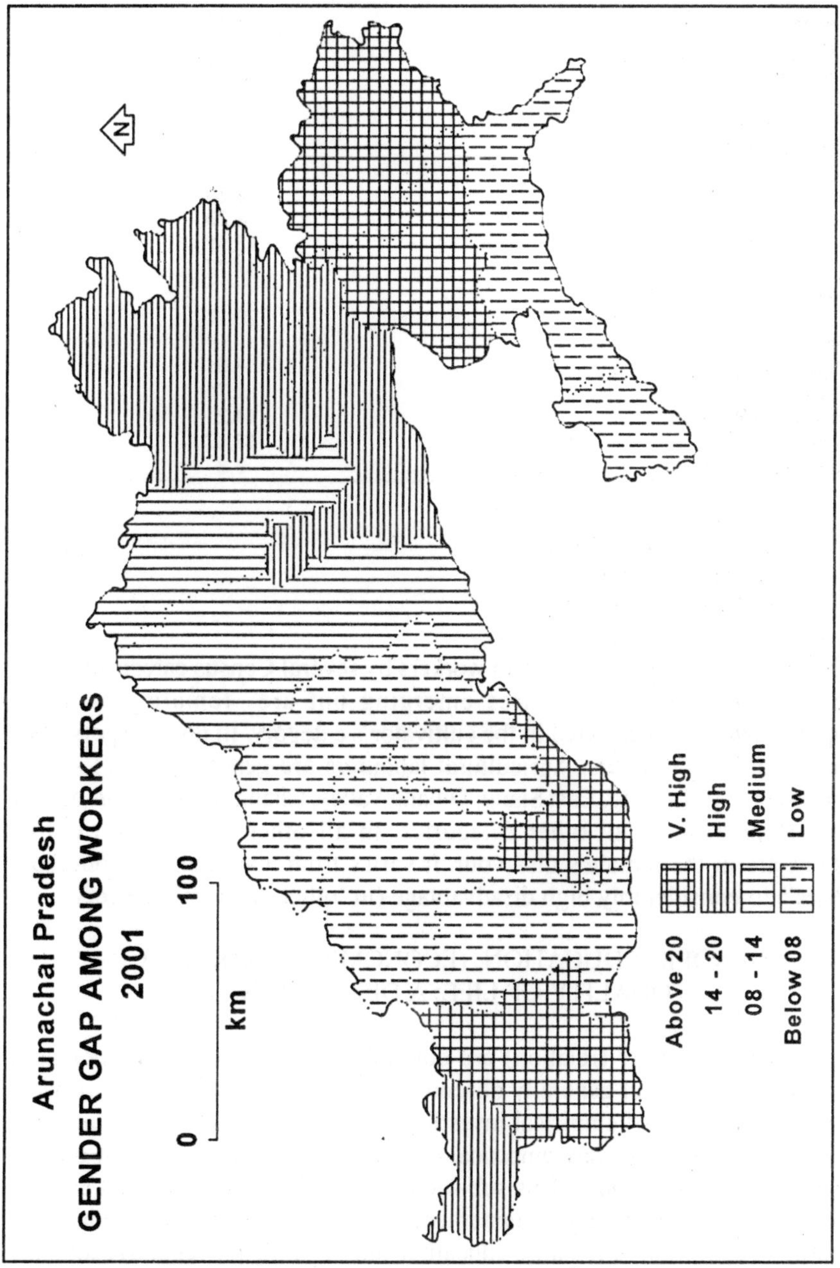

Fig. 6.4: Arunachal Pradesh: Gender Gap among Workers, 2001

Table 6.6b: Gender Gap among Workers, 2001

District/State	Gender Gap
1. Tawang	19.31
2. West Kameng	28.88
3. East Kameng	6.44
4. Papum Pare	21.86
5. Lower Subansiri	3.10
6. Kurung Kumey[1]	
7. Upper Subansiri	7.85
8. West Siang	12.24
9. East Siang	14.23
10. Upper Siang	13.11
11. Dibang Valley	17.77
12. Lower Dibang Valley[2]	
13. Lohit	20.17
14. Anjaw[3]	
15. Changlang	7.01
16. Tirap	5.71
Arunachal Pradesh	14.21
Mean	13.67
Standard Deviation	7.3

Notes: 1. Included in Upper Subansiri.
2. Included in Dibang Valley.
3. Included in Lohit.

Source: Compiled by the author.

The distribution of gender-gap in workers by several Census categories too is interesting. The general features emerging out are female workforce disproportionately concentrated in the cultivator's category. In this category, they dominate male counterparts. Agricultural labourers are generally males still in some districts (e.g. Tawang, East Siang, Dibang Valley, Changlang) females appear outnumbering them in all other categories. In all other categories, existing conditions are in the female's disfavour. It varies from marginal (in 'household industries') to considerably high disadvantage (in 'other services' category).

GENDER, EDUCATION, (ECONOMIC) WORK AND QUALITY OF LIFE: A DISCUSSION

Social issues like gender (relation) are qualitative dimensions of the practised reality and quantification generally obscures the reality we introspect into. Well, there are compulsions of empirical investigations. The purpose of this statement is to confess limitation of any empirical exercise (including the present one) in conversing issues like gender. This sub-section is attempted to provide a broader picture of points of agreement/disagreement on the connection that is believed to exist between condition of females, education, and (earning power and) economic role outside the private domain. Precisely speaking, the whole issue is about the female-male dialectics and said inferior position of females in that.

Recent empirical studies, not to single out anyone of them sufficiently highlight that women's well-being is strongly influenced by their ability to earn (independent income), ownership right, literacy, etc. (cf. Sen, 1999:191). These different aspects may at first sight appear to be rather diverse and disparate. But what they all have in common is their positive contribution in adding force to women's voice and agency, through independence and empowerment (Sen, *ibid*). This observation might be true with reference to the experience of some societies and regions (e.g. Kerala), yet in cases like ArP their validity is doubtful. Here in the light of above discussion; despite a favourable sex-ratio situation, absence of dowry system, participation of females in agricultural and many other activities, women are deprived. They are deprived as they have strikingly inferior social status. In majority of the ethnic communities of ArP women are not allowed to perform sacred rituals and treated virtually as commodities owned by a male person or household. The primordial tribal economy is based on *jhooming* ('the practice of shifting cultivation'). The mode of cultivation has typical bearings upon the family size and gender relations. Cultivation in ArP being largely conducted by family labour requires more working hands within domestic boundary. That is how women are valued for reproduction. In the cultivation process they are to play large role — outcome of unequal distribution of farm work. Men folk clear forest and prepare the land for sowing; rest of the activities from sowing to harvesting is women's responsibility. Thus, she is pivotal in (agricultural) production too. Curiously enough, her value for production and reproduction encouraged the institution of polygamy, of course, to restricted section for the simple reason of bride-price system. That is, how larger number of wives becomes symbol of social status for men! (Das, 1995). It is worthwhile to note in none of the ethnic communities of ArP the women enjoy the property rights. Their non-inheritance is serious particularly in view of the excessive load of domestic and outside works (economic and non-economic both) they share (cf. Singh, 1999). The conclusions of Hariss *et al.*, 1990 and Rana, 1996 quoted in Maharatna (2000) somehow fit here which is "greater female work participation *per se* does not appear to guarantee greater female status and autonomy in tribal societies" (p. 3046). Similarly, how far Miller's hypothesis of a link between female work and female worth (1989; Chapter 6) is valid is a question to be pondered upon.

Admiringly it is difficult to make conclusive comment as how and up to which extent varied identified socio-cultural and economic correlates of gender affect the status of women. The Sen's framework to understand the quality of (women) life appears convincing however accepting that as all embracing perhaps in not possible as that undermines cultural determinants. The cultural moorings exercise greater control over male-females. And, the fallouts of that with regard to gender relations is part and parcel of every society — may that be a traditional or liberal one. However, the degree of enforcement of male/female roles, activities, ways of living and so on necessarily vary from one society to another (cf. Annas, 1993: 280).

Towards Conclusion

Vargas (1996: 344) rightly observes, "To discuss women's interest...is a difficult enterprise.... It is, however an urgent enterprise." Considerable number of works, devoted to analysis of women's status (rather gender relations), prove the urgency of this 'enterprise' felt by scholars. The present exercise is a small part of that.

The details provided above illustrate that a mixed picture of gender reality exists in ArP particularly among the STs owing to the multiplicity of ethnic identities and the rooted diverse cultural systems. On one hand sex-ratio performance is closed to optimal level; on the other, literacy (and education) scenario is evidently in female's disadvantage. Whereas the labour force participation contains a miscellaneous picture. Prevalence of no property rights for womenfolk and commonly no-permission to perform sacred rites by females is important examples of the apparent ways through which they are deprived. The prevalent system of bride price fosters and strengthens the perception that 'women' are commodities which could be bought! The importance of females for their value in production and reproduction surprisingly do not contribute towards her emancipation rather she is treated subordinate, shackled between the domestic responsibilities and farm activities. Even during leisure hours she might be seen weaving to provide clothing to family members. That way she is highly deprived of endowments-entitlements resulting into poor capabilities. One may conclude with the statement that general situations with regard to gender deprivation actually are no different amongst the STs of ArP from other patriarchal societies and to a great extent it echoes the saying that women are "discriminated from womb to tomb"! The *Arunachal Pradesh Human Development Report 2005* rightly illustrates how poor is the gender situation in ArP. One may expect the advocacy for gender sensitive budgeting will bring in desirable results in the interest of Arunachali womenfolk (cf. pp. 113-114). As discussed above, (*access* to) capacity-building, economic opportunity and equality in governance are needed to do more for them.

REFERENCES

Agarwal, Bina (1998) Disinherited Peasants, Disadvantaged Workers: A Gender Perspective on Land and Livelihood. *Economic and Political Weekly*, 33(13).

Agnihotri, Satish Balaram (2000) *Sex Ratio Patterns in the Indian Population: A Fresh Exploration*. New Delhi: Sage.

Ahmed, Aijazuddin (1999) *Social Geography*. Jaipur & New Delhi: Rawat.

Annas, Julia (1993) Woman and the Quality of Life: Two Norms or One. In Martha Nussbaum and Amartya Sen (eds.) *The Quality of Life*, pp. 279-296.

Government of Arunachal Pradesh (2006) *Arunachal Pradesh Human Development Report (2005)* Itanagar: Department of Planning, Government of Arunachal Pradesh.

Bhagat, R.B. and Sharma, S. (2001) Quality of Life, Gender Bias and Fertiltiy Behaviour in Urban Haryana. *Annals of NAGI*, 21(2), pp. 47-57.

Bhatty, Kiran 1998. Education Deprivation in India: A Survey of Field Investigations. *Economic and Political Weekly* 33(27 & 28).

Chattopadhyay, Aparajita and Baishali Goswami (2007). Status of Women in Two Bengals: Evidence from Large Scale Surveys. *Journal of Biosocial Science*, 39:276-286.

Das, Gurudas (1995) *Tribes of Arunachal Pradesh in Transition*. New Delhi: Vikas Publishing House Pvt. Ltd.

Drèze, Jean and Mrinalini Saran (1995) Primary Education and Economic Development in China and India: Overview and Two Case Studies. In K. Basu, *et al.* (eds.) *Choice, Welfare, and Development*. New Delhi: Oxford University Press, pp. 182-241.

Drèze, Jean and Amartya Sen (1995) *India: Economic Development and Social Opportunities*. New Delhi: Oxford University Press.

—— and Amartya Sen (eds.) (1996) *Indian Development: Selected Regional Perspectives*. New Delhi: Oxford University Press.

—— and Haris Gazdar. (1996) Uttar Pradesh: The Burden of Inertia. In Dreze and Sen (eds.) *op.cit.*, pp 33-128.

Government of Arunachal Pradesh (1998) *Statistical Abstract of Arunachal Pradesh 1997*. Itanagar: Directorate of Economics and Statistics.

—— (2006) *Statistical Abstract of Arunachal Pradesh 2005*. Itanagar: Directorate of Economics and Statistics.

Hasan, I. (2000) Sex Composition of Haryana's Population: Some Evidence of Persisting Gender Inequality. Man & Development, Vol. 22(1), pp. 61-68.

——. (2002) Sex Ratio in Haryana's Population – Disaggregated Analysis. *Geographical Review of India*, Vol. 64(3), pp. 154-161.

INDIA. *National Geographical Journal of India* (NGSI, Varanasi), Vol. 47(1-4), pp. 109-122.

Joshi, H. (2003) Gender Related Educational Development index of Rajasthan; A Spatio-temporal Appraisal. *Geographical Review of India*, Vol. 65(3), pp. 251-259.

Kar, B.K. (2002) *Women Population of North East India: A Study in Gender Geography*. New Delhi: Regency Publication.

Lahiri-Dutta, K. and Ghosh, I. (2001) Status of Women in Coal Mining Communities of the Raniganj region. *Annals of NAGI*, 20(1), pp. 36-48.

Maharatna, Anand (2000) Tribal Fertility in India: Socio-Cultural Influences on Demographic Behaviour. *Economic and Political Weekly* 35(34), pp. 3037-3047.

Miller, BD. (1981) *The endangered sex*. Ithaca, N.Y.: Cornell University Press.

Nussabaum, Martha C. and Amartya Sen (eds.) (1993) *The Quality of Life*. New Delhi: Oxford University Press.

O'Neill, Onora (1993) Justice, Gender and International Boundaries. In Nussabaum and Sen (eds.), 1993, *op.cit.*, pp. 303-323.

Raju, S. (2004) Contextualizing critical geography in India: emerging research and praxis. *Geoforum*, 35, pp. 539-544.

—— and Dutta, A. (2004) On not holding half the sky: Gender in Indian Geography. In, H.N. Sharma (ed.) *Progress in Indian Geography 2000-2004: A Country Report*. New Delhi: INSA.

Ramachandran, V.K. (1996) On Karla's Development Achievements. In, Drèze and Sen (eds.) *op.cit.* pp. 205-356.

Samanta, G. (2003) Gender Disparity in Literacy in West Bengal. *Deccan Geographer*, Vol. 41(1), pp. 31-42.

Sen, Amartya (1985) *Commodities and Capabilities*. Amsterdam: North Holland.

—— (1992) Missing Women. *British Medical Journal*, No. 304 (March).

Sen, Amartya (1999) *Development As Freedom.* New Delhi: Oxford University Press.

Singh, Ravi S. (1999) Ethnic minority groups in Arunachal Pradesh, India: A study in Cultural Geography. *National Geographical Journal India*, Vol. 45(1&2), pp. 112-121.

Singh, Ravi S. (2001) *Gender Situation in Mountain Environment: A Case of Arunachal Pradesh.*

—— (2005) *Paths of Development in Arunachal Pradesh.* New Delhi: Northern Book Centre.

Taher, M. (1997) Ethnic Situation in North-East India: A Geographical Perspective. *North Eastern Geographer*, Vol. 28 (1 & 2), pp. 1-15.

Vargas, Virginia (1996) Women's Interests and Emancipatory Processes. In S.C. Chew and R.A. Denmark (eds.). New Delhi: Sage (India Reprint, 1999), pp. 344-354.

7

Development and Environment: A Challenge for 21st Century

SUDESH NANGIA

INTRODUCTION

Development and environment have to be understood in terms of Area/Region, People, Economy and Technology. DEP refers to the material progress made by a geographical area/region which has certain natural resource endowments, social and cultural habitats of people, economic activities and a given level of technology. Referring in the context of a nation, it does not make sense to achieve the status of a 'developed' nation in terms of economy without the balanced development of all economic and social sectors and without proper conservation and management of its environment resource base. Similarly, to talk of development on the strength of a few mega cities, super-star metros and ITs concentration in a few pockets would also be considered myopic. The ultimate beneficiaries of development are the people. Whether the impact is universal or restricted to the creamy layers would be a yardstick for balanced human and regional development.

India is a land of diversity and expanse and whether the impact is exhibited in balanced regional development or in a few city-regions, any development is bound to have differential developmental impact.

DEVELOPMENT—A DYNAMIC PHENOMENON

- Development is a 'dynamic phenomenon'. It is time-specific and space-specific. What was 'development' yesterday may be a mere facility or necessity taken for granted today with the advent of new technology and prosperity of the regions.
- There could be no universal therapy for development for all regions. The resources of regions need to be taken into consideration for a regional development.
- It was apprehended that inappropriate techniques could depict deviant

results. Techniques and methods, therefore, should be carefully selected to secure results close to the real situation.

To understand its spatio-stratal characteristics, development has to be segmented into structure, process and stage.

- *Structure*: The structural parameters of development are both spatial and/or aspatial. While the spatial continuity/discontinuity exposes balanced/unbalanced regional development, the aspatial character highlights disparities in availability and accessibility of opportunities by the people in the regions reaping the benefits of development.
- *Process*: The processes at work may be highly diversified covering fields from environment, economics, geo-politics, infrastructure, social, community-participation, public policies and programmes, information technology, developmental politics and vision of the civil society and its leadership, to name a few. The direct impact of processes is reflected in the structural changes over the space and the social institutions. The indirect impact, on the momentum generated for development, is reflected through the people and their activities.
- *Stage*: Stage indicates the 'performance level' of a region at a given point of time when the policies and programmes have been launched and their impact observed on the ground after a gap of requisite time-interval.

A time-series analysis further indicates whether the stipulated development in a given time-frame has accentuated or reduced disparity between regions/sectors. It also prepares us for reorienting our course of development-trajectory, if it accentuates disparity.

How to distribute the benefits of development more uniformly has been a big challenge to reckon with. Human resource development through education, health and economic opportunity is the need of the hour in order to uniformly distribute the benefits of development. The focus should be to convert the growing numbers into strong asset for the nation. This could also mitigate crimes, terrorism and other such activities which have popped-up on the scene due to inequality and socio-economic deprivation.

ENVIRONMENT—A NATURE'S GIFT

Environment is essentially the resource-base, reflected in quality of land, water, energy, forests etc. The resources may be renewable or non-renewable. Their extraction, exploitation, management, conservation become important factors as they are harassed for material development. So long, the resources are in abundant supply, their utilization is progressive for the community and their use upscales development. Beyond a certain level of extraction, the diseconomies of material development start reflecting themselves in various sectors of economy, society and regions.

DEVELOPMENT ISSUES

- Perfect development is like a 'mirage' with a boundary unreachable/ unattainable. The moment one reaches one's notion of 'perfect development', the shining 'mirage' shifts further.
- *High Consumption and Low Population* versus *Low Consumption and High Population*: Differential spatial and stratal development since the past few centuries has brought extreme form of disparity between the developed and the developing world. The high consumption pattern in the developed world and low population concentration is in marked contrast to low consumption pattern and high population growth of the developing nations.
- Both put together have been the concern for global environmental degradation. The issues of sustainable consumption, checks on population-growth, conservation and preservation of natural resources for a sustained human life on earth have become epilogues to development alternatives.
- *Macro, Meso and Micro Environmental Changes with Development*: Concern about physical environment has increased particularly with space age (1950s) which revealed a worrying increase in Global Environmental Change (GEC) within atmosphere, geosphere, hydrosphere and biosphere attached with a whole series of major ecological problems: ozone depletion, global warming, sea level rise, air pollution, soil erosion, desertification, deforestation, water shortage, toxic waste etc. There is a real fear that global climatic change might provoke large number of environmental refugees causing critical economic and social problems.
- Since the middle of the twentieth century, there has been a serious concern about accelerating population growth on the one hand and growing global inequity in human prospects of economic development, resource use and standard of living on the other, with more developed countries becoming ever richer and using ever more resources and the least developed countries seem unable to escape from their conditions of poverty. The growing gap between the rich and the poor is being brought out by successive UN Human Development Reports. The fate of humanity is further aggravated by geopolitical instability, forcing increasing volumes of refugees and war-affected disabled population. Environmental degradation as a result of use and mis-use of resources remain a matter of grave concern since the middle of last century.
- Development judged in terms of population-environment relationship poses still more complex problems. Not only do population variables include stock elements (like size, distribution, composition) and flow

elements (fertility, mortality, migration and mobility), which influence each other, but also equally environmental variables include inter-related primary elements (air, water, energy, land) and secondary elements (built and non-built inhabited/uninhabited environment). Between population and environment lie many intervening and intermediate variables which affect both (like social and cultural differences, level of technological advancement, development and consumption, types of economic activities and institutional framework, political decisions etc.).

- *What Causes Environmental Degradation*?: A particular difficulty is that population environment relationship may be examined at different scales from the local (e.g. industrial waste, city pollution) through regional, national, continental to the global (CFC emission, acid rains, rising sea level) and there is a perennial problem of linking the explanation at one scale to those at another. The real question is what causes environment degradation?
  (i) Extra Human Population,
  (ii) High resource consumption,
  (iii) Mismanagement of Natural/Human Resources,
  (iv) All the above in combination, and
  (v) Poverty.
- *Sustainable Development*: During 1980s, there was growing acceptance that current rates of population growth associated with increasing international disparities, over exploitation of natural resources and environmental degradation could not continue unfettered. Human betterment was a target not only for today but for future generations as well. International appeal was that conditions should be created for sustainable development. This is not an easy or an uncontroversial concept but perhaps the best has been described as: 'Development that meets the needs of the present without compromising the ability of future generations to meet their own needs' (World Commission, 1987). In simple terms, sustainable development implies that rate of consumption of renewable resources should not exceed their rate of replenishment. The non-renewable resources need extremely careful use and as far as possible alternative resources may be used to minimize the consumption of non-renewable resources, as in the case of energy consumption. It is a worthwhile concept, emphasizing the inseparability of environmental harmony, resource conservation, social, ethical and moral values of the people and economic development.
- It is increasingly accepted that population policies at all levels should be designed with environment in mind; that population activities should be given priorities in geographical areas which are likely to experience environmental impact; that there should be monitoring of key natural resources; that the problems of population and environment can only be

resolved within a comprehensive programme at national and international level to promote social and economic development (UNEP). In other words, there is a growing recognition for a holistic approach to Population, Environment and Sustainable Development.

- *Sustainable Co-operative Development*: How to go for sustainable cooperative development keeping in mind the fragile environmental resource systems of the regions? The natural resources incidentally have common frontiers and cut across political boundaries. The countries of South Asia for instance are joined by:
  - the Great Himalayas, which extend from Afghanistan in the west to Burma (Myanmar) in the east.
  - The Indus river system (draining India and Pakistan).
  - The Ganges and Brahmaputra river system (draining India, China and Bangladesh).
  - Ocean frontiers of India (common with Bangladesh, Myanmar, Srilanka, Maldives, and Pakistan).

Besides, monsoons form a common hydrological resource for south, southeast and east Asian countries. Hence, appropriate inter-regional policies regarding the use of water resources, forest resources etc. could reduce tension in the region and minimize environmental degradation and its adverse effect on human life.

- *Gender Issues*: The next question is how to make policies and programmes on environment and development gender sensitive? Forest, water and other natural resources not only have their global impact but are also of great relevance to the individual households; e.g.:
  (i) forests still provide major fuel source for the rural countryside in this part of the world;
  (ii) their importance as source of timber for house-building cottage and heavy industry, urbanisation and housing can not be ignored;
  (iii) they have also been the traditional reservoirs of medicinal plants, herbs, berries, fruits, floral and faunal bio-diversity; and
  (iv) in the rural areas, forests also serve as places for nature's call and places of worship.

Because of their rich resource diversity and multi-functional use, forests have been a source of innumerable help to the women in the households, who shoulder the major burden of processing wood for fuel and other activities of the household. With deforestation, these women have to walk longer distances, for long hours, carry larger head loads of forests produce with consequential effects on their efficiency and health.

A gender-sensitive approach to forest planning taking care of the requirements of women would go a long way to maintain household peace and efficiency of the region.

Lately, there has been a growing concern at the attitudinal differences towards environment of male and female. Women seem to have a more nurturing and caring attitude towards environmental resources. Hence, it is invariably suggested that common property resources should be maintained and regulated by women. Women should have proprietary rights in forests and water resources to ensure their appropriate use and management. Somehow, women have been left out from the crucial community decisions and the impact of environmental degradation has been felt on their lives.

Apprehensions have been expressed on the reflection on the status of women as revealed in the plan documents like:

- Women are generally clubbed with other disadvantaged groups; children, Scheduled Caste/Scheduled Tribes and minorities and do not seem to have an independent status.
- Even the language used in such documents is more male assertive rather than gender neutral or gender sensitive.
- Considering the fact that 48 per cent of the population of India consists of women, it is felt that the plans must have a gender-positive approach. All the sectors of development, education, employment, health, should have a specific focus on women and girls.

The other issues of gender-concern in Development are the violence against women, rape and other human rights violation (right to live in dignity); economic empowerment, effective child-care schemes for working mothers and other support services; urban poor women and their rights to housing, minimum wages for women, old age security etc. to improve the living and working conditions of women and to empower them and thus promote healthy, social environment in the process of development.

DEVELOPMENT AND SPATIAL DIMENSIONS OF BUILT ENVIRONMENT

God has not promised
Sun without Rain
Joy without sorrow
Peace without pain
How can He promise development without deprivation?

- *Growth of Mega-cities*: At the regional level, growth of mega-cities with huge conurbation of adjoining settlements oriented to their economy and heavy concentration of population due to in-migration, urban-sprawl, extension of urban-rural fringe-zone on one hand; the decline of small and medium towns, the paucity of basic infrastructure—water, sanitation, connectivity—depopulation of rural settlements, lack of basic services of health and education etc. on the other hand, are the development anomalies in space.

- At the same time, each part of mega city is not equally affluent as every micro-region is not equally poor. There are pockets of poverty in mega-cities, mushrooming in the form of slums, which may contain 1/3 to 1/2 of the total population.
- Development leads to accentuation of contrasting paradigms. In our country, development measured in terms of urbanization, industrialization and infrastructural development has led to increased disparity between urban and rural environment.
- *Rural-Urban Fringe*: The urban-rural fringe—a transitional zone is only a small stretch of region extending upto a maximum of 100 kms. in case of the large metropolitan cities in India. This zone too experiences invariably a haphazard growth. The so called urban prosperity exhibited in the fringe zone in the form of land-use change, commercial complexes, multi-story housing, unlicensed household industry is more in the nature of 'invasion' rather than 'succession' process operating on ecological space.
- *Migration*: Migration intensity to the 'developed regions' leading to higher, invariably unmanageable density of population, leading to deteriorating quality of housing, mushrooming pockets of slums with poverty, unemployment, crimes, collapse of physical infrastructure are the other nightmares to reckon with, as is the ineffective governance of unmanageable cities with present technology and administrative skill.
- *Land Values*: The shooting land and property values do not leave even the middle class untouched. Though, the percentage of population in the middle income group has increased, their purchasing power in terms of property values has been adversely affected. Overall, a reduction in the percentage of population below the poverty line conceals a rise in the total number of people living still below poverty line, which is almost equal to the total population of our country at the time of independence. Regional Planners (like Dr. L. S. Bhat) have been advocating the revival of 'economic regions' for development planning and of 'Dispersed Concentration' as a development strategy to ensure balanced regional development.

DEVELOPMENT AND HUMAN VALUES

- A nation is made 'developed' by its people, and therefore, to develop a nation, first the people have to be developed. For this, we need healthy, educated and prosperous people.
- *People's Development*: The development of people is judged by the following indicators:

- Physical quality of life—the health parameters;
- Education including skill-formation;
- Prosperity—including work, income and wealth;
- Equality and equity with respect to gender, caste, religion;
- Accessibility and availability to/of opportunities, services; and
- Last but not the least, the development of people is judged by their moral and ethical values in matters of personal and community behaviour, work-ethics, commitment to social and national interest.

The 'character' of the people sets the tone for development. As goes a saying:

> *"When wealth is lost nothing is lost*
> *When health is lost something is lost*
> *When character is lost everything is lost."*

- The loss of wealth and health in a short term may not be that harmful as that of character, though in the long run, they are all detrimental to human development. The historical accounts of India reveal how she was plundered of her wealth during the fag-end of Hindu period and continued moving towards poverty, starvation, famines, and epidemics. It is not difficult to see the results of chronic malnutrition in the stunted growth of our population (e.g. Orissa). The examples of corruption, kick-backs, graft have become so much a part of hindrance in free and fair development and are instrumental in tarnishing social environment.

There is then a need for character building through moral/ethical education.

EPILOGUE

To conserve, preserve and maintain the environment and natural eco-system is the responsibility of human beings, as they are the main user/exploiter of natural reservoirs of resources. Similarly, if human eco-systems are to be maintained, sustained and developed, mutual co-operation and respect for them from people of different regions, castes/communities and faith is required. Invasion on any of the eco-system, either of the natural on human eco-systems or *vice versa*, results in destruction and degradation with its far-reaching consequences. Hence, the aim should be:

(i) To use the natural resources with the full responsibility of their conservation, preservation and regeneration whichever is needed;

(ii) To inculcate mutual respect and appreciation for human eco-systems to attain a harmonious living and maintain a balanced eco-system;

(iii) To achieve a balance between population, sustainable development and environment, the planning process to be initiated at the grassroots level with full participation of the civil society, and

(iv) To appreciate the role of women in the nurturing and management of environment and involve them in the process of management of resources. Sensitive policies and programmes with monitoring of gender auditing would go a long way in improving the relationship between environment and development.

The development projects should further strengthen the eradication of poverty and upliftment of extremely poor above the poverty-line. How to distribute the benefits of development more uniformly has been a big challenge to reckon with. Human resource development through education, health and economic opportunity is the need of hour in order to uniformly distribute the benefits of development. The focus should be to convert the growing numbers into a strong asset for the nation. This could also mitigate crimes, terrorism and other such activities which have popped-up on the scene due to inequality and socio-economic deprivation.

This is highly relevant in the Indian scenario where more than one quarter of the population still lives below the poverty line. It is rightly said: "It does not make sense to achieve a developed status without a major and continuing upliftment of all Indians who exist today and of many more millions who would be added in the years to come. They should all have a secure and enjoyable present and be in a position to look forward to a better 'future'. Such a development India is looking for" (Dr. A.P.J. Abdul Kalam and Y.S. Rajan: '*India 2020, A vision for the New Millennium*').

REFERENCES

Kalam, A.P.J. Abdul and Y.S. Rajan; *India 2020-A Vision for the New Millennium Year 2000*; Penguin Books, 2002, p.324.

ICPD, 1994; *Cairo Declaration on Population and Development*, International Conference on Parliamentarians on Population and Development (ICPD), Cairo, Egypt, 3-4 September, 1994, p. 5.

Louise Lassonde, *Coping with Population Challenges*, Earthscan Publications Ltd., 1997, p. 173.

Portes, Alejandro, "Institutions and Development: A Conceptual Reanalysis", in *Population and Development Review*, Vol. 32, No. 2, June, 2006, pp. 233-262.

Bhattacharya, Prabir C, "Economic Development, Gender Inequality and Demographic Outcomes: Evidence from India" in *Population and Development Review*, Vol. 32, No. 2, June 2006, pp. 233-262.

Geddes, Arthur, *Man and Land in South Asia*, Ed. By ATA Learmonth, AM Learmonth, CD Deshpande, L.S. Bhat; ICSSR, 1982, p. 215.

Haq, Ehsanul and Sudhir Kumar Singh (Ed.); *Population and Sustainable Development in India*, Authors Press, Delhi, 2006, p. 332.

Khoshoo, T.N., "Sustaining Development in the Developing Countries" published in *The Earth has no Corners* felicitation volume on the 70th Birthday of Dr. Karan Singh' Ed. By K.L. Nandan; published by Shipra Publication, Delhi, 2001, pp. 114-136.

World Bank; "World Development Roport, 2007", *Development and the Next Generation*; IBRD, 2006.

SECTION II
FOOD SECURITY

8

Food Security: Grassroots Concerns

MADASWAMY MONI

INTRODUCTION

Economic growth and poverty reductions were unimpressive during the 1960s and 1970s, as India was weakly integrated into the global economy and had relied heavily on planning and licensing. The accelerated growth, during 1980s, was due to unsustainable public spending and foreign borrowing. Countries that grew rapidly in the 1990s, such as China, India, Vietnam, and Uganda, managed to reduce the share of their "people-in-absolute-poverty" by 5 to 8 per cent per year (World Bank, 2002)[1]. The import of 18,000 tonnes of HYV Wheat Seeds from CIMMYT (Mexico) and the import of Rice Seeds from IRRI (Philippines), along with a policy of assured and remunerated prices through the Commission for Agricultural Costs and Prices (CACP) and procurement through Food Corporation of India (FCI) for foodgrains, was a turning point in India's agriculture. This is what India called "Green Revolution of India" since 1966 A.D.

Food security refers to the availability of food and one's access to it. A household is considered to be "food secure", when its occupants do not live in hunger or fear of starvation. Food Security does not exist, when people are undernourished as a result of the physical unavailability of food, their lack of social or economic access to adequate food, and/or inadequate food utilization. This truncation of human development undermines a country's potential for economic development—for generations to come.

There are strong, direct relationships between agricultural productivity, hunger, and poverty. Eradicating two injsutices: hunger and poverty, requires an understanding of the ways in which they get interconnected. Hunger, and the malnourishment that accompanies it, prevents poor people from escaping poverty, because it diminishes their ability to learn, work, and care for themselves and their family members. Our Prime Minister, Indira Gandhi once said: *"Elemination of Poverty demands frontal attacks on vested interests and causes of poverty"*.

There are many published Research and Study Reports which reveal that rural poor make their living from agriculture, and hunger (and associated child malnutrition) is greater in rural areas. Moreover, the higher the proportion of the rural population that obtains its income solely from subsistence farming (without the benefit of pro-poor technologies and access to markets), the higher the incidence of malnutrition.

Improved agricultural technology has been widely recognized as a prime force for increased agricultural productivity, as well as an engine for accelerating rural economic growth. Agricultural development, among small holder farmers and landless people, provides a livelihood for people, allowing them the opportunity to stay, in their communities. For small and marginal farmers, rice is not just grain: it provides straw for thatching and mat-making, fodder for livestock, bran for fish ponds and husks for fuel. These Agro-products not only have a role in the domestic economy but are often a valuable input to other income-generating enterprises that provide a livelihood for the rural poor. *Improvements in agricultural productivity, therefore, aimed at small-scale farmers, will benefit the rural poor first,* and hence achieving "food security".

While poverty in India is falling, concerns over food security are increasing. In the long term, food security will result from the wider tackling of poverty, which would require improvements in infrastructure and time-limited targeted policies to improve rural farm and non-farm productivity.

FOOD CRISIS: GRASSROOTS CONCERNS

A perfect storm of food scarcity, global warming, rocketing oil prices and the world population explosion is plunging humanity into the biggest crisis of the twenty-first century, by pushing up food prices and spreading hunger and poverty from rural areas into cities (Kate Smith and Rob Edwards, 2008)[2]. As of late 2007, increased farming for use in biofuels, world oil prices at more than $100 a barrel, global population growth, climate change, loss of agricultural land to residential and industrial development, and growing consumer demand in China and India, have pushed up the price of grain (http://en.wikipedia.org/wiki/Food_security). There is no retreat from this Global Tsunami for the poor, particularly rural poor, in India. The Year 2008 was seen as "the Year of Global Food Crisis", a Global Tsunami.

Around the World, protests against soaring food and fuel prices are mounting. The Poor are seeing their incomes squeezed as the global economy enters a slow down. Joseph Stiglitz (2008)[3] suggests that rich nations must reduce, if not eliminate, distortional farm and energy policies, and help those in the poorest countries improve their capacity to produce food. According to Zia Haq (2008)[4], "Between 1993-94 and 2004-05, the percentage of people living below poverty line fell from 36 per cent to 27.5 per cent, according to government data. But a large chunk of people who live just above the poverty line face the risk of sliding back to their earlier status. This is similar to what World Bank said: that "seven years worth of poverty alleviation" could be reversed by rising prices. Globally, the price rise could push 150 million people into poverty, it said. The Asian

Development Bank said "economic progress achieved by many Asian countries could take an about-turn because of high food prices."

Inflation Calmed, not Beaten

"Bucking the global trend, food prices in the domestic market have held up because of sharply higher support prices and continued robust demand. Also, Kharif 2008 output has fallen short of the target. *The poor deserve support and protection from any unfriendly market prices*. The upside risk to commodity prices, especially of energy and agriculture products, is real. The fight against inflation must continue" (*Business Line*, 2009)[5].

Global financial and economic meltdown has hammered commodities, but investors still see rich pickings in agricultural staples such as grains and rice-essentials the world cannot do without (*Business Line*, 2009)[6].

India's Middle Class—A Rising Consumption Sector

"Indians are outraged by President of US Bush's claim that rising food consumption in India and China has sent world food prices skyrocketing. When income rise, people eat more meat, so more grain is fed to animals. Seven tonnes of grain produce only one tonne of beef. The conversion ratio is 4 to 1 for pork and 2 to 1 for poultry. India has a middle class of 350 million, larger than US population. This middle class demand for more food is helping raise food prices. ... Bush is plain wrong", according to Swaminathan Aiyar (2008)[7].

Hungry Mouths and Empty Gas Tanks: A Growing Reality

Concern about Climate Change (CC) has led to biofuels subsidies that pit hungry mouths and empty gas tanks against each other. *This booming commodities market means more famines for the poor*, which the United Nations and the World Bank simply cannot afford to alleviate (Michael Maiello, 2007)[8]. In India, the plan is to have renewable energy sources like biofuels to meet upto 10 per cent of India's transport needs by 2017. In order to achieve that goal, a Group of Ministers (GOM) headed by the Union Agriculture Minister has been entrusted with finalising a national policy, which could see *some 12 million hectares of land harnessed to grow crops* to produce eco-friendly fuels (*The Times of India*, Editorial, 14 April 2008). Agricultural Commodities like maize, sugarcane or vegetable oil can be used either as food, feed or to make biofuels (http:// www.wikipedia.com). In India, the International Crops Research Institute for the Semi-Arid Tropics (ICRISAT), based in Hyderabad, said that 'sweet sorghum is ideal as a "food and fuel" crop for India, based on the plant providing 8 units of energy for every unit of fossil-fuel energy invested' (*Biofuels Digest*, 19 February 2008). It is warranted that *more research* is needed before investing on biofuels.

It shall be understood that "Agriculture is not just a food producing machine, but the backbone of livelihoods". Throughout the World, the poor rely on agriculture for income and sustenance. *In India, the BPL category poor is mostly dependent on the National Rural Employment Guarantee Scheme (NREGS) 2005.* There are many ways to foster development, such as building roads, schools, and health facilities. There are infrastructural investments. But Maize and wheat research is an important path to development, because maize and wheat are pivotal to nutrition, health, income, and environmental sustainability in low-income countries (CIYYMT)[9]. Potato is a safer product, as price is often determined by local market conditions and simple demand and supply, and not by the vagaries of international global market mechanism. The Government of India is planning a series of measures to promote potato crop cultivation by low income farmers at a time when agricultural production is under stress. This move is aimed at ensuring food security for a vast section of the underprivileged population that depends on potatoes as their staple food. It is ideally suited to places where "land is limited" and "labour is abundant", conditions that characterize much of the developing world, including India (*The Pioneer*, dated 8th December 2008).

"White and Blue Revolution [fish]" could give landless labourers and women opportunities for employment and empower them. India is first in milk production in the world. However, falling prices of milk and milk powder worldwide are a worrisome factor (Sharad Pawar, 2008)[10]. Alluding to the risks involved in agriculture and the lack of a *safety net* for the poor, Swaminathan (2008)[11] called for reducing the dependency on agriculture by half and creating employment in other sectors to push up income levels. Given the dependence, it was necessary to protect farmers and the rural people.

Global Hunger Index 2008 Report—India Ranks 66 Out of 88 Countries

India remains a poor country, despite a few years of 9 per cent GDP growth, and India faces severe economic challenges: galloping inflation and a slowdown in growth (due to meltdown somewhere seven seas away). India's economic growth has not reached all sectors of the population, especially those living in rural areas (i.e. economic growth has not trickled down). India ranks 66 out of 88 countries on the 2008 Global Hunger Index (GHI), released by IFPRI, far behind comparable developing countries as well as smaller, less diverse and resource deprived nations.

With over 200 million people who are food insecure, India is home to the largest number of hungry people in the world, according to the findings of the India State Hunger Index (ISHI) 2008. The ISHI findings highlight the continued overall severity of the hunger situation in India, while revealing the variability in hunger across states within the country. The situation for 17 Indian States as per Index are as follows:

Extremely Alarming	1. Madhya Pradesh
Alarming	2. Andhra Pradesh
	3. Uttar Pradesh
	4. Tamil Nadu
	5. Rajasthan
	6. West Bengal
	7. Karnataka
	8. Orissa
	9. Maharashtra
	10. Gujarat
	11. Chhattisgarh
	12. Bihar
	13. Jharkhand
Serious	14. Punjab
	15. Kerala
	16. Haryana
	17. Assam

The Global Hunger Index was based on three leading indicators: *prevalence of child malnutrition, rates of child mortality* and the *proportion of people who are calorie deficient*. India should notice that Punjab is the grain bank of North India. The best-performing state ranked by the India State Hunger Index (ISHI) is Punjab, with an index score of 13.64, although it lies below 33 other developing countries ranked by the Global Hunger Index (GHI). With a population of 24,289,296 (the 2001 Population Census), Punjab's largest industry is agriculture. Punjab is considered to have the best infrastructure in India, which includes road, rail, air and river transport links. For this reason alone, this State is becoming attractive to foreign companies, looking for bases and manufacturing zones for their Indian operations (*http://economictimes.com*). The chief source of income for the Andhra Pradesh's economy has also been agriculture.

Food Security Measures in India

Most states are net importers of foodgrains. Improving agricultural productivity would improve food security. However, even in green revolution states such as Punjab, productivity has declined (Siddu, 2002)[12]. Moreover, agriculture is widely considered to be a part of life rather than an economic undertaking—the continued use of traditional techniques has also resulted in lower productivity. In poorer states, the coverage of irrigation is still very low, and government spending on irrigation has not improved (Debashis Chakraborty, 2004)[13].

India is committed to ensure food security for its citizen, and following a twin-track approach: (a) strengthening productivity and livelihoods, and (b) implementing social safety nets for those unable to provide for themselves (Sharad

Pawar, 2008)[14]. "Right to Food Approach" complements food security, in terms of food availability, accessibility and utilization with human dignity and cultural acceptability.

India is committed to ensure food security for its citizen, and following a twin-track approach: (a) strengthening productivity and livelihoods, and (b) implementing social safety nets for those unable to provide for themselves (Sharad Pawar, 2008)[15]. "Right to Food Approach" complements food security, in terms of food availability, accessibility and utilization with human dignity and cultural acceptability.

Keeping in view the challenges of growing population and the need for food security, the Government of India has launched, during 2007, two major programmes: "National Food Security Mission" (NFSM) and "Rashtriya Krishi Vikas Yojana" (RKVY), to augment food production and availability in the country:

- *National Food Security Mission (NFSM)*: to push both production and productivity of stable food grains such as wheat, rice and pulses on a mission mode.
- *Rashtriya Krishi Vikas Yojana (RKVY)*: to take up agriculture development on priority and in a comprehensive manner with definite action plans.

National Food Security Mission (NFSM)

The National Food Security Mission (NFSM) aims at (a) increasing production of rice, wheat and pulses through area expansion, and productivity enhancement in a sustainable manner in the identified districts of the country through:

- Restoring soil fertility and productivity at the individual farm level;
- Creation of employment opportunities; and
- Enhancing farm level economy to restore confidence among the farmers.

The scheme envisages to increase the production of rice, wheat and pulses to the tune of 10 million tonnes, 8 million tonnes and 2 million tonnes respectively, and has been launched in 311 districts of 17 States, during 2007-08 (*http://www.nfsm.gov.in*). The approach adopted includes:

- active involvement of all stakeholders in planning, execution and monitoring of the programme,
- promotion and extension of improved technologies (seed, nutrients, plant protection, soil amendments, resource conservation, farm machines and tools),
- integration of interventions with district plan, and
- regular monitoring and concurrent evaluation for impact assessment.

In this era of food insufficiency, *SRI (Systematic Rice Intensification) technique*, which was originally introduced in Madagascar and, is slowly spreading to various countries, holds lots of promise in India. According to Suryanarayan (2009)[16], after adopting SRI, the average yield has increased to the tune of 30-40 per cent.

Rashtriya Krishi Vikas Yojana (RKVY)

The RKVY aims at achieving 4 per cent annual growth in the agriculture sector during the XI Plan period, by ensuring a holistic development of agriculture and allied sectors (http://agricoop.nic.in/RKVY). Its main objectives are:

(i) To incentivise the states so as to increase public investment in agriculture and allied sectors;
(ii) To provide flexibility and autonomy to states in the process of planning and executing agriculture and allied sector schemes;
(iii) To ensure the preparation of agriculture plans for the districts and the states based on agro-climatic conditions, availability of technology and natural resources;
(iv) To ensure that the local needs/crops/priorities are better reflected in the agricultural plans of the states;
(v) To achieve the goal of reducing the yield gaps in important crops, through focused interventions;
(vi) To maximize returns to the farmers in agriculture and allied sectors; and
(vii) To bring about quantifiable changes in the production and productivity of various components of agriculture and allied sectors by addressing them in a holistic manner.

This is a State Plan Scheme and the eligibility for assistance under the Scheme depends upon the amount provided in State Plan Budgets for agriculture and allied sectors, over and above the base line percentage expenditure incurred by the State Governments on Agriculture and allied sectors. The list of allied sectors as indicated by the Planning Commission is the basis for determining the sectoral expenditure, i.e Crop Husbandry (including Horticulture), Animal Husbandry and Fisheries, Dairy Development, Agricultural Research and Education, Forestry and Wildlife, Plantation and Agricultural Marketing, Food Storage and Warehousing, Soil and Water Conservation, Agricultural Financial Institutions, other Agricultural Programmes and Cooperation.

Each state is expected to ensure that the baseline share of agriculture in its total State Plan expenditure (excluding the assistance under the RKVY) is at least maintained, and upon its doing so, it will be able to access the RKVY funds. The base line is a moving average and the average of the previous three years will be taken into account for determining the eligibility under the RKVY, after excluding the funds already received. The RKVY fund is provided to the states as 100 per cent grant by the Central Government. The States are required to prepare the Agriculture Plans for the Districts and the State that comprehensively cover resources and indicate definite action plans.

The question is whether the Agricultural Plan is G2G or G2C? If it is G2C, then it is imperative that these plans are expected to be discussed and whetted by the Panchayats and grassroots level Farmers Associations (bottom-up approach). Farmers and their resources mapping are essential for RKVY to usher in the desired result.

Comprehensive District Agricultural Plan (CDAP)

The need for integrated local area plans, based on specific endowments and needs of each area, was stressed from the beginning of planned development. However, despite several reports and studies, only sporadic efforts and isolated cases of such planning could be located. It has therefore been decided by the Government of India that the "District Plan Process" should be an integral part of the process of preparation of State's next Five Year Plan. The Planning Commission Document on CDAP Manual (March 2008) suggested preparation of Vision document with full understanding about, infrastructure and production/productivity of the area, which includes:

- Growth of agriculture and allied sectors including conservation and management of natural resources for sustained production;
- Availability and development of water sources especially irrigation;
- Use of non-conventional energy;
- Agro-based industry including food-processing industry;
- Infrastructure including input output market needs;
- Education including high-tech knowledge in agriculture and allied sectors as well as delivery mechanism and technology transfer to the farmers;
- Veterinary health services;
- Augmentation of livestock, feed and fodder requirements;
- Promoting bio-security to agriculture;
- Poverty reduction and basic needs of Local Bodies;
- Gender issues in relation to agriculture and allied sectors;
- Social justice to SC/ST, persons with disability etc. and cmployment opportunities for the people of the area; and
- Possible local response to the changes taking place as a result of national, state and private development efforts.

Agricultural Technology Management Agency (ATMA)

ATMA is a registered society of key stakeholders involved in agricultural activities for sustainable agricultural development in the district. It is a focal point for integrating Research and Extension activities and decentralizing day-to-day management of the public Agricultural Technology System (ATS). ATMA has the main responsibility of all the technology dissemination activities at the district level, with the objective "to make technology generation/dissemination farmer-driven and farmer-accountable". ATMA is expected to undertake analysis of:

- Existing farming systems
- Research-extension gaps
- Prioritizes the research-extension strategies
- Basis for development of work plans at block/district level

ATMA undertakes District-level Activities, viz.,

- Farmer oriented activities
- Farm information dissemination
- Research-extension-farmer (R-E-F) linkages

It is now a general advocacy that ATMA should propagate only economically viable and proven technologies since it aims to help resource poor families, and ATMA should be a part of an integrated extension system consisting of farm schools in the field of farmers, KVKs, agri-clinics and agri-business centres. The ultimate aim of ATMA should be to make small farmers credit worthy (without collateral).

Krishi Vigyan Kendras (KVKs)

Subsequent to the Kothari Commission on Education, Dr. Mohan Singh Mehta Committee (1973) of the Indian Council of Agricultural Research (ICAR) suggested establishment of Farm Science Centres, instead of Agricultural Polytechnics, later named as Krishi Vigyan Kendra (KVK). ICAR has established, so far, a large network of 578 Krishi Vigyan Kendras (KVKs), in all the rural districts of the country. As per the blueprint, KVKs act as the training centres for agricultural technology transfer at grassroots level, viz., on-farm testing, frontline demonstrations, training of farmers and training of extension personnel.

After three decades, Farmer Information and Advisory Centres (FIACs) were established under the aegis of Agricultural Technology Management Agency (ATMA), as part of the National Agricultural Technology Project (NATP), for effective dissemination of technologies among farmers, in each block of pilot districts, as the existing agricultural extension mechanism within the District had been overburdened due to:

(a) Inadequacy of manpower in line departments;
(b) Non-technical nature of responsibilities for field level staff;
(c) Limitations of the field level extension functionaries to address ground level problems;

(d) Top down extension approach; and
(e) Excessive workload on field level staff.

The problems, as above, continued to impact ATMAs. To overcome these problems, it is reported that ATMAs handed over FIACs to NGOs already conducting different extension services for the farming community in districts. In some districts, KVKs now work as a mentor (viz., resource person, consultant, building rapport with farmers, developing local-need based programme, building up services and inputs, interaction with line departments, and back-up support etc.) for FIACs. The Extension Cycle: KVK→ ATMA→ FIAC→ NGO→KVK is complete. It is also reported that ATMAs have established about 1000 Farm Schools for "farmer-to-farmer" learning, as recommended by the National Commission for Farmers (NCF).

The Planning Commission's Task Group on *Revamping and Refocusing of National Agricultural Research* (TG-RRNAR) 2005, under the Chairmanship of Dr. M.S. Swaminathan, states that "a large component of ICAR funds have been committed to rural development through technology transfer using "KVK" as the focus for programme implementation. A majority of these KVKs have produced little impact on the agricultural growth and rural poverty in the areas of their operation" (TG-RRNAR, 2005)[17].

Agri-Clinics and Agri-Business Centre: Better Farming by Every Farmer—Have They Come of Age?

The Ministry of Agriculture, Government of India, in association with NABARD, has launched a unique programme titled "Agri-Clinics and Agri-Business Centres", to take better methods of farming to each and every farmer across the country, during 2001. This programme aimed at tapping the expertise available in the large pool of Agricultural Graduates (25000 graduates passing out from about 300 Agricultural colleges every year), to provide professional extension services to farmers:

- *Agri-Clinics*: to provide expert services and advice to farmers on cropping practices, technology dissemination, crop protection from pests and diseases, market trends and prices of various crops in the markets and also clinical services for animal health etc. which would enhance productivity of crops/animals.
- *Agri-business Centres*: to provide input supply, farm equipments on hire and other services.

The objectives of the Scheme are: (a) to supplement the efforts of government extension system; (b) to make available supplementary sources of input supply and services to needy farmers; and (c) to provide gainful employment to agriculture graduates in new emerging areas in agricultural sector.

MANAGE (Hyderabad) is the nodal agency to provide "start-up training" to graduates in Agriculture, Horticulture, Sericulture, Veterinary Sciences, Forestry, Dairy, Poultry Farming, and Fisheries, etc. so as to facilitate them to apply for special start-up loans of Rs.10.00 lakhs (*prorata*) for venture. This loan is to repay, within 5 to 10 years, as per easy installment plans, and the respective bank, as per RBI norms, decides the rate of interest, margin and security on such loans. These Centres were envisaged to provide "paid services" for enhancement of agriculture production and income of farmers, through advisory services in respect of: crop selection, best farm practices, post-harvest value-added options, key agricultural information (including perhaps even Internet-based weather forecast), price trends, market news, risk mitigation and crop insurance, credit and input access, as well as critical Sanitary and Phyto-Sanitary (SPS) considerations, which the farmers have to keep in mind. The following high potential areas have been suggested for setting up such centres (*http://www.agriclinics.net/main.htm*):

- Soil, Water Quality and Input Testing Laboratory Service Centre;
- Plant Protection Service Centre (Pest Surveillance, Diagnostic and Control Services including Integrated Pest Management);
- Maintenance, Repairs and Custom Hiring of Agricultural Implements and Machinery including Micro-irrigation Systems (sprinkler and drip);
- Agri Service Centres including at least the above three activities mentioned above (group activity);
- Seed Processing Units;
- Micro-propagation through Plant Tissue Culture Labs and Hardening Units;
- Setting up of Vermiculture Units, Production of bio-fertilizers, bio-pesticides, bio-control agents;
- Setting up of Apiaries (Bee-keeping) and Honey and Bee Products Processing Units;
- Provision of Extension Consultancy services;
- Facilitation and Agency of Agricultural Insurance Service;
- Hatcheries and Production of fish fingerlings for Aquaculture;
- Provision of Livestock Health Cover, setting up of Veterinary Dispensaries and Services including Frozen Semen Banks and Liquid Nitrogen Supply;
- Setting up of Information Technology Kiosks in rural areas for access to various agriculture related portals;
- Feed Processing and Testing Units;
- Value Added Centres;
- Setting up of Cool Chain from the farm level onwards (group activity);
- Post-harvest Management Centres for sorting, grading, standardization, storage and packing;
- Setting up of Metallic/Non-Metallic Storage Structure and Rural Godowns;

- Retail Marketing Outlets for Processing Agri-products; and
- Rural Marketing Dealerships of farm Inputs and Outputs.

NATIONAL RURAL EMPLOYMENT GUARANTEE ACT (NREGA) 2005: A LIVELIHOOD SECURITY IN RURAL AREAS

The National Rural Employment Guarantee Act (NREGA) was notified on September 7, 2005, and its objective is to enhance livelihood security in rural areas by providing at least 100 days of guaranteed wage employment in a financial year to every household whose adult members volunteer to do unskilled manual work. The Goals of the NREGA are:

(a) *Strong social safety net* for the vulnerable groups by providing a fall-back employment source, when other employment alternatives are scarce or inadequate;

(b) *Growth engine* for sustainable development of an agricultural economy. Through the process of providing employment on works that address causes of chronic poverty such as drought, deforestation and soil erosion, the Act seeks to strengthen the natural resource base of rural livelihood and create durable assets in rural areas. Effectively implemented, NREGA has the potential to transform the geography of poverty;

(c) *Empowerment of rural poor* through the processes of a rights-based Law; and

(d) *New ways of doing business*, as *a model of governance reform* anchored on the principles of transparency and grassroots democracy.

Thus, NREGA fosters conditions for inclusive growth ranging from basic wage security and recharging rural economy to a transformative empowerment process of democracy. NREGA covers the entire country, with the exception of districts that have a hundred per cent urban population, since 1st April, 2008 (Phase I: 200 Districts, Phase II: 130 Districts, Phase III: 15 Districts of UP, and Phase IV: through out India). According to the Website (*http://www.rega.gov.in*), through the NREGA Programme, about 4.1 Rural Households have got employment, about 177.52 crore person days of work got generated (SCs—29.63%, STs—25.49%, Women—48.03% and Others—44.88%) and works about 24.24 lakhs have been taken up.

In rural India, over-dependence on land has resulted in high levels of disguised unemployment, although the proportion of the rural population dependent on agriculture is declining (Saqib and Chakraborty, 2004)[18]. Enhancing rural non-farm employment by removing bottlenecks faced by village industries should be the cornerstone of any poverty alleviation scheme. Debroy (2004)[19] noted that there exist various industry clusters with significant linkage effects in the rural areas, revitalization of which is essential for the economy.

Social Safety Net for Household Food and Nutritional security: Need for Food Resources Management Reforms

There needs to be a recognition that food insecurity stems from lack of opportunity and food security results from the wider tackling of poverty. The Government needs to supplement the provision of food security (through a universal or targeted approach) with a mix of short-term and long-term policies (Debashis Chakraborty, 2005)[20]:

- *Short term*: Need to ensure employment opportunities for at least one able-bodied member of a household;
- *Long term*: improvements in infrastructure and time-limited targeted policies to improve rural "farm and non-farm" productivity.

Towards ensuring Social Safety Net (SSN) for food and nutritional security, interventions of the Government cover the "Targeted Public Distribution System (TPDS)" under which, subsidized food grains are being distributed to the poorest of the poor families through the Antyodaya Anna Yojana. It is a well known that "Spending on the Public Distribution Scheme has risen dramatically in recent years, but much of this reflects increasing operational costs". The Committee on Long Term Grain Policy (2002), while acknowledging the extent of inefficiency and economic loss through Food Corporation of India (FCI) functioning, argued that Universal PDS is the only means of addressing food security concerns. The decline in food security was an issue in the 2004 Parliament Election.

Computerisation of the Public Distribution System (PDS) across India is being taken up at a cost of around Rs. 520 crore, during the Eleventh Plan, to improve on the existing ration cards in the States and UTs. The scheme is expected to facilitate transparency and efficiency in implementing distribution of food grains and help in arresting the problem of bogus ration cards. The entire network of PDS from Taluk to State level will be linked. The computerisation scheme is in lieu of Smart Card Scheme, which serves as ration cards, being implemented, on a pilot sacle, in the State of Haryana and UT of Chandigarh. The Government of India has also planned to introduce "Golabal Positioning System" (GPS), to track the movement of trucks carrying the food grains, meant for TPDS so as to curb leakage/diversion of food grains. In this regard, the Five-point Policy of the Government of India are as follows:

(a) Tracking food grains movement up to FPS;
(b) Computerization of PDS;
(c) Streamlining PDS;
(d) Electronic Transfer of Funds; and
(e) Review of BPL and AAY.

The Andhra Pradesh State Civil Supplies Corpration (APSCSC) has introduced "hand-held" devices, as above, to their "e-PDS" system—Integrated Electronic Solution to PDS Management in the State of Andhra Pradesh.

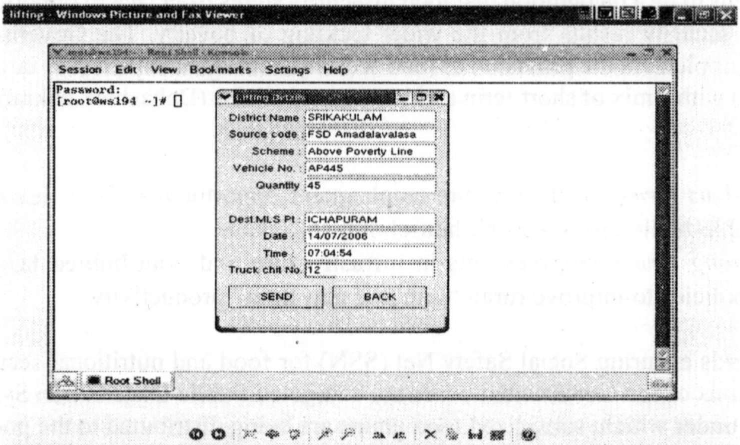

The need of the hour is to have policies to deal with surpluses rather than shortages, i.e. policies relating to food procurement, management of public distribution system and food security, on the output side. Many States have not shown any interest to have larger role in both procurement and distribution of food grains under the Public Distribution System (Naik, 2002)[21]. The Government of India has taken up a pilot project in the State of Haryana to introduce SMART CARD based Ration Card and PDS, which, after successful completion, is likely to be rolled out throughout the country.

Similarly, the Government can make the Farmer's Register detailing his/her agricultural production details, as part of Food Resources Management System.

Agricultural Debt Waiver and Debt Relief (ADWDF) Scheme 2008

The ADWDR Scheme 2008 has covered direct agricultural loans extended to 'marginal and small farmers' and 'other farmers' by Scheduled Commercial Banks, Regional Rural Banks, Cooperative Credit Institutions (including Urban Cooperative Banks) and Local Area Banks (hereinafter referred to compendiously as 'lending institutions'). This would also include such loans provided directly to groups of individual farmers (for example Self Help Groups and Joint Liability Groups), provided banks maintain disaggregated data of the loan extended to each farmer belonging to that group. Direct Agricultural Loans mean:

(a) *Short Term Production Loans*: A loan given in connection with the raising of crops which is to be repaid within 18 months. It will include working capital loan, not exceeding Rs. 1 lakh, for traditional and non-traditional plantations and horticulture;

(b) *Investment Loans*:

  (i) *Investment credit for direct agricultural activities*—extended for meeting outlays relating to the replacement and maintenance of wasting assets and for capital investment designed to increase the output from the land, e.g. deepening of wells, sinking of new wells, installation of pump sets, purchase of tractor/pair of bullocks, land development and term loan for traditional and non-traditional plantations and horticulture;

  (ii) *Investment credit for allied activities*—extended for acquiring assets in respect of activities allied to agriculture, e.g. dairy, poultry farming, goatery, sheep rearing, piggery, fisheries, bee-keeping, greenhouses and biogas.

The implementation of the Debt Waiver and Debt Relief Scheme was to be completed by June 30, 2008. While small and marginal farmers were given a total waiver of their loan, other farmers have been given only 25 per cent relief. The Union Government had further decided to extend the last date of repayment of first installment by the "other farmers" under the Debt Relief Scheme, from September 30, 2008 to March 31, 2009 and further to June 30. The dates of payment of second and third installments remained unchanged, i.e. March 31, 2009 and June 30, 2009. Under the expanded scheme, all farmers, including those with large holdings in the 237 identified districts, would be eligible for debt relief of 25 per cent of the outstanding amount or Rs. 20,000, whichever is higher. A farmer classified as 'small farmer' or 'marginal farmer' will be eligible for fresh agricultural loans upon the eligible amount being waived.

The Union cabinet has created a *Farmers' Debt Relief Fund* with an initial corpus of Rs. 100 billion to be transferred from the Consolidated Fund of India to Public Accounts during the financial year 2007-08, and also gave its approval for augmentation of the Fund required for reimbursing the lending institutions the amount of debt waiver or relief granted by them are as follows: Rs. 100 billion, Rs. 150 million, Rs. 150 million, Rs. 120 million, Rs. 83.14 billion. This scheme of debt waiver or relief was announced in the Budget Speech 2008-09. The implementation of said scheme was expected to mitigate the hardships being faced by the farmers in general, and small and marginal farmers in particular.

The provisional figures so reported by RBI/NABARD show that about 3,69,00,000 small/marginal farmer accounts and about 59,75,000 'other farmer' accounts with an overdue amount of about Rs.60,416 crore and about Rs.31,839 crore respectively are covered under the Scheme. The cash outgo from Central Government towards reimbursement of the amount of waiver/relief to the lending institutions has been estimated by RBI and NABARD at around Rs.60,416 crore for small and marginal farmers and about Rs.7,960 crore for 'other farmers'.

Assuaging the farmers' fears on the need to handle too many papers during the implementation procedure, as per the detailed guidelines available at *http://www.finmin.nic.in,* "the only paper which the farmer has to handle is the paper that he will receive, namely the certificate. The certificate shall be given to each farmer either of debt waiver or debt relief mentioning the amount. Perforated second half of the certificate is the acknowledgement. The bank will give him the certificate and take the acknowledgement. That is the only paper which the farmer needs to take and keep in his possession."

PROPOSED NATIONAL FOOD SECURITY ACT, 2009

In 2009, the Indian Government has planned to bring out the National Food Security Act (NFSA) benefit the Below Poverty Line (BPL) people. Implementing this proposed National Food Security Act, 2009 would be more challenging than the National Rural Employment Guarantee Act (NREGA), 2005. This is a huge challenge because the first concern is that the definition of Below Poverty Line (BPL) has to be clearly made, then comes the issue of financial commitment involved and then the adequate food grain storage to see that this is implemented properly (Thomas, 2009)[22]. The act, one of the main agendas of the United Progressive Alliance (UPA) Government, is to see that every BPL card holder gets 25 kg of either rice or wheat at Rs. 3 per kilogram (kg) every month.

Gender-neutral Technology Development and Dissemination

While rural women are knowledgeable about and use a large amount of traditional technology, they have very little access to modern technology that could benefit them in their farm and household activities. This is due to women's lack of participation in setting research priorities or in generating and disseminating conventional technologies.

Women's lack of access to appropriate technology can have an adverse impact on food security. With the growing feminization of farm labour due to male rural-to-urban migration, women are forced to carry out work previously done by men.

Consequently, women are increasing their workloads and taking care of a wider scope of agricultural tasks.

The problems faced by female-headed households, whether *de jure* or *de facto*, vary according to their degree of access to productive resources, including modern agricultural techniques. This nessicitates "development of technology and dissemination" to be "gender-neutral". Is it happening in India?

The answer is "NOT BIG NO" but "small yes". The Department of Agriculture and Cooperation has launched a website exclusively on "Farm-women" (http://.....). The Ministry of Finance has announced "Financial Inclusion" programme to cover SHGs (mostly women) and made it operational through National Bank for Agriculture and Rural Development (NABARD). The Economic Survey for 2000-01 made a specific reference to the need for "Gender Budgeting (GB)" and the process was initated in the Budget for 2005-06. In the Central Government, the Ministry of Women and Child Development monitors actions taken by various agencies. In addition, States, viz. Assam, Bihar, Meghalaya, Gujarat, J&K, Maharashtra, Rajasthan, Madhya Pradesh, Orissa and Manipur have introduced exercises related to Gender Budgeting. Specific focus on gender based resource allocation is seen from the Eighth Plan (1992-1997) onwards.

The Expert Group (Chairman—Dr. Ashok Lahiri) on "Classification System of Government Transactions", constituted during 2003, among the others, recommeded to establish a "Gender Budgeting Directorate" in the Department of Expenditure. There is a lack of standard nomenclature used by different authorities (Bhatia, 2006)[23].

"Gender Budgeting" is now recognized as a tool for empowering women: socially, politically and economically. "KUTUMBASHREE" Scheme of the Government of Kerala is a progressive and enterprising SHG for "women empowerment" at the grassroots level.

Improving Agricultural Productivity: Integrated Policy Framework

Global Climate Change has considerable implications on Indian Agriculture and hence on food security and farmer's livelihood. Various research publications indicate that major impacts of climate change would be on rainfed crops (other than rice and wheat), which account for nearly 60 per cent of crop-land area. In India, poorest farmers practice rainfed agriculture. The loss in farm-level net revenue would range between 9 and 25 per cent for a temperature rise of 2-3.5°C. Saseendran *et al.* (2000)[24] showed that, for every 1°C rise in temperature, the decline in rice yield would be about 6 per cent.

There is growing need to qualify the effects of rising temperature on yield of crops in different agro-ecologies and agri-production environments. Similarly, various climate change scenarios need to be evaluated for these regions and the specific adoption strategies be evolved. Simulation models may help a long way in linking other biophysical and socio-economic drivers of agri-production with climate change. In India, wheat yields could decrease by 5-10 per cent per 1°C rise in temperature.

Agarwal (2007)[25] suggests for increased support for adaptation research, developing regionally differentiated contingency plans for temperature and rainfall related risks, enhanced research on seasonal weather forecasts, and their applications for reducing production risks, and evolving new landuse systems, including heat and drought tolerant varieties, adapted to climatic variability and changes and yet meeting food demands. There is an urgent need to strengthen crop pest surveillance mechanisms for various pests, and also mechanisms for integrated management of rainwater, surface water and ground water. Farmers require agricultural insurance and weather-derivatives (AGROMET Services) at an early date.

Adaptations to Climate Change, among the other measures, include: (a) New varieties: drought/heat resistant, (b) New farm management practices, (c) Change in land use, (d) Watershed management, and (e) Agri-insurance (Chattopadhyay, 2008)[26].

Most states are net importers of foodgrains. Improving agricultural productivity would improve food security. However, even in green revolution states such as Punjab, productivity has declined (Siddu, 2002)[27]. Moreover, agriculture is widely considered to be a part of life rather than an economic undertaking—the continued use of traditional techniques has also resulted in lower productivity. In poorer states, the coverage of irrigation is still very low, and government spending on irrigation has not improved (Debashis Chakraborty, 2004)[26].

The Greenhouse Gas (GHG) emissions from the forestry and agriculture account for over 30 per cent of the current annual total emissions. Of this, nearly 17.4 per cent emissions emanate from deforestation and forest degradation and 13.5 per cent from agriculture. Where individual GHGs are concerned, about 50 per cent of the total methane releases come from the farm sector, basically from the paddy fields and livestock. Similarly, 75 per cent of the nitrous oxide that goes into the environment annually is emitted from the agricultural fields where nitrogenous fertilizers are applied. Citing these estimates, farmers, especially those living in the already environmentally fragile areas, faced an immediate and ever-growing risk of increased crop failures and loss of livestock. Fishermen could face hardships due to reduced availability of marine and aquaculture fish. The output of forest produce would also decline to the detriment of the forest dwellers.

There are several possible interventions that can help reduce the outflow of environment injurious gases (GHGs) from the agriculture and forest sectors, include the use of more efficient crop varieties, better control of wild fires, improved natural resource management, restoration of land through controlled grazing, organic soil management and conservation agriculture and agro-forestry systems (Alexander Muller, 2009)[29].

The Accelerated Irrigation Benefit Programme (introduced during 1996-97) to generate an additional irrigation potential of 24.0 lakh hectares, the water resource management programmes to restore and rejuvenate water bodies with Command area of 4.0 lakh hectares, the ground water recharge programme to facilitate farmers for diverting rainwater into "dugwells", and the Agricultural Credit provisions were expected to influence farmers' investment in Land and Farm machinery (on-Farm Investment). The Eleventh Plan Document called for increase of agricultural credit, investment in rural infrastructure and speeding up of irrigation projects.

It has been perceived that development of minor irrigation is quite advantageous, as this possess like small investments, labour intensive, quick maturing, and most of all, a farmer-friendly. Our noted Scientist, Dr. M. S. Swaminathan said, "We need more science, both in public and private sectors, related to agriculture, for falsifying the Neo-Malthusian predictions of widespread food and drinking water insecurity."

The question of access, equity, and equality in Water Resources gets directly to the use of irrigation water. Has the expansion of irrigation benefited small farmers? Have the inter-class differences in irrigation widened or narrowed? What is the regional (State) distribution of irrigation by farm size? Deshpande *et al.* (2002)[30] point out that the growth rate of all major sources of irrigation was found to be inversely related with the farm size in majority of the states between 1970-71 and 1990-91. Complex issues of equity and social justice in regard to water distribution are required to be addressed.

The Hashim Committee Report (1999) dealt with various issues related to "Integrated Water Resources Development Plan" in the Country and warrants timely action in respect of: (i) harnessing of the surface flows through major, medium and minor storages, (ii) improving water-use efficiency, and (iii) taking necessary steps for demand and supply. The Nagpur Declaration (2000)[31] on "Natural Resources Planning and Management for Sustainable Development" envisages that for integrated water resources planning and management, both "river basins management" at the macro level and "watershed management" at the micro level, should mutually complement each other. Long term planning needs a clear vision for Land & Water Resources Management at grassroots level.

The All India Soil & Land Use Survey (AISLUS) organisation has delineated the entire country 3237 major Watersheds (6 major River Resources Regions, 35 Basins, 112 Catchments, 550 Sub-Catchments, and 3237 major Watersheds). Each Watershed contains a complex mixture of soil types, landscapes, climatic regimes, land use characteristics, and agricultural systems. Yet, this complexity is not unmanageable, and therefore, can be subdivided into more than one Agro Ecological Regions (AER), on the basis of having similar soil types, landscapes, climatic regimes, crop productivity and animal productivity, and hydrologic characteristics.

Cropping Pattern of an area is determined by many factors, which include: type of soil, climate, rainfall characteristics, farmer's requirements of food grains for self-consumption as well as market supply, and net rate of financial gain, resulting in various alternative crops that can be grown in that area. Each State of the country is expected to concentrate on agricultural products most suited to its agro-ecological and agro-climatic conditions, as it is not possible to hope to be self-sufficient in all the essential commodities (Abdul Kalam and Rajan)[32].

AER planning is useful in conjunction with Watershed Planning for developing a list of priority needs in monitoring, research, education, and implementation activities for various basins (water bodies) in the country. Using the AER characteristics along with existing Water Quality Monitoring Information, it is possible to determine:

- Where the steepest and most erosive landscapes are located,
- Where the water quality problems are most severe,
- Where land use patterns are most conducive to non-point source pollution production, and
- Where the research knowledge base concerning sources of pollution and methods of managing pollution is weakest.

Sustainability in Agricultural Development depends upon the judicious use of natural resources, viz.: soil, water, livestock, plants, fisheries, forests, climate and rainfall, and topography. This requires that (a) both SW and GW supplies are maintained at the desired level, and (b) the quality of Land and Water Resources does not deteriorate with time.

For each major Watershed, it is suggested to engage all stakeholders within the Watershed, in discussions and coordinated planning efforts that cross-state boundaries. In this connection, the following recommendations of the Core Group V Report (2000)[33] on "Agricultural Resources Information System (AgRIS)", of the Standing Committee on Soils and Agriculture (Ministry of Agriculture) are noteworthy:

- "A Decision Support System (DSS) on water allocation in an irrigation system to remove the existing disparities in the availability between the head-reach and tail-end farms and between large and small farms, to achieve "equity and social justice";
- "AER planning is useful in conjunction with Watershed Planning for developing a list of priority needs in monitoring, research, education, and implementation activities for various basins (water bodies) in the country";
- "A DSS on Water Bodies (Basin) using Watershed and AER Planning Concepts is to be taken up"; and
- "National Livestock Policy (NLP) studies classifies the country into four livestock farming system, viz. Cattle Farming System (CFS), Buffalo Farming System (BFS), Sheep Farming System (SFS), and Goat farming System (GFS). To observe the possible linkage between livestock systems and cropping systems, demographic and agro-climatic features, DSS on Cattle Farming System (CFS), DSS on Buffalo Farming System (BFS), DSS on Sheep Farming System (SFS), and DSS on Goat Farming System (GFS) may be developed."

The CMP 2004 recognized that "Irrigation would receive the highest investment priority and Dryland Framing in the Arid and Semi-Arid Regions of the Country". The Central Government has been investing heavily in the Accelerated Irrigation Benefit Programme (AIBP) and the Rainfed Area Development Programme and also in the management and augmentation of Water Resources. An integrated policy framework needs to be formulated to facilitate the increased use of irrigation and the adoption of newer farming techniques. Madaswamy Moni (2004)[34] makes a powerful plea for an Informatics Blueprint for Integrated Water Resources Planning and Management at grassroots level in relation to climate change and sustainable agricultural development. A key recommendation in this context is the setting up of an institution, bringing together the School of Earth Sciences, Colleges of Agriculture, Departments of Geography, School of Environmental Sciences, and Centres of Water Resources Development as well as University Departments specializing in this field.

INTENDED AGRICULTURAL REFORMS

In India, agricultural production patterns are heavily biased towards wheat-rice monoculture. The Government of India has declared, in its Budget Document 2005-06, its policy on agriculture "to diversify into areas such as horticulture, floriculture and oilseeds", and also its intention that "India must become a single market for all products (particularly agricultural produce), and the existing Acts governing Agricultural Produce Marketing Committees have outlived their utility."

National Mission on Horticulture (*http://www.nhm.gov.in*), Horticulture Mission for the North Eastern Region (*http://www.hm4ner.gov.in*) and National Bamboo Mission (*http://www.nbm.gov.in*) are operational in the country. The liberalized Industrial and Trade Policies paved the way for development of export oriented production of cut-flowers and the new Seed Policy had made it feasible to import planting material of international varieties (*http://www.ficciagroindia.com*). However, Indian floriculturists have to resort to distress sales of flowers, in the domestic market, during non-winter seasons due to higher tariff wall in Europe.

Till 2003, private participation in agriculture marketing was limited by regulations such as the Agricultural Produce Marketing Regulations Act and the Essential Commodities Act, which hindered rural regions from more value-added production (Debashis Chakraborty, 2003)[35]. Modifications to the APMC Act in 2003 have paved the way for increased private participation in agriculture through contract farming. Agricultural India requires "further reforms", in the existing back dated regulations for improving agri-business.

The Indian farming community consists mostly of Small and Marginal farmers. Some studies indicate that the Small farmers contribute about 54 per cent of marketable surplus and distress sale by them account for 50 per cent of the marketable surplus. Rural (primary and periodic) Markets, popularly known as "*haat*", "*chanthai*", and "*shandis*" (about 21731) are the first contact points of farmers with the market economy, both for selling and buying. As there have been high price differentials many times between the wholesale markets and the rural markets, there is room for arbitrage, which is being exploited by the traders to their advantage. Therefore, it is imperative to make the wholesale markets as the price discovery point and the rural markets as the price takers with due consideration for transport and other costs. As the rural markets have few traders, the tendency to collude among them is high. In the wholesale markets, as traders are many, one can expect a fair price. Marketing chains are long which results in a plethora of intermediaries leading to high marketing cost and imperfection in these markets. Accurate and timely, information about the market prices of the agricultural commodities is of extreme significance in the interest of farming community.

With a view to disseminate the daily prices and market related information in respect of more than 300 agricultural commodities and 2000 varieties to farmers, the Department of Agriculture and Cooperation (Ministry of Agriculture), with National Informatics Centre as the implementing agency, has implemented the "AGMARKNET" Portal (*http://agmarknet.nic.in*), connecting about 2800 Agricultural Produces Wholesale Markets in the country during 2000-2007. During the next Five Year Plans, the remaining 5000 wholesale agricultural produces markets and about 22000 rural markets are expected to be connected to the portal. The AGMARKNET Portal has emerged as a National Knowledge Portal, linking farmers to both domestic and global markets (Moni, 2008)[36].

RELATIONSHIP BETWEEN FOOD SECURITY AND INFORMATION

Decision-makers at various levels (national, regional, state, district and sub-district) need reliable and timely information on the incidence and causes of food insecurity, malnutrition, improved policy and programme formulation, targeting, and monitoring of progress of interventions aimed at reducing poverty and hunger (*http://www.fivims.org*).

The relationships among sustainable development, food security, gender equality and information have been analysed, making it possible to identify some of the factors that contribute to increased poverty and exclusion (FAO, 2000)[37]. These factors include:

- Limited access for subsistence farmers, particularly women farmers, to all resources. These include: productive resources (land, water, inputs, etc.); technological resources (tools, machines, etc.); educational resources (extension, vocational training, teaching, literacy); social resources (health care, social services and allowances); economic resources (capital, credit, jobs, wages, etc.); and political resources (information, decision-making, management, representation etc.);
- Scarce attention paid to the roles and responsibilities of men and women

when formulating agricultural and rural development plans and policies;
- Inadequate gender-specific data and information, hindering decision-making aimed at improving gender equality and political, economic and social equity; and
- Exclusion of a large part of the population, including rural women, from information flows, communication processes and, thus, decision-making.

The Food and Nutrition Security (FNS) Community of the UN supports India's food and nutrition security goals, by promoting sustainable improvement in food production, reducing malnutrition and poverty, improving implementation and impact of food related social safety-net programmes, food-safety, prevention of food-borne disease, and dietary diversification. Some of the issues covered by this community include:

- Sustainable food production, production resources, post-harvest practices, and livelihood and income generation;
- Food and nutrition security in areas such as food processing, marketing, distribution, food quality and safety;
- Enhancing production and consumption of fruits, vegetables and pulses through farm and dietary diversification;
- Efficacy of current agriculture, food and nutrition programmes and policies; and
- Malnutrition and under-nutrition including micronutrient deficiencies, and nutrition awareness and remedies.

IMPACT OF INDIA'S ECONOMIC REFORMS ON AGRICULTURE

The reduction of capital expenditure in the sector post-1991 led to loss of employment in rural areas, and agriculture became unviable when there was no external support for research in agriculture and market procurement. India's Economic Reforms 1991 have failed to boost the growth of agriculture. Nagaraj (2007)[38] called for a policy that interlinked factors such as credit delivery, investment, pricing and employment to restore the Government support system. The decline of public infrastructure for agriculture in rural areas was one of the reasons for the lag in the sector and there was need for heavy investment in public infrastructure such as roads, railways and power (Ravi, 2007)[39]. Pulapre Balakrishnan (2007)[40] says allocation of financial resources is important but good governance is essential to improve agricultural growth, and cites high food prices in India (compared with developed countries) as one of the reasons for the lag in poverty alleviation.

Closer integration of Indian economy in the global market place, advances in information and biotechnology, enhanced emphasis on privatization and public private partnerships, and domestic reforms have all contributed to considerable changes in production and marketing environment for Indian Agriculture during 1990s and the first decade in the new twenty-first century. Overall, this has brought increased market orientation in the sector and has thrown open a plethora of opportunities and challenges. There has been increased agribusiness activities in the areas of large scale organised retailing, contract farming, futures trading, etc. This has also brought to the fore, the need for a more efficient and strengthened Supply Chain as well as Technology and Institutions to integrate small farmers into these Supply Chains.

Future of agricultural development lies mainly in equipping farmers to adjust and modernize in response to conditions brought about by increasing competition, and changing demands from consumers. In addition, this requires establishing a healthy investment climate to encourage entrepreneurial action in commodities and value chains, supporting human resource development through improved quality and access to social services, and strengthening agricultural technology support services. These Challenges are complex.

Farms output grow in double-digits (11.8-17.7 per cent), in the State of Nagaland, whereas the rest of India's at 2.6 per cent during 2000-05, according to the recent district-wise data compiled by Indicus Analytics—Indian Agriculture Scope 2006-07: District Profile (*Indian Express*, July 12, 2007). Farmers are not getting enough income-rise in the State of Nagaland due to: lack of market access and relevant infrastructure—not enough roads to reach the markets; not enough power to preserve the harvest. This situation prevails in almost every State wherein agriculture has the dominant function. President Pratibha Patil (2008)[41] has said that proper management in marketing agricultural produce at the village level can help end agrarian crisis. The National Initiative: AGMARKNET Portal (*http://www.agmarknet.nic.in*) of the Ministry of Agriculture links farmers to domestic and global markets (Madaswamy Moni, 2008)[42]. Liberalizing Domestic Agricultural Marketing in India needs a lot of attention with respect to the following:

- Granaries Overflow (65 MTs) and Stomach Empty (250 million) (GOSE),
- Price Discovery Mechanism,
- Targetted PDS—uncompetitive in Nature (Too much pilferages, additional transportation cost),
- Poor has the rights over the resources,
- Inter-State Barriers for movement of food grains,
- Integration of local markets with national markets,
- "Levy of fee" by local bodies,
- APMCs previously brought reforms in agricultural sector,
- Agricultural Market Reforms 2002 in 9 key areas,
- ITC e-Choupal and AGMARKNET Portal,
- How to get better returns to the Farmers?

- 35-40 per cent wastages in Fruits and Vegetables,
- Host of intermediaries in the Supply Chain, and
- Insufficient Cold Chains for perishable items.

GLOBALISATION AND SUSTAINABLE URBAN FOOD SYSTEMS

The process of urbanization transforms includes (i) land-use and farming systems, (ii) patterns of labour-force participation, (iii) infrastructure requirements, and (iv) natural resources systems. "Spatial" links refer to the movements of people, goods, money, and information between urban and rural areas. "Sectoral" links describe the interdependence between agriculture and industry and services. Studies show that urban growth rates rise when developing countries favour manufacturing over rural agriculture (Martin Brockerhoff, 2000)[43]. The Urban Agriculture System includes horticulture, floriculture, forestry, aquaculture, and livestock production. Urban Agriculture complements, rather than supplants, rural supplies (Luc Mougeot, 2000)[44]. Regional and global networks are developing, but national and local networks must also be created and supported. Urban food and Nutrition security depend on strong links between urban and rural areas (Cecilia Tacoli, 2000)[45].

EMERGING AGRIBUSINESS FORMATS AND MANAGEMENT

The changing political, demographic and economic features of India such as economic growth, rising incomes and emergence of large middle-class population are changing the preference of demand for food and other agricultural products. Simultaneous changes through the proliferation of brands, changing lifestyles, consumer awareness and improvement in technology have also led to the growth of the Agri-Business Management sector. Newer segments are emerging with specific quality requirements of food and agricultural products. This diversity in demand together with increasing value additions, is posing newer challenges in Value Chain Management (VCM).

The pattern of diffusion of organized food retail chains in India follows that of other regions, with the boom being confined for most part to the urban areas of the country. However, India is at an early stage of modernizing food retailing, with branded and organized food retailing accounting for about four per cent of total retail sales. Due to restrictions on Foreign Direct Investments, domestic capital (rather than FDI) continues to play a major role in the organized retail sector in India.

On the supply side, increasing subdivision and fragmentation of holdings, increasing cost and uncertainty in input markets, new generation technological advancement and weak institutional support have contributed to considerable challenges to farming population. In the wake of these challenges, several alternatives have been tried such as contract farming, commodity futures, privatization of agricultural markets, increased role of private sector, public private partnership, farmers' organization, etc.

Transformation of agriculture into agri-business calls for professional management. The national and international conferences and seminars, organised in recent-past, have found it imperative to address the major issues, such as:

- Value Chain Management (VCM);
- Contract farming;
- Spot and Futures trading;
- Financing value chain;
- Institutional innovations to integrate diverse categories of producers;
- Food safety, quality standards and infrastructure; and
- Information Technology.

IMPACT OF ECONOMIC REFORMS ON IMPROVED FOOD SECURITY

The current process of globalisation of agriculture threatens the three dimensions of sustainable agriculture: ecological security, food security and livelihood security. The new trade liberalisation and globalisation policies are: (i) increasing the centralised control of agriculture, (ii) facilitating the handing over of control over natural resources, production systems, markets and trade, to global agribusiness, and (iii) disempowering and dispossessing small farmers and landless labour in India. Trade liberalisation is leading to external liberalisation, i.e. liberalisation for global agribusiness. What the Indian farmers need is internal liberalisation (Vandana Shiva, 2002)[46].

Agricultural Policies are categorized by the World Trade Organization (WTO), according to whether they have a significant effect on production:

- *Amber Box*—Policies that not have a substantial impact on the patterns and flow of trade;
- *Green Box*—Policies that are not deemed to have a major effort on production and trade: "production retirement" programme, "resource retirement" programme, environmental programme, marketing information and infrastructure; and
- *Blue Box*—Policies that fall in between.

The Agreement on Agriculture (AoA) maintains "protectionism" in the developed countries through the "green box" and "blue box". TRIPs and the AoA, both the part of the WTO, have critical implications regarding "food security" and the "right-to-livelihood". Five Asian Nations (Thailand, Vietnam, Cambodia, Lao PDR, Myanmar) has planned to create a "Rice Cartel", along the similar lines of OPEC, for trading rice in the global market. But if successful, Thomas Fuller (2008)[47] says that it could have far reaching consequences in the global market, and sustaining prices at their current historic highs and worsening a food crisis that is hurting Asia's Poorest Consumers.

The Doha Round was widely touted as "the Development Round". The QUAD Countries (viz., USA, EU, JAPAN and Canada) have conventionally dominated decision making in Doha Rounds. India and other Developing countries have been able to resist unfair deals by forming credible issue-based coalitions viz., G-20, G-33 and NAMA 11. India has shown its disappointments on the revised drafts on Agriculture Market Access (AMA) and Non-Agriculture Market Access (NAMA), circulated by the WTO on May 19, 2008 (*The Economic Times*, 21 May, 2008), and rejected the dilution of Special Security Mechanism (SSM)[48] protecting the livelihood concerns of poor farmers. When shall "Revival of the Weakest" and not "Survival of the Fittest" form the core of the negotiations for reaching an agreement?

During the Uruguay Round, the developed countries had SSMs for 40 products. Agriculture Market Access (AMA) is politically sensitive and food security dominates the discourse in the developing world. The Draft Text having condition of applying SSMs on 3-8 products is unrealistic for a country with more than 23 Agro-climatic zones. This "3-8 products" restriction under which India is expected to block agriculture imports to protect its local farmers. This warrants asking, "Does India need WTO FARM PACT?" Though the Agriculture Text circulated falls short of Indian expectations, it is worth the effort to continue with hard bargaining and strive to achieve an acceptable deal (Prashant Goyal, 2008)[49]. In 2001 also, India had feared that the dismantling of Quantitative Restrictions (QRs) would flood Indian market with cheap agri-imports but these fears were largely belied.

The study results of (Manoj Panda and Ganesh Kumar, A., 2008)[50] provide evidence that a rise in real incomes/decline in income poverty, following trade reforms, need not necessarily translate into, improved food security/better nutritional status for households. India is a country, rich in diversity and in local markets. Strengthening this diversity and these local markets should be the strategy for creating immunity to the globalisation of our food systems.

Globalisation has brought considerable benefits but for many, had become unbalanced, unfair and unsustainable. Trade talks are stalled, financial markets are on the brink, and climate change continues. Any reconstruction will have to find ways to integrate financial, economic, social, labour and environmental policies within a sustainable development approach. International organisations must come together to develop a new multilateral framework for a fair and sustainable globalisation. People must have trust that the economy is working for them (Juan Somavia, 2008)[51]. India can cope with the global fiscal meltdown if it is able to ensure that the policy making is firmly aligned on the side of public purpose, not private greed (Harish Khare, 2008)[52]. Crisis spawns opportunities and progress. The genesis of the next recovery lies in the ruins of the last recession (Robert Samuelson, 2008)[53].

There is no doubt that India's economic fundamentals are strong (Chandrajit Banerjee, 2008)[54], as it is a shielded economy. The swift response of the policymakers and their ability to leverage this global crisis and turn the tides of global wealth in favour of India could re-define the growth story of India for the next decade (Shefali Goradia, 2008)[55]. The year 2009 started showing the sign of impact of "global meltdown" for India.

IMPACT OF AGRICULTURAL REFORMS ON ON-FARM INVESTMENT

While the Indian economy has averaged close to 9 per cent growth annually over the past four years and now averaged to 7.5 per cent (as per RBI estimate 2008), and agricultural sector has been growing just over 2 per cent a year. The National Common Minimum Programme (CMP) of the UPA Government (2004-09) has promised, "Public Investment in the Agricultural sector, rural infrastructure and irrigation will be stepped up in a significant manner". Major initiatives during the Eleventh Plan are as follows:

A. Bharat Nirman: Projected Investment in Rural Infrastructure (at 2006-07 prices): **Rs. 4,35,349 crore**

• Electricity	Rs. 34,000 crore
• Rural Roads	Rs. 41,347 crore
• Telecommunications	Rs. 16,000 crore
• Irrigation (including Watershed)	Rs. 2,53,301 crore
• Water Supply and Sanitation	Rs. 90,701 crore

(*Source*: 11th Planning Commission Document, Volume I, p. 259)

B. Agricultural Sector (11th Plan)	**Rs. 47,380 crore**
• National Horticulture Mission	Rs. 8,800 crore
• National Food Security Mission	Rs. 4,883 crore
• Macro Management of Agriculture (MMA)	Rs. 5,500 crore
• Micro Irrigation	Rs. 3,400 crore
• Rainfed Area Development (New)	Rs. 3,500 crore
• Support to State Extension Programmes	Rs. 2,000 crore
• ISOPAM	Rs. 1,500 crore
• Technology Mission on Horticulture—NER	Rs. 1,500 crore
• Rashtriya Krishi Vikas Yojana (RKVY)—ACA	Rs.25,000 crore

C. Rural Development and Panchayat Raj Institutions

• NREGS (per annum)	Rs. 27,000 crore
• BRGF (per annum)	Rs. 4,700 crore
• NLRMP	Rs. 5,656 crore
• IWDP	Rs. 1,114 crore

D.	**National Rural Health Mission (NRHM)**	**Rs. 90,558 crore**
E.	**Human Resources Development**	
•	Sarva Siksha Abhiyan (SSA)	Rs. 71,400 crore
•	Mid-Day Meal Scheme	Rs. 48,000 crore
•	ICDS	Rs. 44,400 crore
F.	**Fertiliser Subsidy (2009-10)**	Rs. 95,849 crore
G.	**Public Distribution System (PDS) per Annum**	Rs. 50,000 crore

[*Source*: *Hindustan Times*, 18th June, 2009: The annual food subsidy bill could well cross the Rs 50,000 crore mark as the government finalises ways and means to announce the promised Rs. 3 per kg of foodgrains scheme to below poverty line (BPL) families.]

H.	**Agricultural Debt Waiver and Debt Relief (ADWDF) Scheme 2008**	Rs. 71,680 crore

KISAN VISION PROJECT AND THE RAILWAYS

India, at present, suffers an unacceptable loss of about Rs. 35-40,000 crore every year towards wastage of fruits and vegetables. To arrest this trend, the Union Railway Budget 2009-10, presented on 3rd July, 2009 in the Parliament, has proposed to introduce special trains, under the Kisan-Vision project, to carry perishables products (Fruits, Vegetables, Fish etc.) from identified production clusters to consumer centres, by way of maintaining quality and freshness of perishable produce, and also to encourage creation of facilities of setting up cold storage and temperature controlled perishable cargo centres and its transportation through public-private partnership mode.

It has also been proposed that the Railtel Corporation would develop a plan, so as to make that the optic fibre cable network of Railways that runs past various small stations and villages could be leveraged to take information technology up to the door steps in remote areas.

TOWARDS THE IDEAL OF A HUNGER-FREE INDIA THROUGH "GANDHI DISTRICT" MODEL

Achieving the goal of nutrition security for all Indians will need a fusion of political will and action, professional skill, and peoples' participation (Swaminathan, 2008)[56]. In 1981, Indira Gandhi (the Former Prime Minister of India), suggested to convert the "Wardha" district as "Gandhi district"[57], after meeting Vinoba Bhave at the Paunar Ashram in the Wardha district. Swaminathan (2008) says, "Unfortunately, this Plan to dedicate Wardha to Gandhiji is yet to be implemented. Even now, it is worthwhile to update the report and transform Wardha into a hunger-free and poverty-free district dedicated to Gandhiji". How to overcome the curse of malnutrition?

Sustainable agriculture is based on sustainable use of natural resources—land, water, and agricultural biodiversity (including that of plants and animals). This means that ownership and control of these resources shall lie with the decentralised agricultural communities, in order to generate livelihoods, provide food and conserve natural resources.

Financial Inclusion: Mobile Computing Ushered in "Branchless Bank" at Grassroots

Mobile-enabled financial services (m-banking) involve the use of a mobile phone or another mobile device to undertake financial transactions linked to a client's account. M-banking is one of the newest approaches to the provision of financial services through ICT, made possible by the widespread adoption of mobile phones even in low income countries. The roll out of mobile telephony has been rapid, and has extended access well beyond already connected customers in developing countries.

India is the fastest growing cellular market in the world—with ever rising cellular subscribers. Over 260 million people in India now own mobile phones. India's "Financial Inclusion" Programme witnesses use of Mobile Phones at grassroots level (Table 8.1), for providing transactions to members of the Self Help Groups (SHGs). Voice is increasingly becoming a commodity and mobile phones have become a "Branchless Bank" for Corporation Bank, which is one of the India's leading Public Sector Banks. Spoilt by choice, the mobile phone subscribers are beginning to choose their operators on the basis of their Value Added Services (VAS) being offered. The increased importance of VAS makes content developers burn their midnight oil to come up with, better and newer concepts and services.

Table 8.1: Pilot Projects, in the State of Andhra Pradesh, implementing "Financial Inclusion" Programme of NABARD wherein Mobile and Handheld devices are being used

Name of the Bank	*Technology Service Provider*	*Accessories*	*Access Control*	*Card*	*Cost of Card (Rs.)*	*Business Correspondent*
(1)	(2)	(3)	(4)	(5)	(6)	(7)
APGVB (Andhra Pradesh Grameen Vikas Bank)	A Little World	Mobile & Hand held device	Biometric	Non-chip	15-25	Zero Mass Foundation (Section 25 Company)
Corporation Bank	Integra	Hand held device operatable with Backup Battery	Biometric	Chip based	80-100	SHG Members
Axis Bank	FINO	Hand held device and Laptop/Mobile Phone	Biometric	Chip based	100-125	FINO FINTECH Foundation (Section 25 Company)
Rajasthan Grameen Bank, Rohtak Grameen Bank	Source Trace Systems India Pvt. Ltd.	Phones, PDAs, POS Terminals, PCs and Thin Clients				

India is among the fastest growing economies in the world. The power of a billion plus people, all connected via the Internet, will definitely redefine the system of e-Governance. The factors that may drive growth include "National e-Governance Programme (NeGP)" and "Internet on mobile". Mobile phones are the success story of bridging the rural digital-divide, bringing tangible economic benefits and acting as agents of social mobilization through improved communication.

INFORMATICS FOR SUSTAINABLE AGRICULTURAL DEVELOPMENT

The Agricultural Sector requires "grassroots level workers", "technicians" and "para-professionals", capable of handling services like soil testing, seed production, elite planting material, artificial insemination, disease surveillance grading and marketing etc. This necessitates the need for introducing farm education at the school level. It is therefore that the "one-strategy" is definitely creation of agri-polytechnics and ITIs, after minimizing the weaknesses of existing KVKs (Peter, 2008)[58]. Kini (2005)[59] suggests that every Tehsil/Taluka should have an agricultural school, since 60 to 70 per cent of our people depend on agriculture, and agricultural education has to be given greater importance—the use of seeds, fertilizers and pesticides etc.

Agricultural reforms mean land reform plus a package of support services such as credit, marketing, pricing, and rural infrastructure (water, roads, bridges, hospitals and schools). The Agricultural Extension System is expected to be "an Agricultural Knowledge & Information System (AK&IS), using Geomatics Technology". This AK&IS for rural empowerment and improved livelihoods, i.e.

e-farmer, is the need of the hour. ICTs Diffusion and Infusion have many potential applications spanning the breadth of the agricultural industry, at all scales of organization from farmer, to cooperative and professional bodies, from farm machinery vendors, fertilizer and chemical companies, insurance, regulators, and commodities, to agronomists, consultants, and farm advisors. Agriculture has to transcend from the present high material inputs to optimum levels through appropriate use of Information and Communication Technologies (ICTs) and strategies for efficient resource use. Main barriers witnessed for ICT adoption in the agriculture segment are: Power availability, ICT infrastructure, ICT illiteracy, relevant content, and standardization, integration of services, advisory services, and localization. In view of this many ICT projects are lagging progress at grassroots level.

Emergence of ICTs on the national agenda and the announcement of ICTs Policy by various State Governments have recognized the "Convergence of Core Technologies and e-Governance" as the tool for sustainable development and globalization of economy. To achieve this, "Web Service" as a "Service Oriented Architecture (SOA)" has emerged and has to be exploited through localisation for achieving rural prosperity. The Internet, which allows intangible information and ideas to be traded and exchanged instantly, across any distance, is the most recognizable symbol of today's global, knowledge-driven economy. The Agricultural Market Information System must be thought of in both the context of the user's cognitive capacity and also in terms of the means, format, and language of the presentation of the knowledge objects. Rural areas are still not taking benefit of ICT usage in Market Information Services and its dissemination.

Indian farming sector, therefore, needs competent technical manpower in the area of Agricultural Extension to meet the changing needs of the stakeholders (i.e. farmers). The objective of providing technically skilled manpower is to modernize the agriculture. The Agricultural Research System (which consists of Agricultural Colleges, ICAR Institutes, Central and State Agricultural Universities, Krishi Vigyan Kendras and Zonal Research Stations), Agricultural Management and Administrative System of the State Governments (which have up to block level agricultural offices), NABARD System, Public/Private/Cooperative Sector Banks Delivery Systems etc. shall have an "integrated approach" for information delivery to farmers. The present day Agricultural Courses at the Graduate level, being offered by the State Agricultural Universities, are not able to bridge the gap between "Theory and Ground Realities". The farming community is not practicing Agricultural Science and Technology at "the farm level".

The existing database on soil is inadequate to develop micro-level agricultural land use plan in the country, for which the needed scale of resolution is 1:4000/12500. The detailed digital database on soil (physical, chemical and biological) is a prerequisite to address the various issues related to scientific Land Use Planning, soil reclamation; proper diagnosis of soils, judicious use of irrigation water and chemical fertilizers, nutrient deficiencies for maintenance of sound soil health and land productivity. The relevant soil parameters to be considered for such purposes are: soil type, elevation, type of land form, slope, geology (type of parent material), textural class, type of soil structure, soil water retentivity, soil *p*H, Electrical Conductivity (EC), Organic Carbon, $CaCO_3$, Fe per cent, major oxides, available macro and micro nutrients, depth of water table, erosion class, drainage and runoff characteristics, land capability and irrigability etc. The National Informatics Centre (NIC) has already published its village level dataset designed, for its projects for grassroots development:

- *DISNIC-PLAN Project*: IT for Micro Level Planning (*http://disnic.gov.in*); and
- *Agricultural Resources Information System (AgRIS) Project (http://agris.nic.in)* of Department of Agriculture and Cooperation pertains to Soil, Land, Groundwater and Environment parameters. Both these projects, DISNIC and AgRIS are under implementation in identified pilot districts.

An effective rural knowledge society and ICT system needs to be established in each gram Panchayat. This should be involve various stakeholders—farmers, development agents and agencies, knowledge generators and distributors (universities and public and private institutions) for steering a "knowledge-based Soil and Land Resource Management". Village Knowledge Centres (Gyan Chaupals) with extensive rural connectivity, including use of cell phones. This would empower the farmers to access database for site specific natural resource management. Data access through Common Services Centre (CSCs), VKCs and VRCs may be promoted.

The Report of the State Commission on Agricultural Research, Reforms and Development, Government of Jharkhand (2007) recommends "development of Digital Network for the Farmers (DNF)" which will facilitate an integrated approach of "Internet Technology" and "Sustainable Agricultural, Rural and Backward Area Development" with its farm and non-farm linkages and, among the others, recommends the following measures to be given appropriate consideration during the Eleventh Plan period. The following measures are important:

A. Development of Digital Network for the Farmers (DNF)

- *Agrisnet*—an Infrastructure network up to block level agricultural offices facilitating agricultural extension services and agribusiness activities to usher in rural prosperity;
- *Agmarknet*—with a road map to network Agricultural produce wholesale markets and rural markets;
- *Seednet*—Seed Informatics Network;
- *Coopnet*—to network Agricultural Primary Credit Societies (PACS) and Agricultural Cooperative Marketing Societies to usher in ICT enabled services and rural transformation;

- *Hortnet*—Horticultural Informatics Network;
- *Fertnet*—Fertilisers (Chemical, Bio and Organic Manure) Informatics Network facilitating "Integrating Nutrient Management" at farm level;
- *Vistarnet*—Agricultural Extension Information System Network;
- *PPIN*—Plant Protection Informatics Network;
- *APHNET*—Animal Production and Health Informatics Network networking about 42000 Animal Primary Health Centres;
- *FISHNET*—Fisheries Informatics Network;
- *LISNET*—Land Information System network linking all institutions involved in land and water management for agricultural productivity and production systems, which has now evolved as "Agricultural Resources Information system" project during the Tenth Plan being implemented through NIC.
- *AFPINET*—Agricultural and Food Processing Industries Informatics Network;
- *ARINET*—Agricultural and Rural Industries Information System Network to strengthen Small, Micro and Medium Enterprises (SMEs);
- *NDMNET*—Natural Disaster Management Knowledge Network in India;
- *WeatherNET*—Weather Resource System Information Network of India.

B. Mainstreaming of ICT for Collaborative Research Models for Sustainable improvement at grassroots level

- *Agricultural Resource Information System (AgRIS) (www.agris.nic.in):*
  - Proof-of-Concept Pilot projects;
  - Agricultural Polytechnic and Agricultural ITI: Grassroots level Institutions to Operationalisation.
- *ICT for Micro Level Planning (www.disnic.gov.in):*
  - DISNIC Programme.
- *Automation and Networking of Primary Agricultural Cooperatives*
  - *e-Cooperatives and CoopNet*: An Internet Enterprise Development Programme for fostering agricultural and rural industries.
- *Digital SMEs:*
  - A way forward for Reduction of Spatial Disparities and Enhancing Opportunities for Development of SMEs to penetrate into export markets.
- *Automation and Networking of Libraries.*
- ***Empowering Rural Employment.***

C. Development of Appropriate Manpower at Grassroots Level

(i) Two-Year Certificate Course and Creation of Agricultural ITIs (1-2 per District); and

(ii) Three-Year Diploma Courses on Agricultural Science & Technology and Creation of Agricultural Polytechnic (one per District).

The Eleventh Plan of National Informatics Centre (NIC) gives special thrust for ICT based Systems Development and Services in the areas as identified as "Major Challenges" and also aligns with the National e-Governance Programme (NeGP) of the Government of India. In order to realize this goal, and also with its vast experience of "Informatics led developmental services in Government" during the last 30 years, NIC has introduced the following Schemes in its XI Plan:

(i) GRID (Grassroots Level Informatics Development) Programme,
(ii) "Smart Village" Project,
(iii) "Smart Island" Project.

These schemes are envisaged to provide the benefits of Information Communication Technology (ICT) directly to the communities at the grassroots level for promoting need based services related to life-cycle needs of rural population with institutional linkages and capacity building among rural communities. The schemes descriptions are as follows:

(i) *GRID (Grassroots Level Informatics Development) Programme:* This programme is being launched to synergistically combine the efforts and resources of various functionaries at grassroots level, effectively and efficiently, harnessing state-of-the-art ICTs, for bottom up development. It has been decided to implement it on pilot scale and with a mission to roll out at later stage, in 18 district typologies: (1) A tribal people dominated district; (2) A hilly district; (3) A dryland farming district; (4) A socially backward district; (5) A green revolution district; (6) A district dominated by cash crop; (7) A coastal district for Brackishwater Aquaculture; (8) A district where mining/industrial activities are undertaken; (9) A district dominated by forest economy; (10) A dairy farming district; (11) A district dominated by one or two urban centres (Peri-urban); (12) A district in arid-zone; (13) A district, which is flood prone but having vast wasteland that could be used to generate forest cover, (14) A Blue-revolution (Fish Farming) District, (15) A District having urban or rural cluster of Micro, Small and Medium Industries (MSMEs); (16) A District dominated by a Minority Community; (17) A District prone for Natural Calamities; and (18) A Border Area District having international border.

(ii) *"Smart Village" Project:* The Objectives of the "Smart Village" Project is to usher the usage of Information and Communication Technologies (ICTs) for development and empowerment of communities (mostly disadvantaged communities) of the villages. The initiative aims to empower communities (that have limited or no telecommunications access) through the use of latest available technologies, which will help contribute to long-term sustainable and economic development, through Value-Chain and Result-Chain and Input-Chain. The model would work around the human resources at the village level as an individual, family and society; working out the linkages, identification and networking with the right stake holders, creation of necessary infrastructure at the village level, analysis of the services, working out the methodology for digital enablement with digital connectivity in order to reach the un-reached, un-served and under-served.

(iii) *"Smart Island":* This project envisages achieving the objectives of the "Smart Village" in the Islands. NIC proposes to undertake "Smart Island" project in Andaman and Nicobar islands to usher in the usage of Information and Communication Technologies (ICTs) for development and empowerment of communities (mostly disadvantaged communities) of the Island.

To go ahead for implementation of these Schemes, it is felt necessary to undertake "System Development Research Studies" to identify both Digital Layers and Non-Digital Layers which will impact on the "Common Man" at the Grassroots level, so as to affect social engineering and inclusiveness.

Panacea or Not, ICTs can Play a Significant Role for the Rural Poor

The proliferation of Information and Communication Technologies (ICTs), like cell phones and Internet access, has the potential to influence all aspects of development through their effects on governance, markets, media, and public services. IFPRI (2006)[60] addresses the implications of ICTs for poor people. Despite this great potential, however, the opportunities of the digital age are not equally accessible, and poor people have been left behind. This is not to say that poor constituents are passively forgoing ICTs, however. The demand—and at times the struggle—for access by poor people are accelerating in many countries. Successfully harnessing the power of ICTs could make a substantial contribution to achieving the Millennium Development Goals (MDGs), both directly, through the delivery of public services, and indirectly, through the creation of new economic opportunities for the rural poor *via* better links to markets.

Government is an instrument of the people in the development process. For this to occur, the government must open its activities to public scrutiny, provide the public with the information they need to express their opinions to the government, and establish mechanisms to take into account citizens' feedback. Accountability is at the root of the reform process (Nicholas Stern *et al.*, 2002)[61] . The Barcelona Consensus puts the performance of a country's government at the heart of development (i.e. to identify the binding constraints to growth, which, in turn, necessitates recognizing country-specific characteristics and undertaking a more rigorous economic and institutional analysis than a formulaic approach would call for). Former Malaysian Prime Minister Mahathir Mohammad had said, "the quality of an effective government administration cannot be lower than that of its clients—

specifically the private sector." The World has moved away from the so-called Washington Consensus towards the Barcelona Consensus.

There were those who argued for the "trickle down" approach while others argued for a direct attack on poverty. However, it takes some time for the efficiency to "trickle down" whereas Client Charters and Quality Mark, ISO 9000, e-Government, e-Procurement and other similar initiatives represent a direct attack on public sector inefficiency. These are complementary approaches and not substitutes for each other (Prajapati Trivedi, 2008)[62].

CONCLUSION

India is a land of diversity with different types of terrain, various agro-climatic conditions, different levels of socio-economic conditions, and varied levels of regional development. Rural India desires: to take advantage of "knowledge-intensive" techniques in sustainable crop farming and animal husbandry, to get better value-added for their products *via* information links to markets, and to obtain up-to-date, accurate information on entitlements, *viz.* health and welfare benefits, employment opportunities. Innovation is the need of the hour in India's rural sector

NOTES

1. World Bank (2002): "World Bank lauds India for Poverty Reduction" published in *Times of India*, March 14, 2002 and also see http://www.worldbank.org
2. Kate Smith and Rob Edwards (2008): "2008: The year of global food crisis", as published in *Sunday Herald*, March 2008.
3. Joseph E. Stiglitz (2008): Scarcity in an age of plenty", published in the *Economic Times*, 23 June 2008; The Author is the Nobel Laureate and Professor of Economics at the University of Columbia, USA.
4. Zia Haq (2008): "Price rise pushing Indians to poverty", published in *Hindustan Times* (New Delhi), Internet Edition, October 16, 2008.
5. *Business Line* (2009): "Inflation calmed, not beaten", in the Business Line dated 13 January 2009
6. *Business Line* (2009): "Commodity investors see rich pickings in grains", as published in Business Line dated 19th January 2009.
7. Swaminathan S., Ankalesaria Aiyar (2008): "Let others Starve, self-righteously" published in Times of India dated 18 May, 2008.
8. Michael Maiello (2007): "Food Vs. Fuel" in http://www.forbes.com, dated 15th November, 2007.
9. (http://www.cimmyt.org/english/wps/about/index.htm).
10. Sharad Pawar (2008): While speaking in the context of 40th Anniversary of the Green Revolution, New Delhi; Published in *The Hindu* dated 24th November, 2008; He is the Hon'ble Union Minister of Agriculture.
11. Swaminathan, M.S. (2008): While speaking in the context of 40th Anniversary of the Green Revolution, "Need to cut dependency on agriculture", published in *The Hindu* dated 24th November, 2008, New Delhi.

12. Sidhu, H.S. (2002), 'Crisis in Agrarian Economy in Punjab: Some Urgent Steps', *Economic and Political Weekly*, 27, July 27-2 August, pp. 3132-38.
13. Chakraborty, Debashis (2004): "How is the State Functioning? A Comparative Analysis of Growth, Governance and Social Issues during the 8th and 9th Plan Period", in Bibek Debroy (ed.), *Agenda for Improving Governance* (New Delhi: Academic Foundation), pp. 49-104.
14. Sharad Pawar (2008): "India Committed to Ensure Food Security for Every Citizen", while addressing the "World Food Day Celebrations 2007", 16-17 October, 2007, New Delhi; He is the Hon'ble Union Minister of Agriculture, Government of India.
15. Sharad Pawar (2008): "India Committed to Ensure Food Security for Every Citizen", while addressing the "World Food Day Celebrations 2007", 16-17 October 2007, New Delhi; He is the Hon'ble Union Minister of Agriculture, Government of India.
16. Suryanarayan (2009): "SRI technique gaining foothold in TN", as published in *Agriculture Today*, 5th January, 2009; He is a progressive farmer from the Madurai district of Tamil Nadu.
17. TG-RRNAR (2005): Report of the Task Group on Revamping and Refocusing of National Agricultural Research, Government of India, Planning Commission (Agriculture Division) January 2005; Chairman: Dr. M.S.Swaminathan (http://www.planningcommission.nic.in/aboutus/taskforce/tsk_nar.pdf).
18. Saqib, Mohd. and Debashis Chakraborty (2004), 'The Working of Agricultural Cooperatives in India: Is There Any Lesson to Learn from the Chinese Experience?', in Bibek Debroy and P.D. Kaushik (eds), *Energising Rural Development through Panchayats* (New Delhi: Academic Foundation), pp.187-209.
19. Debroy, Bibek (2004): 'Rural Development and Panchayats: An Introduction', in Bibek Debroy and P.D. Kaushik (eds), *Energising Rural Development through Panchayats* (New Delhi: Academic Foundation), pp. 21-34.
20. Debashis Chakraborty (2005): "Food Security in India—Policy challenges and responses", Publication of CHATHAM HOUSE, ASIA PROGRAMME (ASP BP 05/02), February 2005; The Author is with Rajiv Gandhi Institute for Contemporary Studies, New Delhi; also see http://www.chathamhouse.org.uk/files/3218_india_food_security.pdf;
21. S.D. Naik (2002): "Agenda for Agricultural Reforms", Tuesday, Jan 08, 2002, *Business Line* (The Hindu Publications)
22. Thomas, K.V. (2009): Professor K.V. Thomas who is the Minister of State for Agriculture in the Union Cabinet, while speaking at Thiruvananthapuram, June 14, 2009 (IANS).
23. Bhatia, H.L. (2006): *Public Finance* (25th Edition), Vikas Publishing House Pvt. Ltd., New Delhi, pp. 715.
24. Saseendran, S.A.; Singh, K.K.; Rathore, L.S.; Singh, S.V.; Sinha, S.K. (2000): "Effects of Climate Change on Rice Production in the Tropical Humid Climate of Kerala, India", *Climate Change*, 44, 495-514.
25. Agarwal, P.K. (2007): "Climate Change: Implications for Indian Agriculture", *Jaljeevan Sameeksha*, Vol. 22, 2007.
26. Chattopadhyay, N. (2008): "Climate Change and Food Security in India", presented at International Symposium on "Climate Change and Food Security in South Asia", 25-30, August 2008, Dhaka, Bangladesh.
27. Sidhu, H.S. (2002), 'Crisis in Agrarian Economy in Punjab: Some Urgent Steps', *Economic and Political Weekly*, 27, July 27-2 August, pp. 3132-38.

28. Chakraborty, Debashis (2004): "How is the State Functioning? A Comparative Analysis of Growth, Governance and Social Issues during the 8th and 9th Plan Period", in Bibek Debroy (ed.), *Agenda for Improving Governance* (New Delhi: Academic Foundation), pp. 49-104.
29. Alexander Muller (2009): "UN body calls for better farm, forestry practices" as published in *Business Standard*, New Delhi, 5 January 2009; he is the UN Food and Agriculture Organisation (FAO) Assistant Director-General.
30. Deshpande, R.S.; Venkatachalam, L. and Narayanamurthy, A. (2002): "Policies for Access, Equity and Equality: Physical resources and Human Resources", presented as a Theme paper in the 2nd International Conference on "Sustainable Agriculture, Water Resources Development & Earth Care Policies" organised by Bhoovigyan Vikas Foundation (An Earth Care Foundation), New Delhi on 18-20 December 2002.
31. National Association of Geographers India (NAGI)'s Annual Congress at Nagpur in January 2000.
32. Abdul Kalam, A.P.J. & Rajan,Y.S. (1998): *India-2020: A Vision For The New Millennium—Food, Agriculture and Processing* (Chapter-IV), Viking Penguin Books India (P) Ltd, New Delhi, India.
33. Report of the Core Group-V on Agricultural Resources Information System, constituted under the Standing Committee on Agriculture and Soils of the PC-NNRMS, Department of Agriculture & Cooperation and Department of Space, Government of India, 2000.
34. Madaswamy Moni (2004): "Informatics Blueprint for Integrated Water Resources Planning and Management at grassroots level: A Quintessential Requirement for Adaptation to Climate Change and Sustainable Agricultural Development in India", Valedictory Address delivered at the National Conference on "Climate Change and its Impact on Water Resources in India", organized by Department of Geography, School of Earth & Atmospheric Sciences, Madurai Kamaraj University, Madurai, Tamil Nadu (India), 15-17, December 2004.
35. Debashis Chakraborty (2003): "Corporate Participation in Marketing Activities: Scopes and Challenges to Indian Agriculture", in Bibek Debroy and Amir Ullah Khan (eds), *Enabling Agricultural Markets for the Small Indian Farmer* (New Delhi: Bookwell Publishers), pp. 185-234.
36. Madaswamy Moni (2008): "AGMARKNET—A National Knowledge Portal Linking Farmers to Domestic and Global Markets", Presented at the Annual Conference on "Agri-Business Management", organised by Centre for Management in Agriculture (Indian Institute of Ahmedabad and Centre for Public Policy (Bangalore), at Bangalore, from 25-27 September, 2008.
37. FAO (2000): FAO Report on "GENDER AND FOOD SECURITY: The role of information-STRATEGY FOR ACTION", Economic and Social Department, FAO, 2000.
38. Nagaraj, K. (2007): "Economic Reforms fails to boost Agriculture", said at the Seminar on the Impact of Economic Reforms in Agriculture", organised by Ramakrishna Mission Vivekananda College, Chennai (India), published in *The Hindu*, 6th September, 2007. Professor K. Nagaraj is with Madras Institute of Development Studies, Chennai.
39. Ravi, N. (2007): "Need for heavy investment in Public Infrastructure", said at the Seminar on the Impact of Economic Reforms in Agriculture", organised by Ramakrishna Mission Vivekananda College, Chennai (India), published in *The Hindu*, 6th September, 2007. N. Ravi is the Editor, The Hindu Newspaper of India.

40. Pulapre Balakrishnan (2007): "High Food prices in India—a Reason for the lag in Poverty Alleviation", said at the Seminar on the Impact of Economic Reforms in Agriculture", organised by Ramakrishna Mission Vivekananda College, Chennai (India), published in *The Hindu*, 6th September, 2007. Dr. Pulapre Balakrishnan is a Senior Fellow, Nehru Memorial Museum and Library, New Delhi.
41. Pratibha Patil (2008): "Better management in agriculture will help ease the current crisis", while inaugurating a three-day national-level 61st All India Commerce Conference, organised by Dhanwate National College, Nagpur (Maharashtra), as published in *Agriculture Today*, 29th December, 2008.
42. Madaswamy Moni (2008): "AGMARKNET—A National Knowledge Portal Linking Farmers to Domestic and Global Markets", presented at the First Annual Conference of the Indian Society of Agri-Business Management, in collaboration with Centre for Public Policy of Indian Institute of Management (IIM), Bangalore and Centre for Management in Agriculture of Indian Institute of Management (IIM), Ahmedabad, 25th to 27th September 2008.
43. Martin Brockerhoff (2000): "An Urbanizing World" in "Achieving Urban Food and Nutrition Security in the Developing World" edited by James L. Garrett and Marie T. Ruel, *Focus* 3, August 2000, International Food Policy Research Institute (IFPRI), USA.
44. Luc J.A. Mougeot (2000): "The Hidden Significance of Urban Agriculture", in "Achieving Urban Food and Nutrition Security in the Developing World" edited by James L. Garrett and Marie T. Ruel, *Focus* 3, August 2000, International Food Policy Research Institute (IFPRI), USA.
45. Cecilia Tacoli (2000): "Rural-Urban Interdependence" in "Achieving Urban Food and Nutrition Security in the Developing World" edited by James L. Garrett and Marie T. Ruel, *Focus* 3, August 2000, International Food Policy Research Institute (IFPRI), USA.
46. Vandana Shiva (2002): "Globalisation, Food Security and Sustainability" in *Sustainable Agriculture and Food Security* (Eds) Vandana and Gitanjali Bedi, pp. 11-70, Sage Publications, New Delhi, 2002.
47. Thomas Fuller (2008) in his article (printed in New York Times News Service), reprinted in *The Hindu* dated 2 May 2008.
48. Special Security Mechanism (SSM)—Measure for sudden surge of imports.
49. Prashant Goyal (2008): "Why do we need WTO farm pact?", published in *The Economic Times*, 21 June, 2008.
50. Manoj Panda and Ganesh Kumar, A. (2008): "Trade Liberalization, Poverty and Food Security in India", Indira Gandhi Institute of Development Research (IGIDR), Mumbai (India); http://www.igidr.ac.in/pdf/publication/WP-2008-013.pdf; presented at the 11th Annual Conference on Global Economic Analysis organised by Purdue University and UN-WIDER, Helsinki, Finland, June 12-14, 2008; eMail: manoj@igidr.ac.in and agk@igidr.ac.in
51. Juan Somavia (2008): "Time to rescue the real economy", published in *The Hindu*, 25 October, 2008.
52. Harish Khare (2008): "Time to align the Indian State", published in *The Hindu*, 25 October 2008.
53. Robert J. Samuelson (2008): "Good Times breed bad times, and vice versa", published in the *Economic Times*, 24 October 2008. © 2008, the Washington Post Writers Group.
54. Chandrajit Banerjee (2008): "Driving Growth in turbulent times", published in *The*

Economic Times, 24 October, 2008. The Author is Director General, CII, New Delhi.
55. Shefali Goradia (2008): "Financial turmoil and its tax implications", published in *The Economic Times*, 24 October, 2008.
56. Swaminathan, M.S. (2008): "Towards the ideal of a hunger-free India", published in *The Hindu*, 2nd October, 2008.
57. "Gandhi District": It is defined as one where no one is below poverty line and no one goes to bed hungry, but because of doles but because of opportunities for sustainable livelihoods.
58. Peter, K.V. (2008): Suggestions given on the earlier version of this Draft by Dr. K. V. Peter, Former Vice-Chancellor (Kerala Agricultural University), and presently Director, World Noni Research Foundations, Chennai; email: kvptr@yahoo.com.
59. Kini, M.D. (2005): "India Empowered" published in http://community.expressindia.com
60. IFRPI (2006): "Information and Communication Technologies for Development and Poverty Reduction: The Potential of Telecommunications", edited by Maximo Torero and Joachim von Braun and published by the Johns Hopkins University Press (USA), March 2006; also see the website (http://www.ifpri.org). IFPRI Forum March 2006.
61. Manuela Ferro, David Rosenblatt and Nicholas Stern (2002): *Policies for Pro-Poor Growth in India*, Cornell University (USA), April 19-20, 2002;
62. Prajapati Trivedi (2008): "Trickle-Down Accountability" in "gfiles inside the government", Vol. 1, Issue 10, January 2008.

9

Globalisation of Food Prices

GOPAL KRISHAN

RENTING SPACES

A new kind of globalisation is rewriting the territorial limits and sovereignty of individual countries. Imagine China looking for land around to contract in Latin America and Africa to produce the kind and amount of food its thriving population is aspiring for. It has an eye on its neighbour Kazakhstan for the same reason. China's Fuhua Group has plans to invest no less than US$ 4 billion in Philippines to secure the sources of its food supply.

South Korea is making similar moves. Natural Resource Development Company Daewoo Logistics has gone for a lease of 99 years with the distant Madagascar to grow oil palms and corn. Involved therein is no less than one million hectares of agricultural land.

Likewise, Saudi Arabia has invested US$ 4 billion on half-a-million hectares of farmland in Indonesia. It has a similar stake in Pakistan. The country is keen on Ukraine as well. With similar considerations, Qatar has given US$ one million development fund to Vietnam, primarily to promote its agricultural export base.

Certainly most parts of the world today are running out of arable land. Brazil, of course, has a reserve of at least 70 million hectares to plough. Russia, Kazakhstan, and Ukraine are also in a comfortable position on this count. European Bank for Reconstruction and Development is searching ways to facilitate reclamation of agricultural land in these countries. Russia is said to be having 16 per cent of world's arable land but its contribution to the food basket is only 6 per cent.

QUESTION OF FOOD SECURITY

Underlying such developments is the critically growing imbalance between the regular increase in demand for food in quantity and variety and its scarce, fluctuating and uneven supply. This got manifested in recent agflation. June 2008 witnessed a peak in global food prices. The previous three years had marked a price rise by 80 per cent. Rice, wheat and corn, in that order, were noted for the highest price increases. The developing countries were the worst hit.

The surge in food prices pushed millions in the world to the existing pool of the poor. Food First Information and Action Network informs that the number of chronically malnourished, which had increased from 823 million in mid-1990s to 843 million in 2006, reached the 900 million mark in 2009. The low income countries were now paying two times the cost of imported food as compared to what they were doing in 2007.

In this light, it is not difficult to understand the eruption of food riots that took place in 2008 in a number of countries like Haiti, Mozambique, Senegal, Egypt, Indonesia, Yemen, and Bangladesh, to name some. Farming was carried out under the protection of armed guards in ethnic-conflict ridden, post-election Kenya to meet the challenge of food crisis. In Peru, army baked bread for the people at large.

Food and Agriculture Organisation took a note of serious food crisis in as many as 36 countries, among which 21 belonged to Africa. The problem was more acute in countries under authoritarian regimes. After all, democracies do not face famines, as Sen (1981) confirms.

In any case, it was hard to anticipate that the early years of the twenty-first century will witness such a scenario, especially when the race between the field productivity and human fertility had decisively gone in favour of the former for the last about half a century. Of course, the world population had increased from nearly one billion in 1798, when Malthus wrote his classic Essay on the Principle of Population, to 6.8 billion in 2009. He had forewarned that the world would run short of food supply, leading to hunger and famine by the middle of 19th century. This did not happen, by and large. Thanks to development of modern agriculture over large parts of the new world. In 1968, Paul R. Ehrlich, in his book *Population Bomb*, also warned on famines in 1970s and 1980s. Mercifully, the world escaped such calamities. During 1950-1984, the Green Revolution was instrumental in increasing the world food supply by 250 per cent and saving the lives of no less than one billion people (Yunus, 2009, p.151). Notably the prices of rice and wheat marked a sharp decline by one-third from their peak in 1975, in the wake of first world oil crisis.

But by a sharp turn of events, the early years of the twenty-first century experienced a phenomenal rise in food prices, as mentioned above. Only a few could believe that Malthus would resurrect himself, in the manner of speaking. The basic human right to food was seen as having come under threat.

PROFUSION OF LITERATURE

A natural response to the concern for the emerged situation world over was production in plenty of literature on the theme. A spate of writings on the food crisis, surging food prices and food riots followed. Dozens of books, hundreds of articles in journals and magazines and millions of entries on the internet are available for any sensitive soul, research mind or policy maker to browse. A historical perspective of the world food crisis is provided by McMachael (2009) on internet. He finds a similarity of his argument with the thesis propounded by George (1977) in her book, *How the Other Half Dies: The Real Reason for World Hunger*. He observes that the present food crisis, like the one in 1975, has its roots in the colonial phase of world history and it has now been triggered by the neo-liberal capitalist development. A recent book, *Food Inc* edited by Weber (2009) informs us about the dynamics by which the industrial food is making us richer, fatter and poorer. Wilson (2008) expresses a similar concern in his book, *The Last Bite: Is the World Food System Collapsing*? Patel's (2007) book, *Stuffed and Starved: Hidden Battle for World Food System* highlights the contrast between excess food consumption in the developed world *vis-à-vis* its scarcity in its developing counterpart. Robert's (2009) book, *The End of Food*, is a similar treatise on food politics. The book, *Hungry Planet* by Menzel and D'Alusio (2005), also presents a grim scenario as emerging on the food front. All this is listed just as a miniscule sample of the representative writings on the world food wall. There is much more for any curious mind to pursue on the theme.

A longer term review reveals that the focus of food studies has been evolving over the years since the Second World War. The sequence of concerns was from food availability through production or import, to food access in the given context of its affordability, to food consumption in terms of overnutrition or undernourishment, and then to food security since mid-seventies. Food and Agriculture Organisation (2002) defines food security as a condition when all people, at all times, have physical, social and economic access to sufficient, safe and nutritious food to meet their dietary needs and food preferences for an active and healthy life. This is now envisioned as a basic human right.

Today the world has nearly a billion souls who are food insecure. The highest incidence of such insecurity is in Sub-Saharan Africa but South Asia and East Asia carry the largest number of people in this category. Ironical is it that virtually all the agricultural based countries are net importer of food and food insecurity is concentrated in rural areas where food is produced (World Development Report, 2008, p. 95). Added to this is the hard fact that over one billion overnourished obese people today outnumber the undernourished unfortunate one. Overstuffing and starvation are coexisting in this unequal world.

AN EXPLANATORY NOTE

Who is responsible for such a worrisome state of affairs? Mutual accusations are natural for the humans. The developed and developing countries are pointing fingers at each other for the situation. United States believes that the rising demand for food, not only cereals but also meat, poultry and dairy products, by the fast widening base of the middle class in countries like China, India and Brazil is making a much bigger bite at the food basket of the world. On the other hand, the developing countries blame the developed ones for consuming meat and poultry products at a fast increasing pace. The per capita annual consumption of chicken in the United States is reported as having gone up from 20 kilograms in 1980 to 40 kilograms today and a similar trend is observed in the case of beef and pork. Trends in other developed countries are no different.

The production of items like beef, pork and poultry puts a heavy demand on cereals. The conversion ratio of cereals to beef is 7:1, to pork 4:1 and to poultry 2:1. A much hidden consumption of cereals is involved when the food bowl of a society is composed of meat of different variety in an ever increasing quantity.

This factor is only a part of explanation. Most critical is the fact that both food and oil crises have decided to go in tandem with each other. This has impelled many technologically advanced countries to go in for production of ethanol as a biofuel from crops like corn and sugarcane. United States is a ready example of the sort. For years, it used only 5 per cent of its corn production for extraction of ethanol but by the end of 2008, its farms were shipping more than one-third of this crop (one-eighth of the global supply) to ethanol plants (Robert, 2009, p. 325). There is much less corn now to go around for the needy humans in food deficit countries of the world.

The recent big hike in the oil price was not without other fallouts too. It adversely affected the manufacturing and price of fertilizers and also raised the transport cost of agricultural products, among other things. The price tag on the food items naturally experienced an upward revision.

Meanwhile the Green Revolution in developing countries had reached a plateau level under the impact of rising cost of inputs. Yields had started stagnating at the level achieved. On the other hand, liberal subsidies to agriculture in developed countries were blunting any competitive edge of export of agricultural products from developing countries. This got manifest in an increase last year by 11 per cent in agricultural production of the developed world as against only one per cent in the developing one. The terms of trade under the World Trade Organisation regime have evidently tilted in favour of the former. Spending on farming as a share of total public spending in developing countries fell by half between 1980 and 2004 (*Economist*, 2008).

In addition, the reduced allocations to agriculture added to the misery index of agriculture. In 1980, agricultural projects received 30 per cent of the World Bank loans. By 2007, this figure had come down to only 12 per cent. Likewise, in individual countries, which reaped benefits of the Green Revolution, there was complacency on agricultural front, leading to a much reduced allocation to this sector.

Any scarcity situation is generative of excessive holding back or hoarding. To preempt any crisis at home, 40 countries opted to curb exports of their surplus grain production. Prominent among these were Thailand, India, Vietnam, Argentina and Brazil. Speculators also were not to be left behind. The international investors were finding it more lucrative to go in for futures in food or oil or gold than in industrial stocks or dollars. The price curve on the food chart maintained its upward trend. After all, elasticity of demand for food is universally low.

Bad weather had its own additive effect. Two successive droughts in major wheat exporting countries such as Australia and Canada, added fuel to the brewing panic. Recent droughts in wheat belt of Northern China and rice surplus zone of Northwestern India have been equally worrisome. No less was the role of floods in the United States in pulling down the quantum of its corn production in 2008. There is a growing fear that in the coming years, as agriculture will be increasingly threatened by climate warming, demand for food will be gravely outstripped by its supply.

Only a statistical scan will put things in perspective. The world cereal production of wheat, rice, corn, barley and sorghum increased by 17 per cent from around 1.8 billion tonnes in 2002 to over 2.1 billion tonnes in 2007. Meanwhile the world population grew by only 7 per cent and per capita income marked a rise by 20 per cent. The skyrocketing of food prices by 150 per cent during this quinquennium has been most staggering. Putting things together, it seems that the problem does not lie in shortage of food but in its price being on an accelerator. There is lack of access of the poor to food despite its availability.

RESURGENCE OF FOOD PRICES

After some descent from their peak in June 2008, the food prices have again resumed their upward trend. Between December 2008 and June 2009, the food price index rebounded by one-third (*Economist*, 2009). This is something puzzling as the year 2008-09 recorded the highest ever cereal production of 2.2 billion tonnes. There was another contradiction as well. While the price of cereals, which are the staple food in most of the developing countries, recorded a rise, the price of meat, which is the major platter of the developed world, has been regularly declining. How do we explain this?

Reasons are both cyclical and secular. Among the cyclical factors, the return of the poor to the market, in large numbers, following the decline in food prices after June 2008 is cited as one. Also with a fall in the oil price and transport costs, the developing countries were inclined to import food from any available source to replenish their dried up reserves. This increased demand for food was sure to impact on the price. An additional factor could be a further rise in consumption of meat with a decline in its price in the developed world, indirectly impinging on the use of cereals. The contribution of secular factors was no less critical. A continuation of high rates of population growth in developing countries, a rapid pace of their urbanisation, usurping vast stretches of agricultural land, and associated shift from mainly cereals to rising consumption of meat items, all combined together to intensify pressure on food in both national and international markets. The outcome was inevitable.

One cannot miss observing a silver lining on the horizon of otherwise worrisome food front. The rising food prices seem to have created a favourable climate for obtaining higher yields in agricultural countries, thereby improving the living conditions of the farmers. The conversion of opium fields to wheat lands in Afghanistan and of cocaine belt to rice farms in Bolivia is also to be adjudged as a happy development. The rising food prices are also a wake call for the governments to mend their agricultural fences for ensuring food security to their people. After all, food crisis weakens any nation state and opens a gate for interference in its affairs by external providers.

The experience of recent years demonstrates how the food prices are interlinked with non-agricultural sector. May it be the price of oil or components of share markets or priority shifts in development investment or tantrums of weather all impinge on prices of food. All these have a global reach and their operations globalise the food prices at large.

Timely and effective government intervention is always a sure recipe for controlling any abnormal rise in food prices. This is what happened in India which remained largely insulated from the skyrocketing prices of food at the global level (Chand, 2008). An all out effort by the government to regulate oil and fertiliser prices at reasonable levels was effective in checking any undue rise in food prices. Equally important was the role of an uninterrupted increase in food production of the country over the years.

CUBA: A SUCCESS STORY

On such a world map of food scarcity in overall terms, there is a case of Cuba which coped with this difficult challenge with a remarkable success (Steffen, 2007, p. 61). The collapse of the former Soviet Union was an economic disaster for the country. Preferential imports of agrochemicals as also the export of sugar were the first casualty. Equally problematic for it was the embargo imposed by the United States.

Cuba decided to go in a big way to bring under cultivation any available arable land, including in urban places, and to revert back to the traditional organic farming of mixed livestock-crop kind. Urban farming emerged as a prominent dimension of its agricultural system. Several vacant plots in the national capital of Havana were brought under tractor and today 41 per cent of the city area is under crops, raising 51 per cent of the country's vegetable requirements. Whenever there is an innovative response to a challenge, there is birth of a success story.

Some additional facts make an interesting reading. Hardly a century ago, Paris produced about 100,000 tonnes of food, part of which was exported to London. Singapore raises a significant amount of food from its city farms. Green Roofs on Chicago's City Hall are a grand source of garden crops. Time is not far when multi-tiered artificially created vertical land will become a necessity to produce additional food to meet the increasing and varying demand of the humankind at large.

REINVENTING AGRICULTURAL GEOGRAPHY

What is the message of this essay for Agricultural Geography? An answer to this question requires a review of the evolution and present status of this branch of our discipline. Though the study of agriculture in regional perspective or as specific to different parts of the world has a long, indefinite history, it was towards the closing decades of the 18th century that a systematic analysis of land use, cropping pattern and agricultural practices, as influenced by environmental conditions, started taking shape. The colonial interests led to a focus on the study of world distribution of crops and their special relevance to the imperial powers on the one hand, and also on promotion of plantation agriculture on newly reclaimed lands in their colonised territories and international trade, on the other. By the end of 19th century, such a thrust in Agricultural Geography was taken over by a tendency to delineate crop or agricultural regions.

The post First World War Agricultural Geography got interested in detailed land use surveys and typologies of agricultural systems of the world. Subsequently, during the post Second World War phase, the issues of food security, green revolution and environmental degradation drew special attention (Shafi, 2006). The transitions in food systems, as linked to specific stages of development, also emerged as a point of enquiry.

Agricultural Geography came under the influence of a new wave during the 1980s when political economy dimension of agriculture was highlighted. A distinction was made between capitalist agriculture as governed by market forces and socialist agriculture which aimed at crop specialisation at micro-level and food self-sufficiency at regional level, within the context of a nation state, such as the former Soviet Union.

As an offshoot of such developments was the emergence of agro-food geography, which was concerned with the issue of food provision through a direct link among the field produce, its processing industries and the retailing through chain stores. Winter (2003) rightly observes that there was a time, not long ago, when research in the geography of agriculture was concerned about food merely as a raw commodity; now the focus was shifting from production to consumption. A gap in research was getting filled.

The most recent development is in favour of understanding the lineaments of agricultural change under the impact of globalisation, making a surge since 1990s. The role of World Trade Organisation, constituted in 1995, as an influencing factor has been of a special point of study. Along with, the idea of sustainable agriculture was gaining ground, leading to promotion of organic farming, farm forestry and wasteland development. These are now the frequent themes adopted for deliberation at the national and international conferences.

But all this is taking time to enter into the text books and teaching of Agricultural Geography. The issue of food security and that of carrying capacity in terms of food deficit or surplus in different areas may find an occasional mention but discussion on the critical question of food prices is still amiss. What ultimately matters to the people is the price they are to pay for their daily food and herein lies the scope for an extended discourse in Agricultural Geography.

Thus, Agricultural Geography, in its applied version, is obliged to suggest ways to ensure stability of food prices. It may recommend region specific strategies for not only producing food in adequate quantity and of requisite quality and variety but also promising its availability and affordability. A new world order for food is to be in place. It is not to confine its scope merely to the issues of international trade and agricultural subsidies but also to matters relating to conversion of food into non-food items like ethanol and that of cereals into non-vegetarian products. Questions pertaining to harmony between production of food and capacity of nature at local level, hybridisation of cuisines across regions, and food as a human right at large may also be rated as critical for research and action in our fast globalising world.

REFERENCES

Chand, Ramesh (2008): "The global food crisis: Causes, severity and outlook", *Economic and Political Weekly*, Vol. 43 (26-27), pp. 115-122.

Ehrlich, Paul R. (1968): *Population Bomb*. Ballantine Books, New York.

Food and Agriculture Organisation (2002): *The State of Food Insecurity in the World*. Rome.

George, Susan (1977): *How the Other Half Dies, The Real Reason for World Hunger*. N.S. Allenheld, Osmun & G., Montclair, New Jersey.

Malthus, Thomas R. (1798): *Essay on the Principle of Population*. Kessinger Publishing, Whitefish, Montana.

McMachael, Philip (2009): *The World Food Crisis in Historical Perspective*. Internet.

Menzel, Peter and Faith D'Aluisio (2005): *Hungry Planet*. Ten Speed Press, Berkeley.

Patel, Raj (2007): *Stuffed and Starved, The Hidden Battle for the World Food System*. Portobello, London.

Robert, Paul (2009): *The End of Food*. Mariner Books, Boston.

Sen, Amartya Kumar (1981): *Poverty and Famines, An Essay on Entitlement and Deprivation*. Oxford University Press, New York.

Shafi, Mohammad (2006): *Agricultural Geography*. Dorling Kindersley, New Delhi.

Steffen, Alex (2007): *World Changing*. Abrahams, New York.

Weber, Karl Ed. (2009): *Food, Inc.*, Public Affairs, New York.

Wilson, Bee (2008): *The Last Bite, Is the World Food System Collapsing*. Miffin, Houghton.

Winter, Michael (2003): "Geographies of food, agrofood geographies—making reconnection", *Progress in Human Geography*, Vol. 27 (4), pp. 505-513.

World Bank (2008): *World Development Report, Agriculture for Development*. Washington, D.C.

Yunus, Muhammad (2009): "The financial crisis and world hunger" in Karl Weber, ed. *Food, Inc.*, Public Affairs, New York.

Economist (2009): July 4-10

Economist (2008): April 17-23.

10

Livelihood Security Concern in India: Development and Sustainability

K. V. RAMAN

INTRODUCTION

"Sustainable livelihoods", which is the theme of this paper, cover a whole range of sustainable paradigms 'sustainable lifestyles', 'sustainable agriculture', 'sustainable community', 'sustainable economy' etc. The dictionary meaning of sustainability connotes 'keeping an effort going continuously' or 'the ability to last and keeping from falling'. In either case, the concept of sustainability has an element of time span, an infinite time span. Further it is recognized that sustainability is not the end result, but a process of change, concomitant with the current and future concerns. The challenge to respond to the needs of those living in poverty, the desire to help them achieve what is lacking by building on what they have, and the commitment to make it happen, are the core elements of a value system that must be at the centre of promoting sustainable livelihoods. Its primary purpose should be directed towards eradication of poverty.

Drawing on the discussion and writings of Robert Chambers and Gordon Conway, IDS has adopted the following definition: "A livelihood comprises the capabilities, assests (including both material and social resources) and activities required for a means of living. A livelihood is sustainable when it can cope with and recover from stresses and shocks, maintain or enhance its capabilities and assets, while not undermining the natural resource base."

The Brundtland Commission in 1987, introduced Sustainable Livelihoods (SL) in terms of resource ownership and access, basic needs and livelihood security, especially in rural areas. The 1992 United Nations Conference on Environment and Development, in Agenda 21, noted the integrative power of the concept, which offers a way of linking socio-economic and ecological policy considerations in a cohesive policy-relevant structure. The Social Summit linked sustainable livelihoods explicitly to full employment, and the Beijing Platform re-emphasized the importance of women's livelihoods to successful development. Conceptually, livelihoods connote the means, activities, entitlements and assets by which people make a living. Assets are not only natural/biological (i.e. land, water, common property resources, flora, fauna) but also social and political (i.e. community, family, social networks, participation, empowerment human knowledge and creation of skills) and physical (material infrastructure).

Kline (1993) defines a 'sustainable community' in terms of economic security, ecological integrity and empowerment with responsibility. While 'vital signs' like clean water, clean air, safe neighbourhood, jobs, etc., are essential, sustainable communities can develop only if they integrate economic security, ecological integrity, and empowerment with responsibility, with these vital signs.

Sustainable development depends largely on renewable natural resources of water, soil, sunlight, communities of plants and animals. The utility, or the potential of producing goods and services of these natural resources have to be continued if human settlements have to avoid total destruction over time. The poor communities have assets of the basic natural resources that either directly belong to them or the communities in which they live. Assessment by the concerned of the assets, entitlements, the physical material and intellectual resources available to utilize them, should be the basis for the design and implementation of Sustainable Livelihood Programmes.

Food is so basic to human well-being that sustainable agriculture is the oldest and best studied of all managed ecosystems. Sustainable livelihoods especially of the rural population, should, therefore, envisage sustainable development of agriculture by widening employment opportunities, increasing income, improving health and enhancing the quality of life. It is the firm conviction of the author that a systematically structured growth-oriented approach to sustainable agricultural development should form the basis of 'sustainable livelihood opportunities'. Sustainable development in the rural areas can take place only if there is attention paid to sustainable agriculture and the paper will constantly refer to this aspect of development.

Scoones (2000) recognized five key elements as directly related to sustainable livelihoods, the first three focusing on livelihoods linking concerns over work, employment, poverty reduction, well-being and capabilities, and the last two adding the sustainability dimension.

1. Creation of a gainful employment for a certain portion of the year—either on-farm or off-farm, so that they get an economic income to meet their daily requirements of food and other expenses.
2. Poverty reduction based on income or consumption levels, which addresses issues of poverty and inequality.
3. Well-being and capabilities which encompasses far more than the material concerns of food intake or income. This will include such diverse factors as self-esteem, security, happiness, stress, empowerment, etc.
4. Livelihood adaptation, vulnerability and resilience which includes the ability to be able to cope with and recover from stresses and shocks,

coping with temporary adjustments in the face of change or adapt to longer term shifts in livelihood strategies.

5. Natural resource base sustainability.

The concept of sustainable livelihoods is a composite of many ideas and interests, the coming together of a number of different strands. No neat, simple algorithm for objectively measuring sustainable livelihoods is possible, as has been discussed later in the text.

REVIEW OF THE CURRENT STATUS AND ARISING ISSUES OF CONCERN

Government of India's Approaches to the Problem

The Government of India, in its policy proclamation, entitled 'The National Agenda for Governance' has given a high priority to the elimination of the hunger, and has declared "We will ensure food security for all, create a hunger-free India in the next five years." This avowed statement might be a tall order, given the time span specified. However, planning and development efforts in India have always concentrated on economic improvement with social stability. Towards the objective of building a Welfare State, and within the broad framework of the Five Year Plans, the various projects and schemes have addressed the issues of poverty elimination, economic and industrial growth, agricultural improvement and employment generation. For this purpose, new institutional structures have been developed, or where they existed, have been strengthened and social objectives reinforced. It has to be recognized that the local people cannot be divorced from the social structures of which they are a part. The logical approach for development planners is to deal intelligently with existing community structures, including those for handling production and resource management issues. The National Agricultural Policy recognizes the need for providing additional employment opportunities in the rural sector as one of the primary strategies for poverty alleviation.

Poverty alleviation and employment generation schemes have been in operation for several years. From April 1999, several schemes that were operating have been integrated into the Swarnajayanti Swarozgar Yojana. It is conceived as a holistic programme of micro-enterprises covering all aspects of self-employment. The objective is to provide the rural poor with income generating assets, through a mix of bank credits and government subsidy. While the scheme is conceptually very good, proper implementation of the programme will be dependent on the grassroots level planning and the effective utilization of the natural resources of the area.

Fifty years of development experience in our country have yielded some valuable and critical lessons as indicated below:

1. Macro-economic stability is an essential prerequisite for achieving growth needed for development;

2. In largely agrarian societies like India, economic growth should ensure employment generation;
3. Growth does not trickle down; development should address human needs directly;
4. No one policy will trigger development a comprehensive approach is needed;
5. The development orientation should be sustainable; and
6. Sustained development should be rooted in processes that are socially inclusive and responsive to changing circumstances, where local empowerment and institutions matter.

It has further been demonstrated that increasing food production globally or even nationally will not solve the problem of poverty and malnutrition, but agricultural development in regions where poverty is predominantly local will help. The United Nations Hot Springs Conference, as far back as 1943, proclaimed "The first cause of hunger and malnutrition is poverty; and the first cause of poverty is lack of work." Hence the statement of Mahatma Gandhi: "To the poor and hungry, God is bread and appears in the promise of work." No discussion on livelihood opportunities will, therefore, be complete without an analysis of productive employment opportunities. The problem of eliminating hunger, reducing poverty, enhancing livelihood opportunities and improving the quality of life requires the understanding, inventiveness, and interaction of farmers, industrialists, agricultural scientists, educators, environmentalists, health care workers, and policymakers, who share a commitment to development and change.

Sustainable Livelihoods through Rural Employment

About seventy per cent of the 1006 million people in India live in the rural areas and derive their livelihoods directly or indirectly from the 329 million hectares of land resources. Small and marginal farmers dominate Indian agriculture. Of the total number of farming families, more than 78 per cent are small and marginal with less than two hectares of farming land. They cultivate about 32 per cent of the arable land. There are over 111 million cultivators, who are further supported by over 75 million-landless workers. Agriculture will be the primary absorber of this workforce, and this situation is not likely to change much in the foreseeable future. The availability of employment in this important sector throughout the year is dismally poor. Except in about 53.5 million hectares of the irrigated arable land, where the conditions may be marginally better, 90 mha of rainfed arable lands hardly provides 100 days of employment in the year. It is interesting to note that this land area still "produces 90 million tonnes of fob grains out of about 200+ million tonnes that we produce; however, since the activity is highly seasonal, the availability of on-farm work is irregular and uncertain.

It has been estimated that at the national level, the average days worked per adult wage earner in the "agriculture wage work is 137 (145 for male and 24 for female). This figure varies very widely depending on the region and the nature of agriculture that is practised. Thus, in the arid and semi-arid regions with limited rainfall, the work available is highly seasonal and is limited in extent. For example, in Rajasthan, agricultural work is available only for 53 days in a year, while it is about 190 days in the North-East Region. Since crop-based agriculture alone cannot support them, it is necessary for agricultural labour to look for additional income-generating opportunities. Multiple livelihood opportunities, if developed at the farm/community level, help to increase the number of employment days, diversify activities, enhance total income and minimize risks. This is especially true for women who perform multiple tasks at the farm level.

Livelihood security will have to be provided to this huge workforce. The ability to pursue different livelihood strategies is dependent on the basic material and socially tangible and intangible assets that people have in their possession. These include (a) Natural capital of soil, water, air, genetic resources, etc., and environmental services (hydrological cycle, pollution sinks, etc., from which resource flows and services useful for livelihoods are derived, (b) Economic or financial capital including cash, credit/debt, savings, and other economic assets, as well as basic infrastructure and production equipment and technologies which are essential for the pursuit of any livelihood strategy, (c) Human capital—the skills, knowledge, ability to labour and good health and physical capability important for the successful pursuit of different livelihood strategies, and (d) Social capital or the social resources upon which people draw when pursuing different livelihood strategies requiring coordinated actions. In order to create livelihoods, therefore, people must combine the 'capital' endowments that they have access to and control over.

Since this workforce still depends on land and the productivity of the soil that they farm, no attempt at solving rural unemployment can ignore arresting deterioration of the land resource. Since land and water form the basic natural resources, the system has to integrate their development for optimal productivity. In an analysis of youth unemployment in India, Chadha (2000) presents data to show that in rural India, self-employment and casual labour, rather than salaried jobs which is the major employment pattern in urban areas, are the only major avenues of employment, especially for those in the job-seeking age group of 15-29. Planning for what combinations are most appropriate in a particular site presents major challenges. Only a rationally integrated agrarian participation and involvement can identify site-specific problems and develop solutions.

The Eighth Five Year Plan document identified the need to generate approximately 100 million new jobs for the period 1991-2000 to ensure full employment for all based on the number of unemployed at that time and the increments to the labour force during the decade. This meant approximately ten million new livelihoods per year. Impetus was, therefore, provided for creation of a large number of additional jobs both in the on-farm and non-farm activities. However the Government of India's Economic Review recognizes that not more than six million additional workers could be absorbed per year, increasing thus the number of unemployed, especially in the rural sector.

The question is "Where can we create these additional livelihood opportunities?" On-farm employment can be generated only by increasing agricultural activities through increasing cropping intensities, crop diversification, development of horticulture including fruits, vegetables and flowers, as well as from investments in soil and water conservation on watershed-based development programmes. The Vision 2020 document of the Ministry of Agriculture of the Government of India, which the author had the privilege of developing, envisages not only increasing the agricultural production potential but also generating employment.

In his paper on "Sustainable Rural Livelihoods: The Challenge of the Decade", Vijay Mahajan (2000) details some of the activities that would be needed to generate additional livelihoods in the rural non-farm sector (RNFS). Apart from agriculture, allied activities such as dairying, poultry, fisheries, horticulture, floriculture, plantations, etc., provide the basis for RNFS livelihoods in processing, manufacture, storage, distribution, transport and trade. Forests, specially agro-forestry and social forestry, also add to this list, even though timber and timber-based forest produce have declined in quantity. Mining, quarrying and support services such as farm equipment manufacture, supply and repair services are emerging as important activities.

Population Dynamics

India's population, which has already passed the one billion mark in last May, is poised to increase to 1646 million by 2051. This change in the total population will also introduce changes in the demographic age distribution, which will have considerable influence in planning for development. The Population Foundation of India has done a detailed exercise of not only estimating the total population for the next several decades, but also of categorizing them by age, gender, regions, etc. Since the age profile will be directly relevant to employment opportunities, the relevant information is summarized.

One consequence of the decline in fertility will be that the child population will decline and stabilize around 313 million in 2051. This will largely be reflected in the children of the younger age group of 0-4. However an important consequence will be in the children of the school going age group of 5-14; while their percentages may decline, in absolute numbers, this will still be very large. Providing for education and health care of this group, who will be the important leader group in the future, will be another challenge. This will require not only the will to handle the problem but the resources to provide the services.

The most significant increase will be noticed in the working age group of 15-64. The population will increase from 546.1 million in 1996 to 1089.5 million in 2051. Most of them will be in the labour market. Providing employment to such a huge population will be the biggest challenge India will face in the first half of this century. Very significant increase will also take place in the old age population, i.e. in the age group of 65 and over. Their number will increase more than six times from 39.9 million in 1996 (or 43% of the population) to 243.5 million (14.8% of the population). Providing old-age security, in addition, utilizing productively those who are able bodied and in good physical and mental health will be another challenge.

Migration and Urbanization

The demographic distribution pattern between the urban and rural areas, is undergoing a major change all over the world with the people moving from the rural areas and conclaves, to urban areas and urban fringes. In 1995, 46 per cent of the worlds population lived in urban areas. Just after 2000, and for the first time in history, the number of urban dwellers will outnumber the rural population. By 2030, three out of every five persons in the world will be living in cities. In India, the situation will record an even more dramatic change. By 2015, more cities will join the group of cities with a population greater than 10 million, and the number of cities with a population of one million will increase to 29; one estimate puts it at 43. Urbanization is by far the most important social transformation of our times. The consequence of this will be that there will be more charge and pressure for goods and services—more employment and livelihood opportunities will be demanded. This will be especially significant in the developing countries like ours, where we will be faced with the extreme situation of facing not only rural poverty and unemployment, but also the problems of urban slums and their life-styles.

Sustainable Growth Needed

Growth, particularly in the agriculture sector, reduces poverty. But it does not always trickle down to all the poor. Sustainable livelihoods can be ensured only by sustainable growth, which is technologically sound, ecologically compatible, environmentally friendly, economically viable and socially acceptable. For such sustainable growth, in order to be:

(a) *Technologically sound*: improvements in production and productivity should flow from the application of modern and emerging areas of science and technology to finding relevant solutions to problems;

(b) *Ecologically compatible*: will require concern for biodiversity, crop compatibility and climate suitability;

(c) *Environmentally friendly*: will mean conservation and optimal use of the basic natural resources soil and water;

(d) *Economically viable*: will mean focusing: on multiple income-generating activities like choice of crops, with comparative advantage and ready market value, value addition and processing; and

(e) *Socially acceptable*: should be growth with equity that ensures enhanced entitlement and empowerment of resource poor people, especially women and those belonging to the weaker and unreached sections of the community.

Some activities like horticulture and animal husbandry, including aquaculture when practised in common property resources, serve both growth and equity objectives. Such activities are suitable for small farmers and women, for whom they provide additional in come and employment.

Indexing Sustainable Livelihoods

Economists have a singular advantage of having a single measurable indicator like Gross National Product (GNP) to measure progress and monitor changes in progress. Although the measurement of this value by itself may have its restrictions, limitations and lacunae, it reflects a system of checks and balances that will help to develop policy formulations at the macro-level. However to measure 'sustainable livelihoods', or for that matter even 'sustainable development', no single or compounded measurable quantitative parameter is available. However, certain estimates for hunger-free livelihoods and improvements in the quality of life can be made.

Indicators of 'Quality of Life'

- High self-esteem and a sense of fulfilment
- Creativity and enlightenment
- Leadership and vision
- Access to skills, information and resources
- Participation in social and public affairs
- Health, safety and identity
- Command over and access to key goods and services

As has been indicated earlier in the discussion, quantifiable parameters like income, employment, poverty estimates, access to food and clean drinking water, environmental sanitation and hygiene, access to common property resources, literacy, skill-related training, etc., have to be integrated with these quality indicators to have an assessment of the impact of programmes addressing sustainable livelihoods.

WTO Commitments

Under the WTO agreements of which India is a signatory, Quantitative Restrictions (QR) will have to go by April 2001. There are a number of safeguards that are available for member countries to ensure that their trade and domestic social structure is totally disrupted by these concessions. Under Article 6.1 of the

Agreement for Agriculture, these include the "Green" and "Blue" Boxes, which the participating countries can avail of before the removal of QRs come into effect. The "Green Box" includes policies that provide services or benefits to the farming community, stockholding for food security, domestic food aid, and investment subsidies and agricultural input subsidies for low income and resource poor families. The provisions under the "Blue Box" include direct payments to farmers under production-limiting programmes. Further it is also possible to introduce high tariff barriers by increasing import duties. Industrialized nations have availed of these facilities fully and have prepared themselves for the aftermath of the opening up of the global trade.

In our country, we have not been able to provide such support to farming families; in other words, the preparatory precautionary steps that we should have undertaken when we became signatories to such an important trade agreement, is rather low. Part of this may be due to the improper understanding of the entire gamut of implications of some of the proposals; part of it may be due to our fragile political system. Consequently, the apprehension that the removal of the Quantitative Restrictions will further endanger the livelihood systems of poor farm families due to uneven competition is rather real. Seventy per cent of our populations derive their livelihoods from crop and animal husbandry, forestry and agro-forestry, inland and marine fisheries, and agro-processing and agribusiness. Eighty per cent of our farmers belong to small and marginal category.

Dr. M.S. Swaminathan emphasizes that when the WTO agreement is reviewed this year, it is essential that we press for a "Livelihood Box", that would allow us to impose quantitative restrictions. This must be done wherever there is a clear evidence that such imports will kill livelihood opportunities for small and marginal farmers and landless agricultural labour or those involved in small scale agro-processing or agribusiness activities.

POSSIBLE APPROACHES FOR SOLUTIONS

How to Provide Multiple Livelihood Opportunities

All efforts in overcoming poverty at the microlevel the household has to be essentially by the committed efforts of the people themselves, though assisted by community at large. Since most of the ultra-poor are either landless workers or people with very small land holdings that are not economically viable, income enhancement can arise only through, multiple livelihood opportunities. These include:

(a) Primary value addition of commodities at the household level like production of semi-processed foods, pickle making, sun drying and packaging, etc.

(b) Utilization of locally available resources like paddy-straw for mushroom growing, sericulture, goat rearing, dairying and milk production, backyard poultry for eggs and meat.

(c) Community aquaculture, floriculture, horticulture that includes production of fruits and vegetables, etc.

(d) Effective use of common property resources, use of waste and degraded lands, specially community ponds for community aquaculture.

Most of the activities require only the relatively small external financial input, but in terms of income, provide attractive returns. Micro-credit needs to be provided for this activity to initiate action. However, what is probably most important is, ensuring adequate market opportunities for these products, since individual efforts at marketing will not only be difficult and unsuccessful, but also, exploitative of the farmer.

Protecting Community Biodiversity

It is the rural families, with their tradition of farming and conservation activities, who have preserved the rich biodiversity. It is, therefore, necessary to ensure that the benefits of commercial and economic exploitation of these resources benefit the community, specially the poor and the ultra-poor, who might have contributed substantially for their preservation and conservation.

Establishment of Rural Industries

To provide income enhancement and employment, primary industries that utilize the products and by-products arising from the agriculture sector that includes crops and horticulture, animal husbandry, fisheries, poultry and aquaculture. This can be easily accomplished by organization of a consortium of rural industries that can synergise each other to provide for optimal utilization of the resource base of the community.

Strengthening the Capital Formation in the Agricultural Sector

Despite the large increases in production and productivity that the country has recorded in the last 50 years, the capital formation in the rural sector has remained dismally low. Investments in agriculture as percentage of GDP in the 1990s is given below:

Investment in Agriculture (as percentage of GDP)

	Public	*Private*	*Total*
1990-91	0.6	1.6	2.2
1996-97	0.4	1.1	1.5
1997-98	0.3	1.1	1.4
1998-99	0.3	1.1	1.4
1999-2000	0.4	1.1	1.5

Several studies have highlighted the need for enhancement of this activity, if meaningful gains in agriculture sector were to occur. The strategies for this to happen will include:

(i) Investment for development and improvement of land as well as development of efficient water use technologies that will improve substantially contributing to agricultural growth and development.
(ii) Availability of credit for agricultural operations, giving agriculture the status of industry.
(iii) Development of employment opportunities in the rural sector through strengthening the rural industries sectors.
(iv) Establishment of primary processing facilities in the rural areas commodities produced at the farm level.

Agriculture to be Given Industry's Status

One of the reasons for poor development of agriculture including utilization of agricultural by products and establishment of agro-industries, is the lack of adequate capital formation. This can be partly rectified by according an industry's status to agriculture and providing it with the necessary policy support for its development, as has happened in the industrial sector. While ensuring a more equitable treatment for development, this will also mobilize resources, reduce risk and commit the financial resources of financing institutions for overall development. Credit flow for agro-based enterprises as well as micro-credit for farm activities would increase helping stabilization of production.

Market Interface and Promotion of Value Added Agro-food Production

Wide fluctuations in the market prices of agricultural commodities act as deterrent to production of low value agricultural products like cereals, oilseeds and even cash crops like sugarcane and cotton. Demand/supply need to be stabilized so that, over-production in one year does not bring in distress sales, while lower production in another year pushes the prices to unreasonable levels. Market information and demand need to be synchronized through networking systems of information sharing and supply demand projections. Interventions by government agencies to stabilize prices cannot be the only solution. A close to nexus between demand, production, market, availability and economic prices should develop.

Value Addition to Agricultural Products

The Department of Food Processing, Ministry of Agriculture, Government of India, has estimated that turnover of the food processing industry in the country is in the region of Rs. 14,000 crores, more than three-fourths of which is contributed by the unorganized sector. In India, the value addition to food fortification is only 7 per cent, as compared to 23 per cent in China, 45 per cent in Philippines, and 188 per cent in UK.

The scope for value addition to basic food materials is very high. The inherent strength of the country is in the availability of a large and wide variety of raw materials, as well as a ready consumer market for the products. In view of the burgeoning populations and variations in the economic status of the people, any developed product of hygiene and quality will have a viable market. For value addition and agro-processing in the rural areas, the approach should be to create farm level infrastructure and develop capabilities at the rural level. Networking cottage, small and medium industries should viably provide the facilities for the primary and secondary processing for the take-off by the large-scale industries. An integral model is envisaged wherein the cottage, small and medium scale industries act as input conduits for further development of products by the larger industries. For continued sustenance, there should be well-planned backward and forward linkages.

Support Services/Activities for Sustainable Livelihood Systems

As has already been mentioned, sustainable livelihood development is not a single activity but a process of change. It is thus influenced by a number of factors and activities, some of which are indicated below.

Education and Literacy

There is a direct relationship between literacy and livelihood opportunities. Education enables people to get abetter skill orientation, promotes self-confidence and encourages them to recognize their rights and responsibilities. States, which have a higher literacy also generally, have better awareness about their entitlements and rights, which contribute in improving living standards.

Health and Nutrition

Consumption behaviour indicates that 47.7 per cent households have calorie inadequacy and 19.8 per cent households have protein inadequacy. This has caused low birth weight babies, stunting and underweight in children. 40 per cent of the males and 41 per cent of the females have Body Mais Index value below 18.5, indicating chronic energy deficiency. Besides micronutrient malnutrition and vitamin deficiency are manifest specially among women and children. Even though required only in small amounts, their deficiency causes disability impairs work capacity and brings illness, affecting seriously gainful employment opportunities.

Environmental Hygiene and Sanitation

Contaminated drinking water and poor sanitary environment are the causes for many health disorders especially in the rural areas. It has been estimated that less than 18 per cent of the rural households in our country have access to clean drinking water facility through taps. Those having access to safe toilets are even lower. The cascading effect that these have on health and work efficiency, and thus on sustainable livelihoods cannot be underestimated.

Gender Perspectives in Workforce

Women play a significant role in the conservation and optimal use of basic life support systems such as land, water, fauna and flora. They have protected the health of the soil though organic recycling and the first land care movement was initiated by them. They have promoted crop security and preserved biodiversity, exhibiting traditional wisdom and adopting practices, which analyzed scientifically, exhibit pragmatism and simplicity. With increasing migration of men from rural to urban areas, management of agriculture in many cases is done by women. Further, sociologists state that women tend to look at problems in their totality and hence are important promoters of an economically and ecologically sustainable agriculture.

Empowerment of Women

The burden of poverty often falls heavily on women. They have less access to education, remunerative activities, and other supporting opportunities. Agriculture, animal husbandry, health and nutrition, environmental sanitation and a large number of households related activities are attended to by women. Any attempt to development focused on these activities should, therefore, target upliftment of women and their empowerment. Conventional approaches to women's empowerment are based on the twin assumptions that alleviation of poverty would automatically lead to their employment and that the major constraint on programmes for their upliftment is monetary. The results of five decades of development have shown that economic assistance by itself does not necessarily improve the status of women. The most vital inhibiting factor leading to the disadvantaged position of women are gender discrimination, powerlessness, vulnerability and being unorganized. Women belonging to SC and ST are even more disadvantaged because of their social discrimination. Empowerment needs to be human-centred with women and children, who suffer largely, to play the central role. There is a growing need to integrate women into the economic development process. One way to do this is to ensure their access to education, technology, land rights and credit. Credit especially micro-credit for micro-enterprises has proven its value in the alleviation of poverty and in promoting livelihoods. It also provided women the dual benefit of empowerment and better quality of life. Experience till date has shown that micro credit has a powerful role to play in promoting Sustainable Human Development, provided it is linked, to-market-driven micro-enterprises and production-oriented marketing.

Local level institutions play an important role in providing the needed security, self-confidence and handling the local level issues and problems.

Skill Upgradation through Local-specific Training

The primary asset of the rural poor is the human resource. Science and technology should come together to utilize this resource successfully by upgrading their knowledge and skills in specific areas. CAPART, KVK and other organizations have been working on appropriate 'technologies for utilizing local resources' effectively and providing location-specific training. These should be further augmented.

Community Resource Management

The landless people will have to depend upon common property resources like community grazing land, wastelands, community ponds etc. to eke out their livelihoods. Since these resources do not technically belong to any specific individual, there is a general tendency to over-exploit them to get short-term benefits. Also these are most times appropriated by the more vocal powerful sections of the community depriving the needy of even these limited resources. Local level institutions committed to the cause of the community should take leadership to ensure that: (i) a strategic plan for the development of these resources is prepared and implemented; (ii) sustainability concerns are properly reflected in the development of the plan; (iii) the disadvantaged and un-reached sections of the community, specially the women, have access to them.

Traditional Wisdom, Indigenous Technical Knowledge and Practices

Traditional wisdom and indigenous knowledge have preserved agriculture as the oldest living activity. They reflect years of practical field-based experience and the local conditions under certain activities and practices have survived. This is especially valuable during periods of stress and shocks like drought, floods, natural catastrophes, etc. Since most of these practices are cost-effective and socially acceptable, modern science should analyze these practices and knowledge and should see how they can be improved upon to suit local conditions.

Social Organization and Formation of Self-Help Groups

Since organization of micro-credit and micro-enterprises are important to address the issues of poverty, social and cultural dimensions of local-level problems, at the same time attending to the needs of the community organization of the unorganized group are very relevant and shown to be a very succcssful attempt.

Social mobilization represents a collective effort to bring about social changes and establish a new order of social thought and action. Above all, intensive efforts will have to be made in the area of technological and skill empowerment of women, so that there is greater economic value to their time and labour. Self-Help Groups (SHGs) is an informal credit delivery system where its members are able to generate their own capital and lend it among themselves in times of need with low interest rates and easily payable policies. Today for any development work to be initiated in any village, it is imperative to route the activities through SHGs.

Advantages of SHGs

- The SHGs provide a degree of security to the members, protect them from the exploitation of moneylenders, and enable them to have access to credit in times of emergency and for other household consumption purposes without any collateral security.
- SHGs promote a sense of building together as a group, belonging to each other and develops a bondage among them.
- It provides them an opportunity to be bankable by linking their groups with the formal credit system and prove that they are credit-worthy and bankable.
- It is found that only women SHGs are better able to address the specific needs and problems of the women members.
- SHGs have had a wide range of impacts, economic, social and political on the lives of its members. In some cases, it has given the women members new confidence to express their views on matters of social importance.

Since accessibility to financial resources is the most important limitation for many rural development activities including entrepreneurship efforts, specially by women, a redesigning of the institutional framework for rural lending needs to be done in our country in the context of re-engineering, re-structuring, re-organization of the banking industry. There is also a need for a Special Venture Capital Fund for micro-enterprises.

Organization of the micro-enterprise groups provide market support for the participants by establishing direct linkages with the consumers and by providing them the power of scale in collective bargaining and ensuring that they get the maximum share of the prices paid by the consumer.

Models for the Development of Sustainable Livelihoods

Several models have been tried in different countries and at different locations for sustainable livelihoods. Most of these conceptually correct models have been success stories, which have been developed and implemented by committed people or organizations with community support and governmental patronage. It has also to be recognized that all these projects are location-specific and have taken into account the assets and resources available at the local level. Three such models are discussed in this section.

HUMAN-CENTRED DEVELOPMENT MODEL

Bio-villages Programme at Pondicherry, Implemented by the M.S. Swaminathan Research Foundation

The programme is developed on the concept that asset building and community development have to be the pathways for poverty eradication, which have to be on a genuine partnership with the poor, enabling them to earn their living. The term 'Bio-village' is derived from the Greek word 'bios' which means living, and is thus a human-centred development paradigm. With a pro-poor, pro-nature and pro-women orientation, the programme pays concurrent attention to: (a) Natural Resources conservation and enhancement, (b) Poverty eradication, and (c) Women's empowerment.

The principal components of the programme are:

- Eco-farming leading to the substitution of chemical fertilizers and capital with knowledge and biological inputs like vermiculture, bio-fertilizers and bio-pesticides. This, in turn, creates new eco-jobs in villages.
- Increased avenues for rural non-farm employment based on opportunities for remunerative marketing.

Thus, integrated attention is paid to on-farm and non-farm employment. The new livelihood opportunities are based on an analysis of the resources available to the family. Thus, landless labour families take to household mushroom cultivation, ornamental fish rearing, coir rope making, rearing small ruminants under stall fed conditions and other enterprises which are within their resource capability. Those with a small plot of land take to hybrid seed production, floriculture, dairying, poultry and other high value enterprises. Groups of assetless women take to aquaculture in community ponds. The asset building exercise is based on micro-level planning, and micro-enterprises supported by micro-credit.

Multiple livelihood opportunities help to enhance total income and minimize risks. The key inputs are education and training, social mobilization and producer oriented marketing. The self-help groups operate a Community Banking system, which makes available credit to its members on terms decided by them. The system involves low transaction costs and a high percentage of loan recovery. Over a period of time, the training is done by local women or men. The pedagogic methodology is learning by doing and hence formal literacy is not a prerequisite for admission to the training courses. A fundamental principle guiding the bio-village movement is inclusion and not exclusion. The women and men who become trainers are inducted into Bio-village Corps of Rural Professionals. Most of the nearly 100 Bio-village corps members inducted so far, are either semi-literate or even illiterate. They are the prime-movers and doers of the bio-village movement. They have demonstrated that the rural poor can take to new technologies like fish to water, provided they are enabled to learn through practical work experience and not through class-room lectures.

The Bio-village model of sustainable human development helps to bridge at the same time the demographic, digital, economic and technological divides. It promotes harmony with nature and with each other. It is based on ecotechnologies which are environmentally benign, economically viable and socially equitable. It shows the path to an ever-green revolution in agriculture, where productivity advances can take place in perpetuity without associated ecological or social harm. The choice of technologies is flexible depending on local desires, capabilities and opportunities. While the concept has certain ground rules like "a pro-nature, pro-poor and pro-women" orientation to technology dissemination and a partnership and not a patronage approach to poverty eradication, the precise action plan is developed by the people of the village in partnership with professionals.

The programme funded by several organizations, but primarily by the Government of India and the UNDP, operated in 19 villages in Pondicherry. The bio-villages project was a rich and exciting learning experience for all those involved in the programme, viz. farm families especially farm women, scientists associated with the implementation, the Pondicherry Government, the financial institutions and other NGOs. Its success can be measured in terms of the following achievements:

(a) Creating awareness among farm families on their rights and responsibilities,
(b) Improving income and employment at the village level,
(c) Access to improved technologies in crop and animal husbandry and associated activities,
(d) Natural resources conservation and management,
(e) Belter utilization and management of common property resources,
(f) Better health and environmental sanitation,
(g) Better organization within communities and formation of micro-enterprise and microcredit self-help groups (SHGs),
(h) Building up of self-confidence and empowerment of women as well as creating an entrepreneurship spirit in them.

In view of the success of the programme, the Government of Pondicherry is interested in extending the programme to the entire State and a Detailed Development Plan has now been prepared. Details of the operational design of the programme and methodology are given in greater detail in Annexure II.

RURAL ENTERPRISES-ORIENTED MODELS OF DEVELOPMENT

The Spark Programme of the Government of China

The Government of China launched a very significant programme of rural employment towards rural prosperity in 1978 and the progress of the programme has been remarkably successful. It was realized that if the economic conditions of the rural areas were to improve, then processing of agricultural commodities at the primary level will have to be undertaken at the village level. Rural industrial development was put on the top of the national developmental agenda. Between 1978 and 1992, the number of rural enterprises increased from 1.52 million to 20.78 million, the number of employees increased in the sector from 2.8 million to 10.23 million and the share of rural industries to GIMP from 7 per cent to 31.0 per cent. It has been claimed that Rural Enterprise has become the backbone of the rural economy as well as a mainstay of small and medium enterprises. Further, besides providing rural employment to many who were in the throes of hunger and poverty, the development of rural enterprises has strongly supported agricultural modernization through the process of capital input. The benefits that have accumulated from the promotion of rural industries have been many.

It is interesting to note that, when the programme was initially started, the bureaucrats and the urban planners were not too supportive of the programme and were deeply apprehensive about its success. However, the farmers themselves took up the programme with a conviction and commitment because they saw clearly the many kinds of benefits that can result from it. Now it has become a movement.

The Bio-industrial Watershed Model

A 'Bio-industrial Watershed Model' was developed by J.S. Bali, and the Ministry of Rural Development, Department of Soil Conservation. This has some notable features in promoting rural employment. The concept aims at a dynamic convergence between Land and Water Development, the Biomass Production System (Agriculture, Horticulture, Animal Husbandry, Forestry, Agro-forestry, etc.), and Processing and Marketing of surplus biomass within the area. The programme has to be backed by infrastructure (roads, transport, communication, power, market information facilities, etc.) and People's Institutions at the grassroots level (Panchayat Raj, Gram Sabha, Self-Help Groups, etc.).

For ensuring sustainable livelihoods, 'sustainable production systems of plants and animals' will have to be developed. These include, Agriculture, Horticulture, Agri-horticulture, Animal Husbandry, Forestry, Agro-forestry, Agrostology, Aquaculture, Sericulture, Apiculture, Mushroom Production, etc. Home processing and value addition to marketable biomass products, where employment will be available mainly to women, Central Bio-Processing units with backward linkages with farmers and labour, and forward linkages with the Marketing Enterprises will be established within the community.

Soil and Water Conservation Programmes in the States (including Centrally sponsored Schemes of Soil Conservation in Catchments of river-valleys, Drought-prone and Desert Development programmes, and National Watershed Development Project for rainfed area) have generated over 13,000 million man-days of rural employment. As a matter of fact, this is the largest employment generation scheme of the government, despite its problems in implementation due sometimes to improper administration.

Visions of the Future

1. In rural India, sustainable livelihoods can arise only from management of sustainable agriculture.
2. Sustainable agriculture will require efficient management of the basic natural resources of land and water.
3. Policies and programmes of the government should support multiple livelihood opportunities to enhance income, increase employment and improve quality of life. They should be rooted and planned at the local level and operated through local institutions, which should be empowered sufficiently for this purpose. Patterns of agriculture and resource use, which undermine the livelihood opportunities of the rural communities and deny them the right to decide their own future and the means to do so, will never be viable.

ANNEXURE I

Projected Changes in Population of the Country

Year	*Projected Population (in millions)*	*Population Age Group*	
		15-64 years	*Above 65 years*
1996	934.2	541.6 (58.0%)	39.9 (4.3%)
2001	1011.8	618.4 (61.1%)	45.8 (4.5%)
2006	1092.4	706.8 (64.7%)	52.8 (4.8%)
2011	1176.8	783.2 (66.6%)	62.1 (5.3%)
2016	1264.0	844.0 (66.7%)	74.4 (5.9%)
2021	1344.8	901.7 (67.1%)	89.7 (6.7%)
2026	1413.9	957.2 (67.7%)	108.9 (7.7%)
2031	1472.9	1010.0 (68.6%)	131.1 (8.9%)
2036	1526.5	1050.7 (68.3%)	156.5 (10.3%)
2041	1577.5	1077.9 (68.3%)	181.6 (11.5%)
2046	1619.5	1091.7 (67.4%)	207.9 (12.8%)
2051	1646.3	1089.5 (66.2%)	243.5 (14.8%)

Source: K.S. Natarajan & V. Jayachandran: "Population Growth in 21st Century India" In *Population-Development Nexus in India—Challenges for the new millennium*, (K. Srinivasan & Michael Vlassoff (Editors), Tata McGraw-Hill Publishing Company Limited, New Delhi, January 2001.

ANNEXURE II

Biovillage: A Pro-nature, Pro-poor, Pro-women Development Paradigm to Sustainable Agriculture and Rural Development

The term "bio-village" is derived from the Greek word bios which means living. This is another term for human-centred development. Poverty persists under conditions where the human resource is undervalued and land and material resources are over-valued. There- fore, the Bio-village model of rural and agricultural development is based on the foundation of sustainable human development. It pays concurrent attention to:

- Natural resources conservation and enhancement
- Poverty eradication
- Women's empowerment

Sustainable agriculture and rural development calls for a paradigm of development which is pro-nature, pro-poor and pro-women in approach. The Bio-village approach encapsulates this paradigm of development by employing interventions integrating the principles of ecological sustainability and economic profitability with equity, and linking conservation with development in a socially non-disruptive manner. It facilitates the optimal utilization of the production potentials, of both biophysical and human resources, for maximizing income and employment through harnessing the possibilities opened up by science and technology, by blending harmoniously the production opportunities offered by the modern technologies and the ecological security built in the traditional technology; by pursuing the holistic systems approach to the use and management of resources; and by enabling the resource-poor to translate the skills acquired into production and income generating activities through accessing to capital, support services and fostering group action. The health and happiness of the rural families being the goal of development, its objectives require a pro-nature, pro-poor and pro-women orientation to a job-led economic growth activity. In this model:

Pro-nature orientation is reflected through ensuring the sustainability of productivity of the biophysical resource base and employing environmentally compatible interventions.

Pro-poor orientation is validated by employing interventions that improve the livelihood security of the resource-poor through empowering them with technology to enhance their access to income and skilled employment.

Pro-women orientation is ensured through empowering women with skills and access to income, and reducing the drudgery of work at home and outside.

Conceptual Framework

Bio-village paradigm addresses concurrently the twin problems of development, viz. degradation of the resource base and endemic persistent rural poverty: the former by ensuring the sustainability of the resource base through fostering integrated resource management systems [which would maximize income and employment per unit of resource—land and water, and not a specific commodity, per unit of land], and the latter through empowering the resource-poor with technology.

Sustainability of the resource base is fostered through integrated management of the resources. Conceptually, biophysical resource base refers to land, water and micro and macro flora and fauna. Integration should lead to the maximization of biomass directly and income and employment indirectly, and not specific commodities (crop or livestock or tree products) per unit of resource (square metres of land and cubic metres of water) within a time-frame. The process is not confined to primary products but also to product conversion and value addition with the increasing use of human resource (labour). Integrated management of the resource base for sustainability demands a holistic perception of the resource base. Spatially there are two categories of resources, viz. common property resources (village commons, neighbourhood forests, various types of water-spreads etc.) and individually possessed (crop lands/ground water sources). Sustainability of the resource base cannot be ensured unless both are seen as a single mutually dependent resource entity. Spatially, delineation could be natural entities such as watersheds and socio-economic entities as the community (spatially a village) which often transcends the natural boundaries.

Technological empowerment of the resource-poor is an integrated process which involves the identification and adoption of environment-friendly and economically efficient technologies and interventions, adaptating them to the socio-economic conditions of the participants, skill upgradation of the participants through training, internalization of the technology through on-production training, facilitating the transformation of the technology into self-sustaining production activity by accessing to capital, providing infrastructure support and fostering activity-specific group action in securing common services.

Operationalization of the Bio-village Paradigm

Sustainability concerns are addressed through integrated resource management:

Firstly, by taking holistic perspective of the biophysical resource endowment, both the common property resources and privately owned resources;

Secondly, by enhancing the productivity of the common property resources through conservation of soil and water, regeneration of natural vegetation, biomass production for value addition, fostering biodiversity, and productive use of water spreads through aquaculture-I;

Thirdly, by pursuing a systems approach (farming systems identified for different biophysical resource endowments and socio-economic conditions) to use and management of privately owned resources (land and water) for maximizing the productivity, in terms of total biomass and not specific commodities; and

Fourthly, through productivity increasing interventions such as integrated plant nutrient management systems, water management systems, and environmentally compatible interventions such as organic farming and integrated pest management systems.

Poverty concerns are addressed primarily through empowering the resource poor with technology and ensuring social equity in interventions by:

- Identifying and promoting a basket of enterprises that generate income and employment, especially for women;
- Enhancing income and employment through value addition and product conversion by adopting integrated resource management systems;
- Development of common property resources and accessing the infrastructure exclusively for the resource-poor;
- Improving the quality of rural life through promoting environmental sanitation, making available adequate drinking water, improving household nutrition and accessing elementary education; and
- Fostering group action to achieve the power of scale, both in the production and marketing phases of the enterprises chosen for strengthening livelihoods.

Gender concerns are addressed primarily by empowering women through interventions that:

- Enhance the skills of women;
- Improve access to income through promoting income and employment generation activities;
- Reduce drudgery of labour by introducing new tools;
- Make easy access to fuel and water by developing common property resources; and
- Foster group action for improved work environment and mitigate social disabilities.

In brief, the principal components of the programme are:

- Eco-farming leading to the substitution of chemicals and capital with knowledge and biological inputs like vermiculture, bio-fertilizers and bio-pesticides: this, in turn, creates new eco-jobs in villages.
- Increased avenues for rural non-farm employment based on opportunities for remunerative marketing.

Thus, integrated attention is paid to on-farm and non-farm employment. The new livelihood opportunities are based on an analysis of the resources available to the family. Thus, landless labour families take to household mushroom cultivation, ornamental fish rearing, coir rope making, rearing small ruminants under stall fed conditions and other enterprises which are within their resource capability. Those with a small plot of land take to hybrid seed production, floriculture, dairying, poultry and other high value enterprises. Groups of assetless women take to aquaculture in community ponds. The asset building exercise is based on micro-level planning, and enterprises supported by micro-credit.

Multiple livelihood opportunities help to enhance totel income and minimize risks: The key inputs are education and training, social mobilization and producer oriented marketing. The self-help groups operate a Community Banking system, which makes available credit to its member on of terms decided by themselves. The system involves low transaction costs and a high percentage of loan recovery. Over a period of time, the training is done by local women or men. The pedagogic methodology is learning by doing and hence formal literacy is not a prerequisite for admission to the training courses. A fundamental principle guiding the bio-village movement is inclusion and not exclusion. The women and men who become trainers are inducted into a Bio-village Corps of Rural Professionals. Most of the nearly 100 Bio-village Corps members inducted so far, are either semi-literate or even illiterate. They are the prime-movers and doers of the bio-village movement. They have demonstrated that the rural poor can take to new technologies like fish to water, provided they are enabled to learn through practical work experience and not through class-room lectures.

The Genesis and Development of the Bio-villages Programme

An interdisciplinary dialogue on 'New Technologies: Reaching the Unreached'. 'Biotechnology' organized in January 1991 by the Centre for Research on Sustainable Agricultural and Rural Development (CRSARD) of the M.S. Swaminathan Research Foundation (MSSRF), Madras, attempted to look 'at the possibility of resource neutrality in technology development and dissemination' and to undertake 'a proactive analysis of the potential benefits and adverse impacts of biotechnological research not only from the economic angle but also from the ecological and equity perspectives'. The dialogue identified that biotechnology offered possibilities for improving the productivity, profitability, stability and sustainability of small-scale agriculture and aquaculture. It recognized that it is possible for the resource poor rural families to take advantage of the applications of biotechnology (for that matter any other technology) through technological empowerment. Further, the dialogue developed the concept of 'Bio-village' for taking the benefits of biotechnology research to the rural poor.

As a follow-up of the 'Dialogue', it was proposed to test the feasibility of applying the Bio-village approach in a few villages, especially to improve the livelihood security conditions of the resource-poor in the rural areas of India.

The concept of Bio-village paradigm was translated into an action programme. A few technologies (mushroom, biofertilizer, vermicompost, hybrid vegetable production, and pisciculture in community ponds) were tested, evaluated and adapted to the specific biophysical conditions and socio-economic conditions (resource-poor landless households). The process of technological empowerment of the resource-poor to improve their livelihood security was successfully demonstrated with respect to mushroom technology, accessing common property resources to the resource-poor with a community fish pond and transforming illiterate resource-poor into self-reliant women entrepreneurs (coir rope unit). The process of technological empowerment was got refined further, especially with respect to mobilizing group action. This initiative also demonstrated the feasibility of transforming technologies (vermicompost and mushroom spawn production) into self-reliant, economically viable small rural enterprises to which rural youth could be attracted. It has also helped to bring out the innate talents of the illiterate resource-poor participants.

The initiatives undertaken in the three villages of Pondicherry proved that the Bio-village approach is feasible and it was opportune to operationalize the Bio-village paradigm as a pathway to sustainable agriculture and rural development. Translating the Bio-village approach and pursuing the strategies outlined, an action programme, was evolved against the identified potentials and constraints in nineteen villages (twelve revenue villages) in Pondicherry, representing three biophysical resource endowments (uplands, lowland and low wetland) and two socio-economic conditions (high incidence of landlessness, and significant presence of small and medium farmers). The action plan envisaged the sustainable development of the land and water resources for improving the livelihood security of the communities inhabiting these villages. The programme covered a land area of 3680 hectares inhabited by a population of over 24,000 in 5,000 households. The Plan envisaged the following four basic components:

- Testing and adapting technologies, especially biotechnologies, including organic farming and integrated resource management systems;
- Facilitating the initiation of a set of production activities suited to the resource-poor, based on the technologies tested and adapted to utilize local resources;
- Establishing two Biocentres which would serve as focal points for the technology dissemination activities including adaptation, demonstration, training, repository of information, support services; and
- Disseminating the experiences gained from the demonstration of the Bio-village paradigm through organizing workshops and seminars.

The UNDP in July 1994 extended its support in implementing the project. Apart from UNDP, support for the project is sought from the participants themselves through labour, the financial institutions (Commercial Banks) by making available the investment and working capital for production activities. The Government of the Union Territory of Pondicherry provided infrastructure support and channelled assistance rendered generally under the poverty alleviation and employment generating programmes.

Since its inception in 1991 as a concept, the Bio-village paradigm has been under continuous scrutiny with respect to sustainability and replicability, and many of its integral components have been subjected to verification and validation. Most of the individual elements of the paradigm by themselves are not novices. Strength is drawn from the synergy in combining of the various elements, and in their emphasis and adaptation under specific biophysical and socioeconomic environments. Sustainability of the resource base (land, water and natural vegetation), addressed through the integrated resource management systems and poverty alleviation through technological empanelment of the resource-poor by accessing them to a set of income and employment generating activities, continued to be the focus. Common property resources (grazing lands, village forests, water-spreads such as ponds and tanks) give some opportunities for enhancing income and employment enhancement. Given the socio-political context of the present itmes, it may not be possible to bring about a redistribution of the productive assets in the rural areas. But certainly some relief to the resource-poor could be afforded by developing these resources for fodder, fuel-wood, aquaculture, etc. and by giving exclusive access to the resource-poor for the infrastructure. Fostering group action in the management, sharing infrastructure, enabling mechanisms to access to capital and technology are issues that need resolution for sustainability.

Group action is fostered by organizing a network of activity-based groups and integrating them vertically to minimize overheads in procuring inputs, marketing outputs and sharing the infrastructure; and horizontally to share common experience and mutually supportive activities. Building up capacity of the groups to manage the institutions and support services, and the common property resources is another strategy to ensure sustainability of the interventions and the institutions built to serve them.

Accelerating the pace of spread of the movement has been facilitated by the following institutional structures:

- A Bio-village Council comprising two members from each village (one female and one male) provides the overall policy oversight and undertakes the strategic planning.
- A Biocentre serves as a single stop resource centre, providing the needed inputs. Information and training. The Biocentre is the hub of the bio-village movement.
- A computer aided and internet connected rural knowledge centre provides the information needed by the rural families in the areas of health, education, entitlements, ecotechnologies and marketing. At the Knowledge Centre, owned and operated by the local village community, trained women help to convert generic into location specific information.

The knowledge centres also provide information on the population supporting capacity of the village ecosystem and on culturally and socially compatible family planning methods.

Thus, the Bio-village model of sustainable human development helps to bridge at the same time the demographic, digital, economic and technological divides. It promotes harmony with nature and with each other. It is based on ecotechnologies which are environmentally benign, economically viable and socially equitable. It shows the path to an ever-green revolution in agriculture, where productivity advances can take place in perpetuity without associated ecological or social harm. The choice of technologies is flexible depending on local desires, capabilities and opportunities. While the concept has certain ground rules like "a pro-nature, pro-poor and pro-women" orientation to technology dissemination and a partnership and not a patronage approach to poverty eradication, the precise action plan is developed by the people of the village in partnership with professionals. The virtual colleges linking scientists and rural families help to hasten the spread of such symbiotic partnerships. Under UNESCO's Asian Ecotechnology Network, the bio-village paradigm of sustainable human development is now being spread to other parts of India and to other nations. The Bio-village programme has led to the emergence of many new voices and leaders in the villages.

Micro Enterprises Suitable for Income Enhancement and Employment Generation

Several technologies are adopted to improve the socio-economic conditions of the rural poor, but they should also be capable of utilizing locally available resources for income and employment generations through value addition. This will involve development of most appropriate and environmentally compatible technologies and these technologies should be tested and codified. They should have demonstrable superiority over the conventional technologies being practised in the villages, in terms of higher productivity, value addition, employment generation and environmental sustainability. This development of interactive and appropriate technology packages including frontier biotechnology as appropriate is the crucial component of the project and the technology packages included enterprises like:

- Mushroom production
- Vermicompost production
- Goat rearing
- Poultry
- Aquaculture in community pond
- Fodder grass production
- Dairying
- Flower production
- Vegetable production

The above micro enterprises were chosen on market demand and were capable of being supported by micro credit arrangements.

1. Multiple livelihood opportunities to add value to time, labour and knowledge of the rural poor.
2. Economic level of each pilot intervention.
3. Non-intervention linkages.
4. Monitoring mechanism by a well-established MIS (Management Information System) to record life-style changes of the participants in respect to income generation.

The micro-enterprises were identified through preparation of Village Resource Profiles (VRP), followed by Perspective Action Plan (PAP), ensuring that they are economically viable and replicable. Integrating economic viability with environmental soundness and equity is not an easy task at the field level. It is a process of learning by doing and close partnership with the stakeholders. Hence, the Bio-village project implementation was on a participatory action mode with resource-poor farm families, scientists and financial institutions working and learning together. The micro-enterprises lent themselves for decentralized production and centralized marketing services. The distinctive feature of encouraging micro-enterprises at the village levels is a desegregated approach to imparting new income generating skills for women belonging to landless families with utmost attention. Multiple channels of income insulate the family from total deprivation even in adverse years of crop failure, inadequate rainfall, seasonal and uncertain wage employment and exploitation by the moneylenders. The diversification of employment opportunities and creation of multiple channels of income for the families of landless labour, marginal and small farmers are identified from a comprehensive feasibility report prepared for a Bio-village programme. The feasibility report, which was prepared at the initiation of the programme included the following components:

- Participatory survey and resource inventories.
- Farming system survey regarding use of land, water, energy, credit and labour.
- Pre-testing of technological options through on-farm trials and experiments.
- Technological empowerment of the poor through on line production training.
- Joint identification of micro-enterprises by the participants and staff of the project.
- Eco-friendly, socially equitable and economically viable enterprises.
- Activities, which would enhance production efficiency on a sustainable basis, are pisciculture in brick kiln lands that will increase water use efficiency and convert degraded resource, to productive use. This will suit resource-endowed entity.

Through technological empowerment, the resource poor are accessed with new market oriented skills to strengthen their livelihood security. Towards this end, two kinds of activities-on-farm research and demonstrations, that will help the rural poor to understand, and equip with new trends in agricultural production, leading to enhanced farm income; and secondly, income and employment generating micro-enterprises were undertaken.

Types and Nature of Micro-enterprises

The micro-enterprises will vary for resource-poor (landless and women of poor households), limited resource endowed poor (marginal and small farmers and rural women) and resource endowed rural families. The micro-enterprises that can suit different groups specified above are given hereunder.

Rural Families	*Micro-enterprises*
Landless agricultural labourers	1. Mushroom-production 2. Vermicompost production 3. Community aquaculture 4. Goat rearing 5. Poultry
Small and Marginal farmers/ Farm women	1. Flower production 2. Vegetable production 3. Fodder production 4. Dairy 5. Poultry

Impact of the Bio-village Movement

The bio-village project was a rich and exciting learning experience for all those involved in the programme, viz. Farm families especially farm women, scientists associated with the implementation, the Pondicherry Government, the financial institutions and other NGOs. Its success can be measured in terms of the following achievements:

(i) Creating awareness among farm families on their rights and responsibilities;
(ii) Improving income and employment at the village level;
(iii) Access to improved technologies in crop and animal husbandry and associated activities;
(iv) Natural resources conservation and management;
(v) Better utilization and management of common property resources;
(vi) Better health and environmental sanitation;
(vii) Better organization within communities and formation of micro-enterprise and microcredit self-help groups (SHGs);
(viii) Building up of self-confidence and empowerment of women as well as creating an entrepreneurship spirit in them.

11

Food Security in Five Year Plans of India

MRITYUNJAY M. JHA

INTRODUCTION

For India, the second decade of the Twenty-first century is going to be more challenging than ever before in terms of food security for the country at all levels, covering aspects of production for self-sufficiency, sustained employment opportunities for accessibility to food, sustained income for access to nutrition for all and food absorption in the households. The struggle for it will become daunting in the light of sustaining the economic growth momentum, trade liberalization, and declining subsidies among others. The rising food prices, encompassing a wide spectrum of food items, is expected to affect both food and nutrition security. Hundreds of millions in the country, who were food secure and enjoyed healthy life may lose their status and would perhaps fall in a different category, posing bigger challenge to the government, planners and policy makers. The challenges are manifold and multidimensional in nature. Sustained increase in food production, meeting the requirements of the ever growing population and rising standard of living of a certain class and also in the context of globalization and energy security, poses the biggest challenge. With stagnating yield of foodgrains and hardly any scope of expanding land for cultivation, combined with the vagaries of the monsoon, the problem will compound. Economic access to sufficient food has acquired significant dimension, despite economic growth witnessed during the last three decades. Eliminating poverty and the problem of hunger from the rural areas remains the biggest challenge. Its spillover effect has emerged as urban poverty. Providing urban population, especially the urban poor with adequate food and nutrition will be a gigantic task. With the level of poverty still very high according to the Tendulkar Panel (TOI, 11th December 2009)[1].

This paper is an attempt to review different aspects and efforts of our Five Year Plans that determined and influenced food security in our country. It briefly discusses the basic concepts of food security and related issues and then moves on to review food security related aspects mentioned in Five Year Plans.

CONCEPTS AND ISSUES

Food is the most basic need of human needs and is central to the discussion of human rights, social development and sustainable development (Drèze and Sen, 1981, 1995; FAO, 1996; Swaminathan, 1987). Food security has been a consistent theme raised in specific contexts in a number of world conferences convened by the United Nations. The Conference on Environment and Development held in Rio in 1992 emphasized the need to ensure food security at all levels, within the framework of sustainable development, as defined in Agenda 21. The World Conference on Human Rights (Vienna, 1993) emphasized the need to ensure that everyone enjoyed a right to food. ICPD (Cairo, 1994) highlighted the linkage between population growth and food production and the need to evolve global, measures to satisfy the ever growing food needs. The World Summit on Social Development (Copenhagen, 1995) made a strong commitment to the campaign against hunger through its emphasis on poverty eradication.

The concept of food security as understood now has been evolved over decades and has been considered at a number of levels: global, regional, national, state, household and individual. While the ultimate concern may be at the household and individual levels, it is important to realize that food security at the levels outside the household has a strong bearing on the performance at the household level. The World Food Conference of 1974, which was organized in the wake of the World Food Crisis of 1972-74 was largely concerned with global food security and it had recognized the world food security as a common responsibility of all nations and that international approaches were needed to achieve improved world food security.

A wider definition of food security incorporates what is often referred in the quality of life indicators. Accordingly, food security implied livelihood security at the level of each household and all members within, and involves ensuring both physical and economic access to balanced diet, safe drinking water, environmental sanitation, primary education and basic healthcare. Sustainable food security involves strengthening the livelihood security of all members within a household by ensuring both physical and economic access to balanced diet, including the micro-nutrients, safe drinking water, environmental sanitation, basic health care and primary education (Swaminathan, 1999).

The World Food Programme (WFP, 2001) provided multidimensional concept of food security and identified four principal areas concerning food security. These areas are: availability of food, accessibility to food, utilization of food and vulnerability of households to various hazards.

Despite global food surplus, almost half of the world's less developed countries suffer significant problems concerning food. Most social science and policy discussions of food security make the "food availability" assumption that increased food supply is the key to reducing hunger. Critics argue, however, that increased food supply has little impact on hunger and that primary culprits are entrenched inequality and militarism.

EXPLANATIONS OF FOOD SECURITY

Modernization, economic dependency, urban bias, population pressure and militarism are some of the important aspects that are considered the development specialists.

In some formulations, economic development, economic savings and investment in physical capital are the key to an industrial take-off, while others believed in human development and felt that investment in human capital *via* increased education creates a labour force with motivation, skills, social mobility and adaptability to modern technology. Modernization theorists disagree over the role of state because it is state, which prepares pathways for development through plans. Some proponents focus solely on investment and industrialization, as a means to develop the society, ignoring political institutions and processes. During the last 5 decades, there has been two divergent views on the political democracies *vis-à-vis* quality of life. One section argues that political democracies are vulnerable to political instability, and that strong authoritarian are better at regulating new demands and introducing the economic interventions needed for industrialization.

Others argue that political democracy is positively correlated with improved physical quality of life, basic needs fulfilment, more balanced urban-rural development and lower income inequality, which may also promote food security. The centralized development planning has been debating of its merits and demerits. There is no doubt that development is a complex process. It is multidimensional in nature and must work upwards, downwards and sideways simultaneously. It is not a question of bottom-up *versus* top down. It is a question of a judicious blending of the two meet the challenges faced by the developing societies[2].

Modernization and economic development also leads to urban bias. This leads to sectoral disparity in investment, resulting into lower productivity of rural sector. This bias is not only inequitable, producing rural urban income inequality and a significant social welfare gap, but is also inefficient, undermining agricultural development and food production (Jenkins and Scanlan, 2001).

India, being a democratic country, adopted the Five Year Plan route and considered it to be the basis for all development efforts that would lead to economic growth and well-being of its people, removing regional and sectoral disparity.

Food Security Issues Addressed in Five Year Plans

After gaining independence in 1947, the objective for the new Nation was to construct a just and economically strong state, while addressing the deep-rooted problems in society. It was felt that the political independence provides the needed opportunity. It is, therefore, normal that improvement in economic and social conditions through the acceptance of more progressive ideas and through suitable institutional changes is regarded as the practical test for judging the adequacy of the new political system. Therefore, it was unanimously agreed that a national plan has to be an expression of a basic unity of purpose in the community. It is this unity which would constitute the ultimate sanction behind the plan, give it driving force and evoke the necessary sacrifice and effort on the part of members.

The Nation began its journey on the basis of Soviet model of centralized economic planning and a 'think tank' was created to carry out the tasks of planning in the name of National Planning Commission (Sundaram, 1999: Planning Revisited—Rural Area Development in India: Vision and Reality, Professor R.N. Dubey Memorial Lectures—1999). Planning in a democratic state is a social process in which, in some part, every citizen should have the opportunity to participate. To set the patterns of future development is a task of such magnitude and significance that it should embody the impact of public opinion and the needs of the community. The Constitution of India has guaranteed certain Fundamental Rights to the citizens of India and enunciated certain Directive Principles of State Policy, in particular, that the State shall strive to promote the welfare of the people by securing and protecting as effectively as it may a social order in which justice, social, economic and political, shall inform all the institutions of the national life, and shall direct its policy towards securing, among other things—that the citizens, men and women equally, have the right to an adequate means of livelihood (Preface, First Five Year Plan Document).

First Five Year Plan (1951-56)

In July 1951 the Planning Commission presented a draft outline of a plan of development for the period of five years from April 1951 to March 1956. Owing to the greater urgency of the programmes for agriculture and irrigation, the provision made for the development of industry in the public sector was insufficient (Fig. 11.1). Village industries, small-scale industries and handicraft, whose importance for the economy as a whole can scarcely be exaggerated, have been given greater emphasis in the Plan.

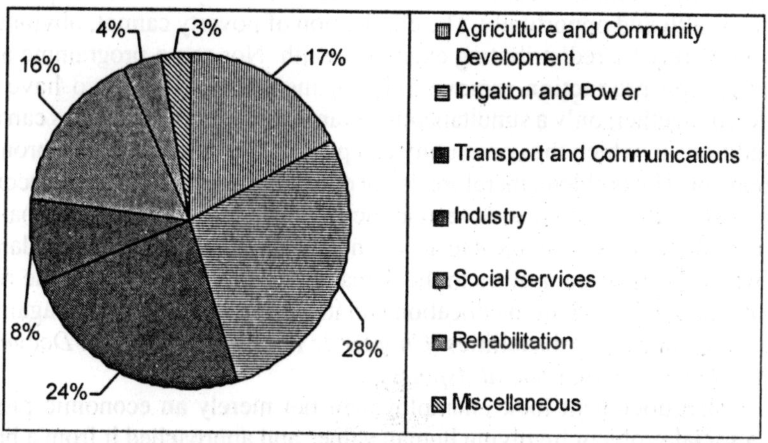

Source: First Five Year Plan Document, Planning Commission.

Fig. 11.1: First Five Year Plan Allocaiton

Clearly the focus of this plan was to pay adequate attention to the sectors impacting large segment of population and the traditional core of the economy. This was an important policy direction. It covered the important aspects of improving agricultural production, to the land problem, and the food security through adequate finance for agriculture, common production programmes for small-scale and large-scale industries, selection of irrigation and power schemes. In making its recommendations, the Commission was conscious that the framing of social and economic policies in different fields is a continuous process and that, within the framework of priorities and objectives now formulated, such changes as may be necessary in the interest of national development will be made as further experience is gained and ideas are tested in practice. This became the guide for all subsequent plans.

Policy Directions

Agriculture was the mainstay of life for about 70 per cent of the population, and productivity in this sector was exceedingly low. The size of agricultural holdings even at that point of time was progressively diminishing; the old cottage and small-scale industries had decayed, and the rural population which constituted about 83 per cent of the total suffers from chronic underemployment and low incomes. Population had increased by more than fifty per cent in the last fifty years, but the growth of alternative occupations either in the rural areas or in the was not on a scale which could absorb this growing population.

The First Plan took into cognizance the underdeveloped economy characterised by the co-existence, in greater or less degree, of unutilised or underutilised manpower on the one hand and of unexploited natural resources on the other. The past decades of uncertainty in agricultural production and its consequences loomed large on the thought process of planners. The urge to economic and social change under present conditions came from the fact of poverty and of inequalities in income, wealth and opportunity. The elimination of poverty cannot, obviously, be achieved merely by redistributing existing wealth. Nor can a programme aiming only at raising production remove existing inequalities. The two have to be considered together; only a simultaneous advance along both these lines can create the conditions in which the community can put forth its best efforts for promoting development. The problem, therefore, is not one of merely re-channelling economic activity within the existing socio economic framework; that framework has itself to be remoulded so as to enable it to accommodate progressively those fundamental urges which express themselves in the demands for the right to work, the right to adequate income, the right to education and to a measure of insurance against old age, sickness and other disabilities (*Chapter 1: First Five Year Plan Document—Planning Economic and Social Aspects*).

The plan document took unemployment not merely an economic problem, but as a social problem involving human values and approached it from a broader view-point. In framing employment policy in relation to development, the following criteria was recommended:

(a) Unemployed manpower should be drawn upon to the maximum for the development programme;
(b) Money incomes in the initial stages should be expanded as little as possible;
(c) Capital formation should be speeded up and technical efficiency improved so as to increase productivity of labour;
(d) The rate at which equipment in established indigenous industries, especially those which employ large numbers, is allowed to be competed out and discarded must be adjusted so as to safeguard against excessive unemployment in the process of technological change; and, lastly,
(e) The distribution of capital in new lines should be planned keeping in view the need to increase employment opportunities in the short run as well as the larger pattern of development necessary for an expanding economy.

Considerations for Food Policy

The frequent failure of monsoon and in the 1940s and the disastrous Bengal Famine gave serious food for thought for planners in the post independence phase. This remained the subject of discussion and debate for more than a decade, and several expert committees have reported on the various aspects of the problem. The Bengal Famine Commission reviewed in detail the long-term trends in the economy as well as the several short-term factors which culminated in the food crisis of 1943. The report of that Commission enunciated the principle that "food for all" must be accepted as the basis for Government policy in this field. In a planned economy, this objective inevitably acquires added importance and has to be effectively implemented. Foodgrains occupy a pivotal place in the price structure, and if this latter has to be safeguarded, as it must be, the prices of foodgrains must be held stable at levels within the reach of the poorer sections of the community. Even a moderate shortfall in the supply of foodgrains is likely, under Indian conditions, to raise their prices more than proportionately, and a rise in food prices leads directly to a rise in the cost of living and in production costs, all round. The Plan recognized the food production deficit of about 5-7 per cent on the basis of net imports of foodgrains during 1946-50.

Price Rise

The attention was paid to the large sections of the community which live near the margin of subsistence, a certain minimum supply of foodgrains at reasonable prices constituted the rock-bottom of the standard of living, a fall in which would be seriously detrimental to health and efficiency. This Plan realized that the consequences of any untoward development in the food situation are too obvious to need stressing. It is important to note that even at that point of time the price rise was an important issue, as it is today. Hence, one can say that the price rise has remained constant *vis-à-vis* the food security for poor households. A policy which might raise prices all round and jeopardise the investment programme itself is, therefore, of no ultimate benefit to the producer. It proposed a policy of price stabilisation. Because if the trend of prices is persistently downward, a system of controls with defined procurement prices can be used—and indeed should be used—to safeguard the interests of producers by preventing prices from falling unduly. Judicious purchases by Government at defined prices are thus an excellent device for stabilising prices and for evening out to some extent inter-State disparities.

Thrust on Supply and Sufficiency

The planners maintained that if "food for all" is to be the effective basis of policy and if the investment targets in the Plan are to be adhered to, the basic structure of food controls has to be kept intact during the period of the Plan. It stressed the need to step up domestic production to the extent of 7-5 million tonnes. The focus was also given to the transportation of foodgrains from one part of the country to another, in order to provide timely emergency relief and for controlling the price. The idea of constant supply and sufficiency was necessitated by the fact that at that point of time several parts of the country were subject to periodical droughts and scarcity. Some areas were underdeveloped and yet so thickly populated that special efforts were considered to be necessary to create new avenues of employment for the people in these areas in order to provide them with the minimum purchasing power necessary for sustenance.

Second Five Year Plan (1956-61)

The First Five Year Plan laid the foundations for achieving the socialist pattern of society—a social and economic order based upon the values of freedom and democracy, without caste, class and privilege, in which there will be a substantial rise in employment and production and the largest measure of social justice attainable. The Plan document recognized that there has not been any marked change in the occupational pattern in India over the last three or four decades in spite of considerable increases in industrial production. Broadly speaking, agriculture and allied pursuits continued to absorb about 70 per cent of the working force (*Chapter 1, Second Five Year Plan Document*)[3]. The Second Five-Year Plan focused on industry, especially heavy industry. Domestic production of industrial products was encouraged, particularly in the development of the public sector. The Plan followed the Mahalanobis model, an economic development model developed by the Indian statistician Prasanta Chandra Mahalanobis in 1953. The plan assumed a closed economy in which the main trading activity would be centred on importing capital goods.

The focus related to food policy remained unchanged in terms of supply and sufficiency in principle. However, in terms of allocation, the major chunk of planned resources went to industrial development and mineral resources. It also laid emphasis on the integrated development of the water and land resources of the country and became of fundamental importance to its economy and programmes for achieving this. The total river water resources in India were computed a few years ago at 1356 million acre feet. The objective was to tap water for irrigation purpose. Of the available supplies, it was estimated that approximately 450 million acre feet could be put to beneficial use (*Chapter 17, Second Five Year Plan: Irrigation*).

Objectives

This Plan was formulated with reference to the following principal objectives:

(a) a sizeable increase in national income so as to raise the level of living in the country;
(b) rapid industrialisation with particular emphasis on the development of basic and heavy industries;
(c) a large expansion of employment opportunities; and
(d) reduction of inequalities in income and wealth and a more even distribution of economic power.

These objectives are interrelated. The Plan document says:

> A significant increase in national income and a marked improvement in living standards cannot be secured without a substantial increase in production and investment. To this end, the building up of economic and social overheads, exploration and development of minerals and the promotion of basic industries like steel, machine building, coal and heavy chemicals are vital. For securing an advance simultaneously in all these directions, the available manpower and natural resources have to be used to the best advantage. In a country in which there is relative abundance of manpower, expansion of employment opportunities becomes an important objective in itself.

The focus of this Plan gets reflected in its plan outlay, as given in Figure 11.2. Besides focusing on the industry and transport facilities, it paid due importance to the social services. This was result of the thought process subscribing to the idea that the development should result in a diminution of economic and social inequalities and should be achieved through democratic means and processes. Economic objectives cannot be divorced from social objectives and means and objectives go together. It is only in the context of a plan which satisfies the legitimate urges of the people that a democratic society can put forward its best effort.

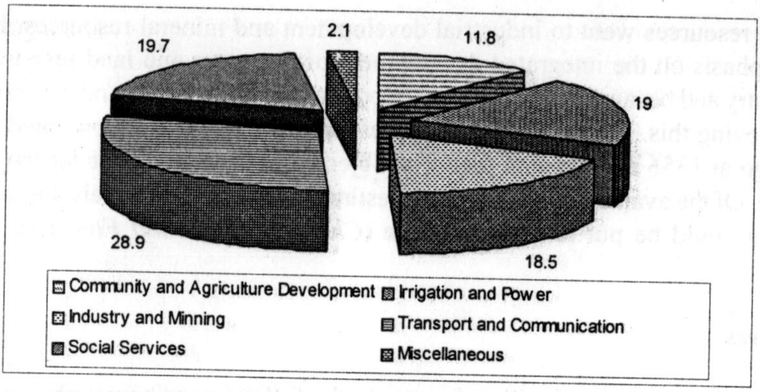

Source: The Second Five Year Plan (1956-61), Planning Commission.

Fig. 11.2: Allocation in Second Five Year Plan.

Agriculture: Sustained Production of Foodgrains and Diversification

During the First Plan period, the production increased by 20 per cent. Over the second plan period, agricultural production was estimated to increase by 18 per cent. The lines on which efforts have to be made for increasing the productivity of land are already familiar. The provision of irrigation facilities, better seeds, fertilizers and the spread of improved techniques of cultivation was considered to offer scope for expansion for many years to come. In addition to carrying forward these programmes, the Second Five Year Plan. The plan brought the role of diversification of crops including cash crops and production of subsidiary foods such as vegetables, fruits, dairy products, fish, meat and eggs. The target for additional production of foodgrains in the Second Plan was placed at 10 million tonnes, i.e., an increase of 15 per cent from 65 million tonnes in 1955-56 to 75 million tonnes in 1960-61. During the Second Five Year Plan 21 million acres of land are expected to receive irrigation, 12 million acres from large and medium irrigation schemes and 9 million acres from minor irrigation works. The provision for minor irrigation is made in part in the agricultural programmes of States and in almost equal part in the national extension and community development programmes.

Unique Features: Panchayat and District Plans

The methods adopted for preparing the Second Five Year Plan have provided valuable training both to the rural people and to rural officials associated with development. It was realised that the pattern of district administration envisaged in the national extension and community development programme will remain incomplete unless village institutions are placed on a sound footing and are entrusted with a great deal of responsibility for carrying out local programmes. The development of village panchayats on the right lines has significance for several reasons. Under the impact of new developments, including the growth of population, land reform, urbanisation, spread of education, increase in production and improvements in communications, village society was in a state of rapid transition. It emphasized that:

> "The interest of the community as a whole and in particular the needs of those sections which are at present handicapped in various ways, village panchayats along with cooperatives, can play a considerable part in bringing about a more just and integrated social structure in rural areas and in developing a new pattern of rural leadership."

District Plans were proposed to be the first step in the direction of decentralization covering the aspects of the community development and national extension programme, social welfare extension projects, agricultural production programme and allied activities in the field of rural development such as animal husbandry, soil conservation etc., development of co-operatives, village and small industries, schemes for utilising effectively resources developed through State projects for irrigation, electricity, communications, industrial development and expansion of training facilities, housing and urban development, the programme of small savings, aiding construction projects through labour co-operatives and *shramdan*, programmes for the welfare of backward classes, land reform and dissemination of information. It was felt that the land reform and other programmes initiated would bring in equality and create greater employment opportunity and food security to the rural population.

Third Five Year Plan (1961-66)

The first two Five Year Plans of independent India, with contrasting focus helped strengthen the foundations of economic and social life and stimulated industrial and economic growth and scientific and technological advance. The Third Plan represented the first phase in a scheme of long-term. In the course of this period, Indian economy strived to expand rapidly, become self-reliant and self-generating. This long-term approach was intended to provide a general design of development for the country's natural resources, agricultural and industrial advance, changes in the social structure and an integrated scheme of regional and national development. This Plan continued with maximum investment in transport infrastructure, industry and minerals. It continued with it commitment in the providing social services with one-fifth of resources allocated for this sector (Table 11.1).

One of the major features of this plan was the concept of 'balanced regional development'. There was profound belief that the balanced development of different parts of the country, extension of the benefits of economic progress to the less developed regions and widespread diffusion of industry should be the objective of planned development. The increasing capacity to achieve a better balance between national and regional development became the motto. It reasoned out the need for such a development approach:

Table 11.1: Third Five Year Plan—Distribution of Plan Outlay by Major Heads

Sectors	*Total provision (Rs. crores)*	*Per cent*
Agriculture and Community Development	1068	14
Major and Medium Irrigation	650	9
Power	1012	13
Village and Small Industries	264	4
Organised Industry and Minerals	1520	20
Transport and Communications	1486	20
Social Services and Miscellaneous	1500	20
Total	**7500**	**100**

Source: The Second Five Year Plan (1956-61), Planning Commission.

> "As resources are limited, frequently advantage lies in concentrating them at those points within the economy at which the returns are likely to be favourable. As development proceeds investments are undertaken over a wider area and resources can be applied at a large number of points, thereby resulting in greater spread of benefits. In the interest of development itself, the maximum increase in national income should be achieved and resources obtained for further investment. The process is a cumulative one, each stage determining the shape of the next."[4]

Large projects were considered as nuclei of regional growth, based on the principle that the benefits of a large project accrue in greater measure to the population of the region in which it is located if certain related or complementary programmes and schemes are undertaken. Therefore, as an essential feature of planning, every major project should be regarded as a nucleus for integrated development of the region as a whole. Such possibilities of development was envisaged in all large regions, in which new resources will be developed during the Third Plan, such as Dandakaranya, the Rajasthan canal area, among others. The philosophy behind this approach was linked with equitable growth, increase in income and livelihood security of the masses in the backward areas of the country.

This Plan targeted to achieve increase in foodgrain production. It was reasoned that the programme of economic development with special emphasis on heavy industries which the Plan embodied would demand a larger increase in agricultural production than had been at first envisaged. The target for production was kept at 80.5 million tonnes. Self-sufficiency continued to the buzzword in the planning parlance, as it gets reflected from the following:

> "In view of the production trends during the Second Plan, it is of the highest importance that in the Third Plan, besides achieving self-sufficiency in foodgrains, substantial increases should be secured in commercial crops, specially cotton, oilseeds and jute. With the growth of the economy and increase in domestic demands as well as the need to

step up exports, success in increasing the production of commercial crops is as vital as increase in the production of foodgrains."[5]

In formulating agricultural production programmes for the Third Plan, the guiding consideration were that the agricultural efforts should not be impeded in any manner for want of financial or other resources. In order to achieve the sufficiency and increased availability, efforts were made to strengthen agricultural administration in the States, and stress was placed on the closest possible coordination between different agencies, notably, those concerned with agriculture, cooperation, community development and irrigation. Supplies of credit through cooperative agencies, emerged as critical for linking credit with production and marketing.

Fourth Five Year Plan (1969-74)

This plan believed that there is an urgent need to modernize agriculture at the same time strengthen and diversify industrial sector. Though the Five Year Plans by then had contributed to achieve a significant increase in the national income in the past eighteen years and laid the foundations of technological advance. Another important feature of this plan was nationalization of banks. The nationalisation of the fourteen big banks was evidence of determination to bring a greater volume of resources within the area of social decision. It has effected a major change in our economic structure. It enabled to pay more attention to the "small man's" needs, and it restricts the scope for the monopolistic operations of the privileged few. Among other areas where social considerations have still to make a comparable impact are the enforcement of land laws, the management of public sector enterprises, and the toning up of the administration as a whole.

In addition to the fight against poverty and economic inequalities, this Plan sought to enlarge the area of self-reliance in terms of financial resources and technological inputs. Here, too, the public sector has an important part to play. Besides striving[5] to set an example in better management methods and ushering in a new pattern of worker management relations, the public sector should increasingly base itself on domestic know-how. The resource allocation to different sectors suggests that the industries, transport and power took away more than fifty per cent of the allocation (Fig. 11.3).

The Fourth Plan provided a necessary corrective direction to the earlier trend which helped particularly the stronger sections in agriculture as well as in industry to enable them rapidly to enlarge and diversify the production base. In the long run, the full potential of growth cannot be realised unless the energies of all our people are put to profitable use. The emphasis on spreading the impetus and benefits of economic growth to the weaker sections is thus necessary in the interest of equality as well as growth. The Plan assisted the less prosperous sections of farming population to improve their position and make a yet bigger contribution to the national economy. The Plan linked modernization of agriculture and industrial growth to increase productivity and generate more employment.

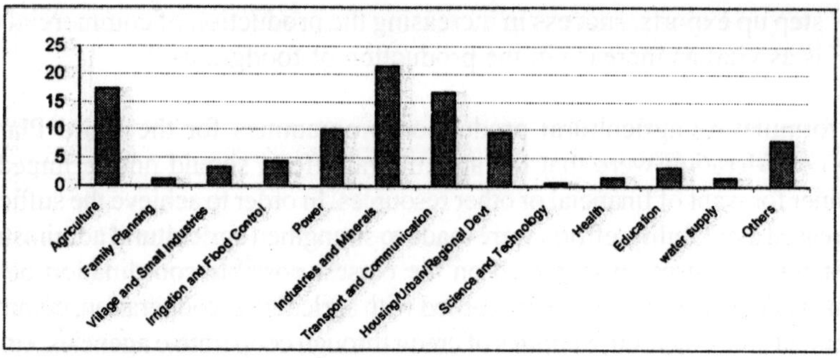

Source: Fourth Five Year Plan, Planning Commission.

Fig. 11.3: Fourth Five Year Plan Outlay.

Greater industrial activity and the modernisation of agriculture such as is proposed through the wider use of electric power and the adoption of intensive methods of cultivation in both irrigated and dry areas, would mean that a larger proportion of young people seeking jobs could find employment nearer home. At the same time, there are some new schemes, i.e. for a network of service centres in the rural areas, which will open out opportunities for young entrepreneurs.

Chapter Ten of this Plan focused on food and nutrition. The Foodgrains Policy Committee (1966) postulated three objectives of food policy: to achieve self-reliance in production, to ensure equitable distribution, and to bring about price stability in the context of both production and distribution. The Committee went on to suggest that the latter two objectives could be achieved by planned management of food supplies involving such measures as procurement, control of inter-State movement of foodgrains, a system of public distribution and the building up of buffer stocks. Some of the measures recommended and indeed actually in operation—such as control of inter-State movement of food grains—were related to a situation of grave shortage coupled with the necessity of maximum procurement. It advocated to be prepared to tackle any situation. As it mentioned:

> Thus, changes would obviously be called for in the management of food supplies if the envisaged rate of growth in the production of food grains materialises in the Fourth Plan period. Food policy has to be so formulated as to meet different situations, whether of deficits or of surpluses. It must have a certain amount of flexibility. It must, at the same time, fit into the broad framework of economic policy.

The main objectives of food policy in the Fourth Plan were:

(i) to ensure that consumer prices are stabilised and, in particular, that the interests of the low income consumers are safeguarded;
(ii) to ensure that the producers get reasonable prices and continue to have adequate incentives for increasing production; and

(iii) to build up an adequate buffer stock of foodgrains with a view to ensuring both the objectives mentioned above.

Spelling out the instruments of food policy, it remained focused on availability of food in different parts of our country. The instruments included a number of measures:

(a) the continuance of the public distribution system;
(b) the acquisition by the public sector of a sizeable percentage of marketable surplus of foodgrains with a view to meeting the commitments under the public distribution system and maintaining the buffer stock at the desired level;
(c) the imposition of such restrictions on the movement of food grains as may be necessary to help the attainment of procurement targets or to prevent, in a condition of shortage, an excessive rise in prices throughout the country;
(d) the regulation of private trade to curb speculation and hoarding;
(e) the regulation of bank advances against foodgrains; and
(f) the continuance of the ban on forward trading.

The principal agency for the implementation of the food policy was the Food Corporation of India. Since its establishment in January 1965, the Corporation was envisaged to expand further, as it has extended its functions in all States except Maharashtra, Jammu and Kashmir and Nagaland. The functions of procuring, moving, storing and handling of foodgrains at the ports and in the interior have been handed over to the Food Corporation by the Food Department.

An integrated nutrition programme was also envisaged for under-nourished. The following requirements were kept in mind as given below:

(i) since resources are limited, it is necessary to establish priorities with reference to needs, classes and areas;
(ii) it is important to improve the efficiency, and extend the coverage, of the organisations which serve the needs of the priority age-groups, classes and areas; and
(iii) programmes of distribution should be supported wherever this is necessary, by programes of production, processing and supply.

Fifth Five Year Plan (1974-79)

By the time Fourth Plan was getting completed, Planning had become an inseparable part of national life. The Fifth Five Year Plan coincided with a major upheaval on the international economic scene which profoundly affected developed and developing countries. Economists and political leaders all over the world were reminded of the collapse of the international economic order in the thirties. The sharp increase in the prices of food, fertilisers and oil seriously upset the assumptions on which the draft Fifth Plan had been framed. These new developments also lent urgency to a time-bound programme of action in order to achieve a measure of self-reliance in food and energy. This Plan had the twin objectives of increasing production and promoting social justice. The provision of fuller employment was one of the surest means of promoting greater social justice. The Planning Commission's document devoted some thought to this problem. Its study shows that a dent can be made on rural unemployment by augmenting agricultural productivity and vigorously implementing land reforms, as envisaged in the 20-Point Programme.

As mentioned earlier, the inflationary pressures was nullifying several development efforts. The pressures came in 1972-73, thereafter these pressures gathered strength in 1973-74 and continued unabated right up to September 1974 food articles and industrial raw materials accounted for about two-third of the price increase. The prices of machinery, transport equipment and manufactured goods contributed to a little over one-fourth to the overall increase in prices. These pressures were first felt as a result of severe drought conditions in 1972-73, followed by shortages of various essential consumer goods and critical raw-materials and inputs. Shortage of power together with higher international prices of imported inputs and their inadequate availability led to the stagnation of industrial production during 1973-74. The price situation was aggravated by continued expansion in money supply partly due to large deficit financing and partly due to excessive expansion of bank credit to the commercial sector.

The balance of payment position also came under severe strain. Large quantities of foodgrains and essential wage goods had to be imported. The four-fold increase in oil prices and increase in prices of cereals, fertilisers, machinery and equipment, non-ferrous metals and other imported goods severely eroded the resources.

Therefore, the resource allocation to different sectors of this Plan also gave thrust on social and community services, in addition to its continued thrust on industry, mining and irrigation. Education also got due importance during this plan (Fig. 11.4). Yet, removal of poverty hogged the limelight along with self-reliance in the planning parlance. It sought to delineate a desirable profile of development, indicating magnitudes which will help to determine options for long term investment and outlining strategies which will help to overcome the constraints in achieving the objectives. The strategies relate to growth in the three leading sectors, viz., agriculture, energy and critical intermediates and the creation of additional employment opportunities.

This Plan set the target of increase in food grain production based on growth in yield by 3 per cent per annum (Chapter 2). The increases in yield depended on the increases in input. Somewhat conservative assessments were stipulated for yield level possibilities for each crop separately for differing agronomic conditions.

It also laid emphasis on successful local planning. The priorities for land reforms in the 20-Point Programme were observed and the measures implemented. Grant of proprietary rights or ensuring security of tenurial arrangements to the small farmers and share croppers together with production support through agricultural and, more particularly, through special programmes, were of great importance. Agricultural planning carried out on the basis of a comprehensive area approach proved effective in generating additional employment through ancillary activities involving animal husbandry, better utilisation of conventional waste materials, etc.

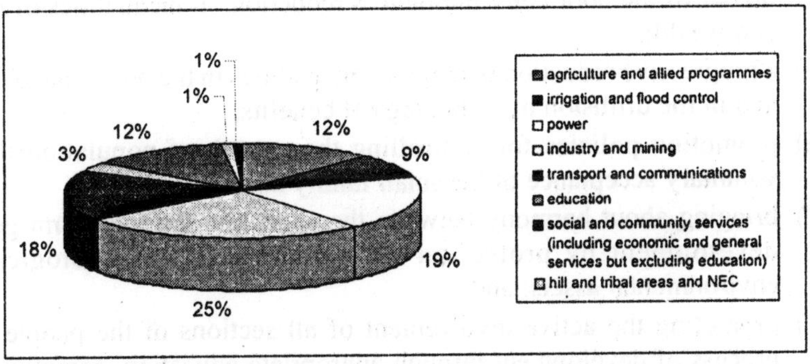

Fig. 11.4: Plan Allocation—Fifth Five Year Plan

Sixth Five Year Plan (1980-85)

In the introduction to the Third Five Year Plan, Jawaharlal Nehru said "Planning is a continuous movement towards desired goals". Therefore, this plan continued some of the efforts of employment generation schemes and other rural development programmes, in addition to the thrust on increasing productivity and production of foodgrains. The final size of the public sector outlay was fixed at Rs. 97,500 crore. This outlay is in real term 80 per cent higher than the outlay in the Fifth Five Year Plan. Keeping in view Plan objectives, an initially consistent and feasible inter-sectoral allocation was adopted to achieve a growth rate of 5.2 per cent. While the outlays on all major sectors of the economy was estimated to at least be double in nominal terms compared to the Fifth Plan, the growth rate of outlays in rural development and irrigation were even higher (Fig. 11.5). Energy sector got the maximum share of resource allocation, followed by industry and transport.

The objectives of the Sixth Plan included:

(i) a significant step up in the rate of growth of the economy, the promotion of efficiency in the use of resources and improved productivity;

(ii) strengthening the impulses of modernisation for the achievement of economic and technological self-reliance;

(iii) a progressive reduction in the incidence of poverty and unemployment;

(iv) a speedy development of indigenous sources of energy, with proper emphasis on conservation and efficiency in energy use;

(v) improving the Quality of life of the people in general with special reference to the economically and socially handicapped population, through a minimum needs programme whose coverage is so designed as to ensure that all parts of the country attain within a prescribed period nationally accepted standards;

(vi) strengthening the redistributive bias of public policies and services in favour of the poor contributing to a reduction, in inequalities of income and wealth;

(vii) a progressive reduction in regional inequalities in the power development and in the diffusion of technological benefits;

(viii) promotion policies for controlling the growth of population through voluntary acceptance of the small family norm;

(ix) bringing about harmony between the short and the long term goals of development by protection and improvement of ecological and environmental assets; and

(x) promoting the active involvement of all sections of the people in the process of development through appropriate education, communication and institutional strategies.

This plan also reviewed the growth performance of all previous plans and depicted the continued growth in terms of GDP/National Income (Table 11.2).

Table 11.2: Targeted and Actual Growth Rates (Percentages)

Sl. No.	*Plan*	*Target*	*Actuals*	*Growth rate for*
1.	First Plan	2.1	3.6	National income
2.	Second Plan	4.5	4.0	National income
3.	Third Plan	5.6	2.2	National income
4.	Fourth Plan	5.7	3.3	Net domestic product
5.	Fifth Plan	4.4	5.2	Gross domestic product

Source: Chapter 1, Sixth Five Year Plan.

The tasks of modernisation and structural change in agriculture were even more daunting at the start of the planning era. The outmoded land tenure system, the primitive technology of cultivation and lack of an infrastructure for raising productivity proved formidable barriers to agricultural advance. The fact that these barriers have been overcome to an extent is one of the major successes of our planning effort. Zamindari and other intermediary tenures have been almost eliminated. The technology of cultivation has changed substantially with the spread of high-yielding varieties and the extension of irrigation, a change which was facilitated by the elaborate network of agricultural research and extension set up during the planning era.

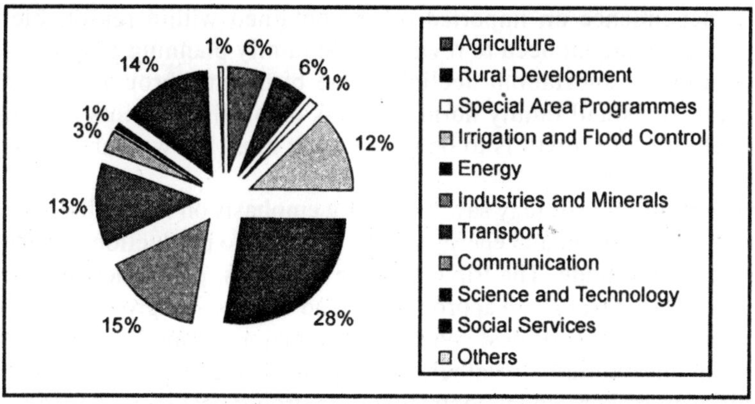

Fig. 11.5: Plan Outlay in Sixth Five Year Plan

An assessment of growth in foodgrain production till Fifth Five Year Plan brought to the fore that area under foodgrain started declining in the early seventies, however, the production witnessed increase during the same period owing to increase in yield (Table 11.3).

Table 11.3: Growth Rate of Area, Production and Yield

Sl. No.	*Item*	*Foodgrains*		*Non-foodgrains*	
		1949-50 to 1964-65	*1964-65 to 1978-79*	*1949-50 to 1964-65*	*1964-65 to 1978-79*
1.	Area	1.4	0.6	2.5	0.8
2.	Production	3.0	3.4	3.5	2.6
3.	Yield	1.4	2.3	1.0	1.3

Source: Chapter 1, Sixth Five Year Plan.

With regard to growth and modernisation the first lesson is that we must mobilise resources to maintain and increase the tempo of investment and protect the size of the Plan both against inflation and external disturbances. The second is the paramount need to improve efficiency in key infrastructural and industrial sectors. The third is that we must reduce the variability of the growth rate and ensure that weather abnormalities and inflation do not lead to undue cutbacks in public or private investment. The fourth is the need to extend the agricultural revolution to all areas and farming systems and in particular to ensure that the incomes of the poor are raised in the process of agricultural development. The fifth is the need to ensure a vigorous expansion in exports and a rapid increase in domestic production of oil, steel, fertilizers and vegetable oils so as to restrain growth of imports in order to maintain viability of our external payments. Sixth, we must develop effective domestic substitutes for imported energy so that our dependence on imported oil is contained within reasonable limits. Finally, there is urgent need to revitalise the family planning programme so as to bring about a substantial decline in me birth rate through the voluntary adoption of the small family norm. Success on all these points is essential if the overall rate of growth is to be raised, as it must be, well above the levels reached in the past.

The agricultural strategy saw increasing emphasis on integrated approaches to pest control, nutrient and energy supply, and also to production, conservation, consumption and trade. The triple alliance of weeds, pests and pathogens will have to be fought through an appropriate blend of genetic, agronomic, biological and chemical methods of pest control. Three major groups of factors influence stability of production—weather, pest epidemics and public policies. Pest epidemics can be kept under control through proper pest surveillance and plant protection measures. Public policies in the area of agrarian reforms and pricing, marketing and distribution can also be tailored to stimulate production. Weather aberrations are, however, beyond human control. Therefore, it was essential that contingency plans are developed, particularly in areas which were prone to drought and floods for meeting different weather probabilities. The overall strategy for minimising the adverse impact of aberrant weather will be: (a) to introduce crop life-saving techniques, (b) to popularise alternative cropping patterns based on weather conditions; and (c) to introduce compensatory production programmes in irrigated areas and in off-seasons. Steps will have to be taken during the Sixth Plan period to systematise efforts in the field of disaster management with regard to human, animal and plant populations.

The Sixth Plan envisaged many challenges and opportunities. It felt that since food occupies the first place in the hierarchical needs of man, we can neglect agriculture only at the risk of economic instability.

Food security remained an important dimension for the agricultural sector and also for self-reliance. The aims of the agricultural programmes during the Sixth Plan period included:

(a) to consolidate the gains already achieved;
(b) to accelerate the pace of implementation of land reforms and institution building for beneficiaries;
(c) to extend the benefits of new technology to more farmers, cropping systems and regions and to promote greater farm management efficiency through concurrent attention to cash and non-cash inputs;
(d) to make agricultural growth not only an instrument of maintaining an effective national food security system but also a catalyst of income and employment generation in rural areas;
(e) to promote scientific land water use patterns based on considerations of ecology, economics, energy, conservation and employment generation; and
(f) to safeguard the interests of both producers and consumers by attending

to the needs of production, conservation, marketing and distribution in an integrated manner.

The relevance of rural development for overall food security and the development of country was considered to be significant. The major thrust of the Five Year Plan 1980-85 was on on strengthening the socio-economic infrastructure of development in the rural areas, alleviating rural poverty and reducing regional disparities. The specific programmes and strategies adopted during the Plan period to achieve these. The concept of an Integrated Rural Development Programme was first proposed in the Central Budget of 1976-77, and a beginning was made. This programme was intended to assist the rural population to derive economic benefits from the developmental assets of each area. The programme with some modifications was introduced on an expanded scale in 1978-79.

A Food for Work Programme was initiated in 1977-78, aimed at creation of additional employment in rural areas on works of durable utility to the community, with the use of surplus foodgrains available in the buffer stock for payment as wages. Beginning somewhat haltingly, the programme gained momentum in 1978-79 when over 12 lakh tonnes of foodgrains were utilised creating 372.8 million mandays of employment. During 1979-80, the utilisation has been provisionally estimated at 23 lakh tonnes of foodgrains inclusive of the special allotments which were made to the States affected by drought in that year, resulting in about 600 to 700 million mandays of employment as estimated on incomplete reports. The programme, besides creating substantial additional employment in the rural areas during lean employment periods, more particularly in areas affected by the widespread drought of 1979, has made a favourable impact on stabilisation of wages in the rural areas and also helped check the rise in prices of foodgrains. Notwithstanding, however, its very substantial achievements in respect of employment generation and even more so its popularity and promise, the programme suffered from severe limitations in respect of planning and supervision of works. The operation of this programme on a year-to-year basis had resulted in uncertainty about its continuance for the full Plan period.

Food security is directly linked with the purchasing power of the poor. Hence, employment becomes critical to food security. This brings in the aspect of accessibility to food. The Sixth Plan focused on this aspect with the National Rural Employment Programme. The problem of employment in rural areas is mainly of seasonal unemployment and underemployment. NREP was implemented as a Centrally sponsored scheme on 50:50 sharing basis between the Centre and the States. The Centre provided its share in the form of food grains to the extent surplus food grains are available, and the rest in cash. Inter-State allocation of food grains was made on a rational criteria related to the population size of the target group, i.e. a State's population of marginal farmers and agricultural labourers and its rural population below the poverty line. The States were encouraged to procure sorghum, millets and other locally grown food grains and utilise them under the scheme. This envisaged besides, making additional food grains available for NREP, help in insulating the producers from uneconomical sale of their produce and also save substantially on cost of movement of food grains from distant godowns to the work-sites. For the storage of food grains so procured, rural godowns programme and other programmes for building up storage capacity in rural areas were considered. Some other programmes also helped rural people and indirectly impacted food security positively. These were: DPAP, DDP, TRYSEM, Cooperative Credit, Cooperative Marketing, Processing and Storage, among others.

Seventh Five Year Plan (1985-89)

Former Prime Minister of India, Indira Gandhi once described "*planning in our country is a charter of orderly progress. It provides a framework of time and space that binds sectors, regions and States together and relates each year's effort to the succeeding years*" (*Preface, 7th Five Year Plan*). She also went on to add that the measure of a Plan is not intention but achievement, not allocation but benefit. It is a statement of universal validity. Like previous plans, the Seventh Plan kept its central planning concern as removal of poverty.

Removal of poverty remains a central concern of planning in India. Consistent with this objective, the Seventh Plan's development strategy and the pattern of growth emerging from it were expected to lead to reduction in poverty at faster rate than in the past. The Plan envisages an expanded coverage under the various anti-poverty programme. Taking into account the highly comfortable position of food stocks with the public sector, it was deemed possible to expand the employment-oriented anti-poverty programmes at a still faster rate than envisaged in the Plan document. The plan advocated to put in efforts to plug various loopholes in the operation of anti-poverty programmes and to integrate these various sectoral and area development programmes into a comprehensive design of integrated development of each area. Promotion of efficiency and higher productivity have been another major concern in the preparation of this Plan increased and more efficient utilisation of existing assets both in agriculture and industry were considered to contribute to increasing efficiency of resource use and also help in containing the rise in the capital output ratio.

In retrospect, the plan mentions that since the launching of the Fifth Five Year Plan the Indian economy has moved to a higher growth path. The successful implementation of the Sixth Five Year Plan has been a major contributory factor to this welcome shift in the growth curve. On the whole, the Sixth Plan has been fairly successful in sustaining and further strengthening the impulses for growth, modernisation and social justice. The satisfactory implementation of the Plan has enhanced our ability to deal with chronic problems of poverty and underdevelopment. This was based on the assessment of Sixth Plan's targets and achievements (Table 11.4).

Table 11.4: Sixth Plan Growth Rates: Targets and Actuals

(per cent per annum)

	Sixth Plan targets	*Anticipated actuals 1979-80 to 1984-85*
Agriculture	3.8	4.3
Mining and manufacturing	6.9	3.7
Other sectors	5.5	6.6
Total	**5.2**	**5.2**

Source: Seventh Five Year Plan, Planning Commission, 1985.

The aggregate growth target set for the Sixth Plan could be achieved mainly because of good agricultural performance and a rapid growth in the services sector. The rate of growth of income generated in mining and manufacturing was well below target, and this is one of the weak points in the growth record in the Sixth Plan. Poverty declined from 48.3 per cent in 1977-78, to 37.4 per cent in 1983-84. The main reasons for this welcome trend are the higher rate of economic growth and the increases in agricultural production. The Sixth Plan also witnessed a massive expansion in the Integrated Rural Development Programme which was extended to cover all development blocks in the country, and a substantial effort at providing employment on rural works through the National Rural Employment Programme (NREP) and, in the last two years of the Plan, the Rural Landless Labour Employment Guarantee Programme (RLEGP). The targets set for the coverage of poor families under IRDP and for employment generation under NREP and RLEGP were met. Various evaluation studies of the IRDP programme including the one undertaken by the Programme Evaluation Organisation (PEO) of the Planning Commission have analysed the process of implementation of the programme, identified several weaknesses and suggested corrective measures which would help reduce leakages, enhance the impact of the programme and improve the viability of the individual schemes.

Now, banking on the success achieved earlier, this plan continued its thrust on the previous programmes and initiated programmes in the areas of education, health care and family welfare in terms of coverage in a targeted manner. It recognized the need for special attention must be paid to the quality of service provided in these sectors, and the performance measured in terms of ultimate effects on literacy, educational status, incidence of diseases, mortality rates, nutritional status and fertility rates. As evident from Fig. 11.6, the plan outlay laid emphasis on social services programmes (15%), to strengthen its base in the areas mentioned above, which would impact people's living standard and help them in leading healthy life. However, the maximum share of the plan allocation to the energy sector (27%).

This was the plan, which looked beyond five years and kept the perspective of the next 15 years. The aim was to make India a modern, technologically

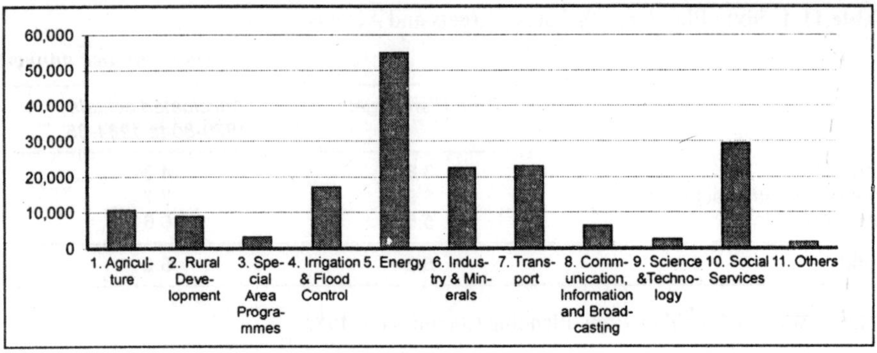

Fig. 11.6: Seventh Plan Outlay (Rs. Crores)

progressive economy with expanding capacity to provide the basic material and cultural requisites of well-being for all people. It recommended that the attainment of these goals would require:

1. action to sustain and enhance the momentum of economic expansion and technological development;
2. adoption of effective promotional measures to raise the productivity and incomes of the poorer sections of the population, poorer regions and poorer states;
3. expansion and qualitative improvement in facilities for health, education and other basic civic amenities; and
4. measures for bringing about a sharp reduction in the rate of population growth.

Continued Thrust on Self-sufficiency in Food Production

The significance of population stabilization was realized as it stated that the fairly high rate of growth of population neutralises to a significant extent the fruits of economic growth and affects food security. Its agricultural perspective sets targets for increasing foodgrain production. Given these developments, the foodgrains requirement by the year 2000 has been estimated around 240 million tonnes. The achievement of this target will be made possible by increased use of fertilizer and irrigated area, and by improvement in technology. For achieving the target of food grains and other crops, the requirment of fertilizer by 1999-2000 was estimated at around 20 million tonnes, and that of irrigation around 100 million hectares. This goes on to show that the country still required infrastructure expansion in this sector and investment in agricultural extension services. The perspective plan for agriculture development aims at maintaining self-sufficiency in foodgrains and attaining self-sufficiency in respect of pulses, oilseeds, and fibre. Its other objectives are to maximise employment opportunities and to promote conservation and environmental protection measures so as to arrest the degradation of the natural endowments of soil, water and other resources.

With its previous programmes and interventions bearing fruits, the plan kept its focus on the rural development and poverty alleviation programmes. Poverty alleviation programmes was viewed in the wider perspective of socio-economic transformation in the country. While the present strategy of direct attack on poverty through specific poverty alleviation programmes is justified on account of insufficient percolation of benefits to the poor from overall economic growth, it should be appreciated that the strategy of direct attack on poverty cannot be sustained and would not yield the desired results, if the overall growth of the economy itself is slow and the benefits of such growth are inequitably distributed. The programmes for poverty alleviation should thus be regarded as supplementing the basic plan for overall economic growth, in terms of generating productive assets and skills as well as incomes for the poor. However, it admitted the deficiencies in the implementation of the poverty alleviation programmes. The special programmes for income generation for the poor through assets endowment and wage employment for them continued at an accelerated pace during the Seventh Five Year Plan.

NREP, Rural Landless Employment Guarantee Programme (RLEGP), TRYSEM, DWCRA and IRDP continued even during this plan with renewed vigour. The total impact of the programme depended on the degree to which the different poverty alleviation programmes, including the Minimum Needs Programme (MNP), are integrated with one another and with the overall development of the area.

Measures Proposed in the Seventh Plan

The National Rural Employment Programme continued in the Seventh Plan as an important component of the anti-poverty strategy. As indicated earlier, this was viewed as an integral part of the total package, which would imply that an effort would have to be made to direct and monitor the wage employment opportunities accruing through this Programme to members of the target group including those indentified for assistance under the IRDP. For purposes of the Seventh Plan, Community Development and Panchayati Raj was viewed to break free from the conventional methodology of including a large number of small schemes through minimal budget provisions. What goes by the name of Community Development in the documents would have to be viewed now more in the nature of a scheme for village development which would imply the planning and implementation of a number of residual activities at the village level which do not get covered in the normal sectoral plans and special programmes, e.g. village paths, drainage and sanitation. This in turn would have to be done on the basis of local, decentralised planning at the village and block levels for which block funds, both in the nature of outright and incentive grants, would have to be placed at the disposal of Panchayati Raj and Community Development bodies rather than by forming sectoral plans for the villages at the State and National levels.

Agriculture occupies a key position in the Indian economy because of its contribution to overall economic growth through supplies of food, raw materials and exports. It is a source of livelihood for a majority of the population and provides a large market for non-agricultural goods and services. This plan focused on the extension of new technology and procurement of foodgrains at remunerative prices. Major problem identified was crop-wise disparities in growth, between food grains and non-food grains on the one hand, and among different food grains themselves on the other. Part of this inter-crop imbalance derives from regional imbalances.

Eighth Five Year Plan (1992-97)

By the time this plan came into place, a third of our population still lived in conditions of poverty, denied of the basic minimum needs. It said that *we cannot have the ambivalent attitude of the developed market economies which can afford to provide social security to its people. We do not have those kind of resources. So, we have to move with caution. Those very processes, which stimulate growth, sometimes tend to neglect the poor.* Preface of the Plan cautions against the opening of the market and trade and said that this could lead to wider disparities within the society. Though the objective and focus remained the same, the Plan tried to look different with some of its features:

- This Plan concentrated on building a long-term strategic vision of the future and sets forth the priorities of the nation. While for the public sector, the Plan goes into the details examining the alternatives and identifying the specific projects in various sectors, for the rest of the economy it works out sectoral targets and tends to provide promotional stimulus to the economy to grow in the desired direction.
- The Plan recognised "human development" as the core of all developmental effort. It is only healthy and educated people who can contribute to economic growth and this growth, in turn, will contribute to human well-being. The priority sectors of the Plan that contribute towards realisation of this goal are health, education, literacy and basic needs, including drinking water, housing and welfare programmes for the weaker sections. In the Eighth Plan, Governments at the Centre and in the States will expand their role in this sphere.
- This is an integrative Plan. If the results of our developmental activities so far have not been commensurate with the investments made, one of the main reasons has been our fragmented approach. Too many agencies trying to do too many things with a thin spread of resources has led to poor results. If we can integrate our developmental efforts, the results can be much more impressive even with these levels of investment. I think the time has come for us to take a close look at the structure of the Government particularly in the priority areas of Rural Development,

Energy and Transport and bring together the various departments/ agencies dealing in each of these areas under one umbrella for coordinated policy formulation and implementation.

The Eighth Plan had the following focus:

(i) Clear prioritisation of sectors/projects for investment in order to facilitate operationalisation and implementation of the policy initiatives taken in the areas of fiscal, trade and industrial sectors and human development;
(ii) Making resources for these priority sectors available and ensuring their effective utilisation; and completion of projects on schedule avoiding cost and time overruns; and
(iii) Creation of a social security net through employment generation, improved health care and provision of extensive education facilities throughout the country.

The resource allocation of the Plan suggests that the manufacturing and services sectors were given due importance (Fig. 11.7). Considering self-sufficiency in food production as prerequisite, agriculture was paid attention, as the pressure to cope up with the population growth kept mounting. About 19 per cent of the Plan allocation went for this sector.

The strategy for agricultural development in the Eighth Plan aimed at not only achieving self-sufficiency in food but also generating surpluses of specific agricultural commodities for export. Though the progress of agriculture in the recent period was satisfactory, there were striking regional and crop imbalances. Productivity varies considerably from one region to another. The plan envisaged to transfer the benefits of Green Revolution to the eastern and north-eastern region of India, which have adequate rainfall, fertile soil and unlimited scope for stepping up agricultural production. Since two-third of the cultivated area is still unirrigated, a more balanced regional development was call for a greater emphasis on dry land farming. The plan emphasized that maintaining food security and relative self-sufficiency in food production is a strategically desirable long-term goal for the country.

A reasonable degree of food self-sufficiency or supply of "wage goods" is seen to have a very positive influence on stability and growth even in our limited experience of development. It may be largely due to the factor of relative food self-sufficiency, among others, that India achieved a higher rate of growth and better economic stability and resilience during the Eighties. This was the only decade as a whole when we felt somewhat comfortable on the food front. Hence, it seems appropriate that food self-sufficiency remains an important element of the strategy of development even in the perspective of a period of next fifteen years or so.

Benefits to remunerative benefits to farmers and provisioning employment for the poor was set as targets for this plan. Poverty remained a problem of considerable magnitude. Incidence of poverty varied very much across the States. The States with high per capita income and highly developed agriculture (Haryana and Punjab) were virtually able to eliminate poverty. The same was not the case for states where industry is highly developed (Gujarat, Maharashtra). Thus development of agriculture and production and supply of food grains seemed to be highly favourable factors in eliminating poverty. The target was to eliminate poverty by the turn of the century.

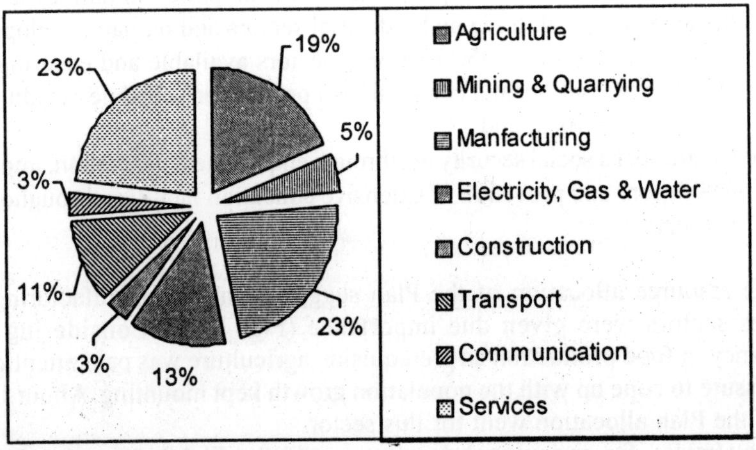

Fig. 11.7: Eighth Five Year Plan Outlay

Food requirements for the country was estimated in the plan: India will have an estimated 941 million people by the year 1997. This will increase to 1102 million by 2007. With this population and given improvements in consumption levels associated with growth in incomes, the estimated foodgrain requirement for 1997 and 2007 will be around 208 million tonnes and 283 million tonnes respectively. The foodgrain production has to match this level of demand. The required production levels of foodgrains by 1997 and 2007 are 210 million tonnes and 285 million tonnes respectively.

Integration of Poverty Alleviation Programmes for Rural Development: District Plans

Important feature of this plan was the emergence of the view that the sectoral plans in isolation would help the cause. Hence, a high degree of convergence was recommended in this plan, in a few districts on a pilot basis by an integration of the poverty alleviation programmes, the area development programmes and sectoral schemes. Taking a district as a unit of planning, a district plan was considered to incorporate the felt needs of the people and the funds available. For planning and implementation of the district plan, the responsibility would vest in the Zilla Parishads where they exist and/or in the DRDAs. However, this should not preclude the involvement of people's representatives both elected and non-elected and voluntary organisations from taking on the planning and implementation of various schemes and programmes. The Integrated Rural Development approach the details of which would vary from place to place. It is proposed in the Eighth Plan that one district per state is selected for the implementation of this programme in the manner described in earlier sections. It also recommended a greater emphasis on the role of voluntary organisations in rural development. Creation of a nation-wide network of NGOs was also suggested.

Ninth Five Year Plan (1997-2002)

The Ninth Five Year Plan, launched in the 50th year of India's Independence, took the country into the new millennium. The plan called to redouble efforts at development, especially in the social and economic spheres, so that the country will realise its full economic potential and the poorest and the weakest will be able to shape their destiny in an unfettered manner. The Approach Paper to the Ninth Five Year Plan, adopted by the National Development Council, had accorded priority to agriculture and rural development with a view to generating adequate productive employment and eradication of poverty; accelerating the growth rate of the economy with stable prices; ensuring food and nutritional security for all, particularly the vulnerable sections of society; providing the basic minimum services of safe drinking water, primary health care facilities, universal primary education, shelter, and connectivity to all in a time bound manner; containing the growth rate of population; ensuring environmental sustainability of the development process through social mobilization and participation of people at all levels; empowerment of women and socially disadvantaged groups such as Scheduled Castes, Scheduled Tribes and Other Backward Classes and Minorities as agents of socio-economic change and development; promoting and developing people's participatory bodies like Panchayati Raj institutions, co-operatives and self-help groups; and strengthening efforts to build self-reliance. These very priorities constitute the objectives of the Ninth Plan. The plan reviewed the growth performance in all previous plans and found that the actual progress was better than the target in the First, Sixth, Seventh and Eighth Five Year Plans (Table 11.5).

This plan focused on improving the household food security. Launching on to the successes achieved during the previous plans, this plan went ahead with its objectives of generating adequate productive employment and eradication of poverty; accelerating the growth rate of the economy with stable prices; ensuring food and nutritional security for all, particularly the vulnerable sections of society; providing the basic minimum services of safe drinking water, primary health care facilities and sustainable development. The plan outlay gave once again importance to the social services besides Energy and Transport sectors (Fig. 11.8). The total outlay stood at Rs. 186315.2 crore (*Economic Survey,* 2008-09).

Table 11.5: Growth Performance in the Five Year Plans

(per cent per annum)

Sl. No.		*Target*	*Actual*
1.	First Plan (1951-56)	2.1	3.61
2.	Second Plan (1956-61)	4.5	4.27
3.	Third Plan (1961-66)	5.6	2.84
4.	Fourth Plan (1969-74)	5.7	3.30
5.	Fifth Plan (1974-79)	4.4	4.80
6.	Sixth Plan (1980-85)	5.2	5.66
7.	Seventh Plan (1985-90)	5.0	6.01
8.	Eighth Plan (1992-97)	5.6	6.78

Source: Ninth Five Year Plan, Planning Commission.

Social Services Sector combined with rural development programmed focused on several poverty alleviation and employment generation programmes. These programmes targeted to improved accessibility to food, and therefore, aimed at improving the food security at the household level. At the beginning of this plan the magnitude of the problem was still quite staggering. Thirty-six per cent of the Indian population was below poverty line (BPL) in 1993-94. The incidence of poverty declined from 54.9 per cent in 1973-74 to 36 per cent in 1993-94. But the absolute number of poor did not decline much over this period of 20 years. There were 321 million poor in 1973-74 and 320 million in 1993-94; in the rural areas the corresponding numbers were 261 million and 244 million. The main determinants of poverty were identified as: (i) lack of income and purchasing power attributable to lack of productive employment and considerable underemployment and not to lack of employment *per se*; (ii) a continuous increase in the price of food, especially foodgrains which account for 70-80 per cent of the consumption basket; and (iii) inadequacy of social infrastructure, affecting the quality of life of the people and their employability.

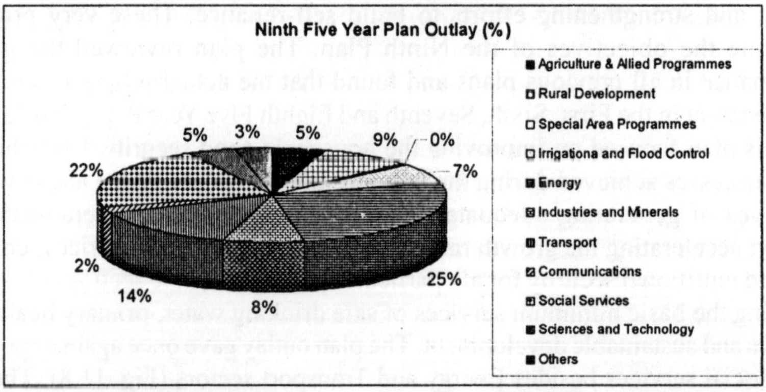

Source: *Economic Survey* 2008-09.

Fig. 11.8: Ninth Five Year Plan Outlay

Rural poverty alleviation was considered to be vital for the overall development of rural India. Integrated Rural development Programme (IRDP) and Allied Programmes considered to be core of self-employment and rural prosperity. Since the inception of the programme till 1996-97, 50.99 million families have been covered under IRDP. Of the total families assisted under this programme 44.75 per cent were Scheduled Castes/Scheduled Tribes and 27.07 per cent women. This plan recommended that the direct poverty alleviation programmes should continue, with the orientation towards strengthening the productive potential of the economy and providing more opportunities for involving the poor in the economic process. The Integrated Rural Development Programme (IRDP) continued to be the major self-employment programme targeted to families living below the poverty line in the rural areas of the country. In the Ninth Plan it would be implemented through an integrated approach under which the existing schemes of Training of Rural Youth for Self-Employment (TRYSEM) and Supply of Improved Toolkits to Rural Artisans (SITRA), Development of Women and Children in Rural Areas (DWCRA) and Ganga Kalyan Yojana (GKY) would be subsumed into the main programme.

New Initiatives under IRDP

- IRDP as a holistic programme covering all aspects of self-employment, namely, organisation of beneficiaries and their capacity building, planning of activity clusters, infrastructure, technology, credit and marketing.
- The existing sub-schemes of TRYSEM, DWCRA, SITRA and GKY to be merged into IRDP.
- Progressive shift from the individual beneficiary approach to the group and/or cluster approach.
- To facilitate group approach SHGs will be formed and steps will be taken to nurture them.
- For cluster approach each district will identify 4 to 5 activity clusters in each block based on local resources and occupational skills of the people. The infrastructure needs for the identified activities will be met in full.
- The Banks to be closely involved in the planning and preparation of projects, identification of activity clusters, infrastructure planning as well as capacity building and choice of activity of the SHGs.

Food Security Objectives Set for this Plan

- Freedom from hunger through increase in food production, effective distribution, improvement in purchasing power of the population;
- Reduction in undernutrition and its health consequences through: universalisation of ICDS, screening 'at risk groups', growth monitoring, better targeting of food supplements to those suffering from undernutrition,

close monitoring of under-nourished persons receiving food supplements; effective intersectoral coordination between health and nutrition workers to ensure early detection and management of health problems associated with or leading to under-nutrition;

- Prevention, early detection and effective management of micronutrient deficiencies and the associated health hazards.

Food Security For All, emerged as new *mantra* as part of the National Agenda for Governance, creating a hunger free India in the next five years and reform and improve the PDS so as to serve the poorest of the poor in rural and urban areas. Hence, there was significant departure on the focus and direction of food security, i.e. from macro level self-sufficiency to household level sustainable food security. However, the plan also suggested a judicious combination of domestic production and food trade can provide a reasonable degree of stability in food availability, especially in a situation where food production is characterised by seasonal and annual fluctuations. The plan took stock of the growth in foodgrain production over the five decades, showing significant increase during Eighties and early Nineties (Table 11.6).

Table 11.6: Production of Food Grains—Average Annual Growth

(*Million Tonnes*)

Year	*Rice*	*Wheat*	*Coarse Cereals*	*Pulses*	*Total Food Grains*	*Compound Annual Growth (Per cent)*
1950-51	20.58	6.46	15.38	8.41	50.82	—
1960-61	34.58	11.00	23.74	12.70	82.02	3.22
1970-71	42.23	23.83	30.55	11.82	108.42	1.72
1980-81	52.63	36.31	29.02	10.63	129.59	2.08
1990-91	74.29	55.14	32.70	14.26	176.39	3.54
1997-98*	83.52	66.38	31.15	13.08	194.13	1.73

*Estimated

Source: Economic Survey 1997-98.

This plan focused on the food security system, especially on revamping the public distribution system (PDS). The successes in terms of self-sufficiency in production and relative price stability have not, however, been without significant costs to the economy. The system of food security, as it evolved over time, tended to consume substantial budgetary resources on account of high levels of subsidies. A significant proportion of food subsidy represents the cost of carrying buffer stocks. The cost of carrying buffer stocks in recent years has been on an average about 25 per cent of the food subsidy bill. However, these costs have to be seen against the cost of food insecurity which is incalculable.

Self-sufficiency in production of foodgrains is often advocated as a first step towards attaining food security for a country of India's size for a number of reasons. First, the world foodgrains market is narrow as compared to India's domestic production and consumption.[6] Second, the strategy of self-sufficiency in food subserves the goal of national security dependence on food aid or largescale imports may entail unacceptable compromises on national security policies. Third, the country is thickly populated and food production is the predominant means of livelihood for a large section of peasant cultivators and agricultural labourers. Last, but not the least, the country continues to produce most of the times cheaper foodgrains, particularly cereals, as compared to the cost of imports. So, except during the years of severe shortfall in production, imports could not be a normal supplement to domestic supplies. On the other hand, there have been hardly a few years of surplus production supporting a sustained level of exportable supplies.

Universal PDS was done away with. Fall all out of the universal PDS has been that the States with the highest incidence of poverty, viz. Orissa, Bihar, Madhya Pradesh and Uttar Pradesh were the once whose per capita PDS off-take was the lowest. It thus became clear that the PDS, which existed, did not serve the poor well, especially in the poorer States. In view of the mounting food subsidy in recent years, coupled with the fact that the PDS did not reach the poor, a view has emerged that the universal coverage of the PDS is neither sustainable nor desirable. Price of foodgrains determine how much the poor will spend on food items and in a way influence the poverty line.

In view of the fact that the poor devote a substantial part of their expenditure on foodgrains, it is essential to protect them from a continuous upward pressure on foodgrains prices, a phenomenon in-built in our system of procurement prices which need an annual increase as an incentive for increasing production. If the poor are not protected from the impact of the ever increasing pressures on prices of foodgrains through a subsidised PDS, the impact of many of the poverty alleviation measures and programmes would get neutralised. Open ended coverage, however, could not be continued, not only because of its massive implication for the total volume of food subsidy but also because of the enormous price distortions that is implicit in an open ended, heavily subsidised PDS.

TPDS

The logic of a targeted PDS described above was enunciated in the Report of the Working Group on National Policy on Public Distribution System (June 1996) set up in the Planning Commission in August 1995. The Working Group after discussing various forms and experiences of targeting, such as, through wage employment programmes (JRY, EAS etc.), area-based targeting (ITDP, RPDS), exclusion of non-poor and the system of food stamps prevalent in some countries, suggested a scheme of allocation of foodgrains out of the Central Pool to the States at two sets of prices, namely, a highly subsidised price for the allocations meant for the poor and near open market prices for the non-poor. The recommendations of the Working Group are given in Box.

For strengthening the operational machinery of the PDS, the Planning Commission provide funds under its plan programmes for the following schemes:

- Construction of Godown
- Purchase of Mobile Vans/Trucks
- Training, Research and Monitoring.

Paradigm Shift: Special Attention to Nutrition Security

Though nutrition related programmes existed in earlier plans, the focus was more on self-sufficiency and food availability (Annexure 1: List of Nutrition Intervention Programmes). This plan came out with Nutrition Policy (Table 11.7) and reviewed related programmes undertaken earlier.

The Policy also prescribed a series of action points/initiatives to be undertaken by various Ministries/Departments of the Government. Accordingly, a National Plan of Action on Nutrition (NPAN) was formulated in 1995 with sectoral commitments to be undertaken by the 14 nutrition-related Ministries/Departments, viz., Agriculture, Food Production, Civil Supplies and Public Distribution, Education, Forestry, Information and Broadcasting, Health and Family Welfare, Labour, Rural Development, Urban Development, Welfare, Women and Child Development etc. (Annexure 2).

Table 11.7: National Nutrition Policy

Direct Short Term Interventions	*Indirect Long Term Interventions*
• Universalisation of ICDS	• Ensuring household food security
• Nutrition education of mother	• Improving dietary pattern
• Better coverage of expectant women	• Improving purchasing power
• Reaching the adolescent girls	• Strengthening PDS
• Control and elimination of micronutrient malnutrition	• Land Reforms
	• Better health and family welfare coverage
• Popularisation of low cost nutritious foods	• Basic nutrition and health education
• Fortification of food	• Nutrition surveillance
	• Information, education and communication
	• Research
	• Education and literacy
	• Improving status of women

Source: Ninth Five Year Plan.

Tenth Five Year Plan (2002-2007)

In addition to the focus on sectoral investments and on schemes and programmes, which has been integral to every Plan, the Tenth Plan laid emphasis on policy and institutional reforms that are required for each sector, both at the Centre and in the States. In other words, the full reform agenda that is considered to be essential for attaining the targets. Privatisation came in limelight during this plan. Preface of this plan highlights the significance:

The other major challenge lies in creating the conditions for vibrant and dynamic private activity in practically every sector of the economy. There are numerous barriers to the free expression of entrepreneurial energies in the country; some of which are in the Centre and some in the States. In particular, our agricultural sector is hamstrung by a plethora of controls which prevent our farmers from realising the full value of their efforts. Considerable reforms in the industrial arena over the past decade were brought, but the agricultural sector continues to be governed by regulations which were framed during an era of shortages. This must change.

Employment generation with higher growth emerged as one of its unique features. It gave explicit recognition that the Indian economy is in a phase where the growth process alone will not to be able to provide adequate work opportunities for the emerging workforce, let alone reduce the backlog of unemployment. Even at an average annual growth rate of 8 per cent, the economy is likely to generate 30 million work opportunities during the Tenth Plan period as compared to the estimated 35 million people who will be added to the workforce. The plan recognized there has been perceptible increase in regional imbalances over the years. The shape of things to come in the coming years was revealed by this plan in the unregulated economic scenario. It was brought to the fore that India was in the midst of transforming an agrarian economy into a modern multi-dimensional economic power-house and a traditional stratified society into an egalitarian society through consultative politics.

The last decade of the 20th century witnessed a visible shift in the focus of development planning from the mere expansion of production of goods and services, and the consequent growth of per capita income, to planning for enhancement of human well-being. Outlay of this plan clearly indicates two major areas, viz., energy and social services. Energy sector occupies the pivotal place once again with 32 per cent of the outlay dedicated to this (Fig. 11.9). Though social services occupy the second place, its allocation is half of the energy sector. The outlay share for agriculture was only five per cent of the total. However, it increased by 58 per cent from its previous plan's allocation. Increasing irrigation capacity and water management were another dimensions given importance in this plan, besides rural infrastructure which support agricultural and non-agricultural economic activities. This Plan recognised that economic growth cannot be the only objective of national planning and indeed, over the years, development objectives are being defined not just in terms of increases in GDP or per capita income but more broadly in terms of enhancement of human well-being.

This Plan identified specific and monitorable targets for a few key indicators of human development:

- Reduction of poverty ratio by 5 percentage points by 2007 and by 15 percentage points by 2012;
- Providing gainful and high-quality employment at least to addition to the labour force over the Tenth Plan period;

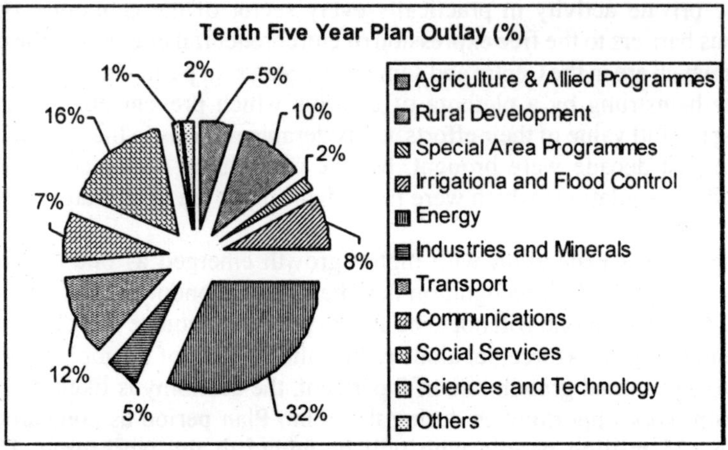

Fig. 11.9: Tenth Five Year Plan Outlay

- All children in school by 2003; all children to complete 5 years of schooling by 2007;
- Reduction in gender gaps in literacy and wage rates by at least 50 per cent by 2007;
- Reduction in the decadal rate of population growth between 2001 and 2011 to 16.2 per cent;
- Increase in Literacy rates to 75 per cent within the Plan period;
- Reduction of Infant Mortality Rate (IMR) to 45 per 1000 live births by 2007 and to 28 by 2012;
- Reduction of Maternal Mortality Ratio (MMR) to 2 per 1000 live births by 2007 and to 1 by 2012;
- Increase in forest and tree cover to 25 per cent by 2007 and 33 per cent by 2012;
- All villages to have sustained access to potable drinking water within the Plan period; and
- Cleaning of all major polluted rivers by 2007 and other notified stretches by 2012.

Unemployment was another area of concern in this plan, which impact food security at household level:

The current backlog of unemployment at around 9 per cent, equivalent to 35 million persons, is too high, and every effort needs to be made to not only arrest the rising trend, but to actually reduce it during the Tenth Plan period itself. The Prime Minister's vision of creating 100 million employment opportunities over the next ten years is taken as the basis for targeting the creation of 50 million employment opportunities during the next five years, which is about 14 million higher than the target mandated in the Approach Paper on the basis of additions to labour force during the Plan period. If this target is achieved, the unemployment rate is likely to decline significantly to 5 per cent by the end of the Tenth Plan. Similarly, the mandated reductions in the poverty rate of 5 percentage points during the Tenth Plan and another 10 percentage points during the Eleventh Plan, as stipulated in the Approach Paper, will still leave more than 11 per cent of the population, or about 130 million people, below the poverty line in 2012. Every effort, therefore, needs to be made to reduce the poverty rate even faster. It is estimated that with a proper sectoral and regional focus, it may be possible to reduce the poverty rate by nearly 7 percentage points over the Tenth Plan period if the growth target of 8 per cent is achieved through the state-wise break-down that has been drawn up in consultation with the States (*Chapter 1, Tenth Five Year Plan*).

The plan aimed at achieving food security through sustained growth in foodgrain production and targeting household level access to food through various rural development and employment generation programmes. It recognized that the main factors for the all-round success of agriculture have been: increase in net sown area; expansion of irrigation facilities; land reforms, especially consolidation of holdings; development and introduction of high yielding seeds, fertilizers, improved implements and farm machines, technology for pest management; price policy based on MSP and procurement operations; infrastructure for storage/cold storage; improvements in trade system; increase in investments, etc. However, the deceleration in rate of production was noted by the plan. During the 1990s (1989-90 to 1999-2000), the growth of agriculture decelerated as compared to the 1980s (1979-80 to 1989-90). An assessment of plan outlay for agriculture and allied sector was made and the result depicted the declining trend over the last 6 five year plans (Fig. 11.10).

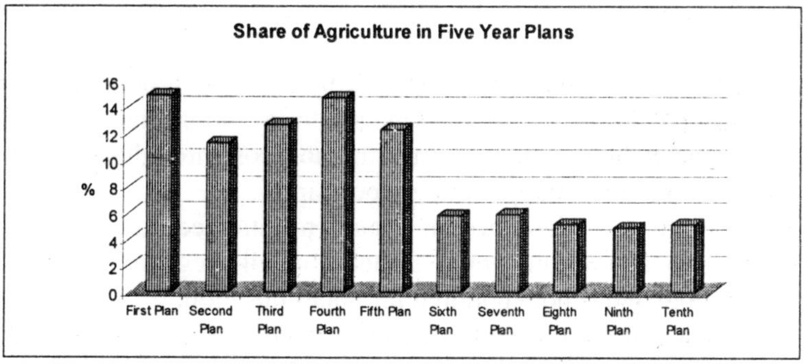

Fig. 11.10: Share of Agriculture in Five Year Plans

The Tenth Plan continued with the regionally differentiated strategy based on agro-climatic conditions and natural resources as adopted in the Ninth Plan. These were:

- increase in overall employment and incomes by raising farm productivity and the growth of other economic activities in the rural areas;
- provision of gainful supplementary employment through poverty alleviation schemes; and
- distribution of food grains through the public distribution system at subsidised prices to those living below the poverty line.

Food security got its latest dimension added in this plan. Three major departures were included for implementation:

- household food security and freedom from hunger to nutrition security for the family and the individual;
- untargeted food supplementation to screening of all the persons from vulnerable groups, identification of those with various grades of under-nutrition and appropriate management; and
- lack of focused interventions on the prevention of over-nutrition to the promotion of appropriate lifestyles and dietary intakes for the prevention and management of over-nutrition and obesity.

This plan envisaged to identify vulnerable groups/families, undernourished individuals and provide them with well-targeted subsidised food items through TPDS. In addition to the supply of rice and wheat, locally procured coarse grains, pulses and iodised salt may be provided; choose appropriate modalities for making optimal use of available subsidies to meet the needs of the vulnerable segments of the population; ensure that there is no duplication of schemes for improving nutrition security to vulnerable groups. It recommended management of transient food scarcity due to drought, on the basis of early warning systems. Major interventions proposed in this plan include:

- Adequate availability of foodstuffs by ensuring production of cereals, pulses and seasonal vegetables to meet the nutritional needs, making them available throughout the year at affordable cost through reduction in post-harvest losses and appropriate processing;
- Prevention of under-nutrition through nutrition education;
- Operationalising universal screening of all pregnant women, infants, preschool and school children for under-nutrition;
- Operationalisation of nutrition interventions for the management of under-nutrition promotion of appropriate dietary intake and lifestyles; and
- Nutrition monitoring and surveillance to enable the country to track changes in the nutritional and health status of the population.

Though not included in the plan document, the plan period witnessed one of the most significant steps taken by the government to ensure food security by providing livelihood opportunities for the rural poor. This step is famously known as National Rural Employment Guarantee Act (NREGA), which was launched in 2006. According to the Ministry of Rural Development, a staggering 17.92 lakh of works mostly relating to water conservation and rural connectivity were taken up in the rural areas. This scheme is operational in all the 670 districts in India with an estimated rural households of 450 million since April 2008 (*The Financial Express*, June 9, 2008). This has been considered a major step in providing livelihood opportunity round the year.

Eleventh Five Year Plan (2007-12)

In the background of 7.7 per cent growth during the Tenth Five Year Plan, this Plan expressed its concern for agriculture and rural development sector. This plan has incorporated the revival of agriculture sector alongside the ongoing reforms. Its Preface brings out the core element of this plan as given below:

The Tenth Plan marked a historic breakthrough on the aggregate GDP growth front. The challenge before the Eleventh Plan is to improve upon this growth performance and also ensure greater sustainability and inclusiveness so that the development process being unleashed has the widest possible spread of benefits. In the search for inclusion, the Plan pays special attention to the needs of the weaker sections including the Scheduled Castes, Scheduled Tribes, OBCs, and minorities.

The slowdown in growth of foodgrain production owed it to many challenges faced. Indian agriculture has faced a number of severe challenges, superimposed on the long-term demographics. Recent trends that have raised concern regarding food security, farmers' income, and poverty include widening economic disparities, increased vulnerability to world commodity price volatiiity following trade liberalization, lack of adequate incentives and appropriate institutions, degradation of natural resource base and rapid and widespread decline in groundwater table, with particularly adverse impact on small and marginal farmers. Sectoral allocation has the bearing of the above scenario. About 74 per cent of the total central allocation for this plan has been put aside for the priority sectors. Their share was only 55 per cent in the Tenth Plan (*Chapter 3, Eleventh Five Year Plan*). Overall, the social sector has been accorded priority with 31 per cent allocation (Fig.11.11). The plan envisages to get private investment in the energy and transport and other infrastructure development. This reflects a conscious shift owing to the magnitude of problem faced by the country. One of the new innovations that is likely to gain importance in the Eleventh Plan period is the concept of investment in infrastructure through Public Private Partnerships (PPP).

According to the latest NSS figures (61st Round), agriculture continues to employ 70 per cent of our rural workforce, industry (14.4%), and services (14.8%) make up for the rest. However, in view of the decline in agriculture's contribution to GDP and the near constant proportion of workers dependent on it, there is need for rapid generation of off-farm employment. In the light of this, the Eleventh

Plan has suggested strengthening of small and medium enterprises mainly in the unorganized sector. Unorganized sector enterprises generally suffer from weak marketing. They need better market infrastructure, professionally organized exhibition of products at the international level, efficient system of supply chain management, brand promotion, and standardization. Efforts are needed to establish better linkages with different parts of the chain.

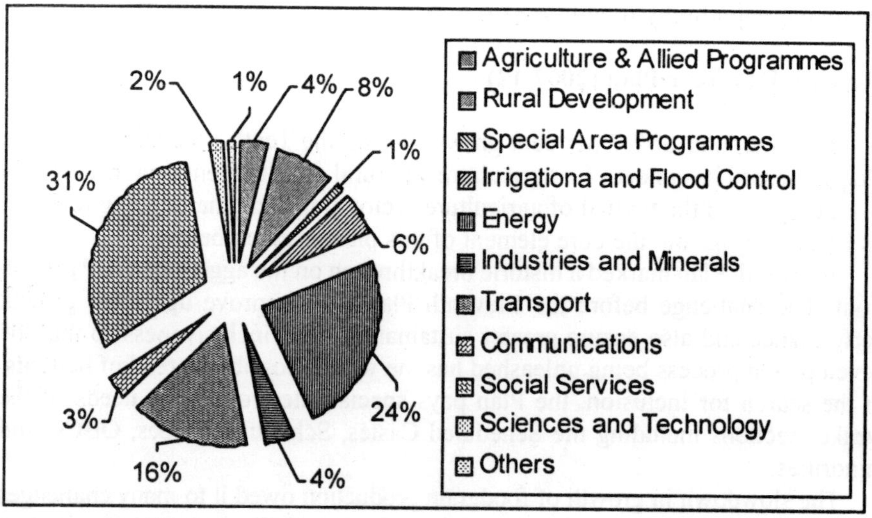

Fig. 11.11: Eleventh Five Year Plan Allocation

Considering the persisting poverty and large concentration of poor population this plan aims at targeting the poverty through various programmes, and with a multi-pronged strategy, with a view on multidimensional nature of poverty in India.

It also noted that there are identifiable occupational features of the poor: they are concentrated in agricultural labour and artisanal households in rural areas, and among casual labourers in urban areas. Casual labourers in urban areas are essentially distress migrants from rural areas in States where agricultural land-man ratio is very adverse. The plan also gives consideration to the spatial disparity in terms of employment and livelihood opportunities. It says that the poor are geographically concentrated in India. Another important feature noted and for which planning has been proposed is a large proportion of the chronic poor is dependent on wage labour. A safety net becomes quintessential for the majority of the poor residing in rural areas. The wage employment programme called NREGA has been given emphasis in the planned document.

The significance of NREGA lies in the fact that it creates a right based framework for wage employment programmes and makes the government legally bound to provide employment to those who seek it. In this way the legislation goes beyond providing a social safety net, and towards guaranteeing the right to employment. The experience with NREGA so far suggests that it is one of the main planks of rapid poverty reduction in the Eleventh Five Year Plan. Starting with 200 districts across the country in Phase I during 2006-07, NREGA was extended to additional 130 districts in Phase II during 2007-08. From 1 April, 2008 onwards the Act will cover the whole of rural India. As a district is notified under the Act, Sampoorna Grameen Rozgar Yojana (SGRY) is automatically merged in the NREGA and would, therefore, cease to exist with effect from 1 April, 2008 (Chapter 4, 11th Five Year Plan).

NREGA has emerged as an important form of social and livelihood security in rural areas. It is especially important for women, who make up half of the NREGA workforce. The biggest challenge is to end delays in wage payments. Under the Act, workers are entitled to payment within 15 days. In reality, workers wait for weeks for the payment. This in fact defeats the purpose as the labour force do not have the back up to wait for the payment. However, the successful implementation of NREGA has the potential to ensure food security for the poor. M.S. Swaminathan (2009)[7] recommends much needed convergence for human development at NREGA sites. Arjun Sengupta, chairman of the National Commission for Enterprises in unorganized sector, whose report found that 77 per cent of the population lives on Rs. 20 or less per day, argues for a new development paradigm, which focuses on job creation[8]. With foodgrain prices rising steeply, even at subsidized rates, a majority would be left out as they do not have the purchasing power, making them food insecure and nutritionally deprived. The real problem lies in the lack of purchasing power. All our development plans have strived towards creating employment generation and also met the emergency situation with aplomb in most cases. Yet, the planners are up against the large chunk of youth in the working age group, as a result of population momentum caused higher population growth during 1960s and 1990s. Any sustainable food security in this country will continuously depend on our capacity to remain self-reliant in terms of foodgrain production and creation of employment opportunities on sustainable basis with a focus to improve in human development.

SUMMARY AND CONCLUSION

India's journey for achieving overall development and food security during the period of Five Year Plans has been challenging. During the course, we have achieved many milestones and witnessed stumbling blocks, blocking the path of reducing the number of poor. From being food deficit to food surplus country for over a billion population is no mean achievement. We have been able to tackle the question of availability of food and moved on to addressing the needs of accessibility to food and further progressed to formulate policy for nutritional requirements. The period is marked by long term planning and short term interventions. The journey is depicted below (Table 11.8).

Table 11.8: Food Security in Five Year Plans: Salient Features and Achievements

Five Year Plans	*Focus of the Plan*	*Important Features Related to Food Security*	*Food Security—Major Thrust and Impact*
First	Irrigation/Transport Agriculture	Expand area under irrigation Increase in area under cultivation Increase foodgrain production	Move towards Self-Sufficiency—Production increased during this plan period
Second	Industries/Irrigation/ Energy	Increase in area under irrigation Universalisation of PDS	Strive towards Self-sufficiency
Third	Industries/Transport/ Regional Development	Targeted to achieve increase in foodgrain production Large projects were considered as nuclei of regional growth Removal of regional disparity through industrial development and trickle-down effect.	Sustained increase in production remained the mantra
Fourth	Indutries/Transport/ Agriculture	Modernisation of agriculture Improved transport network and facilities essential for transporting foodgrains in all parts of the country Modernisation of agriculture Benefit to small and marginal farmers Foodgrain Policy Committee constituted FCI came into existence Ban on forward trading of foodgrains Seeds of Green Revolution sown	Increased production of foodgrains Improved availability and physical access to food through buffer stocks and PDS
Fifth	Industry/ Irrigation/ Power	Emphasis on improved yield of crops Improvement of socio-economic infrastructure in rural areas Impact of global oil crisis and import of foodgrains Green Revolution	Food availability remained the central theme Oil crisis and price rise reduced the economic access to food items and nutrition
Sixth	Energy/Transport/ Irrigation	Improved food situation due to Green Revolution Thrust on modernization of agriculture Stagnancy in net sown area Rural development schemes for improving food security FFW/NREP/DPAP etc.	Improved availability of foodgrains. However, the self-sufficiency still eluded Employment generation in rural areas for improving economic access to food. Contained drought of 1979

(*Contd.*)

(*Contd.*)

Five Year Plans	*Focus of the Plan*	*Important Features Related to Food Security*	*Food Security—Major Thrust and Impact*
Seventh	Energy/Social Services/Industries	Removal of poverty remained central concern Agriculture sector grew robustly Continuance of rural development and employment generation programmes Introduction of new schemes pertaining to education, health and family welfare	Food self-sufficiency at the national level remained the pre-requisite for food security Improved access to food also acquired attention
Eighth	Manufacturing/ Service/ Agriculture	Looked beyond self-sufficiency Targeted to generate surpluses of specific agricultural commodities for export Transfer of green revolution benefits to eastern and north eastern of the country Focus on dryland farming Integration of poverty alleviation programmes	Relatively food self-sufficient Employment oriented schemes helped improving accessibility
Ninth	Energy/Social Services/Transport	Economic reform Combination of social sector schemes and rural development programmes Employment generation Price rise Sustained production of food and effective distribution Launching of new schemes for reducing undernutrition-ICDS Revamping of PDS-TPDS National Nutrition Policy Watershed development programmes	Moved towards food for all Household level food security came into planning parlance and implementation Nutrition security came into focus

(*Contd.*)

Five Year Plans	*Focus of the Plan*	*Important Features Related to Food Security*	*Food Security—Major Thrust and Impact*
Tenth	Energy/Social Services/ Transport	Economic reform continued Focus on employment generation and higher growth Rural infrastructure development TPDS Surplus foodgrain production Nutrition monitoring and surveillance Thrust on commercial crops Declining growth in crop fertility related to foodgrains noticed at the fag end of the plan	Self-sufficiency achieved Household level food security got the attention Nutrition for children and women Need for environmentally sustainable green revolution called for
Eleventh	Social Services/Energy/ Rural Development	Slowdown in foodgrain production Tackling unemployment emerged the greatest challenge NREGA Strengthening of SMEs Safety net for poor Nutrition for tribal population	Sustained increase in foodgrain production back in focus For improved accessibility focus on vulnerable group

It is amply clear that we have succeeded in long term interventions in terms of increasing availability of foodgrains. We are yet to succeed in another dimension of food security, i.e. accessibility to food. The planned interventions have avoided major crises and mitigated disaster. The basic question of addressing the economic access to food for more than 250 million population still persists. The Indian government has traditionally maintained buffer stocks as a means to stabilize domestic foodgrain prices. In the scenario of liberalized external trade in foodgrains, the examination of the cost effectiveness of variable levies on trade as an alternative option to stabilize domestic prices becomes necessary. Government's buffer stock policy plays an important role in tackling transitory food insecurity through price stabilization by transferring resources from the periods of plenty to those of scarcity. The transitory food insecurity is caused by fluctuations in agricultural output, which are mainly due to uncertain weather conditions. Price stabilization achieved through buffer stock operations helps both consumers and producers. Importantly, consumption levels of food are prevented from falling to low levels during bad crop years, by disallowing prices from taking higher values. The efficacy of buffer stocking policies in dealing with transitory food security is reflected in the stability of foodgrain consumption and prices.

In order to improve the accessibility to food, we have banked on the Food for

Work Programme and similar programmes with different nomenclatures. The problem of access to food and nutrition has compounded in the last 2-3 years owing to the steep price rise of food items. Owing to the globalization and our own liberalization policies, the adverse impacts are immediately felt. Therefore, the government has been in the emergency containment mode all the time. NREGA is improved version of Food For Work Programme. The fate of hundreds of millions remain depended on these programmes. The successive plans have though achieved success tremendously in foodgrain production, the number of BPL families have not come down. The planners have to come out with a long term programme for skill development of hundreds of millions in diverse sectors, who can earn their livelihood on their own, linking it up with the market.

Annexure 1

Nutrition Intervention Programmes (1951-1992)

Period	*Nutrition Situation*	*Nutrition Services*
1950s	Food Shortages	Food Production Phase: Technological advancement to improve food production Food fortification measures to improve nutritive value.
1960s	Malnutrition most prevalent in lower economic strata. IDD as a Public Health problem	Community Development Phase: Launching of Applied Nutrition Programme Mobile Food and Nutrition Extension Services Iodisation of salt
1970s-early	Recognition of Chronic Energy Deficiency Anaemia, Vitamin A deficiency and IDD as major nutritional problems of public health importance	Direct Nutritional Interventions: Special Nutrition Programme Prophylaxis against Anaemia and Vitamin A deficiency
Mid-1970s	Recognition that infection and undernutrition were major causes of morbidity and mortality among infants and children	Multi-Sectoral Indirect Interventions Phase: Integrated Child Development Services (ICDS) Universal Immunisation Programme (UIP) Oral Rehydration Therapy (ORT) Nutrition Promotion through poverty alleviation, Public Distribution of Food, Health and Family Welfare measures, Adult Education.
1980s	Felt need for nutritional bias in Sectoral policies and programmes	Efforts for adoption of a National Nutrition Policy
1990s	Recognition that Malnutrition is an impediment to national development; its use as indicator of Development Process	Finalisation of the National Nutrition Policy

Source: Department of Women and Child Development, Government of India, New Delhi.

Annexure 2

Sectoral Commitments under National Plan of Action on Nutrition (NPAN)

	Sector	Sectoral Commitments in the NPAN
1.	Agriculture	To ensure national level food security including buffer stocks and nutritional considerations in Agricultural policy.
2.	Civil Supplies & Public Distribution	To ensure food security at the household level by making the essential foods available through the Public Distribution System to the people particularly to the disadvantaged sections.
3.	Education	To provide convergent services under Education Sector to enhance the nutritional and health status of the community with special emphasis on girls' education and improved status of women.
4.	Forestry	To popularise the growing of plants/trees supplying food stuffs/fruits with special emphasis on Beta carotene (Vitamin A) rich species in the social forestry programmes with a view to create nutritional awareness and promote the consumption of nutritious foods.
5.	Health	Prevention and control of infections, micronutrient malnutrition, diseases related to inappropriate diets, creating health awareness among the people and ensuring adequate primary health care for all.
6.	Family Welfare	To improve the nutritional status of women and children through nutrition prophylaxis programmes, health and nutrition education and promotion of small family norm.
7.	Food	To ensure food security in the country.
8.	Food Processing Industries	To meet the nutritional needs of the people by giving nutrition orientation to the projects in food processing sector.
9.	Information and broadcasting	To create a climate of awareness in the country about the importance of nutrition for the well being of the people and ways and means of preventing various forms of malnutrition through its different units.
10.	Labour	To protect and promote the nutrition of various types of labour-agricultural, construction, industrial etc. with special emphasis on children and women at work, through formulation and enforcement of appropriate labour laws.
11.	Rural Development	To improve purchasing power of the people in rural areas through employment generation and poverty alleviation programmes with a view to improve food security at the household level.
12.	Urban Development	To ensure access to social services relating to health care, nutrition, women and child development, preschool and non-formal education and physical amenities like potable water supply, sanitation, sewerage, drainage etc., with a view to improve the nutritional level of the urban poor.
13.	Welfare	To improve nutrition of the disadvantaged sections of society by ensuring implementation of nutritional components of various welfare programmes.
14.	Women and child development	To ensure appropriate development of human resources both through direct nutrition interventions for specially vulnerable groups as well as through various development policy instruments for improved nutrition as laid down in the National Nutritional Policy. Improving nutrition and health of women and children through strengthening and extension of ICDS programme and setting up of appropriate systems for monitoring the follow-up actions under National Plan of Action for Children

Source: National Plan of Action on Nutrition (NPAN), Dept. of WCD, Government of India, New Delhi, 1995.

NOTES

1. An Expert Group headed by Former Chairman of the Prime Minister's Advisory Council, Suresh Tendulkar brought out that the overall poverty figure is 37 per cent and not 27 per cent as was estimated in 2004. In this new poverty line, the Panel has added expenditure on health and education, in addition to the calories norm set in 1973-74.
2. R.P. Misra, *Development Issues of Our Time*, Concept Publishing Company, 1984, p. 50.
3. Chapter-1, Development of the Economy: Achievement and Perspective, Second Five Year Plan, Planning Commission, Government of India.
4. Balanced Regional Development, Chapter-9, Third Five Year Plan, Planning Commission.
5. Agricultural Production, Chapter-19, Third Five Year Plan, Planning Commission.
6. For example, the size of the international rice market at that point of time was about 12-13 million tonnes. Though the world wheat market is comparatively large at 110-120 million tonnes, it is cartelised. India produces about 65 million tonnes of wheat and 80 million tonnes of rice. Under such a situation, large scale imports of say 10 per cent of its requirements can make India vulnerable to sharp rises in world prices of foodgrains.
7. M.S. Swaminathan, "Synergy Between Food Security Act and NREGA", *The Hindu,* June 1, 2009.
8. *Economics Times,* August 22, 2009.

REFERENCES

Dev, Mahendra (1996): "Food Security: PDSvs EGS", *Economic and Political Weekly*, Vol. 31, No. 27, 6 July, pp. 1752-1764.

Dreze, Jean and Amartya Sen (1989): *Hunger and Public Action*, New York, Oxford University Press.

Economic Times, August 22, 2009.

George, P.S. (1999): "Some Reflections on Food Security in India," *Indian Journal of Agricultural Economics*", Vol. 54, No.4, October-December 1999. pp 465-489.

Government of India, *Eighth Five Year Plan*, Planning Commission, 1992.

Government of India, *Eleventh Five Year Plan*, Planning Commission, 2007.

Government of India, *Fifth Five Year Plan*, Planning Commission, 1974.

Government of India, *First Five Year Plan*, Planning Commission, 1951.

Government of India, *Fourth Five Year Plan*, Planning Commission, 1969.

Government of India, *Ninth Five Year Plan*, Planning Commission, 1997.

Government of India, *Second Year Plan*, Planning Commission, 1956.

Government of India, *Seventh Five Year Plan*, Planning Commission,1985

Government of India, *Sixth Five Year Plan*, Planning Commission, 1979.

Government of India, *Tenth Five Year Plan*, Planning Commission, 2002.

Government of India, *Third Five Year Plan*, Planning Commission, 1961.

Jenkins J. Craig and Stephen J. Scanlan (2001): "Food Security in Less Developed

Countries, 1970 to 1990", *American Sociological Review*, Vol. 66 (October) pp. 718-744.

Kothari, Ashish (2002): Environment, food Security and Natural Resources—Lacune in Tenth Plan Approach Paper, *EPW*, Vol. 38, No.4, pp. 289-292.

Mishra, Baidyanath (2005): "Food Security in India", pp. 29-38, *Man and Development*, Vol. XXVII No. 1, March 2005.

Misra, R.P. (1984): *Development Issues of Our Time*, Concept Publishing Company, New Delhi.

Radhakrishnan, R. (2001): "Food Security: Emerging Concerns", pp. 102-121, published in *Social and Economic Security*, S. Mahendra Dev *et al.* (ed.): Institute for Human Development, Vol I, Sage Publication, New Delhi.

Sainath, P. (2001): And There was The Market, Seminar, No. 497, pp. 101-103.

Srinivasan, P.V. and Shikha Jha (1999): "Food Security through Price Stabilisation", *EPW*, Vol. 34, No.47, November 20, pp. 3299-3304.

Sundaram, K.V., (1999), *Planning Revisited—Rural Area Development in India: Vision and Reality*, Professor R.N. Dubey Memorial Lectures, Allahabad.

Swaminathan, M. S. (2009): Synergy Between Food Security Act & NREGA, *The Hindu*, June 1, 2009.

Swaminathan, M.S. (1987): *Building a National Food Security System*. Indian Environmental Society, New Delhi. p.124.

Swaminathan, M.S. (1999): *Science and Sustainable Food Security*, 31st Jawaharlal Nehru Memorial Lecture, New Delhi.

World Food Programme (2001): *Enabling Development Food Assistance in South Asia*, Oxford, New York.

12

Food Security in South Asia: Demographic Policy and Regional Cooperation Issues

MRITYUNJAY MOHAN JHA

INTRODUCTION

Judged by the criteria of food insecurity and poverty, South Asia has the distinction of being the worst affected region. A large majority of the poor and the food-insecure people live in this part of the world, where the incidence of malnutrition is very serious. The region is also backward in terms of other social development indicators. Any effort of ensuring food security to the poor households should naturally look at the countries of this region. The countries covered by this study (Bangladesh, India, Nepal, Pakistan and Sri Lanka) apart from their geographical proximity, share a common history. Mainly due to the hegemony of British Colonial power for nearly two centuries these countries have common structures and socio-political institutions. There are marked similarities in their judicial and bureaucratic systems, as well as in their approach to education and health services and several other fields of public intervention.

Throughout the developing world and specially in the South Asian countries the population growth has been regarded as the most vital parameters in the development process. In the recent years, food production has increased satisfactorily and, kept both Malthus (1798) and Ehlrich (1968) at bay. South Asia as a whole has managed to keep its food production ahead of population growth. The margin is not large. Despite the marginal advantage in food production there is wide nutritional gap which has led to hunger. A country like India, which has achieved the level of self-sufficiency in food production, is still facing the problem of accessibility to food in ear of globalization and liberalization (Chopra *et al.*, 1992). Pakistan has almost achieve self-inefficiency but mal-distribution and malnutrition is prevalent Bangladesh has emerged as a country which has almost reached self-sufficiency in rice production (Goletti, 1994). Though poverty and malnutrition and its associated problems are posing serious challenges. Most of the countries in this region are struggling to check their high population growth. In the entire region, high population growth along with deep rooted poverty is biggest stumbling block in the socio-economic development process (Khadka, 1990).

While food security at the national level is a necessary condition, it is not sufficient to ensure automatically that all the people have enough to eat. With increasing pressure over the limited usable land and non-farm employment very hard to find the problem of food insecurity get accentuated (Osmani, 1989). Since poverty is taken as the root cause of food insecurity and malnutrition, one has to analyze these two.

Prof. Amartya Sen (1987) and John W. Mellor (1987) stressed the need for increasing the purchasing power to households to improve the household food security as well as national food security. The problem has to be attacked from both ends, food supply and fertility (Sen, 1989). There are examples of grain surplus and widespread hunger, this confirm that lack of purchasing power leads to under-nutrition; malnutrition and chronic food insecurity (Swaminathan, 1987).

The need for mustering food grain stocks and reaching them to the places where they are needed, is highly desirable (Acharya, 1983; Alam,1992). The examination of the population pressure on land and its impact on agricultural productivity is inevitable (Chaudhary, 1986). In another attempt (1988) he stressed the need for subsidized rationed shop to provide accessibility to food. Overpopulation in South Asia with high incidence or poverty and widespread under-nutrition, are closely inter-linked. Therefore, the countries should remain cautious against the declining land/person ratio (FAO, 1996). A proactive approach is needed to bring changes in the political, policy, and institutional factors responsible for development failures, which can be debated.

This study attempts to analyze the population and food imbalance in South Asia. It reviews the existing population, food-nutritional/agricultural policies with special reference to India, and assesses regional cooperation dimension for food security in this region.

Concepts

Food Availability

This depends upon agricultural production in a sustainable environment. Meaning that food crops, cash crops and livestock should be sustained without exhausting the resources keeping the needs of the future generation in mind. Availability is always seen *vis-à-vis* the requirements of the current population. In a food deficit country, the import of foodgrains ensures the physical availability of food.

Accessibility to Food

This refers to the ability of the households to secure food at a reasonable price. One of the major factors influencing food security in most of the developing countries is deep-rooted poverty. Therefore, improving accessibility always rests on improving purchasing capacity of poor households. This relates to income poverty. There are other dimensions of poverty such as shelter, housing clothing, education and health, which influences access to food.

Utilization of Food

This relates to food absorption in the households, which is linked with several socio-economic factors. It is a mistake to view hunger in terms of food deprivation only: the capability to be nourished depends crucially on other characteristics. These other factors include nutrition practices, metabolic absorption and intra-households distribution (Drèze and Sen, 1989). Nutrition practices include dietary practices, child care, nutrition knowledge depending on female literacy. Metabolic absorption requires safe drinking water, sanitation and adequate health services. Intra-household distribution of food deals with the gender dimension of food insecurity and influences health and education of women.

Vulnerability

It refers to natural calamities like floods, drought, cyclone etc., which may lead to transitory food insecurity of a particular region. In some regions calamities occur frequently and in some others these are infrequent.

In India, removal of poverty and ensuring food security has been addressed by planners ever since the beginning of the planned era. High poverty levels are synonymous with poor quality of life, deprivation, malnutrition, illiteracy and low human resource development. Article 47 of the Indian Constitution also expresses its commitment towards this and states that the state shall regard raising the level of nutrition and standard of living of all its people and improvement in public among its primary duties.

Population Dynamics

Population growth has been an important factor in the developing countries determining food imbalances at macro level, and also the course of our planning for development. Population growth will be by far the most important determinant of growth in demand for staple foods during the next few decades. In future, demographic growth will be the only reason why Indian farmers will grow more cereals for direct human consumption[1].

POPULATION DYNAMICS & FOOD AND NUTRITION STATUS

There is a two way interaction between population and food resources, the extent and complexity of which may vary in time and context. The size and composition of the existing population and its growth over time has its impact on various aspects of development, socio-economic and food security. Food security, obviously is the basis of social and economic security (Rodgers, 1989). At a given level of living, any increase in population generates increased demand for resource including 'food' which is the minimum requirement.

During the last few decades the world as a whole has experienced tremendous increase in population of human being, mainly in the poorer parts of the world (*Population Bulletin*, 1994). A rapid decline in mortality and slower decline in fertility rates have been responsible for rapid population growth. In the developing countries of Africa and Asia, large population live in several areas which are poverty stricken. The Data relating to population and food growth clearly explains that in spite of the currently existing balance between the above mentioned, the magnitude of food insecurity persists.

Demographic Trends

Population size and rates in different Regions of the world (UN, 1988) clearly suggests that South Asian Region has to go few notches up in controlling its birth rate, which significantly high. In all countries of South Asia, population has been increasing quite significantly since 1950. With decline in mortality rate due to improved medical facilities and almost unchecked fertility in some parts, it is going to exceed the East Asian Region by 2025. With Indian population already past one billion mark on May 11th, 2000 and large population of Bangladesh and Pakistan (UN, 1988), this 'region' is going to take longer time to stabilise. With around 75 per cent of the total population residing in India, a serious implementation of population policy becomes imminent.

Population of South Asia grew continuously because of the faster decline in death rate (World Demographic Estimates and Projections, 1995-2025). As per the earlier United Nations projections, in case of India it has come down from 25 in 1950-55 to almost 10 in 1995-2000 (projected), Bangladesh and Pakistan are following India. Whereas Sri Lanka has the least death rates. Average Annual growth rates in the countries (World Demographic Report, 2000) indicated that it is slowing down. But due to large population in the reproductive age group its momentum will continue. Declining average annual growth rates in a country like Bangladesh is a pointer towards the success of Family Planning Programme (NIPORT, 1997). South Asia as a whole and other less developed regions, fertility began to decline from 1965 and mainly form 1980 onwards. In this region Sri Lanka registered lowest growth rates and is expected to slow down further.

Indian population registered unprecedented growth in the last five decades. Many parts of India have shown fertility decline in recent period. Projection made by the Population Foundation of India (PFI) suggests that India will reach the replacement level fertility (1.6 TFR) by the year 2026 (Natrajan and Jayachandran, 2000). Some of larger states like Uttar Pradesh will not be able to achieve this even by 2051. At that point of time UP's population will cross 40 crores and total fertility rate would be around 2.4. Considering this within the holistic framework of South Asian Region its implications on food security, environment and development are larger. The past trends in fertility and mortality in South Asia in general and India and Bangladesh in particular have shaped the typical population age structure, which has tremendous in built potential. Even if the total fertility rate comes down below replacement level, yet, absolute number will keep on increasing. Therefore, even after reaching NRR by 2010 both in cases of India and Bangladesh (World Demographic Report, 2000), it would take even longer time to stabilise.

Food Production

The "begging bowl" image of South Asian countries has been erased, as far as 'food grain production' is concerned. With 'evergreen revolution' in past decades and 'gene' revolution round the corner, we are in a position to draw a balance sheet and chalk out a strategy for the future (Swaminathan, 1999). The food grain situation has improved considerably. In most cases growth of cereal production has been steadily increasing (UN Statistical Year Book, 1999).

Being an essentially agricultural region of the world, the entire economy and life of people heaving depend on agriculture. The desired average annual growth rate should be around 4 per cent in South Asia, as set by World Food Conference. In contrast this falls below target (World Development Report, 1994). Here both projected rate is also not that encouraging.

This kind of trend does not give a positive signal and here arise the question of per capita availability of food direct human consumption which can be termed as 'per capita food supplies'. So, how far South Asian region has reached towards per capita food supplies is a pertinent question. Region-wise per capita food supplies for direct human consumption (FAO, 1997) prepared by Food and Agriculture Organization projects South Asia as number two from below. This has propelled incidence of chronic under-nutrition. There is tremendous pressure on the available arable land. In Bangladesh, almost all cultivable land have been brought under cultivation and there is no scope for further expansion (Islam,1991). Arable land hectares per capita is continuously declining from 0.10 to 0.07 in Bangladesh and 0.24 to 0.17 in India and 0.24 to 0.17 in Pakistan. This also gives an indication of declining farm sizes.

In Asia, yield growth contributed the bulk (about 80%) of food production increases, particularly in rice and wheat. There are, however, marked differences across countries, partly reflecting differences in factor endowment and policies. Yield improvement in cereal represented over 70 per cent of the observed growth in China, Indonesia, Philippines, India, Bangladesh, and Sri Lanka (FAO, 1997). On the other hand, both yield improvement and area expansion contributed about equally to cereal production growth in Pakistan, Nepal, and Thailand. In the case of India and China, as well as Bangladesh and Sri Lanka, yield improvement more than offset the effect of area contraction on cereal output. For many of the developing Asian countries, the end of the land frontier came as early as the 1970s for example, mid-1970s in the Philippines and about 1980 in Thailand (FAO, 1997).

Question of Accessibility to Food

While India, Bangladesh and Pakistan continue to maintain the self-sufficiency in food availability marginally, these countries are facing more difficult task of providing economic accessibility. Although data on below poverty line shows decline, yet absolute number is still very high (World Development Report, 1999-2000). Both India and Bangladesh have managed to bring it down to approximately 30-35 per cent. Their absolute figures remained almost unchanged. Nepal still has above 40 per cent of its population below poverty line. If we look into the distribution in the income/consumption at the country level, it almost homogenous (World Development Report, 1999-2000). Highest 30 per cent of the total population is consuming more than 60 per cent, in India, Bangladesh and Sri Lanka, whereas in Pakistan it is more than 70 per cent. This clearly depicts the inequality in the distribution of income. Lowest 30 per cent consumes only round 10 per cent in all countries. This makes a case for the provision of employment-oriented strategy. Gross inequality in consumption pattern has its implications. Country-wise data on percentage of infants with low birth-weights indicate pathetic situation—Bangladesh with 50 per cent; India 33 per cent; Nepal 26 per cent and both Pakistan and Sri Lanka at 25 per cent. These figures are quite higher than South-East Asian countries.

With one-third of its population living below poverty line, the inaccessibility to safe drinking water further accentuates the problem of food and health insecurity. Around 85 per cent of Indian Population do not have access to safe drinking water in 1995 and this figure was 54 per cent in 1982 (World Development Report, 1999-2000).

Infant mortality is another indicator reflecting the prevailing health condition and accessibility to food and nutrition. Almost all countries in this region have brought down their IMR, it is still significantly high. This, in turn, becomes one of the factors why rural populations go for large family size. So, here it shows cause and effect relationship.

Challenges Ahead

Following issues are going to emerge as serious problems in the coming decades:

(1) Meeting increased demand for food with declining safe water and arable land,
(2) Removing inequality in income,
(3) Increasing urbanization would influence/enhance consumerist culture,
(4) Preserving bio diversity, protecting land from further degradation such as salinity and alkalinity,
(5) Providing non-farm employment, and
(6) Aging population.

POPULATION AND AGRICULTURAL POLICIES

To have food and nutritional security in South Asia one must think of reduction of population growth rate as the basic necessity. Considering the number of malnourished and undernourished persons in this region its essential to think in terms of demographic sustainability *vis-à-vis* food security. Problems of food and nutritional security is multidimensional in nature. Its close relationship with population growth, poverty and socio-economic inequality cannot be ruled out. Depending on the situation prevailing in each country with regard to the population—natural resource equation, suitable population policy has to be implemented.

India has the distinction of being the first country in the world to launch a nation-wide family planning programme with full government support (Bhende *et al.*, 1985). Main goals were to control population growth by reducing fertility, decreased morbidity and mortality. The Indian government adopted 'national population policy' in 1976 with unnecessary coercive measures. The earlier programme focused on sterilization, as the main method of family planning, whereas; the latter came out with enactment of some far reaching consequences. All these policies lacked teeth as proper ground was not prepared for creating awareness among rural masses. Without proper rural infrastructure and opportunities for employment these drew flat low level of political commitment of these programmes along with illiteracy and poor health care it did not yield any positive result in some states.

The National Population Policy, 2000 has set 14 National socio-demographic goals, which is to be achieved by 2010 (GOI, 2000). This covers wide ranging issues of literacy (focusing women), immunization, institutional deliveries and access to information, plus convergence in impiementation of related social sector programmes.

Most of the countries in this region also introduced price incentives by subsidizing inputs and guaranteeing remunerative minimum support prices. With an improvement in minimum support prices, the terms of trade between agriculture and non-agriculture sector which were heavily biased against agriculture started improving. The macro economic reforms, particularly since the beginning of the 1990s, also contributed to this process. Favourable agricultural prices and guaranteed minimum support prices created a conducive environment for the adoption of input-intensive high-cost technology. This indirect effect of price policy was more important than the direct impact of the rise in agricultural prices on agricultural production.

Throughout the world there is a broad commitment to reduce hunger and malnutrition. Increased food production is essential to achieve this objective. Reducing hunger involves food distribution, food consumption and human nutrition. To address these issues, in South Asian Region 'agriculture' was brought to the centre of planning. Initially, it aimed machete at increasing gain production.

NEED FOR AN INTEGRATED POPULATION FOOD DEVELOPMENT POLICIES

One must look beyond demography as to search for a truly effective population control strategy. While population policies focused mainly on family planning and sterilization our agricultural policies focused on to increase food production. Non-food sectors have to take care of education, safe drinking water and infrastructure development. National policies should include effective participation of rural people in decision making, specially women. All countries talk about reaching net reproduction rate of (NRR) one and health for all. For this, policy maker should adopt rural-centric and women-centric development policies. And population education and awareness progrmmes have to be integral.

Fast spreading science and technology has proved to be significant gene revolution can still increase food production manifold as suggested by Prof. M.S. Swaminathan. Our yield per ha in many corps is one-third of other developed agrarian economies. Preserving our rich bio-diversity can be done through by using space technology to greater effect. The fast breeding information technology has to be taken to the villages. The space technology and 'Geographical Information System' can be very effective for future land use planning; crop forecasting and also to assess natural resource management. India has to take leading role in the South Asian Region. Because changes or alteration in the natural resources and environmental degradation in its neighbourhood has its impact on India with damaging consequences.

Public Distribution of Foodgrains in South Asia

The South Asian countries have a long tradition of public food distribution to poor households. All countries in this region have instituted Public Distribution Systems (PDS) to achieve this objective. PDS is run through food procurement in the domestic market at a pre-announced procurement price, although imports have been resorted to in some countries, e.g., Bangladesh and Sri Lanka. Foodgrains are distributed through PDS (or 'fair-price' shops) at the "issue price" which is generally lower than the market price. As the gap between procurement and issue prices is usually narrow, the State subsidizes the PDS operations.

The food, usually procured in the domestic market—although recourse to imports is not uncommon in some countries—is distributed through a public distribution system (PDS) or "fair price" shops at an "issue price" which is generally lower than prevailing market price. In the early years of the programme, the gap between the procurement price and the issue price was usually low, resulting in large government subsidies to the PDS operations. The supply was not also well targeted to poor households, making the PDS arrangement not quite different from a "universal" one in which anyone, rich or poor, is entitled to receive the subsidy. In the end, it was the non-poor urban households and civil servants who benefited the most from the programme. The huge cost of running such a programme exerted severe fiscal pressure, thereby leading the governments in these countries to eventually curtail budgets for food subsidies.

REGIONAL COOPERATION FOR FOOD SECURITY

Considering the size of population *vis-à-vis* existing temporary and chronic food insecurity in the South Asian region, regional action is inevitable. The realistic assessment of regional food requirements to overcome chronic food insecurity fostered a kind of interest towards creation of regional food reserve. Basically, the seven member countries of the South Asian Association for Regional Cooperation agreed to maintain a regional food reserve of about 200,000 metric tonnes for the use in emergencies at their 1987 summit level meeting in Kathmandu.

Generally speaking, this kind of idea was motivated by improved grain situation in India since India has already achieved what we call 'self-sufficiency' in foodgrain production and has got a huge buffer stock. The idea was mooted by the then Indian Prime Minister, Mr. Rajeev Gandhi. He said, "Where twenty years ago many of us were still dependent on food imports for survival, our remarkable achievements in agriculture have made it feasible to counter scarcities and unexpected shortages by recourse to our resources. Our national self-reliance could be reinforced by a framework of regional self-reliance" (Government of India, 1987).

This act was justified by a series of natural disasters that caused considerable damage in three countries, India, Bangladesh and Nepal, in 1988. Besides the plan to fight natural disasters through concerted effort, there are also strong political and economic reasons for maintaining a food security reserve for each of the member countries.

South Asia is a disaster-prone area. Large parts of the region are subject to floods and droughts, sometimes both. Volcanic eruptions, fire and frost are common occurrences. There is a view that deforestation and extension of cultivation on marginal lands have increased the incidence of natural disasters. The countries of the region have perfected the art of coping with natural disasters to a great extent, but each country has to fend for itself, even when a calamity is spread over more than one country. The region will benefit from an early warning system that will forewarn the countries about the impending calamity. With modern advances in techniques and instruments of surveillance, this would be a manageable undertaking.

Considering the complex political situation in the South Asian region, the major challenge in a regional food reserve system is posed by its implementation. There are very few regional schemes for maintaining regional reserves of food. One World Bank report has rightly observed that without agreement on domestic policies, on emergency buffer stocks, and on sharing the financial burden, any regional scheme will dissolve.

All countries in this region have implemented a variety of rural development and poverty alleviation programmes. They have made several innovations in their programmes on asset distribution, employment generation, social security and public distribution. Many of these innovations have succeeded while quite a few have failed. Other countries can learn valuable lessons from these successes and failures. Experience in targeting the programmes, in involving people in identification and management, and in making the projects and the schemes financially viable, are of relevance to the countries with similar objectives.

Basically to have a regional food security system or to formulate a course of action for regional cooperation, political commitment is desirable. And to have political commitment, political unity is required. Moreover, the decision to set up such a regional reserve is not based on a realistic assessment of the regional food requirement and the potential of the member countries. The managerial and economic problems regarding its implementation are additional constraints.

Baring instability in food availability and instability in food production, political instability in South Asian region along with disturbed relation between India and Pakistan, make the situation worse. In the light of the needs to achieve food security in the region on the one hand, and the complex problem associated with its achievements on the other, we have to evaluate the establishment of regional food insecurity and regional action required to overcome chronic food insecurity.

So far availability and reserves are concerned, the highest degree of instability in the region was experienced by Nepal, Sri Lanka, Bangladesh, Bhutan and Pakistan. India experienced less fluctuation in foodgrain production.

Since the possibility of stabilizing food supplies through intra-regional trade in food and agriculture is limited, one effective measure to solve temporary food insecurity problems could be to set up domestic buffer stocks. The growing self-reliance in some countries and growing food unavailability in others would surely provide some form of regional insurance against shortfalls in food availability. So, the region must have some reserve.

But the reserve requirement in South Asia depends on many factors. First of all, the size of the regional reserve should be based on the annual fluctuations in food availability rather than on chronic food shortages. Secondly, such reserve should be over and above the member countries' domestic food reserves. Thirdly, it should not be expensive. Lastly, there has to be a 'political commitment' on the part of the comparatively better off countries to contribute to the cost of holding the reserve. Reserve composition should include combination of rice, wheat, and maize. Two other important issues arise in connection with the implementation of the regional food agreement. These are about the location of the reserve and its pricing mechanism.

Apart from these measures, other measures must be taken to enhance the purchasing power of the ordinary people. The SAARC member countries could gain considerably in terms of combating malnutrition, poverty and hunger through some form of cooperation. Besides setting up an emergency food reserve there can be some other areas of cooperation. These include:

(i) setting up an early warning system;

(ii) flow of food by both limited and regulated trade and intergovernmental lending;
(iii) encouraging research and extension in agricultural technology and processing; and
(iv) increasing agricultural productivity through cooperation in developing the most important factor of production including the protection of the environment.

Permanent food security can be achieved through the creation of a Regional Food Reserve. But this would not serve the purpose to those sections of population, who lack accessibility. This is where Bangladesh can take lessons from past experiences of India and exchange planning schemes. Lack of employment opportunities and maldistribution lends to chronic food insecurity. To overcome that situation, efforts at the individual country level and multilateral level is required.

One of the permanent features in the South Asian countries is flood, which ravages agricultural land and causes enormous suffering, especially in Bangladesh, Nepal and some parts of India. This leads to food insecurity. Protection of forestland resources and environmental resources could be another area of cooperation. Population pressure on land is the principal cause of deforestation and soil erosion, which in turn causes flooding. Enhanced cooperation in protecting the environment and forest resources will definitely help in achieving food security.

A number of issues related to the location of the reserve, the kind of grain pricing mechanism, sharing of costs and conditions of release of the reserves are yet to be resolved given the bilateral political problems.

But, without improving the bilateral relations between India and its neighbouring countries, nothing substantial can be done.

CONCLUSION

The rapidly increasing population with large reproductive base along with structural poverty is the root cause of food inaccessibility in the South Asian Region. On the population and food production front countries have improved. But issues like malnutrition among women and children, safe drinking water and unemployment still need serious attention. Due to large population base pressure on land and environmental resources is likely to increase. In a country like India, democratic decentralization which has come through 73rd and 74th Constitutional Amendments, raising some ray of hope. Lack of employment opportunities in the rural areas may trigger migration towards urban centres, resulting increased urbanization with poor health and sanitary conditions. In Bangladesh, growing population is likely to force them to go out in the neighbouring country which will have its regional and political implications and ramification. Considering the recently introduced structural changes in this 'region' the role of 'state' needs to be evaluated in the changing food security system. The main challenge for the coming years will be to sustain the process of economic growth and reduction of poverty in the sub-continent 'Green Revolution' is a matter of past. 'Sustainable gene revolution' and 'evergreen revolution' is an ecological and economic necessity in India as well as in South Asia.

The option of importing food grains in any but marginal quantities is not an easy option for most of these countries, due to the foreign exchange constraint which can be relaxed in most non-oil exporting economies only by a higher level of agricultural production and export. At their present stage of development, substantial foodgrains imports would drain their meagre foreign exchange earnings. Added to this is the inadequate and poor state of infrastructure, e.g. port, transport, warehousing, etc., which result in higher cost of imported food.

From the point of view of availability and to ensure stability, major reliance will have to be placed on government stocks. The countries need sufficient quantities in "buffer stocks" to support stabilization programmes in the face of fluctuating production. Fluctuations in food grains production would put a severe pressure on the poor households. Importing food grains would drain the meagre foreign exchange resources. Within the countries, food grains production will have to be given high priority in inaccessible regions which face serious problems in the event of production shortfalls in any particular year.

Apart from domestic reforms, countries in this 'region' should also review their agricultural and pricing policies. These days, protection of environment from degradation should be one of the important areas of co-operation. This has regional as well as global implications, because a serious environmental crisis in one country may affect the environment of the entire region. Facing common problems, countries of this 'region' should co-operate at the highest level to eradicate poverty and combat chronic food insecurity. These countries will have to focus on the urgent humanitarian issues than other issues because after all human being is going to be our prime focus in the twenty-first century.

NOTE

1. Tim Dyson and Amresh Hanchate, *EPW*, Vol. 35, No. 46, 2000). Mari Bhatt, P.N., Demographic Estimates for Post Independence India: A New Integration, *Demography India* 27, 1 : 23-57.

REFERENCES

A.K. Sen (1987): "Poverty and Entitlement" in J. Price Gottinger, Joanne Leslie and Casoline Hoisenglen (eds) *Food Policy*, The World Bank, The Johan Hopkins University Press, p. 200.

B.M. Bhatia (1985): *Food Secruity in South Asia,* Oxford & IBH Publishing Company, New Delhi-16.

David Norse (1994): "Multiple Threats to Regional Food Production: Environment, Economy, Population", *Food Policy*, Vol.19, No.2, p. 146.

Durham, David Fandrem, Jain, C. (1988): " The Food Surplus: a strapple illusion of economics, a cruel illusion for population", *Population and Environment*, Vol.10, No.2, New York, pp. 115-125

FAO (1997): *Report of the Eighth Session of the FAO Regional Commission on Food Security for Asia and the Pacific*, APCFS/97/REP.

Francesco Goletti (1994): "The changing public role in a Rice Economy Approaching self-sufficiency: The case of Bangladesh", IFPRI Research Report.

Government of India, *India and Foreign Review*, New Delhi, August 1987, p.19.

Hennan Ezekiel (1998): "An approach to a food and strategy: world development," Vol.16, No.11, Washington D.C., p., 1378.

John W. Mellor (1987): "Food and Development the critical Nexus" in *Economic Impact*, No.61.

K.C.S. Acharya (1983): *Food Secruity System of India*, Concept Publishing Company, New Delhi, p.3

M.S. Swaminathan (1987): "Building a National Food Security System". Indian Environmental Society, New Delhi, p.124

M.S. Swaminathan (1999): "Science and Sustainable Food Security", 31st Jawaharlal Nehru Memorial Lecture, New Delhi.

N. Choudhary (1988): "Accounting for subsidized food resources distributed in statutory rationing in Bangladesh", *Bangladesh Development Studies*, Vol.16, No.4, December.

Natrajan, K.S. and Jayachandran, V. (2000): "Population growth in 21st century—India," Paper presented in the Millennium Conference on Population, Development and Environment Nexus. Organised by IASP, PFI and UNEPA, New Delhi, February 14-16.

Nurul Islam (1995): "Population and Food in the early twenty first century: Meeting future demand of an increasing population", IFPRI, Washington D.C.

Population Bulletin, Vol. 49, No.1, 1994.

R.H. Chaudhary (1981): "Population pressure and agricultural productivity", Bangladesh Development Studies, Vol. 9, No.1, March.

Rathindra P. Sen (1989): *Demographic Change and Levels of Living*, Daya Publishing House, Delhi, pp. 71.

S. Alam (1992): "Have supply responses increased for major crops in Bangaladesh". Bangladesh Development Studies,Vol. 20, No.1, March.

Sanderson, Fred H. (1984): "World Food Prospect to the year 2000", *Food Policy*, Vol. 9, No. 6, p.373.

UN World Demographic Estimates and Projections, 1995-2025, New York, 1988.

UN, FAO,WFS 96/Tech 1 (1995): "Food Agriculture and Food Security." The Global Dimension, p. 1.

UN, *United Nations Statistical Year Book 1992*, New York.

UNEPA (1991): *Population Resources and Environment: The critical challenges*, London.

United Nations System in India (1997): *India Towards Population and Development Goals*, Oxford University Press, Delhi

World Bank, (1995): *World Development Report-1994.*

World Bank, (1999): *World Development Report-1999/2000*, Washington, D.C.

World Bank,(1986): *Poverty and Hunger: Issues and Options for Food Security in Developing Countries*, Washington.

SECTION III
RURAL-URBAN DEVELOPMENT

13

Evolving Tribal Space in Rural India: Some Reflections

KRISHNA MOHAN

INTRODUCTION

There has been continuous effort towards holistic development of tribal population ever since the beginning of planned development in India in 1951. In all 245 communities were identified in 1950 for extending special privileges. These communities were called Scheduled Tribes. There were the following immediate requirements of the planners: population size, geographical location, and nature of distribution of these identified communities. None was available. An estimate based on 1931 census, where castewise data exists, indicated their total population as 17.9 million sharing 7.8 per cent of the total population (Table 13.1). A reservation of 7.5 per cent for Scheduled Tribes was arrived at on this estimate at the time of enacting the Constitution on January 26, 1950. On the conduct of nationwide census in 1951 for the 245 communities, their total population was recorded as 19.1 million. It was only 5.36 per cent of the total population of India. Hence one may argue to reduce the reservation based on the actual figures. However it did not happen.

Contrary to it, the schedule was revised in 1956 to include more communities. However, the basic problem on inclusion of any community in any list will revolve around working out their population size, geographical location and nature of distribution. It was assumed that the newly included comminutes will bring up the proportion of scheduled tribes from 5.36 to 7.5 per cent. It was perhaps necessary to defend the decision of the government. In the absence of any data, once again the estimates were worked out using 1931 census. Unfortunately, the figure arrived at indicated the scheduled tribe population of 22.5 million that constituted only 6.25 per cent of the total population of India. Was the reservation brought down?

Table 13.1: India: Scheduled Tribe Population, 1950-2001

Year	*Total Population (million)*	*Total Population (Per cent)*	*Growth Rate*
1950*	17.9	7.80	
1951[1]	19.1	5.36	
1956*	22.5	6.25	
1961	30.0	6.87	51.3
1971	38.0	6.90	26.3
1976**	41.10	7.50	
1981	51.6	7.60	35.8
1991	67.8	8.08	31.4
2001	84.3	8.20	24.3

Note: Years with asterisk are not Census Years.
1 Government of India (1952): First Five-Year Plan, p. 636.
* The List of Scheduled Tribes was revised.
** Scheduled Castes and Scheduled Tribes Orders (Amendment) Act 1976—Area restriction, for Scheduled Tribes, was removed.

The census of 1961 was awaited with a hope that the actual figures may be more than the estimates and the government will be able save its face. However, the census count of 1961 for all the listed communities of tribes placed a total population at 30 million. It was 6.87 per cent of the total population of India.

The attention of planners was deviated from these technical issues and directed towards war with China (1962), Pakistan (1965 and 1971) and severe drought (1965-67). The census of 1971 reported a total of 38 million Scheduled Tribes sharing 6.9 per cent of the total population of India. There were once again deliberate attempts to reach the magic figure of 7.5 per cent. The government removed the area restriction in 1976 and the Scheduled Tribe population was exactly 7.5 per cent of the total population of India. What a great magic?

Ever since 1976, there has been continuous inclusion of communities in the schedule. The Scheduled Tribe population in 2001 census was reported 84.3 million. It is 8.02 per cent of the total population of India. The journey of 1950-2001 remained by and large peaceful. However, Ninety Third Constitutional Amendment Act, 2005 effective from 2006 provided a reservation of 27 per cent to OBC. It is not difficult to understand the under currents in the context of limits to reservation up to 50 per cent. However, the rising share of Scheduled Castes (16.2), Scheduled Tribes (8.2) and persistent demand for inclusion of more castes or communities in the existing schedules is enough evidence as warning of possible constitutional crisis ahead.

The objective of this paper is limited to know the evolving tribal space in India in the backdrop of the above discussions and in the context of changes in the schedule of tribes in last nearly six decades. It attempts to reconstruct the tribal space in historical and geographical context.

Methodology

The historical records were traced and the tribal space constructed using the raw data. The reports of various committees were gleaned to know the criterion of demarcation. The inclusion of new tribes was considered and the new tribal space was reconstructed for 1961 onward. Some spurious elements were identified.

Evolution of Term

The Census of India right from the 1891 refers, with varied nomenclature, to a group of population as 'forest tribes' (1891), 'animists' (1901), 'tribal animists' (1911), 'hill and forest tribes' (1921), ' primitive tribes' (1931), 'tribes' (1941) and 'scheduled tribes' since 1951. Government of India in 1950, listed these communities, which were 245 in number, in a schedule for special privileges in the Constitution hence they are known as 'ScheduleTribe' (Government of India, 1952, p. 636).

The identification of Scheduled Tribes is broadly based on primitive traits, distinctive culture, geographical isolation, shyness of contact with the wider community and backwardness. However, these are very subjective in nature and open for political twisting.

There is an ongoing and perhaps never ending scheduling of tribes. There were 245 tribes scheduled in 1950, 360 in 1991 census and over the years this number has reached above 700 (including sub-tribes) by 2003-04. There is no religious bar. There are state specific area restrictions. The identification of Scheduled Tribes is a state subject.

Table 13.2: India: Chronology of Terms

Census	*Term*
1891	Forest Tribes
1901	Animists
1911	Tribal Animists
1921	Hill and Forest Tribes
1931	Primitive Tribes
1941	Tribes
1951	Scheduled Tribes

SCHEDULED DISTRICTS TO SCHEDULED AREAS: A CHRONOLOGY

During the British period, areas predominantly inhabited by the tribal were identified and named as 'Scheduled Districts'. The Scheduled District Act, 1874 provided for the appointment of special officers to administer Civil and Criminal Justice, superintend the settlement and collect revenue within the 'Scheduled Districts'.

The Government of India Act, 1919 separated the tribal areas covered under the 'Scheduled Districts'. The tribal areas were confined in the north-eastern part of India. The remaining area under 'Scheduled Districts' was divided in to two categories namely (i) Wholly Excluded Areas and (ii) Areas of Modified Exclusions.

The Government of India Act, 1935 renamed these areas. The 'Wholly Excluded Areas' and 'Areas of Modified Exclusion' were renamed as 'Excluded Areas' and 'Partially Excluded Areas' respectively. The term 'Excluded Area' denotes an area excluded from the scope of the control and provincial legislatures (Ulrich, 1968, p.168). These were often considered as problem areas by the British administration.

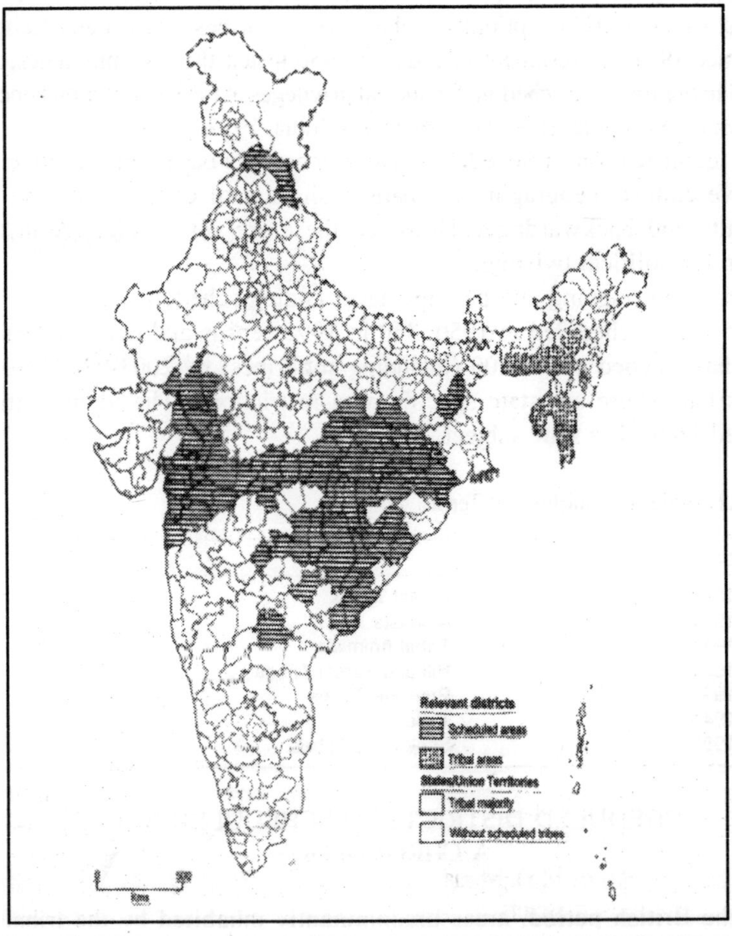

Fig. 13.1: India: Scheduled Areas and Tribal Areas as Listed in the Indian Constitution

Table 13.3: India: Trends in Territory Based Tribal Area Concepts

Year	*Concepts*
1874	Scheduled Districts
1919	Wholly Excluded Areas
	Areas of Modified Exclusions
1935	Excluded Areas
	Partially Excluded Areas
1950	Scheduled Areas
	Tribal Areas

After Independence, the Constituent Assembly paid special attention to the tribal situation and appointed two sub-committees: one for the North-East Frontier (Assam) Tribal and Excluded Areas, and another for Excluded and Partially Excluded Areas (other than Assam).

The sub-committee on 'excluded and partially excluded areas' recommended that these areas be called as 'Scheduled Areas'. There were in all 59 districts partly or wholly covered under scheduled areas that rose to 236 districts in nine states in 2001 (Burman, 2006, p. 3646). These are covered under Fifth Schedule to the Constitution (Table 13.4).

Table 13.4: India: Fifth Schedule Areas, 2009

Sr. No.	*States*	*Per cent Area*	*Per cent Population*
1.	Andhra Pradesh	11.4	4.0
2.	Bihar*	26.6	12.2
3.	Gujarat	15.0	12.3
4.	Himachal Pradesh	42.5	2.9
5.	Madhya Pradesh**	33.7	24.9
6.	Maharashtra	15.1	6.2
7.	Orissa	44.7	28.0
8.	Rajasthan	5.5	7.8
	States Total	21.3	12.4
	India	12.6	6.2

* Including Jharkhand
** Including Chhattisgarh

Source: Report of the Eleventh Finance Commission, 2000, Akalank Publication, Delhi.

Besides, the Sixth Schedule to the Constitution refers to the 'Tribal Areas'. This concept applies to Tribal Areas in the states of Assam, Meghalaya, Mizoram and Tripura (included in 1986). These enjoy full autonomy in respect of all matters falling within their jurisdiction. Hence, some scholars term these as 'states within a state' (Verma, 1995, p. 143). Managed independently by the tribal councils there are nine autonomous districts in Meghalaya (3), Mizoram (3), Assam (2) and Tripura (1), each representing a particular scheduled tribe. In case, there are more than one scheduled tribe, the district is sub-divided into 'autonomous regions'.

Notably, in Tripura one such district has been constituted to cover tribal areas spreading over three revenue districts and several tribes (Table 13.5).

Table 13.5: India: Sixth Schedule Areas, 2009

S. No.	States	Per cent Area	Per cent Population
1.	Assam	19.5	3.6
2.	Manipur	90.0	35.4
3.	Meghalaya	100.0	98.8
4.	Mizoram	18.8	14.5
5.	Tripura	68.0	32.2
	States Total	44.5	14.3
	India	2.1	0.5

Source: Report of the Eleventh Finance Commission, 2000, Akalank Publication, Delhi.

Chronology of Evolving Tribal Space

There are following stages in evolution of tribal space. These are: (i) identification/ selection of a community as tribe, (ii) estimation of numerical strength using caste based 1931 census/sample, (iii) census enumeration for arriving at actual figures, (iv) mapping of population data by administrative units to know the spatial spread and finally, the construction of regions that give birth to tribal space.

The history of enumerating tribes begins in 1891 census. A common class 'Forest Tribes' was used in this census. In all, 44 communities distributed in different parts of the country were grouped under Forest Tribe. Their total population was 15 million (Census of India, 1891, pp.193-195).

A schedule of tribes consisting of 245 communities (First Five Year Plan, 1952, p. 636) was prepared in 1950. All erstwhile Part A states except United Provinces (Assam, Bihar, Bombay, Madhya Pradesh, Madras, Orissa, Punjab, and West Bengal) and six out of eight Part B states (Hyderabad, Madhya Bharat, Mysore, Rajasthan, Saurashtra, and Travancor-Cochin) and eight out of eleven Part C states had prepared separate schedules. Some tribes were scheduled for the whole states whereas some tribes had area restrictions. Inter- state restrictions were already there.

The schedule of tribes was the longest for Orissa with 42 tribes and the smallest for Punjab with one tribe. States where tribes were not notified included United Provinces from Part A states, Jammu and Kashmir and PEPSU (Patiala and East Punjab States Union) from Part B States, Bilaspur, Cooch Behar and Delhi from Part C states, and Andaman & Nicobar Islands from Part D states.

The linguistic reorganization of states in 1956 not only reorganized the states but also schedule of tribes. A state specific list of tribes for reorganized states was prepared. In addition, list of scheduled tribes was modified by different states. The schedule of tribes was longer in number and larger in population size as compared to 1950. The modified list had in all 354 tribes (Raza and Ahmad, 1990, p. 6) against 245 in 1950.

Table 13.6: India: Tribal Space

Category	*Number of States and Union Territories*	*States and Union Territories*	*Tribal Sub-Plan*	*Remark*
A. Tribal Majority States	Four States and Two Union Territories	I. States 1. Arunachal Pradesh 2. Meghalaya 3. Nagaland 4. Mizoram II. Union Territories 1. Lakshadweep 2. Dadar & Nagar Haveli	Not Applicable	
B. Scheduled Areas	Delineated in eight states	1. Rajasthan 2. Gujarat 3. Madhya Pradesh 4. Maharashtra 5. Orissa 6. Andhra Pradesh 7. Bihar, and 8. Himachal Pradesh	Applicable	(i) Delineated under Indian Constitution. (ii) Concept of Tribal majority does not apply
C. Tribal Areas	Delineated in four States	1. Assam 2. Tripura 3. Megha-laya,and 4. Mizoram	Applicable except those included in category A of this Table	(i) Delineated under Indian Constitution (ii) Concept of Tribal majority does not apply
D. Tribal Majority Administrative Units	Identified in eighteen states and two union territories	All states and union territories, excluding those included in category A and E of this Table	Applicable	Concept of Tribal majority applies

(*Contd.*)

(*Contd.*)

Category	Number of States and Union Territories	States and Union Territories	Tribal Sub-Plan	Remark
E. No Tribal Population	Two States and Three Union Territories	I. States 1. Punjab 2. Haryana II. Union Territories 1. Delhi 2. Chandigarh 3. Pondicherry	Not Applicable	Tribal Population has not been identified by these states and union territories

Source: Compiled from various documents of the Government of India.

In 1961, thirteen out of 15 states and eight out of 12 union territories had prepared their schedule of tribes. Tribes were not notified in two states (Jammu & Kashmir and Uttar Pradesh), and four union territories (Delhi, Goa, Daman & Diu, Pondicherry and Sikkim).

A schedule of tribes for Uttar Pradesh was prepared in 1967 that included five tribes (Bhotia, Buksa, Jaunsari, Raji, and Tharu). In addition, Punjab was reorganized and Chandigarh was declared a union territory in 1966. Consequent to these developments, three states (Haryana, Punjab and Jammu & Kashmir) and four union territories conducted 1971 census without any schedule for tribes.

A schedule consisting of two tribes (Bhutia and Lepcha) was notified in 1978 for Sikkim. Hence all states and union territories except (Punjab, Haryana, Jammu & Kashmir and union territories of Chandigarh, Delhi and Pondicherry) carried out census 1981 with an independent schedule of tribes.

A separate list of schedule tribe for Jammu & Kashmir was notified in 1989. It carried eight (now twelve) names of tribe. In 2001 census the newly formed states that is Jharkhand, Chhattisgarh and Uttarakhand also made their list of scheduled tribes.

It means the tribal space over the years has spread covering 543 districts out of 593 in 2001. There are only two states and three union territories (Punjab, Haryana and union territories of Chandigarh, Delhi, and Pondicherry) where Scheduled Tribes are not enumerated (Table 13.3). Of this 77 districts are tribal in majority.

TRIBAL SUB-PLAN

The concept of tribal sub-plan was introduced in 1974 with the objective of covering entire tribal population in the ambit of development. There was a need to prepare a distinct plan indicating the flow of funds for the tribes. It aimed at programmes exclusively to tribal people. The task, apparently simple, was actually very complex. The territorial jurisdiction of tribal sub-plan was to be defined by excluding the tribal majority states (states or union territories recording 50 per cent or more of its population as Scheduled Tribes). The argument was that states with tribal majority need not prepare a separate plan rather the whole plan should focus on tribes. Hence the tribal majority states and union territories were identified.

There are four states and two union territories with tribal majority. The states are Mizoram (94.5), Nagaland (89.1), Meghalaya (85.9), and Arunachal Pradesh (64.2). The Union territories are Lakshadweep (94.5) and Daman and Diu (62.2). These are not covered by tribal sub-plan (Table 13.3).

Of the remaining states Punjab and Haryana do not enumerate scheduled tribe population. Similarly, the union territories of Delhi, Chandigarh and Pondicherry do not enumerate Scheduled Tribe population.

Hence 22 out of 28 states and 2 out of 7 Union territories are covered under tribal sub-plan. These states share 93.47 per cent of the total tribal population of India. On the other hand, Scheduled Tribes living in this huge territory constitute only 15.8 per cent of the total population of 22 states and 2 Union territories. There are many development programmes for sub-plan areas, however, they are beyond the purview of this paper.

EMERGING TRENDS

The proportion of Scheduled Tribe population in total population at the national level increased from 5.36 per cent in 1951 to 8.2 per cent in 2001. The state level proportion of scheduled tribe population in total population reveals increase in some states and decrease in others. The states recording decline in the proportion of Scheduled Tribe population during 1961-2001 were Arunachal Pradesh, Nagaland, Mizoram,

Table 13.7: India: States Recording Proportional Decline in Scheduled Tribe Population, 1961-2001

States/Union Territories	*Scheduled Tribe Population as Per cent to Total Population*		*Decline (per cent Point)*
	1961	*2001*	
Dadra & Nagar Haveli	88.4	62.2	26.2
Arunanchal Pradesh	89.1	64.2	24.9
Andaman & Nicobar Islands	22.2	8.3	13.9
Nagaland	93.1	89.1	4.0
Mizoram	98.1	94.5	3.6
Lakshadweep	97.0	94.5	2.5
Orissa	24.1	22.1	2.0
Himachal Pradesh	4.8	4.0	0.8
West Bengal	5.9	5.5	0.4

Source: Census of India, 1961, Vol. (1), Part V A (ii), Special Tables for Scheduled Tribe.

Orissa, Bihar, Tripura, Himachal Pradesh, Andaman & Nicobar Islands, Dadra & Nagar Haveli etc. (Table 13.5). Dadra & Nagar Haveli recorded the highest decline in the tribal population during 1961-2001. The tribal population of Arunanchal Pradesh is decline from 89.1 per cent in 1961 to 64.2 per cent in 2001.

On the other hand, the states recording proportional increase in their Scheduled Tribe population during 1961-2001 were Andhra Pradesh, Maharashtra, Manipur, Meghalaya, Gujarat, Rajasthan Karnataka, Assam, Tamil Nadu, etc. (Table 13.6). Karnataka has recorded 5.8 per cent point increase in their tribal population during 1961-2001.

Table 13.8: India: States Recording Proportional Increase in Scheduled Tribe Population, 1961-1991

States	*Scheduled Tribe Population as Per cent to Total Population*		*Increase (Per cent Point)*
	1961	*2001*	
Karnataka	0.8	6.6	5.8
Andhra Pradesh	3.7	6.6	2.9
Maharashtra	6.1	8.9	2.8
Manipur	31.4	34.2	2.8
Meghalaya	83.1	85.9	2.8
Assam	10.8	12.4	1.6
Gujarat	13.2	14.8	1.6
Rajasthan	11.8	12.6	0.8

Source: Census of India, 1961, Vol. (1), Part V A (ii), Special Tables for Scheduled Tribes.

The trend of tribal population at the district level is highly variable. In 1961 census 242 districts out of 340 districts were enumerated with tribal population. This number increased to 303 in 1971 census, 356 in 1981 census, 418 in 1991 census and 543 in 2001 census. However, there are districts, which have almost negligible share of tribal population in the total population of the districts.

In 1961 census 71.17 per cent districts had recorded the tribal population. The percentage increased to 84.87 per cent in 1971 census, 88.55 per cent in 1981, 89.69 per cent in 1991 census, and 91.56 per cent in 2001 census. This shows the continuous process of inclusion of new tribes or the recognition of tribal communities in the different districts.

Ever since, the formation of a separate Ministry of Tribal Affairs in 1999 and introduction of National Tribal Policy, 2006, there has been a rapid change expected in socio-economic development of tribal population. The efforts of five decades reveal unbelievable disparity in scheduled tribe population (Table 13.9).

This disparity raises many questions on treating the tribal population uniformly. Consequent to it, relatively better groups of some specific areas are the only beneficiaries. The most deprived of the deprived can be developed only by differential treatment of tribes based on the level of deprivation. This requires a strong political will to ensure meaningful social justice.

Table 13.9: India: Socio-economic Development Disparity Among Tribal Population, 2001

Criteria	*Indicators*	*Highest value (per cent)*	*Lowest Value (per cent)*
Social Development	Female Literacy	96.4 (Aizawl)	4.87 (Lakhisarai)
Modernization	Urbanization	98.28 (Sershhip)	0.02 (Lakhisarai)
Economic Transformation	Non-agricultural Workers	99.77 (Andaman)	0.04 (Araria)

CONCLUSIONS

- The tribal space is expanding by virtue of politico-economic decisions. The increase in their population size from 5.36 per cent in 1951 to 8.2 per cent in 2001 of the total population should be viewed in the context of the continuous inclusion of new communities rather than their natural growth in population.
- There are three categories of space based on presence or absence of tribal population. These are: (i) Tribal majority states, (ii) Tribal sub-plan areas, and (iii) Areas where tribes are regarded as historically absent.
- The spurt in competition for inclusion is a danger signal in the context of strong resistance against inclusion.
- Scheduled Tribes are not a homogeneous group. They vary by region and within a region among themselves. Internal disparity indicates a need for categorization of Scheduled Tribes on the basis of relative deprivation.
- Increase in tribal population share of India is a possible ground of demand for increase in proportion of reservation. Similar demand on the pretext of larger share in total population among Scheduled Castes may invite constitutional crisis.
- Out of 593 districts only 50 districts has not recorded tribal population in 2001. In other words, spatial spread of tribal population exists in 543 districts. However, the spread indicates their preponderance on rural space. The distribution pattern reveals their dominance over some spaces in spite of being small in number. However, analysis by social scientists at larger administrative units hide their spatial identity.

REFERENCES

Burman, B.K. Roy (1994): *Tribes in Pespective*, Mittal Publiations. New Delhi.

Burman, B.K. Roy (2006): *Creating Consternation,, Economic and Political Weekly,* August,26, pp. 3645-3647.

Census of India (1991): *Primary Census Abstact, Scheduled Tribe Population, Series I India, Part II B (iii)*, Registrar General and Census Commissioner, India.

Ghurye, G.S. (1995): *The Scheduled Tribes*, Popular Prakshan, Bombay.

Government of India (1981): *Report on Development of Tribal areas*, NCDBA, Planning Commission, New Delhi.

Government of India (1984): *Report of the Working Group on Tribal Devlopment During Seventh Plan*, Planning Commission, New Delhi.

Government of India (1997): Evaluation Report on Integrated Tribal Development Projects, Programme Evaluation Organisation, Planning Commission, New Delhi.

Raza, M. and Aijazuddin Ahmad (1990): *An Atlas of Tribal India*, Concept Publishing Company, New Delhi.

Ulrich, S. (1968): The Problem of Nagaland in Fisher, Charles A. (ed.) *Essay in Political Geography*, Methuen & Co. Ltd., London, pp. 161-176.

Verma, R.C. (1995): *Indian Tribes through the Ages*, Publication Division, Ministry of Information and Broadcasting, Government of India.

14

Urbanization and Tribal Development: A Case Study of Ranchi District, Jharkhand

AMIT KUMAR SINGH

SECTION I

1. Introduction

Tribal's are the earliest inhabitants of Jharkhand. Before independence, they remained comparatively isolated and enjoyed a more or less self-sufficient economy. All of their primary necessities were fulfilled from the forest resources. But after independence, industrialization and urbanization started hand in hand in this region and many of the tribal areas were opened up for the outsiders and the process of change started influencing even the remotest corners of Jharkhand. This caused enormous uprooting of tribal population from their habitats and they lost their agricultural and forest based occupations. According to 1951 Census, tribes constituted 41.42 per cent to the total population of Jharkhand, but in 2001 they were only 26.35 per cent. The rapid process of urbanization and industrialization also created a huge gap between wage income of workers in cities and that of agricultural labourers and traditional service workers in rural areas. This forced the tribals to seek jobs in urban areas and develop cultural contacts. On one hand, it brought gradual improvement in the standard of living of some of the tribes, but on the other, most of them were forced to work in very low wage jobs and as a result of this they had been impoverished day by day. In such a situation, today, the tribes are finding themselves at crossroads; firstly, in rural areas they often lose their ancestral habitat and traditional occupations. Moreover, the high cost of living in cities, changed income structure and exposure to the glamour of the urban culture are disorganizing their socio-economic structure.

Against this background, the paper tries to reflect the growing disparity between tribes living in Ranchi city from those who are living in the hinterlands. In the present research tribal development has been mainly considered as function of various physical and social aspects of development. In physical aspects of development, availability of electricity, toilet, drinking water, types of houses, transport and communication and in social aspects of development, access to primary health centre/private clinic, primary, and secondary schools have been considered. In order to find out the intra-district variation in tribal development, village and town level study is essential. But it is a known fact that Census of India does not provide information regarding many of qualitative development indicators. So such data at village and colony level has been collected with the help of primary survey.

2. Objectives

Keeping the theoretical background in view, a detailed empirical investigation has been undertaken in this paper with a view to analyse the following objectives:

1. To examine the regional disparity in the availability of housing amenities and infrastructure in Jharkhand.
2. To study the degree of variations in the distributional pattern of housing amenities and infrastructure among the different social groups of Jharkhand.
3. To identify the salient causes resulting in tribal underdevelopment.

3. Database and Sample Design

The study incorporates Ranchi city and its hinterland as a distinct geographical unit where the tribal population constitutes the majority rural areas. The data for the present study has been collected from the three villages (Marwa, Tigra and Latma of Ranchi district) and two colonies (Seram Toli and Nayak Tola) of Ranchi city. These three villages have been selected on the basis of their location and the concentration of tribal population. A village with more than 50 per cent tribal population has been taken in order to observe the impact of urbanization. As far as location is concerned, villages have been selected on the basis of their distance and connectivity from the city. They are catogorised as (a) *Village adjoining the city*, (b) *Village distantly located but on road*, and (c) *Village distantly located away from road.* The data at city and village level has been collected from secondary sources and the information regarding the standard of living at household level has been gathered through primary survey. For the analysis of standard of living of tribals, firstly, the households are stratified on the basis of their location. Next, a total of 150 households (30 households from each village and 60 households from two housing colonies of city) have been surveyed. For the selection of households a simple random sampling has been used. Further, this study has been based on different selected variables for analysis, which require a systematic approach; therefore, certain standard statistical techniques have been used in this paper.

4. Study Area

Ranchi District is situated almost at the centre of the Jharkhand State. It contains an area of 7574.17 sq. km. which form about 10.52 per cent of the whole state. According to 2001 Census, the total population of Ranchi district was 26.90 lakh out of which 43.55 per cent were tribals. According to the Village Directory of Ranchi District (Census of India, 2001), Latma village is located at the fringe area of Ranchi city, Marwa village is 24 km. away from Ranchi city and situated along a road, and Tigra is also a distantly located village away from road. Seram Toli is a tribal dominated colony located at the heart of Ranchi city and Nayak Tola is a slum area and mostly inhabited by tribals.

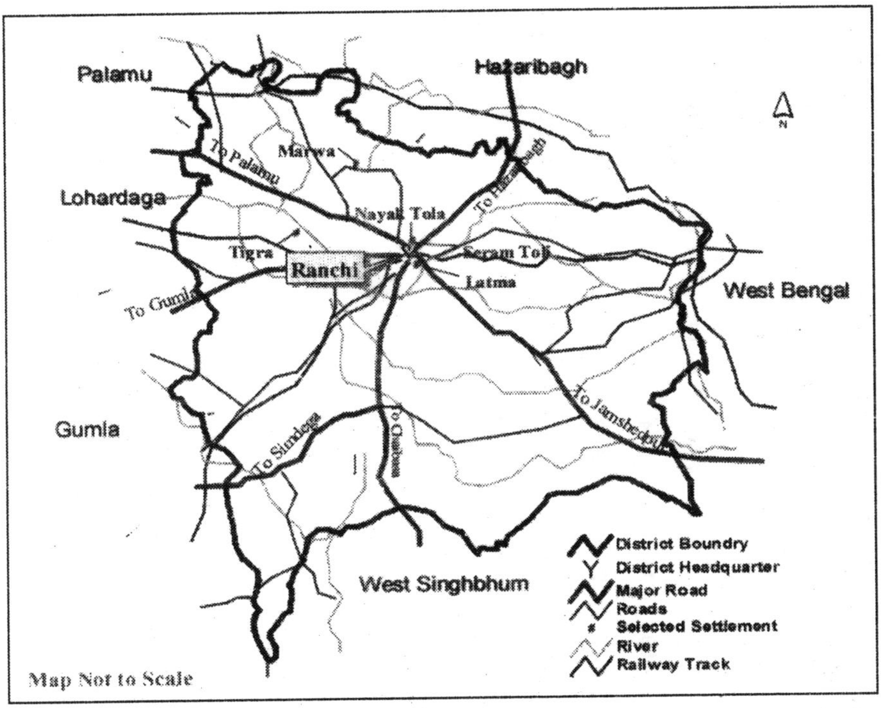

Fig. 14.1: Location Map of Study Area: Ranchi District

SECTION II: HOUSING AND HOUSEHOLD AMENITIES OF JHARKHAND

1. Availability of Housing and Household Amenities

In general, presence of household amenities such as drinking water, toilet and electricity in the house indicates the living conditions of residents. The data presented in Table 14.1 clearly shows that availability of electricity and tap

Table 14.1: Availability of Housing and Household Amenities to the Different Communities, Jharkhand

Social Groups	*Rural*				*Urban*				*All*			
	Elect.	*Toilet*	*Drink. Water*	*Pucca House*	*Elect.*	*Toilet*	*Drink. Water*	*Pucca House*	*Elect.*	*Toilet*	*Drink. Water*	*Pucca House*
S.T.	3.48	2.97	35.12	3.68	53.29	43.73	52.13	45.51	7.84	6.54	36.61	4.34
S.C.	8.60	4.85	37.59	11.71	67.54	44.49	70.21	56.81	20.70	12.99	44.29	21.00
Other	14.52	9.32	35.21	23.51	80.39	73.92	70.31	86.70	33.38	27.82	45.26	65.68
All	9.99	6.57	35.51	15.12	75.61	66.68	68.20	68.20	24.30	19.67	42.63	28.79

Source: Housing and Household Amenities, Census of India, 2001.

water supply to the households of rural areas are far below that of other urban centres of Jharkhand. As per the data, in 2001 the per cent of households having safe drinking water in rural areas of Jharkhand was only 35.51 per cent but the corresponding figure for urban Jharkhand was 68.20 per cent. This gap becomes more prominent in case of electricity and toilet facilities. The percentage of households having electricity in urban Jharkhand was 75.61 per cent but on the other hand it was only 9.99 per cent in rural Jharkhand. It means till 2001 more than 90 per cent households of rural Jharkhand did not have the electricity.

In case of toilet facility, rural Jharkhand again showed a very poor picture as compared to urban Jharkhand. It is remarkable that in 2001 Census, only 6.57 per cent households of rural Jharkhand had toilet facilities in their houses. Therefore, the rural population of Jharkhand has to go outside for their sanitary obligations. Every morning, this is easily discernible in these villages. Again, the percentage of households living in *pucca* houses was much higher in urban areas than in rural Jharkhand. Table 14.1 shows that about two-third (66.68%) of the households of urban areas of Jharkhand had *pucca* houses and were living in their own houses; whereas in rural areas only 15.12 per cent households had *pucca* houses. Rest of the population was living in either mud-built houses or in huts.

The data concerning the availability of these facilities among the different social groups showed a very dismal picture of Scheduled Tribes in Jharkhand. The per cent of tribal population having electricity and toilet facility in their households were very less. It is surprising that more than 92 per cent of tribal population of Jharkhand were still not availing the facilities of electricity and toilet and more than 95 per cent of them were living in either *kutcha* houses or semi-*pucca* houses. Table 14.1 shows that in rural areas, the situation of Scheduled Castes and other communities were also not very much different; but it is noteworthy that their living conditions were better than the scheduled tribes. On the other hand, in urban areas, each social group had better accessibility to these amenities. It will be worthwhile to mention that those tribals who were living in urban areas of Jharkhand had better accessibility to these amenities.

2. Spatial Disparity in the Availability of Housing and Household Amenities

In order to examine the regional accessibility of these amenities among the different social groups, the districts of Jharkhand has been taken as the unit of analysis. As observed in Table 14.1 that even though on the whole 24.30 per cent households of Jharkhand had electricity, there had been districts that had less than 10 per cent households with electric supply. Dhanbad had the highest percentage (66.64) of households having this facility, followed by East Singhbhum (47.39) and Bokaro (44.63). Gumla reported the lowest percentage of households having electricity (5.13). In Garhwa, Chatra, Pakur, Giridih, Sahibganj and Dumka, electricity connection was also less than ten per cent. In case of toilet facilities, the situation was not much different. Only 19.47 per cent households had their own toilets.

Data on toilet facility shows that unlike electricity, only few districts had higher per cent of households with toilet. For instance, only Ranchi (55.99%), Eastern Singhbhum (43.98%), Dhanbad (39.97%), and Bokaro (35.22%) had relatively higher percentage of toilet facility. Apart from them rest of the districts had smaller percentages of households having toilet facilities. In the case of safe drinking water, the situation was very grim. The main source of drinking water in Jharkhand was the well (51.76%) followed by hand pump (26.98%). But well is not a safe source of drinking water and there are districts such as Pakur and Gumla, where more than eighty per cent of households are compelled to drink unsafe water.

Table 14.2 indicates that rural areas of Jharkhand are lagging behind in amenities than the urban counterparts. Only those districts which were more urbanised had comparatively higher percentage of households with these amenities. For example, in the case of electricity the lowest urban connectivity was found in Gumla (52.98%) and this value was even much higher than highest rural connectivity of Dhanbad (46.81%). Detailed information regarding toilet facility in rural areas showed that Dhanbad (18.82%) had the highest percentage of households having this facility in their houses followed by Ranchi (10.22%). Again only 29.79 per cent of houses in Jharkhand were *pucca*. The housing condition was much worse in rural areas. In Gumla, Lohardaga, Garhwa, Palamau, Sahibganj and Pakur, more than ninety per cent of houses were *kutcha*. In the urban areas of Jharkhand 74.27 per cent households had *pucca* houses. Surprisingly, despite the higher level of urbanisation, Ranchi district had only 54.19 per cent *pucca* houses. Actually, a large number of tribal population living in the adjoining villages of Ranchi city had *kutcha* or semi-*pucca* houses.

An analysis of the availability of housing and household amenities across different social groups reveals that except Ranchi, Dhanbad, Eastern Singhbhum and Bokaro, living conditions were poor for all social groups (Fig. 14.2). But within the different social groups, the Scheduled tribes had been the most deprived communities of Jharkhand. According to the computed graph of composite index, the availability of housing and household amenities was very less among the tribals of Lohardaga, Gumla, Chatra, Garhwa and the districts of Santhal Pargana Region. It is a matter of fact, that in these districts the concentration of tribal population was much higher than the other districts of Jharkhand and most of them were living in the rural areas. So the low index value reveals that till now in these Districts, the State Government has not been able to provide a minimum level of basic amenities to their inhabitants.

Analysis also reveals that those districts which were least urbanised had minor differences among Scheduled Tribes and other communities, but this gap had become more prominent in those districts of Jharkhand which were highly urbanised. It is evident from the Fig. 14.2, that in the districts of Santhal Pargana region and Western Jharkhand which had very less urban population, the availability of housing and household amenities were very less in all communities. Among the rural areas of each district, the lowest index value of housing and household

Table 14.2: Availability of Housing and Household Amenities in Jharkhand (2001)

Social Groups	Rural				Urban				All			
	Elect.	*Toilet*	*Drink. Water*	*Pucca House*	*Elect.*	*Toilet*	*Drink. Water*	*Pucca House*	*Elect.*	*Toilet*	*Drink. Water*	*Pucca House*
Deoghar	8.29	4.29	35.70	16.13	72.56	74.10	28.90	76.13	16.86	13.60	34.80	26.05
Dumka	4.32	4.08	40.14	12.08	60.87	58.34	40.26	67.01	7.66	7.29	50.11	15.68
Godda	6.69	6.52	50.73	15.13	64.35	66.80	43.98	68.87	8.48	8.39	40.25	17.12
Sahibganj	3.77	6.80	55.52	9.32	50.79	61.44	59.46	58.69	8.14	11.66	55.88	14.02
Pakur	3.39	3.59	66.58	7.28	62.04	59.22	67.62	67.30	6.02	6.18	13.79	10.19
Giridih	5.33	5.12	10.64	21.69	61.97	66.60	41.64	75.02	9.59	7.88	66.63	25.11
Dhanbad	46.81	18.82	37.21	43.77	83.99	58.50	76.61	73.96	66.64	39.97	58.22	60.43
Bokaro	16.28	7.46	26.24	28.18	76.74	66.67	81.44	77.27	44.63	35.22	52.12	52.12
Hazaribagh	18.68	8.42	14.04	23.99	84.37	68.52	64.68	79.44	34.66	23.04	26.37	38.57
Kodarma	14.90	7.04	19.99	22.84	55.39	50.35	25.73	65.99	21.70	14.31	20.95	30.70
Chatra	4.00	5.65	30.69	10.36	58.65	61.73	51.92	45.81	6.43	8.14	31.64	12.15
Garhwa	4.03	3.12	46.05	5.92	56.34	53.30	83.57	59.68	6.00	5.01	47.46	8.55
Palamu	4.79	7.32	41.92	9.38	59.14	65.02	81.65	63.37	7.76	10.48	44.09	12.92
Gumla	2.80	3.60	15.98	5.12	52.98	54.35	33.34	53.56	5.13	5.96	16.79	7.48
Lohardaga	4.58	5.50	26.45	7.37	55.69	59.66	33.54	61.27	10.20	11.45	27.23	13.85
Ranchi	14.94	10.52	39.06	11.84	70.32	71.71	54.19	72.71	39.86	55.99	36.24	31.53
Pas. Singh.	7.04	4.84	51.81	8.32	66.94	59.36	74.46	66.22	16.51	13.46	55.39	17.39
Pur. Singh.	13.03	7.75	45.04	15.09	79.39	77.73	75.84	80.22	47.39	43.98	60.98	49.57
Jharkhand	9.99	6.57	35.51	15.12	75.61	66.68	68.20	74.27	24.30	19.67	42.63	28.79

Source: Housing and Household Amenities, Census of India, 2001.

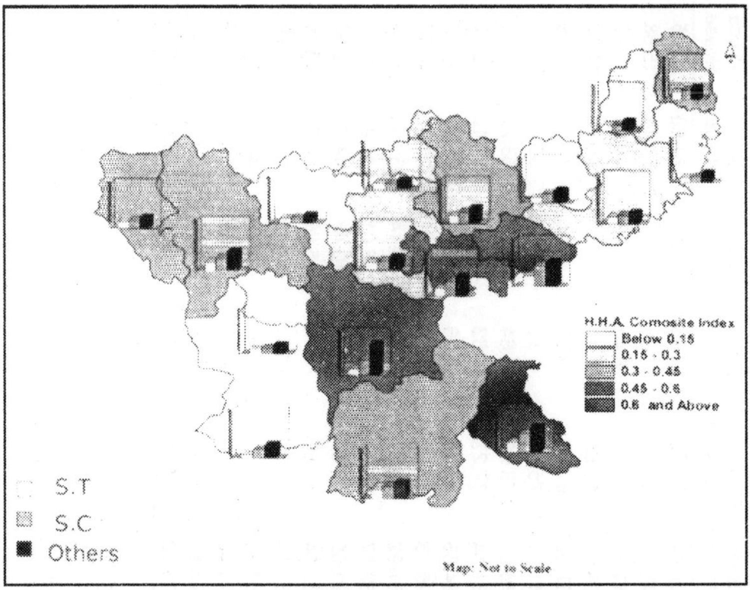

Fig. 14.2: Availability of Housing and Household Amenities Among the Different Social Groups of Jharkhand

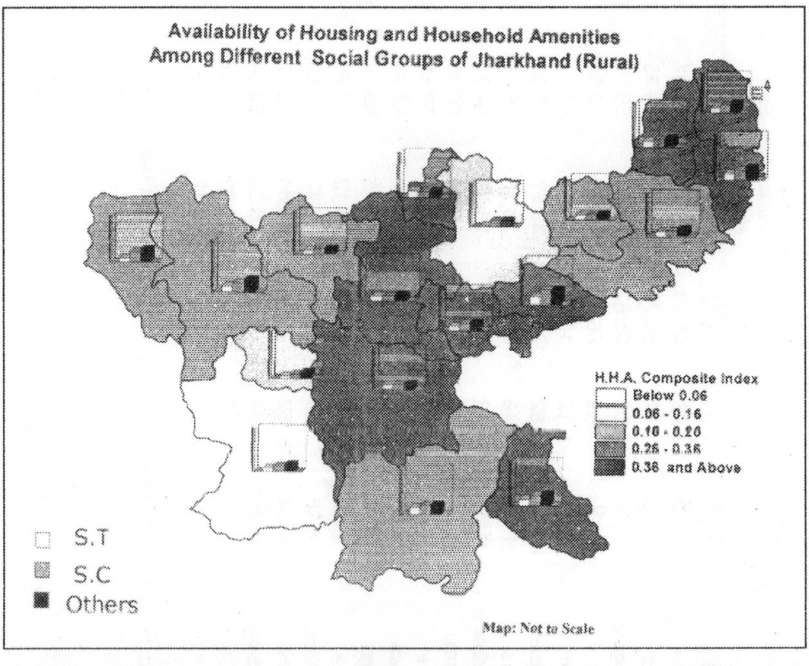

Fig. 14.3: Availability of Housing and Household Amenities Among Different Social Groups of Jharkhand (Rural)

amenities among the scheduled tribes were found in Giridih (2.69) followed by Gumla (4.87) and Lohardaga (7.74) and the highest index value was found in Dhanbad (17.42) and West Singhbhum (15.29). On the other hand, in the case of other social groups the lowest index value was found in Gumla (13.82) and Kodarma (13.71), and this is almost equal to the highest index value of Scheduled Tribe groups of Jharkhand. In this category, the highest index value was found in Ranchi (37.70) and Dhanbad (33.08). Basically these two districts had been the most industrialized and urbanized districts of Jharkhand and they had attracted migrants from the all parts of the state as well as from other parts of India. Most of these migrants had been engaged in well paid jobs. However, big towns, such as Dhanbad, Ranchi, and Bokaro are located in these two districts and obviously they have better infrastructure and basic services than other parts of the state. Therefore, these groups had been availing better living conditions than other social groups.

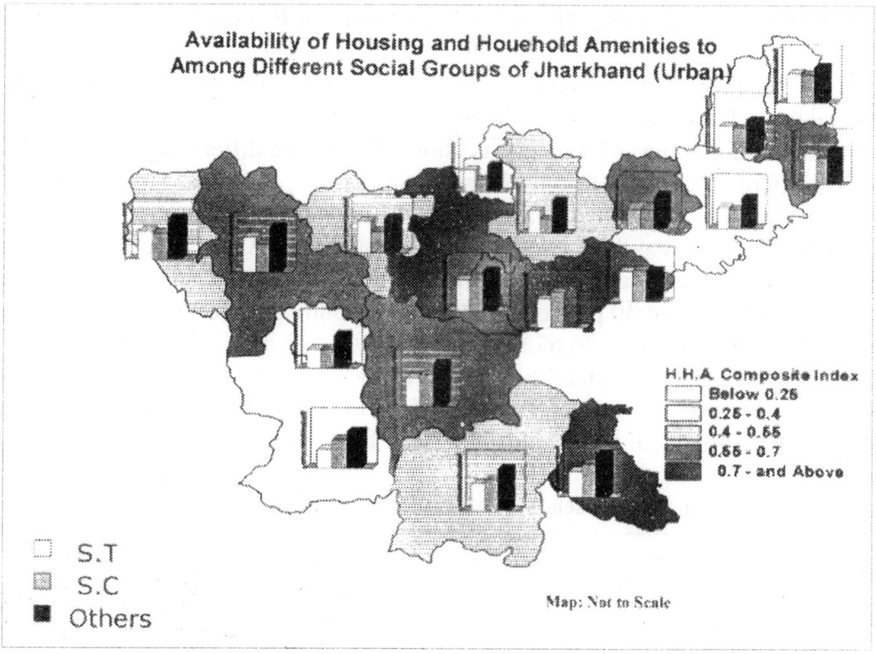

Fig. 14.4: Availability of Housing and Household Amenities Among Different Social Groups of Jharkhand (Urban)

Another significant feature is that in most of the urban centres of Jharkhand the index value of housing and household amenities of Scheduled Tribes people was higher than scheduled caste people. It is also evident from Fig. 14.3 that differences between them and other social groups reduced considerably in the urban areas. Surprisingly, index value of Scheduled Tribes people in the least urbanised districts was also higher than Scheduled Caste people. On the contrary, districts like Ranchi, East Singhbhum Bokaro and Dhanbad which had higher level of urbanisation was marked by higher index value for Scheduled Castes rather than the Scheduled Tribes. The combinations of these two things are quite confusing, but once we analyse the social composition of these districts, we find that most of the scheduled caste population of these districts had been migrants and many of them were engaged in secondary and tertiary sectors, therefore, their living condition had been better than scheduled tribes (Appendix 2). Despite that, it may be said that urbanisation had positively affected the tribals, as far as housing and household amenities is concerned. Best example is Dhanbad district, where index value of all three social groups had been almost the same.

SECTION III: HOUSING AND HOUSEHOLD AMENITIES IN RANCHI DISTRICT

1. Availability of Housing, Household Amenities in Ranchi District

Table 14.3 clearly shows that on a location basis, a comparatively low percentage of rural households had housing and household amenities. On the other hand, the selected urban colonies of Ranchi city showed a marked difference, where better availability of amenities was only found in Seram Toli. In the case of Nayak Tola which is basically a slum area, availability of housing and household amenities were almost as below as other two rural villages of Ranchi. As per the data presented in Table 14.3, the per cent of household having electric connection in Tigra and Marwa was 26.67 and 30 per cent but the corresponding figure for Latma, Nayak Tola and Seram Toli was 76.67, 43.33, and 93.33 per cent. This gap was more prominent in case of toilet facility. The average value for rural Ranchi district was 10.52 per cent and it was clearly reflected in Tigra and Marwa where 6.67 per cent and 16.67 per cent households had toilet facilities within housing premises.

Table 14.3: Housing and Household Amenities in Five Surveyed Settlements

Village/ Colony	*Nature of Settlement*	*Electricity*	*Toilet*	*Drinking Water*	*Pucca House*
Tigra	Rural	26.67	6.67	26.67	10.00
Marwa	Rural	30.00	16.67	36.67	13.33
Latma	Urban Fringe	76.67	43.33	46.67	40.00
Nayak Tola	Urban	43.33	20.00	23.33	16.67
Seram Toli	Urban	93.33	93.33	76.67	63.33

Source: Computed from Primary Survey Data (December 2005).

On a location basis analysis of availability of safe drinking water within houses did not reflect very much variation. Within the study area, Seram Toli had the highest figure (76.67%) followed by Latma (46.67%) and Marwa (36. 67%) (Table 14.3). Apart from these three, other areas had values lower than 30 per cent. The lowest percentage was found in Nayak Tola and it was only 23.33 per cent, followed by Tigra. So it is surprising to see that a residential area of city had lower drinking water facility than rural counterparts. Actually most of the residents of this colony were living below poverty line and they were not able to have separate tap water connection. So they had to use water either from distantly located tap or a hand pump. So it makes it obligatory for women to fetch water for their family. Every morning, this can be seen in this colony. The residents also reported that in summer seasons these taps and pumps also supply less water.

It is notable that of the five settlements only two had more than 40 per cent households with toilet facilities and both of them were located in Ranchi city. The highest availability of toilet was once again found in Seram Toli. Here about 93 per cent households had toilets in their houses. It is evident from Table 14.3 that tribals of rural Ranchi had been facing severe sanitation problems. In Tigra only 6.67 per cent households had toilet facilities in their houses followed by Marwa (16.67%). The availability of toilets in Nayak Tola is also extremely poor. Only 20 per cent households had their own toilet. It was quite surprising that here within the colony, a public toilet was constructed for the residents but it was never properly managed. So people had to go to a public toilet, which is one and half km. away from their residence. In rural areas people had option to go to the open places for sanitation but in urban areas people particularly women have little choice. Therefore, they had been facing severe sanitation problems. It is apparent from Table 14.1 that about eighty-five per cent population of rural Ranchi had been living in their *kutcha* or semi-*pucca* houses. Among the households living in *pucca* houses, the highest percentage was found in Seram Toli (63.63%) followed by Latma (40%). In Nayak Tola only 16.67 per cent houses were *pucca*.

2. Availability and Accessibility of Neighbourhood Facilities

The development of any region is primarily dependent on a variety of services that are available to the residents of all sections and areas. Further, not only the number of services is important but its convenience with respect to accessibility is also essential. So if we assess the facilities in terms of both availability and the distance of accessibility, then it will give a real status and character of development. For this, eleven services had been taken. They are Primary Health Centre (PHC)/ Private Clinic, Hospitals, Primary School, Secondary School, Post Office, P.D.S., P.C.O., Market, Bank, Bus Service, and Railway Station. Table 14.4 summarises the availability of neighbourhood facilities among the tribals of selected settlement of Ranchi Districts.

Analysis reveals that out of the five surveyed areas, not a single area had all the eleven services together. It is evident from the Table 14.4 that Seram Toli had the highest number of facility, i.e. six. Yet again, very less number of facilities was available in rural areas. The lowest number of facilities was available in Tigra, i.e. only two. It is noticed that out of all the eleven services, P.C.O. was easily available to all these settlements. So this is the only one basic service which is available in the entire study area surveyed and it is also remarkable that on average each area was in the range of 280 metres from the P.C.O. booth.

Table 14.4: Average Distance to Neighbourhood Facilities

Number of Facility	*Name of Facility*	*Tigra*	*Marwa*	*Latma*	*Nayak Tola*	*Seram Toli*	*Average Distance*
1	P.H.C./ Clinic	5	2.5	1 (√)	0.5 (√)	0.3 (√)	1.86
2	Hospital	25	20	6	2.5	1	5.5
3	Primary School	.5 (?)	.75 (√)	.5 (√)	.5 (√)	.5 (√)	0.55
4	Secondary School	5	8	1	1.5	1 (√)	45
5	Post Office	5	1 (√)	1.5	1.5	1 (√)	2
6	P.D.S.	.5 (√)	1 (√)	1 (√)	2	1.5	1.2
7	P.C.O.	.4 (√)	.5 (√)	.2 (√)	.1 (√)	.2 (√)	0.28
8	Market	5	3	1.5	.2 (√)	.5 (√)	2.04
9	Bank	11	8	3	2	2	5.2
10	Bus Service	4	8	1.5	1	.5	3
11	Railway Station	35	32	2.5	1.5	1 (√)	14.4
	Total Facility	2	3	4	4	6	3.65

Where (✓) = Available in their Residential Areas.

Source: Computed from Primary Survey Data.

A public health centre or private clinic is an essential service. Unfortunately the tribal population of the rural Ranchi district did not have adequate health facilities. They had to travel on an average three to five kilometres for even minor health problems. Conditions worsen when a patient needs an urgent medical care of hospitals. Hospitals in general are located only in Ranchi city which is twenty to twenty-five kilometres away from these villages. On the other hand, even in the low income group colony of Ranchi city, such as Naik Tola, private clinics had been located just outside the colony. In the case of Seram Toli also clinics and hospitals were located in the neighbourhood of the settlement. As far as Latma is concerned, it is a resettled village of Heavy Engineering Corporation (Government of India Undertaking Industry). Therefore many of their residents prefers to go to the H.E.C. hospital, which is six kilometre away from the colony.

Schools are essential for development of any society. Table 14.4 indicates that primary schools were available in all five surveyed settlements. However of these, only Seram Toli and Latma had secondary schools in their neighbourhood. On the other hand, not a single secondary school was located near Tigra and Marwa settlements. So the students of these villages everyday have to face difficulties in travelling almost twenty kilometres. Post office is another important basic service. But it is noteworthy that post office was found only in Marwa and Seram Toli and except Tigra, in the rest of the sampled villages these were located within a range of 1.5 kilometres.

Graph 14.1

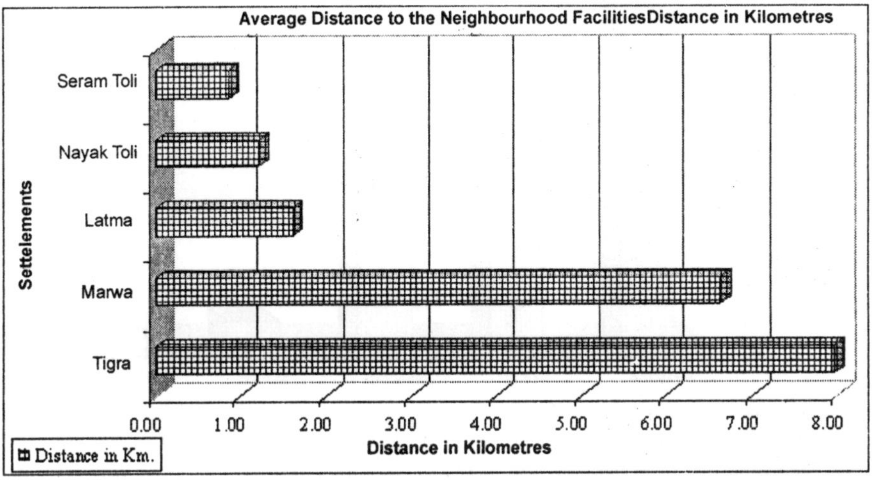

Source: Computed from Primary Survey Data.

It has been noted that only three of the surveyed settlements had a Public Distributions System shop for their residents, viz. Tigra, Marwa, and Latma. In India, P.D.S. is an important facility at least for the population below poverty line. But it is interesting to note that many tribal families of these settlements who are immensely in need of a P.D.S. card; did not have this facility. And for those who had the card, their P.D.S. shops were located in other villages or colonies. Residents of these villages also reported the irregular supply and lack of ration from their P.D.S. shops. Next to the P.D.S., a market centre is essential for any residential area, where one can buy day to day households items. It has been found that no rural village had either a small or a big market centre. As far as Latma is concerned, it is an urban village and distantly located from the Ranchi-Chaibasa Road. So market centre had not been developed here.

Analysis of transport facility revealed the absence of bus service in Tigra and Marwa villages and their nearest railway station is Ranchi which was almost thirty kilometres away from their village. It has been also found that out of five surveyed areas not a single settlement had banks in their neighbourhood. However, in urban areas banks are located within the range of three kilometres, but in Tigra and Marwa banks were the distantly located facilities. So it is clear that there are serious deficiencies in the availability of basic services in the tribal villages of Ranchi District. As a result, population of this area has to go to other distant places. But because of higher transportation cost they often cannot afford to avail up these services.

Graph 14.2

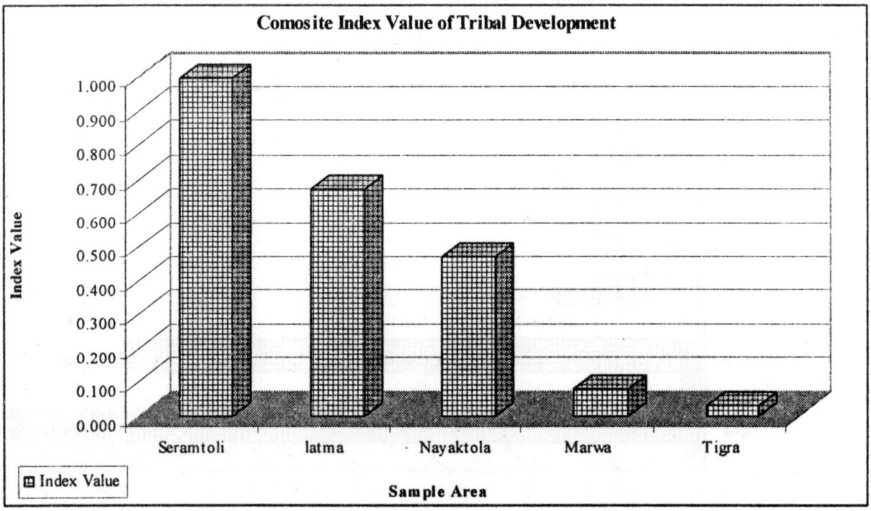

Source: Computed from Primary Survey Data (December 2005).

SECTION IV: LEVELS OF TRIBAL DEVELOPMENT

On the basis of effective use of seven selected indicators, level of tribe's socio-economic development of Ranchi District have been analysed. After that, a composite index worked out for each of the five settlements has then been ranked in order to determine the levels of development. These seven indicators are: percentage of literate, above matriculate population, population treated by doctor, delivery in hospital, households using electricity for lighting, households using toilet, population drinking safe water. Table 14.5 and Graph 14.2 clearly indicate that level of socio-economic development of tribals of Ranchi District vary widely according to the different geographic locations. Population living in rural areas have less availability of different amenities and facilities than those living in urban areas. It is a matter of fact that accessibility to electricity, toilet facility, modern medical services and educational facilities is very much related to the household's economic conditions; if government fails to provide all these facilities in this region, it will surely lead to overall backwardness. On the other hand, tribals of urban areas have certain advantages; despite their economic backwardness they can use all the above facilities more conveniently because of their nearby locations.

Thus the level of development among tribal population is significantly higher in the urban areas of Ranchi city.

Table 14.5: Levels of Tribals Socio-economic Development

Sample Regions	*In per cent*							*Index Value*	*Rank*
	Literate	*Above Matric. Pop.*	*Doctor's Treat-ment*	*Delivery in Hospital*	*Electricity for Lighting*	*Using Toilet*	*Safe Drinking Water*		
Tigra	45.59	23.33	26.67	10.00	26.67	6.67	36.67	0.028	5
Marwa	42.68	16.67	33.33	13.33	30	16.67	43.33	0.079	4
Latma	73.68	53.33	90.00	76.67	66.67	43.33	73.67	0.673	2
Nayak Tolal	68.35	36.67	83.33	63.33	43.33	76.67	63.33	0.469	3
Seram Toli	85.35	73.33	96.67	96.67	90	93.33	86.67	1.000	1

Source: Computed from Primary Survey Data (December 2005).

A close inspection of Table 14.4 and Table 14.5 would perhaps reveal the basic problem in the provision of such services and resulting tribal development. It is apparent that except primary school, P.D.S. shop and Public Call Office (P.C.O.) booth, all other facilities had been distantly located in each of the surveyed villages. Certainly, it is not a coincidence that the percentage of population taking modern medical services was smallest in villages. This is a shocking fact that two-third of the rural tribes had been still visiting 'Jhola Chaap Doctors', or 'Bhagat' the so called 'Ojha', for their health complications. This is to be expected as both villages did not have any kind of hospitals in their locality. It was also found that not a single registered medical practitioner was found in their surrounding areas. Again, in the case of the delivery of a child, conditions of tribals were quite pathetic. More than eighty-five per cent of rural women had given births in their own houses under the supervision of local maid or *Dais*. It is quite surprising that these *Dais* are completely untrained and work only on the basis of their traditional knowledge. On the other hand, delivery conditions are much better in urban areas. A negligible per cent of people were not availing modern medical facilities. Even the data of the slum area (Nayak Tola) showed a better condition than all rural villages.

The survey also showed that a fair number (66.67%) of tribals living in urban slums were using toilets for their sanitary purposes, despite the fact that only twenty per cent households had toilet facilities. Actually this gap is compensated by the use of the public toilet. But on the other hand, in rural areas no public toilet had been set up by the Government and hence the people of these regions had no other option. The percentages of households using safe drinking water also increased in urban areas as they have option to take water from public taps. In contrast, in rural areas only few hand pumps had been installed by the Government and they also had not been properly managed. So after sometime they had become non-functional and often had dried up.

SECTION V

Conclusion

It is well known that tribals are the most disadvantaged section of the Indian society. For a long period of time, they had spent their life in complete isolation, even the earlier development works that were started in their homeland, was only for the exploitation of their resources. Till now, after sixty years of independence they have not been the beneficiaries of our development processes. Development works have not properly reached to them; their living condition is very much poor as compared to other social groups of the Indian society. Jharkhand, one of the ancient heartland regions of tribal concentrations is no different from this. Here, most of the tribal population is living in the rural areas, and are denied access to minimum basic amenities and social services. Schools and hospitals like essential basic services are distantly located to them. Most of them do not have permanent electricity connection. Even in rainy season they have to go outside their houses for sanitation.

It becomes clear from the above discussion that the use of amenities and basic services very much depends on their availability and accessibility. That is why in many districts of Jharkhand, those tribals living in urban areas have better availability of housing and household amenities than the scheduled caste population. But in rural areas, even though all communities have lesser connectivity and availability of these facilities, tribals are the most underdeveloped. In this respect a comprehensive Rural Development Programme was announced by the President of India (Dr. APJ Abdul Kalam) on the eve of 54th Republic day of India. It will be an important roadmap of tribal development of rural Jharkhand. This programme was named as PURA—Provision of Urban Amenities in Rural Areas and it involves identification of rural clusters with growth potential and creating four types of connectivities in them: (i) road, transportation and power connectivity; (ii) electronic connectivity in the form of reliable telecom, Internet and IT services; (iii) knowledge connectivity in the form of good educational and training institutions; and (iv) market connectivity that would enable "*kissans*" and others to get the best price for their produce. Furthermore, while implementing these programmes Government must ensure that the benefit of our socio-economic progress will definitely reach the deprived section of our society. In fact, development of any society should not be conceived as a process limited to the individual efforts, but also as a fundamental responsibility of every Government.

Appendix 1

Availability of Housing and Household Amenities Among the Scheduled Tribes of Jharkhand (2001)

Social Groups	Rural				Urban			All				
	Elect.	Toilet	Drink. Water	Pucca House	Elect.	Toilet	Drink. Water	Pucca House	Elect.	Toilet	Drink. Water	Pucca House
Deoghar	1.43	1.93	40.77	4.79	21.02	49.86	46.45	37.39	2.70	3.10	40.26	1.07
Dumka	0.77	2.16	37.66	3.68	46.24	36.94	34.87	48.14	1.10	2.46	50.53	2.17
Godda	1.65	2.90	50.57	2.71	39.53	43.87	43.08	61.19	1.86	3.10	37.67	7.07
Sahibganj	0.75	1.92	42.34	1.43	67.78	51.99	42.41	57.18	1.45	2.53	42.68	20.79
Pakur	0.39	1.36	57.96	1.02	71.35	34.96	46.08	79.35	0.57	1.58	12.99	26.01
Giridih	0.35	2.76	2.98	4.66	11.60	22.96	75.06	72.99	2.36	0.84	58.03	5.44
Dhanbad	16.75	6.78	31.66	14.49	69.08	71.93	38.83	52.56	29.21	14.02	40.11	6.05
Bokaro	6.26	4.19	21.90	10.81	70.95	54.04	41.06	43.87	19.27	14.23	35.25	2.92
Hazaribagh	16.14	4.52	13.21	10.71	56.66	76.38	46.30	49.04	29.21	13.59	22.64	2.08
Kodarma	10.71	6.99	25.03	16.69	44.52	50.97	45.16	34.10	16.70	12.67	27.93	1.19
Chatra	5.16	5.39	22.06	6.43	55.22	71.64	67.16	40.78	5.93	6.11	22.44	4.02
Garhwa	0.59	2.01	30.57	0.63	75.07	41.74	34.20	52.41	1.08	2.40	31.10	23.05
Palamu	1.61	3.21	34.82	1.49	60.42	57.50	56.64	49.15	2.41	3.99	35.48	21.25
Gumla	1.27	2.39	14.03	1.76	20.87	34.43	34.43	44.56	2.17	3.26	14.22	10.66
Lohardaga	1.83	3.57	23.64	1.92	20.43	40.87	36.09	38.09	3.61	5.05	23.49	3.57
Ranchi	5.41	4.31	27.67	3.86	31.65	47.18	47.71	28.04	11.98	14.43	26.24	2.48
Pas. Singh.	3.53	2.78	51.22	2.82	71.23	47.12	36.61	40.24	6.28	4.91	52.48	5.18
Pur. Singh.	6.35	3.17	41.43	4.56	61.30	52.98	45.43	43.36	16.89	12.72	45.92	14
Jharkhand	3.48	2.97	35.12	3.68	52.13	53.29	43.73	45.51	7.84	6.54	36.61	7.34

Source: Housing and Household Amenities, Census of India, 2001.

Appendix 2

Availability of Housing and Household Amenities Among the Scheduled Caste of Jharkhand (2001)

Social Groups	Rural				Urban				All			
	Elect.	*Toilet*	*Drink. Water*	*Pucca House*	*Elect.*	*Toilet*	*Drink. Water*	*Pucca House*	*Elect.*	*Toilet*	*Drink. Water*	*Pucca House*
Deoghar	7.99	3.58	38.28	1.73	50.02	40.70	34.15	29.32	11.62	6.79	37.92	21.00
Dumka	3.92	2.99	41.40	2.40	36.71	32.62	51.55	27.19	6.74	5.54	56.53	2.35
Godda	3.90	5.25	57.00	5.12	53.95	58.47	40.96	18.45	4.80	6.21	41.39	3.17
Sahibganj	2.57	4.33	59.92	13.76	37.88	32.85	73.13	66.22	8.11	10.19	61.99	5.38
Pakur	3.79	3.75	70.71	13.61	36.26	41.68	90.57	27.25	7.42	7.00	15.22	24.32
Giridih	9.96	3.64	24.47	17.58	22.57	28.67	28.50	31.76	6.77	7.35	72.93	15.35
Dhanbad	50.82	17.18	47.17	13.90	80.73	34.86	76.55	49.46	67.87	27.26	63.92	18.08
Bokaro	11.71	5.53	37.27	12.20	69.62	53.69	76.76	60.45	35.78	25.54	53.68	16.97
Hazaribagh	11.80	4.82	18.82	9.09	77.94	50.93	66.96	39.52	25.11	14.11	28.52	13.06
Kodarma	10.35	4.24	25.73	9.91	24.85	17.60	28.19	28.78	12.20	5.95	26.04	13.86
Chatra	2.03	2.78	35.62	17.66	32.19	31.65	58.37	36.55	2.64	3.35	36.08	12.02
Garhwa	1.55	1.45	45.95	39.44	25.07	27.39	80.42	57.45	2.08	2.03	46.73	19.28
Palamu	2.00	4.07	41.72	24.26	29.14	28.76	71.95	65.02	2.84	4.83	42.66	49.71
Gumla	2.48	2.94	20.19	9.37	53.85	51.74	44.77	55.53	5.16	5.48	21.47	41.20
Lohardaga	4.55	2.70	39.11	4.72	31.87	30.99	46.81	27.03	8.22	6.51	40.15	27.27
Ranchi	13.39	9.28	45.95	3.21	60.04	56.10	55.87	46.04	29.37	54.22	42.54	7.72
Pas. Singh.	7.96	4.23	58.07	7.38	52.74	41.32	77.12	47.20	19.17	13.51	62.84	5.44
Pur. Singh.	12.88	7.34	50.22	18.69	65.69	58.19	73.68	66.18	44.56	37.85	64.29	17.35
Jharkhand	8.60	4.85	37.59	11.74	67.54	44.49	70.21	56.81	20.70	12.99	44.29	47.18

Source: Housing and Household Amenities, Census of India, 2001.

Appendix 3

Availability of Housing and Household Amenities Among the Other Social Groups of Jharkhand (2001)

Social Groups	Rural				Urban				All			
	Elect.	Toilet	Drink. Water	Pucca House	Elect.	Toilet	Drink. Water	Pucca House	Elect.	Toilet	Drink. Water	Pucca House
Deoghar	9.94	5.00	33.95	9.54	75.78	78.68	28.56	67.69	20.75	17.10	33.06	41.76
Dumka	7.74	6.09	40.99	16.59	66.46	64.12	38.07	72.93	13.47	11.76	48.65	13.48
Godda	9.30	8.28	49.80	15.89	65.97	68.43	44.38	51.96	11.39	10.92	41.14	22.07
Sahibganj	5.79	10.11	63.11	30.95	52.74	66.27	56.84	92.26	11.79	16.84	62.31	18.34
Pakur	6.85	6.17	76.30	26.66	67.09	62.72	64.54	72.46	11.78	11.09	13.62	48.19
Giridih	9.23	5.81	15.48	27.60	71.08	70.28	46.05	80.65	11.26	14.03	75.34	35.43
Dhanbad	53.06	22.14	36.02	21.08	85.49	65.69	77.03	16.17	71.40	46.77	59.21	31.60
Bokaro	20.39	8.91	24.68	21.84	80.26	71.47	83.30	72.18	51.43	41.34	55.07	33.31
Hazaribagh	20.96	10.13	12.98	14.25	86.83	75.33	65.54	66.62	37.98	26.97	26.56	24.45
Kodarma	15.95	7.64	18.66	13.01	59.96	55.25	25.11	74.87	23.71	16.04	19.80	20.84
Chatra	5.13	7.44	28.31	19.48	63.59	67.46	50.63	75.77	8.72	11.12	29.68	17.88
Garhwa	6.16	4.21	50.58	57.94	63.35	59.55	84.72	88.78	9.11	7.07	52.35	25.05
Palamu	7.72	10.90	45.00	38.03	65.29	72.89	83.69	89.34	12.52	16.07	48.23	75.89
Gumla	7.41	7.38	20.48	19.59	66.89	69.82	41.03	86.23	13.26	13.52	22.50	65.35
Lohardaga	9.64	9.45	29.82	14.95	62.77	70.13	36.85	70.33	20.57	21.93	31.27	46.82
Ranchi	39.76	29.30	70.78	10.96	79.42	81.79	61.51	70.70	46.19	170.71	44.35	26.54
Pas. Singh.	13.06	8.58	51.83	14.40	75.27	69.17	75.09	79.02	30.04	25.12	58.18	16.20
Pur. Singh.	20.66	13.03	48.43	24.51	85.49	85.49	78.62	91.91	63.17	60.54	68.22	29.38
Jharkhand	14.52	9.32	35.21	23.51	80.39	73.92	70.31	86.70	33.38	27.82	45.26	65.68

Source: Housing and Household Amenities, Census of India, 2001.

REFERENCES

Das, V. (1977): Tribals of Jharkhand and the Question of their Survival, *Social Action*, Vol. 27, July-September.

Kumar, N., (1970): *Bihar District Gazetteers-Ranchi*, Government of Bihar, Patna.

Reddy, G.P. (1991): HRD in Tribals, *Social Change*, Vol. 21, No. 2.

Singh, A.K. (1993): *Tribes and tribal life, Approaches to development in tribal context.* Vol.3, Sarup & Sons Publications, New Delhi.

Sinha, U.P. (1990): Demographic profile of tribal population in India. In *Demography of Tribal Development* (eds. Bose *et al.).* B.R. Publishing Corporation. Delhi.

Srivastava, B. (1984): *Urban Land Use in A Tribal Area: A Case Study of Ranchi and its Environs*, Classical Pub. Com., New Delhi.

Verma, R.C. (1990): *Indian tribes through the ages*, Publication Division, Patiala House, New Delhi.

Vidyarthi, L.P. and Rai, B.K. (1977): *The Tribal Culture of India*, Concept Publishing Company, Delhi.

15

Exploring Sustainable Urban Development: A Regional Planning Approach

NISHITH SRIVASTAVA

It is the very basic nature of human beings to search for a better quality of life. The entire human civilization evolved on the desire to achieve a better quality of living. The people living in the rural areas today are no exception and they move to the urban centres in quest of better livelihood options. There has been a rapid increase in the urban population all across the world in recent past. Almost half of the world's population today is living in urban areas as compared to only 43 per cent in 1990 (World Bank). This has been the trend in both developed and developing countries. There are the push and pull factors that instigate migration of the population from rural to urban areas. The lack of alternative employment opportunities for the rural populace is the prime factor and the primary resources in the rural areas are under increasing pressure from the rising population.

The aim of this paper is to discuss how a regional planning approach can ensure a sustainable urban development. To begin with, the rate of urbanization in India and its ill effects are discussed. This is followed by the case study of Raipur city which is now capital of the newly formed state of Chhattisgarh. This is followed by a discussion on the regional planning approach with reference to the selected case study.

URBANISATION IN INDIA

India is in middle of an economic boom and the urban areas are rightly described as the engines of economic growth. Out of the country's total population of 1027 million as on 2001, about 742 million live in rural areas and 285 million in urban areas (Census, 2001). The net addition of population in rural areas during 1991-2001 has been to the tune of 113 million while in urban areas it is 6 million. The percentage decadal growth of population in rural and urban areas during the decade is 17.9 and 31.2 per cent respectively. According to the estimates by UN, by the year 2030, 40.76 per cent of the country's population will be living in urban areas compared to about 28.4 per cent now (www.ubdp.org). The growth of urban population in India over the last century is depicted in Table 15.1.

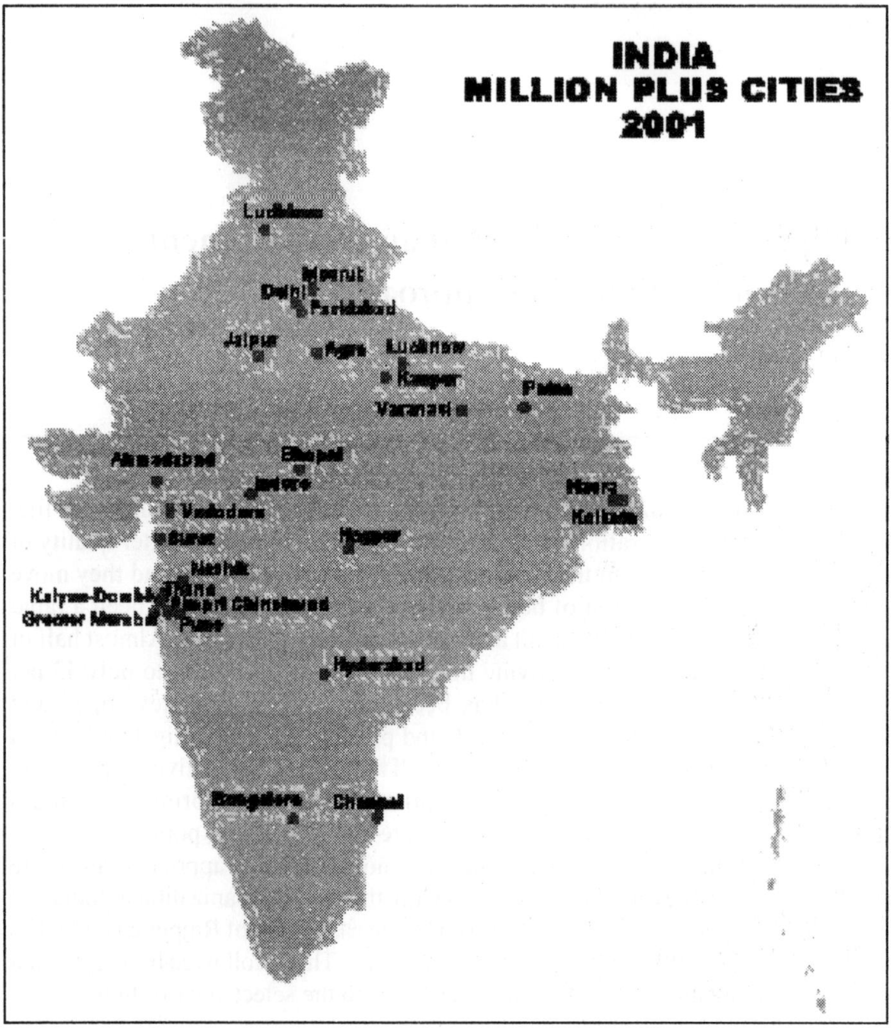

The percentage of urban population to the total population of the country stands at 27.8. The percentage of urban population to total population in the 1991 Census (including interpolated population of Jammu & Kashmir where Census could not be conducted in 1991) was 25.7 per cent. Thus, there has been an increase of 2.1 percentage points in the proportion of urban population in the country during 1991-2001.

Among all the States and Union territories, the National Capital Territory of Delhi is most urbanized with 93 per cent urban population followed by Union territory of Chandigarh (89.8%) and Pondicherry (66.6%). Among the major States, Tamil Nadu is the most urbanized state with 43.9 per cent of the population living in urban areas followed by Maharashtra (42.4%) and Gujarat (37.4%). The proportion of urban population is the lowest in Himachal Pradesh with 9.8 per cent followed by Bihar with 10.5 per cent, Assam (12.7%) and Orissa

(14.9%). In terms of absolute number of persons living in urban areas, Maharashtra leads with 41 million persons which is 14 per cent of the total population of the country. Uttar Pradesh accounts for about 35 million followed by Tamil Nadu 27 million.

Table 15.1: Growth of Urban Population in India, 1901-2001

	Urban population (million)	*Percentage of Urban to total population*	*Decadal growth rate (per cent)*
1901	29.9	10.8	—
1911	25.9	10.3	0.4
1921	28.1	11.2	18.3
1931	33.5	12.0	19.1
1941	44.2	13.9	32.0
1951	62.4	17.3	41.4
1961	78.9	18.0	26.4
1971	109.1	19.9	38.2
1981	159.5	23.3	46.1
1991	217.6	25.7	36.4
2001	306.9	30.5	41.0

Source: Ministry of Urban Developemnt, Government of India.

Table 15.2 below shows that there are 4378 urban settlements in India in which 393 are the Class I cities with a population of over 1,00,000.

Table 15.2: Urban areas in India

Class	*Population Size*	*No. of UAs/Towns*
Class I	1,00,000 and above	393
Class II	50,000-99,999	401
Class III	20,000-49,999	1,151
Class IV	10,000-19,999	1,344
Class V	5,000-9,999	888
Class VI	Less than 5,000	191
Unclassified		10*
All classes		4378

Source: Ministry of Urban Development Website—www.urbanindia.nic.in

The Impacts of Urbanisation

Though urbanization is associated with higher income, better facilities etc., these benefits come at the cost of environmental and social ills. The social ills are apparent in the form of high crime rate, crime against women and lack of social support system which was intrinsic in the traditional society (Dhirendra Kumar, 2007). The environmental ills are physically visible in terms of the rapidly deteriorating quality of environment primarily caused due to inadequate waste disposal facility and sanitation. The recent history has shown that health hazards and epidemics spread at a rapid pace in the urban centres. The impact on environment quality incurred by an urban centre is felt in the rural hinterland as well. The pollution of river or ground water due to discharge from urban areas is one such example.

Urbanisation and Growth of Slums

People move towards the urban areas in search of better economic opportunities. But they find themselves in poor living conditions, often in the periphery of the cities often squatting on the public land. Slums are characterized with an extremely poor people living in sub-standard living conditions. They are often squatters, living on land that they do not officially own. The land is often owned by the government and likely to be vacated by them at some point of time or other. The houses in slums are often temporary construction, made of any materials at hand, like mud, sticks, sheet metal, cartons, and other waste materials. Slums are characterized by overcrowding with entire families living in one-room structures, and very little space between them. Sanitation is generally non-existent and the main cause of spread of diseases such as cholera, typhoid, tuberculosis and diphtheria. Utilities such as electricity, water and sewage disposal are either not available. There is a dearth of employment opportunities due gap in demand and supply wick results in more and more unemployed youth who often get engaged in criminal activities. Slum conditions make maintenance of law and order extremely difficult these areas emerge as the safe centres of organized criminal activities and social evils.

According to the report, over 90 per cent of slum-dwellers in the world live in developing countries with China and India accounting for 37 per cent of them. About 56 per cent of the urban population lives in slum conditions. Nearly 640 cities/towns in India are reported to have slums and have a slum population of over 17.7 million. Greater Mumbai Municipal Corporation with 6.5 million slum dwellers has the highest slum population among all the cities followed by Delhi Municipal Corporation (1.9 million), Kolkata (1.5 million) and Chennai (0.8 million). As the cities are growing in size, so is the slum population. Over 6 million children are reported in the slum areas and are deprived of a decent quality of life. The sex ratio in slum areas is 876, lower than that of non slum areas of 905. The literacy rate in the slum areas is 73.1 which is lower than that of non-slum urban areas of 81.0 per cent.

The growth of cities can have significant impact on the surrounding environment not only within the cities but also the rural hinterland. Due to high concentration of heat sources, cities tend to be warmer than surrounding rural areas. Large cities become 'regional heat islands', which can alter local weather patterns. One of the most obvious differences between an urban and a rural area is the air quality. Due to heavy motorized traffic, energy production, a blanket of smog hangs over many cities. This polluted air is, in addition to being quite ugly, a public health problem. Urbanisation leads to reduction in the ground water table and deterioration in the water quality. Once the rains fall, instead of being absorbed by the ground, the water is channelized into the run-off systems. Moreover this contaminated with the polluted discharge of city.

CASE STUDY OF A GROWING CITY —RAIPUR

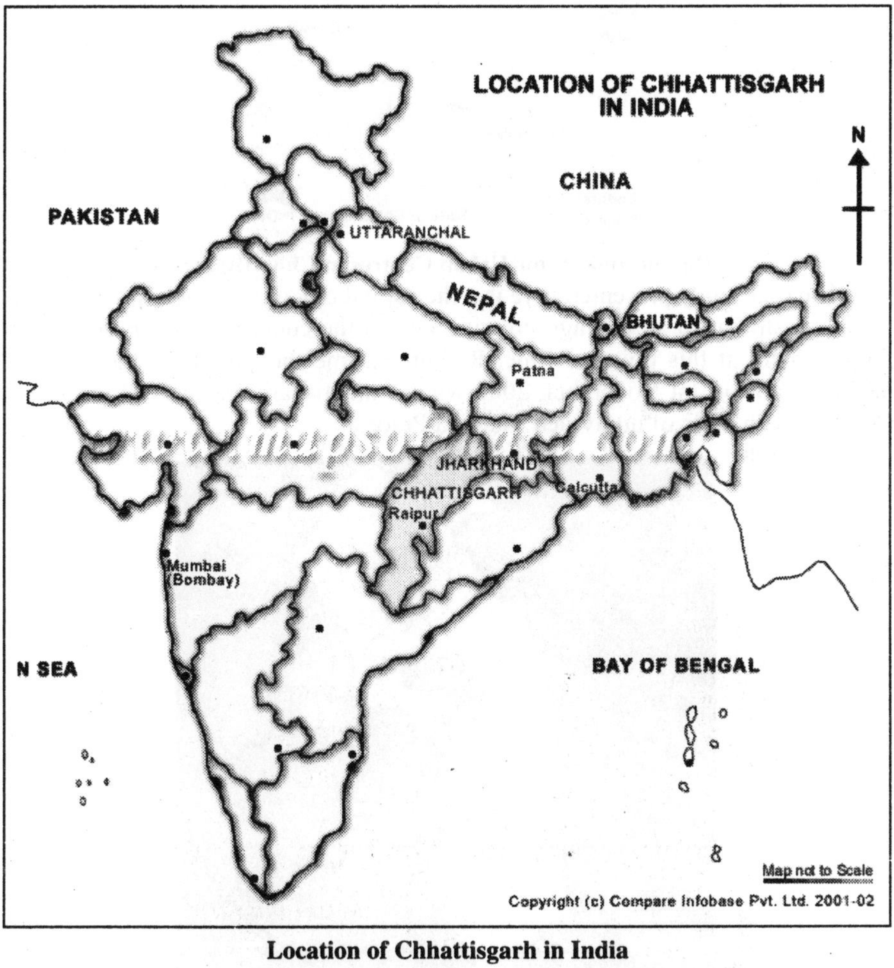

Location of Chhattisgarh in India

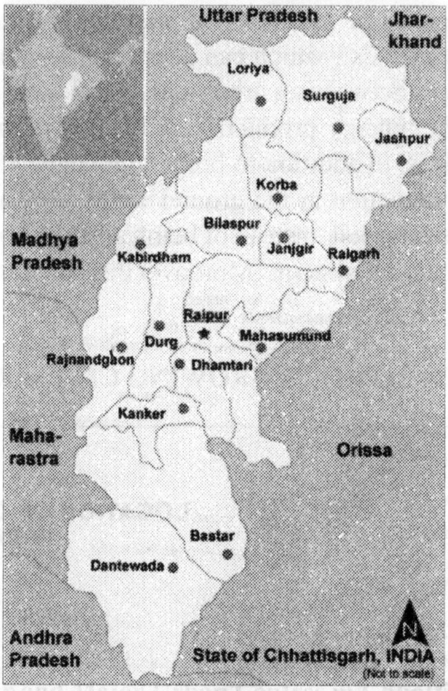

Raipur and Major Urban Centres in Chhattisgarh

The case study presented here is a the capital city of the newly formed state, which is similar to an average growing city in the country, and experiencing a high growth at this point of time. Raipur became the capital of the State of Chhattisgarh on 1st November, 2000 when Chhattisgarh was carved out of the south-eastern parts of undivided Madhya Pradesh.

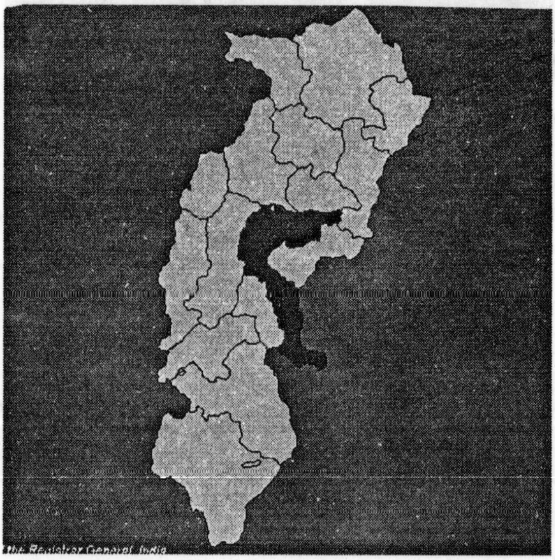

Location of Raipur District in Chhattisgarh

It is bound by Uttar Pradesh and Jharkhand in the north, Orissa in the east, Andhra Pradesh in the south and by Madhya Pradesh and Maharashtra in the west. The rate of urbanization in this region has been slow over the past. Fig. 15.1 shows that there is no single million plus city in the region. If the trend in the other parts of the country is any indication, the region is likely to see urbanization in a large scale in the near future.

Population Growth in Raipur

The population of Raipur District as per the 2001 census was 3016930 in which 917618 is urban population. In 1991 the urban population in the district was 24.2 per cent of the total population whereas in the 2001 it became 30.4 per cent. Over the same period, the population density increased from 193 to 230 persons per square kilometre and the average land holding size decreased from 1.78 to 1.47 hectare. The total employment in agriculture sector decreased from 76 per cent to 62 per cent over the same period. These statistics indicate how the process of urbanization is affecting the demographic and the livelihood pattern in the urban areas. Table 15.3 gives the demographic profile of Raipur district.

Table 15.3: Profile of Raipur District

Population	3016930
Urban Population	917618
% Urban Population	30.4
Sex Ratio	980
Sex Ratio in Urban Areas	927
Literacy Rate	68.5
Urban Literacy	79.6
Mineral Production-Lime (MT)	6027

Source: www.raipur.nic.in, Census of India, 2001.

Population of Raipur City

The population of Raipur city as per the 2001 census is 700113. The population growth in the city has been phenomenal over the recent past. Table 15.4 below shows a population growth rate of 52 per cent over the last decade.

Table 15.4: Population and Growth Rate in Raipur City

S. No.	*Year*	*Population*	*Growth Rate*
1.	1981	338000	—
2.	1991	461000	36.4
3.	2001	700113	51.9

Source: Census of India, 2001.

Migration Pattern

The urbanization and migration are interrelated phenomenon. The close relationship in the two is discussed in subsequent sections in detail. This section presents the migration pattern in the Chhattisgarh state. The data reveals that 32.6 per cent population in the state was born outside the place of enumeration and have migrated either within the state or from outside. 20.4 per cent population is reported to have migrated within their own districts mostly from the rural hinterland to the urban centres and 7.3 per cent from one district to another. 4.7 per cent population in the district has migrated from other states in the country.

Table 15.5: Migration Pattern in Chhattisgarh State

	Total	*% of Total*	*Male*	*Female*
Total Population	20,833,803		10,474,218	10,359,585
Born in India	20,782,945	99.8	10,447,448	10,335,497
Within the state of enumeration	19,813,453	95.1	10,015,311	9,798,142
Born in the place of enumeration	14,048,866	67.4	8,720,820	5,328,046
Born elsewhere in the district of enumeration	4,252,002	20.4	826,688	3,425,314
Born in other districts of the state	1,512,585	7.3	467,803	1,044,782
States in India beyond the state of enumeration	969,492	4.7	432,137	537,355

Source: Census of India, 2001.

Poverty Assessment

Over 38.9 per cent of the population of the state lives below poverty line (BPL) as estimated by the Government of Chhattisgarh. The communities all along the project corridor earn a living from agricultural pursuits. Otherwise, they do not have adequate accessibility to economic opportunities and are thus not empowered to influence the institutions for their development. The average per capita income in the state is Rs. 7,072. According to the Human Development Report for Chhattisgarh prepared by the Government of Chhattisgarh, 2005, the majority of the states tribal population which is 32 per cent of the total population of the state, is poor.

The primary sector, more specifically agriculture and allied activities, forms the base of the State's economy and provides livelihood to 78 per cent of the rural population. The rural economy has a diversified base with agriculture and allied activities as the mainstay, accompanied by a thriving rural non-farm economy. The

Table 15.6: Occupation Pattern in Chhattisgarh

Sl. No.	*Worker Type*	*Per cent Workers*
1.	Farmers	78.01
2.	Shopkeepers	3.10
3.	Wage Labour	18.74
4.	Skilled Worker	0.15

Source: Human Development Report, Government of Chhattisgarh, 2005

About 18.74 per cent of households are workers or wage earners. Around three per cent of the rural households run shops. It is important to note that this figure refers to those households that are completely dependent on wages and other work. A sizeable proportion of agriculturists live on the margins. During the lean season, or when they face a shortage of food grain, they look for wage labour. Wages are an important source of livelihood. Within the wage labour category, there are several sub-categories like agricultural wage labour, wage labour for forest produce collection and wage labour in cattle rearing. Wage earners are engaged in cottage industry, manufacturing industry, construction work, mines, and transport related activities and in small hotels and *dhabas*. About 82 per cent of rural wage earners find employment in agricultural activities. Cattle-rearing is second in importance to agriculture and provides employment to 6 per cent of all rural wage earners. However, wages from cattle rearing are largely contractual in nature. About five per cent of the rural wage earners get wages from forest-based activities. Construction labour provides employment to about 2.7 per cent of wage earners. Table 15.7 gives the Categorywise distribution of wage earners.

Table 15.7: Categorywise Distribution of Wage Earners

Sl. No.	*Type of Wage Earner*	*per cent Workers*
1.	Agriculture	81.98
2.	Forest	4.96
3.	Cattle Rearing	6.01
4.	Fishery	0.97
5.	Cottage Industry	1.18
6.	Petty Industry	0.33
7.	Construction	2.72
8.	Mine Worker	0.86
9.	Transport	0.59
10.	Big Industry	0.19
11.	Dhaba/Restaurant	0.22

Source: Human Development Report, Government of Chhattisgarh, 2005.

Tribal Population in Raipur and Chhattisgarh

Almost one-third of the total population in the state is 'Tribal'. Table below shows that as per Census of India data for 2001, over 66 lakh people in the state are reported as Scheduled Tribes which is 32 per cent of the total population. At the national level the tribal population is only 8 per cent of the total population.

Among the project districts, Dantewada reports exceptionally high tribal population at 78 per cent. Thus, the project road section from Dantewada to Sukhma passes through highly sensitive tribal region of the country. Table 15.8 shows that 12.1 per cent population in the Raipur District is tribal.

Table 15.8: Tribal Population

District/State	'Total ST Population'	'Percentage ST'
Raipur	365273	12.1
Mahasamund	232485	27
Durg	348801	12.4
Kawardha	121957	20.9
Dhamtari	185515	26.3
Dantewada	564931	78.5
Chhattisgarh	6616596	31.75
India	67758380	8.08

Source: Census of India, 2001.

Major Tribes in the State are Gonds, Abhuj Maria, Bison Horn Maria, Muria, Halbaa, Bhatra and Dhruvaas/Parjaas.

Growth of Slums in Raipur

The growth in urban areas has been associated with the rise in poverty levels. In spite of Raipur's prominent role in the economy of the region, urban population and especially the urban poor faces serious problems due to population pressure, deterioration in the physical environment and quality meet the infrastructure and social and economic development needs to their quality of life.

Raipur has 52 slums sprawling the city and constitute one-third of city population, i.e. about 32 per cent of population resides in slum, squatters and other poor settlements in the city and surrounding villages. In the RMC they are mostly concentrated on the central part of the city. Their contribution to city's economy has been growing over decades. With soaring land prices and absence of clear policy framework to address their problems, the poor suffer without access absence of clear policy framework to address their problems, the poor suffer without access to basic services, like housing, livelihoods, education and health services, etc. there is need to clearly articulate policies and programmes to address these concerns and meet the infrastructure and social and economic development needs to their quality of life (CDP, Raipur, 2006).

Raipur urban agglomeration is characterized by a very significant presence of the urban poor, with growing poverty profile. Slum settlements have multiplied over years and the living conditions of the poor have not improved much. Environmental decline, inadequate basic services and infrastructure in poor settlements hit the poor hardest. Slums are scattered across the city in different wards. It is estimated that many slums are located on private lands without access to basic services.

The poor, not only habitat the slums of the city but are spread in squatters and informal settlements in small groups near 68 City Development Plan, Raipur City Basic Services to the Urban Poor residential colonies, market places, industrial areas, etc., deprived of basic services. This makes them more vulnerable to vicissitudes of nature and periodic threats of eviction, ejection and demolition. No authentic data is available on the number of such settlements and their population. Another feature is that the Raipur urban agglomeration consists of out growths, which are presently not part of the corporation area but inextricably linked with the city both spatially and economically. In all these areas the poor population is very high and all these as per the 2005 survey it stands at 369929 an increase of about 53 per cent a development plan 2011 areas can be considered to be slums without basic infrastructure both physical and social.

The number of slums and slum population in Raipur Municipal Corporation are increasing at a faster pace over the decades. The slum population as per 2001 census is over 159120 and is presented in Table 15.9. The slum population has gone up substantially over the last few years and which is very high.

Table 15.9: Slums in Raipur

Sl. No.	Slum	No. of Slums	Dwelling Units	Population	Area in Ha
1.	Declared by Government	135	22777	13821	290
2.	Undeclared	19	4122	20699	—
3.	Total	154	26899	159120	—

Source: City Development Plan for Raipur, Jawaharlal Nehru National Urban Renewal Mission, 2006.

Economic Development

The economy of the district is primarily based on the primary sources. In addition to agriculture, people in the district depend on animal husbandry, traditional occupations, and the collection and sale of forest produce. As many as 68 per cent villages in the district depend only on agriculture for their livelihood. About 63 per cent find employment only for the part of the year. The Human Development Report of Chhattisgarh indicates that the education and health facilities in the Raipur district are inadequate. People want the government programmes to be implemented more effectively and *they are keen to be partners in the process of change and development* (Human Development Report, 2005).

Mineral Resources in Chhattisgarh

Chhattisgarh is rich in Mineral resources. It is the largest tin ore producing state and is a major coal and Iron ore producing state. Chhattisgarh, along with two other Indian States has almost all the coal deposits in India. All the tin ore in India is in Chhattisgarh. A fifth of iron ore in the country is here, and one of the best quality iron ore deposits in the world is found in the Bailadila mines in south Chhattisgarh, from where it is exported to Japan. Rich deposits of Bauxite, Limestone, Dolomite and Corundum are found in the State.

Table 15.10 presents the production of important minerals in the state. It shows that the production of coal, bauxite, iron ore, dolomite, limestone has increased steadily over the periods of time.

Table 15.10: Production of Important Minerals

Sl. No.	Mineral	1998-99	1999-2000	2000-2001
1.	Coal	41774	44723	50227
2.	Bauxite	479	444	557
3.	Iron Ore	17150	20582	20106
4.	Dolomite	739	663	695
5.	Silica Sand	14	14	02
6.	China Clay	04	02	02
7.	Lime Stone	9093	12130	13954
8.	Quartzite	01	17	08
9.	Tin (Concentrate) in Kg	39391	22812	12979

Source: Chhattisgarh at a Glance 2002, Government of Chhattisgarh, http://chhattisgarh.nic.in

The Regional Planning Approach

The need of delineating regions for the planning purpose was realized as early as year 1955 by the Planning Commission (TCPO, 1982). It recommended delineation of whole country into planning regions for development purpose and preparation of development plan for each identified region. More than 50 years later, the progress made in this direction is left wanting. The concept of regions and method of delineation has been a subject of debate for more than half a century with little headway. The lack of consensus has seriously hampered the progress towards adopting the overall regional planning approach towards development of the country.

The first step towards adopting a regional planning approach is to delineate a region for planning purpose. The planning region should be such that it achieves the plan objectives, maximizes the utilization of resources in order to achieve a minimum desired development objectives. To ensure this, it is necessary to consider the natural resources available, socio-economic status of target population and the development potential of the region. With the reference to the case city of Raipur city, the different factors that influence the development of the city and its region are discussed here.

Push and Pull Factors

The push and pull factors define the growth dynamics of the region. The Raipur city has recently become the political capital and become a city of strategic importance. Being the capital of the state which is rich in mineral resources and huge growth potential, the city promises to act like a string magnet. Due to attaining the status of capital city, there has been increased flow of funds and a visible improvement in the urban infrastructure and services. However, it is worth mentioning that the population in the city has grown at an even faster rate. Though the state is rich in mineral resources, the livelihood of the rural population is primarily based on agriculture. With growing population and diminishing land holding size, the pressure on agriculture land is increasing and people are left with no option but to search for alternative sources of livelihood.

The regional disparities between the urban and rural areas are growing. The rural areas near Raipur, particularly towards south in Dantewada district is densely populated with tribal population, a socially disadvantaged and economically backward population. The rural areas are lagging behind in the provision of basic amenities. The advanced as available in the rural areas is a far of dream for the poor villagers. Table 15.11 below shows an example of scarcity of potable drinking water in the villages of Raipur district.

Table 15.11: Drinking water problem in Raipur District Villages

Drinking water facility in the villages in Raipur District		
1.	Problem Villages	2042
2.	Villages with tap water supply	95

Source: http://www.raipur.nic.in

Regional Linkages

The functional linkages act as lifelines for sustaining a region. The functional linkages include transport links like the roads and highways, essential commodities like agriculture produce, vegetable and milk supply zones, education and higher education linkages, hospitals and health facilities linkages etc. In case of Raipur, which is a new capital city and likely to emerge as a big market place in the near future particularly for the rich mineral resources available here, the mineral extraction zones form another important linkage.

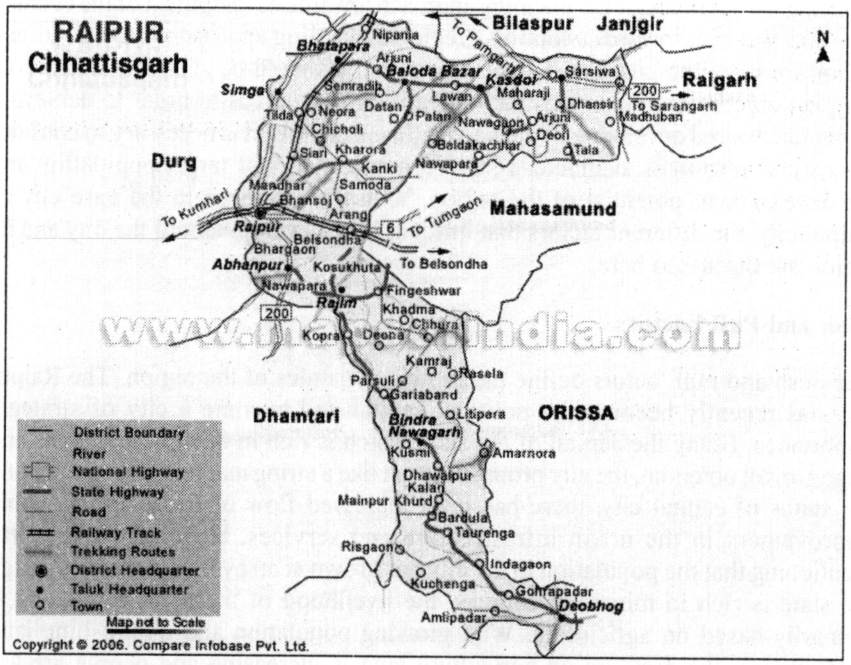

Regional Transport Links of Raipur

Settlement Pattern in the Region and Rural Urban Migration

The growth and development of a large urban area trickles down in the nearby smaller settlements specially those which are well connected through roads and highways. These settlements experience faster growth than the rest of the region. The presence of another large settlement serves as a counter magnet and may lead to a more even distribution of the growth. Raipur is such case, where the industrial city of Durg is located close to the city. Being an industrial city Durg serves as another regional centre. Probably, in the present date it is a stronger regional centre than the new capital city due to the availability of more alternative employment opportunities. Statistics reveal that this migration is the largest contributor in the population growth and growth of slums. The population growth in turn has resulted in the lack of adequate infrastructure, amenities, services and employment and leading to the ill effects of overcrowding and overall degradation in the quality of life.

Alternative Livelihood Opportunities

As discusses in the previous sections the lack of employment opportunities in the rural areas is one of the prime causes for the rural to urban migration. India is a primarily agrarian economy. The Raipur city region is again an agrarian economy with not enough development of secondary sector. This illustrates how the lack of employment and alternative livelihood options is leading to a poor quality of life for both rural and urban population.

The small and medium industries based on the agro products and available natural resources can be an effective means of provision of alternative employment. In the case of Raipur and Chhattisgarh, for example, the region is agriculture based economy and very rich in mineral resources. Encouraging the small and medium industries based on these primary sources can bring the benefits of value addition to these raw products to the non-urbanized population.

The Integrated Regional Development Approach

The integrated regional planning essentially addresses the issues of regional disparity. An easy connectivity between the urban centres and the rural hinterland is the key towards a balanced regional development. The planning approach should be effective in checking rate of population growth in urban centres. One of the possible ways of achieving this is can be providing the alternative employment opportunities in the rural areas. Also it is imperative to reduce regional disparities by providing infrastructure and amenities in the rural areas and providing good connectivity with the urban centres and the market places. The reduction in the population growth in the urban areas is essential to ensure sustainability of development interventions. It is important that the rural population should not be deprived of the basic amenities like the potable water or hygienic conditions as these factors act as a strong force propelling the rural population towards the urban centres. Second most important factor is that the development interventions should not be concentrated in urban but also trickles down in the rural hinterland. The contribution of the rural population in regional economy needs to be appreciated and acknowledged by sharing the profits of value addition in the raw produce from the rural areas.

CONCLUSION

People have been moving from the rural areas towards urban centres in search of better livelihood options. A careful observation of facts and ground realities will reveal that the idea of the people leaving the rural areas and moving to the urban centres is not paying off. It has led to an excessive pressure on the urban infrastructure, overcrowding, pollution or in a nutshell, a deteriorated quality of life for migrants as well as the host community. The growth of slums is one visible implication that has its own environmental and social ill effects. Moreover, the people living in these slums are subjected to a highly sub-standard quality of living. The urban services and amenities in most of the urban area are under a sustained pressure and adversely affecting the sustainability of development interventions. An integrated approach for the development of the urban centres and its rural hinterland is the possible solution of addressing the issue. It is important to delineate the economically viable region for the planning purpose considering the social fabric and the economic growth pattern of the areas. The regional linkages, both existing and the likely should be a key factor as these determine the key future growth dynamics in the region. Analysis of the settlement pattern both urban and rural and the likely impact of the different urban centres as the magnets and counter magnets and the resulting trickle-down effect of development process from the urban centres to the rural hinterland form the basis for the regional development approach. The development approach should essentially address the root of the regional issues like the lack of livelihood opportunities, development of rural economy and reaping the benefits of the development of the urban centres for the development of the rural hinterland and thus enduring a sustainable development of both the urban as well as rural areas.

REFERENCES

Census of India, 2001, Office of Registrar General of India.

Chhattisgarh at a Glance, 2002, Government of Chhattisgarh.

Chhattisgarh Human Development Report, Government of Chhattisgarh, 2005.

Chhattisgarh, 2010, Vision Document, Government of Chhattisgarh

City Development Plan for Raipur, Jawaharlal Nehru National Urban Renewal Mission, 2006.

Environmental Management Systems—An Exemplary for Urban Local Bodies, Dhirendra Kumar, 2007.

Government of Chhattisgarh—http://chhattisgarh.nic.in

http://www.raipur.nic.in

Ministry of Urban Development—www.urbanindia.nic.in

Regional Planning Efforts in India, Town and Country Planning Organisation, Government of India, 1982.

Report on UNDP initiatives in Chhattisgarh, UNDP, 2002.

The Hindustan Times, 7th December 2007, Chetan Chauhan, 'Urbanisation in India Faster than the Rest of the World'

www.bbc.co.uk

www.mapsofindia.com

www.ubdp.org

www.worldbank.org

16

Representing Towns of Coimbatore District by GIS

M. SAKTHIVEL, R. SUNIL KUMAR and
K. S. GOPALAKRISHNAN

INTRODUCTION

Representing urbanization and towns is always a challenge in medium and small scale mapping. Traditionally towns and cities are shown by mono dot or multi dot symbols in paper maps. If large metropolitan/urban areas are involved those areas are provided as insets for details. When changes over a period of time are represented, series of located thematic maps or a located histogram map is the normal option of the cartographer.

The representation of towns and cities and their changes over periods of time are equally a challenging task in GIS. It involves (a) Preprocessing statistical analysis, (b) Choice of either point or area symbolization (under GIS), (c) Incorporating in the result of statistical analysis to the symbols, and (d) The representation of such theme in conjunction with other elements of digital map.

Coimbatore is one of the Metropolitan towns of Tamil Nadu. Coimbatore district has about 9.5 per cent population of 832 towns of Tamil Nadu as per 2001 census. Lot of changes has taken place both in the status and size of the towns of the Coimbatore district for the past two decades, viz. 1981-2001. This presentation is centred around the representation of towns of Coimbatore district during the census period of 1981, 1991 and 2001 as well as to analyse the distribution pattern in terms of functional hierarchy.

THEME AND OBJECTIVES

The point features representing of urban centres is classical in nature. However, this seems to be a well understood and widely practiced method of representation of towns and therefore, can be a methodology of representation to summarise statistical analysis of urban centres.

Obectives

1. To run a preprocessing statistical analysis to bring out the classification of Towns of Coimbatore District—Factor analysis.
2. Use the multi dot symbolization to project the statistical results into thematic maps.
3. To bring out the changing pattern of Coimbatore towns in the past two decades.

OUTLINE OF COIMBATORE DISTRICT

Coimbatore forms the North-western margin of Tamil Nadu Deccan and is highly industrialized district. A total population of 4,271,856 (2001) is spread over the region. The district has a literacy rate of 76.97 per cent and a sex ratio of 963. The overall population density of the district is $572/km^2$.

Problem Statement and Objectives

The total personality of the towns and the degree of importance of the role that they play in the overall economy of the region is to be analyzed through the objectives given below.

The objectives of the study are to identify the distribution pattern of towns in Coimbatore district for the years 1981,1991 and 2001. Establishing the functional hierarchy of towns in the district based on their urban facilities for the years 1981 and 2001. And finally, comparing the classification of towns between the distribution pattern and functional hierarchy of towns for the corresponding years.

METHODOLOGY

Data

In this study, townwise population data of Coimbatore District for the year 1981, 1991 and 2001 have been collected. To establish the functional hierarchy (1981-1991) of the towns in the district and number of services in the towns has been obtained from the census of India.

Techniques Used

Methodology on GIS Representation is presented using Coimbatore District. The towns have been classified to identify the distribution pattern and locations of class I-VI towns have been shown. To establish the functional hierarchy of

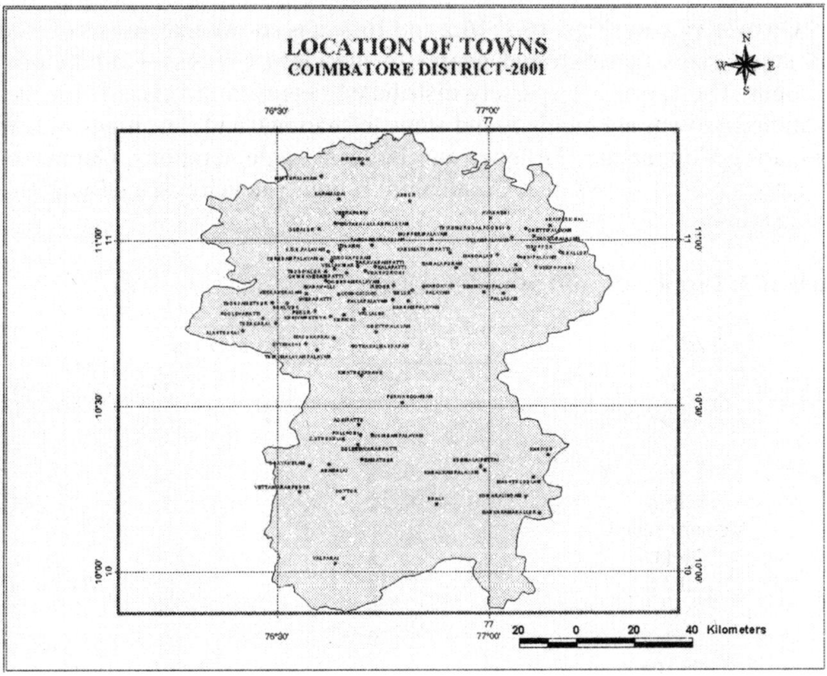

the towns in the district, the list of services like primary school, middle school, high school, colleges, bank, churches of 17 variables have been taken for the factor analysis techniques. The hierarchical clustering technique has been applied for the selected factors using dendrogram to find the functional hierarchy of the towns. The factor analysis and hierarchical clustering techniques has been used SPSS package. The georeferenced map has been digitized using Arc map software. And further analysis has been made spatially using Arc view 3.2 GIS.

RESULTS AND DISCUSSIONS

Distribution of Towns

Towns are classified based on population as class I, II, III, IV, V and VI sizes. There were 36 towns in Coimbatore district in the year 1981. The towns were 40 in the year 1991. It shows there is only a slow growth in urbanization for a decade from 1981 to 1991. In the census year 2001, there were 79 towns in Coimbatore district. Size classes and distribution pattern of towns are shown in Table 16.1.

From the analysis, it shows that number of class I cities decreased from the year 1991 to 2001. Medium towns of class II and III are increased in number from 1981 to 2001, and small towns of IV, V and VI are also increased in majority of numbers from 28 to 52.

On over viewing Figs. 16.1, 16.2 and 16.3, it is known that, towns of medium and small sizes concentrated nearer to the class I cities—Coimbatore and Tiruppur. The towns are sparsely distributed nearer to the class II towns. The locations of towns are highly found along the national and state highways. When comparing Coimbatore, Tiruppur and Pollachi agglomerations, Coimbatore is the largest one. It shows that, Coimbatore is highly developed agglomeration in urbanization.

Table 16.1: Distribution of Towns: 1981-2001.

Size Class	*No. of towns*		
	1981	*1991*	*2001*
Cities			
I	3	3	2
II	3	4	6
III	2	5	19
Medium Towns			
(II+III)	5	9	25
IV	14	12	27
V	9	13	25
VI	5	3	0
Small Towns			
(IV+V+VI)	28	28	52
Total	36	40	79

Source: Census of India.

Characteristics of Towns (1981)

The original data matrix consists of 17 variables for which principal component analysis was computed after obtaining means and standard deviations. From Table 16.2, it is shown total percentage of variance of the components.

Percentage of variance is high for the component 1 (67.9%) and for component 2 it is 15.7 per cent. Therefore, component 1 is more significant than all other components. The component or factor loadings derived in Table 16.3 is the measure of the degree of closeness between the variables and the components. The factor-loading matrix was subjected to varimax with Kaiser Normalization rotation so as to attain simple structure and the result is presented in Table 16.4. From Table 16.4, it is clear that the most of the variables are having high loadings on anyone of the component. It is advocated that the largest loading either positive or negative suggests the meaning of the dimension.

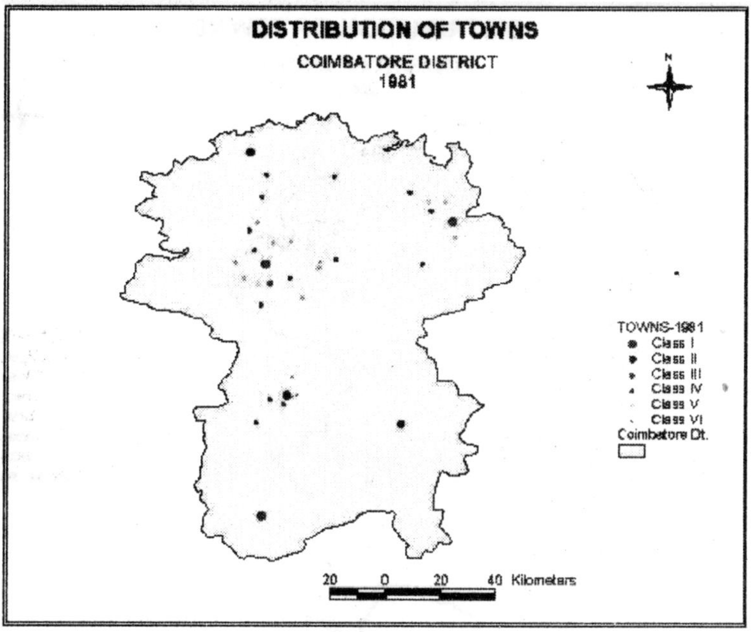

Fig. 16.1: Distribution of Towns in Coimbatore District (1981).

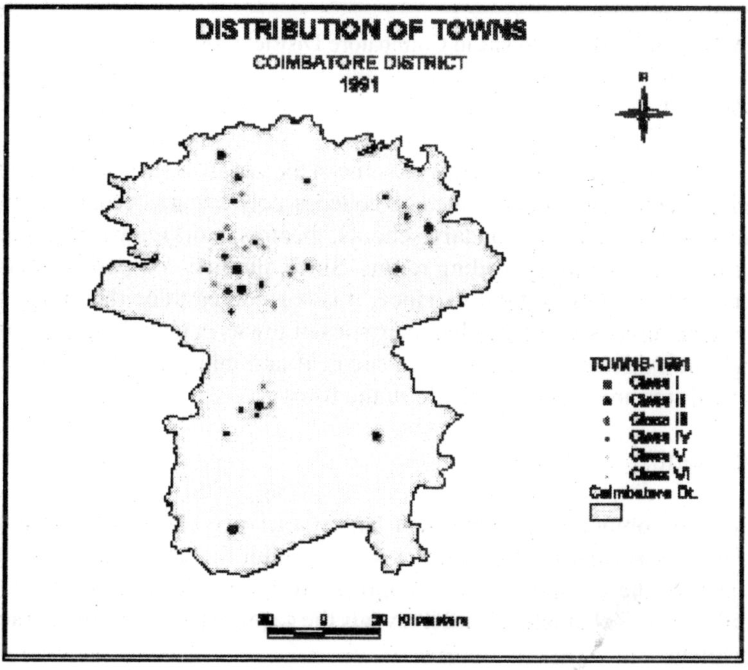

Fig. 16.2: Distribution of Towns in Coimbatore District (1991).

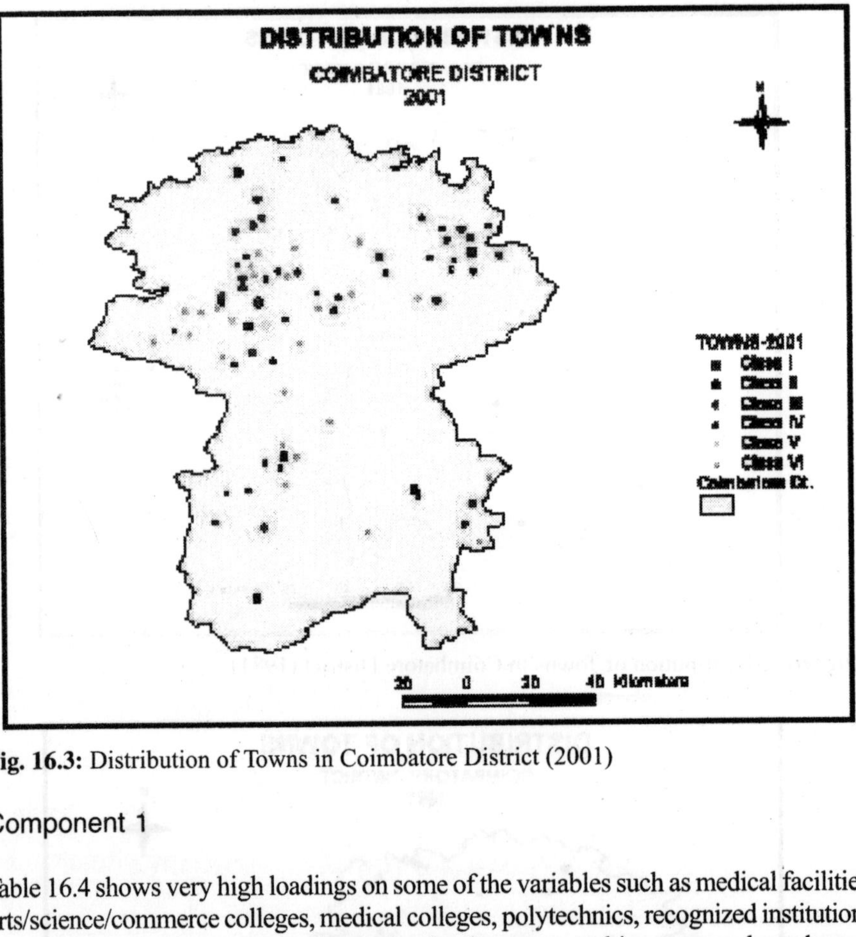

Fig. 16.3: Distribution of Towns in Coimbatore District (2001)

Component 1

Table 16.4 shows very high loadings on some of the variables such as medical facilities, arts/science/commerce colleges, medical colleges, polytechnics, recognized institutions and all kind of primary, secondary schools, theatres, working women hostels and public libraries including reading rooms. Since, the first component accounts for the largest proportion of total variance, it is considered to be the most important single basic dimension of the characteristics of towns in Coimbatore district. This component exhibits a very strong in medical and educational facilities. Hence, these facilities are more significant in the towns.

Component 2

The second component has the next largest variance (15%). High loadings are found to be associated with variables namely adult literacy centres, stadium, and auditorium. The component may appropriately be called as "recreational and cultural facilities characters" and it reveals the second dimension of characteristics of the towns.

Table 16.2: Total Variance Explained

Component	Initial Eigenvalues			Extraction Sums of Squared Loadings			Rotation Sums of Squared Loadings		
	Total	*% of Variance*	*Cumulative%*	*Total*	*% of Variance*	*Cumulative%*	*Total*	*% of Variance*	*Cumulative%*
1	11.859	69.757	69.757	11.859	69.757	69.757	11.545	67.914	67.914
2	2.357	13.863	83.619	2.357	13.863	83.619	2.670	15.705	83.619
3	.989	5.816	89.435						
4	.879	5.171	94.606						
5	.460	2.708	97.313						
6	.228	1.341	98.655						
7	8.498E-02	.500	99.154						
8	6.876E-02	.404	99.559						
9	3.102E-02	.182	99.741						
10	2.081E-02	.122	99.864						
11	8.113E-03	4.772E-02	99.911						
12	4.876E-03	2.868E-02	99.940						
13	3.915E-03	2.303E-02	99.963						
14	3.353E-03	1.973E-02	99.983						
15	1.876E-03	1.103E-02	99.994						
16	7.646E-04	4.498E-03	99.998						
17	2.667E-04	1.569E-03	100.000						

Extraction Method: Principal Component Analysis.

Table 16.3: Component Matrix

	Component 1	2
V1	.961	-.172
V2	.960	-.193
V3	.924	-.149
V4	.958	-.194
V5	.260	-.171
V6	.970	-4.155E-02
V7	.972	-.118
V8	.973	-1.933E-02
V9	.994	1.075E-02
V10	.802	9.147E-02
V11	.920	.121
V12	3.732E-02	.821
V13	.957	-.189
V14	.365	.824
V15	.973	.164
V16	.338	.856
V17	.867	.112

Extraction Method: Principal Component Analysis.
a 2 components extracted.

Hierarchical Clusters of Towns (1981)

A dendrogram is a 'tree like' diagram that summarises the process of clustering. Similar cases are joined by links whose position in the diagram is determined by the level of similarity between the cases. A measure distance between pairs of cases, the distance between the values of the cases is the sum of the squared difference between the values of the cases. After applying regression score to the factors, selected factor scorings (factor 1) has been applied for the hierarchical clustering technique (shown in Appendix B, Graph1). Based on the clusters, ranks could be derived and shown spatially in Fig.16.4. Total variance of the components has been shown in Table 16.5.

Component 1 has 61.6 per cent of variance and second component has 19.4 per cent variance. Hence, component 1 is more significant than the others.

Component 1

In component 1, medical hospitals, number of beds in the hospitals and educational institutions are more significant functions in the towns of Coimbatore and also cinema theatres, public libraries are the important recreational centres found in the towns. Hence component 1 resembles the basic functions of the towns.

Table 16.4: Rotated Component Matrix

	Component	
	1	*2*
V1	.976	5.775E-03
V2	.979	-1.535E-02
V3	.936	2.121E-02
V4	.978	-1.665E-02
V5	.287	-.121
V6	.961	.135
V7	.978	6.009E-02
V8	.960	.158
V9	.976	.191
V10	.772	.236
V11	.883	.286
V12	-.112	.815
V13	.975	-1.205E-02
V14	.209	.877
V15	.927	.338
V16	.177	.903
V17	.832	.268

Extraction Method: Principal Component Analysis. Rotation Method: Varimax with Kaiser Normalization a Rotation converged in 3 iterations.

Hierarchical Clusters of Towns (1981)

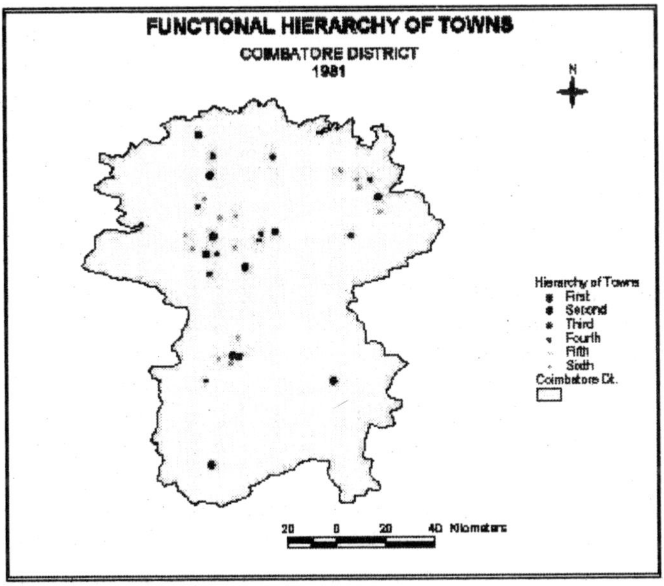

Fig. 16.4: Functional Hierarchy of Towns (1981)

Table 16.5: Total Variance Explained

Component	Initial Eigenvalues			Extraction Sums of Squared Loadings			Rotation Sums of Squared Loadings		
	Total	*% of Variance*	*Cumulative%*	*Total*	*% of Variance*	*Cumulative%*	*Total*	*% of Variance*	*Cumulative%*
1	11.790	69.353	69.353	11.790	69.353	69.353	10.477	61.629	61.629
2	1.996	11.743	81.096	1.996	11.743	81.096	3.309	19.467	81.096
3	.980	5.763	86.859						
4	.795	4.675	91.534						
5	.584	3.438	94.972						
6	.406	2.390	97.361						
7	.162	.953	98.314						
8	.147	.868	99.182						
9	5.572E-02	.328	99.509						
10	3.813E-02	.224	99.734						
11	1.755E-02	.103	99.837						
12	9.025E-03	5.309E-02	99.890						
13	7.974E-03	4.691E-02	99.937						
14	5.649E-03	3.323E-02	99.970						
15	3.377E-03	1.986E-02	99.990						
16	1.694E-03	9.967E-03	100.000						
17	-2.382E-16	-1.401E-15	100.000						

Extraction Method: Principal Component Analysis.

Component 2

In component 2, adult literacy classes, working women hostels, stadium, auditoria, theatre/community halls are highly significant functions. These functions resemble the secondary characteristics of the towns in Coimbatore district for the year 1991.

Hierarchical Clusters of Towns (1991)

After applying regression scores for the factors, hierarchical clustering (Appendix B, Graph 2) has been done for selected score (factor 1). By giving the hierarchies to the clusters, the towns are classified as shown in Fig. 16.5.

Table 16.6: Rotated Component Matrix

	Component	
	1	2
V1	.909	7.822E-02
V2	.935	.201
V3	.970	.119
V4	.969	7.901E-02
V5	.969	7.901E-02
V6	-1.386E-02	-.229
V7	.970	.162
V8	.879	.423
V9	.929	.342
V10	.789	.295
V11	.819	.431
V12	-3.190E-02	.691
V13	.371	.825
V14	.463	.778
V15	.897	.399
V16	.248	.794
V17	.932	.189

Extraction Method: Principal Component Analysis. Rotation Method: Varimax with Kaiser Normalization.
a Rotation converged in 3 iterations.

Comparison of Distribution and Functional Hierarchy of the Towns

Distribution of towns and functional hierarchy of towns may not be same in the classification. Distribution of the towns depends upon the population of that towns, where as the functional hierarchy of the towns depends upon the characteristics of those towns. Hence, class I towns may not rank first in functional characteristics. This has been known from the obtained results in Fig. 16.1, Fig. 16.4 and Fig. 16.2, Fig. 16.5.

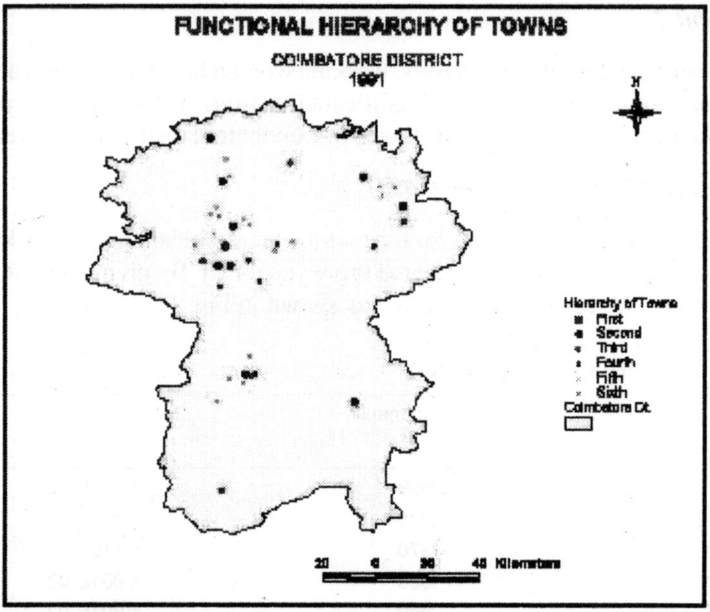

Fig. 16.5: Functional Hierarchy of Town (1991)

LIMITATION OF THE STUDY

For hierarchical clustering technique, the regression score of Coimbatore town has not been included for both the decades (1981 and 1991) because of its very larger score when comparing to other scores and to get the precise clustering in the result. Another limitation is the non-availability of data for functional hierarchy of town in the year 2001.

CONCLUSION

GIS Methodology for Representation of Urban Centres

From the analysis, the distribution pattern of towns in Coimbatore district during the past three decades 1981, 1991 and 2001 reveals that there is heavy growth of the urban population from the past to present decades. In the functional hierarchical analysis, an attempt has been made by services as parameters to identify the existence of hierarchical order of the towns in Coimbatore district. In the six level hierarchical order, first three order centres are found more in urban agglomerations whereas the fourth, fifth and sixth order centres serve the needs of rural and more or less they are distributed throughout the district. From the distribution and functional hierarchy of towns, it is clearly known that there existing relationship between the population and the number of functional establishments in the towns of Coimbatore district, and it is also known that, with an increasing population there is also a proportionate increase in the status of the district. Thus, in the present paper, the analysis on distribution pattern and functional hierarchy will possibly reveal the total personality of the towns and the degree of importance of the role that they play in the overall economy of the region.

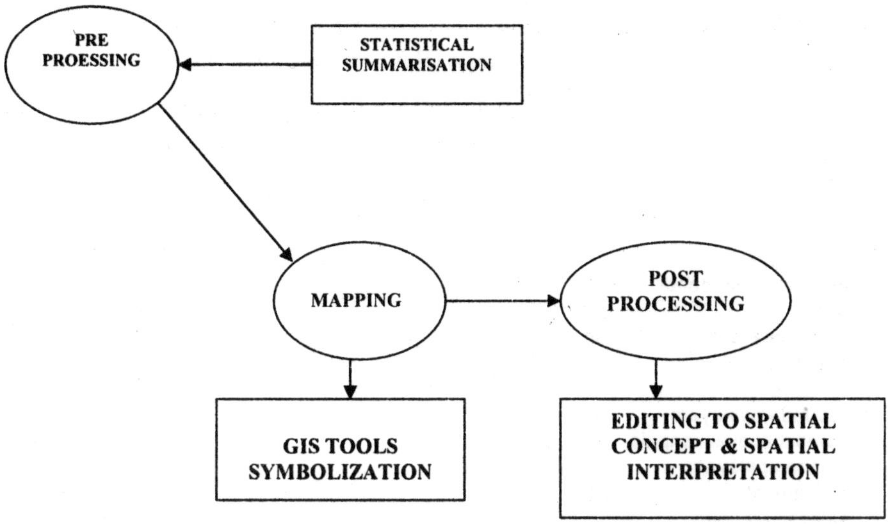

Appendix A

List of Variables Used in the Analysis of the Functional Hierarchy of Towns (1981 and 1991) in Coimbatore District

V1	— Hospitals/dispensaries/t. B. Clinics	V 11	— Primary Schools
V 2	— Beds in Medical Institutions	V 12	— Adult Literacy Classes/other Centres
V 3	— Arts/Science/Commerce Colleges	V 13	— Working Women Hostel
V 4	— Medical Colleges	V 14	— Stadia
V 5	— Engineering Colleges	V 15	— Cinema
V 6	— Polytechnics	V 16	— Auditoria/Drama/Community Hall
V 7	— Vocational Training Institutions	V 17	— Public Libraries Including Reading Rooms.
V 8	— Highr Secondarty Schools		
V 9	— Secondary/Matriculation		
V 10	— Junior Secondary and Middle Schools		

Appendix B
Graph 1

Dendrogram plot, for the hierarchical clustering of towns in Coimbatore district for the year 1981

1981* * * * * * Hierarchical Cluster Analysis is * * * * * *
Dendrogram using Average Linkage (Between Groups)

```
                                   Rescaled Distance Cluster Combine

Case                          0         5        10        15        20     25
Label                   Num +-----------+---------+--------+----------+--------+
chinnavedampatti          3  □□

zaminuttukuli            28  □□
thirumuruganpoondi       31  □□
perur                    14  □□
velampalayam             34  □□
veerakeralam             17  □□
vellalore                18  □□
kavundampalayam           5  □□
narasimanayakkanpala     11  □□
chinnampalayam           23  □□
puliyampatti             26  □□
suleeswaranpatti         27  □□
vilankurichi             19  □□
avanashi                 29  □□
veerapandi (tua)         33  □□
muthukoundampudur        10  □□□□
pallapalayam             12  □□ □
anamalai                  1  □□ □
kurudampalayam            8  □□□
chettipalayam            30  □□ □
kurichi                   7  □□ □
karamadai                20  □□ □□□□□□□
palladam                 22  □□ □      □
kuniyamuthur              6  □□ □      □
annur                     2  □□ □      □
madukkarai                9  □□ □      □
periyanayakkanpalaya     13  □□ □      □□□□□□□□□□□□□□□□□□□□□□□□
perurchettipalayam       15  □□□□      □                       □
makkinampatti            24  □□        □                       □
sulur                    16  □□        □                       □
mettupalayam             21  □□□□      □                       □
pollachi                 25  □□ □□□□□□□                        □
tiruppur                 32  □□□□                              □
udumalaipettai           35  □□                                □
valparai                 36  □□□□□□□□□□□□□□□□□□□□□□□□□□□□□□□□□□
```

Graph 2

Dendrogram plot for the year 1991 functional characteristics

* * * * * * Hierarchical Cluster Analys is * * * * * * 1991
Dendrogram using Average Linkage (Between Groups)

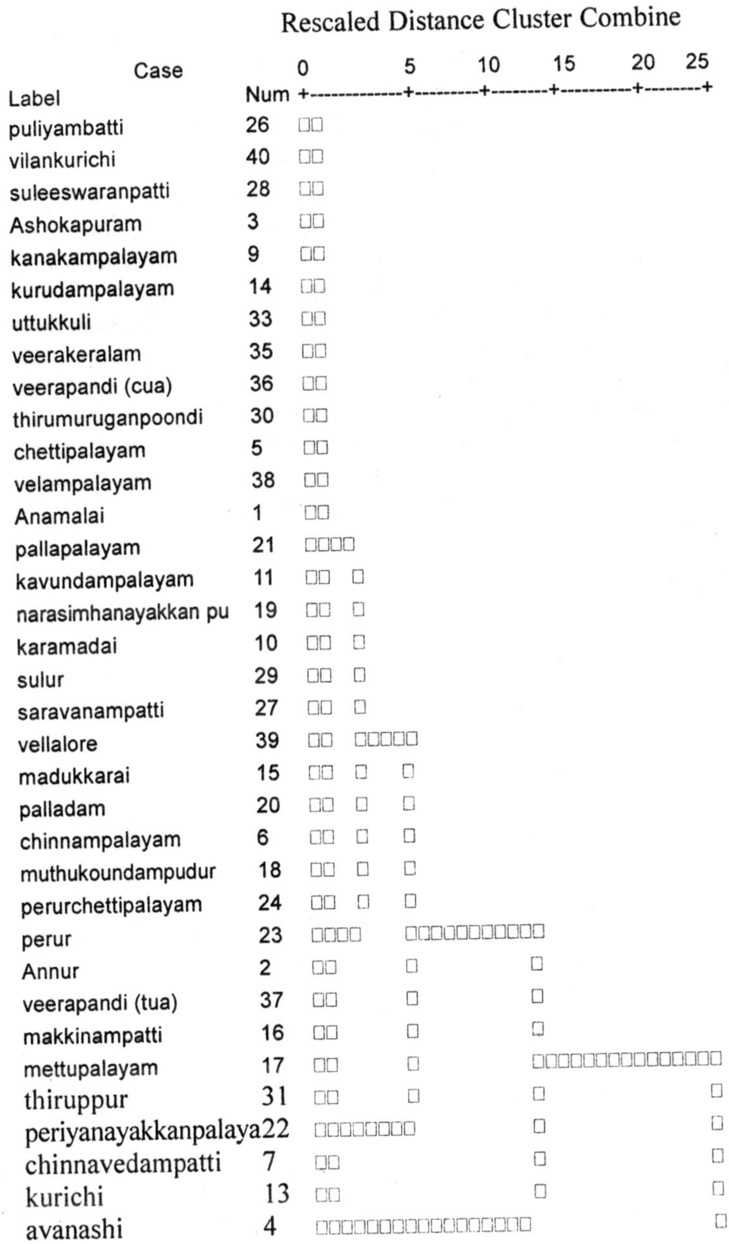

Rescaled Distance Cluster Combine

```
                 Case         0         5        10        15        20   25
Label                  Num +-----------+---------+---------+----------+--------+
kuniyamuthur           12   □□                                                □
pollachi               25   □□□□□□□□□□□□□                                     □
udumalaipettai         32   □□□□          □□□□□□□□□□□□□□□□□□□□□□□□□□
valparai               34   □□□□□□□□□□□□□
```

REFERENCES

1. James Jackson, C., (March 1974), "*The structure and functions of small Malaysian Towns*", Institute of British Geographer, Transaction no. 61, pp. 65-79.
2. Karan, P.P., and Mohammed Carami, S.G., (June 1988), "Urban systems and Urban regions of Saudi Arabia", *The Annals*, Vol. VIII, No.2, pp. 31-40.
3. Laurence Ma J.C. and Ming Ran (December 1994), "Urbanization from Below The Growth of Towns in Jiangsu, China", *Urban Studies*, Vol. 31, No. 10, pp. 1625-1645.
4. Nagarajan, V. *et al.*, (February 1977), "Small towns of Coimbatore and Thanjavur District: A Comparative Study of Pattern, Characteristics and Hierarchy", *Places of Small Towns in India*, the National Geographical Society of India, BHU, pp.127-142.
5. Pothana, V. (1980), "Urban Growth in Andhra Pradesh: An Economic Analysis", *Indian Journal of Regional Science*, Vol. XII, No.2, pp. 113-119.

17

Use and Management of Natural Resources for Sustainable Agriculture and Rural Development of Jharkhand

S.K. PAL and N.N. SINGH

The State of Jharkhand, which became a separate administrative entity, was formed on November 15, 2000 out of the erstwhile state of Bihar. According to the 2001 census, Jharkhand has a population of about 27 million people with the density of 338 persons per sq. km. The State has a total geographical area of 79,714 sq.kms. The word 'Jharkhand' means the land of plants and trees. True to its name, the forest area of the State is about 29 per cent of the land area and is among one of the few states with extensive forest and mineral resources. Agriculture and related activities are the primary sources of livelihood for the people in this State. About 75 per cent of the population resides in rural areas and about 67 per cent of the total workforce is dependant on agriculture. As per revenue records, about 38 lakh hectares are available for cultivation but at present net area sown is 18.04 lakh hectares. Despite the fairly sufficient rainfall in the region, only 11.3 per cent of the total net sown area is under irrigation.

The State has a fairly high potential for development for agriculture and for cultivation of certain high value agricultural crops including fruits and vegetables in view of the salubrious and favourable climatic conditions. Despite these advantages, development of agriculture and adoption of modern technologies have not really taken off in this state. Consequently, productivity is below the national average in the case of most annual, cereal and commercial crops. The milk yield per cattle is abominably low and despite the large area under forests, the value of its forest is one of the lowest in India. One of the redeeming pictures, however, is that in the case of vegetable, the state enjoys a pre-eminent position of not only high productivity but also high production and is the number one agricultural export commodity of the state. The potential for development is, however, very large provided appropriate resources are made available, modern production and development technologies are adopted and committed supportive policies are available.

AGRICULTURAL CROPS AND CROPPING SYSTEMS IN JHARKHAND

Background Information

Jharkhand a newly created (15 November, 2000) state having net sown area 18.1 lakh ha with cropping intensity 114 per cent is rich in natural resources such as minerals, coal, soil, water, forest cover (29.3%), biodiversity but deficient (50%) in food grains production because of meagre irrigation facilities (<10% of cultivated area) in absence of perennial rivers. This state is primarily rainfed and crop production largely depends on monsoon. The southwest monsoon contributes nearly 85 per cent of rain water. Accordingly, success or failure of crop production is closely linked with the onset, progress and withdrawal of monsoon. Delay in onset, intermittent dry spell (1-3 weeks), early withdrawal are also usually observed. Failure of Hathia Rain has adverse impact on the reproductive phase of rainy season crops. Sometimes high rainfall (140 mm/ day) coupled with light soil texture and undulating toposequence provides congenial environment for soil erosion with run off. This also offers opportunity for water harvesting. In fact, soil and water are the two basic natural resources which must be conserved and utilized efficiently for long term basis.

Agro-Climatic Features

Jharkhand having total geographical area 79.72 lakh hectares forms a part of Agro-climatic zone VII of the country known as Eastern plateau and hill region. Based on rainfall, temperature, terrain and soil characteristics, the state has been divided in to three agro-climatic sub-zones, i.e. IV-Central and North Eastern Plateau comprising districts of Hazaribagh, Chatra, Dhanbad, Bokaro, Giridih, Kodarma, Jamtara, Deoghar, Godda, Dumka, Pakur and Sahebganj; V-Western Plateau comprising districts of Ranchi, Palamu, Gumla, Lohardaga, Garhwa, Latehar and Simdega and VI-South Eastern Plateau comprising districts of East Singhbhum, West Singhbhum, Saraikela. The agro-climatic conditions of the sub-zones have been summarized in Table 17.1.

Climate

Water is one of the most important natural resources vital for economic development of any region. The source of all water is precipitation. This state receives rainfall from both the streams of monsoon, i.e. Southwest monsoon and Northeast monsoon. In normal years, pre-monsoon rains are received in the month of May, which helps for summer ploughing. Monsoon usually breaks in mid June (±5 days). Late arrival as well as early cessation is not uncommon. In fact, distribution of rainfall is also uneven and erratic. Some times rain occurs as high as 140 mm in 24 hours. Dry spells of 2-3 weeks or even more usually occur in July-August.

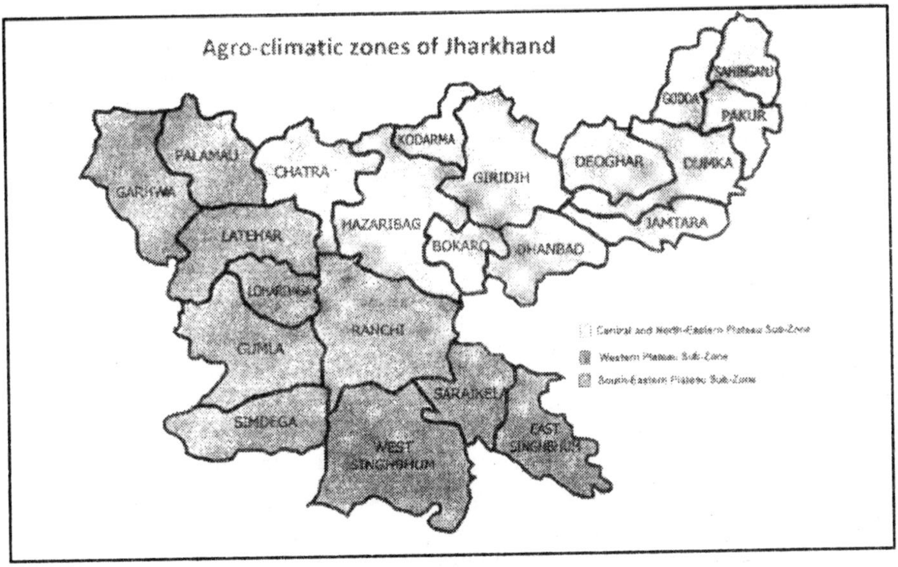

Failure of Hathia rain (late September to early October) is observed once in four years, which not only adversely influence the grain growth of standing crops but also affects establishment of second crop in winter season. Occasional winter rains during December to January is very helpful to winter crops. Climate is classified as sub-humid, mega-thermal with large winter water deficiency.

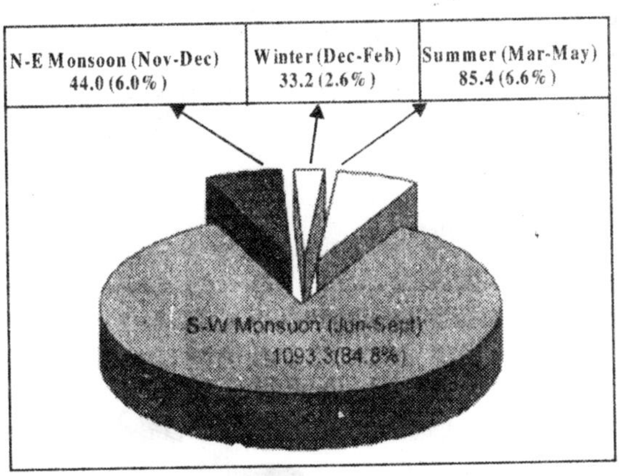

Fig.17.1: Seasonal rainfall (mm) distribution of Jharkhand

On an average annual rainfall of Jharkhand is 1289 mm and it varies from 1285 to 1308 mm between different sub-zones, out of which 85-86 per cent is received during four monsoon months (June-September), where potential evapotranspiration is far behind precipitation. This offers opportunity to harvest run off water (surplus water) and its recycling as per need of crop during dry spell. In the remaining 8 months, evapotranspiration is much higher than precipitation, which requires supplemental irrigation for raising crops. Seasonal rainfall distribution in state has been depicted in Fig. 17.1.

In fact, the fate of rainfed cropping in Jharkhand oscillates with the quantity, onset, progress and spatial distribution of the Southwest monsoon. Hence, rainfall and potential evapotranspiration may be taken into consideration for planting crops. Knowledge of the beginning and end as well as intra season progress of the Southwest monsoon is considered essential for crops and cropping in the rainfed region. The period between the beginning and termination of rainfall sets the duration of the rainy season crops where as the span of post rainy season crops is established by the volume of stored soil moisture and amount of rain water harvested during monsoon as well as availability of North-east monsoon rain and Winter rains. In fact, quantum of seasonal rainfall determines the selection of crops and cropping system. Rainfall pattern of a place guides crop management,

Table 17.1: Agroclimatic conditions of three sub-zones in Jharkhand

Parameters	*Central & North Eastern Plateau*	*Western Plateau*	*South Eastern Plateau*	*Jharkhand*
Number of Districts	*12*	*7*	*3*	*22*
Name of districts	Hazaribag, Chatra, Giridih, Dhanbad, Godda, Pakur, Deoghar, Sahebganj, Dumka, Bokaro, Koderma, Jamtara	Palamu, Garhwa, Gumla, Latehar, Simdega, Ranchi, Lohardaga	East Singhbhum, West Singhbhum, Saraikela	
Altitude (mmsl)	275-670	222-1142	250-1000	222-1142
Latitude (°N)	23.25-25.30	22.30-24.30	21.28-23.36	21.28-25.30
Longitude (E)	84.25-87.40	83.22-85.06	85.05-86.54	83.22-87.40
Rainfall (mm) South-West monsoon (June-September)	1093 (85%)	1101 (86%)	1053 (81%)	1093 (85%)
Rainfall (mm) North-East monsoon (October-November)	79 (6%)	70 (5%)	69 (5%)	77 (6%)
Rainfall (mm) Winter (December-February)	22 (2%)	52 (4%)	58 (4%)	33 (3%)
Rainfall (mm) Summer (March- May)	91 (7%)	62 (5%)	122 (9%)	85 (7%)
Total rainfall (mm)	1286	1285	1308	1289
Maximum temperature °C	44.2	43.6	44	44
Minimum temperature °C	4.8	5.3	6.6	5.6
Average temperature	25.2	25.8	27.2	26
Relative Humidity% Maximum (7 AM)	62.5	56.5	63	60.7
Relative Humidity% Minimum (2 PM)	47.5	42	45	44.8
Cropping intensity	112%	112%	129%	114%
Major Crops	Rice, wheat, maize	Rice, maize, arhar	Rice, maize, niger	

i.e. land preparation, seeding to harvesting. The planting time has a considerable effect on crop productivity and water-use efficiency if it is adjusted to the pattern of rainfall available soil moisture.

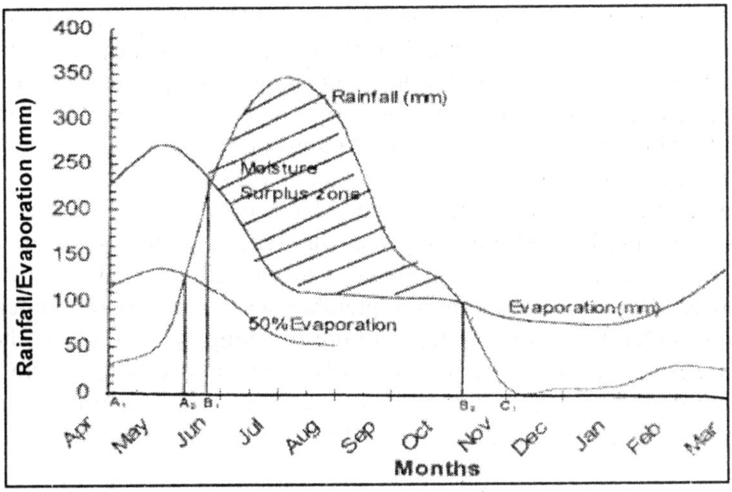

Fig. 17.2: Period of moisture availability

Rainfall pattern of Ranchi has been depicted in Fig. 17.2 clearly indicates, pre-monsoon rainfall is markedly inferior to evaporation during pre-monsoon period. This period begins with the first rain (point A1) and ends when rainfall equals to evaporation (point B_1). In the period between A_1 and A_2 (i.e. preparatory period, 3rd week of April to 3rd week of May), deep tillage (summer ploughing) is recommended which provides a strong foundation for rain water conservation *in-situ* and also minimizes weeds and soil borne pests. The final land preparation must be completed in between A_2 to B_1 (i.e. pre rainy period, May end to 1st fortnight of June) particularly in upland situations. Seeding with earliest opportunity must be completed by end of June otherwise soil wetness with subsequent rain will delay the seeding operation of upland crops. During this period, rice nursery also be raised in staggered manner (2-3 phases at the interval of 5-7 days) so that suitable seedling availability will be prolonged to overcome labour pressure for transplanting and availability of water for puddling.

Monsoon period, i.e. B_1 to B_2 (mid-June to first week of October) starts and ends when rainfall is equal to evaporation. In this period, evaporational loss is far behind rainfall received, indicating availability of surplus water as 85 per cent rain water is received in four monsoon months. Issue here is its conservation as well as management, holds the key to tide out the weather and make rainfed cropping a success. A significant quantum of rain water, 20-25 per cent of Southwest monsoon (250 mm) can be harvested through small scale interventions like watersheds (Watershed is a land area that drains surface water through a single outlet). This intercepted water can effectively encounter intermittent dry spell related crop failure. Rain water harvesting offers tremendous scope to augment water availably. There is no alternative to capturing the run off water and recycling it during current season as well as to establish the stand of succeeding season crops and thereafter.

Post-monsoon period starts from B_2, i.e. mid-October where rainfall is less than evapotranspirational demand. In this period, soil should be disturbed minimum, minimum tillage followed by planking is recommended for seeding and establishment of post- monsoon crops to utilize residual soil moisture efficiently. This region also receives post monsoon rain of about 125 mm during October-March which is very useful for winter crops.

Temperature starts to increase from March onwards and reaches its peak (43.6-44.6°C) in May and June. July and August are the active monsoon months during which, mean temperature remains around 28-29°C. With the start in withdrawal of monsoon from mid- September, a second peak of temperature is observed in October, with day temperature touching up to 35-40°C, however, nights are cooler. From November onwards a gradual decrease in both day and night temperature is observed. In winter season, low temperature occurs in January with mean temperature around 14°C while minimum temperature 4.8-6.6°C.

Atmospheric humidity plays an important role in plant growth as it not only influences the crop water need but also decides the congenial environmental conditions for build up of pests and diseases. Relative humidity exhibits seasonal variation and is influenced by monsoon air mass movements to a greater extent. As monsoon advances, relative humidity increases and it decreases with the withdrawal of monsoon current. Relative humidity values are maximum (76.5-90.9%) during August and the lowest (25.5-59.9%) during April. Its values are usually high in morning and lowest during afternoon. Sunshine hour greatly influenced by the presence or absence of clouds in the sky. Presence of clouds reduced the sunshine hour whereas absence increased it. Sunshine hour varies from 3.5-5.5 hrs/day during Kharif season, 7.4-8.7 hrs/day rabi season and 8.5-8.6 hrs/day summer season. Highest sunshine hour (8.7 hrs/day) is being recorded in February and the lowest (3.5 hrs/day) in July.

Soil

Soil is the base for terrestrial life supporting system. The farming situation in this state is based on type of the land. The land located on the upper slope is called Tanr land and the land following it is called Don land. These two classes have been again sub-divided into three sub-classes, viz. (a) Tanr I, Tanr II and Tanr III, (b) Don I, Don II and Don III. These classes and sub-classes have been regrouped under three categories of land for technology generation. Upland consisting of Tanr I and Tanr II, Medium land Tanr III and Don III and lowland consisting of Don II and Don I. This region having undulating topo-sequences and being primarily rainfed poses several problems, e.g. massive soil degradation (about 30 lakh hectare constituting 40 per cent of total geographical area), diverse agricultural practices with low productivity. The soils of upland and medium land are red and lateritic, highly permeable, course textured, shallow depth with low base saturation, cation exchange and water retention capacity, acidic in reaction (about 16 lakh hectare constituting 19 per cent of total geographical area), low organic matter with low nitrogen status, deficient in phosphorus. Deficiency of potassium is on increase. The lowland soils (5-8 per cent cropped area) have excessive wetness and stickiness after rice harvest (Don I) due to heavy texture associated with poor drainage, which restricts tillage operation and thus fields remain fallow in winter season. In this situation, surface-seeding technique provides an elbow space for growing wheat, eliminating tillage. Crack formation on surface layers with depletion of moisture is usual feature of lowland soil.

Table 17.2: General characteristics of up land, medium land and low land are given below:

Characteristics	*Up land*	*Medium land*	Low land
Colour	Red or Brown red	Yellow or yellowish	Grey or Greyish
Texture	Light textured (Sandy loam)	Medium textured (Sandy clay loam)	Heavy textured
Drainage	Well drained	Moderately drained	Poorly drained
Soil reaction	Low *p* H	Moderately acidic	Neutral *p* H
Soil fertility	Poor in organic carbon, Ca, Mg, N, P&S	Poor in organic carbon, N, Ca, Mg	Medium in N and organic carbon

Land use Pattern

Total geographical area of Jharkhand is 7970.08 thousand hectares out of which forest covers in 29.27 per cent, land put to non-agricultural use is 8.56 per cent, barren and uncultivated land is 7.19 per cent, cultivable waste land is 3.44 per cent, permanent pasture and grazing land is 1.10 per cent, lands under miscellaneous trees is 1.42 per cent, and net crop sown area is 22.68 per cent. In this state, 260.58 thousand hectare area is sown more than once with cropping intensity of 114.

Geographical area of sub-zone IV is 3518.34 thousand ha, out of which 28.13 per cent is covered under forest and 20.24 per cent area is put to cropping. Area sown more than once is 82.81 thousand ha with a cropping intensity of 112. Geographical area of sub-zone V is 3095.12 thousand ha, out of which 29.87 per cent, area is covered under forest and 25.88 per cent area is put under cultivation. Area sown more than once is 93.1 thousand ha with a cropping intensity of 112. Whereas sub-zone VI is comprised only 1556.62 thousand ha, out of which 28.67 per cent area is under forest cover and 18.93 per cent area is put under cultivation. Area sown more than once is 84.67 thousand ha with highest cropping intensity of 129.

Table 17.3. Land use pattern of different agro-climatic sub-zones ('000 ha)

	Sub-zone IV	*Sub-zone V*	*Sub-zone VI*	*Jharkhand*	*% Area*
Geographical area	3518.34	3095.12	1556.62	7970.08	—
Forest area	989.68	896.55	446.32	2332.55	29.27
Land put to non-gricultural use	308.29	179.62	194.97	682.88	8.56
Barren and uncultivated land	260.10	199.74	113.25	573.09	7.19
Cultivable waste land	120.18	99.49	54.79	274.46	3.44
Permanent pasture and other grazing land	71.97	8.33	7.16	87.46	1.10
Land under misc. trees	54.16	41.04	18.24	113.44	1.42
Net area sown	712.31	800.90	294.69	1807.90	22.68
Total cropped area	795.12	894.00	379.36	2068.48	—
Cropping intensity (%)	112	112	129	114	—

Source: Directorate of Statistics & Evaluation, Government of Bihar, Patna.

Water Resources

There are 11 river basins in the state-namely (i) Gomani, (ii) Mayurakshi, (iii) Ajay, (iv) Shankh, (v) South Koel, (vi) North Koel, (vii) Barakar, (viii) Damodar, (ix) Kharkai, (x) Subernarekha and (xi) other streams which originate or drain outside the state. The state has total water resources of 28,781 million cubic metres (MCM) including 23,789 MCM (82.66%) of surface and the rest 4,992 MCM (17.34%) ground water. The total utilization of surface and ground water achieved in the state so far is 4776 MCM and 1328 MCM, respectively. The unutilized water resources workout to be 19103 MCM surface water (80%) and 3664 MCM ground water (73%). This is not a happy situation so far as the useful utilization of precious water resources is concerned and speaks of "scarcity amidst plenty".

Source-wise Extent of Irrigation

The total created potential of irrigation in the state during 1997-98 was 4.32 lakh hectares. Out of this, as much as 1.94 lakh hectare was brought under irrigation. This was 10.73 per cent of the total net sown area. Source-wise extent of utilization of created irrigation during 1997-98 is presented in Table 17.4.

Total rainfall of the state is more than sufficient to raise 2-3 crops satisfactorily, but its distribution is highly skewed, with more than 80 per cent of the rain occurring during four monsoon months (June-September) restricting the farmers with no other choice except to grow only one rainy season crop and rest of the year their land remain fallow in absence of the irrigation water. Therefore, rain water harvesting and aquifer recharge have become essential for ensuring the stability of water supply. It should be made mandatory for all the farmers to harvest and conserve each drop of water fall on their land. Besides effective management of surface water including rivers, canals, water bodies, lakes, ponds and rain water can reduce ground water dependency for irrigation.

Table 17.4: Annual availability of water resources and their present utilization in Jharkhand

Water Resources and Utilization	Amount (MCM)
1. Availability of 75% dependable surface water	23789
2. Availability of ground water	4992
Total	**28781**
1. Utilization for irrigation	
a. Surface water in major and medium irrigation project	3373
b. Surface water in minor irrigation project	591
Total	3964
c. Ground water	772
2. Utilization for domestic purpose	
a. Surface water	82
b. Ground water	556
3. Utilization for cattle (surface water)	59
4. Utilization for industries and railways (surface water)	671
5. Utilization for non-irrigation purpose	
a. Surface water	812
b. Ground water	556

Table 17.5: Source-wise extent of utilization of created irrigation (1997-98) in Jharkhand

(Figures in lakh ha)

Source	*Created potential*	*Irrigated area*	*% of utilization*
Surface	2.42 (56.02%)	1.13 (58.25%)	46.69
Ground	1.90 (43.98%)	0.81 (41.75%)	42.63
Total	4.32	1.94	44.91

Table 17.6: Sources of irrigation in different sub-zones

Sub-zone	*Total irrigated area (ha)*	*Irrigated area as % of total cropped area*	*Source-wise irrigation (ha)*			
			Canal	*Tank*	*Tube well*	*Well and others*
IV	11,237	6.58	1,888	3,433	534	5,516
V	21,956	9.65	3,732	801	3,228	14,381
VI	15,510	4.58	10,211	2,156	409	2,733

In Jharkhand the total annual rain water availability is 1289 mm, out of which 80-85 per cent is received during four monsoon months (June-September) which is equivalent to 10310-10960 m^3 water per ha of land. Out of this rain water, evaporation loss during four monsoon months is approx 50-55 per cent which is equivalent to 5250-5750 m^3 water. Again, approximately 12-15 per cent of this rain water is lost through seepage and percolation which comes to around 1260-1575 m^3 water. Further, 8-10 per cent of rain water is utilized for recharging the soil profile which is equivalent to 840-1050 m^3 water. Thus, remaining 20-30 per cent of rain water which is equivalent to 2100-3150 m^3 water is lost through run off which can be collected by construction of on farm reservoir of size 40 m length × 20 m wide × 4 m deep for each hectare of land. This harvested rain water through OFR can be utilized to provide 2-4 irrigation each of 5cm depth for growing crops during succeeding rabi season considering 50 per cent losses of water from the pond through evaporation, seepage, percolation etc.

Therefore, it is essential to construct OFR for higher cropping intensity by utilizing harvested Liquid Gold to increase income and production per drop of water. In addition, exhausting ponds, wells and other water bodies need renovation for efficient rain water harvesting and its utilization. For *in situ* rain water harvesting, trenches around the field needs to be dug out and it will be recycled during lean period of monsoon as well as for growing succeeding rabi crop.

Crops/Cropping Systems

Major Crops

Sub-Zone-IV: Rice, Wheat, Maize and Greengram.
Sub-Zone-V: Rice, Maize, Niger, Chickpea, and Pigeonpea.
Sub-Zone-VI: Rice, Maize, Linseed and Niger.

Efficient Cropping systems for different land situations are as follows:

Upland: Rainfed ecosystem having water retention capacity 180-200 mm per metre soil depth

Existing	*Diversification*
• Rice/ Maize-Fallow	• Pegeonpea + Groundunt (1:2)
• Ragi/Gundli-Fallow	• Pegeonpea + Blackgram (1:2)
• Arhar/Blackgram-Fallow	• Pegeonpea + Rice (1:3)
• Fallow-Niger/Horsegram	• Pegeonpea + Maize (1:1)
	• Maize + Blackgram (1:2)
	• Maize + Soybean (1:2)
	• Blackgram-Safflower/Linseed/Lentil/Chickpea/ Niger/Horsegram
	• Maize-Safflower/Linseed/Lentil/Chickpea
	• Soybean
	• Safflower/Li nseed/Lenti l/Chickpea

Medium land: It is very potential land situation having limited to adequate irrigation facilities for sequential cropping.

Existing | Diversification

Existing	*Diversification*
• Rice/Maize-Chickpea/Lentil/Peas	• Maize + Blackgram - wheat
• Rice/Maize-Barley/Mustard/Linseed	• Maize - Early potato late wheat
• Rice/Maize- Potato/Wheat	• Maize - early potato - Late peas (green pods)
	• Maize - Wheat - Green gram
	• Maize - Potato - Green gram
	• Maize - Potato - Onion
	• Maize - Toria - Wheat
	• Maize - Early Potato/Toria- Late wheat - Green gram
	• Maize - Wheat + Lentil (4:2)
	• Maize - Wheat + Mustard (8:2)
	• Maize - Lentil + Mustard (5:1)
	• Maize - Potato + Wheat (1:1)
	• Rice - Wheat - Green Gram/Black gram
	• Rice - Potato - Green Gram/Blackgram
	• Rice - Early Potato - Late Wheat
	• Rice - Toria - Late Wheat
	• Rice - Early Potato - Late Peas
	• Rice - Early Potato - Onion
	• Rice - Berseem
	• Deenanath Grass - Berseem - Maize + Cowpea
	• Rice - Early Potato/Toria - Wheat
	• Rice - Early Potato/Toria - Wheat - Greengram
	• Rice - Wheat + Lentil (4:2)
	• Rice - wheat + Mustard (8:2)
	• Rice - Potato + Wheat (1:1)
	• Rice - Lentil + Mustard (5:1)

Lowland: Excessive soil witness after low land rice does not permit tillage operation till January-February. Consequently, land remains fallow. Under this condition, surface seeding of wheat utilized residual soil moisture efficiently and increases cropping intensity as well.

Existing	*Diversification*
• Rice-Fallow	• Rice - Wheat (surface seeded on wet soil)
	• Rice - Summer vegetable
	• Rice - Summer rice
	• Rice - Berseem

Small Farm Diversification in Rainfed Rice Areas

Out of 44 m Ha of rice in India, eastern region comprising eastern Uttar Pradesh, Bihar, West Bengal, Assam, Jharkhand, Orissa on north eastern states occupy 27.0 m ha. Rainfed rice area in eastern India is 5.3 m ha. In upland and 14.0 m ha. In medium and lowland out of 7.0 m ha. And 17.5 m ha. in the country respectively. The rainfed rice area constitutes 56 per cent for the country and 72 per cent in eastern India. Even though rainfed yields are low (less than 1 tonne/ha.) and unstable, rice is being cultivated to meet the food demands of small and marginal farmers who constitute 75 per cent of total farm holdings. Replacement of rainfed upland rice with low water requiring high value crops may be one of the best option to increase the production, productivity, income and employment in rainfed upland rice areas in eastern India. It is generally recognized that second green revolution in India could be realized through small farm development and diversification, particularly in rainfed areas, which have been bypassed by the first green revolution. Emphasis on crop diversification and integrated development of both farm and non-farm sectors is crucial from the point of view of alleviation of rural poverty. India will continue to be a small farm dominated agricultural economy and therefore, we have to plan for viability and sustainability of small farms through diversification. It is difficult to think of viable small farms, without synergistic development of farm and non-farm activities particularly in the context of rainfed agriculture.

Second Green Revolution Through Small Farm Diversification

Because of sub-division and fragmentation of holding, the per capita availability of land has declined from 0.5 ha to 0.15 ha. During the period 1950-51 to 2001-02. From this small holding it is not possible to sustain a family of five members with single crop production enterprise. Hence the small farmers have to integrate various other enterprises to generate additional employment opportunities and income from declining per capita availability of land.

Improved Agricultural Technology even when considered as technically sound, are of limited value if the farming community does not adopt them. In the absence of adequate attention to the understanding of the agro climatic and socio-economic milieu in which the farmers operate, generated and transferred technologies are found inappropriate to the needs and circumstances of the practicing farmers. The potential beneficiaries, particularly those farmers with limited resources, operating in less favourable natural environments, often do not adopt the new technologies due to various reasons like (i) lack of awareness about the new technology, (ii) ineffective extension services, and (iii) non-representation of their conditions by the research stations where the technologies re-development.

Lack of Resources to Invest on the Required Inputs

A less frequently heard explanation is that the recommended technologies themselves are simply not appropriate to farmers and their environment. Farmers, generally, seek those technologies, which increase their income while keeping risks within reasonable bounds under their own circumstances and management practices.

The first green revolution strategy mainly concentrated on "better-off" farmers and "better-endowed" areas with greatest potential for increasing agricultural production. The traditional technology generation and transfer models adopted have been found inadequate to meet the specific needs of a vast majority of farmers in developing countries. Research is mostly conducted at research stations under the conditions not representative of farmer's fields, with little or no farmer involvement. Hence is the necessity to conduct Farming System Research.

There is need for commercialization and diversification of small farms within and outside agriculture and their proper integration with local and global markets. This is indeed not only to liberate the small and marginal farmers from the poverty trap but also to meet the country's growing demands for fruits, vegetables, milk and milk products, meat, fish, eggs, etc. Which generally show rising trends with increasing levels of per capital income in the country. To achieve this goal of diversification of small farms we have to overcome various technological, infrastructural, institutional and policy constraints.

Crop Diversification in Rainfed Uplands

Technological options for rice substitution and crop diversification in rainfed uplands are rain water management, off-season ploughing, early sowing, closer spacing, early weeding, timely fertilizer application, plant protection measures, early harvesting and proper soil intercultural practices.

Other relevant technologies are selection of crop varieties and cropping systems in relation to rainfall pattern and crop growth period, some of the parameters relevant to upland farming are:

- The crops to replace rice should be of short duration, low duty and/or deep rooted which can extract soil moisture from deeper soil layers during dry spell.
- Some of the promising crops for rainfed upland rice area are maize, ragi, black gram, pigeon pea, cowpea, groundnut, sesamum, niger, castro, cotton, mesta, sweet potato etc.
- Inclusion of legumes in the cropping system improves soil fertility besides providing food and nutritional security.
- Pulses have inherent quality to trap the moisture from the lower strata of the soil, therefore, they are considerably moisture stress tolerant and fit well in rainfed condition.
- Adopt dry land horticulture and agro-forestry systems in sloppy upland.
- Suitable forage crops may be grown to sustain dairy industry.
- In all crops there must be emphasis on integrated weed management,

nutrient management, rainwater management, plant protection measures and post-harvesting technology.

Integrated Farming Systems in Uplands

In Eastern India a small farmer usually has a farm pond in the homestead land and possesses 0.5 to 1.0 ha of upland around this farm pond. The farm pond is meant to collect rainwater from the watershed. This rainwater could be utilized in giving a life saving irrigation during the dry spell to various upland crops, such as vegetables, groundnut, pigeon pea, maize, cowpea, mung bean, urad bean etc. fruit crops, viz. papaya, banana, pine apple etc. could be raised on pond embankments.

A cow dung gas plant could be installed to provide fuel (methane gas) for cooking food for the family, compost for manuring the adjacent farm land and slurry to the farm pond to encourage growth of phyto-plankton and zoo-plankton which serve as fish feed in the tank. Catla, rohu, mrigal and shrimp could be cultured in layers of water body for nutritious food and income to the family, ducks could be reared on the pond/tank which not only keep water body clean by eating the aquatic weeds but also increase the fertility of the water body of the tank by providing dropping/excreta through out the tank. A poultry cottage could be erected at one corner of the farm pond and these birds kept in the cottage should preferably be layers so that the farm family can earn extra money through sale of eggs. One or two dairy cows could easily be managed by the family with the help of feed, green fodders raised from the farm. Daily monetary income is ensured from the sale of milk, milk products, eggs, fish and vegetable grown in the farm. Such an experiment on Farming System Research at OUAT paid dividends.

Profitability of small and marginal farmers who have diversified their activities in selected village of Birbhum district of West Bengal has been recorded. Vertical integration of dairy with fodder crops can increase income and employment on a sustainable basis. Structural changes in consumption pattern of vegetable, meat, egg and fish, growth of income results in diversification in favour of non-food grain crops and livestock products, which can generate adequate employment and income for small farmers.

Integrated Farming System in Lowlands

Threats of water logging and high rainfall and excessive ground water resources can be converted to poverty alleviation opportunities in many parts of Eastern India. Diversification of rice monoculture into integrated farming system will be environmentally sustainable, economically viable and risk avoiding strategy. Keeping this is view, the farmers in Cuttack district were involved in testing various models of IFS. The most popular models preferred in India and suitable for waterlogged situations are mainly (a) Pond-dyke integration, (b) Fish-rice-duck/

poultry and vegetable, and (c) Fish-cow/pig-duck/Poultry and vegetable. In addition to economic return these systems are based on multiple recycling of carbon energy and nutrients from biomass to livestock—poultry/piggery/fishing etc. and minimize environmental loading with pollutants. The over all system is most efficient for the absorption of inputs and production of goods and services. In these systems marginal lands, wastelands are generally brought into productive use where pond serves as a focal point for direct and indirect links with other components.

Policy Intervention/Initiatives for Viable Small Farmers

Policies are needed for making sub-marginal, marginal and small farmers economically viable and environmentally sustainable. Well defined guidelines are needed for assisting such families with assured and remunerative marketing opportunities, particularly in the case of perishable commodities and crops like wide range of millets, tubers, pulses and oilseeds. Traditional food habits in rural and tribal areas include millets, tubers, grain legumes and leafy vegetables. Livestock and livelihoods are very intimately connected and crop-livestock-poultry-fishery-horticulture-agro-forestry, integrated farming systems is the pathway for farmers' well-being. It should be noted that suicides by farmers are rare in areas where there are multiple livelihood opportunities.

- Can price protection be extended to fruits, vegetables and other crops which are proposed to be selected for diversification?
- What will be the role to subsidies for promotion of small farm diversification?
- In view of high variability of income and high risk in the production of some of the so-called high value crops and enterprises, what will be role of crop insurance?
- Is there any need to modify the ceiling laws or tenancy laws for small farm diversification? If that is so, how did small holder agriculture in Korea, China, Japan and Indonesia witness diversified growth with smaller sizes of holdings? Can we draw lesson from them?
- Is there any need to change the policy of technology generation and technology transfer, particularly for defining the role of private sector research and extension and if there could be any complementarily between National Agricultural Research System and Private research agencies?
- Since infrastructural facilities are grossly lacking in greater part of rural India, can government augment its public investment in infrastructure, particularly in backward regions? Alternatively, is it true that the present strategy of diversification, based on existing unequal infrastructure facilities will further accentuate regional disparities in development?
- Can Government withdraw regulatory measures from the co-operative

sector and help promote the real autonomous growth of co-operative organization for small farm diversification?

- What will be policy requirement for integration of small farm with non-farm development?

Factors Causing Deceleration in Productivity of Crops

The analysis of agro-climatic regions specific factors contributing to deceleration in productivity of crops has indicated that some of the factors are common across the regions while there are certain factors which are very specific to individual region. There are:

(a) Common factors causing deceleration in productivity:

(i) The decline in total factor productivity in most of the agriculturally advanced and intensive regions.

(ii) Soil fatigue to over exploitation of soil nutrients reserve and organic matter in high cropping intensity regions like trans-Gangetic, upper Gangetic and southern plateau regions due to non-adoption of recommended crop rotation/replenishment of micro-nutrients, e.g. repeated cultivation rice after rice consecutively, i.e. kharif rice-summer rice in Haryana and Punjab and Kharif rice-rabi rice-summer rice in peninsular India.

(iii) Improper water management practices like flooding and submergence especially in command areas which has led to over exploitation and wastage of ground water and increase in slat content of soil surface and sub-soil which affect the crop growth and the productivity.

(iv) There has been imbalance and sub-optimal use of fertilizer nutrients in general. The ratio of N:P:K: has been distorted due to more use of nitrogenous fertilizers with little use of P and K fertilizers. The use of micro and secondary nutrients is almost non-existent.

(v) A sizeable area in the country is under soil salinity/alkalinity and toxicity of aluminium. Due to faulty method of choosing crops for cultivation/repeated cultivation of same crop over years the realized productivity is very low.

(vi) In rainfed areas in absence of protective irrigation at critical crop growth stage, the agriculture is at sustenance level only.

(vii) Non-availability of certified/quality seed of recommended cultivars resulting in low Seed Replacement Rates (SRRs) across the regions, poor level of fertilizers application in rainfed crops and inadequate plant protection measure are the gap in the availability and use of critical inputs which has led to deceleration in productivity over a period of time.

(viii) Continuous cultivation of same genetic material over years has eroded the genetic potential of the crops and their varieties which need to be enhanced.

(ix) Lack of technology breakthrough to break the yield barriers is the major bottleneck in achieving acceleration in the productivity.

(x) Breakdown of extension services and lack of dissemination of improved knowledge on package of practices based on scientific knowledge and field experience at state level has led to low adoption of improved production practices and lower productivity.

(xi) Inadequate or non-existent post-harvest management infrastructure at farm level; lack of price incentives, market distortions; low access to credit due to cumbersome procedures and high transaction cost involved in institutional credit at a very high interest rate are also the reasons which have affected the growth in productivity;

(xii) Decreasing holding size and predominance of small and marginal farmers, that generates small quantity of production with little marketable surplus.

(xiii) Lack of marketing infrastructure, limited access to markets and information; low value addition, inadequate public and private investment in agriculture and regional disparities in investment, technology adoption are also causing deceleration in productivity.

(b) Region specific factors for deceleration in productivity.

There are several region specific constraints which limit the opportunity of realizing full yield potential of the crops. These constraints have basically emanated due to ecological distortions, i.e. soil, water and climate. The most critical region specific constraints which are responsible for deceleration of productivity in Jharkhand region are: Moisture stress, drought and soil acidity, Iron toxicity low SRRs, non-availability of electricity, high population growth, poor road and communication infrastructure.

Major Initiatives Required

Improved agricultural technology, irrigation, timely supply of electricity, livestock sector and literacy are the most important instruments for improving the productivity and nutritional security of the farm-households. There is a need to improve the efficiency of delivery systems for agriculture development by empowering the elected institutions. Education, skill development, livestock, irrigation, diversification, rural infrastructure and credit support have tremendous impact on productivity. Science-led and knowledge based productivity growth need special attention in future. Several ecological problems have cropped-up as a result of past growth processes. These emerging threats in the irrigated agriculture systems call for greater emphasis on research supported by extension, infrastructure and education. Over irrigation and alarming rates of groundwater depletion have been causing land degradation and other environmental problems. Introduction of water-saving technologies and establishment of secure water rights to users, the decentralization and privatization of water management functions upto certain appropriate levels, pricing reforms, markets in tradable property rights may help in enhancing the productivity. Higher investment in education and skill development in low-growth areas will accelerate growth.

Address Socio-economic Constraints

- Consolidation of holding
- Land tenure system
- Rural infrastructure
- Credit support system
- Timely support of electricity
- Improved input delivery system
- Ensure remunerative price to the farmers
- Cold storage facilities for perishable agricultural products

Biophysical Constraints-water Related

- More than 60 per cent of cultivated area is rain dependent.
- Aggressive technology delivery system for small and marginal farmers in rainfed areas.
- Conservation of natural resources.
- Water harvesting structures to store rain water.
- Adoption of dry farming technology.
- Completion of minor/medium irrigation projects.
- Construction of field channels in irrigated areas.
- Desalting of reservoirs within command areas.
- Repair and renovation of water bodies.
- Increase water productivity.
- Multiple use of water.

Soil Related Production Constraints

- Acid soil amelioration.
- Management of waterlogged soils.
- Management of soils under shifting cultivation, soil/water conservation measures, agronomic and engineering.
- Soil fertility management.
- Balanced use of fertilizer.
- Role of S, Zn, B in addition to NPK.
- Al and Mn toxicity in uplands.
- Fe toxicity in low lands.
- Soil health pass books.

- Soil testing by soil-testing laboratory, KVK and the schools having science teachers.
- Use of green manure.
- Recycling of crop residues.
- Organic manure and inorganic fertilizers.
- Integrated plant nutrient management systems.

Seed Production, Certification and Distribution

- Stringent and stringent measures for restricting the proliferation of spurious and misbranded seeds and exploitation of the farmers.
- Strengthening the infrastructure for seed production, certification and distribution.
- Pricing policy of the seeds of different crops.
- Seed replacement rations.
- Strategy for hybrid seeds production.

Matching Production Technology for High Yielding Varieties of Seeds

- Genetic enhancement through molecular biology, application of biotechnology, space technology, biodiversity to usher in second green revolution.
- Adoption non-monitory low or no risk production technology.
- Timely seeding planting, adequate plant population and intercultural operations.
- Weed management.
- Integrated pest management.
- Post-harvest management of crops.
- Precision farming.

Major Concerns in Irrigated Agro-eco System

- Diminishing and deterioration of land and water resources.
- Natural resource degradation.
- Plateauing of yield.
- Decline in total factor productivity.
- Deterioration in soil health.
- Increasing biotic and abiotic stress.
- Threatened loss of biodiversity.
- Incidence of weed infestation.
- Declining water table.
- Productivity, profitability and sustainability.

- Global climatic change.
- Issues relating to intellectual property rights.
- Intensification of competition for quality and cost of inter-natural trade.
- Widening economic inequality.
- Burgeoning population.

Agricultural Extension and Transfer of Technology

- Responsive and dedicated agriculture extension services with commitment.
- Right type of extension agents:
    - Multi purpose extension agents.
    - Appropriate extension messages.
    - Impact points of key messages.
    - Targets for all extension officers.
    - Updating the knowledge of extension agents.
    - Rewards and punishment to the extension staff.
    - Research-extension-farmer-market linkages.

Contingent Crop Planning for Aberrant Monsoon Conditions in Jharkhand

Understanding of intra-season rain fluctuations helps in evolving contingent crop plans and mid-season corrections. The yearwise state annual rainfall pattern and its deviation from normal depicted in Fig. 17.3 shows that out of 51 years (1956-2006), 29 years had less rainfall than normal while 6 years had rainfall less than 75 per cent of normal which is considered as meteorological drought year. Further, it is also clear from rainfall pattern that in Jharkhand every after 8-9 years, there is a probability of occurrence of meteorological drought. Hence, contingent crop planning is a must to mitigate the aberrant weather condition.

STRATEGIES UNDER DIFFERENT MONSOON SETTING SCENARIOS IN JHARKHAND

I. Normal Onset of South West Monsoon (2nd week June)

- Follow the packages of practices of different crops recommended for upland ecosystem, i.e. direct seeded rice, maize, ragi, gundli, pigeon pea, blackgram, greengram, cowpea, groundnut, niger, sesame etc.
- Legume based intercropping, system like pigeon pea + groundnut, pigeon pea + blackgram/greengram in 1:2 row ratio and pigeonpea + maize in 1:1 row ratio have been proved successful.
- For very traditional rice farmers who cannot afford to leave rice even in upland, partial substitution of rice through rice based intercropping like pigeon pea + rice (1:3), rice + blackgram (3:1) is recommended.

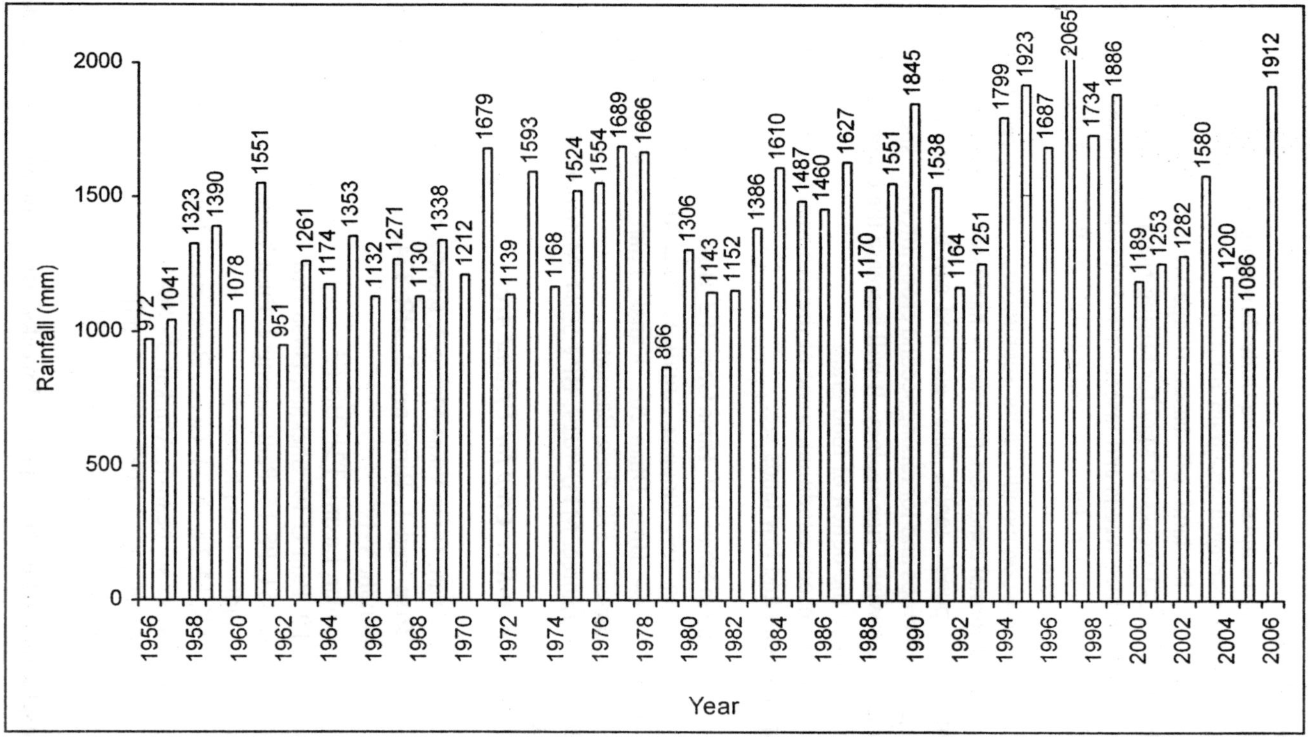

Fig.17.3: Yearwise annual rainfall (mm) and its deviation from

- Analyzing rainfall, 3rd week of June found feasible for sowing of direct seeded upland crops like rice, maize, ragi, gundli, pigeon pea, blackgram, greengram etc.
- Double cropping in upland can be done through gundli/ragi/blackgram/ green gram/maize-niger/horsegram rotation.
- For medium and lowland, off-season tillage with pre-monsoon shower can be done in 2-3 weeks of May for raising rice nurseries. This tillage will not only reduce weeds and insect-pests but will store more water in soil profile and rice can be sown immediately on that land after onset of South-West monsoon.
- As during 4 monsoon months (June-September), > 80 per cent of rainfall occurs under normal condition, this may be harvested to maximum possible extent *in situ*, ponds, tanks, lakes etc. and can be recycled during dry spell to kharif crops and for raising second crops after rice specially under medium and lowland rice ecology. It will increase the cropping intensity and will reduce the deficit of food grain.
- For normal monsoon condition, some of the rice varieties recommended for up, medium and low lands are:

Upland	Birsa Dhan-101, Birsa Gora 102, Birsa Dhan 108, Birsa Vikas Dhan 109, Vandana, Anjali, Kalinga III
Medium land	IR 64, Birsa Dhan 201, Kanak, Lalat, Swarna, Sugandha, Basmati 370, Pusa Basmati
Lowland	Rajshree, MTU-7029, BPT 5204, Mahsoori, Tulsi

Suitable Varieties of non-Rice Crop for Upland Are

Maize	Suwan, Birsa Vikas Maize-2, Kanchan
Ragi	Birsa ragi-1, Birsa ragi-2, HR 374, A-404 Gundli: Birsa gundli, V-17
Pigeonpea	Bahar, Laxmi, T21, BR 65
Blackgram	T9, Pant U 19, Shekhar, Birsa Urd-1
Greengram	K 851, PS 16, Pant moong 2, Pusa Vishal
Horsegram	Madhu, Birsa Kulthi 1
Groundnut	AK 12-24, JL 24, GG 2, Birsa groundnut 1, Birsa Bold-1
Soybean	Birsa soybean-1, Alankar, JS 80-21
Niger	Birsa niger l, Birsa niger 2, IGP-76, N5
Sesame	Kanke Safed, Krishna, TC 25

II. Timely Onset Followed by Dry Spell (1-3 weeks) after Sowing (Early Season Drought)

This situation arises when sowing of upland crops like rice, maize, jowar, ragi, gundli, pigeon pea, urd, moong, groundnut, sesame etc. have been completed due to timely onset of monsoon but thereafter dry spell of 1-3 weeks or even more occurs. It adversely affects the early establishment of crop stand because of sprouting drought and/or seedlings mortality. Besides this,. the transplanting of paddy also gets delayed. To overcome this situation, farmers are advised to adopt the following practices.

Upland Condition

- If direct seeded rice/non-rice crops damaged due to sprouting drought/ seedlings mortality, re-sowing of crops should be avoided till sufficient rains have been received.
- In case of unavailability of good quality seed, locally available seeds may be used after proper germination check.
- Upland crops may be gap filled and re-sowed with subsequent rain rather than allowing sub-optimal plant stand to grow.
- Diversification of cropping system and deploying crops according to land capability will be helpful. For example, if drought resistant early maturing crops are allocated to light textured soils which encounter moisture stress early, the stress can minimized to certain extent.
- Weeding and interculturing should invariably be resorted to for eliminating moisture loss through weed competition.
- Light interculture operation should be performed to break soil crust in order to check the soil moisture loss through capillary.
- Mulching with locally available forest leaves or grasses help in soil moisture conservation.
- One life saving irrigation should be given if irrigation water is available.
- Top dressing of nitrogen (urea) should be delayed till field has sufficient soil moisture.
- Maize crop being at knee high stage needs nitrogen application in the form of urea. This can be delayed and single top dressing of urea should be done at 45-50 days after sowing before earthing up operation is done, provided land has sufficient soil moisture.
- Under moisture stress condition, termite infestation aggravates. To check the hazards, soil should be wetted with 0.1 per cent chlorpyryphos solution.
- Ridge and furrow land configuration technology may be adopted at 3 weeks after sowing as *in situ* soil moisture conservation practices for non-rice crops.
- Water harvesting and recycling can make significant contribution in sustaining the crop production level. While applying harvested water, preference should be given to stress-sensitive crops.

Medium and Lowland Condition

- If the dry spell coincides with transplanting, it will be better to go for direct seeding rather than wait for proper conditions for transplanting.
- Stand by seed and rice seedling should be set aside for re-seeding or transplanting if the situation so warrants. Community nurseries raising of rice is recommended for transplanted rice.
- Rice transplanting can be delayed up to end of August with certain agronomic management.
- In case of delayed transplanting beyond 15th August, up to 50 days old seedlings with 4-5 seedlings/hill in medium duration varieties and up to 60 days old seedling with 5-6 seedlings/hill in long duration varieties and closure spacing (15 cm × 10 cm) should be followed.
- Regarding fertilizer management in case of delayed transplanting, recommended dose of fertilizer should be reduced to 25-30 per cent, 2/3 of nitrogenous fertilizer and full phosphorus and potash be applied as basal at transplanting and the remaining l/3rd nitrogen be top dressed 20-25 days after transplanting after weeding the field under sufficient moisture condition.

III. Timely Onset But Early Withdrawal (3rd Week of September) — Late Season Drought

Under normal condition, southwest monsoon rain continues up to last week of September or even first week of October. Under such situation, winter crops are sown successfully on residual soil moisture reserve and the crop grows satisfactorily. Sometimes under aberrant weather, monsoon rain ceases early as "Hathia Rain" (26 September to 10 October) fails or even before it. This not only adversely affect the reproductive phase of kharif crops but also affects preparatory tillage operations/sowing of successive winter crops. To overcome this situation, farmers are advised to consider following points:

- Development of ridge and furrow across the slope will be effective for soil moisture and rainwater conservation for direct seeded crops like upland rice, maize, jowar, ragi, groundnut, sesame, niger, pigeon pea, blackgram, greengram, cowpea etc. to overcome late season drought.
- Use of locally available forest leaves as mulching materials to conserve soil moisture is recommended. The practices of intercropping minimize the risks of aberrant weather in upland.
- Thinning of standing crop followed by interculture operation should be done in dry fields to check/minimize soil moisture loss.
- If fertilizers are to be top dressed, foliar application (2% urea solution) is recommended.

- Harvesting of crops like maize for cob/fodder, cowpea as green pod vegetable, greengram as fodder purposes and harvesting of upland rice at physiological maturity when late season drought is anticipated.
- Fields should be levelled for uniform water distribution within the sub-plot. Cover crops like greengram, cowpea can be adopted to restrict the soil moisture loss from the field.
- Repeated intercultural operations and integrated weed management practices should be adopted to make the field weed free. Lowland rice will be at tillering to dough stage, so harvesting of excess runoff water due to normal onset of monsoon and utilizing it for protective irrigation will be effective.
- After harvest of early paddy and maize for green cob, field should be ploughed, planked and sown with kulthi, niger or even toria immediately to avoid further soil moisture loss.
- Do not allow accumulated rain water to drain out from the rice field.

IV. Delay in Onsets of Monsoon (3-4 Weeks Delay from Normal)

- Shifting from traditional crops/varieties to short duration low water requiring crops in upland by substituting rice crop is recommended.
- The recommended dose of fertilizer application should be reduced by 30 per cent under rainfed situation and should be applied as basal.
- The field should be free of weeds for efficient utilization of water and nutrients by the late sown crops. Furrow sowing of kharif crops at closure plant to plant distance with wider interrow spacing is recommended.
- Frequent interculturing to facilitate effect of loose soil as dust mulch.
- Summer ploughing and use of organic manures to recharge the soil profile is recommended.
- Emphasis should be given on *in situ* rain water conservation, harvesting excess runoff for its recycling to make provision for protective/life saving irrigation at later stage of crops.
- Making trenches across the slope in the field is suggested to harvest rain water for soil water conservation.
- Seed treatment and proper plant protection measures should be taken to avoid any germination failure and disease pest infestation as sowing will be already delayed because of late onset of monsoon.
- In the event of late arrival of monsoon, the pulses like cowpea, blackgram, greengram can be sown up to last week of July in Jharkhand but direct seeded rice, maize, pigeon pea and groundnut are not recommended to be sown after 3rd week of July. Horsegram can be successfully sown up to August whereas niger up to September. Sowing of maize, cowpea, greengram, blackgram after first week of August can be done only for the purpose of fodder.

V. Advance Rabi Crop Planning

Sometimes failure of monsoon adversely affects Kharif crop production in many parts of the state. In order to minimize the adverse effects of drought on total food production it is imperative to increase rabi crop production through advance crop planning. In this context, farmers of the state are advised to consider following points:

- To best utilise Hathia rain water, bunding, levelling followed by deep ploughing must be undertaken to conserve soil moisture.
- Ploughing should be done across the slope to enhance the retention of water *in situ*.
- After cessation of monsoon, plough the land immediately followed by planking to minimize the loss of conserved moisture from the field. This will ensure good germination and plant stand.
- To minimize the risk of failure, different crops/varieties suitable for early sowing should be spread over the farm.

Suitable Rabi Crops and their Varieties Recommended for the State of Jharkhand

Crops	*Varieties*	*Remarks*
Wheat	C 306 K 9107, NW 1012, HD 2733, HUW 468	If availability of irrigation is: One: Irrigate crop between CRI and maximum tillering Two: CRI + Boot Three: CRI+Boot+Milk
Wheat + lentil (4:2)		2-3 irrigations are required
Wheat + mustard (8:2)		2-3 irrigations are required
Potato	Kufri Ashoka, Kufri Prabhat, K. Chandramukhi K. Jawahar, Ultimus	Mulching will minimize irrigation requirement, weeds and incidence of blight Irrigate at stolonization and tuber initiation.
Gram	Radhe, BG 256, C 235, H 208	Irrigate at flower bud initiation and pod filling stage.
Pea	Arkel, Swarnarekha, Rachna, BR 12	Irrigate at flower bud initiation and pod development stage
Mustard	Shivani, Jai Kisan, Varuna, BR 40 Pusa Bold, Kranti	Irrigate at flower bud initiation and siliqua filling stage
Linseed	T 397, Shekhar, Padmini, Shweta	Irrigate at flower bud initiation and capsule filling stage
Lentil	PL 406, PL 639	Irrigate at flower bud initiation and pod filling stage

VI. General Contingent Plan Relevant to all Crops

(a) Special Package of Practices

Making fields free of weeds for full utilization of water and nutrients by the crops reduction of plant density: In case of mid season drought the crops should be suitably thinned out. In case drought occurs at very early stage, it is always better to re-sow with subsequent rain rather than allowing sub-optional poor plant stand to persist. For drought conditions anticipating prolonged dry spell breaks the practices of inter-row cropping helps in risk distribution. This can be achieved by including a companion crop like green gram, cowpea than the main crops like maize, pigeon pea.

The recommended dose of nitrogen application should be reduced by 20-30 per cent under un-irrigated conditions and should always be applied at sowing/ planting.

Full recommended dose of P and K should be placed as basal dose. Resorting to maximum possible use of organic bulky manures.

Recommended plant protection measures to be adopted for kharif millets and pulses.

Seed of pigeonpea, mung bean, cowpea, groundnut and sunflower must be treated with Thiram or Captan @ 2-2.5 g/kg seed.

(b) Soil and Water Management Practices

Seedbeds should be kept ready so as to facilitate sowing immediately with the onset of rains. Fields should be properly levelled for uniform water distribution within the sub-plot.

Broad bed and furrow, ridge and furrow, compartmental bunding and contour trench land configuration may be adopted in shallow alfisols as moisture conservation practices.

Furrow sowing of kharif crops at closure plant-to-plant distance with wider inter-row spacing.

Frequent inter-culture to facilitate effect of loose soil as dust mulch.

Wherever economically viable, mulching should be practiced in between crop rows using locally available mulching material.

Wherever possible run-off may be harvested to make provision for protective irrigation at later stage/crop ripening.

Major emphasis on *in situ* rainwater conservation, harvesting excess run-off for re-use and groundwater recharge.

(c) Some other useful Irrigation and Water Saving Practices

Conveyance losses should be reduced while irrigating the light textured soils. A simple and cheap technique is to spread a polythene sheet in the field channel before irrigating the field and then roll it back for irrigating the other field.

Wherever possible, the crops should be sown on ridged plots and irrigating every alternate furrow on rotation.

Best use of rainwater should be ensured. In case a rainfall of about 3-5 cm occurs near to irrigation date, the irrigation may be avoided.

Lighter irrigation may be applied during initial growth stages when root growth is limited.

Poor rainfall means lesser recharge to the groundwater. Since groundwater is the most dependable source of irrigation, its indiscriminate exploitation must be avoided. In hard rock areas, for improving well yields, long and continuous pumping should be substituted by intermittent operation of pumps.

(d) Resource Conservation Technologies (RCTs)

- *Zero Tillage* (*Z-T*): Zero tillage can be practiced to establish winter crops for efficient utilization of residual soil moisture. This technology suits well for growing timely as well as late sown crop of wheat. Under timely sown conditions, it can save field preparation cost of around Rs. 3000 per hectare. Under delayed sowing in addition to saving on tillage cost, this technology has the potential to give higher productivity due to advancing the sowing by a few days. The Z-T technology is suitable for various type of soils. The sowing should be done at optimum moisture level to slightly wet conditions depending on soil types.
- *Furrow Irrigated Raised Bed Planting (FIRB) System*: The FIRB system is a method where wheat crop is planted on raised beds. Under such conditions, this system of cultivation helps in saving on account of field preparation, substantial amount of diesel, irrigation water and it is also sustainable. A saving of more than 25 per cent seed has been observed. Saving of nitrogenous fertilizer was more than 25 per cent and water 10-40 per cent depending upon soil types.
- *Seed Priming*: In most cases seed can be primed by soaking in water overnight and simply surface-dried and sown.
- *Laser land levelling*: Saves water by 15-20 per cent and increases the yield by 5-10 per cent.

Recommendations

- Sustainability of small holder agriculture should be investigated with horizontal and vertical diversification involving few high yielding, high income generating eco-friendly crop and non-crop enterprise.
- Research efforts should be concentrated on export oriented crops and non-crop enterprises like fruits, vegetables, flowers, livestock, dairy, poultry, fishery etc.

- Substantial investment may be required for research on agricultural policy formulations and human resource development involving training of scientists, extension workers and farm leaders on the needs and methods for planned agricultural diversification.
- Development of appropriate technology for small farmers for field and horticultural crops with low gestation period would help farmers to diversity.
- Development and transfer of technology, viz. bio-fertilizer bio-pesticides and organic farming would be helpful for small farm diversification because of their cost-effectiveness.
- Strong industry-agriculture linkage through development of agro-processing units and contract farming would be required to help promote small farm diversification.
- Institutional facilities of credits by banks, co-operatives and agribusiness consortium would be necessary for small farm diversification. Development of marketing facilities and ensuring remunerative prices are keys to success of the programme.
- Cold storage facilities for the perishable agriculture products is a must for economic upliftment of the poor farmers.
- Road connectivity and transport facilities from the production centres to regulated markets/Krishak bazar are of prime necessity. Dynamic price and crop insurance polices should be adopted without further delays.
- Consolidation of holdings should be completed in rainfed and irrigated lands without further delay.
- Development of agri-business and agro-processing would be necessary conditions for small diversification.
- The Gram Panchayats which are already statutory bodies should be recognized as cooperatives and empowered to jointly process and market the produce of the small farmers.
- In each Gram Panchayat there must be a full time multipurpose Agricultural extension worker equipped with latest knowledge to transfer the technology. An extension Agent must be effective in communicating best available technology with low risk to the farmers. Farmers training programmes should be strengthened focusing on Integrated Farming System involving crop husbandry, animal husbandry, dairy, poultry, fishery, agro-forestry etc.
- There must be mini but many demonstrations on farmers' fields to familiarize, demonstrate and evaluate new technology by the farmers themselves.

Annexure

Table 1: Jharkhand State: Basic Information

State Formation	*15 November, 2000*
Population (1991)	21.95 million (2.6% of India population)
Population (2001)	26.91 Million (+4.96 million)
Annual increase	0.50 Million (5 lakh)
Growth rate per cent annual	231
Sex ratio (Female per thousand male)	941 (933 India)
Population density	338 persons/km^2
Population (2006)	30 million
Population engaged in agriculture (%)	77.00
Population in rural areas (%)	73.00
Tribal population	7.1 Million (67.7 million: India)
Tribal Population (%)	26.35 (8.1 % India)
Schedule caste population	3.1 million (138.2 million: India)
Schedule caste Population %	11.25 (16.5% India)
BPL Population	46.00 (26% National)
Per capita annual income (2001-02)	Rs 11,100 (Rs. 18,500 India)
Literacy (%)	54.10 (65.4 % India)
Male literacy	67.90 (75.8 % India)
Female literacy	39.40 (54%: India)
*Cultivators (lakh): 2001	39.1
* Agricultural Labourer (lakh): 2001	28.6

Table 2: Jharkhand State: Agricultural Information (2003-04)

Indicators	*Unit*	*Figure*	*Remarks*
Geographical Area	lakh ha	79.70	
Area Available for Cultivation	Lakh ha	25.95	
Gross Cropped Area	Lakh ha	20.7	
Net Area Sown	Lakh ha	18.1	22.6%
Area sown more than once	Lakh ha	2.6	
Area Under Irrigation	Lakh ha	2.05	(10.6%)
Forest Area	Lakh ha	23.33	(29% total area)
Land under non- agricultural use	Lakh ha	6.82	
Fallow land	Lakh ha	20.98	26.3%
Cultivable wasteland	Lakh ha	2.74	3.4%
Permanent pasture and grazing land	Lakh ha	0.87	
Barren and uncultivated land	Lakh ha	5.73	
Land under miscellaneous trees	Lakh ha	1.13	
Fertilizer consumption	N.P.K kg /ha-	44	(85 National)
Cropping intensity	(%)	114	134 % India
Average land holding	ha	1.58	
Contribution of Agriculture to State GDP	(%)	28.60	

Table 3: Food and nutritional Security in Jharkhand State (2004)

Food	Production (Lakh tonnes)	Minimum requirements (Lakh tonnes)	Deficiency %
Food grains	24.0	49.0	–51
Vegetables (2002)	21.2	28.0	–24
Fruits (2002)	4.52	12.5	–64
Milk	13.3	23.3	–43
Meat	4.33	6.7	–55
Fish	0.27	5.3	–97
Egg (lakhs)	6,980	8,380	–20

Source: Mishra and Jayram, 2006.

Table 4: Major Crops in Jharkhand State (2004-05)

Sl.No.	Crops	Area (ha)	% of Cropped area	Production in Jharkhand	Average Yield (kg/ha)
1.	Food Grains	1,823,079	87	2,481,266	1,361
2.	Cereals	1,532,167	80	2,291,170	1,495
3.	Pulses	290,912	7	190,096	653
4.	Vegetables	224,120	7	3,401,340	15,176
5.	Oilseeds	94,268	3	53,198	564
6.	Fruits	32,700	2	388,572	11,655
7.	Sugarcane	400	—	—	—
8.	Others	29,000	1	—	—
	Total	2,366,000	100		

Table 5: Food grain (Cereals and Pulses) Area, Production and Productivity in Jharkhand

Year	Area ha	Production tonnes	Productivity kg ha^{-1}	Remarks
1999-00	1,801,470	2,192,880	1,217	Drought
2000-01	1,877,490	2,142,160	1,141	Drought
2001-02	1,937,516	3,222,953	1,663	Max production
2002-03	1,854,790	2,624,580	1,443	Drought
2003-04	1,934,150	2,790,300	1,443	Drought
2004-05	1,841,120	2,491,940	1,354	Drought

Table 6: Cereals Area, Production and Productivity in Jharkhand

Year	Area ha	Production tonnes	Productivity Kg ha^{-1}	Remarks
1999-00	1,657,030	2,074,830	1,252	Drought
2000-01	1,686,550	2,544,250	1,508	Drought
2001-02	1,725,870	3,057,130	1,771	Max production
2002-03	1,622,980	2,464,130	1,518	Drought
2003-04	1,639,050	2,582,130	1,575	Drought
2004-05	1,550,200	2,301,830	1,485	Drought

Table 7: Area, Production and Productivity of Cereals Crops in Jharkhand (2004-05)

Crops	*Area (ha)*	*Production (tonnes)*	*Yield (Kg/ha)*
Rice	1,276,421	1,908,446	1,495
Maize	1, 85,870	2, 68,400	1,457
Wheat	64,504	104,136	1,615
Ragi / Marua	17,370	10,350	596
Barley *	12,147	10,751	885
Jowar	351	163	464
Bajra	305	136	452
Total Cereals	1,550,200	2,301,830	1,485

* For the year 1999-2000.

Table 8: Typology of land holdings in Jharkhand State

Land holdings (ha)	*Typology*	*Percentage*
0	Land less	9.3
Up to 0.4	Sub-marginal	49.8
0.41-1.0	Marginal	22.8
1.01-2.0	Small	12.5
2.01-4.0	Medium	4.4
>4.0	Large	1.2

Table 9: Jharkhand State: Agricultural Information on Soils

Indicators	*Unit*	*Figure*
Soils with Phosphorus Deficiency	(%)	66.00
Acid upland soils	(%)	71.00
*p*H (<5.5)	(%)	49.00
Soil typed: *p*H (5.5-6.0)	(%)	22.00
Red and Lateritic (Tanr 2, 3 and Don 3)	(%)	78.00
Alluvium (Don 1 & Don 2)	(%)	19.00

Table 10: Districtwise and average rainfall in Jharkhand, 2001-2005

Sl. No.	*Districts*	*Actual Rainfall (mm)*					*Average Rainfall*
		2001	*2002*	*2003*	*2004*	*2005*	
1.	Ranchi	1504.5	1102.0	1502.8	1198.9	896.9	1241.0
2.	Gumla	1063.6	852.7	1167.0	941.0	743.9	953.6
3.	Simdega	1278.9	967.8	1167.3	826.0	995.6	1047.1
4.	Lohardaga	1126.5	805.6	1540.4	932.2	724.3	1025.8
5.	East Singhbhum	1152.1	901.9	1170.9	834.2	858.2	983.5
6.	West Singhbhum	877.5	890.4	1042.4	922.1	820.2	910.5
7.	Saraikela	738.1	790.8	873.5	856.5	718.2	795.4
8.	Palamau	1089.7	774.4	914.1	688.4	608.7	815.1
9.	Garhwa	1109.0	876.2	1089.0	470.2	745.6	858.0
10.	Latehar	1274.3	895.9	1184.4	756.6	670.8	956.4
11.	Hazaribag	1288.7	951.7	1120.7	974.7	832.5	1033.7
12.	Chatra	1008.8	1009.7	1003.4	570.4	594.2	837.3
13.	Koderma	1071.2	1099.9	816.8	709.0	715.3	882.4
14.	Giridih	1311.1	1189.4	1121.8	859.5	637.7	1023.9
15.	Dhanbad	1533.8	1330.5	1486.4	945.8	778.4	1215.0
16.	Bokaro	1135.0	1337.3	1331.0	615.7	751.6	1034.1
17.	Dumka	1381.1	1591.5	1211.9	928.1	913.2	1205.2
18.	Jamtara	971.1	1476.6	1060.1	1067.6	1305.7	1176.2
19.	Deoghar	1600.2	1750.6	974.8	1108.6	734.2	1233.7
20.	Godda	1221.4	1219.6	1126.6	861.9	936.8	1073.3
21.	Sahebganj	1234.9	1595.8	1489.4	923.3	956.2	1239.9
22.	Pakur	1576.7	1912.6	1280.0	1425.6	1450.0	1529.0
	Average	1206.8	1151.0	1167.1	882.6	835.6	1048.6

Table 11: Classification of districts based on average rainfall (2001-05)

Sl. No.	*Average rainfall (mm)*	*Number of districts*	*Name of districts*
1.	> 1500	1	Pakur
2.	1200-1300	5	Ranchi, Dhanbad, Dumka, Deoghar, Sahebganj
3.	1100-1200	1	Jamtara
4.	1000-1100	6	Simdega, Lohardaga, Hazaribag, Giridih, Bokaro, Godda
5.	900-1000	4	Gumla, East Singhbhum, West Singhbhum, Latehar
6.	800-900	4	Palamau, Garhwa, Chatra, Koderma
7.	700-800	1	Saraikela

REFERENCES

Mishra, R.K. (2004), *Agricultural Statistics of Jharkhand at a Glance*, 2004. Birsa Agricultural University, Kanke, Ranchi, Jharkhand, 111 pp.

Mishra, R.K. (2004). *Planning for food and nutritional sector in Jharkhand.* Birsa Agricultural University, Ranchi, Jharkhand.

Mishra, R.K. and V. Jayram (2006). *Agricultural Development of Jharkhand at a glance through figures.*

SECTION IV
INFRASTRUCTURE CONCERNS

18

Land Use Planning for Sustainable Development

MRIDULA SINGH

INTRODUCTION

Land is normally defined as a physical entity in terms of its topography and spatial nature. A broader integrated view also includes natural resources: the soils, minerals, water and biota that the land comprises. These components are organized in ecosystems which provide a variety of services essential to the maintenance of the integrity of life-support systems and the productive capacity of the environment. Land resources are used in ways that take advantage of all these characteristics. Land is a finite resource, while the natural resources it supports can vary over time, management conditions and uses. Expanding human requirements and economic activities are placing ever increasing pressures on land resources, creating competition and conflicts and resulting in suboptimal use of both land and land resources. If, in the future, human requirements are to be met in a sustainable manner, it is essential to resolve these conflicts and move towards more effective and efficient use of land and its natural resources.

Land is the basic unit of all material production. It is a scarce and inexpansible resource which has to be used very judiciously to meet various competing demands. The natural resource base particularly land would be able to support the likely increase in population and provide better standard of living is a serious issue for consideration. Land which includes soil, water and associated plants and animals is a complex and dynamic combination of factors like geology, topography, hydrology, soils, micro climates and community of plants and animals that are continuously interacting under the influence of climate and people's activity. The use, to which land is put, is determined by owners, farmers, government institutions etc. according to their own perception. Such decisions are influenced by factors like—soil and climate, technology and socio-economic aspirations of the community.

Need for Land Use Planning

Land resources are used for a variety of purposes which interact and may compete with one another; therefore, it is desirable to plan and manage all uses in an integrated manner. Integration should take place at two levels, considering, on the one hand, environmental, social and economic factors and, on the other, all environmental and resource components together (i.e., air, water, biota, land, geological and natural resources).

A vast majority of households, especially in developing countries, depend on land and other natural resources for satisfying their immediate needs and achieving their long-term livelihood ambitions. Agriculture remains a major activity in most countries except in the industrialized world. Hence, crop production, use and commercialization of forest products, wild food gathering and fishing as well as extensive grazing are substantially contributing to the Gross National Product (GNP) of these countries. At present more than 44 per cent of the economically active people in the world are still employed in agriculture. For Africa this is even more than 57 per cent (against more than 74 per cent in 1965).

In traditional societies the concept of land extends beyond the production purpose but holds also important social and spiritual values. Land is often the only available resource on which rural families can rely to build their lives. With the growing population and limited land resources, the relevance of Land Use Planning assumes significance. Land use planning ensures the use of land resources in an organized fashion so that the needs of the present and future generations can be best addressed. Land use planning has as its basic purpose to ensure that each area of land will be used so as to provide maximum social benefits, including food production, with least damage or loss of the resource. Land use policy is part of the national policy for promoting objectives including economic development, social justice and equity, and political stability.

LAND USE PLANNING

The concept of optimal land use is basic to land use planning which aims at balancing the competitive demands in a scientific manner so as to ensure sustainable development of economy. The purpose of land use planning is to regulate uses on scientific-ecological basis to curb misuse or abuse of land. The management of plants, animals, land and water as an integrated system has assumed a lot of importance and relevance to overall environmental security. Integrated physical and land use planning and management is an eminently practical way to achieve this. By examining all uses of land in an integrated manner, it makes it possible to minimize conflicts, to make the most efficient trade-offs and to link social and economic development with environmental protection and enhancement, thus helping to achieve the objectives of sustainable development. The essence of integrated approach finds expression in the coordination of the sectoral planning and management activities concerned with the various aspects of land use and land resources.

To achieve equitable distribution of income, social parity as well as self-reliance for all regions of country as well as all sections of society, it is imperative to improve the living condition of people especially in rural India. The land use policy should aim at optimizing returns on long term basis rather than meeting short term requirement on *ad hoc* basis.

An appropriate land use plan has to take into account the only suitability and capability of land. Zero Soil Loss (ZSL) should be the sole objective. It is only at micro level that soil capability can be assessed and decision about land use can be taken. Therefore, the land use plan will be operationally meaningful if it is workable and feasible at micro level. The diversion of prime agricultural land for non-agricultural purposes should be strictly regulated and should be permitted only under unavoidable circumstances. The concept of SAZs (Special Agricultural Zones) has to be taken up earnestly for conservation and protection of prime agricultural land. Then there is the question of motivation and pursuance as far as adoption of land use plan is concerned. The committee of experts on Draft Out line of National Land Use Policy (1988), Ministry of Agriculture, Government of India has aptly observed, "Land Use on private land cannot be dictated by legislation alone. This problem has to be tackled through price incentives and other fiscal mechanism." In short, society should be resource literate and should be able to endorse the idea that land is non-renewable base which supports all primary production systems and fulfils all essential needs in terms of shelter, food, fibre, infrastructure, roads and other facilities.

Sustainable Development

Sustainable development is a pattern of resource use that aims to meet human needs while preserving the environment so that these needs can be met not only in the present, but also for future generations. The term was used by the Brundtland Commission which coined what has become the most often-quoted definition of sustainable development as development that "meets the needs of the present without compromising the ability of future generations to meet their own needs.

The gradual deterioration of the environment lends compelling weight to the need to find a balance between human development and exploitation of natural resources. The many frightening but illustrative examples of some of the consequences are:

- Only half of the world's population breathes healthy air;
- Less than half of the world's rural population has clean water;
- Annual increase in the world's food production is only half the world's population growth;
- Millions of tonnes of hazardous waste flood the environment every year; and
- A hundred species of plants and animals are predicted to disappear everyday.

Some of the major problems that mankind is facing today are:

Shrinking resources of prime lands, deforestation and accelerated erosion, deterioration of soils—physical environment, increasing water-logging and salinity in canal-irrigated areas, declining water-table in well irrigated areas, poor management of rain-water, lower productivity of dry land areas, lower efficiency of inputs of water, fertilizer and agro-chemicals, rapid industrialization coupled with pollution and environmental degradation and hazards.

Obviously the pattern and system of development that is being followed today is conducive to a healthy and sustainable growth so it is absolutely essential for planners and decision makers to reconsider and change the framework of the policies concerned. After all in today's world, quality of life and environment are two most important factors which define growth.

There is a need for a new paradigm of development that encourages the most sustainable, productive and appropriate use of land, water and genetic resources. It is evident that land degradation, economic growth and poverty are interactively linked. Moreover, environment and agriculture are intrinsically linked. So, agriculture research focus must shift from increasing productivity to enhancing sustainability, recognizing that agriculture can be an important solution to environmental management, land use must match land quality and appropriate national policies must be implemented to ensure that land uses are not out of balance with environmental potential.

One must understand that the difference between growth and development is central to the concept of sustainable land use. Growth refers to increase in quantity, whether in terms of goods, wealth, housing, resource extraction or other measures. Development, on the other hand, refers to the increase in quality of goods and services, as defined by their ability to increase human well-being. Coordinated planning on both public and private land is a key factor in sustainable development and the achievement of local economic development and land use objectives.

The separation in practice of the climate change and development agendas has distorted the global debate on the two biggest policy challenges facing the international community. According to the World Economic and Social Survey, 2009, an integrated approach based on the concept of sustainable development is urgently needed. The key to such an approach is a low-carbon, high-growth transformation of the global economy—a transformation that can keep temperature increases consistent with environmental stability as identified by the scientific community, while at the same time fostering the strong growth and economic diversification in developing countries that would allow convergence of incomes worldwide. The greening of catch-up growth will have to be further tailored so as to meet the adaptation challenges facing vulnerable countries and communities whose economic security will be threatened even if climate change is kept within globally manageable limits.

Moreover our efforts for food security through land resources management and sustainable agriculture can be greatly augmented by combining space technology and bio-technology advances. Information obtained through remote sensing data on land use practices, soil condition and water resources can be used for sustainable development and for conservation of this precious resource.

Conclusion

Following are some of the important issues for land use planning and sustainable development:

- Appropriate land reforms including consolidation of holdings and community participation;
- Rehabilitation of wastelands through horticulture and forestry techniques;
- Adoption of holistic watershed approach;
- Bio-industrial watershed approach which advocates soil and water conservation, micro irrigation, land development with biological measures and bio-industries for livelihood at the micro level is the need of the day;
- Scientific and modified terrain-oriented approach for land use planning;
- For planning purposes accurate scientifically devised land use classification maps are essential. It should consider agro-ecological/agro climatic zone, geological and geo-morphological factors as well as cultural heritage of the region;
- State Land Use Boards should be suitably strengthened and made effective to undertake an integrated approach towards management of natural resources in the region;
- It is necessary to document existing land use in this region, identify physical and biological mechanisms responsible for the faulty land use practices and provisions made for alternative land use practices, i.e. revival of vegetation cover both on public and private lands, adopt measures to check the soil loss etc.;
- The participation and involvement of local people especially women are the key to sustainable management of land resources. The lands of local people need to be protected from inappropriate and unsound practices not only from the point of view of environment but it is essential socially, economically and culturally also;
- Land and water resource management on sustainable basis can only be achieved through watershed management approach where all the components of ecosystem are integrated;
- Suitable land use policy should be framed region-wise and planning should be location specific accordingly;
- Success stories have to be popularized and role of NGOs duly recognized and encouraged; and
- People's participation at every level of planning is essential for sustainable management of natural resources. With regard to this cultural traditions of local people should be understood and accordingly policy package should be developed.

19

Planning for Future Residential Developments in a Growing Urban Centre: A Case Study

SHAHAB FAZAL

INTRODUCTION

The last few decades have recorded population of the world increasing tremendously. Significantly the urban population growth rate is much higher (4 times higher) than the rural population growth rate. By the year 2025, world's urban population is expected to cross 5 billion (almost two-thirds of world population). An estimated 90 per cent increase will occur in the developing and underdeveloped countries. India although known as land of villages but here also a steady growth since independence in the size and proportion of the urban population as well as number of urban centres is recorded. India's urban population in the last fifty years has more than tripled (62.4 million to 217.2 million) at an average rate of 3.09 per cent per annum. But these figures do not tell the whole story; there is evidence that urban growth is increasingly dispersed and more significantly, the absolute increase in urban population is very large. Urban sprawl is widespread, which promotes the spread of urban land use especially the residential land mostly into the urban fringe affecting large population from urban interface (Observer 1998).

The city's fringe has been placed under pressure increasingly with increased demand due to rapidly changing social, cultural and economic values associated with land and its resources. The rapid sprawl of cities, outside its political boundaries and beyond its real physical-cultural domain possesses several attendant conflicts and stresses and has also stimulated various adaptations of human activities. These are reflected through diverse facets, such as changing suburban, peri-urban and adjacent or interstitial rural land uses. India is passing through a transitional phase where the urban centres are the focal points of change (Fazal, S., 2001). Urban areas have become centres of all the activities, they are exploding in size, land use is changing quickly and constantly intensifying urban lands and large-scale land transformation is taking place due to substantial increases in urban land value. The real expansion, growing size of cities and the resulting invasion of the rural land by urban forces have caused a succession of land uses in a discordant and disassociated way (Fazal, S., 2004).

Concerns about development around urban areas are not new, but have arisen periodically during most of the last century (Heimlich, E.R. and Anderson, W.D., 2000). The urban fringe literature has many different manifestations in terms of the way it is conceptualized and delimited. Wehrwein (1942) was probably the first to use the term rural urban fringe in his study for cities in USA. Webster (2003), very appropriately stated as "urban fringe is the zone where rural areas are located on the outskirts of cities, become more urban in character in physical, economic and social terms, often in piecemeal fashion." There is also some diversity in the terminology, ranging from rurban fringe (Schenk, 1997), rural hinterland (Kundu, 1991), city's countryside (Bryant *et al.,* 1982) peri-urban fringe (Swindell, 1988) and peri-urban areas (Dupont, 1997), deskota region (McGee, 1991). There are many studies where researchers implying different delimitations and levels of analysis including Ramchandran (1989), Thakur (1991), Nangia (1976), Yadav (1987) and (Fazal, 2001), etc. have dealt with various issues related to urban fringe.

This urban fringe of developing countries, in recent times has been the most dynamic zone. Many efforts and methods have been done to understand the urban fringe development process. Fringe urbanization has raised new challenges for urban development policies. Considering the complex and dynamic character of urban fringe, modelling is a unique tool to understand its process thoroughly and it can provide a suggestive way of exploring actual as well as optimal patterns and plans. As a primary part of urban expansion, the residential expansion is becoming a more and more important issue. Keeping this in mind the present paper try to investigate the trends of urban expansion of Saharanpur city, the residential land transformation in the city and modelling residential land on the basis of current trend and future demand in the study area.

STUDY AREA

The study area lies between 29°55′ to 30° north latitude and 77° 30′ to 77° 45′ east longitude. It is situated in western part of Uttar Pradesh (India), in the fertile tract of Upper Ganga-Yamuna doab (inter-riverine plain) (Fig. 19.1). Saharanpur city is the district headquarters and second largest city in Meerut division. It is well connected by several state road highways to the important cities. City is having nodal location between the hilly state of Uttarakhand (in the north) and plain region (in the south) of Uttar Pradesh. The city is spread over 4,030 hectares (Municipal boundary). In the past few decades, Saharanpur city has experienced significant changes in its economy, where tertiary activities have gained momentum and economy has a whole recorded significant growth. This growth has its bearing on increase in urban population as well as expansion of the urban areas. This expansion indicates a transformation of agricultural land use to construction of urban fabrics especially residential, commercial and industrial development (Fazal, S., 2001).

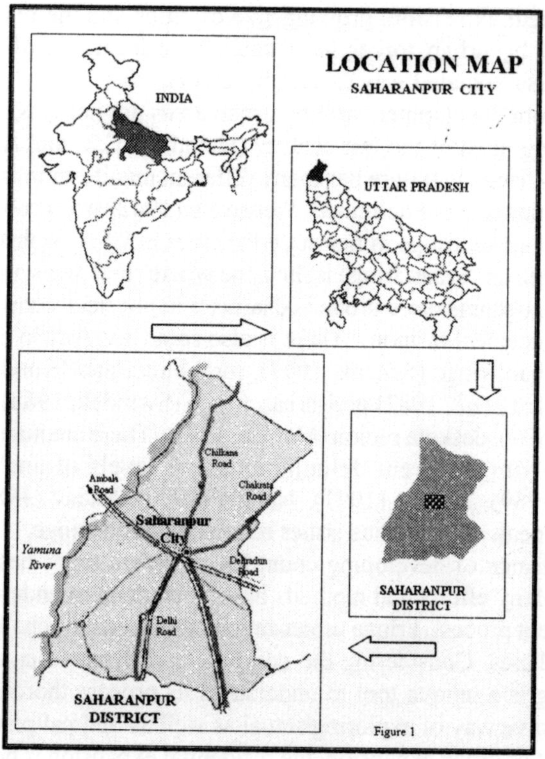

Fig. 19.1: Saharanpur District

Social environment of the study area: The total population of Saharanpur city according to 2001 census is 455754 (241508 males and 214246 females). The city has recorded a gradual increase in its population. The growth rate was 21.89 per cent during 1991-2001 census period. The number of people added to total population was 81850 persons during this census period. The average density of population is about 112 persons per hectare. The city has 76430 households with average family size of 5.96 persons.

Economic environment of the study area: The development and growth of any city depends on its economic base. Traditionally Saharanpur city has agro based economy where its initial development was also because of its rich agricultural hinterland as the city acted as service and distribution centre. However, lately many industrial units (330 registered industrial units) have come up. This includes major industries such as paper, strawboard, tobacco and cigarette, hosiery, motor transport etc. and more than 400 small scale household industries (many of them are world famous wood sculpture industry) are functioning. The city has 27.03 per cent of its population categorized as workers of which 60.6 per cent are engaged in tertiary sector (23.6% commerce, 17.5% communication, 19.5% others) while share of secondary sector was 36.14 per cent (28% manufacturing, 6% household industries and 2.14% construction).

Data

The present study is based on both primary and secondary sources. Secondarv sources includes published data from different governmental agencies, the land use data were acquired through Survey of India maps and IRS (Indian Remote Sensing) 1D Satellite imagery which was processed in GIS environment to extract land use and land transformation information. For spatial allocation for residential area in the study area a *Land Transformation Model* was developed estimating future demand for residential land in consideration. The model was applied to stimulate land use changes in the study area.

Discussion

Urban Land Use of Saharanpur City: Saharanpur City is named after one Sufi Saint Shah Harun Chisti. It was ruled by Mughals and also by Britishers, who in 1903 made this city as district headquarters. In 1926 when the city received electric supply its economic development got a boost and city started to develop at a faster speed. After independence a good number of refugees came to this place and settled here. Although the municipal area of Saharanpur city is only about 4,030 hectare but due to the objectives of our study we are dealing with 8627 hectares of land. It includes the changes and urban expansion of the city and its fringe are where the future expansion is expected. From the perusal of Table 19.1 and Fig. 19.2, it is clearly evident that land use of Saharanpur city not very well planned. With time, the older part of the city has became more and more congested while on the other hand the city has expanded outward in a haphazard manner and swallowed the agricultural land in the fringe area. The residential area has increased by 1149 hectare recording a growth of 201 per cent during the study period (1974-2004).

Land Transformation in Saharanpur City: Land transformation is the process of identifying differences in the state of any phenomenon by observing it at different time periods. During the study period of (1974-2004), Saharanpur city has not only expanded from its original size but there was significant interchange of land among various land use classes. Table 19.2 and Fig. 19.3, which is prepared applying GIS technique, shows the changes in various urban land use class of the city. Importantly, the area under residential use has increased from 1135 hectares to 2285 hectares gaining land from agriculture (812 hectares), vacant land (250 hectares), plantation (27.4 hectares), but it also lost area for commercial development (50 hectares) and 39 hectares for institutional establishments. The study shows that main land transformation was of agricultural land (loosing more than 1200 hectares) from the city's fringe, which was used for urban development.

Modelling for Future Residential Development: Modelling is basically to reduce uncertainty. It means that by modelling for certain phenomenon, our understanding about it enlarges and reduces uncertainty. This way fringe modelling and simulation means, on reducing uncertainty and increase our understanding for complex urban system. Here fringe modelling is future oriented activity, which is strongly conditioned by the past and present trends. The modelling will facilitate scenario building and provide an important aid to future directed decision making. This way urban planning can be more scientific and reduce the subjectivity so prevalent with the decision makers in India.

Table 19.1: Saharanpur City: Area under different land use classes (1974–2004–2015)

Land Use/Year	*Area (1974)*	*Area (2004)*	*Estimated Area After Simulation (2015)*	*Change in area (2004–2015)*
Residential	1135.6	2285	2706.3	+ 421.3
Villages	102.2	192.2	220	+ 27.8
Commercial	40.3	121.6	150.2	+ 28.6
Industrial	133.9	233.9	270.2	+ 36.3
Agricultural Land	5397.2	4163.9	3718.4	–445.5
Tree Plantation	326.4	281.9	265.4	–16.5
Vacant Land	592.7	393.9	321.3	–72.6
Others	298.4	354.3	374.9	–20.6
Restricted Area	600.3	600.3	600.3	—
Total	8627	8627	8627	—
Total Built up Area	2310.7	3787.3	4321.9	+534.6

Note: Area in hectares.

Source: Based on Saharanpur City, Guide map (Survey of India) and IRS 1D Satellite Imagery.

Land Use Modelling: The rising awareness of the need for spatially explicit land use models (Lambin, 1997; Turner & Meyer, 1994) has led to the development of a wide range of land use change models. Most models were originally developed for deforestation, however, some recent efforts address other land use conversion such as urban land transformation and agricultural intensification. Here two land use models need to be mentioned, first is the CLUE model (The conversion of land use and its effect modelling framework (Veldkamp and Fresco, 1996 and Verburg *et al.*, 1999), which is spatially explicit approach based on simulation of land use change as a function of land use in the neighbourhood with a set of user specified relations with driving forces. The second model is DPSIR model, which is a *"process or behavioural"* model, establishing the functional and structural relationships among its elements. This model explains the cause and effect relationships between interacting components of a social, economic and environmental system (Sharifi, 2004).

The Land Transformation model basically based on CLUE model, but modified to suit the prevailing conditions of the present study. The model was developed to stimulate land use change using empirically quantified relations between land use and its driving factors in combination with dynamic modelling of competition between land use types. The model is subdivided into two

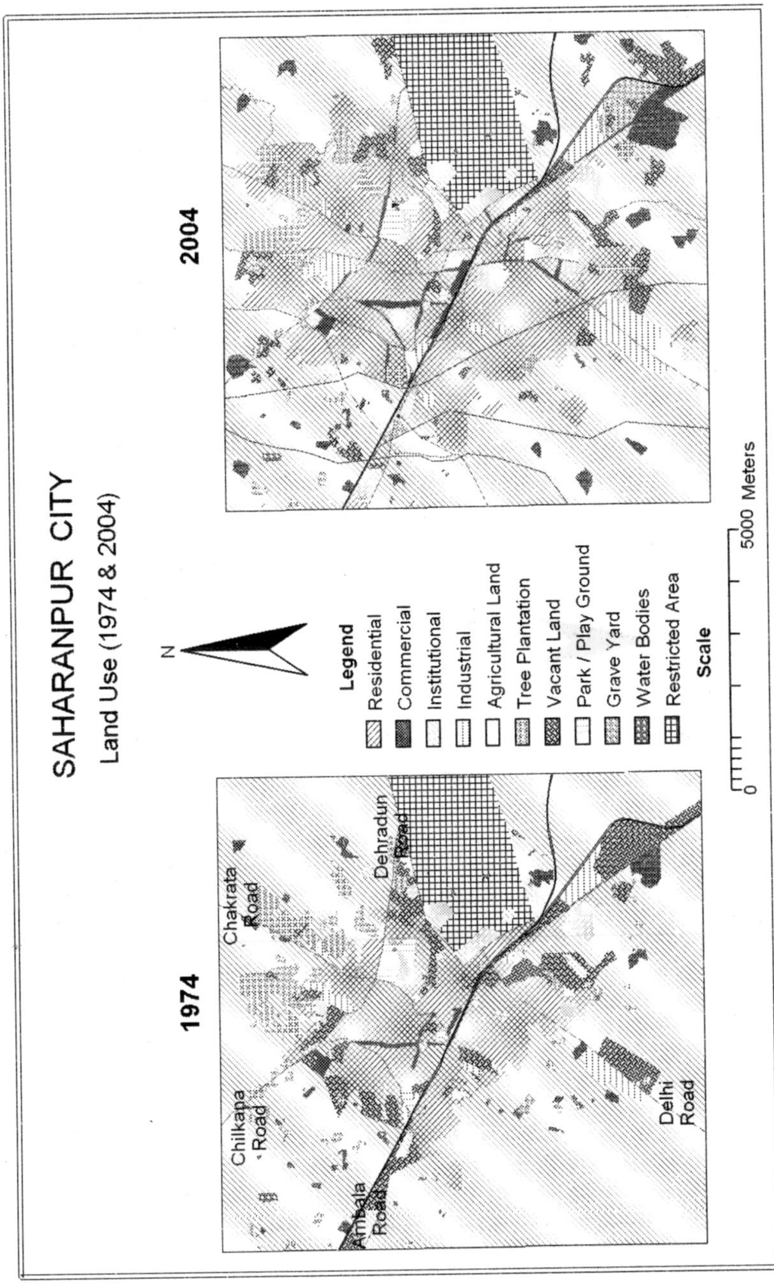

Fig. 19.2: Saranpur City: Land use (1974 & 2004)

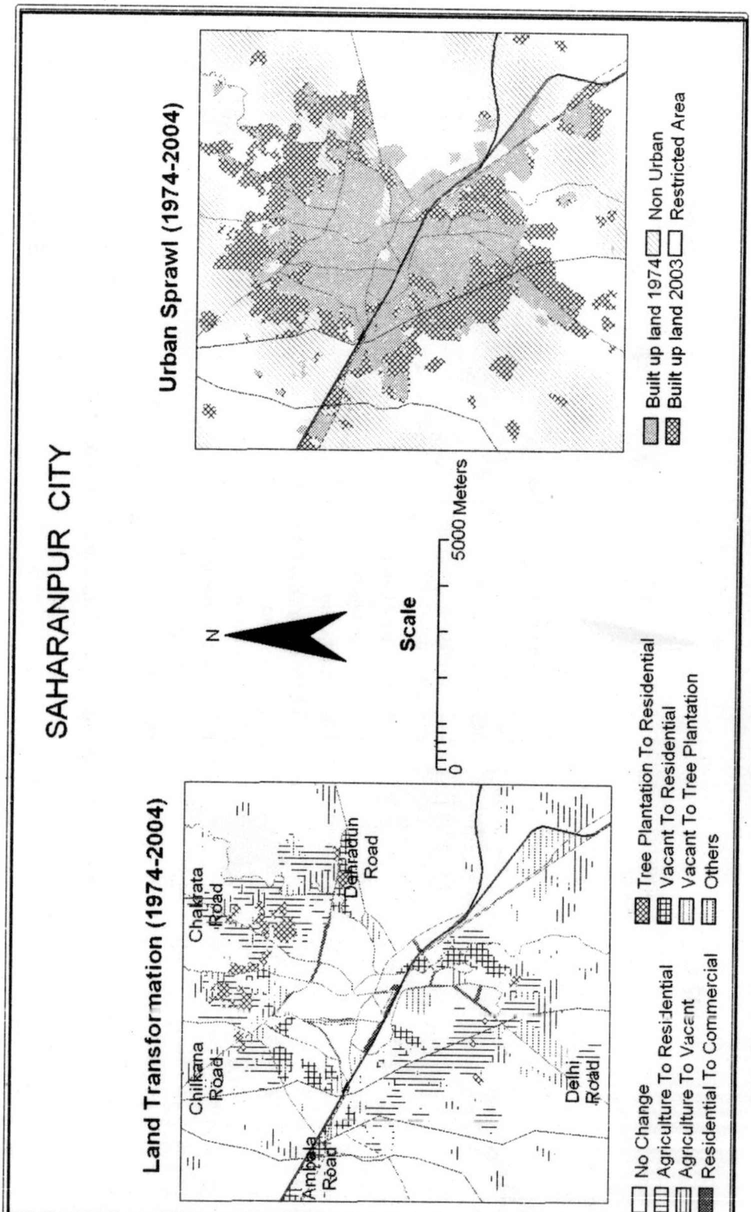

Fig. 19.3: Saranpur City: Land Transfamation (1974-2004) and Urban Sprawl (1974-2004)

distinct modules, namely a non-spatial demand module and a spatially explicit allocation procedure. The non-spatial module calculates the area change for land use types at the aggregate level. The second part of the model, where these demands are translated into land use changes at different locations within the study region. The model is for spatially allocation of land use changes while the land use demand module calculated from simple trend extrapolations.

Multiple regressions are used to derive comprehensive model that describe the pattern of land use as a function of a combination of explanatory factors. A stepwise regression procedure was used to select only the factors that yield a significant ($P < 0.01$). For reasons of simplicity, we have only evaluated linear regression this approach although decrease the explaining power of regression models as some explanatory factors will be related to land use in a non-linear way. However, relationships that are non-linear at fine scales tend to be flatter. An exploration of the data set indicated that at all scales considered in this study the relations are well represented by linear model.

Driving Forces for Residential Expansion: Residential expansion is a complex spatial changing phenomenon in urban system that is closely woven with urban expansion. Although urban growth is a global phenomenon, but the driving forces are greatly varied which also differs with time and space.

The following driving factors were considered for instigating changes for increases in area under residential class (Box 19.1).

Box 19.1: Driving forces for spatially explicit land use change

Land Use Change Drivers	*Representation as Variables*	*Description*	*Source*
Population Growth	PDEN	Population Density	Census Data (2001)
Land Value	LVAL	Municipal Land Evaluation	Saharanpur Nagar Nigam (2001)
Mobility	MBL	Distance to Roads	Land Use Map (2004)
Accessibility to Public Facilities and Utilities	DPF	Distance to Public Facilities and Utilities	Land Use Map (2004)
Accessibility to Market/Commercial Centres	DMC	Distance to Market/Commercial Centres	Land Use Map (2004)
Accessibility to Parks/Play Ground	DPP	Distance to Parks/Play Ground	Land Use Map (2004)

Population Growth: The population of Saharanpur city is increasing at 2.3 per cent annual growth rate and estimated population in 2015 would be about 6,06,152 which means addition of 1,50,398 persons to 2004 population.

Land Value: As the population increases the demand for land also increases, which obviously results in higher land values. But since we cannot anticipate precise land value for future but only anticipate the trend. Thus we presume that land value would increase in same proportion everywhere corresponding to present land value. So we used the current land value and added 7 per cent increase per annum for estimating land value for year 2015. The land value data were acquired from Saharanpur Nagar Nigam, which assign land value for the city and its surrounding areas. Presently, the land value in the central part of the city is higher than the peripheral areas. The entire study area has been classified into three zones of high, medium and low on the basis of estimated land value.

Mobility: Mobility in urban areas has great importance for influencing the use of land in urban areas. Road Transport is the most efficient and popular mode of transport in Indian cities because it needs lesser capital. Thus distance from roads was considered as one of the driving factors for residential land development. Buffers along roads have been drawn at the distance of 250 metres each, with first buffer assigned as high mobility and farthest buffer as poor mobility, while the intermediate buffer assigned with moderate mobility.

Distance to Market/Commercial Centre: Another driving factor considered was distance from market place, as easy accessibility to it would be preferred location for residential purpose. Buffers around main market and commercial centres have been drawn at the distance of 250 metres each, with first buffer assigned as high accessibility and third buffer as poor accessibility, while the second buffer assigned with moderate accessibility.

Distance to Parks/Playground: Similarly, proximity to parks and playgrounds would also be preferred location for residential development. Thus, distance to parks/playground was also taken as a driving factor. Buffers around parks/playground have been drawn at the distance of 250 metres each, with first buffer assigned as high accessibility and third buffer as poor accessibility, while the second buffer assigned with moderate accessibility.

Distance to Public Utility and Facilities: Another driving factor considered was distance from public utility and facilities, such as school, hospital, railway and bus station etc. Easy accessibility to these facilities would be preferred location for residential purpose. Buffers around existing major facilities and utilities have been drawn at the distance of 250 metres each, with first buffer assigned as high accessibility and third buffer as poor accessibility, while the second buffer assigned with moderate accessibility.

Statistical Regression: The variables which were driving residential land development in the study area were put under stepwise regression, using 0.01 significance criterion for independent variable.

The six selected driving factors were statistically evaluated for their impact on future residential expansion, the regression equation was expressed as:

$$\textbf{P(residential land)} = \beta o + \beta(PDEN) + \beta(LVAL) + \beta(MBL) + \beta(DPF) + \beta(DMC) + \beta(DPP)$$

Where P is the probability of a land for the occurrence of residential land, β is the constant value for each explanatory variables—PDEN, LVAL, MBL, DPF, DMC and DPP (Box 19.1). A positive value in the equation means that the explanatory variable will help to increase the probability of change while a negative value indicate a decrease in probability with an increase in the independent variables. The regression equation calculated as:

$$\textbf{P(residential land)} = -2.021 - 0.812(\text{PDEN}) - 0.729(\text{LVAL}) - 2.765(\text{MBL}) + 4.217(\text{DPF}) + 6.149(\text{DMC}) + 3.148(\text{DPP})$$

The main determinants with the negative value were the mobility (distance to roads, meaning the nearer the higher mobility, which will be preferred location and thus showed greater probability), population density (the lower the better and greater probability), land value (the lower the better location and greater probability) all these independent variable have showed lower values in the fringe areas of the city, meaning that the statistically this would be preferred location. While the positive values were showed with distance with markets and commercial establishments, public facilities and utilities and parks and play grounds (which suggests the farther the better and all of these variables are located in the inner part of the study area).

Model Implementation and Analysis: For estimating the land requirement for residential usage in the year 2015 was calculated on the basis of growth of population and the trend of land transformation recorded during 1974-2004. Thereafter, simulation for residential land allocation was performed on land use map of 2004. The simulation was performed on the non-built upland of the study area (lying in the fringe areas of the city, believing that future residential expansion would only possible on these lands). Six driving forces (Box 19.1 and Flow chart) were simulated and their impacts were spatially mapped dividing them into three categories of low, moderate and high. This way we had prepared six aspect maps and from these six maps a composite score map was simulated to identify prospective residential land. This composite score map was also categorized in three categories of most likely prospective residential land, moderately prospective residential land and least prospective residential land. The result shows that 442.3 hectares of land comes under most likely prospective residential land, 1049 hectares under moderately prospective residential land and 2813.8 hectares land under least prospective residential land.

The results reveal that by 2015, the estimated demand for residential land would be of 2706.3 hectares (a demand of another 421.3 hectares) and this demand can be met by highly prospective category lands (442.3 hectares). This means that 21 hectare of land will still remain unutilized from most likely prospective lands. The result also shows that these most likely prospective lands capture land mainly from vacant (59 hectares), tree plantation (14.5 hectares), agriculture (347.8 hectares).

CONCLUSIONS

India although an agrarian country where still 70 per cent of its population live in rural areas and dependent on primary activities but here also a steady growth since independence in the size and proportion of the urban population has been observed and urbanization process is widespread. In fact urban areas have become centres of all the activities, they are exploding in size, land use is changing quickly, constantly intensifying urban lands and spread of urban land use especially the residential land mostly into the urban fringe. The city's fringe has been placed under great pressure and a primary part of urban expansion, the residential expansion is becoming a more important issue.

The study area, Saharanpur city has also recorded a gradual increase in its population and has experienced significant changes in its economy. These changes have its bearing on the expansion of urban areas. The urban land use of the city is characterized by increase in residential area by 1149 hectare recording a growth of 201 per cent capturing land mostly from agriculture (812 hectares), vacant land (250 hectares), plantation (27.4 hectares). The study shows that urbanization process has swallowed fertile agricultural land which lost more than 1200 hectares lying in the city's fringe, where most of this transformation has taken place.

The rapid growth of population of the city associated with the socio-economic changes, which are creating an emergent middle class, have caused a proliferation of squatter settlements in the interstices and fringes of the city. It has resulted in invasion of the rural land by urban forces causing a succession of land uses in a discordant and disassociated way. The unplanned and uncontrolled city expansion produces a patchwork of different developments. This uncontrolled physical growth impacts most on an immediate hinterland around the city. Much of this cannot be described as urban or suburban and yet much of it is no longer rural. However, most of it lies in the designated urban corridor.

The regression analysis for future residential expansion for year 2015 was estimated of 2706.3 hectares (a demand of another 421.3 hectares to the 2004 land under residential use). Here, significantly, mobility (distance from roads), population density and land value have responded negatively, meaning lower the value greater would be the probability for residential use. While distance to markets, public facilities and parks have responded positively meaning that nearer these location, the probability of residential use would be lesser. On the basis of statistical analysis, spatial allocation for residential land showed that 442.3 hectares of land comes under most likely prospective residential land, 1049 hectares under moderately prospective residential land and 2813.8 hectares land under least prospective residential land.

The main determinants with the negative value were the mobility (distance to roads, meaning the nearer the higher mobility, which will be preferred location and thus showed greater probability), population density (the lower the better and

Table 19.2 : Land Transformation in Sharanpur City (1974 to 2004)

Land Use	*1 Res.*	*2 Vil.*	*3 Com*	*4 Govt.*	*5 Ind.*	*6 Agr.*	*7. Tree.*	*8. Vac.*	*9. Oth.*	*10 Rest.*	*Area in 2003*
1. Residential Area	1135.6	33.5		811.9	128.7	264	10.1				2285
2. Villages		102.2			120.1	3.4					192.2
3. Commercial Area	50.2		40.3		3.4	27.7					121.6
4. Government Institutions	39			182.5		4.3	20.2				246
5. Industrial Area	9.6				133.9	15.4		75			233.9
6. Agricultural Land						5397.2					4163.9
7. Tree Plantation					27.4		326.4	93.4			281.9
8. Vacant Land					249.3	32.2		592.7			393.9
9. Others					1.5	1			115.9		108.3
10. Restricted Area										600.3	600.3

Note: 1. Area in hectare.

2. Figures in bold letters (diagonally) are area under that particular land use in 1974, while figures in the same column is sh ift in area to other classes and figures in same fow are increase in area, captured from other land use classes.

Source: Based on Saharanpur city, Guide map 1974 (Survey of India) and IRS 1D Satellite Imagery 2004.

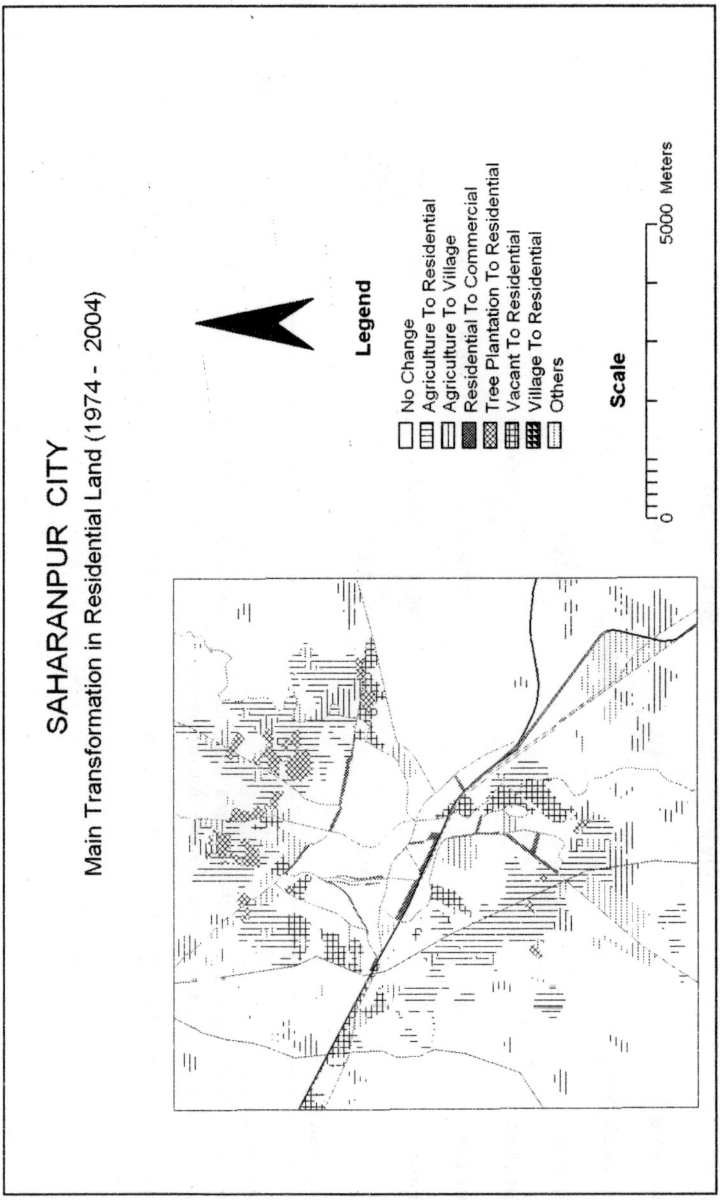

Fig. 19.4: Saharanpur City: Main Transformation in Residential Land (1974-2004)

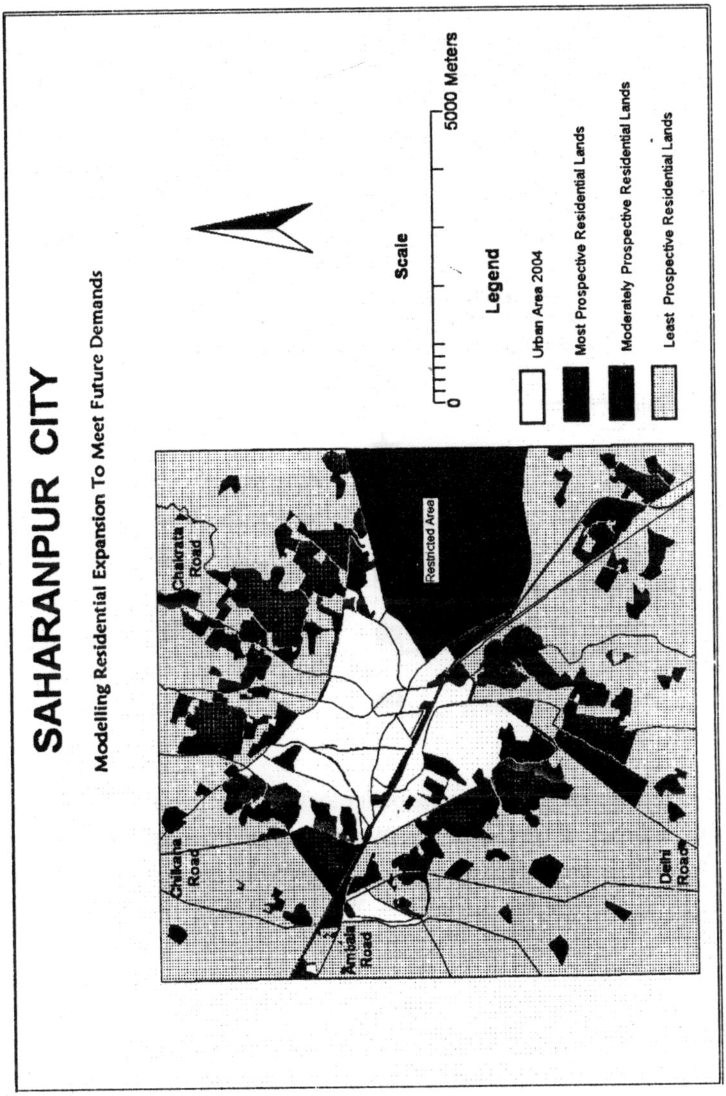

Fig. 19.5: Saharanpur City: Modelling Residential Expansion to Meet Future Demands

Flow Chart – Spatial modelling for Residential Expansions.

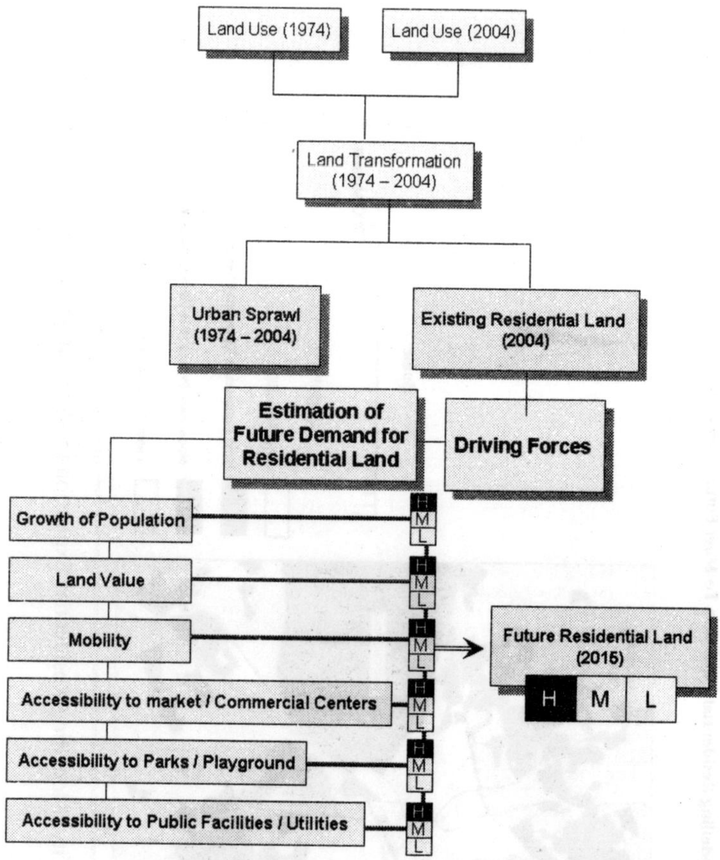

greater probability), land value (the lower the better location and greater probability) all these independent variable have showed lower values in the fringe areas of the city, meaning that the statistically this would be preferred location. While the positive values were showed with distance with markets and commercial establishments, public facilities and utilities and parks and playgrounds (which suggests the farther the better and all of these variables are located in the inner part of the study area).

The result shows that 442.3 hectares of land comes under most likely prospective residential land, 1049 hectares under moderately prospective residential land and 2813.8 hectares land under least prospective residential land. This means that the estimated demand for residential use can be met entirely from most likely prospective lands and this way we can also preserve the remaining fertile agricultural land.

The land transformation model is the simplified representation of reality and seems to be theoretically promising for estimating residential expansion and demonstrates its suitability for using it for understanding complex urban land transformation. This model can be used for estimating future requirements for residential expansion and spatially allocating land in response to the driving forces responsible for it. However, the efficiency of this model needs to be tested when more complex urban forces are included and their resultant responses are evaluated.

REFERENCES

Bryant, C.R., L.H. Russwurm & A.G. McLellan (1982), *The city's countryside: land and its management in the rural-urban fringe*. London: Longman.

Dupont, V. (1997), Les 'rurbains' de Delhi, espace, populations, societes, 2-3, pp. 225-240, Paris: ORSTOM.

Ecological Modelling 116: 45-61.

Fazal, S. (2001) "The Need For Preserving Our Farm Lands. A Case Study from a Predominantly Agrarian Economy". *Landscape and Urban Planning*, Vol 55, No.1, Elsevier Science Publication, United Kingdom.

Fazal, S. (2004) The Role of Accessibility in Land Transformation: A GIS Based Study of a Growing Urban Centre in a Developing Economy. *Asian Profile,* Vol. 32. No.1. Canada.

Heimlich, R.E. and Anderson, W.D., 2001, "Development at the Urban Fringe and Beyond: Impacts on Agriculture and Rural Land," *Economic Research Service*, U.S. Department of Agriculture. Agricultural Economic Report No. 803.

Kundu, A. (1989), The dynamics of city hinterland relationships: the Indian case. In: P. Vennetier, (ed.), *La péri-urbanisation dans les pays tropicaux,* Centre d'Études de Géographie Tropicale, Valence., pp. 306-325.

Kundu, A. (1997), *Urban land markets and land price changes: a study in the Third World Context*. Aldershot: Ashgate.

Lambin, E.F., (1997). *Modelling and monitoring land-cover change processes in tropical regions.*

McGee, T.G. (1991), The emergence of Desakota regions in Asia: expanding a hypothesis. In: N. Ginsburg, B. Koppel & T.G. McGee, (eds.), *The extended metropolis, settlement transition in Asia*. Honolulu: University of Hawaii Press, pp. 3-26.

Nangia, S. (1976), *Delhi Metropolitan Region, a study in settlement geography.* New Delhi: K.B. Publishing House.

Observer Research Foundation (1998), India 1998. *Observer Statistical Handbook*, New Delhi.

Progress in Physical Geography 21: 375-393.

Ramchandran, R. (1989), *Urbanisation and Urban Systems in India*. Delhi: Oxford University Press.

Schenk, H. (1997), The rurban fringe: a central area between region and city: the case of Bangalore, India. In: M. Chatterji & Y. Kaizhang, *Regional Science in Developing Countries*, New York: MacMillan, pp. 212-223.

Sharifi, 2004, *Spatial Decision Support Systems*, ITC, Enschede, Netherlands.

Swindell, K. (1988), Agrarian change and peri-urban fringes in tropical Africa. In: D. Rimmer, (ed.,) *Rural Transformation in Tropical Africa*. Ohio University Press, pp. 98-115.

Thakur, B. (1991), *Land Utilization and Urbanization, the Rural-Urban Fringe*, Deep & Deep, New Delhi.

Turner, B.L. and William B. Meyer (1994), *Changes in Land Use and Land Cover: A Global Perspective*, Cambridge University Press, USA.

Veldkamp, A., Fresco, L.O., 1996. CLUE-CR: an integrated multi-scale model to simulate land use change scenarios in Costa Rica. *Ecological Modelling* 91: 231-248.

Verburg, P.H., De Koning, G.H.J., Kok, K, Veldkamp, A., Bouma, J., (1999a). A spatial explicit allocation procedure for modelling the pattern of land use change based upon actual land use. *Ecological Modelling* 116: 45-61.

Webster, D. (2003) *Emerging third stage peri-urbanization: Functional specialization in the Hanzhou peri urban region*. Stanford University.

Wehrwein, E.G. (1942), The rural urban fringe. *Economic Geography*, Vol. 18, pp. 217-228.

Yadav, C.S. (1987), *Rural-Urban Fringe*. New Delhi: Concept Publishing Company, New Delhi.

20

Waste Disposal and Management: A Case Study of Darjiling Town

SUSHMA BOMJAN

INTRODUCTION

Established by the Britishers in late ninetenth century, the population of Darjiling since 1921 has been growing significantly. From 22 thousand in 1921 to 1.07 lakh in 2001, apart from taking the burden of lakhs of tourist every year, it is entirely dependent on natural springs for its water requirements and *jhoras* for waste disposal. Increasing urban population and unplanned urban growth have also resulted in increasing pile of wastes and, hence, its disposal has become a major problem. Waste disposal problem has two aspects: firstly, considering the large number of wards and its inhabitants but number of disposal baskets and central community vats is very less. Garbage and wastes disposed mostly in jhoras (natural channel) and litter all around city too due to the lack of basic urban infrastructure. Secondly, topography and physical contour of the town accentuate the problem since many municipal wards do not have any access to vehicular means of waste disposal.

Solid waste management is one of the most challenging issues in cities, which are facing a serious pollution problem due to the generation of huge quantities of solid waste. The sanitary methods adopted for disposal of solid waste are, therefore, a serious health concern. The poorly maintained landfill sites are prone to groundwater contamination because of leachate production. Open dumping of garbage facilitates the breeding of disease vectors such as flies, mosquitoes, cockroaches, rats, and other pests, (CPCB 2000). The municipalities in India, therefore, face the challenge of reinforcing their available infrastructure for efficient MSW management and ensuring the scientific disposal of municipal solid waste by generating enough revenues either from the generators or by identifying activities that generate resources from waste management.

Even in smaller cities, where most of the municipal solid waste generated may be collected, it is merely dumped in the outskirts of the city without any treatment or precautionary engineering to protect air, soil and water (Krishna *et al.*, 1996).

The disposal of solid waste has always been an intractable problem throughout the hilly areas of Darjiling. They are generally operated below the standards of sanitary practice. Municipal budgetary allocations for operation and maintenance are always inadequate. The result is substandard and unsafe facilities which pose public health risks and aesthetic burdens to the citizens they are meant to serve. Generally, the widespread prevalence of uncontrolled dumping reflects the weak capacity of districts and municipalities and given the lack of resources for dealing with the problem.

Venkateswaran (1988) outlined the requirement of infrastructure for the hilly areas of the Himalayan region. He maintains that in terms of industries, tourism and basic amenities like water, electricity, health, transport and communication it is essential to have proper and rapid infrastructural facilities and its growth. Pickford (1994) and others discussed several aspects of water, sanitation, environment and development. These included a wide range of current development issues relating to subject including community management, ground-water, health and disease, institutional development, irrigation, sanitation, solid waste management, water quality, water sources, water supply and water treatment. This study emphasised on the low-cost methods of improving quality of life and to communal methods of development. It presents over forty papers presented at the 19th WEDC (Water, Engineering and Development Centre) Conference held in Accra, Ghana, in 1993, which was drawn from countries from all parts of the world. Different criteria and ways of management regarding drinking water supply and sewerage works in the various parts of U.P. have been narrated by Jaffer (1993).

While talking about waste management, Bavaska (1987) has laid emphasis on the mechanization in solid wastes at local bodies. He says that removal of solid and liquid wastes from sewage system and septic tank in most of the urban areas is accomplished in a traditional methods by using manpower and outdated equipments which are neither productive nor economical. Garg (1987) has formulated views to manage the solid wastes mechanically. Due to the inadequacies of technology to collect and transfer the wastes creating lots of environmental problems has been detected. Thus, solid waste disposal and management needs to be improved with the proper use of modern means and technology, which also requires public and political awareness.

Objective

This paper has attempted to analyse the waste disposal system in Darjiling town and has discussed the problems, perceptions and management issues.

METHODOLOGY

The household survey was conducted to draw the samples from randomly selected households, considering house owners spread with uniformly and spatially diverse residential environments of the town. Considering certain norms of the prevalent socio-economic classes within the spatially diverse locations, samples are randomly chosen from each of the high, middle and low socio-economic groups. A total of 320 sample households are covered and all the 32 municipal wards are included as sample subdivisions. Data have been drawn mainly by means of questionnaire responses and also on secondary bases of information. These were separately designed for the consumers and managers waste disposal in Darjiling town.

The Study Area

Darjiling city is one of the famous hill-resorts of Eastern India and the world's tourist resort. It is in the lower Himalayas within latitude 27° 03′ N and longitude 88° 16′ E at a distance of 656 km by rail from Calcutta and 78 km from Siliguri (Fig. 20.1). It is situated at 2134m above sea level and covers an area of 10.57 km^2. The Darjiling hills lie in the outlying hills of lower Himalayas. The months from February to April and October-November are very cool and pleasant. Heavy rainfall occurs during June to August and snowfall occurs generally between the end of December to first week of February. In summer maximum temperature reaches to 20°C and minimum 9°C. In winter maximum temperature is about 7°C and minimum 3°C. The average annual rainfall is generally 2320 mm.

Darjiling owes its present urban structure to colonial origin. It started settling since 1835, acquired by the East India Company. Captain Lloyd was attracted by its advantages as a site for a sanatorium and convinced Governor General Lord William Bentick about its natural beauty and for health resort. Then, this town eventually grew up as an important tourist hill-resort. According to the 2001 census, the population of Darjiling was 1.07 lakh, though a large number of holiday seekers mainly from West Bengal, Bihar, Orissa and other parts of the country and abroad are attracted by Darjiling's scenery and ethnic diversity.

WASTE DISPOSAL SYSTEM

The waste disposal system can be studied through solid waste handling and disposal of liquid waste in Darjiling municipal area. It is necessary to know about the waste disposal system and sewerage and sanitation, because it is also an important utility service and community facility along with water supply for the existing population of Darjiling town.

Sources of Solid Waste Disposal

In Darjiling, major sources of solid waste generation are dwellings, markets, hotels and restaurants. The sample survey was conducted which found that the wastes comprise water products of house keeping, food preparation, fuel residues, food wastes, empty containers, sweepings, old clothings, packaging materials, wooden pieces and garden clippings and vegetable and perishable materials. Various sources of solid waste are shown in Fig. 20.1.

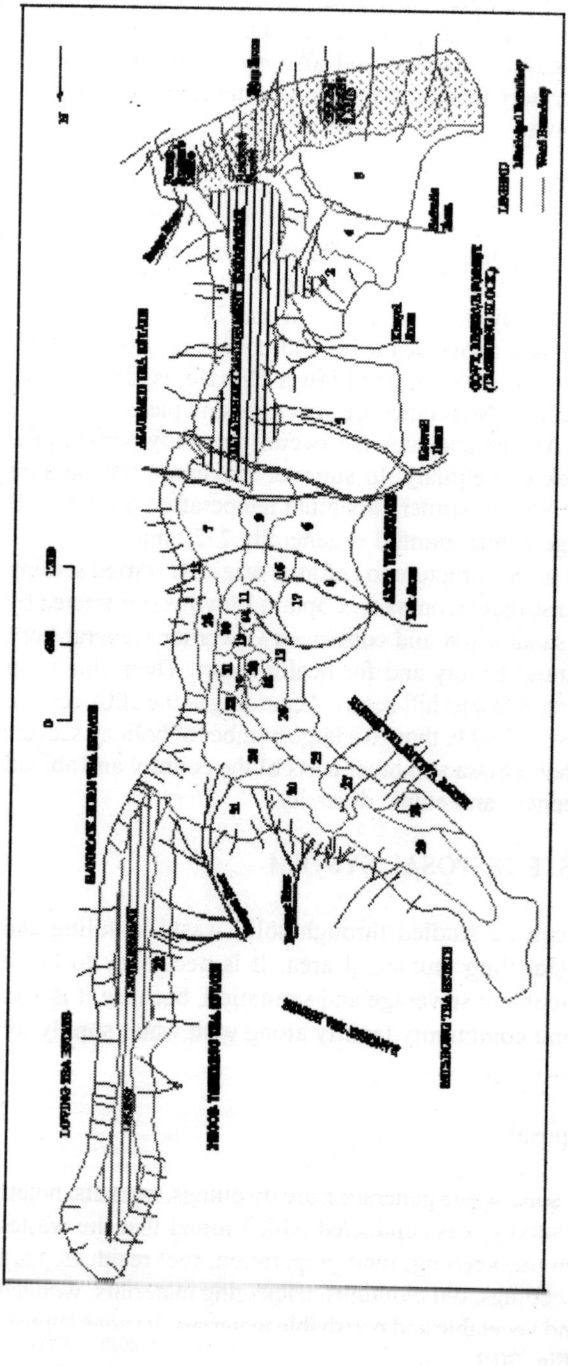

Darjiling City: A Study Area

With a view to develop a rational approach for collection, transportation and disposal system for the municipal area, it is required to assess correctly the present quantity of solid wastes that is being generated daily in the municipality. Table 20.1 shows per day production of solid wastes and the total wastes being handled in Darjiling municipality.

From Table 20.1 present daily generation of solid wastes and the present population in the town, the per capita daily production of solid wastes in Darjiling works out to 613 gm which covers only 60 per cent wastes of the city.

Table 20.1: Darjiling City: Daily Production and Disposal of Solid Wastes

Quantum of solid wastes	*Darjiling*
Daily production of solid wastes in tonnes	50
Solid wastes disposed of daily in tonnes	31

Source: Darjiling Municipality 2002.

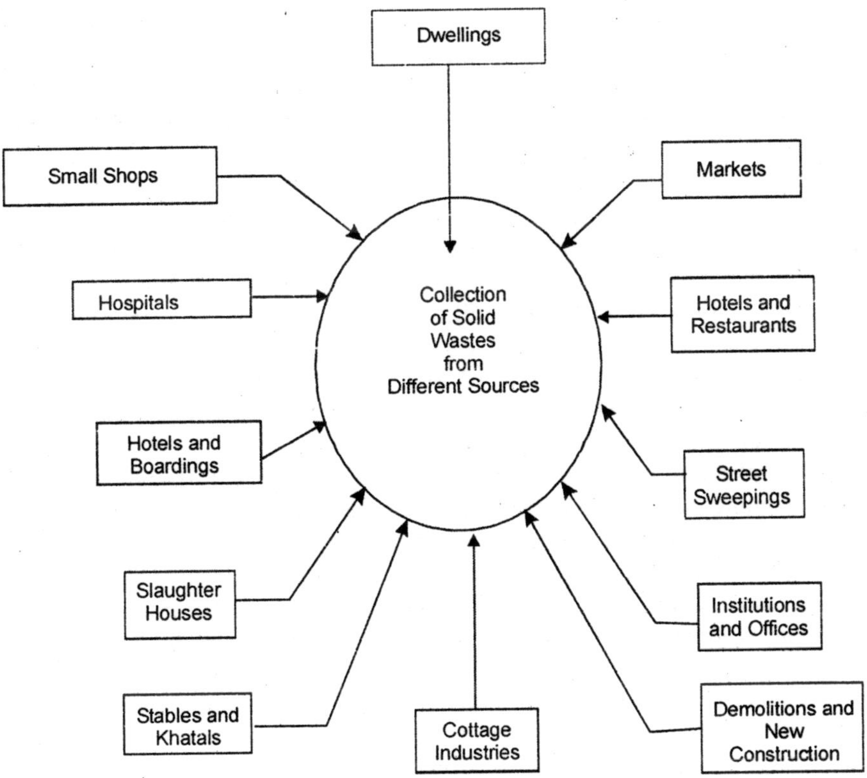

Fig. 20.1: Various Sources of Solid wastes

The present system of collection of solid wastes in Darjiling municipal area has seven conservancy sections (zones), viz. Kagjhora, Collinton, Lower Rockwood and Upper Rockwood, Market, Singamari Bhutia Busty and Chawrasta. Presently, there are 194 dustbins for daily collection of garbages and solid wastes of which 94 dustbins constitute as community central vats. These central vats are situated on nearby roads or road sides of the locality; and transportation of daily accumulated garbages and solid wastes is done by conservancy tractors from the central vats to disposal grounds. More than 50 to 60 tonnes of solid wastes are produced everyday in the entire municipal zones. These bulky amount of wastes are collected by 150 labourers.

Collection of Solid Waste Disposal

There are a number of villages within the municipal limits, where even hand-cart cannot be used, because there is hardly any road and the location is very steep. Such areas are most of the lower regions of Ghum and Jorebunglow, Alubari, Bhutia Busty, Nimkidara, Bloomfield, Lasha Villa, Shyam Cottage, Rajbari, Bhaktay Busty, Haridas Hatta, Singmari, Toongsong, Ging and eastern regions of Collinton location. The residents of these areas dispose their solid wastes to the nearby jhoras. The daily production of garbage in these areas is estimated at 4-5 million tonnes. For conservancy workers, it is a formidable task to transport garbage on hand-load through steep roads to the nearest central vats which is at a distance of 1 km. Besides these places, various new slum areas have come up, such as Rockwood, Shiva Gram, Mangalpuri, Navin Gram, Burn's Gram, Jawahar Busty, Bucher Busty (Dr. Zakir Hussain Busty) etc. Here, municipality has yet to provide collection facilities of solid garbage. The daily production of garbage in these new areas is estimated to be 4 to 5 million tonnes and they do not have any other alternative except to dispose to the nearby jhoras or drains. Consequently, with existing infrastructures only about 12 to 15 million tonnes of solid wastes are transported daily from 94 community vats to the disposal grounds and another 5 to 6 million tonnes are discharged to nearby Jhoras.

In the existing system of collection and transportation of solid wastes in Darjiling municipality there are more than 40 wheel barrows and 13 tractor-trailer. Each wheel barrow has a capacity of 5 cubic ft. only. The ward-wise allocation of wheel barrow varies in a range of 1 to 4 and the distance travelled by a mazdoor with the carrier varies from 0.5 to 1 km. The capacity of tractor-trailer is about 3 tonnes and at present each tractor-trailer makes 3 trips a day and 6 numbers of loader are given to each tractor-trailer. The average speed limit of a tractor-trailer is restricted at 15 km per hour owing to hilly terrain with winding roads and steep slopes.

Disposal of Solid Wastes

Presently, the method for disposal of solid wastes is open dumping at the site near slaughter house in the downhill areas beyond the market place. The daily solid waste produced in Darjiling municipal areas in the 94 community central vats (at least 20 wards) is estimated to be 30 million tonnes of which 50 per cent is transported everyday for disposal at the dumping chute by utilising the services of three conservancy tractors each performing 3-4 trips a day. The dumping ground is situated at a distance of 4 km below the Cart Road near Hindu Burial Ghat and the road is very narrow and steep.

Table 20.2: Darjiling Town: Location of Community Vat in each Zone and the Disposal of Solid Waste by Conservancy Tractors

Sl. No.	*Name of zone*	*No. of community central vats*	*Daily collection in million tonnes*	*Daily disposal*	*Mode of transportation*
1.	Market (Chowk Bazar)	10	6	3	Chowk Bazar 10-8 (d)+2 (w)
2.	Kakjhora	7	3	1	Lower Beechwood 9-5 (d) + 4 (w)
3.	Collington	11	3	1	Kakjhora 7-1 (d)+4 (w)+2 (f)
4.	Upper Beechwood	23	4	2	Upper Beachwood 23-13 (d)+ 9 (w)+2 (f)
5.	Singamari	15	4	1	Collington 11-6 (d)+2 (f)+3(w)
6.	Lower Beechwood	9	4	2	Chawrasta 19-5(d) + 10(w) +4(f)
7.	Chowrastha	10	4	2	Singmari 15-15 (w)
	TOTAL	94	30	12	

Index: d for daily; w for weekly; f for fortnightly

Source: Darjiling Municipality, 1995.

Besides, the people are in habit of throwing or disposing domestic solid wastes in the slopes, nearby jhoras and drains. The average amount of such wastes is about 2 to 3 million tonnes per day, which is causing clotting of jhoras and drains and even causing pollution of jhoras at various places. Even in the dumping ground, ultimately, the solid wastes are disposed of to Sidrabong Jhoras. Thus, the lack of sufficient land for dumping the wastes is an acute problem.

Liquid Waste Disposal (Sewerage and Sanitation)

An old sewer network exists in skeleton form in the municipal area and discharge into jhoras (shown in Plate 2). There are about 109 community type latrines around 32 wards owned by the municipality. These community latrines can be broadly

Plate 1: Solid waste dumping in Darjiling

classified into three categories, viz., latrines with sewerage facility, latrines with individual septic tanks and soak pits and the service privies. Out of 109 community latrines, 55 latrines are connected to 5 major septic tanks located in 5 different locations, which are presented in Table 20.2. Additionally, the sewerage system has also 2900 domestic connections.

Plate 2: Sewerage discharge into jhoras

Table 20.3: Darjiling City: Estimated Community Latrines with Sewer Connection

Location of Septic Tank	*No. of Septic Tank*	*No. of Community Latrines Connected*	*No. of Domestic Connections*
Kagjhora	13	18	1250
Bazar	54	31	2853
Wilson Busty	38	16	1040
Bhutia Busty	42	14	550
Tukvar	11	8	110

Source: Darjiling Municipality, 2002.

The existing sewerage system comprises 150 mm diametre sewer lines. The sewer lines were mostly laid more than 80 years ago for the then population of 20,000 persons. Obviously, the carrying capacity of the sewer lines as well as the treatment capacities of the old septic tanks have become inadequate due to rapid increase in population during the past decades. During field investigation, it was observed that the sewer lines in most places are choked and at certain location they are in a dilapidated conditions. Due to rapid rate of urbanisation with haphazard buildings and mushrooming hotels have been erected over sewer lines keeping no scope for inspections, cleaning, repair and renovations of lines. It has been revealed that the chokage is caused to the sewer lines due to want of adequate quantum of water for flushing arrangement and also ingress of solid wastes through open joints in the sewer network.

The per capita water supply during the peak season is only 41.5 litres/day and during lean season is only 25.5 litres/day. Hence, after meeting all the demands of domestic, commercial and institutional sectors, adequate quantum of water is not available for flushing the night soil. During the survey it was found out that most of the residents used waste water through washing of dirty utensils, clothes, etc., for flushing. Hence, the extension of sewerage system may not be feasible because of this meagre rate of water supply.

Thus, the existing sewer lines are not favourable for proper sanitary sewage with constant choking due to the following reasons:

(i) Worn out condition of sewer network due to old age;
(ii) Blockage for want of water for regular flushing as the habit of using papers instead water by local people;
(iii) The entire sewer main, right from hill top to septic tank has got a uniform diametre pipe as such the load it carries from hilltop with great velocity are often seen overflowing at different inspection pits, situated lower level; and
(iv) Due to the increase in population and holdings, the existing sewer mains and its tributaries are always overloaded.

WASTE DISPOSAL: PERCEPTION, PROBLEMS AND MANAGEMENT

This section provides an insight into the perceptions and attitudes of the sample population and the management authorities with respect to waste disposal in Darjiling town. Waste disposal is an important issue, over which certain responses were also sought regarding the knowledge concerning the location of waste disposal in different parts of the town. Considering the impact of waste disposal on environment it was decided to investigate the response of sample population on the methods of both liquid and solid wastes disposal and also to know the frequency of solid waste disposal. Major sources of solid waste in the study area are domestic, commercial and institutional sectors. The roadside dustbins and community central vats are provided by the municipal authority but these are located only around the market area or motorable roads. This facility is provided to ward numbers I, III, V, VI, IX, XXV and XXVI. People prefer to throw solid wastes on the road sides inside the surface drains, and nearby jhoras or nallahs.

An old sewer network exists in Darjiling Municipality within skeleton form. There are only five septic tanks to cover 10.57 km^2 and 72 thousand to 1 lakh population. These septic tanks are also provided to those areas where the vehicle/wheel barrows are possible to reach. The effluents from these septic tanks are discharged directly to the streams or jhoras at the lower level; likewise, the outskirts or steep areas have independent sewerage which discharge into jhoras. Thus, a good portion of night soil is dumped directly into the jhoras and on the hill slopes causing health hazards to the people residing in down hill areas (Fig. 20.2).

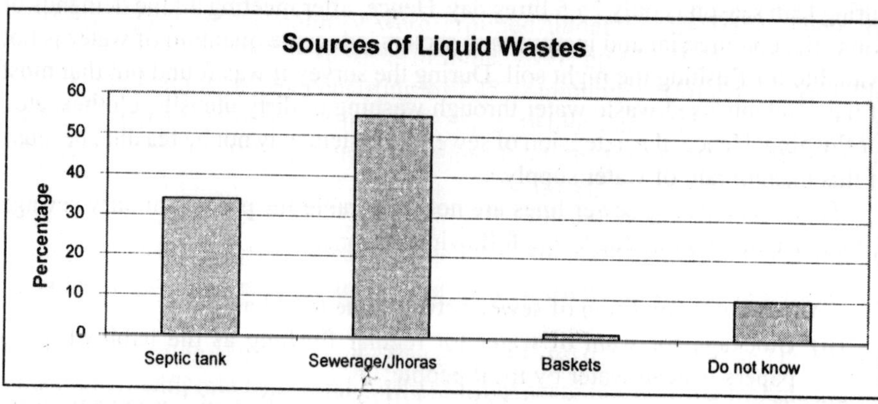

Source: Personal Survey

Fig. 20.2: Darjiling Town: Perceptions of Sources of Liquid Waste Disposal

The frequency of solid waste disposal in different wards is shown in Fig. 20.3. It has been divided into seven categories: Daily, 3 times a week, 2 times a week, once a week, twice a month, every month and rarely. Regarding the disposal of solid waste the authority seems very careless as per people's perception. Only in the market areas, V.I.P. areas and places where the piling up of wastes can be observed, are cleared everyday or twice/thrice a week. Wastes are collected weekly from those areas where people are aware, but are collected rarely or once a month which are inaccessible by the officials. Similarly, areas located on steep terrain throw wastes in the jhoras.

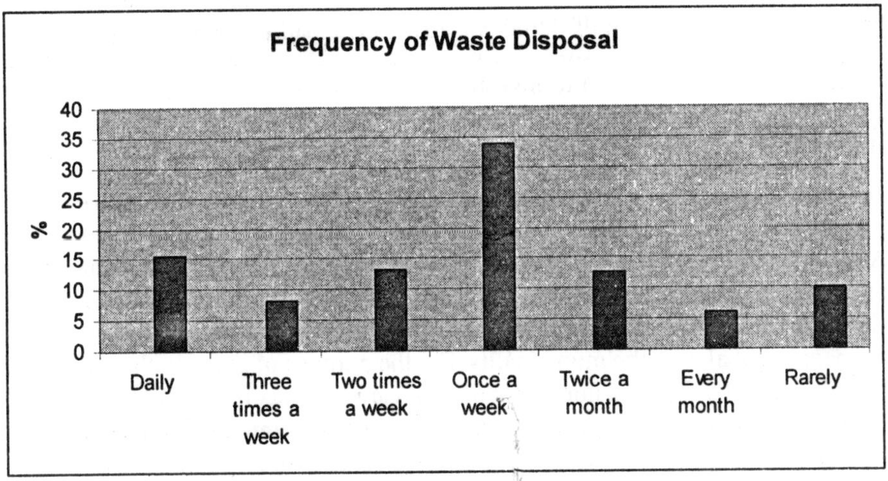

Fig. 20.3: Frequency of Solid Disposal

Eventually, they pollute the human health. Such areas include major portion of Ghum-Jorebunglow, Batasia, Bloomfield, Lasha Villa, Nimki Dhara, Rajbari, Baktay Busty, Jawar Busty, Pandam, Alubari, Tungsong and some parts of other wards too. The frequency of waste disposal is entirely dependent upon the mazdoor rather than officials and is determined by the awareness and ignorance of the public.

Deficiencies of Solid Waste Management

The number of dust bins and community vats are inadequate and placement of these provision also not made properly which has not been designed to meet the situation-specific requirements. Transportation of solid wastes by headload from narrow lanes in place of suitable type of handcarts have to be adopted. Due to inadequate number of mazdoors/staffs the clearance of solid waste is not regular. Non-availability of specific types of tools and plants, makes it obvious. Disposal of solid wastes by individuals directly into jhoras and roadside drains has to be checked by proper management and motivation. Some revenue should be collected to maintain management which are lacking in terms of realisation.

Deficiencies Observed in Terms of Liquid Waste Disposal (Sewerage System)

The disposal of liquid waste is creating problem due to unorganised and improper planning. The municipal authority neither care the community latrines nor different sewer lines which cause frequent logging/damping of the area. Indiscriminate dumping/discharging of night soil/liquid waste in the jhoras or streams poses problems of health hazards. The economically weaker section suffers lot in this manner. Lack of water supply creates problem of flushing and anal cleaning. The capacities of old sewer lines are inadequate to carry the rising sewage and night soil which are damaged and in dilapidated condition as well in certain areas. The practice of transportation of liquid wastes by headload is obsolete, inhuman and unhygienic. The management is absolutely poor and practically no maintenance.

Managerial Perceptions of Waste Disposal

To have a clean township, locality and ecologically sound environment it is essential for planning infrastructure, economic support and access to different localities. An attempt has been made to collect the views and perceptions of the management officials regarding waste disposal management both solid and liquid. In urban situation where there is more pressure on limited land is not only the concern of the people but also of the municipality. For the purpose of gauging the perception of management officials, a number of official views are incorporated. The managers are of the opinion that even the people should co-operate with management in certain aspects as they are also in some ways careless and ignored the matter.

Key Gaps

Generally level of research and documentation of experiences is very low. Experiences with resource mobilization for solid waste management within local authorities requires improvement.

Monitoring and control of waste disposal by local authorities need consistent focus. The financial constraints, institutional problems within the departments, fragile links with other concerned agencies, lack of suitable staff, and other allied problems have prevented the urban local bodies from delivering and maintaining an efficient waste management system. In this context, it is also necessary to harness and integrate the role of three other emerging actors in this field—the private sector, NGOs, and rag pickers—into the overall institutional framework.

CONCLUSION

The haphazard growth along with high rise buildings' construction has to be restricted strictly and there should be a proper co-ordination between stakeholders and managers. It is necessary to minimize waste generation to save on precious land resources required to dispose the waste. It is, therefore, necessary to practise waste segregation at the primary collection centre so that the waste can be sent for recycling or for waste-to-energy applications. This entire multi-faceted problem should be fought with a multipronged strategy, which should consider people's perception, augmentation of new schemes, improvement in infrastructural facilities, co-ordination between different governing bodies and educating people regarding the usages of water into the consideration.

REFERENCES

Bhaskara, M. (1987) "Mechanisation in solid waste management in local bodies", *Civic Affairs* 34 (8): 29-32.

CPCB (Central Pollution Control Board). (2000) *Management of Municipal Solid Waste*, Delhi: Central Pollution Control Board.

Darjiling Municipality. Project on Collection, *Treatment and Disposal of Solid and Liquid Wastes for Darjiling Municipal Areas*, Government of West Bengal, Consulting Engineering Services (India) Pvt. Ltd., January 1996.

Krishna Shyamala and Banerjee, D.K. 'Life Cycle Assessment of Plastic Waste and their fate in the environment' published in the proceedings of the International Seminar on Biodegradable Polymers organized by the National Chemical Laboratory, Pune, India. (November 1997).

Garg, G.C. (1987) "Solid waste management: its arts of mechanisation", *Civic Affairs*, 34 (7): 23-28.

Kakar, K.N., (1988) Modernisation of Solid Waste Management, *Civic Affairs*, Vol. 36, pp. 4-44.

Pickford, J., *et al.* (1993) *Water, Sanitation, Environment and Development*, London Intermediate Technology Publication and the Water Engineering and Development Centre, Loughborough University of Technology, U.K.

Papola, T.S. *et al.* (1983) Development of Hill Areas: Issues and Approaches, Himalayan Publishing House, Bombay.

Subramaniam M.K., (1984) Solid Waste Management, *Civic Affairs*, Vol. 32, pp. 17-24.

Venkateshwaran, R.J., (1988) Darjiling Needs Rapid Infrastructure Growth, *Economic Times*, 15th September, p.4.

Index